The Thought of
Rudolf Bultmann

OTHER WORKS BY ANDRÉ MALET

Personne et amour dans la théologie trinitaire
de S. Thomas d'Aquin, Paris: Vrin, 1956

Jean Calvin, Commentaire sur la Genèse:
Texte établi par A. Malet, Geneva: Labor et Fides, 1962

Le Traité théologico-politique de Spinoza
et la pensée biblique, Paris: Les Belles Lettres, 1966

Bultmann et la mort de Dieu, Paris: Seghers, 1968

ANDRÉ MALET

The Thought of Rudolf Bultmann

translated from the French by
RICHARD STRACHAN

preface by RUDOLF BULTMANN

DOUBLEDAY & COMPANY, INC., GARDEN CITY, NEW YORK 1971

ABBREVIATIONS

Works of Martin Luther:

WA   *Werke . . .; Weimarer Ausgabe (Kritische Gesamtausgabe)*, Weimar, 1883 ff.

Works of Rudolf Bultmann:

GV   *Glauben und Verstehen*, Tübingen: J. C. B. Mohr, 1 (2nd ed. 1954), 2 (1952), 3 (1960), 4 (1965).

KM   *Kerygma und Mythos*, Hamburg-Volksdorf: Herbert Reich, 1 (3rd. ed. 1954), 2 (1952).

EJ   *Das Evangelium des Johannes*, Göttingen: Vandenhoeck & Ruprecht, 14th ed. 1956.

TNT   *Theologie des Neuen Testaments*, Tübingen: J. C. B. Mohr, 3rd ed. 1958.

GST   *Die Geschichte der synoptischen Tradition*, Göttingen: Vandenhoeck & Ruprecht, 3rd ed. 1957.

JS   *Jesus*, Tübingen: J. C. B. Mohr, 3rd ed. 1951.

HE   *History and Eschatology* (Gifford Lectures, 1955), Edinburgh University Press, 1957. *Geschichte und Eschatologie*, Tübingen: J. C. B. Mohr, 1958.

JCM   *Jesus Christ and Mythology*, London: SCM Press, 1960. "Jesus Christus und die Mythologie" in *Glauben und Verstehen* 4, 1st ed. 1965.

CP   *Le christianisme primitif dans le cadre des religions antiques*, translation by P. Jundt (Paris: Payot, 1950) of *Das Urchristentum im Rahmen der antiken Religionen* (Zurich: Artemis-Verlag, 1949).

Works of Karl Barth:

RB   *Rudolf Bultmann—Ein Versuch, ihn zu verstehen*, Zollikon-Zurich: Evangelischer Verlag, 1952.

KD   *Die kirchliche Dogmatik*, Zollikon-Zurich: Evangelischer Verlag, 1948–1953.

TKD   French translation of the above, by F. Ryser, Geneva: Labor et Fides, 1953.

Works of Martin Heidegger:

SZ   *Sein und Zeit*, Tübingen: Neomarius Verlag, 6th ed. 1949.

Works of Karl Jaspers:

PH   *Philosophie*, Berlin: Y. Springer, 1932.

KJRB   *Karl Jaspers—Rudolf Bultmann, Die Frage der Entmythologisierung*, Munich: R. Piper, 1954.

When other works of these authors are referred to, the full title is given.

PART ONE

PART TWO

PART THREE

THEOLOGY AND ONTOLOGY

PREFACE

Dear Dr Malet,

I have read your book with great interest and above all with great joy. You set yourself the task of explaining in detail the purpose behind my theological work. Let me assure you that you have done so with a thorough understanding such as I have rarely been privileged to encounter. You admirably grasp the inner cohesion linking ideas that I have set forth in separate works (each on a particular occasion) and present them as an organic whole.

In Part One ('Bultmann's Categories') you rightly single out the principles that underlie my thought, thus dispelling a good deal of misconception about my writing. Particularly important for what follows, you clarify the relation between subject and object, the ontic and the ontological, and thereby the concepts of transcendence, history and historicity, precomprehension and self-comprehension.

Thus you are able to show how the various concerns of theology can be understood in terms of those concepts. You luminously distinguish true comprehension from comprehension in the eyes of rationalism, orthodoxy and liberalism, and establish the differences which set apart the biblical, Greek and modern ideas of transcendence, the world, man and history. In all these respects your study is more than a descriptive exercise. For the whole is steeped in things which I have at heart—things, I may be permitted to say, which we have at heart.

Need I descend to particulars? Especially important is your way of showing that it is impossible to speak about God as an object, your elucidation of the paradoxical bond between God's present and future, your insight that 'we do not have to choose between the absolutely other God and the absolutely intimate God; he is absolutely intimate only because he is absolutely other', the way you present the historicization of eschatology and the essence of the Church as an eschatological phenomenon.

You do very well, in Part Three, to inquire how my work relates to that of Heidegger, Jaspers and Barth. Here, indeed, you clarify my intentions once and for all. You show that my theology does not

depend on Heidegger's 'philosophy'; that on the contrary the significance of his existential analysis, so far as I am concerned, is that it
provides an adequate terminology (*Begrifflichkeit*) for setting forth the
New Testament and the Christian faith. You define freedom and
decision, authenticity and unauthenticity, in their ontological sense—in
the meaning, that is, which they have for the human being as such,
not as they apply to ontic phenomena. Thus you can explain the
ontological sense of decision as distinct from the decision of faith, which
is an ontic phenomenon. You make this weighty statement: 'The idea
of authenticity and unauthenticity manifestly belongs to the ontological
order, not the ontic order, so that ec-sistential analysis remains strictly
neutral'. I am especially indebted to you for exploding the legend of
Heidegger's 'atheism'.

As to Jaspers, you show that the differences between him and myself
flow from his basically idealist conception of transcendence. Finally
you amply establish that Barth misunderstands me because he is unaware of the problem of adequate terminology, and because he is
imprisoned in the 'armour' of a philosophy which misconstrues the
true relation between subject and object—contrary, indeed, to his real
intention, so that you are actually able to say, 'It is scarcely a paradox
to find Bultmann more Barthian than Barth'.

Whom shall I congratulate the more heartily? *You* for writing a
major work with such intellectual precision and vigour? Or *myself* for
finding so perspicacious an interpreter?

                                                        Rudolf Bultmann

PART ONE

Bultmann's Categories

THE PROBLEM STATED

Most of the criticisms levelled at Bultmann—they have been many and sometimes savage—are based on a garbled idea of his thought. If he has often complained of being misunderstood, the reason is not some persecution complex; the reason is that he has in fact been wrongly read.

Why? Innovation is of two kinds: one happens within the world shared alike by the opponents of the innovation and by its supporters, whereas the other sets things in a context hitherto unknown. As an example of the first kind we may cite the problem of subject and object in Western philosophy. One whole era dwelt upon the object and another on the subject, and all that was involved was the two poles of the same universe.

Most readers of Bultmann have supposed that he was founding a neo-liberalism by turning theology from the object to the subject. Certain others, like Karl Jaspers, think of him instead as neo-orthodox. But both sides agree in assuming that Bultmann remains within the framework of the classic problem. Themselves prisoners of that problem, they judge in terms of it. What has never dawned on them is that to understand Bultmann they must re-examine their deepest presuppositions, those principles which they have taken as axiomatic; that they cannot be guided by those presuppositions when reading him.

The original feature of Bultmann's thought is that it changes our horizon. To grasp it we must get beyond the philosophical and theological categories to which we are accustomed. It is innovation of the kind Goethe refers to: 'If a man appears with something new, something that contradicts the credo we have droned through for years and handed on to others in our turn, something likely to capsize it, then every passion is whipped up against that man, we move heaven and earth to crush him. We set up our bristles as best we can, we feign not to hear or not to understand, we speak scornfully of the new thing . . . Thus it may be a good long time before a new truth makes any headway.'*

*Conversation with Eckermann, 30 December 1823.

CHAPTER ONE

What is 'Objectivity'?

One need not read far in Bultmann's critics to perceive that what they really charge him with is undermining the *objectivity* of God and God's Word. Just what is the position, and how does Bultmann envisage 'objectivity'?

I may have a purely abstract knowledge of things, be able, that is, to give an objective description of them—a sociological, intellectual, moral, spiritual one if persons are concerned—or I may know them through the love I bear them. In the first case I look at them from outside, I stand aloof and in that sense am superior, I master them.

Let us at once use a key word in Bultmann's vocabulary and say that I make an *Anspruch*, make a claim or assert a right, in their regard: the right to remain myself, to go on controlling myself by controlling them. For me they are objects of interest which satisfy my desire for knowledge and enrich me on the plane of theory or of practice. Thus man subjects the world to himself through science and technology. Thus too he seeks to rule the world of persons, by making them serve his ends. Now the hallmark of ec-sistentiell[1] knowledge is that it lays no *Anspruch* upon another. I go forth from myself to submit to the other, to let him be himself. He becomes my 'lord'.

Now what is the 'objectivity' of the other; or, more accurately, what is his true reality? We say that a man who loves is not objective in his judgment of the person he loves, which implies that for him the beloved has ceased to exist in himself, has become subjectified. On the other hand we also say that one only knows a person *for what he is* when one loves him, because then one knows him from within, as one only knows a house or a country when one has visited it. Well then, when is the other most 'in himself'—when I love him or when I look

---

1. We write 'ec-sistence' for the following reason. Latin *ex-sistere* means *stand forth from*. But the English derivatives 'existence' and 'existential' have come to indicate either—in ordinary parlance—an objective thing (one says 'I am certain that exists', meaning that one is not the victim of an illusion), or else—in cultured parlance—a subject in its intimacy. Throughout this book, whether we refer to ec-sistence, the ec-sistentiell, or the ec-sistential, the reader must think of movement forth (from oneself) towards (another). Hence ec-sistence is opposed to every form of subjectivism and objectivism—the two being one and the same thing, as we shall see.

on him 'as a proposition' (Pascal)? The whole of Bultmann's thought is based on the conviction that the other only exists as another when I give up any *Anspruch* over him.

Objective and scientific knowledge claim that ec-sistentiell knowledge is mere subjectivism, and that a thing is its real self only when one looks at it from outside. In fact science has but one end in view: to gain mastery over the world. To make the world an object is a refusal to be subject to it in any way, is to analyse it and seek to discover its laws; there is a certain submission to the world, but only as a man who takes an unfamiliar machine apart in order to understand and control it begins by yielding to the demands of the machine.

Science masters an object so completely as to be able to deduce it. From one law or a set of laws science is able to conclude that the object exists. Did not Le Verrier discover Neptune by sheer calculation? The very existence of technology proves that objective knowledge will not let the other exist as something other. It is not by accident that scientific knowledge issues in technology, but perforce. A tree is known by its fruit and the fruit of science is mastery of the world. More and more the universe is becoming the universe of man; it exists less and less as transcendence.

What is true of things is also true of persons. When is another most himself: when he is my 'lord' or when I am his 'lord'? When I meet with a person in the train who is nothing to me, towards whom I reserve my *Anspruch*, whom I keep at arm's length, whom I can observe, trying to guess what his social background is, what he does for a living, how his mind works, whom in short I look on as an object—does he really exist in himself, as transcendence? By objectifying him do I not really subjectify him, stripping him of his true reality? Here common sense—of whose sins with regard to Christian faith we shall speak presently—strays far afield. It assumes that what is objective must be real, and that nothing else is real. It fails to see that to speak of a thing as an objective reality is necessarily to speak of myself as something independent of it, and therefore to speak of it as dependent on me. For there can be no neutrality, and the principle that 'Whoever is not with me is against me' also applies to knowledge. To know is always to take up an attitude towards what I know.

Man does not like mystery. Historians of the primitive mind have amply shown how long men lived in terror of the unknown and at its mercy. The same is true of each of us: things and events that do not fit into our reasoning and our familiar world cause us anxiety. The riddle of life and death torments modern man as much as ever it did ancient man. And so knowledge is a *battle*, a wrestling with darkness, a means of neutralizing the other insofar as it is 'alien'. Even the most contemplative of knowledge is always an attempt at conquest, to set the other (though it be God himself) where it belongs in the scheme of things—where, consequently, it will lose its alarming otherness. Belief in the disinterested character of science or intellectual contemplation is a delusion; or rather, it is an alibi. Knowledge is always an expression of man's will to power, a manifestation of his *Anspruch*. There is nothing more natural than that things should elude the net which knowledge would cast over them all, but knowledge cannot reconcile itself to the fact. In hopes of capturing the unmanageable phenomenon it re-examines its own principles (the familiar 'substructural crisis' which every science undergoes) and works out a new plan to embrace everything this time (GV 3, pp. 118–19).

But all that we have said applies only to objective knowledge. Ec-sistentiell knowledge respects the otherness of the other. Instead of referring the other to myself, trying to fit it into the world of my thought and life, I give up any *Anspruch* over it, I enter into communion with it. I hear it saying to me: '*Du musst dein Leben ändern*' (Rilke; see GV 3, p. 107). Now it is really itself, it really exists as a transcendence—in Bultmann's language, as a *Dass*. For throughout his work Bultmann uses the distinction between the *Dass* and the *Was*. The *Was* is what (a thing is), what it has in common with others; whereas the *Dass* expresses the *that*, sheer otherness. The 'what' is the conceptual content, the nature, the essence, the substance. The 'that' expresses advent and event. Every being is at once *Was* and *Dass*. What Peter and John have in common is that both are men, not trees or animals (the plane of the *Was*). But at the same time they are two beings absolutely irreducible to each other; each one is unique (the plane of the *Dass*).

What we have said of intellectual and objective knowledge shows that it ignores the *Dass*, that at heart it is domination of the other, that it is concerned with conquering the world or conquering persons. Its proper object is the *Was*. Reason exists in order to know the nature of things. It states *what* they are. Thanks to reason there is physics, astronomy, biology, psychology, economics, sociology—in a word, all the vast range of the natural and rational sciences. But reason cannot reach to the *Dass*.

I might acquire an objective knowledge of the unknown man opposite me in a railway compartment by an exhaustive study of his origins, his family life, his working conditions, his philosophic, political, social and religious ideas—in short, of his *Was*—but doing so I would not arrive at his *Dass*. Instead I would have destroyed it so far as it can be destroyed. For by my methodical, rational investigation I would have taken possession of this man as science takes possession of its objects. I would have submitted to him only so as to subject him to me. 'Submission to facts' is only a *List der Vernunft* whereby one subjects them to oneself. But suppose the unknown man we have been speaking of becomes a friend of mine. Then everything changes. Now he is *primarily* a *Dass* for me. The abstract investigation I have made of him remains valid but acquires an altogether different meaning, because henceforth the *Was* is integrated into the *Dass*. My friendship causes me to give up any *Anspruch* over him, makes me his 'servant' from now on (in the evangelic sense of the word). I recognize him in all his transcendence by at last allowing him to be himself.

The phenomenonology of rational knowledge and ec-sistentiell knowledge which we have just sketched presupposes two diametrically opposite anthropologies. Rational knowledge is based on a naturalist, substantialist view of man. We have said that it does not reach transcendence. It is not ec-sistence towards the other but conquest of the other. The intellect explains, situates, fixes, classifies essences or natures (the *Was* of things); it overcomes the unknown, the obscure, the enigmatic, the disturbing. It does not like the wholly other. Intellect hungers and thirsts to see everything, lay hold on everything, understand everything, and then so far as may be to tame everything. Man as the subject of this knowledge, therefore, will be a cognitive substance.

Substance is equivalent to what Bultmann calls *Gegebenheit* or *Vorhandenheit*. *Gegebenheit* is a datum. *Vorhandenheit* also designates the world of things, of what man controls. The subject of rational knowledge is thought of as a substance, because it need not go forth from itself in order to know the other's *Was*. This kind of knowledge reduces the non-rational to rational terms, dismisses transcendence so far as possible, and wants no dealings with the *Dass*—only with the *Was*, the intelligible essence. Thus it does not have to withdraw from itself, to become as it were a stranger to itself. On the contrary, it reduces the unknown to the known, the unaccustomed to the familiar, things that disturb us to things that reassure, the extraordinary to the ordinary, outward things to inward, the heterogeneous to the homogeneous, darkness to light, chaos to order, disparates to identity, the transcendent to the immanent. It does not forsake itself to wander in countries to which the price of admission is a complete transformation of itself. It does not leave its country; it only expands the frontiers of its country. That is why it is best defined as a *res cogitans*.

The subject of ec-sistentiell knowledge is altogether different. We have said that that knowledge is an opening and an exodus. It allows itself to be scrutinized by the other. So here a man leaves his own country. He does not expand its frontiers, he crosses them, he responds to the call of the wholly other. Accordingly he is not a substance but a *freedom*, which we must think of not as a quality but as the capacity to become something other than what I am while yet remaining what I am. Since by definition the other, as other, is to the core what I am not in any way, then if I am to reach it I must wholly forsake myself, become what I am not, without losing my identity—that is, my otherness with respect to the thing which calls me. Such a feat is possible only if I am constituted by freedom, freedom to abandon what I am and become what I am not while yet remaining what I am. Thus man is that 'being who is not what he is and is what he is not' (Sartre). In other words man is the opposite of substance (material or spiritual), which is only what it is. That is why Bultmann often defines him as *Sein-Können* (aptitude for being). Man is not being, he is aptitude for being, ability to become what he is not, to be torn from himself in order to receive a new being.

In the same sense Bultmann constantly says that man is *Geschicht-lichkeit* (history or historicity). This idea must not be confused with becoming, growth or evolution. The becoming of substance is perfectly consistent with the identity by which we have defined it. Physical and chemical transformations in a body, changes in the cosmos that never wears the same face twice, growth in living things, the ceaseless evolution of all nature that science makes it its business to study—none of this entitles us to speak of historicity.

The πάντα ρεῖ exhibits not a shred of historicity. Nature undergoes transformations but has no history; because change as it may, it is always nature and nothing else. Whatever it is going to be it has always been. It has no past and no beginning, absolutely speaking. Of these, freedom alone is capable, because only freedom can be what it is not. It does not grow like a seed, which already is what it will presently be thanks to many metamorphoses. At the starting-point it is in no sense what it will be, for it makes its way not only from *Was* to *Was* but also from *Dass* to *Dass*. It becomes the other *qua* other. Its future is a true future, a clean break with the past (which it nevertheless continues to be). An encounter and a friendship make me entirely different. I had other friends, of course, but I did not have *this* one. This *Dass* which opens to me and to which I open is for me an absolute future.

So it is of the utmost importance to distinguish the history of things—the evolution of nature or of man as a being determined by biological, psychological, sociological and other factors—and the historicity of freedoms: only the latter is a genuine history. In French [and English] we have only one word for the two things. In German the noun *Geschichte* and the adjective *geschichtlich* are often used to designate the history of freedom, and the noun *Historie* and adjective *historisch* to designate history in the ordinary sense, the evolution of things or of man as a determinate being. We shall cast back to these problems in our chapter on history. Let us say here and now that we shall write history and historical when referring to history in the hackneyed, objective sense; whereas 'historicity', 'history', and 'historical' in inverted commas will indicate that we refer to history in the true sense, the history of freedom.

To say that man is 'historicity' is to affirm his *temporality*: he is not the eternal present of the homogeneous, he makes his way from pasts to futures. Substance is not temporal, because although it has an evolution it has no 'history'. Its future is already there in germ in its present, and that present is only the development of its past. So whatever adventures it may have, it is only an unending present. At bottom its death is the same thing as its birth. Freedom is temporality, because its future is not germinally there in its present, nor its present in its past. The tenses are discontinuous, broken apart, for freedom's privilege is an ability to be what it has *never* been before (while still remaining what it is). As Bultmann never wearies of repeating, man is perpetually open.

Then again man may be defined as *Entscheidung* (decision), which is not to be understood in the active sense which the word has in objective parlance, as rule and mastery. While Bultmann does not admit that human acts are predetermined, decision to his mind is decision to submit to the 'moment'.[2] What is more, it is the 'moment' that sets me free by delivering me from my past and opening me to the future, as we shall see when discussing the matter of grace and freedom. For the other is not a mere *Was* but a *Dass* (a *Thou* irreducible to the *I* that I am), it faces me with a problem of recognition: shall I accept or reject its *Anspruch*? The decision is mine to make when it has summoned me to answer, tearing me from my present being and offering me a new opportunity to ec-sist. Obviously, then, Bultmann's *Entscheidung* does not at all mean a man's supposed ability to determine himself by the autonomous power of his will; it means a man's free response to (or free rejection of) the encounters that stand out as landmarks in his life. It is a species of otherness.

Man is also a *Wie* (literally, a 'how'), a way of being. Since man's freedom constitutes him as an *aptitude* for being, he can respond to the call of several othernesses: simultaneously or in turn he can be an

2. The word *Augenblick*, which he much uses, is to be taken in the Kierkegaardian sense. In the *moment*, the 'wholly other' (God, persons, events . . .) discloses itself to me as an unforeseeable summons.

artist, an economist, a political figure, or other things. He is really at home in the very different worlds of art, economics, politics. Whereas a stone is doomed to be forever a stone, a freedom can have several simultaneous or successive 'how's'. In other words, man is the being with manifold options, whereas substance is determined *ad unum*. Hence Bultmann also defines him as *capacity* (*Möglichkeit*) for ec-sistence. Being able to become a craftsman or a teacher, remain single or get married, be a Christian or a non-Christian, adopt this or that manner of life which I find in the past or the present, are for me so many capacities for existence.

Bultmann's *Wie* bears a certain relation to Sartre's *projet*, but only because a gulf yawns between them. In Sartre too man is this freedom able to be what it is not, while still remaining what it is. But Sartrean decision is above all a *self*-decision. It is not a *response* to the call that comes from a *Dass*. In Sartre man sets himself his *projet*. Is it not remarkable that the theme of vocation—of a call received *from else-where*—is entirely absent from *L'Etre et le Néant*? Existentialist though he be, Sartre remains a rationalist at heart. His paradoxical aim is to restore the omnipotence of reason by the device of a philosophy which of itself negates reason. With him *projet* and decision mean that values are built on man, who is built on nothing. With Bultmann they mean that man is *response to* something. He is initiative, certainly, but responsive initiative.

The *Wie* leads us on to *Verstehen* or *Verständnis* (understanding). This concept is quite basic to Bultmann's thought and anyone who disregards or wrongly judges it is ipso facto doomed to misconstrue Bultmann throughout his works. To keep ourselves right it will not suffice to give the term *Verstehen* the sense it has in rational thought whether the spontaneous rationalism of common sense or the rationalism that has been worked out by philosophers. We have adverted above to the imperialism of reason in its desire to know everything and grasp everything—in the possessive sense of the word, which is also the etymological one. (Compare *comprehend*, from *cum-prehendo*.)

Bultmann's grasp, on the other hand, means humility towards otherness (in the widest sense of otherness). For this 'understanding' is only the response to a previous *being-understood*. First I am 'grasped', laid hold on, by the other (which other may be God, a human person, a vocation, a particular situation). Man's initiative is not absolute; his action is never action pure and simple; it is always a reaction, a reaction to his origins, to his temperament, to his family and social surroundings, to the age he lives in—in short, a reaction to the world. Man is the being who is *first* encompassed [d'abord *investi*]. I did not choose either my birth (Chateaubriand speaks of the day when life was 'inflicted' on him), or my character, or my environment, or my era. No man lives just as it suits him to live. First of all we are what circumstances and fate make of us. No doubt we think, we make decisions, we act, but always in *response* to factors and problems thrust upon us from within and from without. So man is first a 'being-understood', a 'being-grasped', a 'being-encompassed'. 'In ec-sistentiell *Selbstverständnis*', therefore, 'the self understands what encounters it, the persons who encounter it, the world that encounters it, at the same time as it understands itself' (KM 2, p. 201).

Obviously my response to this being-understood gives me a new understanding of myself; I am changed by the encounter. Friendship, for example, opens me to a new *Verständnis* of myself; I receive a *Sein* (a being) that I did not have; henceforward I look on myself differently. By the same token a man who accepts Christ's call through faith has a *Selbstverständnis* (self-understanding) of himself and the world altogether different from the unbelieving *Selbstverständnis* that was his up to that point. The meaning of everything has changed; he has a new way of seeing, loving, acting, living.

To define man as we have done is to sketch his ontological or ec-sistential structure. Bultmann has often complained that his critics do not understand and observe the distinction between the ontological or ec-sistential, on the one hand, and the ontic or ec-sistentiell on the other. Now this philosophic vocabulary denotes a deep but simple reality, one moreover that is as old as mankind itself. Luther admits as a matter of course in *De servo arbitrio* that man, however sinful he may be, differs altogether from the vegetable and the animal by his *capacity* for receiving grace. Neither plant nor beast, he goes on, has this power, for 'it was not for geese that God made heaven'.[3] In these terms he acknowledges the ec-sistential; that is, the fact that man *can* become what he is not, that he is a *fallen* freedom which remains a fallen *freedom*, that consequently he has an ontological aptitude for being made altogether different from what he is.

Ec-sistential ontology conveys the formal structure of the human being, who does not 'exist' but ec-sists, who can be himself and also the other. Ec-sistentiell (ontic) ontology refers to his concrete determinations. Unlike a tree, I am a being capable of friendship (ec-sistential, ontological structure). The day that someone offers me his

---

3. *At si vim liberi arbitrii eam diceremus, qua homo aptus est rapi spiritu et imbui gratia Dei, ut qui sit creatus ad vitam vel mortem aeternam, recte diceretur; hanc enim, hoc est, aptitudinem, seu ut sophistae loquuntur, dispositivam qualitatem et passivam et nos confitemur, quam non arboribus neque bestiis inditam esse, quis est qui nesciat? Neque enim pro anseribus (ut dicitur) coelum creavit* (WA 18, p. 636).

friendship and I respond to him by my ec-sistence, I acquire a new concrete being—that of friendship (ec-sistentiell determination). Or again, as Luther says in his *Commentary on the Letter to the Romans*,[4] I am *Dei capax* (ec-sistential structure). When I effectively respond to the grace of God I pass from the unbelieving *Verständnis* to the believing *Verständnis*; I receive a new ontic structure, that of life in faith and love.

Man-freedom (ec-sistential, ontological structure) may have and in fact always does have several ec-sistentiell determinations (he may embrace this state of life or that, this or that profession, this or that religion, and so forth). The ec-sistentiell, then, is based on the ec-sistential as on its *sine qua non*. The ec-sistential is not met with in an 'indifferent', 'blank' state. My freedom is always a concrete freedom, it is always being ontically engaged. Man can never be found in his pure ec-sistential structure; he is forever 'embarked' on concrete choices, if only on the multitude of decisions (to eat, to work, to rest, to speak, and so forth) that make up his days.

The ec-sistential and the ec-sistentiell take for granted the primacy of otherness. It is the other (God, men, events, vocation . . .) that summons me to answer and provokes me to ec-sist freely towards it. The possibility of ec-sistence is the very negation of subjectivism, since ec-sistence consists in becoming what I am not (without ever losing my own identity, of course). I am at once old and new thanks to my freedom, which enjoys the privilege of being not an *attribute* of human nature but at once the same and the other. All that we have said so far shows that Bultmann's thought is the exact opposite of subjectivism. To define man as *Seinkönnen, Entscheidung, Geschichtlichkeit, Wie, Verstehen, Freiheit* (freedom) is to define him as capacity for responding to the other (to God, to human persons, to an infinite variety of concrete situations and encounters).

The reader will at once perceive that all this thought of Bultmann's is dominated by the idea of creation. God being the Creator and the world of men and things his creation, one's first duty is to respect the Creator and creation by not trying to manipulate them. Contrariwise if rationalism, be it spontaneous or scholarly, tends to suppress all otherness it is because it is ignorant of, or rejects, the biblical idea of creation.

We are now in a position to define the relation between the *Dass* and the *Was*, which we distinguished above. What makes the *Thou*

---

4. *Homo, qui Dei capax est et solo Deo saturari potest* (WA 56, p. 373). The whole passage (pp. 372 [27]–373 [22]) shows that it refers to the human ec-sistential, without regard to its concrete state of sin or grace.

altogether different from the *I* is not its *Was* (its essence), for on this plane all beings have something in common, either matter or spirit. The stuff of them is basically one despite all the range of differences in quantity and quality. Without forsaking myself I am able to know that the *nature* of this object here before me is to be a chair and not a table: because I am partly matter, there is a kinship between material objects and myself.

On a different plane I am able to know a priori what friendship is because I belong to the human race, which is capable of friendship. Between others and myself there is a connaturality which enables me to recognize what people are talking about when they speak to me of friendship. So far as the *Was* is concerned the world and man form a homogeneous unit. 'How should the eye see the sun if it were not itself of a solar nature?' (Goethe). In short, I can know essences because to know is to re-cognize. Thus man can speak of beings in general, universal, scientific, theoretical terms.

For example, before I love I can have an accurate *idea* of love; indeed an even more accurate idea (if I am well-read or am a trained psychologist) than a simple-minded person who draws his life-blood from a deep, concrete love. (In another area, a non-Marxist intellectual may have a more searching *theoretical knowledge* of Communism than a worker who *is* a Communist. Or again an unbelieving historian may have a more accurate *conception* of Christianity than a Christian peasant has.) On the day when I enter upon an actual friendship I learn nothing altogether new about its *Was* (its nature). Of course I may now have a fuller and richer knowledge of friendship; but the fact remains that beforehand I already had the *idea* of friendship, however embryonically.

'A man living without friendship, who consciously or unconsciously, avowedly or unavowedly, longs for friendship, knows what friendship is—and yet he does not know. If he finds a friend, what "more" does he know than he knew before in his *Selbstverständnis* without friendship? Can he now define the concept of friendship in a new and better way? No. Not the vital thing about it, at any rate, though now he *may* find that he can speak of friendship more readily and more amply. But the very fact that talk of friendship, which may arise from an actual friendship, can be *understood* by any friendless person shows that knowledge of friendship is also available to any friendless person. What do I know when I am engaged in an actual friendship? What "more" do I know? Nothing. Nothing about friendship. What "more" I know is this: I know my friend and I know myself in a new way, because my understanding (*Verstehen*) of the friend gives my concrete life in work and joy, in struggle and grief, a new quality; the *event* of

friendship makes the *events* of my life new, with a newness that holds
good only for me, that is visible to no eyes but mine, that becomes
visible only in the moment, visible in a way that is always new. So
though I may know beforehand in general terms what a friend is,
and know too *that* friendship must give me a new life, I never know
beforehand and in general terms what my friend is for me.'[5] In order
to know the nature of anything man has no need to forsake himself,
because he is all things.

Thus we end up with Bultmann's notion of *Vor-Verständnis* or precomprehension. We know that *Verstehen* or *Verständnis* means ec-
sistence towards otherness, which otherness then becomes my future.
But we have just seen that before *actually* loving the *Thou* (before it
becomes my *Verstehen,* my life) I have an *idea* of love: this is what
Bultmann calls the *Vor-Verständnis.* Suffice it to recall the saying of
Goethe just quoted. And Goethe is only stating the basis of knowledge,
which can consist in nothing else than an antecedent vital bond between
knower and known. Before I love I have a *Vorverständnis* (an idea) of
love. In the *act* of loving I have a *Verständnis* of it: my life is transformed, I receive a new being from the beloved. Man has a *Vorverständnis* of all things, because 'deep down' he is all things, including
God.

Karl Barth has taken umbrage at this last assertion, seeing in it an
attack on God's transcendence. Yet it is an indisputable fact that anyone
at all knows more or less what is being said to him if the word 'God' is
spoken in his presence, whereas a stone would be none the wiser. How
would this be possible if man had no *idea* of God? It is related that while
he was a prisoner, Sartre carried on very learned discussions of theology
with religious and priests. The mere fact that all the atheists in the
world can understand the language of a believer proves that man has
an idea of God. Not one of Bultmann's critics can or does get by
without what is meant by precomprehension (call it what you will).
All theologians acknowledge that the firmest unbeliever knows what
we are saying when we speak the word 'God' in his presence, whereas
a tree does not know. If an atheist historian can understand the doctrine
of justification in Paul's writing and distinguish it, say, from Johannine
theology, it is because he has a precomprehension of religious things.

Verständnis must not be taken in a narrow intellectualist sense. It is
need, tendency, desire . . . When Bultmann says that without revelation man has only a *Vorverständnis* or idea of God, he means that man
is a *lack* of God. To have only an idea of God is to be absence from

5. R. Bultmann,' Die Geschichtlichkeit des Daseins und der Glaube' in *Zeitschrift
für Theologie und Kirche* 11 (1930) 351.

God. The anguish of death, the burden and the riddle of fate, thirst for some salvation, longing for truth and love, homesickness for the eternal, a sense of the fragility and pointlessness of this world—this is what makes up the precomprehension of God. Because 'deep down', in the shape of absence and desire, man is all these things, all this plenitude, therefore he understands what is said to him when one speaks to him of God; he knows that God is everything of which he feels the want. If then man has a precomprehension of God, says Bultmann quoting Augustine, it is because '*Tu nos fecisti ad Te, Domine, et cor nostrum inquietum est, donec requiescat in Te.*'

Bultmann's critics charge him with anti-intellectualism in his insistence on the *Dass,* on event and act. The truth is that he has always sternly rejected what he himself calls the '*sacrificium intellectus*', and his whole career as a scholar is a living protest against it. It is precisely the idea of precomprehension which enables us to perceive why he is not anti-intellectualist although he is doggedly antisubstantialist and anti-rationalist. We have seen that the intellect is wholly incapable of reaching the other in its otherness: freedom alone can do that.

Whether it be my friend, or God, or the world as God's creation (and as the object of science and technology), I find them only by ec-sisting. Is my act therefore blind and irrational? By no means. When I love my friend actually and ec-sistentially, the conceptual knowledge I had of him before is in no way obscured: the *Vorverständnis* is integrated into the *Verständnis,* the *Was* into the *Dass.* In the experience of friendship I (normally) know my friend even better than I knew him before he was my friend. Bultmann himself says, in the foregoing quotation, that in the *Selbsverständnis* of friendship I can speak of friendship 'more readily and more amply'. It is the same with God. When he has become my *Verständnis* and rules all my life, the pre-comprehension I had of him in my unbelief, far from disappearing, widens and deepens. If the unbeliever can understand conceptually what is said to him about God as truth, life and salvation, a fortiori the believer can, who even on the plane of intellect normally has a sounder and richer knowledge of these things.

Vorverständnis in no way prejudices otherness, as Barth seems to fear it will. To have *Vorverständnis* of the other is to be the *lack* of that other. To say that man has only a *Vorverständnis* of the other is to stress the fact that he *is not* the other.[6] If man has the *idea* of God, that means that he is not *God,* he is an absence of God; just as we have seen that a man with the *idea* of love does not therefore have love, love as an

---

6. Bultmann often makes this point by saying that precomprehension is an unknowing knowledge (*ein nichtwissendes Wissen*).

event. So to admit that there is a precomprehension of God is not to say, Bultmann explains, 'that man bears within him an "organ" open to the divine, a sort of "higher self" attuned in advance to revelation, or some such thing. That is precisely what faith denies; it knows that without revelation man is wholly sinful' (GV 1, p. 297).

Evidently *Vorverständnis* has to do only with the essence (the *Was*) of a thing. The thing itself in its basic reality, in what makes it solitude, selfhood, irreducibility, uniqueness, transcendence, advent and event, altogether eludes *Vorverständnis*. Reason can win through to the *idea* of the other but not to the other *itself*. (The non-Communist intellectual with his splendid grasp of Marxism *is not* a Communist. The unbelieving historian who ably expounds the thought of Paul *is not* a Christian.) In order to reach the other, one must give oneself to it and agree to make it one's 'lord'. Because by definition it is *totally* different from me, the only way I can reach it is by forsaking myself to ec-sist towards it; which is only possible if I am that being which can become what it is not—that is to say, a freedom.

Otherness can also be defined as *Sinn* (meaning). The meaning of a thing is what most radically makes it itself. When the *I*, in virtue of its ec-sistential structure, ec-sists towards the *Thou*, it reveals the meaning of the other, or rather the meaning of the other is manifested to it and becomes its *Verstehen*. So there is nothing 'subjective' about meaning. People ordinarily make the mistake of first considering the thing in itself and then as it were grafting a meaning onto it; as if first there were the *est* and then the *significat*, whereas the meaning is the actual thing.

If my friend is really my friend, if his friendship is not a figment of my imagination, it is because he embodies the meaning of friendship, because he *is* that meaning, which constitutes him in his transcendence as a friend. He is not my friend in virtue of his psycho-logical being, his cast of mind, his character, the work he does—all those things he is for everybody. Everything objective about him is universal. He is my friend because he has a *significance* for me that he has for no one else and that constitutes him in his being, his selfhood, his transcendence for me. Here is the source of his uniqueness. Thus meaning is far more 'real' than objective fact, which as an abstraction has no true being. True being is the meaning of objective fact. Meaning is the other as other, which it conveys as sheer event, sheer 'grace'.

In view of all that has gone before, it can now be stated that *faith* is the ec-sistential structure of man—man, the being who we know is always ahead of himself, who is not his future in germ. No doubt he has a *Vorverständnis* of his future, he knows otherness as a *Was*, he knows *what* friendship is, what God is, and so on, because in a sense he is all things. But the *idea* of friendship is by no means *friendship* and the *idea* of God is by no means *God*. Therefore if man encounters the other as a *Dass* it can only be by a 'leap', the leap of freedom. His reaching the other is an act of ec-sistence, that is, of faith. In this sense Kierkegaard says: 'To be is to believe.'

Man is man (the being whose future is a true future because it is no longer his past except by the mode of not being that past) only when he is act. Since the other as other has no kinship with me insofar as I am myself a *Dass,* to reach it I have nothing to go on—no sign, no proof, no safety, no certitude. My ec-sistence towards it is an absolute act in which I am pure *Entscheidung,* because no grounds will excuse my freedom from making a 'leap'. Of course my act is not blind, I must have the soundest possible reasons for it, worked out as well as possible; but they can never be a footbridge taking me to the other without any need for decision. As a *Dass* the other can only be an object of faith and can only be reached by a being whose structure is faith. That is why Paul says that faith and hope subsist together with love in eternal life (1 Cor 13:13). Otherwise man would no longer be a freedom but a thing.[7]

In the end we must define otherness as *Anrede* or *Appell* (address, summons). By definition, the other is one whom I cannot control. To reach him, therefore, I must forsake my past and everything I am to become what I am not. But how shall I do this, how will the idea of doing it ever enter my head if the *Thou* does not first *address* itself to me? How shall I be roused from my in-sistence and desire to stand forth from myself unless I am first summoned by the other? 'You would not seek me had you not already found me.' If the *Thou,* then, is really a *Thou,* that can only be because it is a being which calls me in question; otherwise it would be no different from myself.

If otherness were not essentially a summons, it would only be a kind of identity with myself. In other words the *Thou* is necessarily an imperative, not an indicative. Here is a person about whom I know everything, objectively speaking: his past, his character, his ways, and the rest. I may know him till doomsday in this fashion, as a datum; but as long as I stick there, all he will have for me is the sham otherness of an object. Only on the day when he offers me his friendship—that is, when he becomes a living summons that compels me to answer

---

7. It is significant that Catholic exegesis and theology, which imply a substantialist view of God and man, cannot admit this interpretation of 1 Cor 13:13, though it is the only one consistent with the grammar and with Paul's thought. Compare Fr Allo's commentary on this passage (E.-B. Allo, *Première Epître aux Corinthiens* [1935], pp. 349–51) with those of H. Lietzmann (*An die Korinther I-II* [1949], p. 66) and Bultmann (CP, p. 152).

yes or no—will he be a real *Thou*. Or again I learn that in the past my father made a staggering sacrifice for me, about which he has never breathed a word. I can take up one of two attitudes: either consider this sacrifice objectively, as an interesting phenomenon of fatherly love, or else be so 'touched' by it that my relations with my father now take an entirely different course. In the latter case his sacrifice is an *Anrede*, because it transforms my life, and that is its real being for me.

Now let us define one last crucial category: *eschatology*. Eschatology is the next world as contrasted with this one, eternity as opposed to time, that which is wholly other than the world and man—in a word, God himself and the things of God. But eschatology is not really such unless it is thought of on the plane of 'historicity'. It does not mean some transcendence that is only a supernature or a superhistory, a higher kind of *Was*.

The eschatological God is not the invisible spiritual being that the Greeks talked of, nor the God of classical Christian theology, nor yet the God of contemporary theology, which defines otherness in terms of the suprahistorical, as we shall see. He must be thought of as the *Thou* which we have described. He is the Wholly Other who is such only because he is our *Selbstverständnis*—that is, our Lord. He is the supreme *Dass*, over which man has no control; that which man's eye cannot see, his ear cannot hear, his thought cannot understand, his heart cannot love, his acts cannot embrace, which can be reached only by faith. Eschatology conveys the most absolute otherness, that of God, who is constituted not by his *in se* but by his lordship.

Let us conclude this examination of 'objectivity'. As Bultmann never wearies of repeating, the only true otherness is that which is an understanding of oneself. Whereupon his adversaries accuse him of subjectivism. To their mind the *Thou* is only the *Thou* insofar as it exists in itself *before* it becomes my *Sichverstehen* (self-understanding). Victims as they are of what we may henceforth call the 'philosophy of natural man', they do not perceive that for me to recognize the other and to allow it to determine my being are one and the same thing.

The other is only *itself*, for me, when it changes me. So long as it does not do so, by becoming my *Wie*, its relation to me is one of identity. In itself, to be sure, it is *extra me*; but the objective relation in which we stand to each other, because of the fact that it does not change me, does away with the *extra me* so far as I am concerned. In its objectivity the other is only an extension of myself. Until it determines me, it is for me only a sham otherness, because it forms part of my world, never oversteps the frontiers of my world. It will only be itself for me on the day when it compels me to exile myself from myself, on the day when it transforms me and thereby ceases to be the phantom that it must be for me so long as I have no living bond with it. Only when it loses all objectivity does it exist, for me, as transcendence.

To put the matter another way, the other does not make me other because it is other—it is other because it makes me other. For me, the only being which can have otherness is the being that alters me, and insofar as it does alter me; failing which, my relations with it are only relations of myself with myself.

Consider the dialectic of sin and grace. Grace is otherness because it has nothing in common with sin, and if it has nothing in common with sin that is because it makes man a new creature. If its essence did not consist in changing man, it would be of the same nature as man and therefore would not be other at all. What happens does not indicate that grace is at bottom a thing *in se,* the salvific character being merely one of its attributes; for if that were so, then grace in its fundamental nature would be an object and I could manipulate it as I manipulate any object. The only real *Thou* is the one that *saves* the *I.* That is why the truly 'objective' Christ is not Christ *in se* but the Christ of the *beneficia:* 'Christum cognoscere, hoc est: beneficia ejus cognoscere, non ejus naturas et modos incarnationis intueri' (Melanchthon).

Most theologians, including Karl Barth (RB, pp. 22–3), think that first there is the objective Christ, who then becomes our Saviour. But this objective Christ is a mere shadow, entirely the prisoner of man. *Christ does not make me wholly other because he is the Wholly Other: he is the Wholly Other because he makes me wholly other.* So long as he does not change me, the relation between us is objective and he is in fact a mere prolongation of myself. Only by his saving relation with me does he reveal himself to be independent of me, to be my lord. He cannot be the Lord *until* he is the Saviour, or the Creator, or the Friend, or the Enemy, or the Judge—in a word, until he stands in a relation with me which makes me dependent on him.

Accordingly the other is only other when it is my *Selbstverständnis.* We know that *Verstehen* in Bultmann is not ordinary understanding but the response to a previous being-understood. To understand is to exile oneself from oneself so as to receive an absolute future; it is to enter otherness in such a way that otherness becomes my life, but a life which I was not before and which, though it is indeed *my* life, is such only as the different life of the other. Far from subjectifying the other, *Sichverstehen* allows it to exist in all its transcendence by submitting to it—nay, by *being* that submission. Doubtless Bultmann's adversaries go astray because they envisage the understanding of oneself as an appropriation of the other. Whereas the fact that the *Dass* becomes my *Sichverstehen* does not mean at all that I subjectify it; quite the contrary,

I ec-sist towards it, so that the understanding of myself which follows upon this ec-sisting is a newness—the very newness of the other. I am created by it.

The believer does not appropriate Christ, Christ makes of him a 'new creature' (2 Cor 5:17). When God becomes man's *Sichverstehen*, man does not humanize God but God divinizes man. In other words: *Christ does not transform believers because he is the Christ, he is the Christ because he transforms believers.* He is the Lord—that is, himself—insofar as we depend on him. The power to save us is not one of his attributes, it is his very being. Only insofar as he is the Saviour is he, for us men, the Wholly Other (see JCM, pp. 73–7)⁸.

---

8. In this chapter we have only considered the *I* in a *favourable* response to the summons of the *Thou*. But the same principles hold good when the *I* turns back on itself, rejecting the future which is offered to it. For a relation of antagonism is still a relation. *Not* to make the other my *Sichverstehen* is still to make it my *Sichverstehen*. My contempt for it determines my being no less than my admiration for it, my ingratitude no less than my gratitude, my hatred no less than my love. 'Even if I do not open myself to love, it produces some sort of ec-sistentiell reaction. Ignorance, shutting oneself in, hatred are also ec-sistentiell reactions. In every case I am affected by the encounter' (KM 2, p. 199).

CHAPTER TWO

The Mind of the 'Natural Man'

I

THE GREEK MIND

All Bultmann's writing, one might almost say his every sentence, is explicitly or implicitly a dialogue with the Greeks. For the Greek is the epitome of the 'natural man'. Greek philosophy represents the triumph of reason and immanence, despite all the conflicts inherent in that immanence (notably the conflict between form and matter) and all the efforts of the Greeks to discern the 'other'. Nevertheless it is true that before the era of the Sophists they had an idea of freedom which exhibits an unquestionable awareness of transcendence.

This theory took shape in the political sphere. In the beginning, men were strangers to the art of politics. Zeus presented them with it by sending them Hermes, the bearer of reverence and right (αἰδώς and δίκη), so that they received political 'virtue'—that is, justice (δικαιοσύνη) and moderation (σωφροσύνη). Thus the City was born.

Henceforth the citizens form a community where the appetites of the individual are restrained by submission to right. The City is based on right (δίκη) and law (νόμος). Hesiod (about 700 BC) and Solon (about 650 to 560) are the harbingers of δίκη:

> Evil doings bring endless desolation upon the City.
> But reverence for the laws (εὐνομίη) begets wholesome deeds,
>   thwarts and strangles those who live lawlessly.
> It tempers pride, allaying covetous desire . . .
> Only on law can man base his well-being and raise a lasting edifice.
> —Solon

By submitting to law the citizens secure their freedom (ἐλευθερία), which is not freedom for each one to gratify his desires but rather freedom for each to obey the behests of law. Thus it is not a matter of individualist freedom but of submitting to a transcendence. Herodotus says of the Spartans in particular: 'They are indeed free, but not free in all things, for they have a master over them: the law. It they fear far more than your people [the subjects of Xerxes] fear you.' Bultmann

22

observes that here, at this very early date, we already find the profound truth which Goethe perceived: that 'law alone can give us liberty' (GV 2, p. 275). The Greeks arrived at the real meaning of freedom, which is freeing oneself from oneself, for the other. And it is in thus giving himself to the other that the individual conquers his real being and his real humanity. The Greeks, then, had a certain experience of man as 'historicity'.

But this was only within the narrow context of the City: man was nothing more than a citizen. Now the City cannot be absolute transcendence, even if it is founded on a deity; for the City's deity is only the hypostatized will of the community of free men. If the City and its laws were regarded as absolutes, the fact remains that they were given their concrete form only by the acts and decisions of the citizenry. Thus there was a danger that they would gradually lose their sacred character, becoming subordinated to the designs of men, their appetites and their interests.

In fact this is what happened. Political life grew profane. Selfishness, ambition and greed were no longer held in check by the supreme authority of the law. The great tragic writers saw the danger and sternly denounced it. They tried to restore the sway of reverence and its sister, fear, the awfulness (το δεινόν) of unwritten law[1] and of the deity; but to no avail. The rationalism of the Sophists carried the day, destroying belief in any norm antecedent to or higher than man. They held that laws do not oblige by nature (φύσει) but by convention: laws are not sacred, they are only useful (Protagoras, Hippias, Antiphon). The tyrant is not subject to them (Callicles and Thrasymachus). Thus the City is made to serve the ends of private life. And in due course man, as the celebrated phrase has it, becomes the measure of all things. Aristophanes' *Clouds* is an extreme caricature of the Sophists, but calls attention to the terrible danger which their attitude represents—that of nihilism.

Socrates too speaks of the useful (συμφέρον), but he seeks what is *truly* useful, not what happens to seem so to the individual. True utility can only be what serves the City; that is, an authority which stands above the subjectivity of the individual and controls it; in other words, the law. This holds good even if in a particular case the law is ill-made or ill-applied. Thus Socrates accepts the mistaken verdict condemning him to death and will not avail himself of a possible

1. When Creon is about to make his will the law of the City, Antigone says to him: 'I did not think your edict strong enough for you, a mortal, to set aside with it divine decrees unwritten and immutable. They are not of today or yesterday: they are eternal; no man knows from what remote antiquity they come to us.'

reprieve. By his death he proves that he acknowledges the authority of
law. But are we dealing here with a real transcendence? No, because
the law exists within man, within the *logos*[2] in which he shares and
which constitutes him. Abandoning the philosophy of nature, which he
studied under Anaxagoras, Socrates takes refuge in the *logoi*: 'I thought
it incumbent on me', he says, 'to take refuge with the *logoi,* trying to
search out in them the reality of what is.'

Plato sets transcendence in the world of Ideas. But man shares in this
world through *logoi,* which grasp the Ideas. Thus the *logos* is the stuff
of which gods, men and things at large are made, all forming a
harmonious, gradated whole: the cosmos (κόσμος means order and
harmony). 'Heaven and earth, gods and men and all things are bound
together by communion, friendship, harmony, moderation and
justice. For this reason they [the wise] call the universe the order of
things (κόσμος), not the disorder or irregularity. . . You have surely
forgotten that mathematical relationships are all-powerful among gods
and men alike.' Thus Socrates addresses Callicles (*Gorg.,* 507e–508a),
revealing to us the fundamental nature of the Greek view of things.
There is no real dualism in that view.

The universe of the Greeks is a rational universe. The *logos* permeates
it from top to bottom. In the cosmos, lower things always participate
to some degree in form. No doubt, from thinker to thinker and age to
age, the relations between matter and form are conceived of in quite
a variety of ways. The point is to observe that at the utmost the
separation never destroys a certain kinship between them (the Idea
being attracted to lower things and lower things imitating the higher);
so that the cosmos (gods and men) is always homogeneous at heart.

Where does Greek philosophy come from? Is there, so to say, a
pattern for it? There is: the pattern is the work (ἔργον) of 'art' (τέχνη).
A work of art is a thing made by man (whether it be a house, a ship,
or what we call today a work of art strictly speaking: a statue or the
like). It is an εἶδος produced in a matter. We know—the point is
worth attending to—that the word ὕλη originally meant wood. The
Greeks envisaged the world of Ideas as something like the form of a
work of art. Similarly they envisaged the lower, indeterminate world
of the ὕλη as something like the matter of a work of art. Moreover
they envisaged concrete beings (man, animals, and so on) in terms of
a work of art, as composed of matter and form. The totality of them
makes up the cosmos. Thus the universe is even called a work of art;
for nothing is such unless it be κόσμιος (harmonious). Greek philosophy,

2. Such is the wealth of its connotations that the word *logos* defies translation. It
means at once utterance, thought, reason, mind.

then, is 'technical' and humanist in origin. Greece is the real native country of humanism.

What of man's position in the cosmos? As an εἶδος he is firmly put into his niche in the hierarchy of essences, where he stands midway between the higher beings and the lower. His εἶδος is defined as καλὸν κἀγαθόν. Only when he has embodied this idea and has been fitted into the objective system of essences will he have found his own country and his security, reached his goal and his perfection, which is to be a member of the cosmos. He is not that from the outset, because he is also involved in the lower world of matter. Therefore he must make himself, as the artist or the artisan produces in 'wood' the ideal that is in his mind. He has to 'form' himself.

He will succeed thanks to ἀρετή (virtue), which is simply the artisan's (or artist's) knack of embodying his ideal. Plato says that three virtues are necessary in order to fashion the human εἶδος of the καλὸν κἀγαθόν: wisdom (σοφία), valour (ἀνδρεία), and moderation (σωφροσύνη), which are summed up in justice (δικαιοσύνη). In proportion as he approaches to his εἶδος, set in its own place in the hierarchy of Ideas, a man becomes 'cosmic'—that is, harmonious (κόσμιος)—well balanced (εὐσκήμων), well proportioned (εὔρυθμος), well adjusted (εὐάρμοστος), well tempered (ἔμμετρος). The ideal is to become 'cosmified' (διακοσμεῖν). It will be noted that all this moral terminology is borrowed from the 'technical' sphere. What we have said of man applies *mutatis mutandis* to other beings: every concrete being (ὄν) embodies a set εἶδος.

We are now able to ask, and in a general way answer, the question that concerns us here: is there any room in the Greek mind for the category of the 'other'? We have seen to what extent there was before the advent of the Sophists. How do matters stand after the Sophists? The Ideas are not each a *Dass,* they are all participations in the *logos.* There is a basic kinship among all forms—that of the *logos.* In Plato it derives from the Good, which therefore lies 'beyond being' but not beyond thought. It is, so to speak, the sum of the intelligible world and as such is the object of direct intellectual intuition (νόησις).

Hence it comes about that with the Greeks 'God is always regarded in the end as part of the world or as the world *simpliciter,* even when he is made that source and formal principle of the world which subsists beyond the world of phenomena. For even in this case God and the world form a unity which the mind can grasp: it is precisely in the idea of God that the meaning of the world becomes clear. That is why the Greek mind tends towards pantheism' (JS, p. 115).

Nor can one say that concrete beings, τὰ ὄντα, are really distinct from the εἶδος which they must embody. They are already the εἶδος *in potentia*. At first sight the Idea of man seems to be a true future, since the individual is set the task of achieving it. But in fact it is nothing of the sort, for the individual has an ἀνάμνησις of the εἶδος. He directs a kind of gaze at the essence, not only seeing it in but reducing it to the ἰδεῖν. The essence is defined as what is conceived by and for the mind, exactly as in a work of art the εἶδος which a man embodies in matter is conceived by and for him. As his own artisan, the individual likewise has an ἀνάμνησις of the human εἶδος. One cannot dwell too much on the 'technical' origin of Greek philosophy, because it clearly shows why the Greeks never got beyond the technical sphere and therefore never knew a true future.

This is what Bultmann means by saying that with them the quest for truth is the quest *nach der unverhüllten Aufgedecktheit des Seienden in seiner gegliederten Ganzheit* ('for a full disclosure of things in their articulated totality'; GV 2, pp. 110–11): in Greek eyes the 'other' is not something of an altogether different nature. Its meaning is revealed a priori because being is made of the same stuff as the human mind. It is made for man, who therefore need not open himself to what he can in no way control. As one might say, the whole game has already been played. In biblical thought, on the other hand, the quest for truth is a quest *nach dem Sinn des begegnenden Augenblicks* ('for the meaning of the moment that encounters us'; *ibid.*, p. 111); which means that what encounters me is a *Dass* really different from myself. I must therefore forsake myself if I wish to reach it. Truth is not already possessed in germ. With the Greeks, man already has truth in germ, *in potentia*. He implicitly controls it, before he explicitly knows it, in virtue of the basic homogeneity of reason and being. So far as the Bible is concerned, man *receives* truth. That is why the biblical man listens whereas the Greek looks. The dictum of Heraclitus that 'the eyes are better witnesses than the ears' states the pith and marrow of Greek thought.

It will now be realized that the Greeks have no acquaintance with history properly speaking. Becoming (γένεσις) is indeed familiar to them. But they look on it with contempt. The world of generation and corruption is the world of what does not really exist (μή ὄν). Stars are the perfect type of being because of their incorruptibility and their undeviating courses. But above all, when the Greeks *are* forced to recognize evolution there is no question of 'history', made up of a true past and a true future. Every being must embody an *eidos* that is rigidly defined and firmly set in the hierarchy of Ideas. But the *eidos,* as we have seen, is not really transcendent. Thus from the outset man is already, in some sense, the form that he must embody. He bears it within him as an ideal. 'Become what you are'—that is the basic maxim of Greek ethics. Accordingly the future is not a true future, it is only a broadened and consummated present. (Likewise in a work of art the form has no true future, because the artist conceives it before making an ἔργον by τέχνη.)

Finally, if the mind became the sovereign power in the human community—and that it shall do so is the aim of Greek ethics—then history would cease. We would have reached the end of those variations (μεταβολαί) which make up the sphere of γένεσις. It is clear why the Greek historians take no interest in evolution for its own sake. Thus Thucydides seeks out the stable factors in history; the eternal, which as such can serve as an example to future generations. He tries to draw the invariable from the variable—the invariable being, to his mind, the appetite for power, ambition. Concrete, unique, individual history that will never be seen twice, does not matter.

The Stoics bring Greek rationalism to its acme. They suppress all 'dualism' of matter and form. In Plato the two 'regions' coexisted; in Aristotle they were joined together; here they are merged. Heaven is equated with earth, λόγος with φύσις—the vital force in nature. The *logos* is matter (a σῶμα) of ethereal consistency, an ether (αἰθήρ), a breath diffused through all things (πνεῦμα διῆκων διὰ πάντων). 'All that exists forms one whole because a breath pervades it all, whereby the universe is sustained and coheres and forms an organic unity' (Chrysippus). The whole universe is a living thing (ζῷον ἔμψυκον). It is the deity itself, totally immanent in nature, of which it is the common law (κοινὸς νόμος φύσεως) and the providence (πρόνοια).

The human being too is immanent in the whole. His *logos* is determined by the universal *logos*. The human *logos* is also the universal *logos*. Therefore man must live at one with nature (ὁμολογουμένος τῇ φύσει). But this oneness is an imperative, not a datum. The *logos* presents itself as a demand: man must affirm the universal *logos* by endorsement (συγκατάθεσις). It is in this that the celebrated freedom (ἐλευθερία) of the Stoics consists. By it a man must be able to bear with equanimity whatever may happen to him: health or sickness, wealth or poverty, position and honours or exile and disgrace . . . He must approve the divine law of the universe and the providence which nothing can elude. By this endorsement he sets himself free of all things, which become indifferent (ἀδιάφορα) and alien (ἀλλότρια) to him. Above all he must emancipate himself from the passions (πάθη), which are bent on chaining him to 'alien things'.

'You must forsake all things, all bodies and possessions, your good name, your books, society, public life, your private life. For wherever your inclination draws you, there you have become a slave, an inferior, you are chained, walled-in; in short, you depend altogether on someone else' (Epictetus).

Man can and must control his passions. The hallmark of Stoicism is this conviction that the most intimate thing in man is the mind and that when a man concentrates on the mind he is free of all the world:

> Would you tempt the wise man with gold?
> He will despise it.
> What are the joys of love or private life to him?
> What does he care for glory or disgrace?
> What for praise? What is death to him?
> He can worst them all.
>
> —Epictetus

If a man cannot change the outside world, the world at least cannot harm him, controlling it as he does by his inward aloofness.

Is Stoic freedom that (Christian) freedom which we have described in the foregoing chapter, freedom *for* the other? Is the Stoic wise man that man who ceases to be what he is so as to become reception of the other? No. Stoic freedom is not openness to the other but independence of it. Thanks to that freedom the Stoic controls his destiny. He is his own master. He is αὐτάρκεια. On the contrary the man who is 'historicity' *receives* his freedom from concrete encounters: every encounter is a sign and a summons of the other, a demand that snatches me from my αὐτάρκεια. The Stoic closes his door to encounters and lives in the timelessness of the *logos,* he dwells on the perpetual present of reason, he lives in the category of the identical, he has neither true past nor true future.

The Christian does not control his own fate, because grace is every moment detaching him from what he is. Instead of holding aloof with Stoic ἐλευθερία from what happens to him, he must respond to the 'moment'. Stoic freedom is an attribute which the wise man acquires in proportion as he becomes *logos*. Freedom for the Christian is not a state but an act. Christian freedom consists in being freed from oneself by and for the other; Stoic freedom consists in being freed from the other by and for oneself.

'The Stoic concept of freedom transfers to the human person what is true of reason itself—the fact that rational thought obeys its own law and is basically independent of events in nature and history. The Stoic is able to make this transference because for him reason is the true essence of man. And so, for him, freedom is the attribute of a man who concentrates on his authentic being—his reason—and regards as alien (ἀλλότρια) whatever may happen to him from without. The Christian concept of freedom affirms that freedom, as freedom of the person, is not an attribute but must be the event of every moment. Freedom becomes possible only in encounter, which by demanding a decision offers freedom. That is why the problem of freedom begins for Christian thought at the point where it ends for Stoic thought. To the Stoic philosopher's way of thinking it is indisputable that man is free whenever his thought obeys the law of reason; whereas the Christian questions man's control over himself in his decisions' (GV 2, p. 279).

Obviously, Greek thought is one of the perfect forms of rationalism. It always more or less merges the category of the other in the category of the same. Because the Greeks did not attain to the idea of creation they were not able to recognize otherness in all its strength and fullness. The hallmark of natural man is that he refuses to let God control him, either directly or through creation. In the eyes of Christian faith, the only sin is the sin of aseity; and Greek rationalism is one of the forms of aseity. The *logos* being the stuff of which the cosmos (heaven and earth, gods and men, higher beings and lesser beings) is made, or the πνεῦμα διῆκων διὰ πάντων (for in the last analysis any Stoic formula applies to all Greek thought), there can be no such thing as real transcendence.[3]

II

THE MODERN MIND

Bultmann carries on dialogue not only with Greek thought but also with modern philosophy. Here we can only indicate the burden of the dialogue. If the Greeks proved unequal to working out a philosophy of otherness, how much better have the moderns done? It is a fact that modern freedom has taken shape by a progressive killing-off of transcendence. The seventeenth and eighteenth centuries were marked by the conquest of individual freedom as against the authority of religious tradition, embodied in the Christian churches; whereby men did not lapse into subjectivism or nihilism but set up the authority of reason. Reason takes the place of revealed religion. Though immanent in man, it rules him as a divine law. If reason is a Deus *in nobis*, it is also a *Deus* in nobis.

3. We shall see presently (ch. 14) how from another point of view Greek humanism can and must be one of Christianity's soundest allies in the fight against modern subjectivism and nihilism, on the one hand, and on the other hand against the dangers involved in the advent of technology.

In the eyes of Idealism, man is still mind but he is also will. We all know how Kant exalted the categorical imperative. He holds that for lack of an *intellectus archetypus* we have no intuition of intelligible things. But practical reason enables us to reach the absolute. Moral life is a struggle against instinct, desire, inclination, appetite (all things that Kant calls *Triebe*), and against *Sinnlichkeit*, which is opposed to duty.

Kant turns original sin into what he calls 'rooted evil'. He says there is in man a bent towards evil which defies explanation but remains a fact. Therefore human life is a conflict between mind (*Geist*) and everything opposed to it (*Triebe und Sinnlichkeit*). Schiller says: 'Good and right are condemned to an endless battle. The enemy will never be conquered.' While retaining the Greek concept of man as mind, Idealism has clearly been influenced by the Christian tradition. 'Man's will is now recognized as an essential part of human nature' (HE, p. 103). Thus 'historicity' begins to be perceived. Nevertheless the absolute is not the wholly other.

Kantian morality, of course, accuses the essentialist moralities of destroying the freedom of the will—by setting man outward goals to attain. Freedom, to Kant's mind, is an absolute beginning in oneself: it is autonomy and autarchy. Free will can will only itself; it must be absolute and infinite. Thus Kant avoids heteronomy by seeing within the will the source of those determinations which were formerly thought to come from outside it. It is not God the wholly other who gives man freedom: the categorical imperative is the essence of the rational will. So there is no true future, which future can only be *received* from without. Man as envisaged by idealism can become more and more of a man by means of his will. His God is a *Deus in nobis*:

> *Nehmt die Gottheit auf in eurem Willen,*
> *Und sie steigt von ihrem Weltenthron.*
> > —Schiller

Bultmann has often demonstrated how liberal theology derives from this Idealist school of thought. It reduces revelation to a few noble religious and moral ideas, to a spiritualist ethic culminating in the great prophets of the Old Testament and in Jesus. Jesus is the supreme manifestation of divine values, the apex and paragon of life according to the spirit. Truth, justice and love most perfectly reveal God and themselves in certain mighty 'religious personalities', the greatest of whom is Jesus. Contact with him makes us better men, inflaming our faith and generosity. Our life can only achieve its fullness if we plunge into the divine stream of which he is the source. Our task is to make his inward experience our own and become capable of the same spiritual heroism and self-sacrifice by following in his footsteps. His religious consciousness rouses and nourishes our own.

Ever since the 1920s Bultmann, together with Barth and Gogarten in particular, has reacted against liberalism by pointing out that Christianity is neither an ethic nor a mysticism. In liberalism all man really discovers is himself, because the God he experiences is not the Wholly Other but a mere transposition of what is best in man: spirit, truth, love . . . Liberals have always been fond of the saying in John 4:24 that 'God is spirit' but they miss its real meaning, thinking as they do that by his spirit man is akin to God. So encounter with Jesus is only a salutary shock which rouses a man's spiritual energies from their lethargy and heightens them to the utmost. Contact with the gospel does not make a man what he was not in any sense before; it only brings out what he already is in germ. Jesus incarnates the spiritual ideal that is already present in every human being, and therefore revelation has only a *pedagogical* significance: it helps man to become the spirit he already is, helps him turn aside from evil and sin to achieve the purity and love for God and neighbour of which Jesus is the supreme example and inspiration.

Liberalism has never perceived that God is not a *Was* (however spiritual you care to make it) but a *Dass*. No doubt God is spirit and love; but these things must not be taken, as liberalism takes them, for general timeless truths the possession of which somehow gives me possession of God. We have seen that the idea (*Vorverständnis*) of love is not love. It is not because I am spirit and God is also spirit that I experience *God*, even supposing I am prompted by the 'religious personality' of Jesus, any more than I can meet a man because we both share the same human nature; for that common nature only enables me to reach the other's *Was* and not the other as other. Of themselves spiritual life and mystical union cannot lead a man to God. God is a *Dass* which as such has *nothing* in common with man; so that when man does in fact encounter God, it is as sheer grace.

To say that God is truth and love and to experience truth and love in myself is no proof at all that I have encountered God. Of course it may be that I have indeed encountered him, but my spiritual experience of truth and love is no evidence of the encounter, much less the foundation of it. The error of liberalism is basing the encounter between God and man on an underlying kinship of spiritual essence which it confuses with faith. Here we see how liberalism derives from the Greek tradition and from idealism. The God of liberalism too is a *Deus in nobis*.

CHAPTER THREE

The Biblical Mind

According to the Old Testament, man is composed of a flesh and a soul that are not antagonistic as in classical dualism, where the soul is an essence which has come from a higher world and been imprisoned in a material body. Here, on the contrary, the soul is the force animating the flesh. The *I* can be called either soul or flesh, they being not true principles but two modes in which the person exists. For the soul is not a rational mind, it is essentially will. Man's true 'nature' is the will, which may be good *or* bad.

The Old Testament knows nothing of the Greek opposition between matter and spirit. Neither, consequently, has it any notion of *eidos*, of humanity as the ideal that each individual must embody by becoming 'well formed', 'harmonious', 'well proportioned', 'well articulated', and so forth. Man finds his true being not in his adaptation to a form but in his concrete history, in the decisions he takes with regard to events. He is relation to the God who comes ever and again in the 'moment', who therefore is not an eternal spirit or a rational law which gives the cosmos a harmonious form perceptible by the mind, but the Wholly Other whose will is never known in advance because he encounters his creature in history. His transcendence is not that of reason but that of freedom.

Man, therefore, is just the opposite of a substance: he is a relation of obedience to this God; he is altered by each encounter he has with God, because each one demands of him a highly personal decision. His past is *his* past because it is the result of an experience of God which he alone has had and no 'fellow' of his has had (no man *has* a fellow, in the sense of his like). His future is truly *his* future; it is not the *eidos* common to all but a 'vocation': man's being is to be constantly called by God, each time in a new way. The encounter between God-who-is-will and man-who-is-will is in every case a singular thing. This keen sense of the 'unique' appears in certain of the psalms, in Job, and in Jeremiah.

Hence moral language expresses itself in what might be called the 'categories of encounter'. Man must be 'upright', 'faithful', 'true', 'without reproach'. His essential duty is to love God and his neighbour. Love in the biblical sense is above all an encounter—that is, a listening to and welcoming of the other. For this reason community too is understood in 'historical' terms.

The Greeks thought of it in terms of mutual education. There is an *eidos* common to all, and each must help the other to attain it by a reciprocal emulation (ἀγών) and by dialectic converse (διαλέγεσθαι), the best instrument for training the mind and gradually embodying the human ideal. In scripture, the community is constituted by love which looks on the other as a man's 'neighbour'. It follows from the gift that a man makes of himself to the rest, in whom he sees the very demand of God. Accordingly it is a community of those who are 'called', 'elect'; which explains why the basic commandments are ones without meaning except on the plane of the *I* and the *Thou*. It also explains why the Ten Commandments are put in essentially negative form: thou shalt not do this or that. What has to be done positively, only encounter with the other will show: if one is heedful enough of one's neighbour one will discover in the concrete case how to love him as oneself.

But it is especially the New Testament that discloses 'historicity' to us. Throughout his book *Jesus*, Bultmann shows how Jesus's conception of the *I* and the *Thou* is diametrically opposed to that of the Greeks and of all forms of humanism. The *I* is not a nature but a will which draws its being from a *Thou*. Man is a relation of obedience and love to God. He is ec-sistence by the grace of the other (God and neighbour) which summons him to forsake his past and receive a new being. 'In very truth only the *Anspruch* [of the *Thou*] brings man into existence as the *I*' (JS, p. 174). But since we cannot say all there is to say and do not wish to content ourselves with generalities, let us consider in some detail how Bultmann discovered the category of 'historicity' in Paul. Analysis of certain anthropolgical concepts in Pauline theology establishes that man is not a free, thinking substance but an 'historical', temporal being. The first of these concepts is that of σῶμα.

(1) Σῶμα

In accepted usage the body means the material element in man, the other element being the soul. For the Greeks the body is 'matter' and the soul is 'form'. Pauline anthropology is normally set forth according to this scheme, which sometimes includes three elements (body, soul and spirit). Now if Paul makes room for this commonplace notion, we also find in his writing another one, quite his own, which treats the σῶμα as the ec-sistential structure of man, who can therefore receive various ontic determinations, above all those of sin and grace. Σῶμα, then, means an aptitude for being.

(*a*) In a certain number of texts the σῶμα is not something belonging

extrinsically to man, as if he only *had* a σῶμα. No, he *is* the σῶμα. Such
a text is 1 Cor 13:13 ('If I deliver my σῶμα to be burned'); 9:27 ('I
pommel my σῶμα and subdue it'); 7:4 ('The wife does not rule over
her own σῶμα'). It will be seen that σῶμα must be rendered by the
personal pronoun: I deliver *myself*, I pommel *myself*, and so forth.
We find the same thing again in Phil 1:20 ('Whether by life or by
death, Christ will be honoured in my σῶμα [=in me]'); in Rom 12:1
('I appeal to you therefore to present your σώματα [=yourselves] as
a living sacrifice . . .'). Rom 6:12f is enlightening:

> Let not sin therefore reign in your mortal σῶμα . . .
> Do not yield *your members* to sin as instruments of wickedness,
> but yield *yourselves* to God . . .
> and *your members* to God as instruments of righteousness.

Here 'your σῶμα' is parallel to 'your members', which in turn is
parallel to 'yourselves'. 1 Cor 6:15 ('Do you not know that your
σώματα are members of Christ?') corresponds to 1 Cor 12:27 ('*You*
are the body of Christ and individually members of it'). In the first
text the subject of the sentence is 'your σώματα' and in the second 'you',
with no difference in meaning. Thus it is clear that the person as a
whole can be called a σῶμα. Significantly, Paul never calls a corpse
σῶμα, although that usage is found both in profane Greek and in the
Septuagint.

(*b*) But in what exact respect is man called σῶμα? As related to
himself; to be more precise, as the object of his own action. Our
examples are plain enough: he pommels *himself* and subdues *himself*
(1 Cor 9:27), he delivers *himself* to be burned (1 Cor 13:13), he yields
himself as an instrument to sin or to God (Rom 6:12ff; 12:1), he spends
himself for Christ (Phil 1:20). Husband and wife must give *themselves*
to each other (1 Cor 7:4). 2 Cor 5:10 declares that everyone will
receive 'good or evil, according to what he has done in the σῶμα'—in
other words according to his deeds, according to what he has made of
himself by them.

In all these cases the σῶμα is the man as the object of his action
insofar as he guides himself, controls himself, rules himself. Thus he is
not a substance but a relation, and a relation of himself to himself.
He is free to change himself, to make himself other than he is, to
become what he is not while remaining what he is. The σῶμα is
neither good nor bad, it simply expresses man's capacity for being good
or bad according as he determines himself for God or for evil.

Thus one can see why Paul jealously defends the resurrection of the
σῶμα against his adversaries at Corinth: if the risen man were no

longer a σῶμα he would no longer be a man. It would not be the same individual who dies and rises again. Such is the deeper meaning of his reply to the Corinthians on this point, although it does not wholly preclude substantialism.[1]

(c) The σῶμα does not mean man only insofar as he makes himself the object of his own acts but also insofar as he is the object of acts by a person alien to himself. In the latter case he in some sense goes forth from himself, but never to the extent alleged by substantialist dualism—Gnosticism, for instance. Wholly alienated though he be, he remains a man. Rom 7:14ff first attributes sin to the flesh (σάρξ) (vv. 14, 18), but then (v. 23) speaks of the law of sin which dwells in my members—that is, in the σῶμα. Hence the cry: 'Who will deliver me from this σῶμα of death?' Here the σῶμα is man as the object of sin's acts. Paul does not ask to be delivered from the σῶμα as such, but from the carnal σῶμα, from the σῶμα as ruled by sin and the flesh.

In spite of everything, such a gulf separates the self which bears man's true will (the 'inmost self' of Rom 7:22) from the self which forsakes that will to fall under the dominion of the flesh—this is the conflict set forth in Rom 7:14ff—that the second self seems practically a stranger to the first and the distinction between σῶμα and σάρξ seems to have disappeared. Yet this is by no means true, because the flesh is dead for a Christian (Rom 8:2ff) and it is shut out of the kingdom of God (1 Cor 15:50), whereas the σῶμα, delivered from the flesh, is the bearer of risen life. The σῶμα is man himself; the flesh is only the power that determines him. That is why Paul speaks of a life κατὰ σάρκα but never of a life κατὰ σῶμα.

To sum up, there are two senses of the word σῶμα in Paul. One is the ordinary sense and the other the strictly Pauline sense, according to which the σῶμα is simply the person—more precisely the person insofar as it makes itself the object of its own thought, attitude or act, or insofar as it is the object of acts on the part of outside forces.

(2) Ψυχή, πνεῦμα

(a) If, as we have just seen, the specifically Pauline meaning of σῶμα is not substantialist, the same must be true of the ψυχή. In fact—except for the trichotomy of 1 Thess 5:23 and 1 Cor 15:44 and 46—ψυχή does not designate a higher principle in man. Paul is unfamiliar with the Greek idea of the immortality of the soul. Just as in the Old Testament, 'soul' means the living man (Rom 11:3 [after 1 Kg 19:10]; 16:4; 2 Cor 1:23; Phil 2:30; 1 Thess 2:8), the person himself (Rom

1. See GV 1, pp. 38–64.

2:9; 13:1; 2 Cor 12:15). More precisely, it is the person as intending to . . ., as willing to . . . ; the proof is Phil 1:27 and a study of the words based on the root ψυχ– (TNT, pp. 205–6).

(b) Πνεῦμα—apart from the frequent use Paul makes of it to designate the Holy Spirit—may be synonymous with ψυχή, likewise meaning the whole man as in Rom 8:16; 1 Cor 2:11. Thus the word may take the place of a personal pronoun (like σῶμα and ψυχή). When we are told in 1 Cor 16:18 that 'they refreshed my πνεῦμα as well as yours', πνεῦμα means me and you. Similarly in 2 Cor 7:13 (Titus's πνεῦμα is Titus) and 2 Cor 2:13, which must be compared with 2 Cor 7:5. The concluding formula of certain letters, 'God be with your *pneuma*' (Gal 6:18, for instance) is equivalent to the usual phrase, 'God (or the grace of God) be with you all'.

Πνεῦμα therefore refers to the person, but under a particular aspect, first of all the same as ψυχή—that is, the person as will . . ., as intending . . . This is the case in Phil 1:27; 2 Cor 12:18 ('Did we not act in the same spirit?'=with the same intention). But the πνεῦμα is also man as aware of . . . (1 Cor 2:11, where *pneuma* verges on the modern idea of consciousness). Thus the πνεῦμα is man knowing and willing, as we see when Paul says that the divine Spirit thinks both as a will (Rom 8:6, 27; Gal 5:17) and as a conscious subject quite clear about the end it has in view (Rom 8:26; 1 Cor 2:10; 2 Cor 3:6).

(c) To sum up, it emerges that to Paul's real mind man is neither a dichotomy (body and soul) nor a trichotomy (body-soul-spirit). He is not, as Greek and Gnostic supposed, made up of several principles. He is not a being but an aptitude for being, a living unity, an *I* which on the one hand is related to itself insofar as it makes itself the object of its own acts (in this aspect man is a σῶμα), and on the other hand is intentionality (in this aspect man is ψυχή and πνεῦμα). It is a rationalist interpretation to see in the Pauline ψυχή and πνεῦμα some kind of higher principle, as if man could be defined as composite of body and soul, or of body, soul and spirit. Σῶμα, ψυχή and πνεῦμα are each the *total person himself* in one of his aspects.

(3) *Noῦς and συνείδησις*

(a) The *νοῦς* is not an intellectual faculty (the 'reason' or 'mind' of Graeco-Western philosophy) but the *Verstehen* we have already defined. It controls no objective knowledge but an ec-sistentiell one, which is an act and therefore includes a will. *Noῦς* designates the whole man insofar as he intends . . . When Paul exhorts the Corinthians (1 Cor 1:10) to be of one *νοῦς* and one judgment, he plainly does not mean a theoretical attitude but a scheme and a will to union. Likewise the exhortation of Rom 12:2 ('Be transformed by the renewal of your νοῦς') does not refer to a change in abstract ideas but to a renewal of the will. This νοῦς, like the one in Rom 1:28, ought almost to be translated 'character'.

In Rom 14:4 νοῦς is judgment about what one ought to do and not do. Thus the word has an intentional sense, it implies a scheme. The νοῦς of Rom 7:23 stands for 'inmost self' in v. 22; accordingly it is the real self as contrasted with σῶμα, here the all but alienated self (see above, §1c). This νοῦς is the same *I* which is the subject of θέλειν in vv. 15, 16 and 19–21, which tends towards good but in fact only contrives to do evil. The νούμενα of Rom 1:20 does not mean theoretical intelligence but knowledge of God's will; so much so that in v. 32 Paul calls the knowledge of God which pagans have a demand, a law—though the point was already quite clear in v. 21 ('Although they knew God they did not honour him . . .'). So the νοῦς is the person himself as a conscious and enlightened capacity for deciding for or against God; it is not a faculty.

(b) The same conclusion forces itself upon us when we consider the derivatives of the root νο-. 2 Cor 2:11 speaks of Satan's νοήματα in the sense of his designs. When 2 Cor 3:14 says that the νοήματα of the Jews were darkened, the intellectual sense seems to be the dominant one; but the following verse clearly shows that νοήματα imply conduct of a given sort, an attitude of mind, the taking up of a position. Similarly in Phil 4:7 'hearts' and minds' form a hendiadys.

The 'voluntary' sense of νόημα is obvious in 2 Cor 10:5 ('We take every νόημα captive . . .') and also in 11:3 ('I am afraid that your νοήματα will be led astray . . .'). Μετανοεῖν (2 Cor 12:21) and μετάνοια (Rom 2:4 and 2 Cor 7:9f) of course refer to an act of the will.

(c) The term συνείδησις (conscience) conveys a relation which a man has to himself, but in a different way from σῶμα. Whereas σῶμα creates a distance between the self properly speaking and that same self insofar as it has become an object, συνείδησις is the knowledge a man has of his own conduct. It is not, like νοῦς, a knowledge that includes a being ahead of oneself; it is a knowledge of that scheme in respect of the judgment to be passed upon it.

Thus συνείδησις is the science of good and evil and of the attitudes appropriate to each. It may have to do with the future or the past. Both aspects are included in 1 Cor 8:7–12 and 10:25–30: on the one hand συνείδησις forbids the 'weak' to eat food that has been offered to idols; and on the other hand, when they have eaten it συνείδησις is thereby defiled. The συνείδησις of Rom 2:15 shows that the requirements of the law are written in the hearts of pagans, so it has to do with future conduct. Rom 13:5 says that one must obey the authorities for the sake of συνείδησις, which here likewise has to do with the future. When Paul commends himself to 'every man's συνείδησις in the sight of God' (2 Cor 4:2), the meaning is that the conscience of those who know him as an apostle forces them to acknowledge his sincerity. The same applies to 2 Cor 5:11, where he hopes not to be misjudged by the Corinthians if they are guided by their conscience (ἐν ταῖς συνειδήσεσιν ἡμῶν). Thus we see that conscience is man as oriented to his future acts. But it may also bear on the past, either to condemn or to approve it: 1 Cor 4:4; Rom 9:1; 2 Cor 1:12.

The existence of conscience is ample proof that man is not a spiritual nature but a being-ahead-of-himself. For συνείδησις is an absolute (a *Dass*). No doubt it may err as to the content (*Was*) of this *Dass*. This has happened in the case of the 'weak' at Corinth who feel that they must not eat food which has been offered to idols. But Paul says that they are bound by the verdict of their conscience and cannot be forced to do a thing which their conscience would condemn. 'Weak' though it be, conscience has an absolute validity as a *Dass*. Again the confidence with which he vindicates his actions (Rom 9:1; 2 Cor 1:12) shows that Paul considers the judgment of conscience to be absolute. In both cases this is because the demand which conscience perceives is rooted in a sphere that transcends man—obviously in God himself, so far as the Christian is concerned.

The point is clearly put in Rom 13:5: authority must be obeyed 'for the sake of conscience'; in other words, as the context shows, out of reverence for the transcendent Authority which stands behind authority. Here, as in 2 Cor 1:12 and Rom 9:1, Conscience takes on a kind of separate existence. It is personified as an authority beyond man and yet related to him since it summons him to answer.

Once again we have the conception of man as 'historicity' and openness to . . . By responding to the absolute Other of Conscience, man acquires his true being—freedom (ἐλευθερία) with regard to all things. 'Why should my liberty be determined by another man's scruples?' (1 Cor 10:29). The verdict of my conscience is an absolute which emancipates me from the judgment of anyone else. It is the transcendence to which alone I owe my freedom.

(4) Καρδία

The Hebrew word for heart is rendered by καρδία or νοῦς in the Septuagint. Paul, too, often uses καρδία in the sense of νοῦς, to mean the self insofar as it wills and schemes. In 2 Cor 3:14f νοήματα and καρδία bear the same sense, and we have seen that they form a hendiadys in Phil 4:7. Just as the νοῦς (νοήματα) can be wayward, callous, blind, corrupt (Rom 1:28; 2 Cor 3:14; 4:4; 11:3), so can the heart (Rom

1:21; 2:5; 16:18). Just as the νοῦς must be renewed (Rom 12:2), the heart must be illuminated (2 Cor 4:6). Since it is called ἀμετανόητος, its business is μετανοεῖν.

Like the νοῦς, the heart designates the *I* and usually stands for a personal pronoun. For it is the subject desiring (Rom 10:1), coveting (Rom 1:24), willing (1 Cor 4:5), deciding (1 Cor 7:37; 2 Cor 9:7), grieving (Rom 9:2; 2 Cor 2:4), loving (2 Cor 7:3, 8:16; Phil 1:7). A comparison of 2 Cor 1:22 (God 'has given *us* the Spirit as a guarantee') firmly establishes that καρδία=*I*. The heart, therefore, is not a higher principle (any more than the νοῦς is); it is none other than the self. It is the ec-sistential structure of man, who can become ontically good or bad, Christian or un-Christian, as Paul expressly declares: the heart doubts or believes (Rom 10:6–10); unbelief is a hardening of the heart (2 Cor 3:14), and faith occurs when God illuminates the heart (2 Cor 4: 6). Thus the heart is the person himself. The difference between νοῦς and καρδία is that cognition dominates in νοῦς, whereas intention or feeling (grief, love) sets the tone in καρδία.

Σῶμα, ψυχή, πνεῦα, νοῦς, ουνείδησις, καρδία, are so many concepts whereby Paul teaches a non-substantialist anthropology. Man is relation. But he never exists in his sheer ec-sistential structure. In fact he always lives in a state of ontic aptitude. On the religious plane this means that he is never neutral. He is always for or against God. His *Wie* is a Christian *Wie* or an unbelieving *Wie*. He is a plan of God's or a plan of the world's. The world is at once the flesh, sin, law and death. But we must not envisage these forces as objective things. They are modes of man's being. Let us establish this point somewhat amply in the case of the flesh and the world, leaving law, sin and death to be examined later.

(5) *Σάρξ*

(a) *Σάρξ* is contrasted, in the first place, with κρέας, which means the flesh of animals that are used as food (Rom 12:21; 1 Cor 8:13). Here we are already given notice that the σάρξ cannot be an objective thing. It is the living flesh of man; not 'matter' as opposed to 'form', but the self in its bodily mode of being.

Just as in the Old Testament, it may mean simply a man (Rom 3:20; 1 Cor 1:29; Gal 2:16), the person himself (2 Cor 7:5 must be rendered: '*I* had not rest'). Together with αἷμα, σάρξ may bear that same sense (Gal 1:16 must obviously be translated: 'I did not confer with anybody') or mean humanity as such, the human sphere as contrasted with the kingdom of God: 'Flesh and blood cannot inherit the kingdom of God' (1 Cor 15:50). But σάρξ alone may also have this latter meaning,

as we see from Rom 6:19 (which says the same thing as Rom 3:5) and
1 Cor 9:8. To 'remain in the flesh' is equivalent to remaining in this
world, in earthly life (Phil 1:23f). The flesh is frail and fleeting in comparison with the next world (Gal 1:16 and 1 Cor 15:50 are particularly
striking instances). It is not the children of the flesh (that is, the humanity of this world) who are the children of God (Rom 9:8).

Thus the flesh means not only man but also what surrounds him,
that in which he lives, the whole realm of earthly and worldly things.
Hence σάρξ can become synonymous with κόσμος. The 'wisdom of
this world' (1 Cor 1:20 and 3:19) is the wisdom of those who are
'wise according to σάρξ (worldly standards'; 1:26). To say that the
world has been crucified by the cross of Christ (Gal 6:14) means that
'those who belong to Christ have crucified their flesh' (Gal 5:24).

Henceforth the turn of phrase ἐν σαρκί (except in Rom 2:28) means
that man is not defined by what he is as a substance (in this sense the
Old Testament says that he is flesh) nor by what he is *in se* (as among
the Greeks) but by the sphere in which he lives and which fixes the
horizon of his opportunities. This is made particularly clear by the
contrast between life ἐν σαρκί and life ἐν πνεύματι: to live in the flesh
(Gal 2:20; Phil 1:22), to walk in the flesh (2 Cor 10:3, Greek text), is
to live in this world. So the expression does not necessarily mean that
sin is involved: Paul speaks of Onesimus as a brother ἐν σαρκί καὶ
ἐν κυρίῳ, that is as a man and as a Christian (Philem 16). But of course
it always implies another 'dimension'—life in the Spirit—and therefore
a certain value-judgment (as we see even in Philem 16). Rom 8:8 does
show that the sphere of the flesh may also be the sphere of sin, as will
become perfectly clear with the expression κατὰ σάρκα. At all events we
see how the flesh designates a *Wie* of man: his 'worldly scheme'.

(b) *Κατὰ σάρκα* may bear the same sense as ἐν σαρκί; that is, may mean
this present world, the realm of human life. In that case κατὰ
σάρκα means 'according to the world'. Thus Paul speaks of Israel
according to the flesh, of Christ according to the flesh, and so forth.
But the latent conflict with the κατὰ πνεῦμα may become the dominant
or even the only sense, so that κατὰ σάρκα comes to mean 'in sin'
(2 Cor 1:17; 5:16; 10:3; Rom 8:5, and *passim*).

But we are not necessarily dealing with 'sins of the flesh', the
disorders of sensuality, 'immoral' living; we are still dealing with a
worldly *Verständnis*, with the mode of existence which the σάρξ makes
its rule of life and which therefore is an ontic determination. We see
plainly enough from Rom 8:5 that what is involved is indeed a
'world': life κατὰ σάρκα consists in φρονεῖν τὰ τῆς σαρκός, in human
freedom's earthly scheme. Thus the two senses of κατὰ σάρκα (which
now means the earthly sphere and now sin) do not conflict: sin

originates in the flesh when the flesh becomes the norm of a man's conduct.

(6) Κόσμος

(a) Common sense looks on the world as an objective reality in which man is present as the contents are present in a container. The Greeks, for instance, pictured it as a global essence in the midst of which man was one particular essence. One occasionally finds this commonplace idea in Paul (Rom 4:13 and 1 Cor 14:10). More often the world for him is the sum of life's circumstances and of man's opportunities on earth. It includes all that goes on in the span between life and death, among things present and things future (1 Cor 3:22). Human life in all its aspects and all its concrete determinations makes up 'dealing with the world' (1 Cor 7:31) and 'the things of the world' as contrasted with 'the things of the Lord' (7:32–34, Greek text). Thus the world is not the physical reality which common sense understands and science studies, but a *Verständnis*.

In a great many texts the word similarly refers to the world of man, to humanity as such (Hellenistic Judaism was also familiar with this sense). Rom 1:8 presents us with a transitional sense, one halfway between the objective use of the word and the 'historical' one: 'Your faith is proclaimed in all the world' means the same thing as 16:19: 'Your obedience is known to all'. When Paul says that he has conducted himself sincerely 'in the κόσμος', he obviously does not mean the objective world but the realm of human relations, as the text itself declares outright: 'more particularly towards you'. The same sense is found in 1 Cor 4:9 ('We have become a spectacle to the κόσμος'). In Rom 3:6, 19 God will judge the κόσμος; that is, man. 1 Cor 11:32; Rom 5:12f; 2 Cor 5:19 and Rom 11:15 also refer to the human world. The wisdom of the κόσμος is the wisdom of man as contrasted with that of God (1 Cor 1:20).

(b) Thus we see that the world is 'constituted' by man, which of course must not be understood in an Idealist sense. By ec-sisting towards the world, man adopts its ways and allows it to become his master. This is what is meant by the expression ὁ κόσμος οὗτος: it has a theological sense, because it implicitly contrasts the lordship which 'this world' exercises over man with God's lordship. The wisdom of 'this world' (1 Cor 3:19) is the diametrical opposite of God's wisdom. Sinners are called the immoral of 'this world' (1 Cor 5:10). We are told that the form of 'this world' is passing away (1 Cor 7:31b). The world is 'this age' as contrasted with the age to come (1 Cor 2:6, 8; 3:18). The wise of this world are the wise of this age (1 Cor 1:20).

The κόσμος is not something spatial but something 'historical'. It is the world-scheme, which at the same time is the sphere of the 'rulers of this age' (1 Cor 2:6, 8) and of the 'god of this world' (2 Cor 4:4), whom we must not think of as objective beings (for if they were, then they would be phantoms). They are 'constituted' by man: by giving himself to them, by disclosing them as his *Wie*, he allows them to exist in all their terrible otherness and becomes their prisoner. We must say the same of σάρξ, which in Paul is a synonym of κόσμος (compare 1 Cor 1:20 and 3:19 with 1:26). The flesh and the world are each a *Dass* because man freely makes himself their slave by embracing their ways and receiving his being from them. Thus the κόσμος is 'constituted' as an independent subject set over the individual subjects whose life it has become.

Paul says that 'the' world did not know God (1 Cor 1:21), that 'the' world has its wisdom (1 Cor 1:20; 3:19) and its grief (2 Cor 7:10). He makes the point that the world has become the master of those who constituted it such, by speaking of the πνεῦμα τοῦ κόσμου (1 Cor 2:12)—an 'atmosphere' that everyone helps to create and that at the same time affects everyone. This meaning of κόσμος is confirmed by the antithetical doctrine that Christians have become lords of the cosmos (1 Cor 3:21f) and will sit in judgment on it (1 Cor 6:2f).

On the formal plane man stands in the same relation to the world and to God.

(a) God is the Christian's determination, his Lord (whereas the objective God of the Greeks is a God whom man controls through reason). He is the Lord because in and through Christ he calls man to be his servant, his son, his friend. The believer receives from God a true future, even to the point of becoming a καινὴ κτίσις (2 Cor 5:17) and crying 'To me to live is Christ' (Phil 1:21). Thereby he wins freedom (ἐλευθερία), which of course has nothing to do with license to gratify the flesh (Gal 5:13).

Freedom is not a deliverance from every kind of norm; the Christian is not free *from* . . . but free *for* . . .; so that his new existence is a new slavery (Rom 7:6)—to the living God (1 Thess 1:9), or to Christ (Rom 14:18; 16:18), or to righteousness (Rom 6:16–18). But what a paradoxical slavery: the δοῦλος χριστοῦ is at the same time an ἀπελεύθερος κυρίου (1 Cor 7:22).

(b) By that very fact he is a being who lives κατὰ πνεῦμα instead of κατὰ σάρκα. The Spirit is not an objective reality but God's world become the *Wie* of man. Just as the σάρξ was the sphere of things visible and corruptible, which the sinner 'set up' over himself as a power of death by living κατὰ σάρκα, so the πνεῦμα is God's kingdom which the Christian has entered in order to live there κατὰ πνεῦμα. The Spirit is

God himself as determining man. For it is at once the eschatological gift and that gift already present as 'first fruits' (Rom 8:23) and as a 'guarantee' (2 Cor 1:22; 5:5)—which is to say that it is 'historical'. One never has it as a possession. It is the perpetual future which always determines the believer 'forensically'. Such is the paradox indicated by the words ἀπαρχή and ἀρραβών, and it can only be understood within the framework of Pauline anthropology.

The 'pneumatic' *Wie* is expressed in several ways. The Spirit is the 'spirit of sonship' (Rom 8:15). By receiving it in baptism we are justified (1 Cor 6:11) and incorporated into the body of Christ (1 Cor 12:13). The life of the Christian is a 'being in the Spirit'. But this being is 'historical': it is at once an indicative and an imperative. In the first clause of Gal 5:25 ('If we live by the Spirit, let us also walk by the Spirit') πνεῦμα designates the Christian's indicative, and in the second clause his imperative (for here πνεύματι means κατὰ πνεῦμα as in 5:16). Since the Spirit as man's indicative means his deliverance from the powers of sin and death (Rom 8:2) and gives him the opportunity to 'reap eternal life' (Gal 6:8), it is simultaneously man's imperative—that is, the norm of his περιπατεῖν.

Only this living dialectic of present and future enables one to understand Paul's thought in regard to the Spirit, which is not a divine person dwelling in me somehow or other but God's speaking to me, whereby he becomes the determination of my being. That is how I can retain my identity and personality, how I am in the world without being of the world, how I live ἐν σαρκί whilst no longer living κατὰ σάρκα; in short, how I am *simul peccator simul justus*. The πνεύματι ἄγεσθαι (Rom 8:14; Gal 5:18) does not mean the moving of one spiritual substance by another spiritual substance but implies a choice between the flesh and the Spirit (Rom 8:12-14; Gal 5:16-18).

True, we do seem to lapse into metaphysics when there is talk of the φρόνημα (Rom 8:6, 27) and ἐπιθυμεῖν of the Spirit (Gal 5:17), as if the Christian were stripped of his responsible self. In fact, however, these expressions mean that the *pneuma*, being the aptitude for eschatological ec-sistence, lays the foundations for a new will which is not of human origin.

In this glimpse of the 'historical' nature of revelation we have confined ourselves to Paul; but the whole New Testament is historical, as will be evident shortly.

CHAPTER FOUR

Myth

We know that rational, objective knowledge reveals man's craving to control things. Scientific knowledge is only a methodical elaboration of this spontaneous knowledge. The purpose behind it is clear: to let nothing escape its clutches, to wrest from nature every last secret. *Oneness* in theory and in practice is the ideal. That is why science will admit no 'gaps' in the world through which the world beyond might intervene among us. Certainly it comes up against the unknown, it is aware of its limitations, and in this sense it is always open. But it never questions the Aristotelian συνεχές, even if knowledge of the laws, structure and unity of the cosmos has to be accumulated indefinitely.

It has been objected against Bultmann that today science no longer holds the strictly determinist view of the world which it did of late; and he has quite fairly replied that the objection is naive. For the probabilist approach in microphysics has never been remotely connected with a return to the mythical world of the primitive mind, which believed in extramundane and supramundane powers and influences. No scientist has dreamed of exploiting the 'determinist controversy' in order to affirm the possibility of supernatural interventions in the world.[1]

Modern science by no means repudiates experience and it perseveres faithfully in the Greek tradition of the ἀρχή and the λόγου διδόναι. It matters little that scientific data are always tentative and that the image of the world is changing. What matters is the scientific attitude and scientific method: 'The hallmark of "modern scientific thought" is not the content of its judgments about nature and the world but this— that no judgment passed on nature and the world can pretend to any validity unless there are plainly adequate reasons for it. It is ignoring

1. See Jacques Merleau-Ponty's exposition in *Panorama des idées contemporaines* (1957), pp. 583–96, where he gives the basic texts of Louis de Broglie, Niels Bohr and Albert Einstein on this matter. He also shows that the most rigid determinist tradition is coming back into favour with young investigators and indeed with Louis de Broglie himself. The latter has established in his book *Nouvelles perspectives en microphysique* (1956): (1) that Neumann's theorem rests on a highly debatable assumption; (2) that a new mathematical solution now enables scientists to return to the idea of the corpuscle as a fixed unit within a wave phenomenon (the evolution of the latter being the only point on which we are fully informed).

the real difference between "mythological" and "modern" thought to contrast the content of their respective world-pictures, pointing out that the "modern world-picture" is in certain respects admittedly "discontinuous", "unclosed", or is even in a state of flux. That is neither here nor there. The unbridgeable gulf between modern thought and mythical thought consists in the difference between unconsciously uncritical judgment and consciously critical judgment, even if the conclusions arrived at by, say, modern natural science (obviously on the basis of consciously critical judgment) change in a few years' time. World-picture yields to world-picture; each arises as an hypothesis, but [these hypotheses are] based on responsible, critical thought'.[2]

In every case, therefore, science presupposes a rational attitude. So long as it does not overstep its own sphere, the world of things and determinism (whether statistical or not), it is of course entirely legitimate. Only when it would lay down the law to the 'human sciences' [*les 'sciences de l'esprit'*][3] are its claims unwarranted, precisely because of itself the 'scientific scheme of things' is a unifying scheme which necessarily tends to reduce the 'other' to the 'same'.

The *purpose* of myth is altogether different. By contrast with rational thought, myth seeks to stress the fact that the world and its events are 'open' to one *Dass*, or more, that are not part of the world. It attributes certain phenomena to supernatural powers, whether envisaged in animist or dynamist fashion, or else to personal spirits and gods. Thus it presupposes the existence of an entire sphere beyond man's control, which he can never fathom or master. It intends to express what is wholly other than man and man's world: there is its real significance. It speaks of demons and gods not only as objective realities but as powers on which man depends, whose succour he hopes for and whose wrath he fears. Thus it has not to do with some Wholly Other which is only a supernatural *Was* (and as such, a sham otherness) but with a Being who is man's Lord, a true transcendence.

For genuinely mythical thought, everything abounds with terrifying enigmas. Man is master neither of the world nor of life, because the world and life are grounded on and hedged in by a power beyond the sphere where man can calculate and control at will. Hence the under-

---

2. C. Hartlich and W. Sachs, cited by Bultmann in KM I, p. 181. Compare Bultmann himself in JCM, pp. 35–8.

3. It was the German philosopher Wilhelm Dilthey who originated the expression 'human sciences and natural sciences' (*Geisteswissenschaften und Naturwissenschaften; sciences de l'esprit et sciences de la nature*). The natural sciences are the exact sciences: chemistry, physics, etc. The human sciences are those that cannot abstract from man and his freedom: psychology, history, etc.

lying purpose of myth is diametrically opposite to the underlying purpose of science. The scientific scheme expresses man's will to grasp everything, to owe everything to himself alone. Contrariwise the mythical scheme expresses man's conviction that he depends on a power to which he owes his being now and in time to come (KM 1, pp. 22–7; 2, pp. 180–84).

But myth never quite lays bare its purpose. It is aboriginally ambiguous (GV 3, p. 52, note 1). The endless controversies provoked by Bultmann's critique of myth are due to the fact that his adversaries have not properly grasped this point.[4] The history of religions shows that man's relation to transcendence is always tainted. What we have called the philosophy of the natural man plays the same role with *homo religiosus* as it does with the 'Greek'. 'Primitive' man is also tempted to take control of himself by neutralizing and taming the power on which he depends, by abolishing the *Anspruch* it lays upon him. This process of objectification ends in mythology. Mythology is the rationalism of primitive man.

Mythological objectification has been much analysed and Bultmann has always declined to propose novelties in that field. The better, then, to understand his thought we shall turn to one of the outstanding historians and phenomenologists of religion: G. van der Leeuw. According to van der Leeuw, mythology subdues power (1) by shaping it, (2) by naming it, (3) by eternalizing it, (4) by celebrating it.

(1) Man feels the need to give power some kind of appearance. He is ill at ease with the extraordinary and the mysterious pure and simple. He does not care for a god so immanent and so crushing that its features cannot be made out, a will so overpowering and so close at hand as to be invisible. He cannot endure the direct lordship of transcendence. So he will try to neutralize it by giving it a shape. By giving it a shape or an image he moves it away from himself. Now he can look at power. Now he can breathe.

'The human experience which accounts for animist doings, the endowing of power with a will and an image, comes down to that very common thing called *solitude*. To live under the dominion of powers is to remain isolated. Whether power be hostile to us and thwart us, or whether we feel at one with it, even know how to manipulate it by

---

4. A striking proof is found in those authors who use the French language. All of them (we, at any rate, are aware of no exception) say and write *démythiser* and *démythisation,* whereas Bultmann invariably says and writes 'demythologize' and 'demythologization' (*Entmythologisierung*). For his purpose is not to destroy the import of myth but rather to restore its transcendence by eliminating the *logos* which strips it of its otherness and makes it a mere supernatural *Was*. To demythologize is to 'derationalize'.

magic—always and everywhere it leaves us at the mercy of our solitude. Man seeks more in his surroundings than company: he seeks his like, a will . . . In that crisis of isolation which may have been a torment to primitive man and which we ourselves are only too familiar with, he contrived to give the powers a will and an image. Thus dawned the possibility of analysis, discourse, impetration, cursing and blessing— the possibility that the hidden god might reveal himself.'[5]

Significantly enough, the classic religion of the image is that of the Greeks, whereas in Israel there is no image.[6] All that we have said about Greek thought will confirm this dominance of the *eidos*. The Greek *sees* the divine *eidos*, thus keeping it at a distance. Israel *hears* the divine will which is its absolute master. 'Out of the midst of the darkness' a voice speaks on Sinai (Deut 5:23). Thus 'man gives the powers of the world an image, the better to master them'.[7]

(2) A name throws the image into sharper relief, 'for the name is not a mere designation, it is an essence'.[8] Thus 'formless power and purposeless will are given intelligible associations which mingle to produce a particular outline'.[9] 'A name gives power and will a clear-cut image and a set content . . . Only by having a name do gods come to have a history and attain to myth. For myth is nothing else than . . . experience of the rejuvenated god, henceforth indirectly perceived, equipped with a structure, shaped. That is why man wishes to know the god's name: only then is he in a position to do anything with the god . . . Moses assumes that the children of Israel will ask him the name of the Being by whom he is sent.'[10] But it is common knowledge that God foiled this desire to control him by answering 'I am who I am' (Ex 3:14).[11]

The Roman distinguishes *di certi* from the *incerti*. The latter are much more disturbing. There is no way of mastering them except to build an altar dedicated to the 'unknown god' (the ἄγνωστος θεός of the Greeks). An Egyptian hymn consists of twenty-nine names, preceded only by two short sentences. Thus mythology uses a name to objectify the deity. By means of the name, the 'soul' of a being, 'men give shape to the being's essence'[12] and master it.

5. G. van der Leeuw, *La Religion dans son essence et ses manifestations* (French edition revised by the author, 1948), p. 79.
6. *Ibid.*, p. 621.
7. *Ibid.*, p. 537.
8. *Ibid.*, p. 142.
9. *Ibid.*, p. 143.
10. *Ibid.*, p. 144.
11. At least this is one of the possible senses of God's reply.
12. G. van der Leeuw, *op. cit.*, p. 144.

(3) The process of rationalization goes a step farther when the power is made eternal. Bestowing eternity on it is often simply a device for getting rid of it. The true God can only be the God of the 'moment' (of the evangelic καιρός). He is the Being who permanently threatens the security of man, who is unforeseeable grace and the perpetual future, who is forever coming along to upset human plans.

Mythology, on the other hand, speaks of God in terms of eternity; it sees him 'at the crossroads of the when and the where' (Dante). It does away with time. 'Myth neatly fits event into its own world. There event becomes eternal, it happens now and always; it behaves typically ... What happens every day in nature—sunrise, for example—happens only once in myth ... Thus mythical event is something at once typical and eternal; it lies beyond the reach of any temporal determination.'[13]

Here we have man's congenital rationalism: event eludes him, so he makes it typical in order to control it. That the sun shall rise every day is a matter of life and death for man. To ensure that it does, he invents a typical sunrise that happens once for all, in a 'timeless time'. 'What men regard today as the god of the "moment" is fixed in myth by an act that happened once in the remote past, whereby it becomes reliable and lasting.'[14] The myth of the dragon-killer is associated with the city of Worms. Its cycle includes events of universal historical import. 'The dragon becomes a monster which existed before time began, ceasing to be a terrible present danger.'[15]

Mythology swallows up 'history', the unforeseeable thing that rules man. Christianity too knows what a temptation it is to eternalize God's will in changeless, timeless laws which provide the believer with security and in fact substitute his will for the will of the Wholly Other. By his mythological behaviour 'man withdraws to a certain distance from the world and at first seems minded to contemplate it; hence the static element in the mythical world, which disregards time, as it were leaving it to stagnate ... The images of the mythical world are eternal, incapable of transformation ... But this control man has of the world, while seeming to contemplate it, is nonetheless control, though of a different sort than that which magic affords. By shaping images, by addressing event and speaking of it in mythical terms, man has placed himself in a position which is the direct opposite of magic. Magical man incorporated himself in the world; mythical man sets the world up outside himself. He projects beyond himself the power which he

13. *Ibid.*, p. 405.
14. W. F. Otto, quoted by van der Leeuw, *op. cit.*, p. 404, note 2.
15. *Ibid.*, p. 407.

has experienced.'[16] He turns it into an *eidos* that is forever the same and therefore harmless.

Thus 'magical autism and mythical imaging agree and complement each other'[17] in neutralizing power. Magic takes it over; myth projects it afar by the objectifying process of investing it with an image, a name and timelessness.

'Those who would understand myth must not regard it as primarily an explanation of certain natural phenomena, but as a mastering of the world which seeks, though less ardently than magical control, to deprive the *Thou* of that which magic wrested from the powers by force'.[18]

(4) Myth must therefore be interpreted first of all by worship, for what lives in myth is what lived in sacred action—that is, in the 'celebration' of event. Moreover myth is a rite, a mighty word (μυθέω) that controls power. 'Strictly speaking, myth is none other than word itself. It is neither a conjecture, nor a poem, nor a primitive explanation of the world, nor an embryonic philosophy (though myth may be all these things and indeed fairly often is). It is an uttered word which by being repeated wields decisive power . . . Living myth parallels celebration; it is itself a celebration. By discovering the close kinship that binds myth and rite together, scholars have recently been able not only to understand a good many myths which hitherto baffled them but also to explain the very essence of myth.'[19]

Thanks to worship, myth becomes a present reality that men experience. The abduction of Cora and her rediscovery, the Mithraic sacrifice of bulls, the death and resurrection of Attis, Isis's search for her lost husband, are objectified and placed at man's disposal in and by rite.[20] Rite is the last word in man's mastery of power, when it has already been neutralized by having an image, a name and eternity imposed upon it. Of course worship may also be sheer thanksgiving; but the history of religions shows that normally, in fact, 'it becomes an action meant to influence the behaviour of the deity, to turn aside his wrath and win his favour' (KM 2, p. 184)—in the Lutheran sense of the word, a 'work'.[21]

16. *Ibid.*, p. 536.

17. *Ibid.*, p. 537.

18. *Ibid.*, p. 538.

19. *Ibid.*, p. 404.

20. See other highly significant examples of the way worship masters power: *ibid.*, pp. 188–201, 338–40 and *passim*.

21. Anyone who would vividly experience the effect of *logos* on the meaning of myth need only read cantos 20 and 22 of the Iliad.

Bultmann has made a special study of the religions contemporaneous with the New Testament. In these religions the *purpose* of myth is what it is everywhere: to speak of a transcendence. But myth itself is man's laying hold on the deity. Bultmann establishes with regard to them what van der Leeuw establishes with regard to religions in general: that they objectify the divine. 'Myth objectifies the other world in terms of this world and thereby makes it a controllable thing' (KM 2, p. 184). This process is particularly observable in the two great forms of religion with which Christianity has had close contacts and which will keep recurring throughout this book: the Hellenistic mystery religions and Gnosticism.

(1) By mysteries we mean a group of religions in the Middle East— the religion of Phrygia with its cult of Attis, that of Egypt with the cult of Isis and Osiris, that of Syria with the cult of Adonis, the religion of Mithras—which took on a new shape in the civilized world. Originally they were tribal cults. Slaves, merchants and soldiers brought them to the West. Thus uprooted from their native soil they became religious communities, constituted by their voluntary adherents, where the ordinary distinctions of the profane world were done away with—differences of nation and race, of rank and social position. Here high and low, freemen and slaves, were brothers; and men were joined by women (except in the cult of Mithras).

These religions are alike in the following respects. One joins them by an act of initiation. It is a solemn rite; secret, of course, and a mystery. The initiates are bound together by this secret, which they take an oath not to reveal and which sets them apart from the uninitiated. Initiation is preceded by various rites of purification: fasts, lustrations (purifications by sacrifice), baptisms, and (at least in Mithraism) floggings. After this preparation comes the handing over (παράδοσις) of the sacred formula (σύμβολον, σύνθημα) and contemplation (ἐπόπτεια) of the deity, in which photic phenomena play a part. During contemplation the initiate experiences union with the deity and has the immortal essence bestowed on him. In many mysteries this union takes place through symbolic sexual union (συνουσία). There are other rites besides. For example, by putting on the clothes of the god the initiate 'puts' him 'on' (that is, is deified). But communion with god or goddess is chiefly established and strengthened during sacred meals.

Salvation (σωτηρία) is the goal to which initiation leads. (Note that the god bears the name of σωτήρ, and the goddess of σώτειρα.) It includes all that a man can wish for: protection against the dangers that threaten his life in either world (everything from shipwreck to disease) but above all the salvation of his soul—immortality (ἀθανασία, ἀφθαρσία). Quite understandably, therefore, the central figure in the mystery religions (except for Mithraism) is that of a young god who dies and rises from the dead.

Originally the gods concerned were gods of fertility, but in the mysteries they lost their naturist character. By uniting himself with the god through worship, the initiate shares in the fate of the god—that is, his death and his immortality. 'Be of good heart, O initiates of the god who is saved, for we too shall be saved from suffering' (a formula recorded by Firmicus Maternus). So it will be seen why in many mysteries the act of initiation represented the death and resurrection of the initiate. Thanks to these rites, he who was called the 'risen one', the 'metamorphosed', the 'deified', the 'transfigured', henceforth bore within himself the 'medicine of immortality' (φάρμακον ἀθανασίας).

The mystery religions express the conviction that man cannot find true life in this world: neither in the City nor in the cosmos. We have seen how, before the rise of these religions, the City and the cosmos were the 'salvation' of the Greek, who received his perfection from his obedience to the laws of the community of free men. Later the Stoic concentrated on his mind, which grasped the cosmos as a rational whole and understood itself in its oneness with the universal *logos*.

All this leaves the man of the mysteries unsatisfied. The god who can come to his aid is neither the power that rules the City nor the *logos* as a rational law that binds the universe together and assigns the individual his niche in it. He trembles at the thought of death, knowing it for a thing he cannot overcome. Therefore he believes in the existence of a supramundane god whose intervention alone can save him. The mystery religions are essentially a withdrawal from the world [*une 'dé-mondanisation'*]. That is why they have so often been compared to Christianity; for it too is first and foremost an eschatology, and its worship displays very striking similarities to the worship of those religions.

On closer examination one finds that the mystery religions never reach beyond the framework of mythology—the sphere, that is, of the *Was* and of sameness. They do not envisage man as temporality; for them he has neither a true past nor a true future, he is neither sinful nor pardoned; he already is in germ what he will be after his deliverance.

These religions are concerned to free a prisoner, not to make a 'new creature' (2 Cor 5:17). Fate (εἱμαρμένη) and fortune (τύχη) only *prevent* a man's being what he should be and what he already is in his prison. Thus the old self does not die; it persists in the will to live, which is only *unbound*. There is neither real death nor real resurrection. Immortality and resurrection are so far confused that the deified initiate is nothing more at bottom than he was before his initiation: he is not *simul peccator simul justus*. His salvation is not a 'being-ahead-of-himself'. He possesses immortality as an attribute. Salvation is a mere indicative; not at the same time an imperative. The 'consider yourselves dead to sin and alive to God in Christ Jesus' (Rom 6:11), the 'if we live by the Spirit, let us also walk by the Spirit' (Gal 5:25), are wholly alien to the mystery religions (see p. 43, above). Accordingly their followers could be libertines without any inconsistency, strictly speaking, since they were already saved whatever they might do. Deliverance was a thing attained to once and for all. They were not called on at every moment to satisfy the constantly changing demands of their god, to live by faith that works through love. The initiate possessed 'grace', he was not possessed by it.

A final proof that the mystery religions were mythological in character is provided by the very structure of their community. As we have seen, this community was supramundane to the extent that all differences of race and class were abolished within it. But there was nothing exclusive about it: belonging to it did not prevent a man's taking part in the official worship of the City or in other mysteries. Thus it was not eschatological through and through like the Christian Church, which is the assembly of those who have received a life wholly transcending the world, because that life is not a mere supernature but the *Dass* which determines them to the very marrow of their being.

(2) Gnosticism is another example of mythological religion, with which we shall have to do explicitly or implicitly from one end of this book to the other. It is a vast religious movement multifarious in form but fundamentally single in structure. Scholars first unearthed it as a phenomenon within the confines of Christianity and it was long regarded as a transformation of the Christian faith into a speculative theology or, as Harnack said, a 'thoroughgoing hellenization' of Christianity. But closer investigation has revealed that Gnosis is an earlier thing in the East and that it penetrated the West, in one form or another, as a rival of Christianity.

The Gnostic communities worked out their rites and doctrines with the help of various mythological and philosophical traditions. Some of them appeared in the region of the Jordan in the guise of baptist sects. Others set themselves up as communities devoted to a mystery cult. Having a strong bent towards syncretism, Gnostic ideas drew their concrete shape from one or other of the cults we have spoken about. Thus the Gnostic redeemer was assimilated to the Phrygian Attis. Gnosis also developed among the religious philosophers of Hellenism —in Philo, for example—and even among the Neoplatonists notwithstanding the objections of Plotinus.

Such being the case, Hans Lietzmann has gone so far as to call Gnosticism a syncretist phenomenon. Yet at bottom it exhibits an astonishing oneness. With countless variations on the theme, Gnostic myth sets forth the destiny of the soul: its origin—in the world of light —its tragic fall, its bondage on earth and in the body, its deliverance by the redeemer, and its return to the heavenly world. The soul—or rather man's true self—is a fragment of a heavenly, lightsome form (the first man) which in the very remote past fell into the hands of the demoniac powers of darkness (accounts differ as to just how this happened). This form was torn up and its lightsome shreds serve the demons as the magnetic forces of cohesion which they need to create a universe out of dark chaos. Building this universe hedges in the heavenly world which is the object of the demons' covetous desire. Were these elements removed, then their world—that is to say, *our* world—would fall back into chaos. And so the princes of this world keep jealous watch over the fragments of light which they have stolen.

Naturally the myth is altogether preoccupied with such sparks as are imprisoned in man, constituting his real self. The demons try either to get men drunk or lull them to sleep so that they may forget their heavenly country. But the supreme God, moved with compassion, sends men his own son to deliver them. The redeemer assumes the garment of an earthly body so that the demons shall not recognize him. He calls 'his own' (a characteristic term that is taken up again in the Gospel of John), wakes those who are sleeping, and teaches them 'the road back'. In particular he entrusts them with the sacred formula that will enable them to rise unimpeded, at their ascension, through the various spheres of the cosmos which are inhabited by demoniac powers. The redeemer reveals himself to be God's envoy. 'I am the shepherd', 'I am truth'—such are the things he says about himself. His task is to free and gather together the captive souls, which will then ascend to heaven in his train to reconstitute the body of the heavenly first man, rent by the demons. Once this redemption has been accomplished, our earthly world will come to an end by relapsing into chaos. Darkness will be delivered to itself as its doom and punishment.

Thus Gnosis is essentially a theology of redemption, with striking similarities to Christianity. And yet it remains thoroughly mythological. First of all the theme of the fall is mythologized (rationalized). It is not a true fall, because the divine spark is only *imprisoned* in this world below, and in the body. It remains what it was, it has only been put to sleep. The idea of freedom and responsibility—and therefore of sin—is nowhere to be found. The fall is not a sin but a fate: it is due to powers outside man. Nor is the world of the fall a *Verstehen*, or a sinful scheme of things, as in Paul (see pp. 41–2, above); it is a mere prison.

The only connection between 'this world' and the spark of light is the wholly extrinsic one between container and contained:

> Who has cast me into Tibil [the earthly world]?
> Into Tibil who has cast me?
> Who has imprisoned me within these walls?
> Who has riveted to my foot this chain-and-ball
> vast as the world and all it holds?
> Who has loaded me with fetters
> heavy beyond all measure?
>
> .   .   .
>
> Who has cast me into the house of darkness?
>
> .   .   .
>
> Why have you driven me forth from the place where I dwelt,
> dragged me to dungeon,
> cast me into stinking bodies?

Such is the unending lament of the self. There is no hint at all of the idea that the self has 'set up' 'this world' by its own free, sinful choice, by making this world its lord and master. The self feels no responsibility for itself; its fundamental being is withdrawn from its control. It experiences the life of its soul, the impulses of its will, as if they reached it from somewhere outside.

Gnostic anthropology is an anthropology of three storeys which have no communication with each other. Man is made of three super-imposed principles: body, soul and self, called by various names in the various traditions. Among the Greek-speaking Gnostics the self is called πνεῦμα. We have already observed that once or twice Paul (1 Thess 5:23; 1 Cor 15:44 and 46) makes a regrettable concession to this substantialist anthropology which contradicts the whole idea of man as freedom. The Gnostic is not a freedom; he is a three-storeyed man, of whom only the top storey—thanks to the grace of the redeemer—will regain his heavenly country, the other two remaining plunged in darkness.

Thus there is no question of conversion, justification, death and resurrection. The self does not cross from a sinful past to a pardoned future, it is a changeless, substantial present imprisoned by powers outside itself. And therefore it is not inwardly affected by the fall: lost, it is but what it will be when saved; saved, it will only be what it now is when it is lost.

Quite understandably, in these circumstances, redemption is looked on as a natural process. The redeemer does not approach *sinners*, in order to transform them by his pardon and his grace; he approaches beings who are already divine. He has only to loose the πνεῦμα from the matrix of soul and body. Between the saviour and the saved there obtains a community of nature (φύσις), in virtue of which his destiny is theirs. To know this—one's true nature, that is, as identical with the saviour's—is redemption in the strict sense. Let the divine envoy but impart to the imprisoned self a speculative doctrine which instructs it about its divine nature, and that γνῶσις arms the self against all the onslaughts of the demons, delivering it from fate and from necessity.

Obviously Gnosis is a religion worked out in terms of what we have called the philosophy of the natural man. 'They [the Gnostics] are forced to classify the self as a substance (as a spark of light) and to understand the destiny of the self as something made up of natural events' (CP, p. 138), including its salvation: 'They can represent its attainment [that of redemption] only in a mythological way—that is, as the separation at death of the elements that are united in man. Leaving body and soul behind it, the true self, that pre-existent spark of light, rises to its own country, the heavenly world of light' (*ibid.*, p. 139).

It will now be seen why ecstasy looms large in Gnostic piety. Since there is a dualism between 'this world' and the self, since the world was made by the evil god of darkness, a radical flight from the world is necessary. This flight culminates in ecstasy, which is possible because the self, though captive, is by nature divine. Christian faith holds that the world is not evil in itself. It remains God's creation, which man has simply perverted by his sin. Thanks to pardon, the believer makes the proper use of the world. He is not to run away from it by asceticism and ecstasy but to live in it according to the ὡς μή (1 Cor 7:29–31). His relation to the world is a dialectical one. Of themselves, asceticism and ecstasy are 'works' and opposed to faith. Thus the Gnostic may quite as well turn to libertinism: since he is saved by nature, what risk does he run? Why submit to an imperative? Whatever his manner of life may be—good or ill—he remains what he is by nature: a divine spark.

How does the New Testament, how do Paul and John in particular, demythologize Gnosticism? We have seen that the *purpose* of Gnostic myth is wondrous deep. It is true that 'this world' is a world of darkness and anguish. It is true that there is a 'prince of this world'. It is true that the real self is alien to the world (a fact which the Greeks did not perceive when they made the cosmos the homeland of men and gods). It is true that man finds himself in a dreadful state of fallenness and solitude. It is true that he needs a redeemer. It is true that this saviour is the Son of God, dwelling in light inaccessible. It is true that he delivers men and brings them in his train into the kingdom of truth. But we have also seen that the sense of all this is a good deal altered by the '*logos*': man, the fall, this world, the next world, the redeemer and redemption are thought of as intramundane realities.

Let us cast back to a familiar category and say that Gnosticism is only a precomprehension (*Vorverständnis*) of true salvation. People often imagine that the original feature of Christianity is a new doctrine, as if it revealed to us hitherto unknown secrets about 'what' God is. Exegetes and theologians do their best to show that the content of the New Testament is not the same as the content of Gnosis (or any other religion). In fact the difference is principally found on the plane of the *Dass*; on the plane of the *Was* the difference is only a consequence, as we shall see.

(1) Paul envisages salvation *geschichtlich*. Since man is a freedom, his fall cannot be an objective fact; it can only be a guilt. He did not succumb in spite of himself to the onslaught of demons, he freely delivered himself to them. Therefore the evil powers are not cosmic powers outside man but are his *Wie*, the determination of his existence. True, in this matter Paul has not altogether shaken off the mythological attitude; he does present the demons in the Gnostic fashion as real beings (Rom 8:38; 1 Cor 15:24; 2:68; Gal 4:3, 9) with Satan as their leader (Rom 16:20; 1 Cor 5:5; 7:5; 2 Cor 2:11; 11:14; 1 Thess 2:18). But this dualism is corrected: the demons are part of creation (Rom 8:39) and God can use an angel of Satan for his own purposes (2 Cor 12:7).

Moreover it is plain that the 'being' of these powers only makes sense to a man who freely 'constitutes' them over himself by making them his *Selbstverständnis*, which is precisely his sin (in Gnosis there is no sin). This is what 1 Cor 8:5–6 means: just as God is not an objective reality but an $\epsilon\hat{\iota}\nu\alpha\iota$ $\hat{\eta}\mu\hat{\iota}\nu$, so are the gods and lords of heaven and earth. Paul adopts this Gnostic terminology in order to make the point that the world becomes a hostile and deadly power for man when he has chosen the world in preference to God, worshipping the creature instead of the Creator (Rom 1:25).

Fate is not, as in Gnosis, a destiny outside man; man's guilt is his fate. 'Every man, then, has his share in constituting the "world"; and being thus made the world becomes a power that rules over the individual, a fate that the individual has forged for himself' (CP, p. 158). Basically, the powers 'owe their power to man himself' (TNT, pp. 258–9). Paul also shows that he has demythologized them when he says that they have been annihilated so far as the Christian is concerned (1 Cor 2:6). Because the believer has chosen God, and his freedom has ceased to make the powers his *Verständnis*, they have become impotence itself—which certainly proves that their true being is not an objective existence but their being-for-man. Once man is living for God they cease to exist: the world is experienced as God's creation.

All the same, the believer's salvation is never a thing that he possesses. We have seen how the initiate of the mystery religions and the Gnostic *were* saved, even if they afterwards lapsed into libertinism. The Christian, for his part, can always cease to be 'God's plan'. He is always in danger of worshipping creatures anew and setting up the world again as his lord and master. It is this constant danger—following from the fact that man is ec-sistence (not a substance as in Gnosis)—that Paul conveys by putting Gnostic mythology right. In his eyes Satan is essentially temptation (1 Thess 3:5) against which one must be ever on one's guard (1 Cor 7:5; 2 Cor 2:11)—a thing that never occurs to the Gnostic, since he is saved once and for all. Satan is the world insofar as man makes it his own possession instead of looking on it as God's creature.

In mythology, contrariwise, Satan is envisaged with the realism of *homo religiosus*: he is only a phantom, because he can only attack the self from without and does not become its *Verständnis*. He leaves the self unscathed because he is dealing with a divine substance which can only be what it is. So the Gnostic is a prisoner but not a sinner. I am only a sinner when I make Satan my way of being and living, my *Sichverstehen*.

(2) John also demythologizes the substantialist dualism of Gnosis. For him, as for Paul, 'this world' is man's way of being and not a fate (the dismemberment of the first man by demons). If the world is darkness, that is the fault of sin. God's creation became 'this world' because man preferred darkness to light. It is the free rejection of light which made the world a world of darkness and therefore a world of lies.

That it is a world of lies can be gathered from Jesus's saying that he has come into the world to bear witness to the truth (18:37). He promises the knowledge of the truth to all who abide in his word (8:31-32), because he himself is truth (14:6). Jesus directly indicates the lying nature of the world when he accuses 'the Jews' of not understanding him because they have the devil for their father and the devil is a liar and the father of lies (8:43-45). Whoever does not acknowledge Jesus as the Messiah is a liar (1 Jn 2:22). Darkness and lies are the fruit of the free, sinful decision whereby man has set up the world as a power that rules him and of which he is the slave. This bondage is indicated when Jesus declares that his word, which is truth, will set man free (Jn 8:32). For John, as for Paul, man's fate is his guilt.

Here we are at the antipodes of Gnosis. No doubt John speaks of the devil as Gnosis does, but in fact he demythologizes the devil even more thoroughly than Paul does. The devil is darkness, lies, sin, death, nothingness. 'To John's mind, does the devil exist in the mythical sense [that is, as an objectified thing]? It is, to say the least, very doubtful whether he does. But be that as it may, he certainly represents the power to whose rule the world is subject, the power of darkness and lies, the power of sin and death' (TNT, p. 369). Not as though the evangelist subjectified the devil. Darkness, lies, sin, death and nothingness are not mere states of mind. But they *are* real only because they affect man's being. If the devil were an objective reality outside man, then he would only be a phantom.

In Gnosis Satan is a sham otherness, because he leaves the true self of the Gnostic unchanged: the worst he can do is imprison it. The devil is only real if he is an aptitude for ec-sistence. For John, the devil is the prince of this world only because man has freely rejected God by refusing to treat the world as God's creation; has made the world his end, his absolute, his god, thereby turning himself into darkness, lies, bondage and death.

When it comes to explaining where darkness, lies, bondage and death come from, John does not give the mythological answer. Darkness comes solely from rejection of the light (God). Lies come solely from rejection of the truth (God). Bondage comes solely from rejection of freedom (God). Death comes solely from rejection of life (God). Darkness, lies, bondage, death and the devil are the meaning (see pp. 16–17, above) that man attaches to the world when he does not acknowledge it as God's creation. One may think Satan a figment of the imagination (as unbelievers do). One may think him an objective reality (as many believers do). Either attitude is a rationalist one.

To speak of the devil as a figment of the imagination is to deny that evil is a fearful otherness. To envisage him as an objective being is to make him a harmless phantom, one more object among the objects which man controls and which leave him unchanged. Such is not the mind of the fourth Gospel: 'For John the world is not, as it is for Gnosis, a cosmic power imprisoning men; an irresistible force of nature alien to their φύσις (which belongs to the world of light). Rather it is a power *geschichtlich* ['historically'] constituted by man in revolt against God. Man does not belong to the world of darkness or the world of light by reason of his fate or his φύσις, but through his own decision. The Gnostic dualism of fate has become a dualism of decision' (TNT, p. 429; see JCM, pp. 20–21, 34).

Thus light (God) is not thought of as an objective reality enlightening man from without. It is one of man's modes of being, as John indicates by speaking of περιπατεῖν or ἐργάζεσθαι in light, or conversely of περιπατεῖν in darkness. Only *in* the light can one walk and act with security; in the dark, man is blind and cannot find his way (9:4; 11:9f; 12:35; 1 Jn 2:11). Light is not that which helps man keep his bearings as he moves among objects (that is how common sense and science look at the matter), but that by which he understands himself in his world and does find his way. The 'true light' (1:9; 1 Jn 2:8) is not the light which enables man to use the external world but the illumination which enables him to find his own authentic being, guides his footsteps, soothes his distress, gives him a clear and tranquil mind. Christ the light is not a metaphysical being (like the Gnostic redeemer) but man's *Selbsverständnis* (his salvation and his life—that is, a true transcendence).

The same must be said of Christ the truth. Johannine ἀλήθεια is not the ordinary objective truth of common sense, though occasionally it does have that meaning (8:45; 16:3). When Jesus says (8:32) that knowledge of the truth sets men free, he obviously does not mean the rational knowledge which frees us of the prejudices and errors we absorb from tradition or convention, but existential knowledge of a truth that transforms man and is not mere objective information about the world or about God.

Johannine truth is not a doctrine taught by Jesus but the very reality of God so far revealing himself in Jesus that he is the truth (14:6) and that anyone who has seen him has seen the Father (14:9). The Father dwells and acts in him (14:10f). Because he is the truth, he is also life (14:6). When he is said to be full of grace and truth, that is a hendiadys meaning that in him God encounters and saves us. If believers are 'sanctified' by the truth (17:17), it is because God's reality, manifesting itself in the truth of his word, snatches from the world those who are still in the world (17:14–16). When God demands worshippers in spirit and in truth, this is again a hendiadys, and means that the only true worship is that produced by the power of God and by his revelation. Finally, when Pilate asks: 'what is truth?' he shows, in John's view, that the world has become indifferent to God. Εἶναι ἐκ τῆς ἀληθείας (18:37; 1 Jn 2:21; 3:19) is synonymous with εἶναι ἐκ θεοῦ (7:17; 8:47; 1 Jn 3:10; 4:1ff; 5:19). Thus Johannine truth is not an objective reality but God's very approach to man, to which man responds by ec-sisting towards God.

This chapter was not meant to embark us upon the subject of demythologization, to which Part Two of this book will be devoted; it was only meant to set forth the *formal* structures of myth, mythologization and demythologization. 'In myth, faith finds an expression of the fact that the known, controllable world in which man lives is not based on man or limited by him—that its foundation and frontier lie beyond the known and controllable, and that the known and controllable are constantly governed or threatened by the disturbing powers which are its foundation and frontier. At the same time myth expresses the knowledge that man is not his own master, that he is not only a dependent within the known world but above all depends on those powers which rule beyond the known, and that it is precisely in this dependence that he can shake off the control of known powers. Thus myth itself calls for criticism of itself, insofar as its real purpose—which is to speak of an outside power that the world and man are subject to—is thwarted and disguised by the objectifying nature of what it says' (KM I, pp. 22–3).

To demythologize, then, is to 'derationalize'. It is to strip away from the meaning of myth the *logos* of natural man, which as far as possible would neutralize and appropriate any otherness that calls it in question—in short, any *real* otherness. Not by chance is demythologization closely bound up with Christian revelation, which being the advent of the Wholly Other cannot be fitted into the mind and life of natural man. In the second part of this book it will be our object to show that the *witnesses* of revelation (the biblical writers) and the *documents* they have left behind them (scripture) are themselves not altogether untainted by the philosophy of natural man; that they have partly mythologized the Word of God.

CHAPTER FIVE

Historie/Geschichte

We have already defined the two senses of history, which may be *Historie* (history) or *Geschichte* ('history'). This distinction must now be explored.

I

HISTORIE

Historie is objective history. Its importance should not be belittled. We have already had occasion to observe that Bultmann will have nothing to do with anti-intellectualism. Knowledge is legitimate and indispensable in its own field, which is the world of objects (GV 2, pp. 76–8). The sciences as a whole give us knowledge of otherness as a *Was*. The same is true of scientific history, which enables us to know the past as a *Gegebenheit*, explaining to us what it was insofar as it is objectified and we can therefore grasp it. We have seen what knowledge is based on: on the fact that man is in a sense all things, so that to know is to re-cognize. This accounts for the agreement among scientists. There can be no conflict of principle over an intelligible world governed by rational laws.[1] There can only be a de facto and tentative disagreement arising from the concrete difficulties which face scientific investigation.

The same must be said of history insofar as it does not interpret facts but merely ascertains them, considering events only in their objective being. We are often told that there is no such thing as 'pure fact'. Quite so. But to say this is to admit that there is something in fact which forms the object of study and which must unite the minds of unprejudiced men. Everyone will agree about the existence of Napoleon, about the major events of his life, and to a large extent about his cast of mind, political ideas, and so forth. If there is no unanimity on these latter points, that is only because full information is in fact hard to come by. There is no problem in principle: Napoleon's cast of mind as a complete reality is a datum that can in itself be as fully

---

1. We have noted what is to be thought of 'indeterminism' in microphysics. Also see Bultmann himself on the subject in GV 3, pp. 108–9.

analysed as any other object of scientific psychology. Whatever in history is part of nature can be subjected to rational investigation.

Thus there is a science of history which studies the necessary and universal on the same footing as other sciences do. The monuments of the past (whether literary or archaeological) are at least in themselves a basis for objectivity as to the events and deeds which they relate. 'Scrupulously methodical research can objectively make out a certain part of the course of history—events, that is, as mere events which take place at a certain point in space and time. For example, it can be objectively established that Socrates drank the hemlock and did so at a given moment; that Caesar crossed the Rubicon and did so at a given moment; that Luther put up his ninety-five theses on the door of the castle-church at Wittenberg and did so at a given moment; or again it can be objectively known that such and such a battle was fought and at such and such a moment, that this empire was set up, or that that disaster happened. From this point of view there is no substance to the objection that the truth of historical statements is only relative in many cases. Of course, many events cannot be verified because the evidence is scrappy or obscure, and also because there are limits to any historian's wisdom and ability. But theoretically that does not matter, because of itself methodical historical research can attain to an objective knowledge in this field' (HE, p. 116).

Insofar as Christianity is an event in space and time it necessarily falls under the scrutiny of the critics. Historical criticism in general and biblical criticism in particular demand the utmost disinterestedness—that is, 'innocence of any preconception about the results' of one's investigations (GV 2, p. 230). For instance, the historian must not yield to 'his hope that a text will uphold a given (doctrinal) opinion or offer valuable guidance as to conduct, which of course has happened in the history of exegesis on many an occasion' (*ibid.*). Obviously we do not mean that the investigator remains passive; on the contrary, all his training, all his energies, all his wisdom, all his sympathy must be concentrated on the object of his study.

In *this* sense science is most 'objective' when it is most 'subjective'; and in this respect Bultmann has often expressed his admiration for the liberal exegetes of the nineteenth and twentieth century. Along with Karl Barth, Eduard Thurneysen, Friedrich Gogarten and others, he is well known as an exponent of 'dialectical theology'.[2] But from the outset he has thought and said that theological renewal must take the fullest account of historical criticism.

2. On this matter see H. Bouillard, *Karl Barth, Genèse et évolution de la théologie dialectique* (1957), pp. 161–221.

It was on this score that Bultmann somewhat diverged from Barth, who to his mind was apt to make light of scientific exegesis (GV I, pp. 38–65). He praises the great liberals for training the theologians 'in criticism—that is, in freedom and truthfulness. We who were bred to liberal theology could never have become or remained theologians if liberal theology had not been marked by a scrupulous regard for truth. The work of the orthodox university theologians, whatever shade of thought they represented, struck us as a feat of compromise which we ourselves would have found soul-destroying' (GV I, pp. 2–3). 'On the plane of historical science any *sacrificium intellectus* to the various orthodoxies must be dismissed out of hand' (*ibid.*, p. 8). In 1941, in his celebrated lecture 'The New Testament and Mythology', Bultmann declared: 'The critical work of earlier generations must not be allowed to sink into oblivion; it must be taken up again in a positive way' (KM I, p. 24).

Bultmann is known as perhaps the major figure in modern New Testament exegesis, one of the founders of the *Formgeschichtliche Schule*, which tries to reach behind the literary sources to make out, as far as may be, the various stages of tradition, from the earliest to the latest. Take the preaching of Jesus, for example. Critical analysis reveals that what the sources give us is first of all the preaching of the Christian community, most of which assuredly goes back to the words of Jesus himself. But that does not prove that he actually spoke every word which the community attributes to him. On the contrary, it can be shown that many of these sayings arose within the community and that others were recast by the community.

In fact the tradition about Jesus which we find in the synoptics is made up of a series of strata which generally speaking can be distinguished with reasonable certainty, though in many a case the task is difficult if not impossible. The reason is that the synoptic accounts were written down in Greek and within Hellenistic Christianity, whereas Jesus and the original community inhabited the quite different world of Palestine and spoke Aramaic. Consequently whatever in the synoptics can only have originated—given the language or the content —in Hellenistic Christianity, must be excluded from the preaching of Jesus. Criticism does show that the substance of the three synoptics goes back to the Aramaic tradition of the earliest Palestinian community. But even within that tradition several strata can still be discerned. Anything that is motivated by the specific interests of the community or indicates considerable development must be judged secondary to the preaching of Jesus. Thus critical analysis can make out the first layer of all with relative certainty.

Of course we have no absolute certainty that even the earliest sayings were really uttered by Jesus. Doubts that he ever existed do not deserve a word of refutation, and he is obviously the origin of the historical movement which to our knowledge first manifests itself in the initial Palestinian community; but determining how far that community preserved an accurate, objective image of his person and his preaching is quite another matter. We shall presently see why and how this critical 'extremism' not only raises no hindrance to faith but on the contrary throws the true nature of faith into high relief. In the first part of his monumental work on the history of the synoptic tradition (GST, pp. 8–223) Bultmann minutely examines the process by which the words of Jesus were handed down. Part Two deals with the transmission of the narratives.

Time and again, in the course of this book, we shall have occasion to use his critical findings, but we shall now cite a pregnant example of his historical method which will be of use to us later. The matter concerned is the problem of Jesus's messianic consciousness.

(1) According to the common opinion, the indubitable belief of the original community in Jesus's messiahship is based on the awareness he himself had of really being the Messiah (or the Son of Man).[3] Such was certainly the mind of the evangelists; but the question is precisely whether they did not themselves introduce this belief into the tradition about Jesus. It is quite arguable that faith in Jesus's messiahship was born of faith in his resurrection. The episode of Peter's messianic confession (Mk 8:27–30), far from discounting this hypothesis, confirms it, for criticism shows that the episode is only Mark's projection into Jesus's life of a paschal narrative.

The same must be said of the transfiguration (Mk 9:2–8). As for the baptism of Jesus, it has a legendary aspect which is as certain as its historical aspect: the actual fact of his being baptized by John the Baptist cannot be doubted; but the account of Jesus's investiture as the Messiah only goes back as far as the period when his life itself was considered messianic, whereas the story of the transfiguration—which, as we have said, was originally a paschal narrative—dates the messianic character of the resurrection. No less legendary is the episode of the Messiah's temptation (Mk 1:12ff); it expresses meditation on the nature of Jesus's messiahship and on the nature of Christian faith in the Messiah. Legend has also coloured the messianic entry into Jerusalem (Mk 11:1–10) and many features of Jesus's passion, for the community which honoured the risen Jesus as the Messiah was automatically convinced that he was also crucified as the Messiah.

---

3. Here we do not enter into the difference there is between the Messiah and the Son of Man, since both terms mean the bearer of eschatological salvation.

Now the synoptic tradition—notwithstanding the changes which it underwent, as we have just seen—shows beyond all doubt that the life and deeds of Jesus were not really messianic. So does Paul: witness the christological hymn he quotes in Phil 2:6–11, where the life of Jesus is regarded as the life of an ordinary human being, without any messianic radiance or glory. The same is clear from Rom 1:4, where Paul evidently uses a traditional formula. Acts 2:36 likewise proves that the earliest Christian community dated Jesus's messiahship from his resurrection. The word Messiah means the eschatological saviour, but it came to have a mere sense of *king* (βασιλεύς is substituted for it in Mk 15:2, 9, 18, 26, 32; Jn 1:49).

There was nothing of the king about Jesus. Rather he appeared as a prophet and a rabbi, and—we may add—as an exorcist. None of the power and glory which to the Jewish mind characterize the Messiah was to be seen in his life, not even in his exorcisms and other deeds of power. Even if miracles are, in Jewish belief, a sure sign of the messianic age, the Messiah himself is not a miracle-worker. If it be objected that according to what he said about the Son of Man Jesus did not think of the Messiah as a Davidic king but as the heavenly judge and saviour spoken of in apocalyptic literature, the case is in no way altered; for he did not manifest himself either as that judge or as that saviour.

(2) Will it be said that on his own authority he changed the traditional idea of the Messiah to something more inward and spiritual? Where in his words do we find him attacking the prevalent idea? Nowhere, any more than he attacks the Jewish conception of the kingdom of God. (Mk 12:35–37 does not question the traditional view of the Messiah.)

(3) Will we be told that Jesus was conscious of being the *future* Messiah? In support of this thesis the texts are cited where he speaks of the Son of Man in the future tense (Mk 8:38; Lk 12:8f and parallels;[4] Mt 24:27, 37, 44 and parallels; Lk 11:30). But he speaks in the third person, not identifying himself with the Son of Man. It is perfectly true that the evangelists—like the community which handed on Jesus's words—themselves identified the two, but by what right can anyone say that Jesus likewise did so?

There is not one word, in the synoptic tradition, of any prediction that Jesus will return some day. The word παρουσία, which means the coming of the Son of Man, was never rendered in the earliest tradition as 'return': quite correctly it was always 'coming'. Besides, how is

4. Parallels here, with reference to Mt and Lk, mean those texts parallel to Mk which Mt and Lk drew from Q (not from Mk itself).

Jesus supposed to have envisaged the connection between his present historical activity and his return as the Son of Man? He must have allowed for being removed from earth before the dawn of God's kingdom, to be able to play his later role on the clouds of heaven. But how did he think of this removal? As a miraculous phenomenon? His words bear not the slightest trace of such a fanciful idea. As a passing away by natural death? His words say nothing of that kind either.

Certainly the prophecies of the passion (Mk 8:31; 9:31; 10:33f) represent his death as an event brought about by God. But how can we doubt that they are *vaticinia ex eventu*? Moreover they do not speak of his parousia, any more than the prophecies of the parousia (Mk 8:38; 12:26f; 14:62; Mt 24:27, 37, 39, 44 and parallels) speak of the death and resurrection of the Son of Man. It is obvious that the prophecies of the parousia and those of the death and resurrection had nothing to do with each other originally. In other words one finds no hint at all, in the sayings about the Son of Man, that this Son of Man is already there in person and that first he must be removed by death so as to return later from heaven.

At this point consider the striking contrast between the prophecy of the parousia in Mk 8:38 and the prophecy of the passion and resurrection that goes before it. They are two entirely different things simply stuck together. Mk 9:1, 11–13 mentions only the parousia (12b is an interpolation modelled on Mt 17:12b); while the story of the transfiguration (9:2–10), which the envangelist has inserted between verses 1 and 11, originally consecutive, mentions nothing but the resurrection. Only Mt 17:12b brings the theme of the suffering Son of Man into the context of sayings about the parousia. Similarly Lk 17:25 combines the theme of suffering with prophecy of the parousia (also compare Lk 17:23–25 with Mt 24:26–27). All this joining up of the two themes was done later. Moreover it is impossible to doubt that the prophecies of the parousia are earlier than the prophecies of the passion and resurrection. Q contains only the former and not a trace of the latter, which are the work of the Hellenistic community, where the title Son of Man was not understood in its original sense, while the prophecies of the parousia probably go back to Jesus himself.

In short the synoptics present three groups of sayings about the Son of Man. The first speaks of the Son of Man to come; the second of the Son of Man who dies and rises again; the third of the Son of Man already present and active. This third group (Mk 2:10, 28; Mt 8:20 and parallels; 11:19 and parallels; 12:32 and parallels) arises from a wrong Greek translation of the Aramaic original, in which 'Son of Man' simply meant, was an alternative form of, the personal pronoun I. The second group comprises the *vaticinia ex eventu* which are missing in Q. Only the first group embodies the earliest tradition; it speaks of the Son of Man in the third person.

As for the material peculiar to Mk and Lk, it has no bearing on the present question. There the term Son of Man has become so much a self-designation of Jesus that Mt can substitute an 'I' for a traditional 'Son of Man' (10:32f as contrasted with Lk 12:8f; compare Mt 16:21 with Mk 9:31 and Mt 5:11 with Lk 6:22) and conversely 'Son of Man' for an 'I' (16:13, contrasting with Mk 8:27).

It is true that the prophecies of the passion do re-interpret the Jewish conception of the Messiah or Son of Man insofar as Judaism has no acquaintance with a Messiah or Son of Man who suffers, dies and rises from the dead. But this amplification of the sense is not the doing of Jesus himself. It was made *ex eventu* by the community. There certainly was an effort to show that Jesus believed he was the Suffering Servant of Isaiah and himself blended the two themes of the Son of Man and the Suffering Servant in the one figure of the Son of Man suffering, dying and rising again. But what we have already said about the unauthenticity of the prophecies of the passion rules out such an hypothesis. Besides which, the authentic words of Jesus that have come down to us reveal no hint of his having considered himself the Suffering Servant of Isaiah (despite recent but quite unconvincing attempts, Bultmann adds, by Wolff, Bieneck, Cullmann and J. Jeremias to show that he did).

(4) It was very soon unthinkable that the life of Jesus had not been a messianic life, at least in the Hellenistic Christian circles where the synoptic gospels took shape. Jesus must obviously have been the Messiah *even* during his lifetime. Consequently the earliest tradition about him was altered in the light of belief in his messiahship—at the cost of a glaring contradiction. That contradiction is ingenuously embodied in the theory of the messianic secret, which gives the Gospel of Mark its special character. The evangelist maintains that the earthly Jesus is already the Messiah, but his messiahship must be kept a secret until Jesus has risen from the dead (Mk 9:9). Therefore silence is imposed on the devils who recognize him as the Messiah (1:25, 34; 3:12). Silence is likewise enjoined after Peter's confession (8:38) and after the transfiguration (9:9).

The disciples are entrusted with a secret revelation, but we are told with an emphasis that is plainly deliberate that they do not understand it; so that the theme of their incomprehension, so prominent in Mark, subserves the equally characteristic theme of the secret. Thus the evangelist's theory of the secret reconciles his conviction that the life of Jesus cannot have failed to be messianic, with the fact that the earliest tradition knows nothing of a messianic life.

An attempt has been made (Schniewind) to show that this secret is not merely a theory of Mark's but answers to an historical reality. The thesis breaks down because the secret is missing from the early tradition, being found only in the editorial contributions of the evangelist. Moreover it assumes that Jesus 'interiorized' and 'spiritualized' the classic idea of the Messiah (since his activities on earth can have been messianic only in secret) and that he regarded himself as the Son of Man in his own heart until his return in triumph should blazon the truth for all to see. But here we once more come up against the difficulty, already explained, of crediting Jesus with a belief that he was the Son of Man to come (TNT, pp. 26–35). Therefore the texts which attribute a messianic consciousness to him are subsequent interpolations into the earliest tradition.

The same must be said of the texts that relate the circumstances of his birth. Countless studies of the infancy narratives have firmly established their legendary character to the satisfaction of any mind which does not confuse faith with the objectification of faith. If there can be no doubt, on the other hand, that Jesus cured the sick and cast out devils (whatever questions be asked about the true nature of these facts), nonetheless most of the miracles recounted in the gospels are legendary or have been embroidered with legend (JS, p. 146). We shall have occasion later to discuss the apparitions of the risen Christ. For the present let it be said that the paschal accounts and the legend of the empty tomb, which are supposed to be proof positive that the resurrection really happened, 'are without doubt later accretions of which Paul knows nothing' (KM I, p. 44), though he himself on one occasion succumbed to this kind of argument.[5]

Generally speaking, higher criticism shows that the divine aspect of Jesus *in its mythological (objectified, rationalized) form* was interpolated afterwards into the earliest tradition. We hope that the foregoing chapters afford a glimpse of exactly what the words in italics mean; to clarify them further will be the sole purpose of Part Two of this book. Of course conservative exegetes and theologians are up in arms against Bultmann. They feel that they oppose him on behalf of scholarship and faith. In due course we shall see that in reality they oppose him on behalf of a spurious scholarship and a spurious faith, both of which result from mixing revelation with the categories of natural man.

---

5. Critical discussion (*a*) of the miracles: GST, pp. 223–60; (*b*) of the infancy gospels: pp. 316–29; (*c*) of the apparitions: pp. 308–16.

II

GESCHICHTE

The essential aim of history (*Historie*) is not to study the past as a datum: history cannot be that kind of mere objective science. To suppose that it can was the error of the Greeks when they invented rational historiography. In accordance with their basic philosophical thinking, they saw the past as a complete thing which could only be the object of a knowledge such as that which tries to make out the essence of any natural phenomenon. The only difference was that historiography dealt with the past. But just as the natural sciences try to discover the structure of things and the laws that govern them—try, that is, to educe the unchangeable from the changeable and the general from the particular—so it was the business of history to formulate the great laws of the present and the future. Such is Thucydides' whole ambition. 'He regards human events as natural events and thus, even as an historian, he is a kind of scientist' (HE, p. 15). To his mind the unchanging element in history is ambition and the pursuit of power.

Therefore the significance of history lies in the useful lessons it gives for the future by showing what the past has been, on the rational assumption that the future is bound to be a repetition of the past. The movement of history is conceived on the analogy of movement in the cosmos, where every change is but a new form of the same thing. Let us add that the Latins had the same idea of history as the Greeks.

The same must be said of the historians of modern times, 'who in fact conceive of history on the analogy of nature. It seems that the business of historiographers is to establish facts and deduce laws from the interconnection of facts . . . They try to eliminate the subjectivity of the historian and to avoid pronouncing any value-judgment. Historiography is simply the science of facts; as to the nature of historical fact, historiography does not raise the issue' (HE, p. 78).

This reduction of history to nature goes back (in modern times) to Vico (1668–1744), who takes up again, if with certain modifications, the ancient theme of cyclical movement. Every cycle passes through three stages: the age of the gods, or barbarism; the heroic age of aristocratic constitutions, represented for Greece by the Homeric age and for Europe by the Middle Ages; and the classical age of monarchies and republics, when thought prevails over imagination, prose over poetry, and so forth. All ends in barbarism and thence a new cycle begins. But it is not a case of sheer repetition. For Vico—and here he diverges from the Greeks—admits a spiral progression: the barbarism of the *ricorso* differs from the barbarism of the *corso*, and so on. In short, if our thinker historicized nature, he naturalized history even more.

As we know, for a long period his work exerted no influence; but it was at least paralleled by that of Herder (*Ideen zur Philosophie der Geschichte der Menschheit*, 1784–1791), who also reduces history to nature. He makes evolution the central theme of his thought: beginning his book with a description of cosmic and geological evolution, he ends it with a description of animal life, of which mankind is the highest species. He does indeed declare that man is reason; but as he does not perceive that man is also freedom, the history of mankind is nothing more in his eyes than an evolution of the mind. Peoples necessarily develop along the lines of their *Volksgeist*, and history as a whole exhibits no oneness.

Herder, together with Rousseau and Hamann, had a tremendous influence on the Romantic movement. The idea of the *Volksgeist*, in particular, led to historical relativism, according to which there exists no natural law, only positive law. There are no moral rules that bind all men. Each age has its own ethics. Men of the Romantic revival are not interested in what is changeless and eternal but only in *Erlebnis*. Thus as they react against the Enlightenment, far from condemning the medieval past, they will find there the same irrational forces that each individual can observe in himself. Hence the interest in the art, the poetry, the popular songs and tales of the Middle Ages and a leaning towards the Catholic Church seen, for instance, in Novalis's *Die Christenheit oder Europa* (1799). At bottom, then, *Erlebnis* is an esthetic attitude towards history as well as towards nature. And in fact the Romantics look on historical events as natural events.

This approach lived on in modern historiography, which was given its naturalist expression par excellence in Oswald Spengler's work *Der Untergang des Abendlandes* (1918). According to Spengler, only particular civilizations exist, quite cut off one from another. The only link between them is sheer temporal succession, so that the science, philosophy, and so forth of each civilization are absolutely its own; different cultures have nothing in common with each other. In every cycle the same process is repeated, from the barbarism of archaic times to the classical age, when science, law and politics arise. A civilization is like a plant that germinates, grows, matures and dies.

No effort is required to perceive the unity in this long tradition of naturalist historiography, from Thucydides to Spengler. It envisages historical facts on the model of natural facts. Whether in the cyclical movement of the Greeks, the *corso* and *ricorso* of Vico, Herder's *Volksgeist*, nineteenth-century positivism, or Spengler's isolated civilizations, always and everywhere historical event is regarded more or less as a complete reality, as a thing. We granted earlier in this chapter that there is certainly some truth to this idea of historical fact and to the science that studies it.

But all the same one cannot stop there. Objective historiography falls short of real historiography, because it insists that historical fact is essentially natural fact and nothing more. In other words, we say that historical event is never finished: it perdures, so that its meaning (see pp. 16–7, above) will not be completely revealed until the end of history. From the spatio-temporal point of view the fact that Socrates drank the hemlock, Caesar crossed the Rubicon, Luther put up the ninety-five theses, are 'finished' facts, 'dead' facts. But their meaning is far from finished and dead, for they have by no means displayed that meaning yet in all its implications and all its depth. It still endures and determines our existence.

Not until the end of history will the meaning of Luther's appearance upon the scene be known, because it is still unfolding its consequences in the world of today and because without Luther (Caesar, Socrates) the world would not be what it now is. So too with the world of tomorrow, which will be determined in part by them and generally speaking by all the history of past ages.

'Historical phenomena are not what they are in their sheer individual isolation but only in their relation to the future for which they matter. We may say that every historical phenomenon has a future of its own, a future in which alone it will be seen for what it really is—or, to be more precise, the future in which it will more and more be seen for what it is. After all, it will not disclose itself in its real essence until history has reached its goal' (HE, p. 120; GV 3, p. 113), for being itself is 'historicity' (pp. 327–8, below).

The past is not merely a dead past, it is also a present; or rather a future that summons us to answer, that still has something to say to us. History lays an *Anspruch* upon us and challenges us to dialogue. It is an *Anrede* (see p. 18, above). So we are responsible for what must be called the to-be of the past. Every Protestant, for example, is responsible for the Protestant past, which is still going on. It is not closed but open and by its very nature it is incomplete as to its meaning—in other words, as to its true being. This meaning can be disclosed only by our ec-sistence, in and by the freedoms that we are, in accordance with all that we have said about man's 'historicity'.

Rich with a meaning whose every aspect has not yet been revealed, the past is an *Anrede* directed to us. The present historical situation is constituted by the appeal which being addresses to us. Our business is to hearken to the καιρός. The Protestants of today are the people responsible for the Protestantism of today. They must respond to the imperative which constitutes the future of their past. The French are in the same position with regard to their French past, the Chinese with regard to their Chinese past, mankind with regard to its human past. 'The present is the moment of decision, and by taking his decision a man plucks the fruit of the past and chooses the meaning of the future. Such is the nature of every historical situation; in it the problem and meaning of past and future are shut up, as it were waiting to be manifested by the decision of man' (HE, pp. 141–2).

Accordingly human freedom does not invent the question which it must answer. If man helps to create the historical situation it is only by his response, which 'allows' this or that aspect of the past 'to exist', the aspect corresponding to the 'historical' moment. Thus there is set up between the past and the future (present) of the past that dialectic of the *Thou* and the *I* which we have described. Historians have indeed perceived the relativity of the present, but they understand it as the relativity of a particular point within a series of causes. The present being wholly determined, it is not a present of decision, whereas that is what it ought to be both for the past and for the future: for the past, because what we are about is disclosing one of the possibilities with which the past is pregnant; for the future, because as the to-be of an incomplete past the future must reveal a new aspect of the past. Today, in the *hic et nunc*, mankind decides the meaning of his heretofore and his hereafter.

The ec-sistential view of history derives from the Bible. It is obviously not by chance that the Greeks were the people who conceived of historical event as a datum and of historiography on the analogy of the natural sciences. That is only a particular instance of their general philosophy. Conversely, the biblical conception of history is only one facet of biblical thought as a whole. To the mind of the Bible, events are not finished things nor are historical periods isolated cycles. Events and periods are connected by a goal, a purpose. A particular episode is never complete; it will only be complete when God's design for the world has been carried out.

Historical fact is weighty with a meaning that transcends it as a mere objective datum. The meaning of each epoch only emerges in terms of the end of history. The people are responsible for the future of their past, which will bring them weal or woe, blessing or chastisement, according as they are obedient or disobedient. Man certainly does not create the future, but he discloses its meaning in this respect or that, according to his attitude. History is an *Anrede* of God, who challenges man to dialogue and awaits his free response.

Biblical historiography is steeped in this conception. The Yahwist takes for his guide the theme of the people's national unity under the leadership of Judah. This unity rests upon God's promise, which binds together the origin and the end of man. For although the Yahwist account ends with the fall of the house of David and the disunion of the twelve tribes, there is still the hope that the future will restore the nation under the sway of Judah and her kings. So the course of events is seen as an advance towards a goal.

Influenced by the great prophets of the eighth and seventh century, the Elohist also sees the course of events as a highly significant whole. History shows us the alternation of God's grace and the nation's sinfulness, of his judgment with their repentance and pardoning. Herodotus too saw the explanation of events in the government of the gods, who punish the evil and reward the good; but to his mind the course of events was not thereby changed, whereas the Elohist sees history moving towards a goal and God's chastisement means that the people are that much nearer the goal. He ends his account with the destruction of Jerusalem and the fall of Judah. While he considers this disaster to be a punishment from God, a door remains open to the future because the dynasty of David has not died out.

The Deuteronomist adaptation of Israel's history is also influenced by the prophets. The meaning of history is the kingdom of God, who has chosen Israel to be his people. Reflection on the past brings to light a series of idolatries, of divine chastisements executed by foreign oppressors, of repentances, and finally of deliverances. Thus understood, the account is a critical history of the past and an exhortation for the present, together with the promise of a salvation to come if the people obey their God. The priestly editor is specially concerned to point out God's revelation in the past. History is divided into the stages of this progessive revelation. The first three stages begin respectively with Adam, Noah and Abraham. Then comes Moses, to whom the author attributes the priestly legislation. Finally he makes the goal of the people's history their return from exile and their reestablishment as a cultic community under the Law.

All these Old Testament representations of history are obviously ec-sistential and not scientific. History follows the course that is assigned to it in God's plan. Thus each event has a future that is not the false future of an object, because it is pregnant with many possibilities which man is called on to disclose. God is not a fate fixing the course of things. That is precisely why he promises and chastises, which otherwise would be absurd. He will keep his promises only if the people are obedient. Man's attitude affects history according as he is faithful or faithless to the *Anrede* which God addresses to him through history. There is no substantialist dualism between history and man but rather a relation of call and response. 'Historiography is determined by the sense of responsibility which the present age has with regard to its inheritance of blessings and curses from the past and with regard to the future which will bring either salvation or death' (cp, p. 19).

According to the Old Testament (excepting Daniel and Ezra 24–27), God's judgment and salvation take place within history. There is no eschatology. Apocalyptic Judaism, on the other hand, distinguishes two aeons and thus envisages history from an eschatological point of view. But the only link between these two aeons is that of bare temporal succession. A cosmic disaster will end the first aeon, with respect to which the second aeon will be a wholly extrinsic event. 'The end is really the end of the world and of its history. The end of history is no longer part of history as such. Therefore this end cannot be called the goal of history, towards which history is advancing by stages. The end does not complete history but abolishes it; it is rather like the world's dying of old age. A new creation will take the place of the old world without there being any continuity between the two aeons' (he, p. 30). Thus apocalyptic Judaism falls back into substantialist (mythological) dualism.

The New Testament preserves Jewish eschatology but thinks of it in ec-sistential terms—radically, that is, on the plane of freedom and true otherness. Jesus's preaching makes the matter perfectly clear. He announces the eschatological kingdom of God, but this kingdom will not come as a fate, regardless of how human freedoms behave themselves. Obvious as it is that man neither creates nor merits the kingdom, it is no less obvious that he must freely decide for or against it. Jesus's preaching is a summons to decision: a man must choose between God and the world. 'Do not lay up for yourselves treasures on earth . . . For where your treasure is, there will your heart be also' (Mt 6:19–21 and parallels). 'No one can serve two masters' (Mt 6:24 and parallels). 'It is easier for a camel to go through the eye of a needle than for a rich man to enter the kingdom of God' (Mk 10:25). Most men become attached to the possessions and cares of this world and when they are called to decision, refuse (Lk 14:15–24 and parallels).

One must be ready to make any sacrifice for the kingdom, like the man who having found a treasure in a field covers it up again and sells all he has and buys that field; like the merchant who, on finding one pearl of great value, sells all he has and buys it (Mt 13:44–46). 'If your hand causes you to sin, cut it off; it is better for you to enter life maimed than with two hands to go to hell' (Mk 9:43, 47). 'No one who puts his hand to the plough and looks back is fit for the kingdom of God' (Lk 9:62). 'Follow me, and leave the dead to bury their own dead' (Mt 8:22 and parallels). 'If any one comes to me and does not hate his own father and mother and wife and children and brothers and sisters, yes, and even his own life, he cannot be my disciple' (Lk 14:26 and parallels). 'Whoever does not bear his own cross and come after me, cannot be my disciple' (Lk 14:27 and parallels).

Thus the kingdom cannot come without the free consent of men. Jesus's preaching is at once a cry of malediction and a call to repentance, a fact which would be inexplicable if a man were not responsible for his eschatological future. Woe to you, scribes and pharisees . . . (see Mt 23:1f). Woe to you that are rich . . . Woe to you that are full now . . . (see Lk 6:24–26). 'The time is fulfilled, and the kingdom of God is at hand; repent' (Mk 1:15). But his contemporaries are an 'adulterous and sinful generation' (Mk 8:38). They say yes to God's demand but do not obey it (Mt 21:28–31). They will not give up the error of their ways (Lk 11:31 and parallels). This brings down upon them God's judgment (Lk 13·1–5) and the fulfilment of the prophecies of woe (Mt 23:34–36 and parallels). In particular, Jerusalem will be destroyed (Mt 23:37–39) and of the temple not one stone will be left upon another (Mk 13:2).

A readiness to repent is found only in the publicans, sinners and harlots, for whom Jesus says he has primarily come (Mk 2:17). Because he has come for those who at first said no but then repented (Mt 21:28–31). God rejoices more over one sinner who repents than over ninety-nine righteous people (Lk 15:1–10). The promise of salvation is for those who really wait on God, who are hungry, who weep, who know that they are poor (Lk 6:20–21).

Jesus, then, takes an 'historical' view of eschatology. The future is the future of a present, of a free decision made for or against God. In the present, man discloses the meaning of his future, which will be life or perdition. By and in his decision he gathers together his past and chooses the meaning of his future, which will be quite different according to whether it is open to the kingdom, like the decision of the sinners and publicans, or closed to it like that of the scribes and pharisees and 'righteous' people in general. We have seen (p. 43, above) how Paul also considers man responsible for his eschatological future. Thus the old aeon has a meaning for the aeon that is to come. Whereas in Jewish eschatology the past was simply annihilated, in Paul's eyes the history of mankind under the law and sin abounds with meaning. Paradoxically, sin is necessary in order for grace to appear (Rom 5:15 and particularly 5:20f; see Gal 3:19–22). So we have a dialectical relation between the two aeons.

Just as the naturalist view of history which was the Greek view endured into modern times, down to Vico and Spengler, so the ecsistential view found in the Bible likewise had a long career—first of all, naturally enough, in the Christian Church. Here the most illustrious name is that of Augustine. Notably in the *De Civitate Dei* he understands the meaning of history to be what is at stake in the struggle between the *civitas caelestis* and the *civitas terrena*, between faith and unbelief.

History is the field where decisions are made for one or other of the two cities. If from many points of view the Middle Ages relapsed into substantialism, all medieval Christians nevertheless assumed as a matter of course that the world is making its way towards the goal which God has set it. Joachim of Flora (1131–1202) distinguishes three ages: that of the Father, that of the Son, and that of the Holy Spirit, which latter is to begin in 1260 and last until the second coming of Christ. Much later Bossuet, in his *Discours sur l'histoire universelle*, will have nothing to add to the traditional Christian view, which presently is secularized in the concept of progress so dear to the heart of modern man.

In our own time the anthropological (but not anthropocentric) idea of history has been taken up again by thinkers like Dilthey, Croce, Jaspers, Heidegger and Collingwood. They all sift out the originality of historical events as against natural facts, of history as against the natural sciences. Like other philosophers contemporaneous with him (Windelband and Rickert, for example), Dilthey's effort is to justify the distinction which he draws between the 'human sciences' (*sciences de l'esprit*) and the 'natural sciences' (*sciences de la nature*). Thus he distinguishes between explanatory psychology and comprehensive psychology. The former treats of psychical phenomena on the purely causal plane whereas the latter tries to reveal their structure and meaning. We are wrong to study human life on a purely objective basis, as though it were simply a datum. In fact it has a primal vitality whose expressions brim over with purpose and meaning.

History is precisely the field where these manifestations take shape: in culture, in the political and social order, in religion, in art, in the various *Weltanschauungen*. Thus life embodies itself in works of which history can only be the interpretation: behind the objectification of life in works, history must search for the teeming seedbed from which they have sprung—for the soul that reveals itself only in them. It is possible to do this, because the interpreter himself shares in human nature. As Dilthey says, there is an original *Verwandschaft* (affinity) between the interpreter and the creator of the work, an affinity heightened by the fact that the interpreter enters into the life of the creator with his own life, so that the experience objectified in the work can be understood by another living soul.

Of course there are different kinds of psychical experience and therefore different kinds of philosophy, art, religion, *Weltanschauung*. So it is not for the historian to raise the question of truth; his only business is to disclose the soul. 'We seek the soul', Dilthey writes. 'That is where we have got to with the long evolution of historiography.' So there is no need to ask what is the goal of history. There are only individual experiences. Man is an 'historical' being only in the sense that the soul constantly brings forth works as so many manifestations of itself. When all is said and done, Dilthey looks at history as an esthetician. It is a spectacle in which the historian delights to reveal man's various possibilities in the past as his own possibilities.

While owing a good deal to Hegel, Benedetto Croce differs from him in one important respect. Hegel thinks of the historical process as embracing the whole of history, from its beginnings to the shape in which it will have hardened at the last stage. Thus he looks on it as a (dialectical) progress. Croce says that mankind remains in some sense the same through all the changes which it undergoes. 'Mankind', he says, 'is a whole within each age and within each human individual.' Each moment, therefore, although it relates to the whole, abounds with a significance of its own, because in it is concentrated the meaning of the whole historical process; whereas for Hegel the present is only a mediation.

No need, then, for us to attempt a knowledge of history as a whole. Historical truth is found in the individual phenomenon, where the whole constantly presents itself anew. It is the business of each 'now' to gather up the heritage of the past by solving the problems that it poses and carrying out the tasks that it allots. So the present is responsible for the future. Mankind exists only in the problems and tasks of the moment.

Being thus 'placed', the historian cannot master history so as to know it in all its range. His business is to disclose the meaning of individual phenomena in the past by reliving them. What field of study he will choose depends on the interest of the age in which he lives, because historical knowledge is born of the need for action in the present. It is the problems of today that open our eyes to the problems of the past. No one can deny the profundity of Croce's thought, which throws Hegelian necessity into bold relief. And so one wonders whether it is not inconsistent for him to maintain that 'reason is the true essence of man'.

Bultmann thinks that the soundest observations made in recent years on the problems of history are those of Collingwood in his study *The Idea of History* (1946–1949). Throughout his work Collingwood shows that he is bent on explaining with the utmost possible penetration the difference between the historical sciences and the natural sciences and between their respective objects. Human acts are the object of historical science. Every event has an inner aspect and an outer one The historian may begin by establishing the latter but he must not stop there. Remembering that the past was an act, he must make it his chief business to reveal the thought of the men who did the act.

The historical process is a process of thought. Now the historian cannot *perceive* ideas as a scientist perceives natural phenomena; he must *understand* them by reviving them and reliving them. Accordingly history is a rebirth (re-enactment) of the ideas of the past in the mind of the historian.

This rebirth of thoughts gone by is obviously not a mere imitation or repetition of the act of the man who thought them. It is that act as 'surviving and reviving' in different times and in different persons—that is, in the life of the historian and in the life of the man whose history he is relating. To put it another way, the rebirth is not a passive surrender to the spell of another mind but an active and therefore critical exploit of thought. 'This critique of the thought whose history he [the historian] is retracing is of no small importance precisely in unearthing that history', Collingwood says. (Translated into Bultmann's language, this means that we reach the past by disclosing those meanings of the past which answer to the tasks of the present.) The critique must not be made as from outside history but as from inside it. For if the conceptual systems of the past remain valid for later generations it is not in spite of their historical character but rather because of it. In our eyes the ideas they convey are things of the past, but that past is not dead. By understanding it we absorb it into our present thought; and by working up and critically examining this inheritance we are able to use it for our own advancement.

Thus Collingwood comes to the point of saying that 'whenever the historian finds that an historical subject is unintelligible, he has discovered a limitation of his own mind'. So the investigator begins by knowing the present of the past. 'Each present', Collingwood continues, 'has its own past and each reconstruction that the imagination makes is meant to reconstruct the past of this present—the present in which the act of imagination is going on—as perceived here and now. In principle the purpose of the act is to use the entirely tangible here-and-now as evidence of all the past whereby it has come into being . . . For even when the events which history studies are events that took place in a remote past, they can be historically known only if "they vibrate in the human mind"—that is, if the evidence for them is present to the human mind and intelligible to it here and now.'

Hence the distinction which the natural sciences draw between subject and object is not a legitimate distinction in history. What makes history objective is its very subjectivity, because the subject and object of historical science do not exist independent of each other.

Historical knowledge is itself an historical event; it forms part of a process in which the historian is as deep as the object that he hopes to disclose. That is why the findings of his research are never definitive. Each generation has to rewrite history. Each new historian must not only give original answers to old questions, he must restate the problems themselves.

This idea of history involves an antisubstantialist view of man, whom Collingwood defines as mind. But to his way of thinking the mind is not an essence underlying the activities of the subject. In the case of a machine, he explains, we differentiate between the structure and its working; but we cannot think in these terms about man, who is action and life. More logical than Croce, Collingwood does not conceive of man as reason, though obviously there is no such thing as a mind without reason. The mind is something more than reason, it is freedom—as Collingwood recognizes when he defines thought as a deliberate effort whereby we realize a thing of which we have an antecedent idea.

A deliberate act is an act that we do on purpose. To judge a person's acts is to judge the person in respect of his intentions. Therefore thought includes the will. It is a decision in which a man's whole being is at stake. 'A historian's thought should spring from the organic oneness of all his experience and be an act of his whole person, with its practical interests as well as its theoretical ones.'

The affinity of outlook between Dilthey, Croce and Collingwood on the one hand and Bultmann on the other, will escape no one. All of them have recognized the 'historicity' of history and man, each in his own way. But they have not all managed to avoid the twofold danger of relativism and nihilism. Dilthey is least felicitous in this respect. True, he half-escapes by seeing the life of the soul as the source and ground of historical events, but only half-escapes; for where is truth, to Dilthey's mind, where is the absolute, if not in man? And then can one still say that man is intentionality and ec-sistence? As to Croce and Collingwood, one wonders whether they have made enough of responsibility for the future. Can Croce's man-who-is-reason be fully 'historical'?

Collingwood says that history exists for self-knowledge. This knowledge of self certainly includes knowledge of the present situation with its inheritance and its problems, but does it adequately include responsibility for the future? Is not Collingwood still too substantialist in this respect? It is only in Heidegger that the problem of history has emerged 'with definite clarity' (GV 2, pp. 226–7; see below, ch. 16, § IV).

Such is the ec-sistential idea of history. Since the idea is of biblical origin, it would be nonsense to try to interpret the two Testaments in terms of an objective history which is entirely alien to them. Yet this is what conservative exegetes do more or less—and more or less consciously—when they treat revelation as an 'objective' or 'supra-objective' divine fact. We shall presently show that such is the case. As was said earlier, Bultmann has devoted a very large part of his life and work to scientific exegesis of the New Testament, but always in the service of the real, specific purpose behind the Word of God. To show what this means in the concrete will be the aim of Part Two of this book.

Bringing the Categories into play

THE PROBLEM STATED

Protestants generally hold that after the time of the ancient Catholic Church, Greek philosophy more or less adulterated the purity of revelation, and that matters went from bad to worse until the Reformers returned to the pure gospel—that is, to the *sola Scriptura*, the *intimior intimo meo* of traditional Protestantism. Now the deepest significance of Bultmann's work is that it calls this idea in question— certainly not, as people often suppose, in the name of the 'religious experience' dear to the heart of liberals; much less in the name of 'modern man'; but in the name of *sola Revelatio*.

What he is about is this: distinguishing between God's Word and the book which contains it, but above all taking this distinction in deadly earnest and carrying it to its utmost consequences. The distinction between scripture and revelation is not his own. Luther set it forth with matchless power, as we shall see. Karl Barth took it up again (TKD, pp. 5, 7–8); but how timidly compared with Luther, how very timidly compared with the thorough and remorseless Bultmann. For Bultmann holds that the 'philosophy of the natural man' lurks not only in ecclesiastical tradition but *even in scripture itself*. We have seen that the philosophy of the object is not the esoteric philosophy of a few rare minds. It is what Bergson called the natural metaphysics of the human mind. From the moment a man is man enough to distinguish himself from things, he is a philosopher.

To be born a human being is to be born a 'rational animal'. As human beings, the witnesses to revelation bore within themselves a graceless cast of mind. Anyone who thought he could exempt them from it by a sort of immaculate conception would have to be answered, '*Nondum considerasti quanti ponderis sit peccatum*'. Those witnesses too exemplify the *simul peccator simul justus*. They were not yet in eternal life. It is a fact that revelation did not miraculously change them, and it is likewise a fact that *quidquid recipitur ad modum recipientis recipitur*. If revelation itself is the pure Word of God, the rendering of revelation which we have in the biblical documents is not, because that has been more or less warped by the objectivism native to the human mind. No doubt, as we have shown, the Bible bursts the categories of natural thought. Had Bultmann said no more than this, he would hardly have called forth objections or excitement. But his special merit has been to lay bare 'an outright contradiction running through the whole New Testament: on the one hand the cosmic determination of man, on the other the summons to decision; on the one hand sin seems to be man's fate, on the other he is to blame for it; cheek by jowl with Paul's indicative we find the imperative, and so on. To sum up, on the one hand man is envisaged as a cosmic thing, and on the other as an autonomous *I* which can gain itself or be lost by its own decision' (KM I, p. 23).

In a word, if the New Testament is absolutely pure as revelation, it is ambiguous as a witness to revelation: the biblical writers did not succeed in quite shaking off a philosophy which tends to make the kerygma a thing that falls within the grasp of reason. We have seen how Jesus, Paul and John demythologized the Old Testament by understanding and uttering revelation on the plane of 'historicity'— that is, by making God the one Lord and the one Saviour of man. But many vestiges of objectifying thought are still to be found in the Bible; even in Paul, even in John. These vestiges reveal the true *purpose* of the biblical witnesses, which is to speak of God as the Wholly Other and of Christ as his Word. *Therefore the necessity for demythologization is engraved upon the New Testament itself.* Demythologization is not an arbitrary business, taken in hand on the strength of some criterion outside the New Testament (criticizing the New Testament in the name of a *Weltanschauung* was the error of theological liberalism, as we shall see): it is carrying on with a task that was begun and in all essentials finished by the New Testament itself.

Bultmann's adversaries have failed to grasp this point. Most of them agree that the Bible must be interpreted in one way or another. But when it comes to deciding what the norm of interpretation shall be they are altogether at a loss. The more faint-hearted make shift with eliminating details that particularly offend the thinking of our day, like baptism for the dead or the idea that to receive Communion unworthily may do one physical harm. They will sometimes be unsure what to do with, say, a resurrection worked by Paul in Acts that is obviously postfabricated. But even those who in principle admit the difference between revelation and scripture hardly know how to apply it and know still less where to draw the line.

The question Bultmann is most often asked is this: 'How far will you go with demythologization?' To ask this question is to admit that one has no criterion for distinguishing between *Scriptura* and *Revelatio*; which leaves one practically defenceless against Catholicism. It has always been the chief illusion of Protestantism to imagine that it can dispose of Catholicism with the *sola Scriptura*. In fact the Catholic principle is already there in scripture, and the Roman Church has every right to invoke the Bible in support of her opinions and of the account she gives of herself. Of course, not everything is in scripture that she says is there (the New Testament contains no trace of the papacy, the seven sacraments, or many another essential article of Catholic faith); but the fundamental principle of Catholicism *is* there—that is, the *objectification* of the divine, the mixture of revelation with the philosophy of natural man or, expressed in Lutheran terminology, of faith with works.

Luther himself, with his matchless integrity and his extraordinary discernment between the things of God and the things of man, was perfectly aware of this truth. He admitted that 'works' are already there in scripture, and consequently that Catholicism is already there in scripture. To those who objected the texts which deal with works, his retort was: 'Christ is the Lord of scripture and of all works . . . I care nothing for texts of scripture, though you should find me six hundred for the righteousness of works against the righteousness of faith, and appeal to scripture against me. As for me, I have the author and Lord of scripture on my side . . . You urge the slave, that is scripture, and not even the whole of it or the principal part but only some passages relating to works. I leave that slavery to you. As for me, I urge the Lord who is the king of scripture . . . He it is whom I have, I cleave to him. Works I leave to you, who have never done them anyhow' (WA 40, I, pp. 458–9).

'He who does not teach Christ is not apostolic, though it be Peter or Paul who teaches. Contrariwise he who preaches Christ is apostolic, though it be Judas, Annas or Herod who does it' (WA, *Die Deutsche Bibel*, 7, p. 385). Luther very often applied this lapidary principle. He applied it to the Letter of James, which 'flatly contradicting St Paul and all the rest of scripture, attributes justification to works . . . It is only an epistle of straw . . . for there is nothing of the gospel in it' (WA, *Die Deutsche Bibel*, 7, p. 385, §§6 and 10). He applied it to the Letter of Jude, which is 'useless' (*ibid.*, 7, p. 386). He applied it to the Letter to the Hebrews, which 'seems to contradict the whole gospel and the epistles of St Paul', which 'seems to be a hotchpotch', 'perhaps of wood, straw and hay' (*ibid.*, 7, p. 344). And finally he applied it to the Apocalypse, which 'my own mind cannot put up with . . . I stick to the books which give me Christ plain and simple' (*ibid.*, 7, p. 404).

Hence to shrink from criticizing the New Testament on the grounds that it is scripture, is an untenable position for a Protestant and we may say a craven one, because it springs from the same need for security which characterizes Catholicism. Such a Protestant forgets that scripture is not the criterion of revelation but that rather revelation is the criterion of scripture. Only the Holy Spirit can be the norm of the Holy Spirit. It must be added that Catholics do not mistake the significance of Bultmann's work. One of them, a German theologian, has gone so far as to say that Bultmann is the most consistent of all modern Protestants. Coming from such a source this is not praise, but it may be the truth.

At any rate it will be obvious that Bultmann is already there in Luther; obvious how wrong people are to accuse him, as they so often do, of making 'modern man' the criterion of New Testament interpretation. They have not understood the import of his celebrated lecture on demythologization (KM I, pp. 15–48). Certainly Bultmann is concerned for the man of today, but as Luther was for the man of his time—solely in order to bring him the unadulterated gospel.

When he says it is absurd (*sinnlos*) to demand that our contemporaries accept as truth those things in the New Testament which are a remnant of mythology, it is not because he would make the modern outlook the norm of faith but simply because 'there is nothing whatever specifically Christian in the mythical picture of the world' (KM I, p. 16). Again when he says that 'a blind acceptance of New Testament mythology would be capricious', he means that to represent it as a demand of the Christian religion would be 'reducing faith to the level of works' (KM I, p. 17).

Possibly Bultmann's readers have been misled by his sympathy for modern man. This man is in a sense nearer to the gospel than the 'Greek', since he is a secularized Christian. We shall see that modern philosophy is in large measure a 'Christian truth gone mad', to quote Chesterton's phrase. As Bultmann says, 'without the New Testament, without Luther, without Kierkegaard, there would be no modern philosophy at all' (KM I, p. 35). What is true of modern philosophy holds equally good of the age which it expresses. Thus 'many New Testament sayings speak directly and with no ado to the man of today, whereas others baffle and defeat him' (KM I, p. 23). The latter are precisely those which derive from mythology.

The sensitivity of our contemporaries to the gospel must therefore be taken into account, but only insofar as they stand nearer to faith in some ways than the ancients did, or are more disposed to accept the real scandal of faith, or insofar as there is a kind of noble 'complicity' between revelation and themselves. This complicity is obvious in the various forms of existentialism. But it also exists, somewhat more negatively, in the philosophies of naturalism and idealism.

The naturalist sees man as a biological-psychical unit and rejects any divine intervention of a mythological kind—one, that is, which would mix with biological and psychical reality on their own ground and as it were compete with them. Here he is right, as we shall see in the chapter dealing with miracles. If he is wrong to rule out God's action, he cannot be blamed for balking at an objectified idea of that action. He does not understand—and quite rightly so—how the Christian *pneuma* can be the same kind of factor, though 'super-natural', as biological and psychical factors.

To the mind of the idealist, man is also a unit, not an aggregate of principles. He is conditioned by his body, no doubt, but in such a way that he remains answerable for it. Only a God who addresses himself to freedom, then, will be acceptable to the idealist. He quite rightly rejects any magico-mythological intervention on the part of God.

In a word, the man of today sees himself as a unit responsible for itself; and in this respect, though he may be unaware of the fact or may deny it, he remains faithful to biblical anthropology. Accordingly when Bultmann speaks of modern man he never for a moment loses sight of the only valid criterion of New Testament criticism: revelation. 'Demythologization does not mean making faith acceptable to modern man by whittling away tradition or the affirmations of scripture in the name of higher criticism; it means clarifying what Christianity is and thus facing modern man with the issue of decision' (KM 3, p. 50).

Now we must set about concretely implementing the ec-sistential interpretation. Bultmann observes that it hardly matters what we call it and that it can also be called the anthropological interpretation, provided—he hastens to add—we do not confuse ec-sistential analysis of the human being with the anthropology of objectifying thought, which treats man as a mere earthly phenomenon (KM 2, p. 184, n. 1). Indeed we must once more denounce the fatal error of imagining that Bultmann makes man the norm of revelation.

We have seen that to define man as ec-sistence is to define him as intentionality. Therefore to interpret the New Testament ec-sistentially is to withhold supremacy from the human subject and the objectifying thought that is native to him. It is to look on God's Word as a *Dass* and not a *Was*. Far from subjectifying revelation, the ec-sistential interpretation proposes to *let it exist* in its radical otherness and absolute lordship.

CHAPTER SIX

God

I

GOD IS NOT AN OBJECT

To talk of God as an object is atheism, just as to talk of love as an object is not to love. Doing so, one talks *about* God and *about* love, not *of* God and *of* love. To talk *about* someone is to discuss him from one's own point of view. Speaking *of* God implies that one has one's being in him, so that one speaks of him from his point of view. Proofs of his existence are mere discourse about him, because by definition they are what one relies on in order to reach him. And so they are revealed as a 'work'. Their inner purpose is to show that starting from himself and without being actually 'irrational' man can believe in God. Whether the point of departure be cosmological, logical, moral, affective or mystical is neither here nor there. In each case one believes in God by starting with the world and man; that is to say, one believes not in God but in oneself.

A knowledge that denies God is not the only atheist knowledge: far more deeply atheist is any knowledge that claims to know anything about God. To state general truths about God is to make affirmations which are supposed to hold good whatever may be the footing of the speaker or the position of the divinity he is speaking about. Such a science of God need not be erroneous but it is bound to be sinful. Luther points out that Adam's sin was not breaking God's commandment but wondering: has God really forbidden this? His sin was the *disputare de Deo*, speaking of God from the point of view of man.

To ask questions about God is to call *him* in question, because it is to turn his lordship into a problem: it is to ask *oneself* whether he exists and whether one is 'right' to believe in him. Doubtless someone will object that there can be a 'good' *disputare de Deo*. Is this not the case when a man asks himself honest questions? But even that is still a sin, for such an attitude implies that one can seek the truth about God as one seeks it about an object; it implies that man, if he is upright, can find God by asking himself questions about God.

The truth is that when I have reached the end of my 'honest', 'sincere' intellectual or moral road and finally believe in God, all I believe in is myself, because I do not believe in God from God's point of view (*aus Gott*). Believing in God *aus Gott* is only possible if God takes the initiative and comes to meet me, so that what I do is a mere response. In other words, I cannot speak of God without at the same time speaking of myself—that is, without being determined by him, regardless of my ec-sistentiell footing. I do not first satisfy myself that God exists and then allow him to rule over me. God is not that kind of being. Such a procedure befits objective knowledge; it does not befit the knowledge of God. To 'see' God, in the evangelic sense, I must give up the attitude of an observer. God is recognized as *extra me* only in encounter itself—that is, when he is my *Sichverstehen*.

Meanwhile to speak of everything from my point of view is not to speak from God's point of view. Is it speaking 'of' God, for instance, to speak out of religious experience and the interior life, or out of piety? Can one find God by relying on the experience which someone else has of him? More to the point, if I rely on my own past experiences to rescue me from my present doubts, is that finding God? Who is to say that those experiences are not illusions and that I am not closer to the truth now in my doubt than I was in the days when I believed? Which is sounder: my present doubt or the past experience by which I hope to overcome it?

Perhaps it will be said that we speak *aus Gott* when we confess him, when we give utterance to our interior life? Of course this *may* be the case. But it does not follow automatically. From the moment we make our confession or our interior life the basis of our trust in God, or think that we can help someone believe by telling him of our own conviction, we are speaking 'out of' ourselves and not 'out of' God. When we speak of ourselves in *this* way we really speak of nothing but ourselves.

The same thing happens when we attempt to experience God for ourselves. By grounding the otherness of the other on the experience I have of it and not on faith, all I win through to is a phantom, because I never for an instant get outside myself. Therefore when I seek God in an experience I remain *gottlos* (without God). God is the Wholly Other (*das ganz Andere*), he is not *some thing* wholly other (*etwas ganz anderes*), a metaphysical being, or the creative source, or the irrational— all of which convey a God who is object. In other words when I speak of myself as a nature (*Was*) I no longer speak of God as anything but a nature, which comes down to saying that I speak only of myself to myself. When I try to put my future into an experience I am lapsing into the sham transcendence of objects. I am at once torn apart and still the same: my future is a counterfeit future and leaves my present life empty of God.

Hence mystical piety, based on an objective representation of this sort, is really a flight *from* God though it fancies itself to be a flight *into* God. The man of mystical piety tries to escape into a supernature, to become something different (*etwas ganz anderes*), forgetting that God is only met with in one's concrete life. The charm of mysticism for *homo religiosus* (pagan or Christian) is quite understandable, for he thinks he has found the way to escape from himself and acquire a new essence. But by fleeing from himself in *this* way he flees from the true God, who can only be a determination of the 'historical' self. To flee from my concrete self and to flee from God is one and the same thing. To attempt to substitute a supernatural self for one's real self is the acme of self-seeking. Here we see the truth of Luther's dictum that the natural man flees and hates God.

The fact that God is not an object will also emerge from consideration of the problem: does God reveal himself in nature and history?

First of all it must be recollected, according to all we have said about *Vorverständnis* in general, that there is a precomprehension of God. If someone objects that it is not possible to know God before he reveals himself, we must reply that 'man can perfectly well know who God is through the question of God . . . In the human being there is an existentiell knowledge of God that lives in the question of "happiness", of "salvation", of what the world and history mean' (GV 2, p. 232). So man can and does put the *question* of God (as is evident from the mere fact that there are unbelievers, agnostics, and religiously indifferent people), which implies that he has an *idea* of God.

What exactly is this idea of God, on which everyone agrees so far as to distinguish him from the world or at least not to make him absolutely identical with the world? In the first place God is the one whom we look on as exalted above all that exists; the one to whom we entrust our heart because nothing is impossible with him. There is universal agreement that God is not a certain power but omnipotence. God is the Almighty. Then he is the one who does not allow man to behave himself just as he pleases, to live in hate, injustice, impurity, sin; because God himself is love, justice, purity and holiness. Whenever men speak of God they speak of holiness, however variously they may conceive of holiness. God is the Holy One. Finally, as a consequence of what has been said, God is distinct from the world and from man. He is the Transcendent One. No form of pantheism makes God's being nothing more than the particular being of earthly phenomena. He is always felt to be beyond phenomena, a reality vaster and deeper than they are.

Even when God is identified with the totality of the world, it is never with the world as a sheer datum: God is called the law of the world, or its soul, or its vital force, or some such thing. Moreover man never encounters the world in its totality, only in one or another of its manifestations. A man who makes God the soul of the world plainly indicates that he himself is only a part of the whole. He admits that in his individuality he is nothing and must try to live *sub specie aeternitatis*. He admits that God is in some sense beyond his human subjectivity. The same is true of the man who speaks of the *Deus in nobis*, by which he does not mean that he is divinized *hic et nunc*, in his sheer facticity, but only in the authentic self which he must acquire, which is the law of his conduct and lies beyond his subjective desires. Thus for all men the idea of God more or less involves the idea of omnipotence, of holiness and of transcendence.

But is this knowledge *about* God a knowledge *of* God? Is one acquainted with God because one has a *Vorverständnis* of him? Obviously not. The knowledge we have described is only a man's knowledge about himself—his limitations, his finitude, his nothingness. It is a knowledge of God gained from the point of view of man, an objective knowledge which merely puts the *question* of God.

The man who speaks of God's omnipotence is only speaking of his own helplessness. He knows that his life is ruled by forces which now favour and now thwart him, forces of nature and history that make game of him, forces of fate and death that remorselessly hem him in. He is left in darkness and disquiet so long as he cannot speak of a force that masters all the rest, that brings him aid and comfort, above all that enables him to conquer death. Then he sets up as a sovereign power one of the forces that he feels closest to and in respect of which all the other forces seem to take second place. It may be the mind, reason. Or else he tells himself that the sovereign power dwells far beyond the powers of this world, in an invisible, unthinkable transcendence. But however he may speak of this omnipotence, he is still speaking only of himself, of his desires, his aspirations, his need for security, protection, salvation. He hypostatizes in an omnipotence the need he has of omnipotence.

We must say the same of the man who speaks of holiness: he is simply expressing his awareness of not being what he should be, his longing for a pure life, his homesickness for lost authenticity. He finds himself set down between good and evil, he knows that there are two warring selves within him. Thus there awakens in him a sense of God's holiness, whereby he invests the demands of good with a sacred dignity, or sums up in one the manifold imperatives of moral life, or else acquires a convincing norm by which to judge himself and others. So this knowledge about God is still a knowledge about man, about the nature of the authenticity which is to be his and which he never attains. This demand for holiness is laid down on man's own initiative, out of his need for perfection. He postulates a holy God.

When man speaks of transcendence and eternity he is only speaking of his contingence, of the limits of the world he lives in. For there is something negative about human acts, as the poet says:

> *Ach unsre Taten selbst, so gut als unsre Leiden,*
> *Sie hemmen unsres Lebens Gang.*[1]

Nothing human can satisfy our human desires. Anguish always gnaws in secret at our happiness; nothingness swallows up all plenitude. Time never brings us one moment worthy to be told:

> *Verweile doch, du bist so schön!*[2]

For

> *Dort, wo du nicht bist, dort ist das Glück.*[3]

It is this desperate situation that gives birth to the desire for eternity—the need for a kingdom where there is light without darkness, good without evil, life without death. Man then decides to flee the world, by contemplation which gives him a share in the timelessness of Ideas, or by asceticism and mystical experience. He proclaims God the numinous being before whom all thought falls silent, and whose fullness fills the heart. He may also declare that the mysterious river of life is a divine thing. In it every individual form is swallowed up like the wave in the rising tide, but the tide is itself the other world. So man must free himself for eternity by detaching himself from anything individual and particular. But always the eternal, transcendent God is nothing but the embodiment of human yearning.

Accordingly the knowledge man has of God is a knowledge of himself, of his limitations, of his 'indigence'. He postulates God as the power that bursts these shackles asunder and gives man his true being. And all he attains to is the *idea* of God. Working from nature and history we shall never find God; because God is neither in nature nor in history. God's omnipotence is not so manifested in the world that man can acknowledge and obey it. Nothing in the world is omnipotent, not even the world as a whole. We have observed that man never encounters the world as a whole; therefore he cannot contemplate the

1. 'Alas, even our deeds, even our sufferings, hinder our life's course.'
2. 'Linger, thou art so beautiful.'
3. 'Where you are not, there is happiness.'

omnipotence of the world as a whole or find salvation by acknowledging it. (If the fate to which man is handed over be called omnipotent, then one is abandoning the idea of a single world. Men speak so when they do not understand fate, when they regard it as a dark thing standing over against us. But this is also to abandon the true concept of omni-potence, which must be *salvific*.)

Following the Greek tradition, man does indeed try to picture the world as a compact whole. Now in so doing man regards the world as a nature and thereby denies its omni-potence, because it becomes a power to which he cannot entrust his heart. Stoicism tried to make the cosmos a saving power by the ὁμολογουμένως τῇ φύσει ζῆν. But if man is the 'historical' being we have said he is, is it credible that he will find his true self by becoming part of nature? So nature is not the omni-potence to which man can surrender himself.

Is God the perfection that man longs to attain? Is the voice of conscience the voice of God? Is God the imperative that holds conscience subject to it? And does actual obedience to that demand lead one to God? No. For we are still dealing with a work of man. God's majesty is something far loftier than obedience to the moral law implies. God is not the moral law but the Holy One. That is why only one whose heart is pure can see him (Mt 5:8).

But whose heart is pure? A man who thinks to find God in the demands of good and is not steeped in the conviction of his own sinfulness is like the Jews who Paul says think they can glorify themselves before God on account of their zeal in observing the law. Such a man would believe that his moral struggles justify him in God's eyes and that he has no need of grace. Thus the holy God is not known simply because a man knows the demands of good, nor is he found by a man's merely satisfying those demands.

Nor can one say that God is revealed in history. History as such does not make known the will of the holy God. It is an illusion to see his kingdom in the movement of history envisaged as an evolution that gathers isolated events into a meaningful whole and is directed towards a set goal. The meaning of history is not visible. Where one man thinks he perceives the meaning of history, another sees only a tangle of error and violence. Besides, we no more encounter history as a whole than we do the world as a whole. Only to one who looks at it as from outside, from a theoretical or esthetic point of view, does it seem to present any unity.

We have seen that history is not a mere datum but a *Verstehen*. The past is at once an inheritance and a task set us. But the inheritance is equivocal, be it the past of an individual, of a people, or of mankind. So one must listen to history with one's wits about one, ready to be faithful to the past and at the same time ready to break with it. In fact all historical phenomena are ambiguous; 'none, as such, reveals the will of God' (GV 2, p. 92). Certainly one must believe in the tasks of the future, but 'such a faith is not faith in God' (*ibid.*). The word that history speaks to us is obscure and of itself by no means conveys the demand of the holy God. To listen to that demand is precisely to silence all talk about the alleged revelation of God in history. Man is a sinner before God; and since the only history is human history, it hides God instead of manifesting him.

Finally, even when speaking of God's eternity man is not really speaking of God. All talk about the transcendent God is illusory if it pretends to do more than confess the divine absence. So long as man sees in eternity a way to escape his contingency and attach himself to the absolute, he is not forsaking himself. To represent the other world as the sphere in which one can take refuge by asceticism, contemplation or mysticism, is to remain this world's prisoner.

From God's absence in this world man cannot conclude that there is another world where he is present. To do so is precisely man's sin, because yet again he hopes to find God by starting with himself. He ought instead to admit that the transcendence he aspires to condemns his godless life. He ought to admit that he can only put the question of God—that he 'can only speak about the other world as a positive reality when the other world gives itself to him' (GV 2, p. 94). Of himself he can only proclaim with Faust:

> *Den Göttern gleich ich nicht! Zu tief ist es gefühlt;*
> *Dem Wurme gleich ich, der den Staub durchwühlt.*[4]

Working from nature and history, then, man has merely a negative idea of God. His knowledge is an unknowing. The underlying reason why he cannot find omni-potence, holiness and transcendence in nature and history, is that he cannot escape himself by himself. Through sin he has become pride and self-centredness, in-sistence and aseity. He can only find God as a *Dass* (that is, as *God*) if God first finds him and forgives him his sins. Only then does he know that God is the Al-mighty, because he understands that omni-potence is the force that is able to crush him, man, instead of exalting him. Exaltation is what he expected of the omni-potence he imagined, which in fact was only the highest expression of his will to power. Only then does he understand what the holy God is: understand that God is not the one who exalts the moral and spiritual man but the one who condemns him, in whose

---

4. 'I am not like the gods—too well I know—but like the worm that worms its way through dust.'

eyes he has no dignity or merits of his own. Only then does he understand what the eternal God is: transcendence that abolishes what is
human.

The Wholly Other is not a *Was*, however inaccessible or even
'numinous' one cares to think of it as being. Make God the irrational
itself; carry apophatic theology to its utmost extreme; still you will
have only a God fabricated by man, who is the mere embodiment of
man's longing for the infinite. Feuerbach's celebrated critique of this
God is unanswerable.

So nature and history do not reveal God, they only put the *question*
of God. Rom 1:19f is no objection. There we read of the pagans that
'what can be known about God is plain to them, because God has
shown it to them. Ever since the creation of the world this invisible
nature, namely, his eternal power and deity, has been clearly perceived
in the things that have been made.' Now *why* does Paul say this? In
favour of a 'natural theology', to open men's eyes to a revelation
outside Christ? Just the opposite; to open their eyes to God's one
revelation in Christ by bringing an accusation against them: 'So they
are without excuse.'

Man *ought* to regard himself as a creature and give up any *Anspruch*
over God. He *ought* to despair of himself: then he would see the world
as creation, and the world as creation would speak to him of God. But
that is precisely what Paul says man does *not* do. He transforms his
negative knowledge of God into a positive knowledge. He thinks to
know God in the light of nature and history, instead of knowing
nature and history in the light of God. Creation summons him to take
stock of his limitations and his dependence on God, but he is unwilling
to be taught these things. That is his sin, from which Christ alone can
deliver him. Thus Paul declares that creation *ought* to make man
despair of himself and that he is inexcusable in rejecting the summons.
But to say this is to say that there is no revelation of God in nature as
nature and history as history—which means in the world as the world.

II

GOD IS LORD

Accordingly God can only be known through his revelation. What
does the Old Testament say about this matter? It shows us God as the
one who eludes man's grasp and is man's master. It has no familiarity
with the Greek problem of the ἀρχή, the origin of the world, ever
present in it, which enables the mind to grasp it as a single thing. God
is indeed the principle of everything, but as the Creator. This affirmation is no cosmological axiom designed to explain the origin of things,

it is an act of man confessing his Lord, to whom he belongs and to whom he owes obedience.

It is a remarkable circumstance that Hebrew monotheism did not spring from theoretical reflection, but rather from an 'historical' encounter. At the beginning the God of Israel is a national god. Round about the year 1000 B.C., when Israel becomes a state and Yahweh a national deity, polytheism presents a problem because of the wars with other countries and other gods. It then emerges that Yahweh is a 'jealous' god who will not endure having anyone compared with him. He is the sovereign Lord with foreign nations at his beck and call as he has Israel. With a 'whistle' he calls the people of the north to execute his judgment (Is 5:26). Assyria is the 'rod' of his anger and the staff of his fury (10:5). Pharaoh is the 'great dragon' that will be given to the beasts of the earth and the birds of the air as food (Ez 29:4-5). The creation of the world is attributed to this Lord. Only in the background of chapters 1 and 2 of Genesis do we find the mythology of the *Fabricator* who works with 'chaos' and dust from the ground as his materials; in fact the idea of formative creation has disappeared. God commands and his command is carried out: 'God said, "Let there be light"; and there was light', and so forth (Gen 1:3, 11, 24). Faith has displaced myth.

Eventually we have the affirmation—worked out little by little: Jubilees 12:4; 2 Mc 7:28—that the world was made out of nothing. Creation, therefore, is not thought of as analogous to a work ($\check{\epsilon}\rho\gamma o\nu$) of manual art ($\tau\acute{\epsilon}\chi\nu\eta$): it is not objectified in a cosmos whose eternal laws can be grasped by the mind. The Greek thinks of God as a 'technician' embodying his idea in a work (in this case, the world). It follows that God, man and the world are mind. The cosmos is the system made up by gods and men. Contrariwise if God is not a 'technician' but creates out of nothing, then he is quite different from man and his work itself is mysterious in character. That is why there is no natural science in the Old Testament. That is why we can speak here, and only here, of a revelation of God in nature; because it is seen as creation, in terms of God, and no longer, as in the idea criticized above, in terms of man.

To the mind of the Bible, nature is not an intelligible whole where each part has its own $\tau\acute{\epsilon}\lambda o s$ and the whole has its $\tau\acute{\epsilon}\lambda o s$ in the organic oneness of the parts. Quite the other way: nature is what man cannot control. Precisely that in nature which eludes man is what reveals God. 'The revelation of God in nature is not grasped at the end of nature's history, a history governed by laws, but in its unusual and alarming events, such as hurricanes and earthquakes. The world is admired as the work of God because it is *not* intelligible to human reason' (CP, p. 15):

> Who has measured the waters in the hollow of his hand
> and marked off the heavens with a span,
> enclosed the dust of the earth in a measure
> and weighed the mountains in scales
> and the hills in a balance?
>
> —Is 40:12

History reveals God in the same way. God is not discerned in the course of a development whose plan man can understand, but in things astonishing, singular, enigmatic—in the opposite of what is ordinarily meant by the revelation of God in history. 'The Lord of hosts has a day against all that is proud and lofty . . . And the haughtiness of man shall be humbled, and the pride of men shall be brought low; and the Lord alone will be exalted in that day' (Is 2:12, 17).

God is the master of history: he chooses and rejects whom he will, victory and judgment lie in his hands (Is 48:11), he directs the course of events in accordance with norms that man cannot fathom. 'My thoughts are not your thoughts, neither are your ways my ways . . . As the heavens are higher than the earth, so are my ways higher than your ways' (Is 55:8f). 'But when I thought how to understand this, it seemed to me a wearisome task' (Ps 73:16). 'Such knowledge is too wonderful for me; it is high, I cannot attain it' (Ps 139:6). Thus it is only when man forsakes himself and his in-sistence and sees himself as a creature, that nature and history speak to him of God, thereby teaching him that he is nothing:

> Woe to him who strives with his Maker,
> an earthen vessel with the potter.
> Does the clay say to him who fashions it,
> 'What are you making?'
> or, 'Your work has no handles'?
>
> —Is 45:9

The prophet hears a voice saying:

> Cry: all flesh is as grass
> and all its beauty is like the flower of the field.
> The grass withers, the flower fades,
> when the breath of the Lord blows upon it.
>
> —Is 40:6–7

Man owes his whole worth to God. He is created in God's image, according to Gen 1:26–27 and Ps 8:5–6:

Thou hast made him little less than God,
and dost crown him with glory and honour.
Thou hast given him dominion over the works of thy hands;
thou hast put all things under his feet.

If God is Lord, then man cannot know God of himself. For the Greeks the otherness of God is that of an essence which is transcendent because invisible. But this invisibility relates only to the senses. God is accessible to intellectual knowledge, though at the cost of strenuous effort.[5]

The Old Testament says that God is by no means essentially invisible. He can perfectly well be perceived by the senses. But to see him is to die. His inaccessibility is not that of an invisible spiritual nature but that of holiness and lordship. If man cannot see God without dying that is because he is a sinner and the sight of God is judgment and annihilation to the sinner. 'You cannot see my face; for man shall not see me and live' (Ex 33:20). Hence Jacob is overcome with astonishment: 'I have seen God face to face, and yet my life is preserved' (Gen 32:31).

On the other hand Manoah and his wife cry out in horror: 'We shall surely die, for we have seen God' (Judg 13:22). And Isaiah: 'Woe is me! For I am lost; for I am a man of unclean lips, and . . . my eyes have seen the King' (Is 6:5). Thus God is not an invisible and mysterious being but the being who controls man and whom man does not control. That is why he is more readily perceived by the ear than by the eye.

Whereas the Greeks, who tend towards an objective view of the world, consider sight the highest sense, the Bible accords that position to hearing.[6] To see another is to lay hold of him, to hear him is to be summoned by him and be ready to do his will:

I will tell thee, O man, what is good
and what the Lord requireth of thee.
                                        —Micah 6:8[7]

Priests and prophets utter the *Word* of God. God's revelation is his Word. Knowledge of God (the 'science of Yahweh') does not bear on

5. Even the Platonic good, which lies 'beyond οὐσία', is attained by direct intellectual intuition (*Republic* 506b and 511d).

6. Under the influence of Greek tradition, Philo of Alexandria characteristically tries to change biblical auditions of God into vision. The voice which speaks out of the dark on Sinai he interprets as an illumination.

7. [Douai version. RSV does not make the author's point.—Tr.]

his essence but on his will. To do God's will is to know him. 'Did not your father do justice and righteousness? He judged the cause of the poor and needy. Is not this to know me? says the Lord' (Jer 22:15ff). 'I will give them a heart to know that I am the Lord; and they shall be my people and I will be their God, for they shall return to me with their whole heart' (Jer 24:7).

When the psalmist says 'Continue thy steadfast love to those who know thee', he repeats the same thing by going on: 'and thy salvation to the upright of heart' (Ps 36:11). To the mind of the Old Testament, truth is not essentially the truth of knowledge but a wisdom, and wisdom is knowing the demands of God, fearing God: 'The fear of the Lord is the beginning of wisdom' (Prov 1:7).

God's lordship also emerges from the remarkable fact that there is no theodicy in the Bible. God is the one with whom man does not bandy words. Suffering and death, natural disasters (famine, earthquakes, and the like), are not problems which make men doubt God's existence. Theoretical denial of God is entirely unknown to the Old Testament. It is familiar only with practical ignorance of God, so often described in the psalms (Ps 14:1 is an example). The wicked man is without knowledge of God when he slays the widow, the fatherless, and the poor, saying 'The Lord does not see' (Ps 94:7) or 'How can God know?' (Ps 73:11).

There is no Hebrew word which conveys the Stoic idea of πρόνοια (providence)—that is, the rational assurance that the cosmos is a harmonious whole in which every element has its organic place and therefore its usefulness. The Bible does not try to justify suffering and misfortune. Neither does it try to show that such things are only appearances because all things are necessary, and therefore good, in view of the whole. Marcus Aurelius's advice, 'Consider the whole', has no standing here. Doubt and distress are coped with not by reason but by faith.

A devout man is particularly oppressed by the problem of why the innocent suffer. Why do so many wicked men live at their ease while the righteous are afflicted? One answer is to commend resignation; we find it characteristically put in Ecclesiastes:

> I saw the wicked buried;
> they used to go in and out of the holy place,
> and were praised in the city
> where they had done such things.
>
> (8:10)

> There are righteous men to whom it happens according to the
> deeds of the wicked,

and there are wicked men to whom it happens according to the
deeds of the righteous.
I said that this also is vanity.

(8:14)

The book of Job sees only one solution: silent submission by the
innocent sufferer to the will of God, whose wisdom leaves men far
out of their depth:[8]

Though I am innocent, my own mouth would condemn me;
though I am blameless he would prove me perverse.

(9:20)

God answers Job's remonstrances:

Where were you when I laid the foundations of the earth?
Tell me, if you have understanding.

(38:4)

Shall a faultfinder contend with the Almighty?
He who argues with God, let him answer it.

(40:2)

Then Job holds his peace:

Behold, I am of small account; what shall I answer thee?
I lay my hand on my mouth.

(40:4)

I have uttered what I did not understand,
things too wonderful for me, which I did not know.

(42:3)

Therefore I despise myself,
and repent in dust and ashes.

(42:6)

Faced, then, with God's omni-potence and unfathomable wisdom man
must hold his tongue. He receives no answer when he asks the meaning
of suffering. But the more difficult it is for the poet to understand evil
and injustice in view of his idea of God, the sounder and the more
necessary that idea becomes for him. Indeed only here is God really

8. The book of Job has been recast in the light of Judaism's belief that God trains
up and rewards man; particularly by the insertion of Elihu's words.

God: his omni-potence and his wisdom are a bottomless abyss. Thus a profound conception of faith takes shape. To believe in God is not to hold that he exists—that is, to know him with an objective knowledge—but to trust in him at the very moment when one has every possible objective reason not to do so.

Again, the very nature of the relations between God and man, which are regarded as an alliance, shows that God's transcendence consists in his lordship over man. Israel's settlement in a given territory and the influence of Canaanite religion might have encouraged the idea that God was bound to that particular territory; in which case the Israelite faith would have lost its distinctive character and sunk to the level of those Semitic religions where the deity was worshipped as a power at work within nature to give it fertility. It is against this evil that the prophets preach. Yahweh is not the God of vegetation, of springs, of fields, of mountains, but of the nation. In this respect Israelite religion has a certain kinship with Greek religion. Nevertheless Israel does not regard itself as a *polis*. For if the City is the norm of personal life and the deity is conceived of as the power that watches over the City, we know that in fact norm and deity alike are only the personified will of the citizens (see ch. 2, §1, above)

In Israel the nation is not conceived of as something that each individual helps to constitute but as the work of history. This history in turn is not a work of man but a gift of God and a proof of his grace, as we are strikingly told in a beautiful passage of Deuteronomy (8:11–18). Thus it comes about that the nation can be spoken of in language that properly applies only to God's acts (whether creation or annihilation). The defeat of the Egyptians is a crushing of the dragon of ancient days (Is 51:9ff) and the disaster that will overtake the people is a return to chaos. Thus the nation is not constituted by the forces now visible within it, it is there because of the deeds God has done in the past: the deliverance from bondage in Egypt, the covenant on Sinai, the crossing of the wilderness, the gift of the promised land.

One can easily understand why the great feasts, originally of an agrarian and pastoral significance, became 'historicized'. Passover, the yearly solemnity when the first-born of the flock were sacrificed, commemorates the deliverance from Egypt. The feast of weeks (Pentecost), which was a thanksgiving for the harvest, celebrates the giving of the law on Sinai. The feast of tabernacles, which originally celebrated the new year, henceforth recalls the days when the Israelites lived in tents in the wilderness. Worship itself loses its character as a magical action to ensure the welfare of country and nation, more and more becoming the means by which the people grow aware of the history of salvation and associate themselves with it.

Yet again, the theme of election shows that God is Lord. Israel has not itself to thank for what it is but God alone, who has given it its history. The people of Israel have not been chosen for their virtues or accomplishments. 'Do not say in your heart . . . "It is because of my righteousness that the Lord has brought me in to possess this land . . ." Know, therefore, that the Lord your God is not giving you this good land to possess because of your righteousness; for you are a stubborn people' (Deut 9:4–6). God's election is not necessary but gratuitous. Consequently Israel has no *Anspruch* upon God; it is at all times subject to his grace, over which it has no control whatever.

What God has done in the past cannot be possessed like an object; the nation must constantly win it anew by observing the covenant— that is, by keeping faith with its history. The prophets attack the self-confidence which inspires a high-flown religious nationalism Just as God has chosen the nation, so he can reject it:

> Woe to those who are at ease in Zion,
> and to those who feel secure on the mountain of Samaria . . .
> to whom the house of Israel come!
> Pass over to Calneh, and see;
> and thence go to Hamath the great;
> then go down to Gath of the Philistines.
> Are they better than these kingdoms?
> Or is their territory greater than your territory?
>
> —Amos 6:1ff

So the covenant is not sealed once for all; it is the choice that a bride-groom makes of his bride, a marriage (Hosea, Jeremiah)—a voluntary faithfulness that must be constantly kept up and renewed on each side. Always the Israelites are tempted to make it their possession, to imagine that belonging to the chosen people is security in itself. The prophets never weary of attacking this idea: by its obedience or disobedience Israel is responsible every moment for preserving or destroying the covenant. Thus the past is a question put to the nation and the covenant is a permanent future.

With Bultmann himself let us sum up the Old Testament conception of God. 'Compared with the tradition of the Old Testament and of Judaism, the idea of God's transcendence has not been thoroughly understood even in Neoplatonism, where the idea of divine transcend-ence is carried so far that the deity is pictured as quite beyond the grasp of man's reason. For even in Neoplatonism the human self is looked on as essentially akin to the deity; and the idea of creation, which embodies that of radical transcendence, always yields to the idea of emanation. God's transcendence can be thoroughly understood only when it affirms that the deity *meets* man as a power that is not only different from and superior to all the powers of the world but above all is different from myself. Now transcendence is given an entirely new meaning, because first of all man's being is not classified, in the Greek manner, under the same heading as the being of natural data but seen in the will of man, in the "historicity" of his being; and secondly, as a result, the relation between God and man is shifted from the horizon of substantial things to that of encounter, of "historical" things. Here transcendence is not the realm of the spirit as opposed to material and sensible things, of timeless eternity as opposed to the waxing and waning of things. On the contrary, God's transcendence is his permanent future, his absolute freedom, which not only means that man can never lay hands on God, never subject him to any constraint or make good any claim upon him on the strength of man's having fulfilled certain conditions, never require anything of him; it also means that human reason can never grasp the things God does. Only on this basis can the idea of God's grace be thoroughly understood. These corollaries are not spelt out in the Old Testament or in Judaism. Protestants hold that they are only spelt out in Luther. But be that as it may, obviously this notion of transcendence is an inheritance from the tradition of the Old Testament and of Judaism' (GV 2, pp. 244–5).

In order to understand Jesus's thought about God we shall have to set forth something which is only alluded to in the passage just quoted: the Jewish conception of God. Judaism enlarged upon the Old Testament tradition. If ancient Israel accepted as a matter of course that it must invoke only one Lord, there was still no denying that other peoples had other gods, though they were no match for Yahweh. But later Judaism considered God the only god, without qualification.

This idea did not spring from philosophical reflection but represented a development of faith. It was perceived that admitting a number of gods made God still an earthly being, because only earthly beings can be thought of as many. What Jewish monotheism affirms is not a philosophical view of the world but faith in a God exalted above the world he has made.

Characteristically, God's own name—Yahweh—fell into oblivion, for like all names it had meaning only insofar as God was considered a subject among other subjects from which he had to be distinguished. God's own name is already missing from the book of Job and from Ecclesiastes. In Judaism God is called King and Lord, the Most High, and the Holy One—all terms which stress his exaltation above the world. Titles are used which convey his transcendence even more forcefully, like heaven, majesty, glory. And we have the avoidance of any title, with the use of a passive construction: 'God has decided' appears as 'It has been decided'. Such expressions are found in the mouth of Jesus: Lk 15:7, 10, 18; 6:38 ('It will be given to you . . . good measure . . . will be put'); 12:20 ('Your soul is required of you'); 16:9.

But this God of the far reaches is at the same time a very intimate God. In his mighty hands he holds the destiny of the world, of his people, and of every individual. This conviction is expressed above all in the idea of creation, not a cosmological theory here any more than it is in the Old Testament but a sense of the utter dependence which a Jew feels in the presence of his God. The theme of the intimate God is found again in the Hebrew faith in God as the master of history, which he governs according to his plan from its beginnings through to its appointed end. Thus man is not lost in an isolated cosmos: he fits into a meaningful history. First he looks back to the past in which the 'God of Abraham, of Isaac, and of Jacob' displayed his blessings and his chastisements. The Jew knows that this history speaks to him and that its demands and consolations directly concern him. He also turns his gaze to the future, since it is God steering the course of things towards a goal, executing his judgment, and manifesting his glory. The remote God is therefore the intimate God; the God of the future is the God of the present.

Judaism, however, never was able to integrate its thought on this point, and here a certain ontological dualism appears. Stress is laid on the God of the future in such a way that one does not quite make out how he can be the God of the present at the same time. It cannot be doubted that in this respect dualist ideas of foreign origin (basically Persian) have exerted an undesirable influence. The whole range of time is divided into two eras: the present aeon (which includes the past and the present), and the future aeon in which God's kingdom will be manifested. The starker this contrast becomes and the more the future is thought of as the time when all God's powerful enemies will be annihilated, the more the present seems to be abandoned by God, as the time when Satan and the evil spirits enjoy unchallenged dominion. God's present lordship over the present world fades into the background. That is to say that his omni-potence is hedged about and his nature changed, since he is no longer the one who determines man in his present existence. The more exclusively revelation is looked for from the future, the more man groans under the sufferings of the present. Thus the future is no longer a true future—a *future of the present*. The 'historical' connection between the two aeons yields to a substantialist overlay.

According to a widespread Jewish conjecture, the goods of salvation pre-exist in heaven, so that the future presents itself as totally extrinsic to the present. Quite understandably, therefore, Judaism fails to establish any real connection between the God of the future and the God of the present, and its affirmations that God is the God of the present tend to become mere theory. Of course we are told that the Creator of the world is the same being as its Judge; that what God decided from the very beginning will only be carried out in the future; that God rules time and all that happens in it. But we are not really told how far the transcendent God directs man's present in such a way that life here and now is governed by God.

Statements about God's present doings are often disjointed and even tend to contradict both the hopes set on the future and the dualist, pessimist judgment which is pronounced on the present. On the one hand God's providence is said to extend even to the birds of the air, but on the other hand the world is handed over to Satan and the powers of evil. On the one hand God judges men's deeds even now, and yet the definitive judgment is put off until the end of time. God pardons us in this world, but his pardon will not be definitive until the day of judgment, when he will bestow it on such as are deserving. Thus the present acts of man are not radical decisions for or against God. The future does not wholly determine the present. From start to finish the dominant theme is that of the two aeons envisaged as two entities instead of two *Verstehen* of man—his sinful *Verstehen* and his reprieved *Verstehen* (pp. 39–43 and 74, above).

Like the God of Judaism, the God whom Jesus preaches has nothing to do with the Greek idea. He in no way belongs to the cosmos and he is not an object of thought. He does not enable us to understand the world, and he does not ensure its oneness. He is neither a metaphysical being nor a power nor a rational law, but a holy, personal will. Jesus speaks of God only as laying an *Anspruch* upon man and as determining man's present existence by his judgment and his grace. The remote God is at the same time the intimate God, because he cannot be perceived outside man's concrete life—only in it.

Jesus does not speak of God in general terms, does not make doctrinal statements about him; he only tells what God is for man and how he acts for man. He does not (like the Greeks) try to work out and describe God's attributes (eternity, immortality, and the rest). On occasion he does indeed say that God is merciful and kind (Lk 3:36; Mk 10:18), but that is only expressing God's way with men. Naturally he does not differentiate between any transcendent, mysterious metaphysical essence in God and the operations which disclose it to man. The remote God and the intimate God are one and the same.

Similarly in the case of man as Jesus conceives of him, no line can be drawn between a basic nature and the acts that issue from it, because man is action (ec-sistence), just as God is wherever he acts. So Jesus brings us no new conception of God, no revelation about nature, but he announces the coming of God's kingdom and God's will. He speaks of God by speaking of man, and teaches man that he is subject to God's demands in the moment of decision.

In short, any idea of God as a higher nature is alien to Jesus's mind. One cannot draw near to God by worship or sacraments that supposedly endow one with new qualities. And just as Jesus does not consider worship a good work, so he does not envisage it as a mysterious means for delivering man from his lower nature. The very idea of a nature is altogether unknown to him. Only the will is good or bad. It is not sacramental ablutions that make man pure but his heart—that is, his will (Mk 7:15).

What significance Jesus attached to John's baptism it is impossible for us to discover at this date. The late tradition according to which he himself baptized (Jn 3:22) is doubtful. Probably the Johannine rite was an eschatological rite; and though a properly sacramental significance may have been attached to it within the circle of the Baptist's disciples, Jesus can hardly have regarded it as anything more than a confession of repentance in view of the kingdom's being at hand. At all events he did not institute the baptism we are told about in the legendary account of Mt 28:19, which merely describes baptismal practice in the Hellenistic communities. The Hellenistic Christians likewise held that Jesus had instituted a sacramental meal, and the account and meaning of his last meal with the disciples was transformed in the light of this belief. Nothing is more alien to the preaching of Jesus and the preaching of the earliest community than the idea of sacrament, because any idea of nature is altogether alien to them both: so far as they are concerned, man is not a lower nature and God is not a higher nature.[9]

Consequently Jesus knows nothing of any mystical relations with God. The great commandment of love (Mk 12:30) is not given in view of that complete union with God which mystical love aims at. It is

9. We use the word sacrament here in the strict sense (the sacrament as it is found in the history of religions and notably in the mystery religions). When men hold that natural objects (baths, meals) or mere words can in certain circumstances be the vehicle of supernatural powers, then we are dealing with sacraments. The necessary conditions having been met (if the formula is correctly spoken, for example, so that the matter is 'consecrated'—that is, charged with supernatural power), supernatural forces are released and conferred on man.—As we shall see, Bultmann does not mean to deny the demythologized Christian sacrament.

addressed to the will, as the very wording of the second commandment makes clear: 'You shall love your neighbour as yourself' (Mk
12:31). True life is not a matter of being engrossed in God. On the
contrary, it is only true life if it is action. If man did not see himself
as the one whose true being consists in his sheer freedom of decision
—that is, in his obedience to the divine *Thou*—God would logically
be an essence or else the Unthinkable. Then one could only enter
into communion with him through meditation, contemplation,
ecstasy.

But Jesus never speaks of God as the Unthinkable, or mentions any
mystical experience or mystical state. We find in his preaching no
trace of the mystics' God, no talk of the soul and its interior life. The
mystical notion of God may go back to dualism or pantheism, but no
suggestion of either one can be found in Jesus; because for him God
exists only in his will and his deeds, just as man does. He does not
differentiate between sense and spirit, between lower and higher. He
does not speak of any divine principle imprisoned in the body, which
would need to be set free and reunited with God. Man is wholly evil
when his eye is not sound, his heart pure, and his will obedient.
Always he is seen as a freedom called to obedience.

Obviously Jesus remains within the framework of Judaism. The
remarkable thing about him is not anything new he says but his
searching grasp and striking presentation of the traditional idea of God.
This point will emerge much more forcefully if we now consider how
he solved the problem of identifying the remote God with the intimate
God—a problem which Judaism, as we have seen, left in suspense.

At first sight it would appear that Jesus does not rise above Jewish
substantialist dualism, and that for him God is not the God of the
present. By teaching men to pray 'thy kingdom come' (Mt 6:10) he
seems to imply that the world more or less eludes the sovereignty of
God: his name is *not yet* hallowed, his will is *not yet* done on earth as
it is in heaven. When he sees the evils fleeing and Satan falling like
lightning, he admits that hitherto the world has been ruled by them.
So it would be idle to assert that unlike his contemporaries he not only
looks for God's coming but sees it accomplished *hic et nunc*, sees that
the end of time has already come and that the power of the kingdom
is manifest henceforth. For real faith in the real God declares that there
never was a time when the world slipped out of God's control.

Would it do to say that since Jesus's faith was not a theology worked
out to all its logical implications, he admitted the existence of other
factors notwithstanding God's unlimited power over the course of
human affairs? This is only an approximation to the truth, for everything depends on how one envisages Jesus's faith in God. If we under-

stand it as a *theoretical* certainty, despite all experience to the contrary, that God is the master of all that happens, then we blunder.

Jesus's faith is not a *general* affirmation that God directs the course of events but a conviction that he is the power which determines the *hic et nunc*. If God is God, he must be man's *Wie*: no instant of human life can escape him. And if someone did not believe that God acts in the *hic et nunc*, if he settled for the certainty that God rules history *in general*, then his faith would be a mere abstraction, a dogma, and all the zeal with which he might cling to it would be only a state of mind or heart; because true faith can only be God's encounter with us in the present moment. That man would be fleeing from the concrete reality in which alone God summons us, and his belief would be only a phantom belief.

Nor must we think that the future aeon merely perfects creation, for then we would be denying its transcendent character. Faith in the Creator would be reduced to a theoretical belief or a general truth. It is making Jesus a 'Greek' to say that he regards this world as already the kingdom of God in germ, which has only to be perfected by his reign. Jesus never put creation and the future kingdom on the same plane. The only thing he may have had in mind is the theme of the Apocalypse, where the end of time restores the age of the original paradise; and in that case creation is not perfected but restored, after the degradation caused by sin. Here, in spite of everything, the transcendence of the future aeon is safeguarded. But nothing that Jesus says allows us to suppose that he shared this view. Indeed the fanciful mythology which Judaism had made of it strongly argues that it was far from his mind.

If we would understand Jesus's preaching we must not in any way diminish God's transcendence the better to reconcile it with his immanence. We must respect the paradox that the God of the present is at the same time the God of the future. Now how can this be done? What is the connection between the two aeons? How can God be both remote and close to us?

(1) We are given a preliminary answer by Jesus's notion of divine providence. His belief in it is embodied in a number of sayings: Lk 12:22–31 (Mt 6:25–32); Mt 10:29–31 (Lk 12:6–7); Mt 5:45. These texts present difficulties as to form and content, but minor ones, as we shall see. We are at once struck by the fact that Jesus does not conceive of providence at all as a divine law ruling nature, that his view is the diametrical opposite of Schleiermacher's, who fancied that in the shifting scenes of nature we could contemplate the reign of life, of the spirit, and of the godhead. It is no less opposed to the Stoic view which we have already discussed. Seneca says, like Jesus (Mt 5:45), that the

sun rises on the wicked as well as on the good; only it does so in virtue of a natural law that operates for everyone. Stoic providence is nothing else than the rational character of events.

The abstract idea of finality and providence is unknown either to Judaism or to Jesus, who moreover have no term with which to render them. The providence that Jesus's words show he believed in is God's personal dealings with things and men, who are not envisaged as parts of a rational whole but as individual beings, each with his own character and his own needs. It is not a theory which consoles the individual with the thought that his life too is controlled by the general law of the universe and therefore escapes the jeopardy Goethe speaks of:

Denn unfühlend ist die Natur:
Es leuchtet die Sonne über Böse und Gute,
Und dem Verbrecher glänzen wie dem Besten der Mond und die Sterne.[10]

But is not Jesus's optimism about the lilies of the field and the birds of the air cancelled out by the suffering and evil that prevail in the world? Is there not something childish about his faith in providence? Has it not to do with the Eastern way of life, where in a shallow unconcern men get by with very little?

Taken in themselves, the sayings to which we have just alluded do derive from the popular wisdom of the East. But even if they are not Jesus's own, the fact remains that the Christian community saw no inconsistency between them and the teaching it inherited from him. In any case their association with the preaching of Jesus suffices to show that he left a number of problems outside his view of things, especially the problem of theodicy. The fact that he did not raise this problem by no means shows that his thought was still that of a child; it merely shows that his idea of faith eliminated the problem.

Jesus was not the naive optimist that Renan considered him. More than once he spoke of man's 'finitude', his 'wretchedness', his 'care', just as many a Psalm (103:15–16; 90:5–6) and the book of Job had done before him:

> Foxes have holes,
> and birds of the air have nests;
> but man has nowhere
> to lay his head.
>
> (Mt 8:20)[11]

10. 'For nature has no heart: the sun sheds light on evil men and good, the moon and stars shine on the blackguard and the saint.'
11. 'Son of Man' is a misunderstanding.

Which of you by being anxious can add one cubit to his span of life?
(Mt 6:27)

What does it profit a man to gain the whole world and forfeit his life?
For what can a man give in return for his life?
(Mk 8:36–37)

Let the day's own trouble be sufficient for the day.
(Mt 6:34)

To him who has will more be given;
and from him who has not, even what he has will be taken away.
(Mk 4:25; see GST, p. 112)

Now obviously these sayings are not questions, prompted either by curiosity or distress, about the existence of evil and suffering. They do not raise the question of theodicy, which will very soon be exercising the ancient Church. Jesus allows man no right to make sense of fate. Just as he offers no explanation for suffering in general, so he offers none for his personal sufferings. We know that the prophecies which represent his passion and death as willed by God and necessary for salvation were put into his mouth by the community.[12] If he really did say, on the night of his arrest, 'Not what I will, but what thou wilt', these words are a rejection of all theodicy and rank with Job's 'I lay my hand on my mouth'.

It never crosses Jesus's mind that the mystery of evil may stir doubt in the soul of the believer; for doubt implies that one lays an *Anspruch* upon God and has some criterion by which to judge what is worthy of God and what unworthy. Man can and *must* doubt only himself, his security, his independence, his natural certainties, his in-sistence. In demanding this, Jesus passes beyond the Jewish attitude of resignation to fate as we find it expressed in Ecclesiastes.

God is not a fate, he is the holy will that lays an *Anspruch* upon man and demands total obedience of him, even in suffering. Suffering is an expression of God's will as real as it is mysterious. It too is a determination of our concrete life by him. He is the God of the present even when we are suffering: 'Not as I will, but as thou wilt' (Mt 26:39). In short, Jesus's faith in the intimate God, as embodied in his belief in providence, is not compensated for by any diminution or objectification of the distant God. His faith in the God who determines the present is such as to be simultaneously a faith in the God of the future,

12. They felt they had to find a *reason*.

whose transcendence is upheld in all its starkness, not degraded into the rationalism of the Stoic πρόνοια. God is the *Thou* that we have described (pp. 19-21, above): at once absolute otherness and the determination of man's life—·it is the latter *because* it is the former, and the former because it is the latter.

(2) This paradox is also exhibited in Jesus's conception of prayer. God is the God of the present in prayer, but here again prayer is not an objectification of God, a way of controlling him and making an attempt on his *Jenseits*. Prayer (public and private) had reached an extraordinarily high development in Judaism. There is nothing surprising or new in the fact that Jesus and his disciples prayed. Thrice daily the devout Jew—doubtless as early as Jesus's time—had to say the prayer called the Eighteen Benedictions. The community set up by John the Baptist also had prayers of its own (see Lk 11:1). Christians had the Our Father. To what extent this prayer really goes back to Jesus, it is no longer possible to make out. There are also difficulties about establishing the original text. But these are problems of a lesser order.

What sets the Our Father apart from the Jewish prayers is neither content nor language but its extreme simplicity and concision. In it Jesus stresses the fact that prayer cannot be an *Anspruch* upon God. To make it such would be to act like the pagans, who think they will be heard by dint of fine speaking (Mt 6:7). Prayer is not a good work which one might vaunt before men; it is a conversation with God that is no one else's business (Mt 6:5-6) and is possible only through his kindness.

If earthly fathers are good to their children, how much more so is God to his (Mt 7:7-11). But man cannot control that kindness. It is not an objective truth, a principle for him to rely on. Only that man can expect it who allows it to rule his own life; only that man who forgives his brethren can ask God to forgive him (Mt 6:14-15). Moreover this readiness to forgive does not of itself create any right to get what one wants from God, as if a man who has forgiven seven times could feel that he has done enough to deserve God's grace (Mt 18:21-22). Nothing can give man any *Anspruch* upon God, as is made abundantly clear in the parable of the debtor servant (Mt 18:23-35).

What Jesus says about prayer relates almost exclusively to the prayer of petition. In this respect Mt 7:7-11 and particularly the two parables in Lk 11:5-8 and 18:1-5 are characteristic texts. They show that to Jesus's mind the prayer of petition is really petition: that its object is to move God to do what he otherwise would not do. It is not addressed to an immutable essence. Of course there is no question of magical coercion. Prayer affects God as one freedom affects another. And of course Jesus has no theory about the way in which prayer can influence God, for that would be to regard him as governed by laws and there-fore to control him. On the other hand if God is free, then obviously he can do this rather than that, or that rather than this. To Jesus's mind, the course the world takes is not laid down by necessity but by the free acts of God[13]. Why, then, should it not be fitting and proper for me to pray?

But is God still the Al-mighty if my freedom can influence his? This question well shows that God's omni-potence must not be treated as a theory, a general truth, a principle for man to rely on, so that he would have no need to ask God for anything. Certainly: for Jesus, God is the Al-mighty and the prayer of petition proves that he is—it proves that man does not control God, because man does not consider God omni-potent at all until he reveals himself to be such.

The pantheist does not ask his god for anything, because he sees the god's omni-potence at work in the world, expressed in the visible course that things take. Why should one ask God to change what one sees him doing, what one already controls? But when dealing with a God who cannot be directly seen at work, one may and must ask him to disclose his omni-potence. If I see what God is doing because nature is divine, I may not wish him to act otherwise: that would be irreligious. But for Jesus God is the *Wholly* Other. So one must beg him to reveal what he is doing. One asks *this* of him rather than *that* because one takes a radical view of his omni-potence.

Now here is another problem. How can we reconcile petition with obedience? Is it not indocile to ask God to do this rather than that? Jesus himself answers the question: 'Not as I will, but as thou wilt.' This is not resignation, and much less is it asceticism. Obedience to God does not mean destroying our desires or acquiescing in fate. It is the act of a freedom—the act of a man who explains his purposes, begs God to accomplish them, and at the same time says 'Not as I will, but as thou wilt'. Obedience, certainly; but also the assurance that God is there for me and acts there for me. He is not a fate, he is a father, and the person praying to him is his son. Thus there is no room for the delusion that one can draw near to God by practising asceticism and annihilating one's desires.

One guise which prayer has often taken in modern times, that of devout submission to whatever God decides, is quite alien to the thought of Jesus (Lk 11:5–8 and 18:1–5). True prayer is a paradox; on the one hand man must be ready to give up his desires for God's sake, and on the other he must confidently ask God to fulfil them. It is 'a

---

13. We shall return to this matter when dealing with miracles.

paradoxical blend of the spirit of sacrifice with confident petition' (JS, p. 158). To hold back from the prayer of petition would be to make God a metaphysical essence—that is, ultimately, a being on whom one does not depend. A man who was not ready to sacrifice his desires would be laying a claim upon God and controlling him. If God is freedom one must simultaneously ask him to reveal himself—since by definition one can never know beforehand what a freedom wants—and be ready to obey his will if it does not fall in with our desires. Plainly, prayer as Jesus conceives of it safeguards and illustrates the paradox of the remote God and the intimate God. God is sheer otherness (which is precisely why one must pray to him; whereas for a pantheist it is nonsense to ask God for anything), and at the same time he is infinitely close to us, the father who gives us what we ask of him when he is pleased to do so.

(3) Closely akin to the theme of prayer, and expressive of the same paradox, is the theme of God's fatherhood. God is the father whose children men are (Mt 5:45). 'Son of God' is the noblest thing that man can be called. For that reason it is primarily an eschatological thing: 'Blessed are the peacemakers, for they shall be called sons of God' (Mt 5:9), and Jesus says of those who attain to the resurrection from the dead (though this saying is of doubtful authenticity): 'They are equal to angels and are sons of God, being sons of the resurrection' (Lk 20:36).

Most religions and religious *Weltanschauungen* likewise call God father. Even the early Stoa did, and much more that of imperial days. Being part of the divine cosmos, man is akin to God; he is his son. Epictetus boldly draws the logical inference from this dignity: he stresses the security that man finds in trusting to his father's providence. Here divine sonship is a general, objective truth. It is part of human nature, an attribute or quality of that nature.

Quite the other way with Judaism and Jesus. Israel is not God's son by nature but because it has been chosen. The same must be said of each individual, whose divine sonship is an absolute future, a 'forensic' determination, a *Verstehen*, and not an attribute. So it is not the prerogative of a few privileged souls. The Father in heaven watches over all men (Mt 6:26, 32) and all men must address their petitions to him (Mt 7:7–11). Observe how sonship of God conveys the paradox of the divine *Thou*. It is sheer grace (in Stoicism, a natural attribute) and therefore changes man, makes him a new creature by becoming his aptitude for ec-sistence.

(4) Jesus's conception of faith again expresses the same paradox. Though the actual words *faith* and *unbelief* do not often occur in his

sayings, they are thoroughly characteristic.[14] They show that faith is not an abstract conviction but an aptitude for ec-sistence. 'All things are possible to him who believes', he says to the father of the epileptic child (Mk 9:23), and to his disciples: 'If you have faith as a grain of mustard seed . . .' (Mt 17:20). In the same way he upbraids men for their puny faith or their unbelief (Mt 6:30; Mk 9:19). Unbelief is refusal to believe in God's omni-potence, his ability to concretely determine the life of man.

Jesus's thought becomes crystal-clear when it is compared with what the author of the Letter of James says: 'You believe that God is one; you do well. Even the demons believe—and shudder' (2:19). In this text we have to do with an objective faith, since the demons have it without God's being their *Verstehen*. Their faith is a mere 'regarding-something-as-true', a general persuasion that God exists. They have faith without living by God. They remain quite unchanged, in every way God's enemies, losing no vestige of their demoniac state. This idea was born of missionary practice. Against polytheism it was necessary to preach faith in the one God. Pagans being those who do not know God (Gal 4:8; 2 Thess 1:16), faith became a mere correct knowledge about God. We read in Hermas: 'First, and above all things, believe that God is one'. Thus he merely invokes a monotheist theory against pagan polytheism, whereas for Jesus faith is a *Wie*: the distant God becomes the intimate God when he reigns over man by determining his existence.

To sum up, it is easy to see where Bultmann parts company with orthodoxy and with liberalism. He repudiates the objectivism of orthodoxy, its rationalism, its general statements about God, its conjectures as to what he is in himself, the idea of faith as a mere 'regarding-something-as-true'. Orthodoxy imagines that it speaks *of* God whereas it only speaks *about* God, never getting beyond a *Vorverständnis* of him. It always tends to forget that 'we cannot say what God is like in himself; we can only say what he does for us' (KM 2, p. 200).

Like orthodoxy, liberalism makes God a datum though in another way—by means of historical pantheism. According to this view, the forces that shape history are spiritual powers immanent in it. Spurred on by them, man passes from nature to civilization. The process is a struggle, in which the true, the good and the beautiful finally triumph. Sustained by these values, man takes part in the struggle. Thus he shakes off the fetters of nature, attains personality, and enters the kingdom of liberty.

14. Mk 1:15; Lk 18:9, and so forth, which deal in the manner of Paul and John with faith in God's salvific coming, are later accretions to the synoptic tradition.

Truth, goodness, love, and the like mould the character of history and give it its divine meaning. God manifests himself in the great personalities which embody these things. Insofar as he is such a personality, Jesus reveals the godhead. But he is only the summit of history, the apex of love, sacrifice, and so forth; for those divine values were already present and operative among the noblest peoples of antiquity, who thus paved the way for the Christian religion. The course of history is one whole in which every moment marks an advance towards the spiritualization and divinization of man.

Obviously this conception leaves no room for a future or for grace properly speaking. Otherness is a closed book to liberalism. '[In liberalism] the divine is not characterized by newness but by eternity' (CV I, p. 8). All that it calls 'new' is those accidents which break the continuity of spiritual progress. Here then, as with the Greeks, newness is a pejorative term. No stage in historical evolution, no era, no person, represents an absolute value. As far back as 1924 Bultmann was praising Karl Barth for his clear perception that this historical pantheism is only a device for sidestepping the scandal of revelation and, ultimately, divinizing man. We have seen that nature and history do not reveal God. Only when God manifests himself in them do they speak to us of him.

CHAPTER SEVEN

God's Action and Miracles

I

In order to understand what God's action is we must first eliminate two mistaken notions about miracles. There is the one that reduces miracles to what Bultmann calls *Mirakel*—that is, an event that can be *verified* as *contra naturam*, nature being taken to mean the normal course of things. A *Mirakel* is what common sense understands by a miracle. We must differentiate it from *Wunder*, which is *God's action*—that is, the abolition of the world as nature.

The *Mirakel*, the unusual but visible event we have spoken of, also claims to be an act of God. But is it really? Can we entertain the idea of exceptions to the laws of nature? No. In the first place we know what to think of the pseudo-scientific argument that nature is open to supernatural interventions. We have seen that indeterminism in microphysics makes sense only in terms of the imperfect means man has at his disposal for observing and measuring things which are infinitely tiny (GV 3, pp. 108–9). If the *Mirakel* is unthinkable today, that is not only because it flies in the face of all experience but because the determinism of nature is not something we can banish at will. It is the foundation, express or tacit, of everything we think and everything we do in this world.

There is no question here of any 'meaning of the universe', any 'value-judgment', any *Weltanschauung*—that is, of a decision on man's part to hold that the world is determined rather than that it is not determined—but of a necessity intrinsic to our 'being-in-the-world'. Everything we do implies that the normal course of things can be taken for granted. When we make plans we never allow for the possibility that the laws of nature may be turned upside down. No architect, for example, has ever thought he should allow in his blueprints for the possible abolition of gravity.

Determinism is not a discovery of modern science, it is as old as man himself. Science has merely thought it through. After all, primitive man based his idea of the miraculous on it. In his eyes, the miraculous is the effect of a higher causality—a reality, therefore, that does not burst the bounds of our rational categories. Normally, primitive man—

like man today—controls nature by relying on the laws that govern it. He knows that what he has sown will germinate, that the sun will rise every morning, and so forth.[1] But he feels helpless when faced with certain more difficult actions. Then it is that he invokes the deity and asks for a miracle. In so doing he does not forsake determinism, he only appeals to a higher causality which, for instance, will effect a cure that man despairs of effecting by ordinary means. This *Mirakel* is in no way a *Wunder*—that is, the abolition of determinism—it does not overstep the earthly framework; because even qua miraculous it can be verified and because its divine nature is inferred from its visible nature.

This is just what modern defenders of *Mirakel* do when they attempt to prove that a miracle has really happened. They say, for example, that a given sudden cure is miraculous because it cannot be *explained* in any other way. From an unusual effect, but a visible one, they infer the *necessary* intervention of God, whom they thus bring into the sphere of causality. They consider his act a verifiable reality, thus incurring the criticism we made in the foregoing chapter of those who fancy they see God in nature and history. It matters little that in the latter case we are dealing with an 'ordinary' natural or historical phenomenon and in the former with a 'miraculous' phenomenon. If what God does is *God's* act it cannot be seen, either directly or indirectly, by working back from effect to cause; for in the latter case one would arrive at a God who was a mere object. To assert that only God can be the author of a given particular event is to take one's stand on the plane of proofs for the existence of God and make him nothing more than a *causa prima*. This is super-determinism; it is not getting rid of determinism.

Another sign that the *Mirakel* is not a *Wunder* is the fact that a *Mirakel* can be worked by devils or even by mere man. If man contrives to wrest the secret of the deity from it, he will do the same works as it. Sorcerers, magicians, prophets and devils can work miracles. There is a white magic and a black magic. To tell whether a *Mirakel* comes from God, the devil or man, one must have some criterion that is higher than it—which means that God is by no means the only possible source. Thus a miracle, as an event unusual on earth, is only an apparent exception to the laws of nature. It must be caused, as its very defenders admit. They christen the cause God, but this god is only a higher-grade technician whose knowledge and power exceed man's. Since one can *infer* the author of the *Mirakel* from the *Mirakel*, that author is not God. Despite its extraordinary character, therefore, the *Mirakel* is not an event *contra naturam* but *intra naturam*.

1. We do not refer to the stage where mankind considers *all* events supernatural.

And so it is not by chance that the number of *Mirakel* steadily dwindles. Nowadays a person who is not a specialist in the history of religions has no inkling how the ancients saw supernatural events on every hand. Compared with them the most rabid Catholic devotee of Lourdes is a high rationalist. What were formerly taken to be miracles, we recognize today as determined events. Thus the *Wunder* cannot be a *Mirakel*; because if it were, then God's action would be an event *intra naturam*, whereas it must do away with nature, must be something man does not control at all, that he can neither verify nor deduce, that will not fit into the categories of causality and determinism. Because it only seems to do away with determinism, the *Mirakel* is not a *Wunder*.

II

Fair and necessary criticism of the *Mirakel* has led many moderns to turn their backs on the idea of *Wunder* as well—that is, the idea of an event that is really *contra naturam*. Their error has been to miss the underlying *purpose* of the *Mirakel*. It is quite true that if God acts, his act must do away with determinism and the world as nature. But, as we have seen, the *Mirakel* only *appears* to do away with them. Not that one need embrace the notion dear to the heart of Schleiermacher that the *Wunder* is, to quote himself, only 'the religious expression of a datum (*Begebenheit*)'. From this point of view all events are miraculous. Here the *Wunder* is not opposed to determinism at all: it is only the religious garment of determinism. As Hermann Schuster wrote: 'The religious concept of the *Wunder* has nothing to do with opposition to the laws of nature. The laws of nature are the forms in and instruments through which God's action takes place' (quoted in GV 1, p. 217).

This view is not far from the Catholic idea, according to which God as *causa prima* acts through *causae secundae*. But it forgets that God's action is the action of the *Wholly* Other, so that it must itself be wholly other—which is to say that it must simply annihilate the natural order. One can only speak of a *Wunder* where the world as nature and determinism are done away with altogether.

People often invoke the idea of creation in support of the view that every natural event is a direct act of God, not realizing that they thereby deny it. If every event is miraculous, then none is. God, creation, miracle are then only pious synonyms for data. One is up to the eyes in pantheism.

This pantheist dissolution of *Wunder* ignores two points. The first is that man cannot know of himself that the world is God's creation. While he is able, working from nature and himself, to arrive at the *idea* of God, he cannot reach *God*, as we have seen in the preceding chapter. Therefore he cannot recognize the world as God's creation until God reveals it to him as such. I do not discover the Creator by deciphering nature: only when the Creator has manifested himself in nature do I know it for his creation. I control the world as nature; I do not control it as creation. God is the judgment of the world as nature. Seen from man's point of view, the world is *gottlos* (without God) and therefore of themselves the events that happen there do not disclose God. Science and man's labour never find him there because they are both 'works'. Faith in creation is not a datum, an axiom, a general truth, but a response to the revelation of God. This fact is overlooked when one considers every datum a *Wunder*; for in so doing one assumes that God is homogeneous with the world, is an objective reality that man can reach by his own powers. In fact I can only understand the world as creation when grace has broken my earthly in-sistence, when I am no longer a sinner but a believer.

So long as God has not become my *Wie*, so long as I have not the eyes of faith, I cannot see the world as his creation and events that take place in the world as so many *Wunder*. Thus creation is altogether misconceived when one tries to make it the grounds for regarding all natural or historical data as acts of God.

Now by that very fact the pantheist view we are criticizing misconceives the world even as the world. If every event is a *Wunder*, the world is divine as nature and as history. God is neither the annihilation of the world as the world nor, consequently, is he the Wholly Other. So far as faith is concerned, the world as nature and as history is not divine but *gottlos*. As a rational datum governed by laws that made it the sphere where science and technology come into play, it is atheist. It is a tool of man, the tool with which he keeps alive and fends for himself. But to see every event as a *Wunder* is to make the world as the world a divine thing instead and to ignore its sinful character. Thus liberal theology works its way back to Greek thought, where the cosmos and its laws were expressions of the divine, as will become yet more evident if we now undertake to examine *Wunder* in itself.

III

(1) *Wunder* cannot be anything objective, it is a *Dass* hidden from the eyes of natural man. Faith relates to *Wunder* as to an act of God absolutely different from any event of this world. Belief in *Wunder* and belief in God are one and the same thing. I only know God when he reveals himself, and this revelation is *Wunder*. We cannot begin by affirming God's omni-potence and thence conclude that he is able to

work a *Wunder*. For it is only through believing in *Wunder* that I can believe in God's omni-potence. I cannot use his omni-potence as an apologetical basis on which to justify belief in *Wunder*; because *Wunder* is itself omni-potence.

Accordingly it is not an event that can be verified in the world, any more than God is. *Wunder* as *Wunder* is hidden from the eyes of anyone who does not believe in God. So neither is it a *Mirakel*, which though unusual is no less earthly on that account. Of themselves a sudden cure, the return of a corpse to life (assuming that such things can really have happened), are not acts of God. Trying to infer from the verifiable existence of such facts that God is their author is, as we have said, turning him into a *causa prima*. *Wunder* is not a basis of faith in the sense that as a visible event it enables one to infer the existence of the invisible God; for such invisibility would only be that of some hidden natural force.

Wunder is a basis of faith, not as a verifiable event but as the revelation of God: so that in the first place the question 'Do I believe in *Wunder*?' is identical with the question 'Do I believe in God?'; and in the second place, though I may *see* a *Mirakel* I must *believe* in *Wunder*.

So *Wunder* demands faith. What happens if I have no faith? What does God's action look like to me then? Well, it no longer looks to me precisely like God's action. I remain the prisoner of my in-sistence: I no longer see the world as creation; I see it only as nature, causality, determinism; as the sphere of my knowledge, my work, and my earthly life. Once cut off from God, man of himself is blind to earthly events as *Wunder*. *Sin* is what spawns the world as nature.

Here is the underlying vindication of what we declared at the beginning of this chapter—that the idea of determinism is ingrained in man as a being-in-the-world. If he cannot shake off at will this conviction (the basis of science and technology) that the world is a seamless determinism, it is because he is a sinner and cannot escape sin by his own efforts. To think of determinism as a postulate in the field of science is to stall on the surface of things. It is the fruit of sin. By cutting himself off from God, man has made creation his own scheme, his mode of existence—that is, the world *as nature*. Man is at the bottom of the world's *Gottlosigkeit*: he has made the world in his own sinful image and likeness. That is why science and technology never find God. They are atheist through and through. The world as determinism is the world in a state of fallenness.

In a searching passage of his *Commentary on the Letter to the Romans*, Luther has shown how the world is a substance yearning to be stripped of what he calls its quidditative being so as to have a future that will be a true future (WA 56, pp. 371–2). The *Wie* of natural man is his being-in-the-world, which explains why he cannot see the world as God's *Wunder*. Sin is that will to aseity which flies in the face of true otherness. The world as nature is the tool with which man has provided himself in order to build his being-in-the-world. Of course there is much toil involved in science and technology; but nature is so made that it offers man a hold over itself and in due course he becomes its master (as our age has shown plainly enough), though at the end of the day his victory is bound to be a pyrrhic one.

It will now be obvious why *Mirakel* is also atheist. However extraordinary it may be, we know that it falls within the framework of earthly phenomena and cannot escape determinism. Even its defenders admit as much when they claim that we must infer from its existence the existence of its necessary cause. Whether they call this cause God is neither here nor there. What matters is the causal connection. By asserting it they amply demonstrate that *Mirakel* is confined within the sphere of determinism and therefore within the sphere of *Gottlosigkeit*. A 'miraculous' cure is every bit as atheist as a 'normal' cure. It cannot be seen for the act of God it is, so long as one attempts to infer its character as such from its character as a verified fact. It can only be known for the act of God it is, if God *reveals* it and if his revelation is *believed*.

(2) Man *ought*, indeed, to see the world as *Wunder*; for being blind is not part of his authentic nature, it is a result of his sin. So *Wunder* can only be defined as that whereby man, no longer sinful, is now pardoned. It can only be God's revelation, which is identical with the forgiveness of sins. Revelation necessarily takes the shape of forgiveness, because it is addressed to sinners. It is not some intellectual illumination bringing new knowledge to a being who is already God's friend. It is an act of God that *transforms* man by giving him a new mode of being. That is why 'there is only one *Wunder*: the miracle of revelation' (GV I, p. 221). Now this point must be enlarged upon so that we may understand two things: (*a*) why justification is a *Wunder*—in other words an event *contra naturam* which does away with determinism—and (*b*) why *Mirakel* and *Wunder* overlap.

(*a*) Why does I Cor 1:22 say that it is the hallmark of the Jews to require a σημεῖον? Because this demand lays bare the essence of their *Gottlosigkeit*. If they are not justified before God, it is not because they fail to acknowledge him in theory (in such acknowledgment they yield to no nation); it is because they think to reach him through ἰδία δικαιοσύνη. Understanding themselves in terms of what they do—that is to say, in terms of something visible and palpable which proves their worth—they likewise understand the *Thou* in terms of what he does. Exactly as they expect to justify themselves before God by their works, they expect God to justify himself by his, to offer some visible proof that he exists and is at work: a sign. Thus one can understand their longing (the longing of natural man) for a *Mirakel*; because, as we have seen, *Mirakel* enables man to prove faith and thus manipulate it.

Seeing a σημεῖον, man thinks he is sure that God exists. He does not realize that it is rank immanence to try to infer the existence of God from a visible sign. So it is obvious enough why *Wunder* scandalizes him. For *Wunder* is not a work. It is impossible to reason one's way from tangible effects to the action of God. For example, the mere fact that I observe a miraculous (*Mirakel-*) cure does not tell me whether it is a real *Wunder*. That is why it is open to the most disparate interpretations. Some will think it the work of the devil; others, the effect of an unknown law of nature; and others will credit God with the doing of it.

The same wide range of interpretation is found when we turn to the world at large, which I am free to regard as nature or as God's creation; as the sphere of my earthly business—that is, in some sort as an extension of myself—or as God's property; as what I control or what God controls. Thus *Wunder* is a crucial question put to man: has he a mind to understand himself, and understand the world and God, in terms of himself; or is he prepared to understand himself and understand the world and God, in terms of God?

But can man answer such a question on his own? Can he of his own initiative decide to understand himself, and understand the world and God, in terms of God? Obviously not; for that would be yet another work. He is locked within a circle and his servile freedom can only be set free by the grace of God. That is why *Wunder* takes the form of forgiveness: because it delivers man from his sin. And that is why forgiveness is necessarily a *Wunder*: because its face is set against the world as nature and as the sphere of human business—that is, against the world as a 'work'.

Even our future deeds in the world are already done before we do them, already past before they become future. They are 'works', because I have thought them up for myself and planned them for myself. Luther keenly perceived that every deed man will presently do is bereft of true future simply on the strength of being man's, because its future is one which man controls· *Semper ita fit, ut opus nostrum intelligamus, antequam fiat, Dei autem opus non intelligimus donec factum fuerit* (quoted in GV I, p. 223). Contrariwise the *Wunder* whereby God justifies man makes the world henceforth an *utterance of God*. The believer no longer regards it as that which he controls but 'as the realm in which we must hearken to God's *Anspruch* and give it effect' (GV I, p 225).

Clearly we are not dealing now with a *Weltanschauung*, a theory about the world; clearly this gaze which faith turns upon the world is every moment bestowed by God's forgiveness. We are constantly tempted to lapse into regarding the world as nature, because that is the whole pull of sin.

Of course the believer must *also* look on the world as nature, insofar as it is the sphere of his doings. No one suggests abolishing science and technology. But faith must transform this profane use of the world, so that the Christian shall live there according to Paul's ὡς μή; or again, as John says, be in the world without being of the world. Man needs the world as nature, for his work. How far he needs it cannot be laid down a priori. But in no circumstances may he regard the world primarily as nature: that would be backsliding into unbelief.

(*b*) We are now in a better position to sift out what is true and what is false in the two views which we have rejected: that of *Mirakel* and that of pantheist *Wunder*. *Mirakel* is a typical instance of mythology. We are familiar with the ambiguity native to myth, the transcendent meaning of which is always more or less rationalized. The case is the same with *Mirakel*. Insofar as it is an extraordinary event (a sudden cure, a virgin birth or the like), it is designed to call attention to the existence and operation of supernatural forces. It is 'a primitive and confused way of saying that one understands God's action as opposed to any earthly event and any earthly act' (GV 1, p. 226). Nevertheless it leads to a sham transcendence and no farther; because man thinks he can reason from the observed fact of a *Mirakel* to its cause, which is nothing else but manipulating faith.

The fact that a cure is extraordinary does not mean that it is of God. Despite its unusual character, as we have pointed out, a *Mirakel* only *seems* to be an exception to determinism. Of itself, it is part of the world as nature. Mythological thought *objectifies* God's intervention, projecting it into the plane of this world's events. It claims to ascertain the existence of *Wunder*, forgetting that 'the transcendence of God's action is safeguarded only if one envisages that action as operating *in* earthly events, not *among* them; so that the unbroken cohesion which those events display to the objectifying eye remains intact' (KM 2, p. 196). Thus a doctor cannot assure us that a given extraordinary cure is a *Wunder*, because a *Wunder* as such is not visible. Try to observe it and you annihilate it. Only as a believer has the doctor any business to declare that God has intervened; but he should also declare—still as a believer—that God has intervened in every cure that is called 'normal'.

This latter point is firmly driven home by the pantheist idea of *Wunder*. By declaring *all* events divine, it shows that *Wunder* is in no way a 'marvel', a 'prodigy', an extraordinary phenomenon. There can always be new *Wunder* so far as faith is concerned, because nothing whatever is exempt from God's control. The pantheist view rightly holds that the extraordinary character of an event does not make it an act of God. But it wrongly supposes that the faith of the believer enables him to regard every event in the world as a *Wunder*. It supposes that there is a Christian *Weltanschauung* in virtue of which all events can be interpreted as *Wunder*. Now that is making faith an attribute or quality of man, whereas it is at every moment a gift from God; forgetting that justification is a perpetual future, that it is always 'forensic'—in other words, that while remaining the justification of man it is always ahead of man, always something granted by God.

Faith is not an infused light which enables me to see the world as *Wunder* when and as I please. We must uphold the *semper credendum*. At every moment, faith is grace. Pantheism believes in a *direct* identity between earthly event and act of God, which is nothing short of manipulating God. Faith, on the other hand, affirms a *paradoxical* identity between the two—an identity, that is, which can only be revealed and believed. Because it holds God to be immanent in the world pantheism is sure a priori that every event is divine. Because it holds that God transcends the world, faith never knows a priori whether an event is divine: it only knows by revelation.

'When I think of earthly events as a closed system—which I must do, after all, not only in order to understand them scientifically but also in order to go about my daily tasks—there is certainly no room left for God's action. But the paradox of faith is that nonetheless it sees an act of God in an event which can be verified in its natural and historical context. The *nonetheless* is inseparable from faith' (KM 2, p. 198).

Thus we see that what makes a *Wunder* is not its 'matter' (the work itself) but rather its meaning (see pp. 17–8, above). Seeing the world as nature and as *Wunder* is seeing the same 'thing' in two diametrically opposite ways: in the first case, the world is what man controls; in the second case, the world is what God controls. Contrariwise to turn a *Wunder* into a *Mirakel* is to make it consist essentially in its 'matter', its visible and tangible nature. That is the time-honoured trick of the *homo religiosus* who manipulates faith while fondly imagining that he has it.

IV

What shall we say of the New Testament miracles? The primitive community was sure that Jesus had worked miracles, and credited him with quantities of them. Most of the miracles related in the gospels are either legend or embroidered with legend, as we have said before. But beyond all doubt Jesus did certain things which in his eyes and the eyes of his contemporaries were real miracles—acts, that is, of which God must be accounted the author. Beyond all doubt he cured the sick and cast out devils.

But our first concern must be with his idea of how God acts. It is diametrically opposed to the idea implied by *Mirakel*; in other words, it is not based on the analogy of the laws of nature. Jesus never thought of God or the world in terms of causality. Invariably he sees any given event as arising from a will, not from an abstract law or objective cause. His belief in miracles does not mean that he accepts the existence of a supernatural causality but rather that certain events must be attributed to God in a very special way.

Then does he not think God al-mighty? We have seen that, to Jesus's mind, God is at work in *all* events, that even the lilies of the field grow because of him. How shall we reconcile this with his belief in miracles? Well, that belief drives home to us his certainty that God is not an object of thought. Far from conflicting with his belief that God is at work in the events of everyday, it confirms and illustrates it. It stresses the fact that God's omni-potence is not a general truth which man applies at will to the world (as is done in pantheism). The affirmation that God is the Al-mighty always goes hand in hand with the avowal that I cannot know him of myself. This point is lucidly made when the father of the sick child cries: 'I believe; help my unbelief' (Mk 9:24). The world's daily round hides God away: I can only see him in *Wunder*.

Jesus does not consider miracles a proof of the existence of God; a miracle is not an extraordinary event which implies that it must have been caused by God. There is no such thing as a general belief in miracles, any more than there is a general belief in God's omni-potence. Those events which Jesus looked on as *Wunder* were not such in their objective and visible nature, as though they could have provided faith with a why and wherefore.

No miracle can ever rescue a man from doubt (contrary to what Christian apologetics very early and very wrongly imagined). A man who is looking for some evidence that God exists will never see *Wunder*; because *Wunder* can be seen only if instead of doubting God one doubts oneself. That is why Jesus always refused to vindicate himself by miracles (Mk 8:11–12), which would have meant manipulating faith. That is also why he attached no particular importance to the miracles he did work; or at least was no enthusiast for miracles, was not intoxicated by his power, as so many other 'saviours', ancient and modern, have been.

If we take Jesus's belief in miracles to be a general conviction that certain events, which today we are in the habit of putting down to natural causes, are the effect of a higher causality, it loses its meaning and contradicts his idea of God. No, his belief in miracles expresses his conviction that God's will is not visible in general but only in certain events—in ec-sistentiell encounters. Thus belief in God necessarily includes belief in miracles, because it is itself nothing but a *Wunder*. Belief in God and belief in miracles are the same thing, because they both abolish the natural way of thinking—which is to say, that of sinful man.

In short, the *Wunder* of Jesus are witnesses to the *ambiguity* of Christian faith. They show that a miracle as a verifiable event will not serve as grounds for faith; for every man is free to put it down to whatever cause he may choose (Mk 3:22; 8:11–12), as the Gospel of John makes abundantly clear. In that Gospel Jesus's miracles are called σημεῖα. With John the word is used in the strict sense, to mean sign. The sign is an ambiguous thing that requires to be interpreted, and can be interpreted in different ways. It is not a proof of anything.

Signs reveal the glory of Jesus (2:11; see 9:3; 11:4) and those who will not be convinced by so many σημεῖα are taken to task for their unbelief (12:37). Yet, on the other hand, Jesus says reproachfully: 'Unless you see signs and wonders you will not believe' (4:48). And the risen Christ has the same complaint to make of Thomas: 'Have you believed because you have seen me? Blessed are those who have not seen and yet believed' (20:29).[2] When the Jews ask 'What sign do you do, that we may see and believe you? What work do you perform?', it is obviously a mark of unbelief (6:30; see 2:18). Their question follows upon the episode of the feeding of the five thousand, which plainly shows that the meaning of this miracle was not to be found in its visible nature as an extraordinary event. Indeed v. 26 had already said as much: 'You seek me, not because you saw σημεῖα, but because you ate your fill of the loaves.'

As signs, therefore, *Wunder* are ambiguous. One can mistake their meaning, just as one can mistake the meaning of Jesus's words. Their being extraordinary events does not make them proofs: the extraordinary character they exhibit merely suggests that the coming of Jesus does away with the ordinary behaviour of things. Their real purpose is to show that revelation is not something objective but the eschatological *Dass* which cannot be demonstrated,

The miracle of Cana, which is an epiphany, exemplifies what happens in everything that Jesus does: his glory is revealed—not that

2. As to the translation, see EJ, p. 539.

of the wonder-worker but the glory of him through whom grace and truth are bestowed (2:1–12). If the healing of the imperial officer's son (4:46–54) and of the paralytic at the pool (5:1–9) have only a general meaning—they drive home the fact that Jesus is the source of life—the feeding of the five thousand (6:1–15), the cure of the man born blind (9:1–7), and the raising of Lazarus (11:1–44) each have a special meaning: they present revelation, respectively, as food, light and life.

John 6:26, 30 alone suffices, as we have seen, to show that σημεῖα as extraordinary events (qua *Mirakel*) do not vindicate Jesus. In the same sense the observation that faith based on miracles is not true faith (2:23–25), is highly characteristic. The whole Gospel of John stresses the fact that miracles give scandal when they are not interpreted as signs. The cure of the paralytic, and that of the man born blind, incense the Jews and provoke them to compass Jesus's death. If miracles are the first shock which draws the attention of many to Jesus—it can be said that they are granted for this purpose—to the leaders of the people, who represent the 'world', they are a scandal which determines them that he must die (11:7; see 12:8f). After the miracle of Lazarus's resurrection there is no turning back (11:53).

Since miracles are signs, they are apt to be misunderstood. After the miracle of the loaves, which raises the question whether Jesus is really the prophet who is to come into the world (6:14), the multitude try to make him king (6:15), because they have eaten their fill (6:26). Jesus's brothers wish him to go to Jerusalem for the feast of tabernacles and make himself known, for 'no man works in secret if he seeks to be known openly. If you do these things, show yourself to the world' (7:3–4). They do not understand the true nature of revelation, which for the world is always a thing ἐν κρυπτῷ although it takes place ἐν παρρησία. For there is nothing visible about this παρρησία: it is hidden in the most commonplace events and only faith perceives it.

If Jesus himself never considered miracles a proof of anything, his disciples were very early given to regarding them as proof of his messiahship, and even a proof shattering enough to convince the devils (Mk 1:24). Indeed this apologetical aim accounts for most of the miracles related in the synoptics.[3] Now it is a remarkable fact that the author of the fourth Gospel, who derived his narratives from one source,[4] transformed their meaning. Miracles which proved their own divine origin he turns into the signs we have just been speaking of. Here is an example of his recasting. Let the reader compare Mt 8:5–13

3. Critical exposition in GST, pp. 233–60.
4. The σημεῖα-source, which Bultmann discusses at length in his commentary on John.

(Lk 7:1–10) and Jn 4:46–54. They deal with the same material. But the author of the fourth Gospel has altered it by adding Jesus's reproach: 'Unless you see signs and wonders, you will not believe' (v. 48).

True, the synoptics also warn men against miracles. But they do so in general terms and outside the framework of any narrative (that is, of the source), whereas John sets it at the very heart of the episode he is relating.

In short, the ambiguity of Jesus's miracles is the ambiguity of his own self. For the historian he is only a fact in the past. The question facing us is whether we wish to regard him as merely one of the great men of history, or as God's *Wunder*, the word of pardon and grace that he speaks to us. Anyone who tried to discern God's revelation in Jesus's historical personality as such, would incur the mockery of Kierkegaard for being stronger than God himself, who sent his Son to us veiled in flesh.

From all the foregoing there follows a weighty conclusion, which we shall have occasion to return to presently. If it is true that miracles, far from being a ground of faith, presuppose it—if, as verifiable facts, they 'have in themselves no religious character at all' (JS, p. 146)—the question whether they are possible and *objectively* real becomes a very minor one. Christian faith has nothing to gain, on the contrary has everything to lose, by trying to prove the possibility and the reality of Jesus's miracles as objective facts (qua *Gegebenheiten*). We must insist on this point 'with the utmost vigour' (GV I, p. 227).

People fancy these days that to question the historical reality of the cures or the resurrections from the dead related in the New Testament is to doubt the divinity of Jesus. Now this is an admission that one bases the invisible on the visible and rationalizes the acts of God. Even if Jesus had really risen from the dead, that would be no proof at all that he is the Word of God; and if he did not rise from the dead, that is no proof that he is not the Word of God. We have seen that *Mirakel* sticks within the framework of determinism and that a God who recalled a corpse to the life *of this world* would as such be no more than a 'higher-grade technician'.[5]

The problem of the historicity of Jesus's *Wunder* must be given over

---

5. As Luther saw. When Christ gave commandments, taught, comforted, went about doing good, worked miracles—all that, says Luther, was not his *officium proprium* but an incidental office. Or again he says that these things are not *proprie Christi opera*. 'Nam prophetae etiam docuerunt et fecerunt mirabilia. Sed Christus est Deus ut homo, qui patitur legem Mosis et tyrannidem externam, Mosen et hanc tyrannidem vincit, pugnat cum lege et patitur et postea resurgens damnavit, sustulit nostrum hostem.' All Christ's other works (preaching, miracles . . .) are *opera vulgaria* (WA, 40, I, p. 568, 9ff, quoted in GV I, 227).

without reserve to higher criticism. Working as an historian, Bultmann has shown that most of the miracles narrated in the gospels are legendary. They sprang from the conviction that Jesus was the Messiah, and from the desire to spread this conviction by making it seem credible (GST, pp. 233–60). Therefore their essential meaning is not to be found in their objective nature.

What we have just said of their origin shows that they are primarily a *confession of faith*. They are not the grounds for faith, they derive from faith: they are not its cause but its effect. That is just what constitutes their value. They show that the Christian community believed Jesus was the Word of God and not a wonder-worker, not one of those 'men of God' who abounded in ancient times. Had they been objective events on the strength of which the community believed in him, its faith would not have got beyond the mythological stage. Jesus would only be a god in the ancient sense. But the fact that they come after faith and spring from it, shows that Christians regarded Jesus as the Word of God. No doubt, the confession of faith which the miracles constitute is *ambiguous*; because the form it took is *mirakelhaft*; because the community yielded to the temptation of proof, as a rule for apologetical reasons. But behind this naive objectification it is easy to discern the deep purpose of the New Testament miracles.

As for those which are historically established (cures, exorcisms), we are by no means forced to believe that they represent an exception to the laws of nature such as *Mirakel* claims to be, and that as visible, objective phenomena they escape the universal law of determinism. Today we have exhaustively thought over the world as nature, and we know that there is no such thing as *Mirakel* in it. Even if a dead man rose again, science would give us a natural explanation of the fact; though for faith it were an act of God and, as such, did away with determinism. We believe that God sows life and death, gives health and sickness; but that in all these things he acts, as has been said (pp. 121–2, above), *in* events, not *among* them.

CHAPTER EIGHT

The Word of God

As we have said, there is only one *Wunder*: revelation, the Word of God, which it is time to examine in itself.

I

In the Old Testament, the expression 'word of God' may mean either God's action—in Ps 33:4 and 145:13 the 'word of the Lord' is synonymous with 'acts of the Lord'—or his commands. Both senses spring from a primitive conception of word as something charged with power; that is, an *act*. We find the king's word (Is 11:2-4) and the prophet's (2 Kgs 1:10ff) envisaged in this way; but above all the word of God, who calls things into being by the breath of his mouth (Ps 33:6; see Is 40:26). His word is declared to be invincibly efficacious and indestructible (Is 40:8; 45:23; 55:10-11).

Obviously what matters here is the *fact* of God's utterance, not what it says: his word is a temporal event and not an eternal truth. It is not a *Was*, but a *Dass*. No doubt it *also* has a content: God says what is to be, and what he has said takes place. His is not a magical word that comes into being merely because it is said and in spite of a content which is wholly unintelligible. Still, the chief feature of the biblical word is its character as *Anrede*. Always it is a word spoken *to* someone. It is not a judgment in the logical sense of that term, but a command:

> For he spoke, and it came to be;
> he commanded, and it stood forth.
>
> (Ps 33:9)

Thus the word of God rules the world; but not like the Greek *logos*, which rules the cosmos by being its immanent law. The word of God is his sovereign power doing what it sees fit to do. It is not only addressed to nature, calling it into existence; but also, through nature, to man. The world as creation '*tells* man something': it teaches him that he is God's creature and that as such he must turn to God in praise (Ps 29 and 145).

But it is not through nature alone that God summons man to

answer. He also speaks to him, in the strict sense, through the prophet and through the priest. His word *says* what is good and what he requires (Mic 6:8). His demands are his words (2 Chron 29:15) and often the ten commandments are simply called the ten words (Ex 34:28; Deut 4:13, and *passim*). Whether God addresses man indirectly or directly, it is always by a word which is a supremely efficacious command. The two kinds of address are clearly conveyed in the following text:

> He sends forth his command to the earth;
>   his word runs swiftly.
> He gives snow like wool;
>   he scatters hoarfrost like ashes.
> He casts forth his ice like morsels;
>   who can stand before his cold?
> He sends forth his word, and melts them;
>   he makes his wind blow, and the waters flow.
> He declares his word to Jacob,
>   his statutes and ordinances to Israel.
>
>   (Ps 147:15ff)

This picture of the word reveals a certain conception of *Dasein*. If one plumbs the depths of the primitive idea that we have called power, searches out what it tells us about man and therefore about the meaning of the expression 'word of God', it will become clear that the word of God is God in his relation to man, as calling man into existence—as the power that limits man and has an *Anspruch* upon man. Just as God's word scatters life and death in nature, so it is life or death for man (Deut 30:19). It is the way of life and the way of death (Jer 21:8). He who keeps it will live, he who despises it will die (Prov 19:16). What it says is clear but the reason for it is unfathomable.

God's commandments can no more be deduced from an ethical theory than his power can be deduced from the laws of nature. In both cases man depends utterly on the will of God. Hence God's word is not a doctrine on God and the world. Biblical man does not achieve *Verständnis* of himself by a θεωρία, but by listening to the word, which is the Wholly Other insofar as it becomes the Wholly Intimate without ceasing to be the Wholly Other.

In later Judaism the formal sense is the same as in the Old Testament. The pseudepigrapha and writings of the rabbis alike hold that God's word is creative. Power is often attributed to it (Wis 12:9; 16:26; 18:15f). It is well known that the Targums speak of God's *Memra*, meaning not a hypostasis but the manifestation of God himself, the *praesens numen.*[1] In Judaism the dominant conception is that of the law as God's word (Sir 24:23; 36:2; Bar 4:1, and *passim*). The fact that this word is action emerges from the very use it was put to as an amulet. The sacred text was inscribed on phylacteries and on the doorposts and gates of the people's houses (Deut 6:4–9; 11:13–21).

Above all, the law is a commandment. God's word is a summons; it does not lie within man's control; it controls him. He cannot deduce it from anything or search out any reason for it. It contains no eternal truths already known to him by implication: it is not a particular form given to some changeless moral law, but the word God spoke to Moses, which constantly summons the Jewish community anew. It is not a synopsis of doctrine or a religious *Weltanschauung*; its business is not with man's reason, but with his will; it is not seen, it is heard; it is not something to be known, but something to be obeyed.

Jesus's interpretation of the word fits within the framework of the Old Testament and of Judaism. He takes it for granted that the Old Testament is the word of God (see Mk 7:13). But he takes it no less for granted that God acts in the present through the word that he, Jesus, preaches. The synoptic tradition makes him the herald of the word, and it is his words that the community collected and handed down. Beyond all doubt, he was conscious of being the messenger of the word. Though it must have been the Hellenistic community which first thought of his preaching as an εὐαγγέλιον, though the expression εὐαγγελίζεσθαι must have been put into his mouth by the disciples, and though the episode of Lk 4:16–30—where he presents himself as the bearer of the good news—is also the work of the community, nevertheless he certainly spoke in the name of God, announcing that God's kingdom was at hand; indeed, had already begun.

Declaring God's word was his peculiar office. He brought neither ceremonies nor practices; he brought the word, which was not a new teaching but a summons to repentance in view of the kingdom that was on the threshold. Jesus preaches the will of God. His word is a summons to decision. Nothing that he says is new: what matters is *that* he says it, that the word is event and advent. 'He who has ears to hear, let him hear. Hear me, and understand' (Mk 4:9; 7:14), whereby we see that hearing is not mere audition but an obedience, a *Verstehen*. A man who listens and does not go on to act is like the man who built his house upon the sand (Mt 7:24–27) and in fact did not hear, although he has ears (Mk 8:18; 4:12). For the word of God is the will of God. Where Mark (3:35) has 'whoever does the *will* of God', Luke says

---

1. Bultmann agrees that the Jewish scholars and Billerbeck are right in denying that God's *Memra* is an hypostasis.

(8:21) 'those who hear the *word* of God and do it'. The exegesis is correct: God's will comes to us in his word.

As we have seen, Jesus refuses to vindicate himself by miracles. Neither does he invoke his own personal qualities. His one wish is to be the word of God, which has the power of life and death and decides the fate of man:

> Whoever is ashamed of me and of my words
>   in this adulterous and sinful generation
> of him will the Son of man also be ashamed
>   when he comes in the glory of his Father with the holy angels.
>   (Mt 8: 38)

Luke has: 'Everyone who acknowledges *me* before men . . .' and 'who denies *me* before men . . .' (12:8), showing that the word of Jesus as it were exhausts his person. In the Bible, therefore, word is a *Dass*.

II

For the Greeks, on the contrary, word is primarily a *Was*. Of course they are familiar with the magic word, the efficacious formula, and also with the oracle—the utterance that is of divine inspiration. Nevertheless λόγος is primarily not utterance as an event, but utterance as something intelligible The original meaning of λέγειν is not 'summon' but 'explain'. Here we see once more how little interested the Greeks were in otherness. Λόγος is essentially ἀπόφανσις (explanation, setting forth): first of all it lays bare a content. The speaking of this content, its being uttered, told *to* someone, is a lesser aspect which may even fade out altogether, as happens when *logos* acquires the sense of motive, reason. Λόγος does not have its full weight in isolation, but only when it is the κοινὸς λόγος, the timeless meaning of the whole. Until this has been explicitly done αἰτίας λογισμῷ, an opinion that is sound enough in itself (ἀληθὴς δόξα) can have only a relative validity (*Menon* 97c–98a). Since the *logos* conveys the intelligibility of an utterance, it does not need a genitive; whereas in the Old Testament a word is always someone's word, always has (expressly or by implication) a genitive complement of person.

Not only is the *logos* not an *Anrede*: it has no business to be such. A man who listens to what a philosopher is saying should assent to the *logos*, not to the philosopher. So to hear the *logos* is not to perceive a demand, issuing from the present situation, that concerns oneself. No doubt the hearer is aware of an *Anspruch*, but in such a way as to understand it only when he knows that ultimately he must lay it upon

himself, so as to get beyond the ἰδία φρόνησις. What he listens to is not
a *Thou* but himself in his authentic being, which is existence in the
logos. Socrates interprets the admonition of the Delphic god, γνῶθι
σαυτόν, as an invitation to *logoi* (*Phaedo* 96ff). So this *logos*, unlike that
of the Old Testament, is never an absolute: it always remains within
the realm of διαλέγεσθαι, which means that it must again and again be
called in question. Hence he who utters the *logos* is devoid of authority:
a man should even listen to trees and rocks εἰ μόνον ἀληθῆ λέγοιεν.

This idea prevailed in Greek thought to the very last. Man as a ζῷον
λόγον ἔχον has his true being in the *logoi* (of the *logos*). He is not an
'historical' being constituted by the dialogue between the *I* and the
Thou. On the contrary, he tries to understand his existence in the
world in terms of thought. All rests on the assumption that the being
of the cosmos is made up by the same *logoi* that make up man. Man-the-
logos finds his bearings in the world, which is his security. The necessity
which pervades thought is at the same time a necessity pervading the
Whole: ἡ ἰσότης ἡ γεωμετρικὴ καὶ ἐν θεοῖς καὶ ἐν ἀνθρώποις μέγα
δύναται (*Gorgias* 507e–508a).

The οὗ ἕνεκα which rules human thought seems to rule the cosmos as
well and give it its τάξις. Thus the *logos* is both an impetus and a
foundation. Not only does it express the coherent structure of being,
it actually is that structure. So one can see why Heraclitus calls the
logos the law of all being and why Parmenides simply identifies being
and thought; why, just as λόγος and ἀνάγκη are one for Leucippus, so
λόγος and φύσις are one for the Stoics.

In Stoicism the process of identifying form with matter has reached
its term. The *logos* is a *pneuma*, matter of an ethereal nature, a fire or
ether. The entire world is steeped in it as in a τονικὴ δύναμις, a λόγος
σπερματικός, so that the intelligible and rational form is none other than
the generative power of nature. This *logos*, which is the κοινὸς νόμος
φύσεως and makes the cosmos a ζῷον ἔμψυχον, is at the same time, as
λόγος ὀρθός, the law which the individual must affirm outright in
συγκατάθεσις so as to become aware of his identity with the world
logos (see p. 27, above).

Nevertheless a distinction, however subtle, emerges within this
identity. Since the individual must affirm the *logos*, he is in a certain
way different from it. Out of this fissure grew the subsequent philosophy of the *logos*, which continued to regard the *logos* as a divine
power immanent in the world but dwelt upon its transcendence over
particular phenomena, notably man—man who can find his true being
only in the *logos* but may not find it at all. Then, under the influence of
the Platonist and Aristotelian tradition, the deity is thought of as more
and more remote from the cosmos. As God and the world travel

farther and farther apart, the *logos* takes up an intermediate position: it partakes as much of the nature of God, whom it represents or displaces, as of the nature of the world, on which it bestows existence and order.

Here we cannot show how the theory of the *logos* evolved from the author of the *Περὶ κόσμου* through Plutarch, Numenius, Plotinus, the *Corpus hermeticum*, and Philo to Gnosis. But two observations must be made. First, we know that Greek thought envisaged the cosmos (of which the gods were part) as a unit: that composed of form and matter. Form and matter did not exist independent of each other.[2] But at the stage which we have now reached a true dualism appears: henceforth there are two *substances*—the divine substance and the earthly substance. The relation between God and the divine forces which are in the cosmos is no longer one of identity but one of emanation.

In the second place the *logos* is thought of as a being intermediate between God and the world, and thanks to the influence of various mythologies it becomes a semi-personal being and finally an altogether personal one. It is given the same status as those divine figures which in myth play a cosmic or soteriological role. On the one hand the *logos* is so to speak the sum of what constitutes the world—forces, laws, forms and shapes—and on the other, it manifests the inaccessible, invisible, unknowable godhead—discloses God.

This evolution lays bare a gradual falling away from the *Was* to the *Dass*. Cornutus, a Stoic of the first century, says that the *logos* is Hermes, sent to men as a *κῆρυξ* and *ἄγγελος* to inform them of God's will. Here we have a revival of the ancient belief in word. The *logos* is envisaged as the mighty, efficacious word of the primal godhead. It becomes the creator of the world. The more the *logos* is thought of as something analogous to the holy word in the mystery religions (which is as much a magic formula as a piece of doctrine), the more the knowledge he reveals ceases to concern the world and its laws and becomes a mysterious doctrine. And the more like a mystery this knowledge becomes, the more the *logos* emerges a person: it is the 'son', the 'messenger' of the supreme God who sits enthroned, unknowable, beyond the world. Thus the *logos* becomes hypostatized.

Can it be said, then, that at this final stage we have a parallel to the word of God as known in scripture? The resemblance consists in this: that in both cases the word is by nature spoken *to* someone; and, once

2. Even in Plato there is no real dualism. See J. Adam, *The Republic of Plato* (1902), II, p. 62, note 13 on *Rep.* VI, 509b.

spoken, reveals to man his position in the world and his road of
salvation.

But there remains a fundamental difference between the biblical idea
and the Greek idea. The *logos* is not *Anrede* in the true sense of that
word. Pride of place always goes to the content of what is said, to the
mysterious wisdom that is imparted. If certain esoteric writings contain
passages where the word of revelation seems to be a summons to
repentance and conversion, still they do not define man as the being
who is constantly under summons. The *logos* is merely the mysterious
source of a gnosis which, it is held, cannot be of human origin. It is
a striking circumstance that the godhead's *logos* is balanced by his
σιγή (his silence). Σιγή is the unfathomable depths of God; it is the
Deus absconditus, whereas the *logos* is the *Deus revelatus*. At bottom, the
Deus revelatus enables man to manipulate faith. Thanks to it man
knows God by means of an objective knowledge, without making God
his *Verstehen*. In the Bible, contrariwise, the word of God is God
himself as revealing himself. The word is only his mode of being. Not
only is he *in* the word that he speaks to man: he is that word.

According to Gnosis, God is not in the *logos*, and much less *is* he the
logos. Hence the eager desire of the Gnostic to pass beyond this intermediary and enter into God's σιγή. Philo says that the *logos* only takes
one to the threshold of seeing God. The goal is the σιγή. In the silence
of worship and ecstasy man is really in God, whereas the Bible says
that man finds God in the word itself. There is no reason for passing
beyond the word; for it is not a step towards God but God himself,
who is one with it. The *Deus absconditus* is the *Deus revelatus*. The *logos*
is God in his relation to man.

III

What the Old Testament and Jesus thought of God's word remains
dominant in the New Testament conception. Now in its original form
and now in an altered one, we find there the primitive notion that word
is endowed with a potent efficacy. As examples of the first type we
have the words through which Jesus worked his cures, and which have
been preserved as ῥήσεις βαρβαρικαί (Mk 5:41; 7:34; see Mt 8:8, 16;
Lk 4:36; Acts 5:5); or again, sacramental formulas (Eph 5:26; 1 Tim
4:5). John 15:3 and 17:17 are examples of the second type. God's word
is his creative word (2 Pet 3:5, 7; Heb 1:3; 11:3) and therefore the
word that judges and annihilates (Rom 9:28 quoting Is 10:22ff;
Heb 4:2; 2 Pet 3:7). It is also his commandment, laid down in the
Old Testament (Acts 7:38; Heb 2:2; 4:2), which is identical with the
promise (Rom 3:12; 9:6, 9; 1 Cor 15:54; and so forth).

The New Testament either declares or implies that God's word contained in the Old Testament is an *Anrede* and not a theological doctrine (Rom 3:19; 15:4; I Cor 10:11). An efficacious word, a creative word, a word of judgment, a word of command, a word of promise, a word of summons: as many characteristics that define God's word as a *Dass*, an ec-sistentiell determination that destroys man's in-sistence.

When the term is used (as generally happens) to mean the noblest thing in the New Testament—the Christian kerygma—it keeps the same sense: we are still dealing with a word of potent efficacy. We are told of its ἐνεργεῖσθαι (I Thess 2:13), its τρέχειν (2 Thess 3:1), its αὐξάνειν (Acts 6:7; 12:24), its καρποφορεῖσθαι (Col 1:6). By nature it must be spoken and listened to.[3] It is a behest, an order; it must be put into practice and kept.[4]

The word's event is not an event of this world, though it takes place in this world. It has its origin in God. Certainly God speaks a human language; but one that comes from him, that is inspired and produced by his Spirit. So his word is not a psychical phenomenon and there is no psychical criterion whereby it could be distinguished from other words. Quite the contrary; any psychical phenomena must be judged by it. It is not the expression of a mood or of a particular personality. When we say that it is produced by the Spirit, we are not alluding to any objective criterion by which an observer could tell that it comes from God.

The primitive mind of New Testament days and the New Testament world puts down any extraordinary phenomenon to the direct doing of a supernatural cause, and therefore speaking with tongues is represented as an effect of the Spirit. But the very fact that the question arises whether it is the work of God or of a devil is an admission that its strange exterior does not prove it to be of the Spirit. The problem has to be resolved in terms of its content, its meaning for the community (I Cor 12).

So the more God's word manifests itself in speaking with tongues, thereby seeming to bear a supernatural seal, the less its unusual form proves it to be of God. Just as in the Old Testament the ecstasy of a prophet is no proof that what he says comes from God, and the Spirit

---

3. Κηρύπτειν: Mk 13:10; 14:9; Rom 10:8, 14, and elsewhere. Κήρυγμα: I Cor 1:21; 2:4, and elsewhere. Κῆρυξ: I Tim 2:7; Tit 1:11. Καταγγέλειν: Acts 13:5, and elsewhere. Εὐαγγελίζεσθαι and εὐαγγέλιον are often met with. Ἀκούειν: Rom 10:14, 18; Gal 4:21, and elsewhere. Ἀκοή: Rom 10:16f; Gal 3:25, and elsewhere.

4. Ποιεῖν: Lk 8:21 (Jas 1:22f); τηρεῖν: Jn 8:51, 52, 55 and elsewhere; φυλάττειν: Lk 11:28; Jn 12:47.

summons men as truly through the dry, plain text of the law, so in the New Testament Paul does not admit that God addresses men particularly through one who speaks with tongues. He restricts glossolalia and subordinates it to speaking ἐν voî (1 Cor 14:19). We know that the πνεῦμα is not a spiritual principle in man but a form of περιπατεῖν (p. 43, above). And therefore not ecstatic speaking alone but all prayer, all song, all prophetic and edifying words, are a gift of the Spirit. Of itself, ecstasy is a mere psychical phenomenon. That in a human utterance which is of God, cannot be ascertained from outside.

God's word is the eschatological *Dass*. Therefore it is only understood when the hearer gives up all reliance on objective or subjective criteria and opens himself to it in faith. Its only vindication is itself, and no one who would remain non-committal towards it can understand it (1 Cor 2:14). Only he can listen to it who gives up all καυχᾶσθαι, all desire to understand it on his own without allowing it to call him in question. For it is the 'word of the cross' (1 Cor 1:18)—that is, the condemnation of natural man.

Evidently, then, the renunciation and death demanded by the word stand on the plane of the *Dass*, not of the *Was*. Revelation is not a set of baffling propositions about God that require a *sacrificium intellectus*. God's otherness is not that of an impenetrable essence, as in the speculations of Gnosis. Revelation gives us no secret doctrine on the godhead. God's transcendence is not that of his hiddenness but that of his lordship. His word is no dogma that requires one to accept the incomprehensible in blind obedience. On the contrary: to define it as *Anrede*, summons and address, is to say that it is perfectly intelligible to man.

Paul stresses this point when he castigates the illuminist tendencies of the Corinthians who have the gift of tongues. He calls attention to the dangers of ecstatic speaking, first for the members of the community and then for unbelievers, who will be sure to label the Christians madmen, whereas speaking with tongues ought to be a sign to them. Accordingly Paul would rather speak five words with his mind than ten thousand in a tongue (1 Cor 14:1–26).[5]

Over the centuries the Christian Church has always been tempted to make God's transcendence a doctrinal mystery: God is God because he is incomprehensible. The celebrated mysticism of the *via negationis* can only be accounted for in terms of a theology that confuses other-

5. See Luther's text on the Apocalypse, already quoted (p. 83, above): 'My own mind cannot put up with it . . . I stick to the books which give me Christ plain and simple.'

ness with the ineffable. In reality, God's word demands no *sacrificium intellectus*. It deals with things that are plain as day: it speaks of σωτηρία or ἀπώλεια, of ζωή or θάνατος, of δικαιοσύνη or κατάκριμα. There is no esoteric teaching on these alternatives: there is the *event* of salvation or damnation, of life or death, of righteousness or judgment. If I am to be able to decide, what is put to me must be clear. *Because* there is no other vindication of the word than its own self, it must be comprehensible. And in fact any man knows what one is talking about when one speaks to him of salvation and damnation, life and death, pardon and condemnation.

The word is the object of faith. Since it is event and advent, the word invites man to give up all he relies on, his security, all he has and all he is—which can only be done by faith. So faith must be as intelligible as the word. It is not some irrational or mystical impulse. If everyone can understand that the word is pardoning, salvation and life, everyone can also understand that faith is being pardoned and reconciled. These are not baffling notions but plain alternatives. The New Testament assumes that every hearer knows *what* faith is. It tells him nothing new about the *nature* of justification, it asks him whether he *wishes* to be saved or not, whether he *wishes* to acknowledge God as Lord or *wishes* to perish in his own autonomy.

The word is intelligible because man has a *precomprehension* of it. Just as I have a *Vorverständnis* of friendship (p. 14, above), of God (p. 88, above), so I have one of the word. 'The "word" of preaching tells me "nothing more" than I already knew or was capable of knowing in my profane *Selbstverständnis*. No believer can explain what revelation in general is, any more accurately or fully than any unbeliever can. Because he knows what death is, any man also knows what revelation and life, grace and pardon, are. What "more" does the believer know? This: that revelation *has* found him, that he *is* in life, that he *is* pardoned and *will* always be pardoned anew. He knows it in such a way that, believing as he does in revelation, his concrete life in labour and joy, struggle and grief, takes on a new quality; the *events* of his life become new through the *event* of revelation, with a newness that exists for the believer alone, that only he can see—indeed, that *is* only visible in the now and will always be visible *anew*. The only new thing that faith can say about revelation is that it has become event and is becoming event.'[6] Since the word assumes that the hearer knows *what* God is, what salvation and life are, it does not try to inform him about them but gives them to him.

6. R. Bultmann, 'Die Geschichtlichkeit des Daseins und der Glaube' in *Zeitschrift für Theologie und Kirche* 11 (1930) 351–2.

This truth is affirmed by the New Testament in countless ways. Take
Acts 2:37–38: 'Now when they heard this they were cut to the heart,
and said to Peter and the rest of the apostles, "Brethren, what shall we
do?" And Peter said to them: "Repent, and be baptized every one of
you in the name of Jesus Christ for the forgiveness of your sins".' Or
again: 'For the word of God is living and active, sharper than any
two-edged sword, piercing to the division of soul and spirit. . . '
(Heb 4:12).

Paul takes the intelligibility of the word entirely for granted,
whether Jews be concerned or heathen. The law served the Jews as
a 'pedagogue'. As such it was the *Vorverständnis* of grace. Without it
grace becomes incomprehensible. He who has not come by way of the
law cannot know what grace is. So 'scripture consigned all things to
sin, that what was promised to faith in Jesus Christ might be given to
those who believe' (Gal 3:22). 'Law came in, to increase the trespass;
but where sin increased, grace abounded all the more' (Rom 5:20). In
Rom 7:7ff, too, Paul shows how the word of grace is intelligible to
a man who remains under the law.

But pagans likewise have a precomprehension of revelation. Paul's
missionary preaching, of which Rom 1:18ff gives us some idea, assumes
that they are able to understand what the judgment of God's wrath
upon them is. For they are well aware of God's will (1:28–32). What
the law requires is written on their hearts and conscience (Rom 2:
14–15). So when the gospel is announced to them, they do not find
its language esoteric: they know what it is about. What the word
brings them is not a knowledge of forgiveness and grace but the event
of forgiveness and grace, a new *Sichverstehen*.

Similarly Paul's struggle with the Gnostic Christians of Corinth
abounds with significance. He reminds them that the word is not the
revelation of a secret doctrine about God, but a 'folly', the '*logos* of the
cross', the death of human pride, giving up owing one's salvation to
oneself. All the Corinthians did was to replace their old knowledge
with a new theory about God, one wisdom with another. Paul
reminds them that they must replace one *existence* with another (1 Cor
1:17ff). John too takes it for granted that the word is entirely comprehensible; it brings us nothing new in the way of ideas. It gives the
hearer the reality of what he already knew. But the Johannine conception of the word calls for separate treatment.

IV

(1) What 'works' are those in the Gospel of John which 'bear witness' to
Jesus (5:36; 10:25)? Are they the miracles? Yes; but insofar as they

are σημεῖα—which really means insofar as they are words. We have seen that the miracles in John are a language, because they need to be interpreted. They have a twofold meaning, according as the hearer has faith or does not have it. The case with them is the same as with the words of Jesus, which are also ambiguous (2:20; 3:4; 4:11, 25; 4:33; 6:34; 12:28-30; 16:17, and so forth).

The miracles are *verba visibilia*. Only on this basis can one understand why the whole of Jesus's activity is presented as a ποιεῖν σημεῖα (12:37; 20:30); whereas throughout this Gospel the σημεῖα are subordinated to the ῥήματα and the final prayer makes Jesus's mission consist in handing on the words that God has given him (17:8, 14).

In fact Jesus's 'works' are his words. When he says: 'The works which the Father has granted me to accomplish, these very works which I am doing, bear me witness that the Father has sent me' (5:36), the preceding text (verses 19ff) shows that the proper activity of Jesus is the κρίνειν and the ζωοποιεῖν which he effects through his word.

A great many texts emphasize the identity of his work and his word—8:28: 'Then you will know that I am he and that I *do* nothing on my own authority but *speak* thus as the Father taught me'; 14:10: 'The words that I say to you I do not speak on my own authority; but the Father who dwells in me does his *works*'; 15:22, 24: 'If I had not come and *spoken* to them, they would not have sin . . . If I had not done among them the *works* which no one else did, they would not have sin'. In 8:38 λαλεῖν and ποιεῖν alternate. In 17:4, 8, 14 ἔργον, ῥήματα and λόγος have the same meaning.[7]

The identity of work and word likewise emerges from what is said about the efficacity of word. Jesus declares: 'The words that I have spoken to you are spirit and life' (6:63), and Peter echoes him: 'You have the words of eternal life' (6:68). A man who listens to Jesus's word and believes in him who sent him, has eternal life, has passed from death to life (5:24). Anyone who keeps his word will never see death (8:51). So the word gives life. The same thing is said in 8:31-32:'If you continue in my word . . . you will know the truth, and the truth will make you free'. Jesus's word makes men clean and holy (15:3; 17:17).

---

7. We read in 10:38 and 14:11: 'Even though you do not believe, believe the works', which seems to imply a difference between word and deed. But the works of 14:11 are the words of 14:10. When Jesus bids men turn from himself to his works, it means that he bids them turn from a faith that is mere knowledge about him to a faith that is willing to be determined by his word. Only then is the word a work in John's sense—a deed that transforms the hearer (see EJ, pp. 298, 471). It is in the same sense that Jesus bids the Jews turn to his works in 10:24f.

Being the word of life for those who believe, it is naturally the word of death for those who will not believe:

> If any one hears my sayings and does not keep them,
>   I do not judge him . . .
> The word that I have spoken will be his judge. [8]
>   (12:47–48)

(2) What then is the content of Jesus's words (or word)? What he has said (or done, in virtue of the identity between word and deed) is what he has seen or heard with the Father. He bears witness to what he has seen (with the Father 3:11; 8:38), what he has seen and heard (3:22), or what he has simply heard (8:26, 40; 15:15; see 5:30). He says that the Father himself has taught him (8:28; see 7:1). He speaks as the Father has commanded him to (12:49). He passes on the words which the Father has given him (17:8). He does what he sees the Father doing and what the Father shows him (5:19–20). Generally speaking, he reveals the Father's name (17:6, 26). In short, as the prologue says, 'No one has ever seen God; the only Son, who is in the bosom of the Father, he has made him known' (1:18; see 6:46).

Now here is the astonishing thing: Jesus's words tell us nothing of what he has seen or heard with the Father. Nowhere does he disclose things or events which he is supposed to have witnessed. He never makes the heavenly world the subject of his discourses. Unlike the Gnostic redeemer, he unveils no cosmic or soteriological secret. The only burden of his words is that the Father has sent him; that he has come as light, the bread of life, the witness to truth; that he will return; that it is necessary to believe in him. He is the event and advent of God.

Such is the meaning of his statements that he says and does nothing on his own authority. Although his words are the words of a man, yet they are not human words: 'No man ever spoke like this man!' (7:46). It is true that the Old Testament prophets were men with their minds under the ascendancy of God. But this similarity only makes the difference the more striking. Jesus is not only inspired from time to time: at all times he speaks and acts in virtue of his oneness with God. Moreover what the prophets said related to concrete and passing circumstances in the life of the people, upon which they shed the light of God's demands. Whether by promises or threats, they taught men

---

8. The end of verse 48 ('on the last day') is an interpolation by the ecclesiastical editor (EJ, p. 262, note).—Let us state once and for all that the author of the fourth Gospel is not an eye-witness of Jesus's life and has nothing to do with the apostle John (see EJ, pp. 4–5; 70, note 8; 76; 127; 369–71; 554).

to recognize the will of God in certain particular cases. But encounter with the person of Jesus bears on the human condition pure and simple: the word sets man as such on the permanent footing of decision for or against God. No Old Testament prophet has an absolute significance. One prophet follows upon another. But no one succeeds Jesus. In him God's revelation is given to the world once for all; and therefore his Spirit will only remind men of what he has said (14:26); or again, as Jesus puts it, 'he will take what is mine' (16:14).

Thus we have a profound identity between speaking and doing, between word and work. Jesus's words have no other conceptual content than this: they are God's words and words of life, which means that they are not God's words and words of life by reason of their tenor but rather because they are words of Jesus. Because they are the words of him who speaks them, they are God's words and words of life. What makes them special and decisive is not their timeless truth but their character as events. That is why the word of Jesus is a work. His deeds are words but his words are deeds.

This explains why all the words he utters in the Gospel of John are words about himself. They are not a set of truths that could be called 'the teaching of Jesus', and here John presents a striking contrast to the synoptics. Very few of the sayings which they record are found in John (2:19; 4:44; 12:25–26; 13:16, 20; 15:20). The difference does not arise, as is sometimes suggested, from the fourth evangelist's unwillingness to repeat his predecessors. It is explained by the fact that he considers Jesus's word an event, not a doctrine. What the Johannine Jesus says about himself does not make up a 'christology'. To think so is to ignore the fact that his ῥήματα are ἔργα: it is following in the footsteps of the Jews who demanded of him a clear doctrinal statement on his messiahship. Now we know what answer Jesus gives them: he refers them to his works (10:24f; see footnote 7, above).

Jesus's word is his own self. What is true of it is true of himself. He says that his words are 'life' and 'truth' (6:63; 17:17); but he also says 'I am the way, and the truth, and the life' (14:6). He says that anyone who hears his word and believes him who sent him, has life (5:24); but he also says 'I am the resurrection and the life' (11:25). He says that his words (12:48; 17:8) and his witness (3:11, 32f) must be 'received', but he says the same of himself (1:12; 5:43; see 13:20). To reject his person and to reject his words is one and the same thing (12:48). To say that his disciples abide in him and he in them is to say that his words abide in them (15:4–7). He is the judge (5:22, 27), but so is his word (12:48). That is why the evangelist calls the Pre-existent by the mythological name of *logos*. Bultmann has shown (EJ, pp. 5–19) that this term does not derive either from the Greek philosophical tradition as a whole or from the Stoic tradition in particular; but from Gnosis, which, as we have seen, hypostatized the *logos* (§11, above).

John 1:1ff does treat *logos* as a proper name. Nevertheless it also means 'word' in the biblical sense which we have explained. John demythologized the Gnostic idea by 'historicizing' it. For he can hardly have begun his Gospel with the formula 'In the beginning was the *logos*' without any thought of the first phrase in Genesis, 'In the beginning' (Gen 1:1), and of the words 'God said' which constantly recur through the story of creation. Our supposition is amply confirmed by 1 Jn 1:1, where instead of the person of the *logos* we find λόγος τῆς ζωῆς. Here there is no hypostasis and accordingly the 'word of life' is called 'that which' was from the beginning (not 'he who' was). The *logos* is not a personal being but a *mode* of God's being, God himself as present and at work.

Nothing could be better evidence that Jesus's words are not abstract propositions but declarations about himself, than the great utterances of the ἐγώ εἰμι:

> I am the bread of life (6:35).
> I am the light of the world (8:12).
> I am the door (10:9).
> I am the good shepherd (10:11, 14).
> I am the resurrection and the life (11:25).
> I am the way, and the truth, and the life (14:6).
> I am the true vine (15:1, 5).

Jesus also uses the ἐγώ εἰμι in an abstract sense: 'Unless you believe that I am [he]' (8:24). 'You will know that I am [he]' (8:28). What attribute are we meant to gather here? Obviously nothing definite: 'I am all that I say'; or better, perhaps: 'I am he on whom life and death, existence and non-existence depend—he whom the world awaits as the Saviour'. For we must observe that in the expressions which have ἐγώ εἰμι, ἐγώ is the predicate and not the subject. The sense is always: 'In *me* such and such is present (life, light, or whatever)'. All these metaphors—bread, light, the door, the way, the shepherd, the vine— signify the very being of truth and life, and therefore what is necessary to every man, what every man longs to have so that he can truly exist. By uttering the 'I am', Jesus presents himself as alone capable of satisfying human expectations and desires (the human *Vorverständnis* in the broadest sense of the word: the craving for light, truth, life, love).

This matter is symbolized in the episode at the well of Jacob. The Samaritan woman says to Jesus, 'I know that Messiah (he who is called Christ) is coming; when he comes, he will show us all things'. And

Jesus replies, 'I who speak to you am he' (4:25–26). When the blind man who has been cured asks him who the Son of man is, he likewise replies, 'You have seen him, and it is he who speaks to you' (9:37).

(3) Thus, when all is said and done, Jesus the revealer of God reveals only one thing: *that* he is the revealer. In other words, he is the one whom the world awaits, the one who offers in his person all that man seeks and has only a precomprehension of: light, truth, life. But how is he all this, and how does he offer it to us? Simply by saying that he is and that he offers it. 'In his Gospel, therefore, John sets forth only the *Dass* of revelation, without explaining its *Was*' (TNT, p. 419).

In Gnostic myth, quite the other way, revelation is essentially a *Was*. The Gnostic redeemer has the task of freeing the human self from its imprisonment in matter. This deliverance is possible because redeemer and redeemed share the same φύσις. Because of that identity, his destiny is theirs. To know this, to know man's true nature and its oneness with the redeemer, is salvation—salvation, therefore, of the 'Greek' sort, based on knowledge. The redeemer is not the Wholly Other, able to give man a *radical future* (which is to say, the only real salvation), because the Gnostic already is what he will be: he is divine by nature.

When the Fathers of the Greek Church presently attempt to work out the Christian theology of the incarnation and the redemption, they will more or less fall back into mythology. As for John, he rules out the naturalist premise of myth—the idea that God and man share a common φύσις. He makes redemption a *Dass*: man really becomes what he was not.

Hence the notion has arisen that John is a mystic. For in mysticism, just as there is absolutely no definable divine essence, so the experience of the soul defies all attempts to give it utterance. Now in fact the author of the Gospel is anything but a mystic. So far as he is concerned, spiritual experience is wholly incapable of reaching God. He shows no interest at all in asceticism or mystical phenomena. His rejection of the world has quite a different meaning from mystical rejection of the world. It has not the slightest ontological connotation. It is a dialectical, 'historical' rejection: believers are not of the world although they remain in the world. Jesus does not bid men flee this world. He says that a man who makes this world his god is already judged—which is not the same thing at all. So to reject the world is to condemn the pride of natural man, condemn his standards and his ways; it is to use the world differently, not escape from it.

The fact that the word is event by no means implies, in John any more than it does in Paul, that the world is unintelligible or unutterable. On the contrary, it is perfectly intelligible. It speaks to man of things that he understands full well: of his salvation or his damnation, of his life or his death. Every man knows beforehand *what* salvation and life are, because he desires them and that desire is the driving force behind his whole existence. So revelation brings him nothing in the way of *Vorverständnis* of these things. And it is not a gnosis but a deed: God's saving deed in Jesus of Nazareth.

Now we understand why Jesus cannot vindicate himself in the way his adversaries demand, by signs that would manipulate faith and turn revelation into an objective reality which natural man could grasp. The signs Jesus gives are identical with that which they signify. Even as signs they demand faith.

Hence the two statements, which seem to cancel each other out, that Jesus does not bear witness to himself (5:31ff) and that nevertheless he does bear witness to himself (8:14, 18). The credibility of his word does not spring from any ascertainable bond between the act of bearing witness and the thing that is borne witness to: it springs solely from acceptance of his word by faith. As Jesus says elsewhere: 'If any man's will is to do his [God's] will, he shall know whether the teaching is from God or whether I am speaking on my own authority' (7:17). The expression 'do God's will' does not bear a moral sense, inasmuch as it is God's will that man shall have faith (6:29). In the eyes of faith, Jesus bears witness to himself; in the eyes of natural man, he does not bear witness to himself. He does signs, but those signs speak only to the believing.

CHAPTER NINE

Jesus Christ

I

LIBERAL 'DEMYTHIZATION'

We say 'demythization' and not demythologization' (see ch. 4, foot-note 4, above). What the liberal solution to the 'problem of Jesus' does is not to interpret the myth, not sift out its transcendent meaning, but get rid of its meaning. Here is how the case is put. The New Testament marks the summit of mankind's religious life. In it the idea of God has reached perfection. God is a spirit and demands to be honoured and worshipped in spirit. He is a will to love, and the only real way to serve him is to live by love. He is the one who clasps the repentant sinner to his bosom.

Liberalism holds that religion is *ein universaler ethischer Gott-Vater-Glaube* (GV I, p. 314), a universal moral belief in the fatherhood of God, which finds its noblest expression in Jesus. Steeped in this belief, Jesus felt that preaching was his special mission. True, ethical monotheism occupied a prominent place even in the Old Testament, which had won through to it after a bitter struggle with ritualism and religious nationalism. It triumphed in the preaching of the prophets, where God is seen to be a universal God whose holiness is a moral will demanding purity and obedience and whose love is pardon and grace. But this sublime doctrine was choked out in Judaism. The work of Jesus was to restore it by stripping it free of legalism, just as the religious geniuses of Israel had disentangled it from ritual in former times. He contributed nothing really new to prophetic religion. He is the term and apex of an evolution that began long before him.

What does specifically characterize the New Testament, the *escha-tology* and *christology* (the pre-existence of Christ, his incarnation, his miracles, his resurrection, Paul's doctrine of redemption and justifica-tion, and so forth), amounts to a dangerous obscuration of essentials. At best it decks out in the finery of myth the pure faith Jesus had in God. This travesty may have been necessary, in New Testament times, for safeguarding belief in the God who is spirit and love; but today we must get rid of it without hesitation. Thus liberalism 'reduces the kerygma to certain great religious and moral ideas, to a religiously motivated idealist ethic' (KM I, p. 25). 'Here everything to do with myth is swept away' (KM I, p. 24).

Liberalism abolishes christology: making 'religious values' the ultimate norm, it eliminates from the New Testament whatever does not harmonize with them. Bultmann has often shown how, by applying outside criteria to the New Testament, the leading liberals came to regard Jesus as nothing more than a great historical and religious figure who most nobly manifests the divine (see ch. 2, §II, above).

Let us, for instance, see how Johannes Weiss (under whom Bultmann studied) reduces christology to the 'personality' of Jesus. He begins by observing that an evolution takes place in primitive Christianity: the man Jesus (with the consciousness he had of being the king chosen by God to rule at the end of time) is turned into a heavenly being who becomes incarnate, dies for man's redemption, rises from the dead, and returns to heaven. It was a rapid evolution, because a major theme in Judaism and pagan religions alike was applied to Jesus: the theme of a divine being who is the saviour of men. Thus christology was put together with the help of such categories as the Messiah, the Son of David, the Son of man, the Son of God, the *Kyrios*, the *Logos*, the virgin birth, the resurrection, and so forth.

Not one of these ideas was new: they all belonged to the hoary patrimony of the ancient world. What was new was the projection of all this mythology upon a particular man: Jesus of Nazareth. But that involved no change in its structure; so that there is *nothing specifically Christian* to be found in New Testament christology. Rather, it unfortunately obscures the personal characteristics of the individual upon whom it is veneered. We have modern critics to thank for giving us back the real Jesus, freed at last from the matrix of mythology in which he was buried.

This historical Jesus must be the object of faith. Faith is the conviction that in his person we are given the noblest religion conceivable and shown the closest possible union with our heavenly Father; it is the realization that we depend on a God with whom one can only deal as a loving child, full of trust and self-surrender. What matters is establishing a personal relationship with Jesus. The vivid impressions conveyed by his interior life, his lofty virtues, his heroic love of neighbour, awaken or revive our conscience, warm our heart and bring it nearer to God. For we are not to believe in him but in God through him, moved by his tremendous religious personality. In him the primitive community were able, as one might say, to touch God. Contact with him made them feel full of God's power and life, brimming over with the Holy Spirit.

Just as parents pass on their feelings and habits to their children by a steady sort of vital contagion, so Jesus imbued the disciples with his own filial attitude towards God. Throughout the long history of Christianity we observe a certain way of living one's relations with God which has its source in Jesus and draws its power and perennial youth from him. So the decisive influence of Jesus upon the souls of his disciples was this: he emboldened them to believe in their salvation because he did not simply talk about a loving heavenly Father but showed them by his example how to live in the serenity and joy of God's love. Thus he *guarantees* our faith and our salvation. He is the ground and vindication of our trust in God.

It is obvious what violence liberalism does to the New Testament. Christ becomes an earthly phenomenon, the noblest example of *homo religiosus*. He is reduced to the plane of psychology, the interior life, mysticism and love. The ambiguity which is peculiar to myth goes unheeded: its *eschatological* meaning is brushed aside. Jesus is no longer the wholly different Word we have spoken of: in him we can see, touch, feel the divine. Faith as ec-sistence, as utter death, yields to 'contact', 'experience', 'piety'. Jesus is looked on as 'the guarantee which spares one real faith' (GV 1, p. 250). He is the divine become visible as the divine. He is a kind of bridge, reaching between God and men, which eliminates every possible hazard. Thus his real otherness is ignored. As to God, he is indeed thought of as spirit, truth and love; but since man can reach him by his own means, or rather by means of Jesus the exemplar of religious living—which, as we have just seen, comes down to the same thing—nothing more can be involved than the *idea* (*Vorverständnis*) of God.

All this is rank religious humanism. To reduce christology to the personality of Jesus is to miss the very heart of the New Testament. For that personality, though it be the most exalted in the world and the holiest, is only a human phenomenon. The New Testament declares Jesus to be the Word of God which, as such, can neither be seen nor touched nor experienced. It can only be *believed* in; whereas liberalism takes one straight to it on the wings of trust and love as mere human virtues (see ch. 2, §II, above).

II

'DEMYTHIZATION'

ACCORDING TO THE HISTORY OF RELIGION SCHOOL

When the liberal attempt broke down, the 'history of religion school' made a fresh effort to interpret the New Testament. It can be studied to best advantage in Wilhelm Bousset's monumental work *Kyrios*

Christos. Here again christology is treated as of minor concern, for it is still thought to enshroud the real religion of the New Testament. But Bousset no longer sees the latter in terms of faith in God the father of men. For this view, which after all is only an optimist and altruist *Weltanschauung*, he substitutes another: religion is a particular manifestation of psychical life; christology actually represents a mystical phenomenon.

Bousset sharply distinguishes Hellenistic Christianity, which gave birth to christology, from Palestinian Christianity, to which all the characteristic notions of Hellenistic Christianity are unknown—in particular the category of the *Kyrios*. Palestinian Christianity contains neither a true christology nor, properly speaking, any faith in Christ. It saw Jesus simply as the Messiah, applying to him the Jewish dogmas on the Son of man—exactly what disappeared from Hellenistic Christianity. The backbone of the Christian religion, the major factor in its evolution, is the cult of the *Kyrios*, which takes a mythological form. That form is always the same: the man Jesus has been turned into a divine being. He has become the pre-existent Son of God, incarnate, crucified, risen from the dead, exalted to the right hand of the Father.

All these christological categories express only one mystical fact: the presence, in the community's worship, of him to whom they are all applied. He manifests himself there by extraordinary phenomena (signs, miracles, visions, ecstasies, enthusiasm), spreading his power there through the sacraments, which bestow a divine nature on believers. This is the reality to which myth gives expression. Christianity now is a cultic religion, and therefore something entirely strange to Palestinian Christianity. The christology in which it is couched does not, as Harnack thought, represent a hellenization of Christianity to be accounted for by the speculative interest that Christians took in Greek thought. Just the reverse is true: christology is the fruit of cultic piety. Therefore it has nothing to do with the historical Jesus. It is the mythological garb of the community's mystical experience at worship. Jesus is the *Kyrios*—that is, God himself present among his own, either in collective experiences or in individual pneumatism. Always we have a religion cast in the mould of mysticism and closely akin to the mystery religions already described.

This is how Pauline and Johannine christology must be interpreted. Paul's religion presupposes the community's cultic piety, from which it is differentiated as the pneumatic mysticism of an individual. His christology is the crucial affirmation: ὁ κύριος τὸ πνεῦμα. The *Kyrios* is the divine *Pneuma* which rules the community and makes its members inspired men by penetrating them to the core and carrying them from δόξα to δόξα. Thanks to this indwelling divine power the pneumatic man works miracles, lays bare the secrets of God's plan, gives authoritative orders, and rises above the contingencies of this world. He is already a divine being.

Insofar as it is an anthropoloy and a soteriology, Paul's theology is nothing but a mythological explanation of this mystical piety, which interprets the whole of life in terms of ecstasy. Insofar as it consists of the doctrine on justification, it is an apologetical theory that Paul needed for his missionary work. In John, Christ-mysticism likewise dominates. Christ divinizes his disciples, thus granting them true life. The word which the God-Man utters is an efficacious word such as we find in the mystery religions: to believe in the word is to gaze on eternal life and possess it.

Such, very briefly, is Bousset's thesis. He regards Christianity as a phenomenon of psychical life, a piety; a piety of redemption, to be precise, based on a dualist *Weltanschauung*. It is a religion born of the consciousness its adherents have of being delivered from the darkness, tribulation, wretchedness and death that are inseparable from earthly, bodily existence. This deliverance is effected by collective phenomena like enthusiasm (divine transports), by the sacraments, by union with God who contains in himself the forces of the heavenly world and imparts them to his own at their worship. It also takes place in individual experiences such as ecstasy. Christology is nothing more than a theoretical explanation of this piety, coloured by the mythology of the mystery religions and of other traditions. Faith is not strictly speaking faith in Christ but the mood (διάθεσις) of piety (Bousset holds that the Pauline conception of faith derives full-blown from Philo). If faith has a special object, it can only be God; but this god is simply the divine in general, because to John's mind faith is identical with vision.

Now the criticism we must make of Bousset's interpretation is the one we have made of the mystery religions and Gnosticism (pp. 50–52 and 52–55, above) and of mysticism in general (pp. 88 and 105, above). In a word, even mystical experience remains an earthly phenomenon confined within the sphere of *homo religiosus*. The Christ of mysticism is not the Wholly Other, the Word of God. Certainly he comes nearer to it than the Christ of liberal theology; for, as we have seen, the mystery religions and Gnosis have a keen sense of transcendence, which is revealed in their dualism and their 'withdrawing' the initiate 'from the world' through worship, the sacraments and ecstasy. All this stands on a much higher plane than the rather jejune spiritualist ethic to which liberalism reduces the New Testament. And yet it does not reach beyond the domain of religion. The initiate does not find God in true faith but in an experience which, however noble it may be, remains of itself a psychical phenomenon. When all is said and done, man still manipulates God. Like liberalism, the 'history of religion school' does not demythologize christology but abolishes it. The *Kyrios Christos* is a 'work'.

III

DEMYTHOLOGIZATION

Thus liberalism and the history of religion school regarded Christ as a reality to be set under the heading of 'religious personality' or mysticism, and thereby objectified him. Nevertheless there can be no doubt that Jesus himself believed he was the word and deed of God. This point needs to be explored at length.

A

We know that the original feature of Jesus's preaching about God was his *radical* idea of the divine lordship: God is the one who completely determines man's existence (pp. 101–12, above). And *now* with himself, Jesus, and *only* now, the eschatological reign of God begins. He preaches its coming. He tells us nothing new about the nature of God: 'His teaching is not new so far as its intellectual content goes; in respect of content, what he teaches is pure Judaism, pure prophetic religion' (GV 2, p. 265). But what is unheard of is his announcement that the kingdom of God is coming *hic et nunc*—the assurance with which he says: Now the time has come; the kingdom of God has begun; the end is here. That is the meaning of his words:

> Blessed are the eyes which see what you see!
> For I tell you:
> many prophets and kings desired to see what you see,
> and did not see it;
> and to hear what you hear,
> and did not hear it.
>
> (Lk 10:23f and parallels)

Now is not the hour of grief and fasting, now is the hour of joy and the bridegroom (Mk 2:18f). And so:

> Blessed are you poor,
> for yours is the kingdom of God.
> Blessed are you that hunger now,
> for you shall be satisfied.

> Blessed are you that weep now,
> for you shall laugh.
>
> (Lk 6:20f)

Satan's lordship is shattered here and now: 'I saw Satan fall like lightning from heaven' (Lk 10:18). Jesus's preaching, his conviction that his task is to announce the event, not the content, of the kingdom, is summed up in the well-known saying: 'The time is fulfilled, and the kingdom of God is at hand' (Mk 1:15).

We have seen, however, that he did not claim to be the Messiah, although the evangelists represent him as such. On the contrary he announced the coming of the Messiah by stating that he himself was not the Messiah (Mk 8:38; ch. 5, §1, above). Here is 'the great problem in New Testament theology' (GV I, p. 266): how can the man who announced the Messiah have been announced as the Messiah; or, as Bultmann puts it, 'how did the herald become the heralded?' (*ibid.*) Why was the Christian community not content with simply repeating what Jesus had said? Why did it announce the preacher instead of his preaching? Why do Paul and John as good as ignore the words of Jesus and fall to preaching his person?

On the plane of the *Was*—of images and concepts—the problem is insoluble. But if instead we shift to the plane of the *Dass*, then the solution can be made out. For Jesus did not simply announce the event of the kingdom: he bound up that event with the event that he is himself in his preaching and in his person. He taught no doctrine about his person but he put forward the 'fact of his person' (GV I, p. 204) as decisive, the fact that he was the messenger of the word; so that to reject the messenger was to reject the message—that is, God himself. He claimed to be the event and advent of God's word: that is to say, the event and advent of God. 'The decisive thing is not the *Was* of his preaching but its *Dass*' (*ibid.*, p. 265). 'What he says, he does not say as anything new or startling; the point is *that* he says it and that he says it *now*' (*ibid.*, p. 204).

Jesus is the divine *Dass*. And therefore to take one's stand against him is to decide against God in person, and to take one's stand for him is to decide for God in person: 'Blessed is he who takes no offence at me' (Mt 11:6).

> Every one who acknowledges me before men,
> the Son of man [the Messiah whom Jesus announces]
> also will acknowledge before the angels of God;
> but he who denies me before men
> will be denied before the angels of God.
>
> (Lk 12:8–9)

> Whoever is ashamed of me and of my words
>   in this adulterous and sinful generation,
> of him will the Son of man [the Messiah whom Jesus
>   announced] also be ashamed
> when he comes in the glory of his Father with the
>   holy angels. ˙
>
> (Mk 8:38)

In bygone days the queen of the South came from the ends of the earth to hear the wisdom of Solomon, 'and behold, something greater than Solomon is here'. The men of Nineveh repented at the preaching of Jonah, 'and behold, something greater than Jonah is here' (Lk 11:31–32). Jesus is the *Anrede* of God himself to men. And so deciding for or against him is not one choice among many choices, but the choice between eternal life and eternal death. So pressing is his demand for our decision that he obviously regards it as an act on which a man's whole fate depends. 'In his person he embodies the demand for decision . . . He is the summons to decision' (TNT, p. 8). 'No one who puts his hand to the plough and looks back is fit for the kingdom of God' (Lk 9:62). 'Follow me, and leave the dead to bury their own dead' (Mt 8:22 and parallels). 'If any one comes to me and does not hate his own father and mother and wife and children and brothers and sisters, and even his own life, he cannot be my disciple' (Lk 14:26 and parallels). 'Whoever does not bear his own cross and come after me, cannot be my disciple' (Lk 14:27 and parallels).

Every man is asked what he will set his heart on: God or the world? 'No one can serve two masters . . .' (Mt 6:24; Lk 13:3). How perilous it is to be rich! (Mk 10:25). For though men are willing enough to be invited to the salvation God has prepared, when it comes to actually deciding then they balk and make excuses (Lk 14:15–21). Because 'where your treasure is, there will your heart be also' (Mt 6:19–21 and parallels). And yet one should be ready to sacrifice everything for the kingdom, like the man who has found the treasure and the merchant who has found the pearl of great price (Mt 13:44–46).

Jesus, therefore, puts forward the fundamental claim that a man's fate is decided by the attitude he takes towards himself, Jesus, and towards the word which he announces. He demands 'decision for his person as the bearer of God's Word' (TNT, p. 46). 'He who is not with me is against me' (Mt 12:30). He represents himself as identical with the very Word of God—as that word, as its *event*. Now it is plain as day that such an assertion 'implies a christology' (GV 1, pp. 204, 266; TNT, p. 46), but of course a christology on a different level from that of the *Was*. We must not imagine that it is 'either a piece of metaphysical speculation about a heavenly being, or a description of his [Jesus's] personality as having any sort of messianic consciousness' (GV I, p. 266). This christology 'is preaching, a summoning men to anwser' (*ibid.*). The important thing about Jesus is 'his person—but not his personality—his *hic et nunc*, his event, his mission, his summoning men to answer' (*ibid.*).

There is no mystery about the vital distinction between person and personality. Personality is a man's character, his outlook; the way he thinks, feels, behaves himself, leads his life; his cast of mind, his failings and his virtues. To say that Jesus was a Jew, a preacher, a prophet, or to say that 'he wrongly expected the end of the world in the immediate future' (CP, p. 79), is to enunciate propositions about his personality, his *Was*. Personality is the biological, psychological, sociological *datum*. Contrariwise the person is the man insofar as he is ec-sistence and deed. Now here is the crucial point: Jesus represented himself to be God's saving deed, and from that point of view not the slightest importance attaches to his personality. In any case it cannot be reconstructed. No one can write a biography of Jesus, for example, evoke his mind or his piety, because our sources paid these things no heed. The first Christians were well aware that the personality of Jesus, whatever it may have been—pedestrian or brilliant, fallible or in-fallible—offered no guarantee at all that he was God's saving deed for men.

The same thing must be said of the celebrated 'messianic conscious-ness'. As we know, Bultmann holds that Jesus did not claim to be the Messiah and that he plainly said as much. But he takes this view in his capacity as an historian doing his best to be fair-minded. In his capacity as a Christian and a theologian, Bultmann thinks the problem is a specious one: 'Whether Jesus believed himself to be the Messiah or not is neither here nor there. If he did, that would only mean that he understood the decisive character of his work in the language peculiar to a contemporaneous Jewish image' (GV I, pp. 265–6).

Of itself, messianic consciousness is only a psychical phenomenon: it has no bearing on the fact that the man with it is the man in whom God encounters us and the deed by which he saves us. It is an objective category that as such proves nothing. What guarantee have we that the consciousness is not a delusion? How many Jews have claimed to be the Messiah and thought they really were! Conversely, there is no reason why the man in whom God encounters us and saves us must believe and say that he is the Messiah. The messianic image is only one possible expression of this *Dass*, which can as well be conveyed by other categories: Son of God, Kyrios, Saviour, or what have you.

Traditional exegetes and theologians are apt to think that all is lost if Jesus did not know he was the Messiah. But supposing he did: what would that have proved? Not a thing, obviously. For 'a messianic consciousness can only lead us to a psychical phenomenon; no farther' (GV I, p. 204, note). And if he did not know he was the Messiah, what proof would that be that he is not the man in whom God speaks and acts? None at all, obviously; for the same event can be conveyed in a thousand other ways. As it happens, Jesus himself did not convey it through the messianic category, but by declaring that he was God's herald and that to reject him as such was to reject God himself.

Thus it is clear that the category of the herald can be fraught with the same eschatological significance as the category of the heralded (of the Messiah). In objectifying, rationalizing parlance, the herald is every whit as supernatural as the heralded (the Messiah). In 'historical', demythologized parlance, the category of the herald shows Jesus to be God's saving word (deed) every whit as well as does the category of the heralded (the Messiah).

B

We can now account for the fact that the primitive community turned the herald of the Messiah into the Messiah himself. They thereby made Jesus no different from and no greater than what he claimed to be. To the Jewish mind, the Messiah was not an image but an event. He was the *epiphany* of God's salvation. Men did not await new revelations about the Messiah, they awaited the Messiah himself in person. For their part Jesus's disciples believed in him as the Word of God; they believed that with him the future aeon had begun. And so they quite naturally looked on his life as a messianic life. The fact that the community turned the herald into the heralded shows that in Jesus they saw God's advent among men.

By what stages was Jesus the preacher of the Messiah turned into Jesus the Messiah?

(1) We know that Jesus believed he was the Word of God. During his lifetime a certain number of his hearers accepted that he really was what he claimed to be, and by that very fact the group of believers considered themselves the community of the last days, the *eschatological* community (see p. 19, above). Had the disciples not regarded him as the Messiah (the Son of God) *to come*, they would only have been a Jewish sect—which indeed they remained from many points of view, as witness the struggle which Paul had to sustain against the Judaizing Christians. But the heart of the matter is that during his lifetime they believed in him—though all the implications and demands of that faith were still far from manifest—as the event and advent of God himself.

The proof is none other than their *Verständnis* of themselves as the eschatological community which we shall describe in due course. Suffice it to observe here that Jesus's eschatological preaching was met by a no less eschatological faith on the part of his disciples which even now distinguished them *toto caelo* from the Jewish community.

A further indication that Jesus was regarded as the eschatological *Dass* in his own lifetime is a whole cluster of sayings that mention his 'coming' and his being 'sent'. These sayings are attributed to him; but in all likelihood most of them were made up by the community. They prove that even before his death and resurrection he was considered God's decisive and saving deed. Jesus has not 'come' to call the righteous, but sinners (Mk 2:17). He was 'sent' only to the lost sheep of the house of Israel (Mt 15:24). He has not 'come' to bring peace, but a sword (Mt 10:34–36 and parallels)—that is, the hour of eschatological decision and separation. Whoever receives him receives him who 'sent' him (Mk 9:37; Mt 10:40). Whoever rejects him rejects him who 'sent' him (Lk 10:16). One could go on adducing texts (GST, pp. 161–76). His 'coming' pronounces judgment on Jerusalem (Lk 13:34f). This is a Jewish prophecy, which was perhaps quoted by Jesus himself but in its present form was re-interpreted by the community and put into his mouth. Thus those who believed in him looked on him during his lifetime as the Word of God. But their faith had to surmount the unutterable scandal of his death on the cross. For in Jewish eyes anyone crucified was necessarily accursed of God (Gal 3:13).

'Thus in a sense the cross once more raised the problem of decision. If the *Was* of his [Jesus's] preaching could not be called in question by the cross, its *Dass* most certainly could. How was Jesus to be vindicated? Was he indeed God's messenger, bearer of God's final, decisive word? Thus the community had to surmount the scandal of the cross, and did so by its Easter faith' (TNT, p. 47). Evidently faith in Jesus as the Word of God was not born of the post-Easter apparitions. However important, the Easter event is only one more expression of the only fundamental event—God's epiphany and work in Jesus of Nazareth.

(2) The clash between the categories of natural man and the thinking of the Bible, which we have defined and illustrated in this study from the outset, should now clarify Bultmann's real attitude towards the resurrection of Jesus. The risen Christ is not an earthly phenomenon. He is not an objective reality. Contrary to what common sense assumes, as we have seen, objectivity is the antithesis of otherness. Just as messianic consciousness as such is only an earthly phenomenon, so is resurrection when one understands it as a return to this world.

In other words, the resurrection of Jesus cannot be a *Mirakel*, which mythologizes the divine and degrades it to the status of a 'work'. Even were it duly established that a dead man had returned to life, the phenomenon would still remain within the framework of determinism so far as concerned the observer. Of itself, a resurrection in this world no more manifests God than does any phenomenon that we call normal. Anyhow, is it possible for a corpse to return to earthly life? Bultmann thinks not (KM 1, p. 45; 3, p. 51). But at bottom, it does not matter in the least whether *Mirakel* in general could and did happen; because *Mirakel*, be it possible or impossible, credible or incredible, real or imaginary, belongs to the realm of data, of things which man controls—that is, to the realm of sin.

To believe in Jesus because he supposedly returned to earthly life is only to believe in oneself. As we have seen, that is what the reproach addressed to Thomas by the Johannine Jesus means: 'Have you believed because you have seen me? Blessed are those who have not seen and yet believe' (Jn 20:29). A return of Jesus to this world, supposing it did happen, could in no way express his *eschatological* character (much less vindicate it).

Thus the resurrection cannot consist in the reappearance which the Easter narratives describe: 'it asserts a great deal more than the return of a dead man to earthly life; because it is an eschatological event' (KM 1, p. 45). The risen Christ, insofar as he is the Wholly Other, can only be a *Verständnis* of man. If he were what the Easter narratives describe (a supernatural being), in what way would his resurrection have changed mankind? There would simply be one more man alive. Now Christ's resurrection means judgment upon the world, the annihilation of sin, and the advent of God's grace. Before Christ and without him, the world is the design of sinful man cut off from God and at enmity with him. The whole human race is nothing but a will to autonomy, nothing but pride, hate, despair and damnation (pp. 38–42, above). Thanks to him the meaning—that is, the being—of everything is changed. The world becomes God's creation once more, sin is forgiven, everlasting life is vouchsafed (pp. 42–3, above).

For this utter transformation to take place, the risen Christ must be something quite different from a being who appears when the doors are shut (Jn 20:19). He must be God's saving deed. There is no real otherness except that which saves by becoming man's *Verständnis*. 'Being the Word of God, Christ is *ante et extra me*; but not as an objectively verifiable fact that could be dated *ante me*, rather as the Christ *pro me* who meets me as the word' (KM 2, p. 206). The risen Christ is only such if he raises me from the dead; *as* raising me from the dead he *is* the risen Christ. Otherwise he is only a phantom, an extension of myself just like any other objective thing, just like the world as nature and as history. So it is because he did not *objectively* rise from the dead that Jesus *really* (eschatologically) rose from the dead. Only insofar as he is man's saviour and Lord is he the risen Christ. 'The resurrection of Jesus does not mean his "translation" into the next world but his exaltation to lordship' (Phil 2:11; TNT, p. 306). Here we must refer back to what has been said about the true nature of otherness (pp. 19–21, above).

It will now be perceived why the resurrection is nothing else than the meaning of the cross—that is to say, its underlying reality. There is nothing eschatological about Jesus's crucifixion as such. In the course of history multitudes of men have been crucified. What matters is the meaning of his death. A detached observer sees in that death only one fact, one that is meaningless or (at the utmost) heart-rending. For the historian, 'there can be little doubt that Jesus was crucified as a messianic prophet, like other agitators' (JS, p. 26). For the unbeliever, the crucifixion simply terminates the career of an idealist. The bare facts are nothing: their real being consists in what they mean. But meaning has always to be disclosed and singled out; which explains why there is complete disagreement about the meaning of Jesus's death, its underlying reality, though all the world accepts the fact of it.

'The resurrection is nothing else than belief in the cross as salvific event . . . The cross is not salvific event because it is Christ's cross: it is Christ's cross because it is salvific event. Otherwise it is only the tragic end of a gallant soul' (KM I, p. 46). This much misunderstood text oₗ Bultmann's only stresses the primacy of meaning over objective fact. The true being of the cross (its *Dass*) is its divine meaning, conveyed by the resurrection, which can only be perceived by the *Sichverstehen* of a believer. The cross is the cross *of Christ* insofar as it is *God's eschatological deed*, hidden as such from the eyes of natural man. The resurrection is the resurrection *of Christ* insofar as it is *God's eschatological deed*, hidden as such from the eyes of natural man. It is not the return of a dead man to this world.

As scripture, to be sure, and as the witness to revelation, the New Testament is not innocent of objectification in what it says about the resurrection. It presents the resurrection not merely as an object of faith but also as a verifiable fact (a *Mirakel*). Acts 17:31, an apologetical text, declares that God is to judge the world 'by a man whom he has appointed, and of this he has given *assurance to all men* [obviously to pagans, therefore] by raising him from the dead'.

The account of the empty tomb is also *evidence* of the resurrection: the fact that the tomb is empty proves that Jesus has risen from the dead. Such is the idea behind the account (Mk 16:1–8). Although the guards have not the faith, they see the angel of the Lord looking like lightning; they see him so clearly that they become 'like dead men' (Mt 28:3–4). The heavenly messenger tells the women that they will 'see' Jesus, who in fact 'meets' them, and they fall down before him, taking hold of his feet (verses 7 and 9). Nowhere is there any question of faith: facts are ascertained. The high priests, though not believers, are obviously assumed to recognize the resurrection as genuine, for in order to deceive the multitude they say to the guards: 'Tell people, "His disciples came by night and stole him away while we were asleep"' (Mt 28:13). The soldiers have told them 'all that had taken place' (Mt 28:11) and the high priests take their word for it. For their own part, the narrative assumes, they are satisfied that Jesus has risen from the dead; otherwise they would not attempt to hush things up. So the apologetical aim behind the episode of the empty tomb is obvious.

Everywhere the disciples 'see', and it is only out of dogmatic prejudice that certain exegetes try to represent this 'seeing' as a 'believing' instead (Mt 28:10, 17). The 'hands' and 'feet' of the risen Christ are 'seen'. The disciples and women 'touch' him, for he is not a 'spirit': he has 'flesh and bones'. He eats 'broiled fish' in his disciples' presence: 'before them' (Lk 24:38–43). He shows them 'his hands and his side' (Jn 20:20). He even says to Thomas: 'Put your finger here, and see my hands; and put out your hand, and place it in my side' (Jn 20:27). True, he is not always recognized at once (Lk 24:16; Jn 20:14); but when he finally is recognized, we are not told that it happens by virtue of an act of faith. On the contrary it is his visible movements that open the eyes of his followers (Jn 20:16; Lk 24:30–31).

The temptation to objectify proves too much for Paul himself in 1 Cor 15:5–8. Here Karl Barth out-Bultmanns Bultmann. In vain Barth makes believe that Paul's only purpose is to drive home the identity of his kerygma with that of the primitive community. If that is indeed Paul's incidental purpose (verse 11), there is no getting round his primary purpose, which is to assert the resurrection outright as a fact verifiable by the senses and verified by them. The meaning of the text is obvious and inescapable. In confirmation of all this, let us recall that the devils (who assuredly have not the faith and are not Christians of any description) are compelled by the evidence of his miracles to confess the divinity of Jesus (Mk 1:24, 34; 5:7).

Bultmann holds (critical study in GST, pp. 308–16; EJ, pp. 528–40) that the accounts of the apparitions and the empty tomb are without the slightest doubt later accretions. Nevertheless these legends are not borrowings from the pagan religious environment. They spring from Christian faith itself, of which they form the *Niederschlag* ('precipitate').

They were already current in the Palestinian community. In no time they had taken on various forms. But the Easter narratives as we read them today bear the stamp of the Hellenistic community (GST, pp. 332–3). Thus the apparitions of Christ are not the source of faith but its *result* and *expression*.

Later we shall see why orthodox exegetes and theologians feel they must defend the 'objectivity' of those apparitions and why, in so doing, they set at naught both historical criticism and the purpose of the texts. Faith has everything to lose by treating the apparitions as so many historical data. Had the resurrection been primarily the *Mirakel* which our accounts say it was, the faith of those who were eye witnesses to it would have been a mere 'work'; for a *mortuus redivivus* is only something earthly.

When the apparitions are made chronologically prior to faith, as having been its source, nothing is left but a sham resurrection and a sham faith. But when the apparitions are seen instead for what they really were, a *subsequent* expression of faith in Jesus as God's word and deed, then it becomes clear that this faith needed no *Mirakel*, no evidentiary sign, no 'work', in order to exist; that he called it into being who alone was able to do so—the Holy Spirit. The Easter narratives, therefore, are *professions of faith*; they reflect the *Verständnis* of the Christian community, not objective events.

Nevertheless, as we have seen, this *Verständnis* has been partly objectified. In its mythologizing aspect it is a fruit of human weakness, of the rationalism instinctive to natural man, who itches to see and touch the divine. Yielding to the temptation of proof, with an eye to apologetics, the community turned the risen Christ into a *mortuus redivivus* and a verifiable object. Here it is that we must demythologize the New Testament in the name of its real intent. After all, that is what the author of the fourth Gospel did, gently but firmly, in rearranging the account of Jesus's apparition to Thomas which he had got from the σημεῖα-source. We know that in a general way he is critical of faith objectified in *Mirakel* (Jn 4:48 and pp. 124–6, above). Here he demythologizes his source by putting into it Jesus's reproach to Thomas: 'Have you believed because you have seen me? Blessed are those who have not seen and yet believe.'[1] In this episode Thomas represents unbelief and the *homo religiosus*, who, Paul also says, has a characteristic craving for σημεῖα (1 Cor 1:22)—though he himself at one point yielded to that temptation, as we have seen, in 1 Cor 15:5–8.

Because Bultmann repudiates the objective resurrection (a phantom

---

1. The sense remains the same with or without the question-mark where the first part of the verse ends.

resurrection, in other words) which is in part that of the legends about
the risen Christ's apparitions, various critics of his have concluded that
he does not believe in the resurrection of the *whole man* or, more
particularly, of man as σῶμα. To lay such nonsense at his door is to
tell the world that one has absolutely no inkling of his thought,
although he has made it plain enough in his interpretation of Paul's
theology of the resurrection of the dead.

Paul has never heard of, and has not the slightest interest in, the
immortality of the soul: the ζωή he speaks of is not an indefinite
prolongation of the soul's life. He defines earthly life as death, which
he obviously would not do if he believed the soul to be immortal by
nature. For then death would only be an event within life, a mere
passing sleep of the soul or a journey taking it into the other world. To
the Greek mind death is only an accident, because the soul is immortal.
The Greeks do not say that the essence of life in this world is death.
Paul says so: this world has death for its prince. Therefore life can only
be an *altogether* future thing. For the Christian, of course, the life to
come is already here, but that is by *grace*; whereas belief in the
immortality of the soul means that man is already saved by *nature*.

Does Paul then see no identity between the man who dies and the
man who rises again? Of course he sees one. The bearer of this identity
is precisely the σῶμα, which, we have shown (pp. 33–5, above), is
not one of the two or three principles making up man, as the Greeks
and Gnostics thought. Man does not *have* a body, he *is* his body. The
σῶμα is the person himself insofar as he is determinable. In this world
he is totally determined by death which is his *Wie*. Man is nothing
but sin and death. The risen Christian naturally remains a σῶμα
(otherwise he would no longer be a man), but a σῶμα wholly determined by God's ζωή.

Thus death and life are not two successive attributes or states but the
person himself under two absolutely different ec-sistentiell determinations. Death is a *mode of being*. Life too is a *mode of being*. That is why
there is a real *resurrection of the dead*. If death merely *happened* to a man,
if he *were* not death, it would not be taken seriously; nor would life,
being only a new attribute. Man would be nothing more than the
substratum of death and life, now to be defined as mere attributes.
In fact the entire person is totally determined by death or by life.

Here Bultmann quotes with approval the beautiful words of Barth:
'The body is man, the body is the *I*; and that man, that *I*, is God's . . .
God is lord of the *body* . . . Trying to be God's without the *body* is
rebelling against God's will . . . The expression "resurrection of the
body" is only a paraphrase of the word "God" ' (quoted in GV I,
pp. 61–2). Thus it is indeed the total man who rises from the dead.

How could the case be otherwise in Bultmann's anthropology, which is the antithesis of dualism between soul and body?

Since the resurrection gives man a future so absolute that it is equivalent to the very being of God, naturally enough the New Testament feels powerless to say what ζωή is and rests content with affirming its *Dass*. There is no description of the *Was*. Jesus was sobriety itself in his teaching about the life to come. Not for him the fanciful images of it presented in the apocalypses. He paints no picture of future glory. For him, everything is, so to speak, subsumed into the one idea that God will reign. Heavenly beatitude he simply calls 'life' (ζωή; Mk 9:43, 45 and elsewhere). True, he speaks of drinking new wine in the kingdom (Mk 14:25), but is there any more here than a metaphor? At any rate he rejects the mythological idea which the Sadducees had—the better to disown it—of the resurrection of the dead: 'When they rise from the dead, they neither marry nor are given in marriage, but are like angels in heaven' (Mk 12:25).

Paul is no less sober. He too refrains from describing the life to come. He could only describe it by idealizing earthly life, which would be a denial of the resurrection as entirely other and a contradiction of the future as μὴ βλεπόμενον (2 Cor 4:18). So he speaks of no more than the 'glory' that is to be revealed (Rom 8:18; 2 Cor 4:17), of the 'being-with-Christ' that will then begin (1 Thess 4:17; 5:10; Phil 1:23; 2 Cor 5:7–8), of seeing face to face (1 Cor 13:12).

While promising eternal life, the Gospel of John never describes it, for 'any representation of the *Was* and the *Wie* of the promised life would perforce speak of mere human possibilities, the noblest of them no better than the crudest so far as concerns the promised ζωή, which as an eschatological thing—as ἀνάστασις καὶ ζωή—lies beyond human possibilities. One prepares for that life by freely accepting earthly death—that is, by relinquishing the human self as one knows and wills it. Thus the ζωή appears to the world in the guise of death' (EJ, p. 308).

(3) What we have said of Jesus's resurrection applies to the other gospel 'legends': the legends of the nativity, the baptism of Jesus (in the synoptic form), his temptation in the wilderness, Peter's messianic confession, the transfiguration, the messianic entry into Jerusalem, the 'supernaturalized' story of the *visible* passion, ascension and parousia. Historical criticism shows (GST, pp. 260–335) that these accounts are a later, objectified expression of faith.

Generally speaking, the Christian community conveyed its faith in Jesus as the Word of God by turning his earthly life into a *Mirakel*, by the same objectifying process which we have described in connection with the messiahship and resurrection. These legends are *eschatological* in their *purpose* and *import*: what they mean to express is the stark (divine) otherness of Jesus. They do not in the least overdraw his person.

It is not as though Jesus were a great historical figure whom the disciples had therefore, by a sort of collective hallucination, turned into the Word of God. Quite the contrary. Not only do the christological legends we are considering not *over*value Jesus, they actually *under*value him in that they mythologize the eschatological *Dass*. In them the Wholly Other has to some extent become an object, *Wunder* a *Mirakel*, the divine *even as divine* a thing of this world; so that if these accounts were authentic history, Christianity would be a religion —even *the* religion, if you will—but it would no longer be God's revelation.

(4) The christological titles also need demythologizing. They fall into two groups: those which go back, so far as we can gather, to the Palestinian community, and those which the Hellenistic community bestowed on Jesus.

To the mind of the Palestinian community, Jesus is first and foremost the *Messiah*. God has raised him up to make him the Messiah.[2] The Messiah is the king of the last days. The expression *son of David* has the same meaning. Genealogical speculations attach to it, but basically it is a royal style. Similarly, in the Palestinian community, the *son of God* is the king. The expression *servant of God*, so far as it was used of Jesus in the primitive community, can hardly mean anything else: Jesus is God's servant as David was.

To these royal styles we must add the title *son of man*, which signifies that the Saviour of the last days is of a nature more than earthly. Jesus received this heavenly title at his resurrection. It is taken as a matter of course that the king who bears the foregoing titles is also a supernatural being, but never on the same footing as God. The primitive community did not make Jesus the equal of God.

In Hellenistic Christianity the title of titles is κύριος. It shows that Jesus is the godhead present at worship and also that he is lord of the world; whence those texts of the Septuagint which speak of the κύριος are applied to him. Being the lord brings him quite naturally into the divine sphere but does not make him God's equal. In the stylized blessings (like 2 Cor 11:31) God is the lord's Father; and if Phil 2:6–11 makes Jesus lord over all the powers by his resurrection, it is 'to the glory of God the Father'.

The expression *son of God* acquired a different sense in the Hellenistic

---

2. We mean the 'real' Messiah, the Messiah who will soon *come*, not the one who will come again. As has been pointed out, the earliest Christian community did not consider Jesus's *earthly life* to have been messianic (see ch. 5, § 1, above).

community. It no longer meant the messianic king but a being who was truly divine: thus at the beginning of the hymn which Paul quotes in the Letter to the Philippians, Christ is spoken of as ἐν μορφῇ θεοῦ. *Son of God* is a name higher than the name of any angel (Heb 1:4). This idea made Christians regard even the earthly life of Jesus as the life of a θεῖος ἀνήρ, a 'divine man', full of power and attended by *Mirakel*. The idea that Christ was the son of God gave rise to the notion of his pre-existence, the later and contradictory notion that he was miraculously conceived by the Holy Spirit, and finally the notion that he became incarnate, suffered, died and rose again. Here we recognize the full outline of the mystery religions. The notion of Christ's pre-existence entails making him a cosmic power, as in oriental mythologies—that is, the instrument of creation (1 Cor 8:6; Col 1: 16–17; Jn 1:3).

All this shows us that Jesus was looked on as a divine being and worshipped as such, but not made the equal of God himself. Christ's subordination to God seems perfectly obvious to the New Testament writers. If he is the son of God, he is only the son of God, subject to the Father. He is the lord, but 'to the glory of God the Father' (Phil 2:11). As the head of a woman is her husband, so the head of Christ is God (1 Cor 11:3). Or again: 'You are Christ's; and Christ is God's' (1 Cor 3:23). Or again: 'When all things are subjected to him, then the son himself will also be subjected to him who put all things under him, that God may be everything to every one' (1 Cor 15:28).

Thus all the titles Jesus bears are distinctly 'subordinationist'. If the New Testament does not make him a second divine Person alongside the first and equal to him, is that not precisely because Christ is sheer *relation to God*, or God himself in his *mode of being*, in his *Wie*, towards men? Is it not the underlying purpose of the New Testament to demythologize? In other words, 'New Testament utterances about the divinity or godhead of Jesus, at least *a parte potiori*, are not designed to convey its nature at all but its meaning; they confess that what he is and what he does is not of earthly origin, does not issue from human thoughts and the doings of this world, that through it God speaks to us, acts upon us and for us. Christ is the strength and wisdom of God; God has made him our righteousness and sanctification and redemption (1 Cor 1:30). But insofar as statements of this kind smack of objectification, I feel that they must be interpreted in a critical spirit' (GV 2, pp. 252–3).

Those New Testament expressions which *identify* Christ with God— not which make him equal to God as a second Person alongside the first—so that Christ becomes God himself in a different mode of being, make it clear that we must not think of Christ as a hypostasis. Paul mentions the grace of God that is given to us (Rom 5:15) and the grace of the κύριος (2 Cor 8:9). The grace of his apostolate he has from God but also from the κύριος (1 Cor 3:10; see Rom 1:5). If he is 'a servant of God' (2 Cor 6:4) he is also Christ's servant (1 Cor 3:5). In Paul we find two forms of the old Jewish saying that there is nothing in the world but 'what God wills' and 'if he wills it': 'by God's will' (Rom 1:10; 15:32) and 'if the κύριος wills' or 'permits' (1 Cor 4:19; 16;7). 1 Cor 7:17 absolutely identifies ὁ θεός and ὁ κύριος. 1 Cor 12:4–6 represents the Spirit as a third mode of being: 'There are varieties of gifts, but the same Spirit; and there are varieties of service, but the same Lord; and there are varieties of working, but it is the same God.' Could Paul possibly make himself clearer?

His view of the judgment confirms what we have been saying. If God is to judge the world (1 Thess 3:13; Rom 3:5), so is Christ (1 Thess 2:19; 1 Cor 4:15). Are we to suppose that man will be called to account before two authorities, two tribunals, two persons? That would be a substantialist and mythological interpretation—one which, it is true, has slipped into the book of Acts (17:31). But Paul is of no such mind. He treats God and the Kyrios as interchangeable.

Rom 14:9 says that Christ is 'Lord both of the dead and of the living' and 14:10 that 'we shall all stand before the judgment seat of God'. In 1 Cor 4:5 we read: '[Wait until] the Lord comes, who will bring to light the things now hidden in darkness and will disclose the purposes of the heart. Then every man will receive his commendation from . . .' Here one would expect 'from the Lord'; yet the text says 'from God'. Who, then, is the judge: God or the Kyrios? The same confusion—if the expression may be allowed—between God and the Kyrios recurs in 2 Cor 5:11. First we have verse 10: 'We must all appear (φανερωθῆναι) before the judgment seat of Christ'. Then verse 11 goes on: 'Therefore, knowing the fear of the Lord, we persuade men; but what we are is known (πεφανερώμεθα) to God'. Obviously φανερωθῆναι is as much a work of God as of Christ. Therefore Paul did not think that we shall have to appear before two persons: so far as he is concerned, our responsibility to the Kyrios is identical with our responsibility to God. God concretely becomes our judge in Christ. In Christ, the world's judge becomes *our* judge. So Paul has 'historicized' the idea of judgment.

The New Testament understands the kingdom of Christ in the same way. The kingdom of God can also be called the kingdom of Christ (Col 1:13; 2 Tim 4:18; 2 Pet 1:11). For its part the Letter to the Ephesians speaks of the kingdom of Christ and God—evidently one and the same kingdom. Thus the attributes with which Christ is invested mean that God encounters and saves us in him and him alone.

Jesus is God's saving deed, God himself insofar as he turns to us. Hence quite naturally, as time went by, the doxologies which originally had to do with God came to be applied to Christ, and so Christians increasingly prayed to him (2 Cor 12:8; 1 Thess 3:12; 2 Thess 3:5, 16).

To sum up, the christological titles (Messiah, son of man, son of God, and so forth) do not mean that Jesus is a divine hypostasis. If we understand them in that way we rationalize God, blind to the fact that '[Christ's] lordship, his divinity, is always sheer event and rules out any sort of objectification' (GV 2, p. 258). The ancient Church went wrong by interpreting the word of God in terms of Greek metaphysics. Bultmann holds that we must keep the fundamental *meaning* of ancient christology but reject the language in which it is clothed (its *Ausdruck*; GV 2, p. 257). It will be recalled that at the Amsterdam Assembly (1948) the World Council of Churches drew up a profession of faith according to which the churches acknowledge 'Jesus Christ as God'. Is this not once more the same rationalist rendering of God's manifestation in Jesus? To Bultmann's mind, 'the formula *Christ is God* is erroneous if God is understood to be something objectifiable, whether in the Arian manner or the Nicene, the orthodox or the liberal. It is correct if "God" here means the event of God's deed' (GV 2, p. 258).

In other words, 'there is not another divine Person alongside God, as though the Jewish belief in one God were now completed by belief in a second divine Person. Faith is not affirming metaphysical speculations about the divinity and the natures of Christ. Faith in Christ is nothing else but faith in God's deed in Christ' (GV 1, p. 331). So it is clear why Bultmann brings a nonsuit against both the orthodox at Amsterdam and liberals, calling them *par fratrum* (GV 2, p. 257); because both alike interpret Christ according to the categories of natural man. Liberalism, as we have said again and again, humanizes him; orthodoxy rationalizes him, as we shall see at greater length.

C

HOW DID PAUL THINK OF CHRIST?

(1) First let us state the problem. Does Paul think there is a Christ *in se*? Are his death and resurrection not historical events that one should begin by accepting as fact? Must one first believe in their objective divine reality and then embrace their saving significance? To quote an adversary of Bultmann's, must one draw a distinction 'between an act of faith which sees God's love revealed in the event of the cross and a second act of faith for which the first has prepared a man . . . and

which consists in a radical change of *Selbstverständnis*?'[3] Can I believe
in Christ before he is, and without his becoming, my *Verständnis*? Is
he my saviour because he is Christ, or is he Christ because he is my
saviour? Must I first believe in the objective Christ and only then in
the Christ of the *beneficia*?

(2) (a) In order to explain what the event of salvation means, Paul
uses a number of images borrowed from this or that *Weltanschauung*
of the day. First the death of Jesus is interpreted in the categories of
Jewish worship—that is, in juridical terms. It is an *expiatory sacrifice*
which procures the forgiveness of sins—that is, cancels a debt that has
been contracted. Christ's death is ἱλαστήριον ἐν τῷ αὐτοῦ αἵματι (Rom
3:25) which echoes Rom 5:9: 'We are now justified by his blood'. The
liturgy of the Last Supper (1 Cor 11:24f) combines the theme of
expiation with that of the covenant (1 Cor 11:24f).

The idea of expiatory sacrifice also underlies those texts which
declare Jesus to have died ὑπὲρ τῶν ἁμαρτιῶν ἡμῶν (1 Cor 15:3; 2 Cor
5:14) or simply to have died for us (Rom 5:6, 8; 14:15; 1 Thess 5:10;
see 1 Cor 1:13), or say that he was given up (or gave himself up) for us
(Rom 4:25; 8:32; Gal 1:4; 2:20). In all this Paul follows the tradition
of the primitive community or Hellenistic Christianity.

(b) Much akin to the sacrifice of expiation is *vicarious sacrifice*, which
also derives from Jewish categories. Like expiatory sacrifice, vicarious
sacrifice may be conveyed by the ὑπὲρ ἡμῶν: we have examples in
Gal 3:13 and 2 Cor 5:21. Rom 8:30 refers to it. Expiatory sacrifice
and vicarious sacrifice are mingled in 2 Cor 5:14–15, where the
phrase 'one has died for all' must be taken in a vicarial sense because
of the 'therefore all have died'; whereas in verse 15, 'he died for all,
that . . .', the ὑπέρ means 'in our behalf' and thus implies expiatory
sacrifice. But be it observed that verse 14 likewise has a *geschichtlich*
('historical') meaning; for in terms of bare vicarious sacrifice the 'all
have died' could only mean 'all are *regarded* as dead', whereas according
to our analysis of Rom 6:3, 5 Paul certainly means that 'all *are* dead'.
Here Jewish categories are overstepped for the first time: Christ's
death is inseparable from the transformation it is meant to effect in
man: 'all have died'. The cross is a relation, a *Verständnis*.

(c) The theme of sacrifice is closely bound up with that of redemption. By his vicarious sacrifice Christ redeems mankind from the curse
of the law (Gal 3:13)—that is, from the chastisement it has deserved by
not keeping the law. Christ's sacrifice of expiation blots out both our
fault and our punishment. But redemption does not confine itself to

---

3. E. Schweizer, quoted in KM 2, p. 202, note 2.

the sphere of penalties. According to Gal 4:4 Christ not only redeems men from the punishment they have deserved for not keeping the law, but from the law itself, because the redeemed are granted divine sonship: 'God sent forth his Son . . . to redeem those who were under the law, so that we might receive adoption as sons'. In Gal 1:4 he delivers us from the wickedness of the 'present aeon'. Now this aeon is the aeon which is subject to the law and therefore also to the power of sin and death. Thus the freedom Christ has bought us not only cancels our punishment but snatches us from the powers (from law, sin and death). In other words, man is not only delivered from sin as a fault and a penalty, as a thing that lies *outside* him, but above all from sin as a power—that is, as a force that eggs him on to evil and *inwardly determines* him.

This interpretation is confirmed by 1 Cor 6:20; the redemption at issue obviously consists in a transformation of man, a new *Sichverstehen*. In the context of 1 Cor 6:12–20, the redemption spoken of in 7:23 is a deliverance from sin, and in the context of 6:12–20 it is a deliverance from ἄνθρωποι—that is, from the human standards and judgments which prevail in this sin-ridden aeon. Thus it is no longer a problem to decide who Paul thinks Christ paid the τιμή to. He paid it to the powers which were man's *Verständnis* (see pp. 39–42, above). Of course the expression is a metaphor. The mythological idea of a bargain struck with the devil is alien to the Apostle's mind.

To sum up, it is clear how Paul bursts the categories of Jewish rules and worship: Christ's death is not merely a sacrifice which cancels the culpability and the penalties incurred through sin, it is also 'the instrument of men's deliverance from the powers of this aeon: law, sin and death' (TNT, p. 292). In other words it is not an objective divine fact which merely does away with fault and punishment (things quite extrinsic to man, after all): it is a *geschichtlich* event which transforms man *from within* by delivering him from the powers that constituted his *mode of being*, and endowing him with a new *Verständnis*. Paul demythologizes Jewish images by raising them to the plane of 'historicity'.[4]

(d) He also used the categories of the mystery religions in order to convey his own thought, but thoroughly transformed them as well.

---

4. So there is no reason to be shocked at Bultmann's saying (during his 1941 lectures) about Christ's death envisaged as an expiatory satisfaction: 'What primitive ideas of sin and justification underlie such images? What primitive ideas of God?' (KM I, p. 20). From this point of view 'sin could only be thought of in juridical terms, as an outward transgression, and there would be no room for any moral standard at all!' (*ibid.*, p. 20). As for redemption, it would be a purely natural operation, as in Gnosis.

The essence of a mystery religion is this: that through baptism and sacramental communion the initiate shares the fate of the deity—participates, that is, in his death and resurrection. By entering upon death he is delivered from death. If we slightly altered the wording of Rom 6:10 and then applied the text to the god and the initiate, it would aptly describe the position: ὅ γὰρ ἀπέθανεν, τῷ θανάτῳ ἀπέθανεν ἐφάπαξ. The god and the initiate (the latter by sacramental participation in the fate of the former) die to death once for all. Only Paul did not write τῷ θανάτῳ, he wrote τῇ ἁμαρτίᾳ, shifting everything from the mythological plane to the 'historical' plane. In his eyes, deliverance from death is at the same time a complete liberation from the power of sin—first for Christ himself (Rom 6:11) and then for all who have been baptized 'into his death' (6:3).

Therefore Jesus's death is not a mere objective reality, like the death of the god in the mystery religions, but a deed that altogether transforms man; and precisely in this respect it is the very doing of God. Otherwise there would be nothing to distinguish the death of Jesus from the death of Attis or Osiris.

(e) In order to convey the salvific meaning of Christ's death, Paul makes use of Gnostic myth, thereby simply continuing a practice which had been begun by the Hellenistic community before his time—as is proved by the christological hymn in Phil 2:6–11. Gnostic myth, as such, speaks only of the coming and ascension of the heavenly messenger in the guise of his abasement and his exaltation. It does not necessarily involve any idea of his departure because of a violent death.

Long before Paul's time, as we have seen, the Gnostic redeemer was apt to be confused with the gods of the mysteries, who did die a sanguinary death (see p. 52, above). It is the burden of the myth that men (Gnostics) and their saviour together form one σῶμα. Just as the heavenly messenger is not really a person but a cosmic figure, so too his σῶμα is a cosmic thing. His fate—to sojourn on earth in human form—is also the fate of his disciples. Just as the redeemer has suffered death, so will those who belong to him (2 Cor 5:14). Just as he has risen from the dead, so they too shall be made alive (1 Cor 15:20–22). Since his return to his heavenly home means his deliverance from the demoniac powers that rule the cosmos, those who are connected with his σῶμα share in that deliverance.

Paul alludes to the Gnostic myth when he says that we have all been baptized into one σῶμα (1 Cor 12:13), that we are σύμφυτοι by baptism into Christ's death (Rom 6:5). Accordingly the whole life of a Christian bears the stamp not only of Christ's death but also of his resurrection. Paul carries in himself the death and life of Jesus (2 Cor 4:7–12; see

1:15). The same is true of all believers: he only speaks of himself as an illustration (Phil 3:10-11).

It is clear how Paul uses myth in order to convey the universal effect of the salvation wrought by God in Jesus Christ. What he is considering is not a mere historical (*historisch*) event, some fact that happened in the past and is done with, but an 'historical' (*geschichtlich*) event which has ended the old aeon and the powers that inhabited it. They are already destroyed (1 Cor 2:6), although for the present the believer's risen life is still hidden under the semblance of death (2 Cor 4:7-12). But the present is a brief interlude (1 Cor 7:29, 31), so that he can cry in triumph: 'The old has passed away, behold, the new has come' (2 Cor 5:17). Christ is the second Adam. The human race sprung from the first Adam was subject to sin and death; the human race sprung from the second Adam is risen and free (Rom 5:12-19; 1 Cor 15:21-22, 44-49).

Now it will be evident why Paul did not use purely Jewish images to explain his idea of the person and work of Christ. Those categories were not the categories of relation and encounter. They could not express the true nature of redemption, which consists in transforming the sinner through and through. Being juridical categories, they conveyed a purely extrinsic salvation which only affected man from without and did not become his ec-sistentiell determination. They were powerless to express the truth which Paul has so much at heart: that the saved and their saviour make up a single body, that his destiny is their destiny, his own country their own country, his life their life, his being their being, his glory their glory. Having once been demythologized (pp. 55-9, above), concepts drawn from the mystery religions and from Gnosticism were much better fitted to make men understand that God's revelation in Jesus Christ is not something metaphysical but an event which ushers mankind into divine life. Christ gives the world a different destiny and all who are his form a single σῶμα with him.

(3) Here let us undertake to settle the question which we asked ourselves above. Does christology come first, to be followed by soteriology? Must I first be convinced that Jesus Christ is the pre-existent Son who became man, died and rose again, before I am in a position to believe in the salvific meaning which those events have for me? Are they first of all *extra me* and only then *pro me*?

Are there two sorts of faith? Does one consist in a readiness to admit as true the incarnation, death and resurrection of Christ, seeing in them the objective reality of God's grace; and is the other the surrender of oneself to this grace, thoroughgoing conversion of one's whole being, giving up the old *Selbstverständnis* for a new mode of being? The answer must be no. The act by which a man acknowledges Jesus as the Son of God and as the saviour is the same act by which he is saved and receives a new *Sichverstehen*. As we shall see, this is the authentic mind of Paul.

(4) One thing is clear. The Paul who speaks of the Son of God who loved him and delivered himself up for him, is and must be the same Paul who gave up his own righteousness and delivered his ἐγώ to death (Gal 2:19f; Phil 3:4–11). He knows Christ only because he understands himself anew: that knowing and understanding are one and the same act. 'Zealous for the traditions of his fathers' (Gal 1:14), he says at the very first that Christ as Lord demanded the sacrifice of his old 'zeal for God' (Rom 10:2), and it is precisely as that demand that he describes his preaching of Jesus. It is not an 'eloquent wisdom', a mysterious doctrine about a metaphysical being, but the 'word of the cross', a 'stumbling-block' and a 'folly' to natural man because it tears him away from himself and from any καυχᾶσθαι (1 Cor 1:18–31; 2 Cor 5:12). A man does not first believe in the divine objectivity of Christ and then become converted: he knows the Lord only in and through the very act of conversion.

Paul's Letter to the Romans is an exposition, to a community with which he is not as yet acquainted, of the major themes in his gospel, designed to vindicate himself as an apostle. Now he does not first give an objective doctrine, such as one finds in the hermetic treatises, which are essentially concerned to teach a soteriology. He begins by speaking of man's condition. He shows that the event of salvation is not an object of knowledge but an object of decision; that it does not exist apart from its relation with man—that is, until the man whom it summons has made Christ his Lord by giving up his own righteousness. In Rom 7:7–8, 11, Paul insists with a kind of passion that a man can only believe in the salvific event wrought by God in Jesus Christ when he despairs of himself, when he recognizes himself as the ταλαίπωρος ἄνθρωπος groaning for deliverance.

That event is to be found nowhere else but in the word of preaching. If the cross and resurrection of Jesus are a saving power, that is solely by virtue of their divine meaning, which preaching alone discloses: their meaning is identical with the preaching and the preaching is identical with their meaning. For Christian preaching is no ordinary word: it contains the thing which it announces to me; in it Christ encounters me. The word is Christ himself. It is God's very deed in men's behalf. It is the *actual event of salvation*. Paul plainly indicates as much when he says that God has set up not only reconciliation but the διακονία τῆς καταλλαγῆς as well, the λόγος τῆς καταλλαγῆς (2 Cor 5:18f); so that in the preaching Christ himself is present and at work for our salvation. Since the νῦν in which it rings out is the νῦν of eschatological event itself (2 Cor 6:2), the latter is essentially relation, as becomes doubly clear if we compare it with Gnosticism.

For the Gnostic, entering the σῶμα was not an ec-sistentiell act, a forsaking of himself: his self was already divine. But the Christian must die altogether to his sinful past and become a 'new creature' if he would become a member of Christ's body. Rom 7:12–19 illustrates this raising of Gnostic categories to the plane of 'historicity'. Post-adamite mankind was wholly unable to escape from sin and death. Logically there should be no escape for them, now that the second Adam has come, except by being a Christian. Gnosticism is built upon just such an objective scheme. A Gnostic is saved or lost in the same way that a thing is a thing, because his redemption is a process of nature. But Paul says that the choice between sin and grace still remains after Christ's coming (verse 17), because Christ's death and resurrection are something 'historical' which does not exist apart from the decision and the design of man. Likewise 1 Cor 15:22 ('As in Adam all die, so also in Christ shall all be made alive') should logically mean: 'All men will live through (in) Christ as necessarily as all die in Adam'. In fact, however, Paul means: all receive that capacity but it is used only by those who are τοῦ χριστοῦ (verse 23).

(5) We can now clarify the true nature of the event of salvation, beginning with the cross.

(a) It will not do to start by recognizing the Crucified as a divine being, so as to believe, on that basis, in his significance for salvation. To believe in the Crucified is to acknowledge him as Lord, which I cannot do without my life's being altogether transformed in and through that same acknowledgment. I cannot confess that Jesus the Crucified is the son of God by an act of faith which leaves me unchanged and merely affirms his divine nature. That would be 'emptying of its power' the '*logos* of the cross' which is a stumbling-block and folly. I cannot acknowledge the Crucified *until* I have allowed myself to be crucified with him (1 Cor: 18–31; Gal 6:14; see 5:24). That is why the apostle bears the death and the 'marks' of Jesus in his body (2 Cor 4:10f; Gal 6:17). He shares abundantly in Christ's sufferings (2 Cor 1:5). We are not dealing here with psycho-somatic, mystical phenomena but with the transformation which a believer undergoes by entering upon the death of Christ, with the determination of his life by the cross, with his new, eschatological mode of being.

(b) What Paul says about Christ's pre-existence and incarnation does not mean that from all eternity there is a second Person, alongside God, who became man. Such mythology would in no way express faith as the forsaking of all καύχησις. God would no longer be believed in

but only speculated about. Christ would no longer be God himself as
summoning us to answer, but a hypostasis thought up in the image and
likeness of natural man. A pre-existent being is neither the word of
God nor the deed of God. If Paul nevertheless uses this theme of pre-
existence—which has nothing specifically Christian about it—it is to
make men understand that the person and destiny of Jesus are no part
of this world, that they are not earthly either in their origin or in their
meaning; but that God acts in them, that Jesus is God's action taking
place 'when the time had fully come' (Gal 4:4).

Thus interpreted, pre-existence does not make it any easier to believe
in the Crucified (as though the divine meaning of the cross were only
credible provided it was God's pre-existent son who died on it), it is
itself an object of faith; it is folly just as the cross is folly, it is part of the
λόγος τοῦ σταυροῦ, because it is only another way of saying that Christ
is God's action.

The same must be said of the incarnation when it is called an act of
obedience and love on the part of the pre-existent Son (Phil 2:8;
Gal 2:20; Rom 8:35, 39). Just as the coming of a divine being into this
world does not at all mean that he is God's salvific action, so his love
for us need not, of itself, be God's love. But the fact that the incarnation
and the love of Christ live on in the Church's preaching shows us that
they are not objective events, bound to a particular time and place,
but rather the ever-present, ever-mighty action of God.

Just as Christ became 'a servant to the circumcised' (Rom 15:8), so
his ministers are the 'ministers of a new covenant' (2 Cor 3:6), 'servants
of God' (2 Cor 6:4), 'servants of Christ' (2 Cor 11:23; see 1 Cor 3:5),
the slaves and servants of Christ (Rom 1:1; Gal 1:10; Phil 1:1), and
thereby the servants of men (2 Cor 4:5; 1 Cor 9:19). Accordingly it is
in these servants that he who took the form of a servant (Phil 2:7)
encounters man. The incarnation endures in the ministers of Christ;
not, of course, insofar as they are men or insofar as their person is
endued with any mysterious supernatural attribute (GV 3, p. 19), but
insofar as God himself summons and saves men through them.

The fact that the incarnation extends beyond the historical Jesus,
shows that it has an eschatological import. Just as Christ delivered
himself to death to win us life, so death is at work in the apostle of
Christ that life may flood into the hearers of the word (2 Cor 4:12).
The love of Christ controls him (2 Cor 5:14). He calls on his hearers
not only to imitate himself (1 Cor 4:16; 11:1; see Gal 4:12; Phil 3:17;
4:9) insofar as he is Christ's ambassador to them (2 Cor 5:20). Thus
the eschatological event lives on in the ministers of Christ. In them
Christ summons and saves men. This is what the incarnation of the
pre-existent Son means: 'What is said of Christ's pre-existence gives

mythological expression to the fact that there exists a divinely-sanctioned preaching of God's prevenient grace and love. By believing in that pre-existence, the hearer declares that it is the Word of God which has encountered him' (TNT, p. 305).

The doctrine that all things were created through and subsist in Christ (1 Cor 8:6) means the same as the doctrine of pre-existence; for the δι' οὗ τὰ πάντα is completed by the καὶ ἡμεῖς δι' αὐτοῦ, which 'historicizes' the role of the pre-existent Christ. For through him the Christian is what he is—one who has passed from sin to grace. Therefore the role of Christ in creation must be understood in ec-sistential, not mythological terms. Creation and redemption are one and the same thing. The fact that the redeemer is the Creator shows that the event of salvation is indeed God's doing, just as creation is; that it is something eschatological and rooted in God himself, that what encounters man in the kerygmatic word is really the love of *God*.

(c) Christ's resurrection is likewise eschatological in character. Before he can perceive it in its true nature, therefore, a man must have abandoned his old *Selbstverständnis*. Despite 1 Cor 15:3–8, it is not an objective supernatural event but an *Anrede* which asks a man whether he is prepared to acknowledge the risen Christ as his Lord. Thus it is possible to believe in the risen Christ only insofar as he is God's word present in the word of Christian preaching. A divine being who has died and is now *redivivus* has nothing whatever to do with God himself summoning and saving us. So belief that Jesus is the risen Christ and belief that he himself speaks to us through the preaching of the Church (2 Cor 5:20) are one and the same belief. The word that proclaims him in the Church is the word that he is: it is identical with him and he is identical with it. Anyone who listens to that word as to the word that is spoken to him and brings him death or life, thereby believes in the risen Christ.

That is why Jesus's resurrection is not his removal to the next world but his exaltation to the lordship (Phil 2:11) that will be his until he delivers it to the Father (1 Cor 15:24). This means that he has it in and for the present, which is given its character by the Church's preaching. It is by his command that the preaching is done (Rom 10:17). It is he who speaks through his ministers (2 Cor 5:20; 13:3) and acts through them (Rom 15:18). When an apostle arrives he does so 'in the fullness of the blessing of Christ' (Rom 15:29), because the risen Christ is present in him: by carrying the death of Jesus he manifests the life of Jesus (2 Cor 4:10f).

In the apostle Christ displays his power. 'For he was crucified in weakness, but lives by the power of God. For we are weak in him, but in dealing with you we shall live with him by the power of God'

(2 Cor 13:4): in the apostle it is the risen Christ himself who encounters men. Accordingly the resurrection is anything but an objective supernatural event. It is infinitely more. And the risen Christ is anything but a divine being *redivivus*. He is infinitely more.

To sum up, christology and soteriology are the same thing in Paul's eyes. For until I myself have died and risen again I cannot perceive Christ who has died and risen again. To fancy that a man can believe in God's action before he has himself been thoroughly transformed by it would be to forget how deep-seated sin is. By that very fact it would be turning Christ into a metaphysical being and redemption into a process of nature.

D

The author of the fourth Gospel demythologized the event of salvation even more thoroughly than Paul had done.

(1) As we know, John says that by sin man has turned creation into 'this world' (pp. 57–9, above). In this world of death, life has appeared (1 Jn 1:2); in this world of darkness, light has shone (Jn 1:5; 3:19). All these things happened through the coming of God's son. It is Jesus who is God's son. As such, he was before John the Baptist although in the order of time he came after him (1:15, 30). He was before Abraham (8:58), before the foundation of the world (17:5, 24). In him the word that was with God in the beginning, became flesh (1:1–2, 14). Thus Jesus is presented in mythological terms, as the pre-existent son of God who became man.

Has this mythological language a mythological *meaning*? We shall presently see whether it has. For the moment let it be observed that the beginning of John's first Letter, which obviously bears the same meaning as the prologue to the Gospel, speaks only of the life which was with the Father from the beginning, and speaks of it as 'that which was from the beginning', not as a person (Jn 1:1f). So the *logos* is not a hypostasis. The evangelist only uses the mythological theme of pre-existence in order to declare that Jesus is the very action of God.[5]

(2) But is God's action in Jesus an objective event independent of the hearer's faith? Can the hearer of the word observe it before he makes it his *Verstehen*? No. With John as with Paul, christology and soteri-

---

5. Ch. 8, §IV, above.—See also O. Cullmann, *Christologie du Nouveau Testament* (1958), pp. 230–31: 'Even though we find here some incidental thoughts about the *nature* (*l'être*) of the *logos*, the author knows that the *logos* only has a nature in view of its action . . . The Bible is not about God as such but about God as he has turned to the world in his revelation . . . The *logos* is God revealing and communicating himself in his action.'

ology are one and the same. Nothing makes this point clearer than the basic Johannine theme of judgment. It is Christ's nature to be a summons which drives man to decision:

> And this is the judgment,
> that the light has come into the world,
> and men loved darkness rather than light.
>
> (3:19)

> For judgment I came into this world,
> that those who do not see may see,
> and that those who see may become blind.
>
> (9:39)

John's 'historicization' of eschatology goes farther than Paul's, because κρίσις and κρίμα have the twofold sense of judgment and *separation*. The judgment happens in such a way that encounter with Jesus separates those who believe from those who do not believe, those who see from those who do not see. The believer is not judged (condemned), whereas the unbeliever remains in darkness and under the wrath of God—that is, he is judged (condemned):

> He who believes in me is not condemned;
> he who does not believe is condemned already.
>
> (3:18)

> He who hears my word and believes him who sent me,
> has eternal life;
> he does not come into judgment,
> but has passed from death to life . . .
> The hour is coming, and now is,
> when the dead will hear the voice of the Son of God,
> and those who hear will live.
>
> (5:24–25)

On sending Jesus into the world, the Father has given him power to wake the dead and execute judgment (5:21f and 26f). Therefore a man who believes in him has life already:

> He who believes in the Son has eternal life;
> he who does not obey the Son shall not see life,
> but the wrath of God rests upon him.
>
> (3:36; see 6:47; 1 Jn 5:12)

> I am the resurrection and the life;
> he who believes in me,
> though he die, yet shall he live,
> and whoever lives and believes in me
> shall never die.
>
> (11:25f; see 8:51)

Thus the judgment is not a cosmic, outward event; it takes place in a man's very reaction to the words of Jesus. It consists in God's *Anrede* and man's decision. In 11:24 Martha expresses the traditional idea, but verses 25 and 26 correct her: the judgment takes place *now*, in the very act of decision.

This interpretation was too profound to be understood by all, as we see from the ecclesiastical emendations of 12:48 ('on the last day') and 6:39–40, 44 ('I will raise it up at the last day'). Even more characteristic is the addition of 5:28–29, flatly contradicting 5:25. Judgment is the major theme running through whole sections of the Gospel (3:1–21, 31–36; 4:43–46, 59; 7:15–24; 8:13–20). Moreover the κρίσις and κρίμα which Jesus and his work execute are thrown into relief by the evangelist's arrangement of his material: chapters 2–12 set forth revelation to the world, and chapters 13–17 (20) revelation to the community of believers. Finally the 'historicization' of Antichrist. He is no longer a mythological being, but the very *Wie* of those who refuse to believe: in short there are as many antichrists as there are unbelievers (1 Jn 4:3 and especially 2:18: 'Now many antichrists have come').

(3) John's view of the incarnation and his stern rejection of Docetism in any form, also show that Christ is not a metaphysical being: Jesus is so much a man that he seems to be nothing but a man. Before one can perceive the Word of God in him one must first be saved. According to the synoptic tradition, the divine in Jesus is visible *before* a man gives up his unbelieving *Selbstverständnis*. While still remaining devils, the devils recognize him as the Son of God (Mk 1:24; 3:11; 4:8 and elsewhere; p. 158, above). Jesus is envisaged as something of a *Mirakel*. We have seen how Paul—at least in all essentials—washes his hands of this approach. John does the same. So well hidden is the Word of God in Jesus that he seems to be only a man like other men; nothing about him gives any hint of his being the Son of God. He is totally human: ὁ λόγος σὰρξ ἐγένετο.

Hence the evangelist has no theory about any miraculous entry of the *Logos* into this world. He has no acquaintance with legends of a conception by the Spirit and a wondrous birth at Bethlehem, which reveal a craving to see and touch the divine and which adulterate the otherness of Jesus. Or supposing he did know of those accounts, then it is the more remarkable that he will not associate himself with anything they say. On several occasions he deliberately insists that Jesus comes from Nazareth and is the son of Joseph (1:45; 7:52), that his origin is known (7:27). He has the 'Jews' say: 'Is not this Jesus, the son of Joseph, whose father and mother we know?' (6:42). It is precisely on the grounds of this purely human origin that 'the Jews' will not believe in him. They would have a more 'Docetist' Jesus—one, that is, who manifests his divinity by an extraordinary birth and by the *Mirakel* he works.

(4) But does the Gospel of John not contain mythological statements which make Jesus a θεῖος ἀνήρ, one of those divine beings, so well known to the Hellenistic world, who are a sort of living *Mirakel*? Doubtless many texts do present him as such. For instance, he as it were sees through Peter and Nathaniel (1:42, 47f). He reads the Samaritan woman's past (4:17f).

But while using this traditional material, the evangelist transforms its meaning. He turns it into *symbols* which show that the believer knows himself to be steeped in God, knows that his true being is finally disclosed when he encounters the Revealer. When we are told in general terms that Jesus 'knew what was in man' (2:24f), there is no question of any miraculous power. His knowledge of man is based on his knowledge of God and his awareness of what a scandal God is to man. The same theme recurs in 5:42; 6:61f. In 16:30 the disciples proclaim Jesus omniscient ('We know that you know all things'); not because miraculous phenomena have proved him such, but because now Jesus has spoken 'plainly, not in any figure' (16:29). His supernatural knowledge in the episode of the raising of Lazarus (11:4, 11–14) was mentioned in the account of the miracle which John received from tradition and did not touch up at this point.

Of course Jesus foresees the betrayal of Judas (6:64, 70; 13:18), but here the main reason seems to be that the possibility of falling is a crucial theme in revelation: even disciples may go astray. There is no guarantee which faith can rely on, and the community must realize that the devil is at work even in their midst. The prophecy that the disciples will flee and the Christians will be persecuted (16:4a, 32; 15:18ff) is to be interpreted the same way: it is a case of foresight based on an exact understanding of revelation. Since Jesus is the revealer, he knows what awaits him (2:19, 21); he knows 'his hour' (13:1; 18:4; 19:28). Obviously his omniscience is not the miraculous knowledge of the Hellenistic 'divine men', but is bound up with revelation itself.

The theme that he was immune from capture before 'his hour' (7:30, 44; 8:20, 59; 10:39) shows how the fate of the revealer is not decided by any human will but rests in the hands of God.

(5) We likewise see that Jesus is not a divine event which can be objectively grasped, from the changes John made in the traditional idea of miracle. These have already been examined. If Jesus himself never considered that his miracles proved anything, we know that the community soon turned them into more or less evidentiary signs and invented many more to the same purpose. John used a σημεῖα-source, but eliminating its apologetical and probative features. He turned *Mirakel* into a σημεῖα that a man can only understand by giving up his old *Selbstverständnis*.[6]

(6) We know that Jesus himself did not claim to be the Messiah and that his life was not a messianic life. We also know that Mark invented the theory of the secret in order to cover up this fact which he quite wrongly thought was awkward: Jesus was indeed aware of being the Messiah during his lifetime, but he only revealed this truth to a handful of people, sternly forbidding them to let it be known (pp. 67–8, above).

John turned this theory inside out. In his Gospel men fail to recognize Jesus as the Messiah because he proclaimed that he was *not* the Messiah, not because he concealed what he was. Instead the *Logos* so truly becomes flesh that everything comes down, for natural man, to this mere Jesus of Nazareth 'whose father and mother we know'. Mark thinks that Jesus's messiahship would be, *of itself, visible*, unless he deliberately concealed it: the devils, though they are the epitome of unbelief, have seen it and Jesus peremptorily bids them hold their tongue (Mk 1:25, 34; 3:12 and elsewhere). In John, the messiahship is, *of itself, absolutely invisible*. All through this Gospel Jesus preaches in vain that he is God's messenger, God's δόξα; 'the Jews' see nothing, because his divine character can only be perceived by one who believes in him and whose *Verständnis* he becomes.

(7) In accordance with all that we have said, John also transformed the widespread and much-favoured Christian idea of the 'facts of salvation': the death and resurrection of Christ. He 'derationalized' them even more thoroughly than Paul had done. Death and resurrection are not of themselves the doing of God. What matters is the person of Jesus. In other words everything about Jesus, or rather the whole Jesus, manifests God's δόξα. That is why John takes no interest in his

---

6. Ch. 7, pp. 122–6, above.—Of course the σημεῖα-source takes for granted the historical authenticity of the miracles it recounts: Jesus actually did change water into wine, cure the man born blind, raise Lazarus from the dead, and the rest. When he made signs out of these *Mirakel*, did the author of the fourth Gospel still believe in their objective reality? Bultmann observes that we can by no means be so sure about the miracle at Cana as people generally say we can (EJ, p. 83, note 4). In any case the matter is of very minor importance (p. 126, above).

death as such, insofar as it is a particular phenomenon, distinct from his birth, for example. Death simply marks the end of Jesus's mission (6:62; 17:5). Hence the crucifixion is first and foremost his ὑψωθῆναι (his lifting up or exaltation; 3:14; 8:28; 12:32, 34) and his δοξασθῆναι (glorification; 7:39; 12:16, 23; 13:31f; 17:1, 5). There is no question of the Pauline σταυρός or ἐσταυρομένος; and where Jesus foretells his death, the being-lifted-up or exalted and the being-glorified have displaced the ἀποκτανθῆαι (being-put-to-death) and the σταυρωθῆναι (being-crucified) of the synoptic prophecies.

Christ's death is not a catastrophe which has to be made up for, as it were, by his resurrection. On the contrary: *as* his death it is the exaltation of Jesus, which means that it is interpreted as the doing of God *in the same way* that all Jesus's life is. The evangelist is not interested in it as a particular event—as suffering willed by God, for example. He speaks neither of Jesus's πάσχειν nor of his πάθήματα. Except for 3:14, the necessity (for the Messiah to suffer and die) of which the synoptics speak (Mk 8:31 and elsewhere) is not found in John; and in that one passage it refers precisely to the ὑψωθῆναι.

The death of Jesus is a particular phenomenon only in the sense that it marks his *definitive* victory. By that death he leaves the world to return to his Father and receive from him the fullness of heavenly δόξα. It only sets Jesus's glory free, so to speak. For even in this world he was the revelation of God, since anyone who saw him saw the Father (14:9–11); but at his death the world is conquered, the veil which hid the revealer is lifted, he receives from God the glory he had with him before the world was made (17:5). The cross is the judgment of the world, the annihilation of natural man—that is to say, the event of everlasting life and glory for Jesus and for all who believe in him.

Now we can see why the notion of Jesus's death as a sacrifice in expiation of sin does not figure prominently in John. At the utmost, a few passages adapt it to the theology which then prevailed in the Christian community. This is the case with 1:29 and 1 Jn 3:5, where the verb αἴρειν does not mean 'take upon himself' but 'take away', 'blot out'.

No doubt the metaphor of the lamb, which the evangelist draws from tradition, necessarily turns the mind to sacrifice. But nothing forces us to suppose that here John saw this sacrifice in the bare act of death and not in all Jesus's acts, as he normally does. On the other hand 1 Jn 1:7 certainly refers to expiation. But there is reason to think this text an editor's gloss; 1 Jn 2:2 and 4:10 are probably the glosses of some editor as well. (On 19:34b, interpolated by the ecclesiastical editor, 6:53–56, and 1 Jn 5:6, see TNT, p. 407.) However that may be, it is certain that the theology of the evangelist is in no way shaped by the theme of expiatory death. Had he taken it up because it was a traditional theme, it would have remained a foreign body in his work.

Significantly, John does not relate the institution of the Eucharist, which does make Jesus's death an expiatory sacrifice. He replaces it with the farewell prayer, in which the phrase 'For their sake I consecrate myself' clearly alludes to the liturgical words used at the Lord's Supper; but it assigns no particular role to the death itself, which is thought of simply as bringing Jesus's mission to an end. For his whole life is a sacrifice, in the sense that God sent him to men (3:16; 10:36). We are not told that this sacrifice is an expiation for sin. In all the Gospel of John the forgiveness of sins is mentioned only once, in a verse (20:23) that quite obviously comes from the source the author is using (EJ, p. 537). When he speaks for himself about the forgiveness of sins, John does it differently: man is delivered by the word of Jesus or by the truth that word conveys: 'The truth will make you free' (8:31) from sin (verse 34). We find the same declaration in 15:3.

Thus John demythologized the death of Jesus more thoroughly than Paul had done. For Paul as for John, of course, Jesus is God's action; but whereas Paul still uses the mythological category of expiatory sacrifice in order to convey this *Dass*, John conveys it without recourse to any mythology at all: Jesus's death has the same salvific import as the rest of his life.

(8) Nor does any special weight attach to the resurrection, since Jesus is already glorified by the cross. He does not need the resurrection to counterbalance his death, as it were; because the cross is already his triumph over the world. The hour of the passion is the judgment of the world (12:31–33). It is over the Jesus of the passion that the prince of this world has no power (14:30). This Jesus it is who overcomes the world (16:33). We are not told (as in Phil 2:11; Eph 1:20f; 1 Pet 3:21) that the resurrection makes Jesus Lord over the cosmic and demoniacal powers. It is not from the resurrection that he derives his power to diffuse life: the Father has granted the son to have life 'in himself' (5:26). Long before his resurrection, he is the resurrection and the life (11:25), the way, the truth, and the life (14:6). Long before his resurrection, any man who believes in him has eternal life (5:24f; 11:25f).

Unlike the synoptic Jesus, the Johannine Jesus does not foretell his resurrection. True, on one occasion the evangelist himself incidentally mentions it (2:22); but we see in 12:16 that what is involved is not any return of Jesus to this world but his glorification. The resurrection as a *Mirakel* can be found only in the editorial gloss of 20:9 and in the epilogue (21:14), likewise the work of an editor. Nowhere in John's Gospel do we find the words ἀναστῆναι and ἐγερθῆναι by which the synoptics designate precisely that kind of resurrection.

We need not wonder that the evangelist, following tradition, includes the Easter narratives. The point is, what meaning does he give them? These narratives are linked with the original ending of the Gospel: 'Jesus did many other σημεῖα' (20:30), which indicates that the apparitions themselves must be taken as σημεῖα, in accordance with John's general approach. They illustrate Jesus's eschatological victory over the world. To the extent that they are objective events,[7] they are like the miracles: no one *should* have any need of them. They are concessions to human weakness. 'Have you believed because you have seen me? Blessed are those who have not seen and yet believe' (20:29). We have already explained the meaning of this text. Let us merely add that the evangelist ends his book with this reproach of Jesus, and must have a good reason for doing so. He means to criticize the sham faith which constantly requires signs, in the sense that 'the Jews' attached to this word. He warns against the temptation to expect more of apparitions than they can give. They are, and can be, only symbols—or rather professions of faith in the risen Christ.

John's refusal to grant the resurrection any special significance also emerges from the farewell discourse. The Easter promise (16:16–24) and the 'I will see you again' are paralleled by another promise: 'I will not leave you desolate; I will come to you' (14:18). The reference is to the parousia: 'I will come', and not 'I will come again'. But the sequel, 'Yet a little while, and the world will see me no more, but you will see me; because I live, you will live also' (verse 19), mingles the two promises. For in John's eyes the resurrection of Jesus and his parousia are the same thing.

A third promise parallels the other two: the promise of the Spirit (14:15–17)—that is, of Pentecost. Easter, Pentecost and the parousia are not three different events but one and the same thing. That is why the language proper to Easter and that proper to the parousia are always being intermingled. On the one hand 14:19 and 16:16, 19, 22 speak of the temporary parting at Easter, and 14:21f of Jesus's manifestation to his disciples. On the other hand 14:3, 18, 23, 28 speak of the coming that is the parousia; 14:20 and 16:23, 26 give us the typical eschatological phrase 'in that day'; and 16:25 another: 'the hour is coming'. In between comes the promise of the Spirit: 14:15–17, 26; 15:26; 16:7–11, 13–15. So there is only one event, which of course is not an objective reality but the eschatological triumph Jesus wins when faith surmounts the scandal that he is to natural man.

The victory Jesus has won over the prince of this world is his having

7. Here again it has not been established that the evangelist himself believed in the objective reality of the apparitions (which he relates as he has them from tradition; GV 3, p. 205).

made possible the faith which sees in him the revelation of God. Jesus's 'I have overcome the world' (16:33) is answered by the believer's confession: 'This is the victory that overcomes the world, our faith. Who is it that overcomes the world but he who believes that Jesus is the Son of God?' (1 Jn 5:4–5). Here there is no question of a supernatural objective event which a man first perceives without giving up his 'insistence' and then believes in. We are explicitly told so in the brief dialogue between Jesus and Jude (14:22–23): the Father and Jesus manifest themselves by dwelling in the believer, and the Spirit does likewise (14:17).

Finally, the parousia obviously cannot be a cosmic event at the end of time if, as we have said, the mere coming of Jesus is already the judgment of the world. This explains why the synoptic prophecies of the son of man's coming in the glory of his Father and on the clouds of heaven (Mk 8:38; Mt 26:27, etc.) are completely absent from John's Gospel.

(9) In short, 'the "facts of salvation" in the traditional sense play no part in John . . . The totality of the event of salvation—the incarnation, death and resurrection of Jesus, Pentecost and the parousia—is reduced to a single event: revelation' (TNT, p. 411). All that the evangelist had it at heart to say was this one thing: that Jesus is the salvific word (deed) of God. And he said it by demythologizing the pre-existence, the incarnation, the life, the death, the resurrection and the parousia more thoroughly than Paul had done.

E

The confession of faith known as the Apostles' Creed in one of the most perfect mythological expressions of the New Testament's underlying meaning, because it stresses the objective character of the 'facts of salvation'. What Paul and John meant to show was that the 'facts of salvation' are not of the slightest importance, because they can be interpreted in a thousand different ways. So far as faith is concerned, what gives them their real 'objectivity' is the fact that they betoken the intervention of God. Consequently the categories of pre-existence, incarnation, expiatory death, resurrection and parousia are only symbols (inadequate ones) of the divine *Dass*.

Without any *objective* incarnation, death or resurrection, Jesus would be no less the one who calls man in question, judges and saves him. All that matters is that in him God summons us as the Lord who condemns us and pardons us. Men, and men alone, have more or less *rationalized* his deed in Jesus of Nazareth: it is their 'work' (in the Pauline and Lutheran sense of the word).

(1) Jesus had no consciousness whatever of being the pre-existent Son made flesh. He never paid the slightest heed to his pre-existence, his miraculous conception, his birth of a virgin, to the angels, shepherds and wise men of Bethlehem. Nothing, absolutely nothing he ever said or did permits us to think that he considered himself the hero of this mythology. Quite the contrary. Everything indicates that he considered himself a man in every sense of the word, a man born in Nazareth, whose father and mother everybody knew, who had brothers and sisters. All these things the unrevised synoptic tradition makes perfectly clear; Paul takes them all for granted and John heavily underlines them.

Are we saying that the idea of the incarnation is meaningless? Certainly Jesus considered himself the 'incarnation' of God, but in the demythologized sense that we have explained (ch. 9, § III a, above). He announced that the time of salvation had begun with himself; that in him, and him *alone*, God encountered men to condemn them or save them. He represented himself as the *eschatological* event which decides the fate of mankind, as the *Anrede* of the Wholly Other, as the grace of God in person. 'Such is the meaning of the ὁ λόγος σὰρξ ἐγένετο: we are told that an historical man and his fate, perceptible as historical phenomena, capable of evocation in our memory, no different as historical phenomena from any other historical phenomena —are the eschatological event!' (KM I, p. 226).

The mythological incarnation was born of the craving which *homo religiosus* has in every age to *control* the divine through prodigies and *Mirakel*. There is *nothing* Christian about the idea of a pre-existent divine being who becomes flesh: that is the very definition of Gnosticism. The theme of a miraculous birth is no less specifically pagan, as historical criticism has amply proved to the satisfaction of any mind that does not confuse faith with the objectification of faith. Plato himself was born of a virgin . . . Jesus is the incarnation of God in the sense that God is so well hidden in him that he seems to be a mere man: no *Mirakel* points him out as the Word of God which judges and saves. He is an utter scandal to natural man. Only one who makes him his *Verständnis* perceives the *Deus revelatus* in him: 'Blessed is he who takes no offence at me' (Mt 11:6).

(2) Jesus attached no particular importance to his death. He did not predict it, much less consider it a sacrifice of expiation for the sins of men (Mk 10:45 is an alteration by the Hellenistic community of an older saying recorded in Luke [Lk 22:27]. Mk 14:22–24 comes from the liturgy of the Hellenistic community, replacing an old text of which traces remain in Lk 11:15–18).

This mythology can only have rationalized what Jesus really was—

and that long before his death: the grace of God in person. Even the most orthodox theologians have always admitted that Jesus's death is only of value because he is the Word of God. The category of expiatory sacrifice is nothing but a highly ambiguous expression of faith in him as the saviour. The bare cross strikes terror into the heart of *homo religiosus*: how shall he believe that the Crucified is God's saving deed if his death is like all other deaths, if it does not, so to speak, bear the sacred seal of expiatory sacrifice?

(3) Jesus did not think he was going to rise again in the *objectified sense* of the Easter narratives. Much less did he predict any such resurrection. If it were taken seriously, and not seen as the *naive* symbol of a higher reality, the mythological idea of the resurrection would be a kind of blasphemy against God, because it would make him ridiculous. Death is the deepest anguish known to man, for in it he sees his whole fate. To give one's life for another is an act of infinite significance, because the one who does so knows that he is giving everything. But a pre-existent divine being who dies knowing that he will rise again on the third day is obviously only playing at death (KM I, p. 20).

Now playing such a game with God must either be mythological naivety or else blasphemy. No, Jesus entertained no such idea of his resurrection. We have seen with what sobriety he speaks of the ζωή which life in the kingdom will be (pp. 160–61, above). Everything militates against his having considered himself the θεῖος ἀνήρ of the apparitions. 'It can hardly be doubted that Jesus did not speak of his death and resurrection as salvific facts' (JS, p. 179); in other words, that he did not attach any special importance to them within the context of his work as a whole. His person was God's saving event; he in person was the Word of God, quite apart from his death and his resurrection *regarded as Mirakel*. Of course the Easter narratives express what he was, but they do so in mythological terms that were altogether alien to him.

(4) To sum up, when the tool of historical criticism is used in a spirit of faith it enables us to distinguish in tradition between what Jesus claimed to be and the semi-mythological idea which his disciples had of him. He represented himself as the Word of God in all its utter purity, otherness and transcendence. And so the labour of demythologization takes us to Jesus as the word (deed) of God, to what he himself thought he was and said he was. Insofar as the Christian community objectified him through the mythological categories of pre-existence, the virgin birth, the expiatory death, and the miraculous resurrection, it did not *over*rate him but rather *under*rated him, by making him more or less a 'work'.

On the other hand when Paul and John demythologize him in the way we have examined, they simply rediscover Jesus himself: so that the Jesus of Paul and John is no mere Jesus of Paul and John. Bultmann has often been accused of giving these latter a kind of priority over the synoptics. In fact the only person Bultmann has any interest in is Jesus, the Word of God, whom he finds first of all in the synoptic tradition stripped of its mythological elements. Paul and John matter to him only insofar as they speak of Jesus, or rather insofar as Jesus himself speaks to us in them unencumbered by mythology, 'plainly' and 'not in any figure' (Jn 16:29).

IV

THE RATIONALISM OF ORTHODOXY

The thesis of Lutheran orthodoxy is best formulated against Bultmann in a collective work under the editorship of E. Kinder,[8] which has been given a kind of official standing in Germany. No one can quarrel with the *purpose* of Lutheran orthodoxy: it wishes to safeguard the transcendence of God and of his revelation in Jesus Christ. But the whole issue is whether the way the orthodox go about upholding that transcendence will not bring it crashing to the ground.

Lutheran theologians make much of what they call the 'facts of salvation'. For they do not mean to get bogged down in the metaphysical dogmatics of the ancient Church. They reject the categories of nature and supernature. They speak of history and suprahistory. Revelation, they say, must be looked at from an *historical* point of view: only so 'do we take the realness of the Bible seriously and bring it to light'.[9] They dismiss all philosophies, ancient or modern, sticking to the 'facts of salvation' alone.

Consequently matters shape up as follows. God acts within history in an objective way. His Son objectively became man. He is the objective manifestation of God's love. He worked objective miracles. The theophanies of his baptism, his transfiguration, and the rest are objective realities. Jesus's sacrificial, expiatory death is an objective event, as are his resurrection and ascension.

Such are the 'facts of salvation', which (our theologians say) have an

---

8. *Ein Wort lutherischer Theologie zur Entmythologisierung* (1952). See also *Für and wider die Theologie Bultmanns, Denkschrift der Ev. theol. Fakultät der Universität Tübingen* (1952), which we shall not examine here.

9. *Ein Wort lutherischer Theologie . . .* , p. 33.

'objective reality', are 'objective' or 'historical truths'.[10] They are 'perceptible', 'verifiable events'. They exist *ante et extra nos*. On the other hand 'genuine knowledge of these events as God's revelation can be had only by faith'.[11] Or again: 'The objective truth of these salvific events cannot in itself be the grounds for faith'.[12] Or again: these events have to do 'with realities which cannot be judged of by historical means'.[13] Or again: 'Revelation is always something more than history, it is not history alone but it does not exist without history'.[14]

Thus on the one hand we are told that 'faith as faith knows itself to be grounded in, produced by, achieved by the *facta*';[15] and on the other hand, that the objectivity of the *facta* cannot be the grounds for faith. The first point must necessarily be affirmed, because otherwise faith would only be a creation of man's; we would be miles away from the New Testament, in which 'fact is the first presupposition of faith, which comes second'.[16] The second point must necessarily be affirmed, because otherwise faith would be a mere 'holding-to-be-true', and without faith a man could accept the facts of salvation.

Orthodox theologians, who accuse Bultmann of philosophizing, think they are not themselves philosophizing when they express themselves in such language as this. Now if there was ever a case where the parable of the mote and the beam applied, this is it. To go on and on about 'objectivity', 'truth', 'reality', or 'history' and 'suprahistory' is to use a vocabulary that necessarily implies a whole philosophy. All these terms cannot be endlessly repeated without attaching a quite definite meaning to them, and a meaning that relates (whether or no the speaker realizes the fact) to a whole conception of the world. Here we come back to the old question: What is objectivity? What is reality? (ch. 1, above). No doubt, the objectivity which Bultmann's adversaries attribute to the *facta* of revelation is of a special kind. It is not, so to speak, purely objective. In Bultmann's terms, it is not sheer *Gegebenheit* since it requires faith in order to be perceived. Accordingly

10. It is hardly necessary to say that the terms *history* and *historical*, in this section (IV), which we devote to a discussion of orthodox theology, must always be understood in the ordinary sense. Where we place them in inverted commas, that is only because they are quoted from Lutheran theologians.

11. *Ein Wort lutherischer Theologie* . . . p. 80.

12. *Ibid.*, p. 48.

13. *Ibid.*, p. 49.

14. *Ibid.*, p. 80.

15. *Ibid.*, p. 51.

16. *Ibid.*, p. 79.

it is *supra-objective*. Revelation is *at once* objective and supra-objective' historical and supra-historical.

The trouble with this conception is evident. Two contradictory things are asserted about the event of salvation: on the one hand its objective reality and therefore its 'historical verifiability' (*historische Fixierbarkeit*), and on the other the fact that 'it cannot be grasped by human thought'[17] and 'is only accessible to faith'.[18] The incarnation, Jesus's miracles, his redemptive death, his resurrection, his ascension, are objective events—since they take place in history—and supra-objective events—since they can only be perceived by faith. Their objectivity proves to be at once earthly and more than earthly. It eludes the grasp of natural man, and in this sense is transcendent; but at the same time it is objective, so that it turns out to be historical *precisely* as being suprahistorical and suprahistorical *precisely* as being historical. For example the risen Christ is a suprahistorical being because faith alone can perceive him, and an historical one because even as risen from the dead he is truly of this world. He is historical precisely as a suprahistorical being, and suprahistorical precisely as an historical being. This, we are informed, is the paradox of the Word made flesh, its objectivity *sui generis*: the suprahistorical qua suprahistorical becomes historical, and the historical qua historical becomes suprahistorical.

In reality this paradox is only a compromise and the rationalist prejudice involved in it is all the more tyrannical for escaping the attention of its authors. This Christ who is at once objective and supra-objective is only a super-hypostasis, a supernatural being. As we have said, orthodoxy claims to reject metaphysical ideas in favour of historical ones. The truth is that it cloaks the old natural metaphysics of the human mind in a pseudo-historical disguise: its very language betrays the fact. Over and over, the authors of the aforesaid book call revelation a suprahistorical event; but the better to show what they mean, they bracket this epithet with the epithet 'supernatural' (*übernatürlich*), put into inverted commas as though they were ashamed of themselves.

Now the instinct which moves them to couple these two terms is a perfectly sound one, for the idea of supra-history goes back to the Enlightenment. The Enlightenment regarded history as the sphere of the contingent and the transitory. Therefore truth was to be sought in timeless things: it was precisely the supra-historical. Evidently this modern notion springs from the same source as the notion of the super-

17. *Ibid.*, p. 20.
18. *Ibid.*, p. 80.

natural in the old metaphysical theology. The difference between them is a purely verbal one. All that orthodoxy does is revive the old theory of the natural and the supernatural: supernature is simply the upper storey of nature, the supra-objective the upper storey of the objective, and the supra-historical of the historical. On this basis the position of Bultmann's adversaries is plain enough. Insofar as Christ is a *supra-historical* being, faith is needed to perceive him; insofar as he is a supra-*historical* being, he is a thing of this world. The whole issue is whether the notions of supernature, superhistory or the superobjective are not a rationalist compromise between the categories of natural man and the thought of the Bible—whether they are not a mythologization.

(1) By maintaining that the objectivity of Christ is a supra-objectivity, orthodoxy acknowledges that faith is necessary in order for one to perceive him. The incarnation, the virgin birth, the theophanies of Christ's baptism and transfiguration, his miracles, his Easter apparitions, are events which must be believed. Thus the orthodox seem to ward off Bultmann's charge that they neglect eschatology. But in reality the faith they talk about is only a sham faith. For they say that a man must *first* believe in the supra-objectivity of Christ, that a man is transformed and saved only on account of that first belief. Giving up his old *Selbstverständnis* is the mere *consequence* of adhering to the supra-objective Christ; the two things do not coincide.

The orthodox thesis is the same as the thesis of Schweizer, who asks Bultmann to draw a distinction 'between one act of faith which sees the cross as the revelation of God's love and a second act of faith, for which the first has only freed a man . . . that consists in a radical change of *Selbstverständnis*' (quoted by Bultmann in KM 2, p. 202, note 2). 'No, not for anything in the world', is Bultmann's answer (*ibid.*). For that would be imagining that a man can assent to revelation before he makes it his *Verständnis* or, in Pauline language, that I can believe in the Crucified before I allow myself to be crucified with him, that I can know him before he has pardoned me. Orthodoxy fails to heed the depth of sin: *Nondum considerasti quanti ponderis sit peccatum*! Man's guilt is such that he cannot possibly perceive Christ as God's deed until he has been pardoned and justified.

The faith that orthodox theologians talk of is a sham faith, because it can exist without one's having first received a totally new *Selbstverständnis* from God. According to them, therefore, one can and must believe in the suprahistorical Christ *before* experiencing his *beneficia*. This is to fancy that I can recognize Christ's divine otherness before I depend on him, before he has become my Lord. It is to suppose that I can think of him as existing *ante et extra me* and at the same time *pro me.* He need not deliver me from every vestige of my sin before I can confess him as the Word of God: on the contrary, it is when I have acknowledged him as the Word of God, by an antecedent act of faith, that he will become my saviour. Now here is rationalizing with a vengeance. Christ can be recognized before he becomes the mode of *being* (the *Wie*) of the man who is in search of him. At heart, orthodox faith is only a watered-down 'work': for it does not require that a man *altogether* despair of himself before he can know Christ. Bultmann reminds us that Luther envisaged faith quite differently from the theologians who nonetheless give out that they are speaking in his name in their 'Ein Wort *lutherischer* Theologie' (see KM 2, pp. 203–4).[19]

(2) And yet do the orthodox not admit that the act whereby I believe in Christ must be the same act whereby he becomes my *Sichverstehen*—the act, that is, by which I am pardoned and justified? For they look on the event of salvation as a supra-history, thus confounding *incarnation* with *objectification* and lapsing into a version of the old Docetist heresy. Docetism consists in fancying that Jesus is not completely human—in other words, that his divinity is not altogether invisible. The Word only pretended to become man, because the miraculous element in him enables us to recognize that he is not exactly like us. As has been pointed out, in the New Testament as scripture (though not as revelation) there are unmistakable traces of Docetism, which John in particular has tried to eliminate. Orthodoxy is Docetist because the supra-objective Christ whom it preaches did not really become incarnate: the divine in Jesus *crops out* in such a way that man can believe in him before being justified by him. The Word did not become altogether flesh; he did not become flesh to the extent of being imperceptible by the kind of bargain-basement faith we have been discussing, which does not reach the length of radically transforming a man's being.

How else, then, could the divine be thought of but as an upper storey of the human? Precisely because the suprahistorical Christ is *supra*-historical, he must be more or less perceptible. He is not eschatological enough, or (what comes down to the same thing) well enough hidden in the flesh, for the divine in him to show no hint of itself. There is something of the pagan θεῖος ἀνήρ about the Christ of orthodoxy.

Bultmann asks: 'Does Christ help me because he is the Son of God or is he the Son of God because he helps me?' (GV 2, p. 252), and all he has ever written replies: He is the Son of God because he helps me.

---

19. See also F. Gogarten's *Die Verkündigung Jesu Christi* (1948), pp. 306–7, to which Bultmann refers.

Orthodoxy, for its part, declares: He helps me because he is the Son of God. This assertion is made out of the unconscious rationalism we have denounced again and again, which fails to see that true otherness only comes into being through what may be called a *redemptive relationship*. For me, Christ is the Wholly Other only because he makes me wholly other. A Christ who was not the saviour by his very being but only by reason of his role or mission, would not be the Wholly Other; for in order to know him man would not have to despair of himself altogether. How can the other be the other if I need not become it in order to reach it? If it can exist for me without my giving up myself, then it must be akin to me and therefore is not sheer otherness.

The otherness of the other is, so to speak, in proportion to the degree of change which it has to effect in me before I can *let it be itself*. Since God is the *Wholly* Other, I cannot recognize him as such until he has made me *wholly* other—that is, until he is my saviour. *He does not save me because he is God, he is God because he saves me.* So far as I am concerned, it is because he is *pro me* that he exists *extra me*. Only when Christ transforms me has he no kinship with me; so only then is he himself. He is Lord only when he brings man to bow the knee before him (Phil 2:10–11). Here we must cast back to what we have said about true 'objectivity' (pp. 19–21, above). By ignoring those principles, the orthodox imprison themselves in monism and self-reliance so far as language goes, whatever their intentions may be.

(3) Perhaps that is why certain of their spokesmen brand Bultmann a dualist. Given their semi-rationalist outlook, the charge is inevitable. As we have seen, Bultmann does not admit that the divine as such can be objectified, even in suprahistorical terms. God is so well hidden in Jesus that he cannot be reached even by that first act of faith of which the orthodox talk. But does this justify the charge of dualism? Not in the least; for we have demonstrated at length that I can only perceive Christ once he has become my *Selbst*-Verständnis.

The criticisms of Bultmann cancel themselves out by contradicting each other. On the one hand the complaint is that he makes God so transcendent as to rule out any possibility of an incarnation. The truth is that his adversaries think of the relations between transcendence and immanence entirely in the naturalist categories which we have criticized. They have not realized that Bultmann sacrifices neither the remote God to the intimate God nor the intimate God to the remote God, but rather labours to clear up the original connection between the two as revealed to us by the New Testament.

(4) Finally one must ask whether orthodoxy does not set up the absurd in place of the mysterious. The event of salvation, we are told,

is an 'objective reality' that can be 'historically verified' and yet 'cannot be grasped by the human mind'. We are dealing with 'an event which is purely and simply suprahistorical but which occurs in history'.[20] The 'history of God is an event verifiable in history, which however cannot be historically grasped in its true nature'.[21] How can that be? What, pray, is 'an event which is purely and simply suprahistorical but which occurs in history'? To make shift with the plea that here we are confronted by a reality *sui generis*[22] is getting off too easily and blinding oneself to the fact that one confuses the incarnation of the divine with its objectification.

V

THE TROUBLE WITH CONSERVATIVE EXEGESIS

No one questions Bultmann's competence as an exegete. Ultra-conservative critics, Catholic and Protestant alike, are guided by his work. Their very clashes with him are the best proof of the hold he has over them. No doubt most New Testament specialists would subscribe to this judgment of Karl Jaspers (whose passages of arms with Bultmann we shall consider elsewhere): 'Bultmann's research as an historian is exceptionally sound and enlightening. His rare honesty enables him to face awkward facts without jibbing—for example, when he admits that Jesus made mistakes. I must say, as one who is not a specialist, that I have learned as much from him and from Dibelius as I have from all the other contemporary theologians put together' (KJRB, p. 53). 'Bultmann is a first-class scholar' (*ibid.*, p. 54). But impressed as they are by Bultmann's authority, conservative exegetes are shocked at his critical radicalism. They revere the keen mind of the researcher and his findings appal them. Why?

It must be said that the work of these exegetes suffers from philosophical assumptions of which they are unaware. They are quite sure they are not philosophizing. Indeed philosophy is anathema to them. With Cullmann they announce their abandonment 'of deep methodological considerations', saying that they recognize 'no other method but the historical and philological method which has stood the test of experience', no other attitude towards a text than 'an unqualified readiness to listen honestly to what it says'. And so, Cullmann goes on,

20. *Ein Wort lutherischer Theologie* . . . , p. 26.
21. *Ibid.*, p. 18.
22. *Ibid.*, p. 52.

'we shall understand and explain a text without any regard to our own philosophical or theological "opinions".'[23]

Such statements only obscure the real problem. In reality any exegete, simply because he is a human being, has a certain way of looking at things and judging them, and his judgments as a philologist and historian are necessarily reached within the categories of this thought. The less those categories are criticized, the more utterly he will depend on them. The more naive one is about one's philo-sophizing, the more truly one does philosophize. It is always the old story of Monsieur Jourdain and his prose in *Le Bourgeois Gentilhomme*: '*Vous faites de la prose sans le savoir*'. For man to philosophize is as natural to him as breathing. If an investigator thinks he has no philosophy, that is because he has the philosophy of the man in the street. His exegesis is all the more 'slanted' for his being unaware that it is. Let us cite one or two examples.

As an historian, we have seen, Bultmann thinks that Jesus did not consider himself to be the Messiah. Conservative exegetes take the opposite view. Do they do this on purely exegetical grounds? Is it not rather out of *anguish*? Do they not fancy that faith is in danger if Jesus had no messianic consciousness? But why do they fancy faith is in danger unless it is because they think with the aid of certain philo-sophical categories which here are hopelessly inadequate? We have seen an exegete of Cullmann's stature declaring in the preface to his *Christologie* that he will disregard his philosophical and theological view so as to understand the New Testament; yet *two* pages later he says that unlike Bultmann he envisages the 'role of Christ' as an '*ontological* christological event'.[24] Now what is ontology? Is it not as plain as day that a man who speaks of ontology is philosophizing? How then can he claim that 'We shall disregard our own philosophical and theological "opinions"?'

If one takes it for granted that belief in Jesus is bound up with the category of the Messiah (son of man), then certainly one is no longer free—if one is a Christian—to doubt the messianic consciousness of Jesus, and exegesis must go along willy-nilly. But what if that bond derived from a set of ideas that are inappropriate to revelation? We have seen that messianic consciousness as such in no way expresses divine otherness. If conservative exegetes have it so much at heart, that is because they turn Jesus into a higher kind of *Was*, thrusting upon him the framework of the philosophy that is instinctive to common sense, that the various Christian orthodoxies take for granted and the

23. O. Cullmann, *Christologie du Nouveau Testament* (1958), p 8.
24. *Ibid.*, p. 11, note 1; my italics.

New Testament itself takes for granted to some extent and in a mythological form.

Now what if purely exegetical considerations forced Bultmann to retreat from his position and admit that Jesus really was conscious of being the Messiah? As a believer, could he accept the change which had been forced upon him as an historian? The answer is obvious. Whether Jesus had a messianic consciousness or not neither adds anything to nor detracts anything from what he really is: God himself as present and at work among men. So Bultmann could perfectly well accept that Jesus had a messianic consciousness. On the plane of exegesis, which is the plane of the *Gegebenheit*, he is as free as the breeze. The conservative exegete is not; because by virtue of unexamined philosophical assumptions he thinks of the divine as a higher kind of *Was* and not as a *Dass*. Consequently to say that the categories of the Messiah, the son of God, and the rest come from the community and not from Jesus himself, is in his eyes jeopardizing faith. But when one has realized that these concepts are possible ways of saying that Jesus is the Word of God, then it matters very little whether he himself used them or not. All that really matters is his *being* the event and advent of God.

Here is another example. Conservative exegetes are always reticent about the profound differences—in some respects the gulf—which the critics cannot help seeing between Palestinian Christianity and Hellenistic Christianity. (We have seen some instances of the differences and shall see more.) It is no accident that Catholic orthodoxy is the firmest opponent of the difference. It is no accident that in Protestantism the various orthodoxies are likewise most set against the difference. It is no accident that the more orthodox the exegete is theologically speaking, the more he insists as an historian that the radical critics have exaggerated the difference and that it must be 'cut down to its proper size'.

Cullmann thinks 'we must discard the strict pattern of a Jewish primitive community versus Hellenistic Christianity. The sharp distinction which it is usual to draw between the theology of the Gentile Christian Church and that of the Church of Jerusalem, is not tenable... It has now been shown that there is no such startling contrast between them.'[25] Generally speaking, over the past thirty years Protestant exegetes have done their best to show that the New Testament is rooted almost entirely in the tradition of the Old Testament and Judaism, as far as possible discounting the contribution made to it by Hellenistic syncretism. They have thought they were doing this for

25. *Ibid*, pp. 282, 283.

purely historical reasons, but in fact their (pseudo-) scientific position is more or less dictated by the religious disquiet we mentioned above: the fear that faith will crumble if too much is made of the pagan contribution.

There is panic because Bultmann attaches such importance to Gnostic myth and the mystery religions, because he says that the sacraments in their definitive form, various legends (like the virgin birth, for example), many sayings and miracles attributed to Jesus, and so forth, go back no farther than the Hellenistic community. This fear is felt because an unconscious assumption makes people envisage the incarnation of the divine as its objectification. So the conservative exegete is not easy in his mind until he has contrived to show that the various images by which the New Testament conveys the meaning of Jesus actually derive from Jesus himself. He lavishes an ingenuity worthy of a better cause on proving what can never be proved—that all the New Testament categories go back in substance to the historical Jesus. It never occurs to him to wonder whether certain themes of pagan origin do not convey what Jesus was and claimed to be, better than certain patterns of Jewish thought do, as Paul and John judged was the case (pp. 55–60 and 168–9 above; pp. 290–96, below).

Protestant exegesis today has generally drawn back from the positions held in the age preceding ours; because most of its representatives, as Christians and as theologians, are supporters of the religious renewal which began about 1920. Obviously it would be naive to suppose that the great investigators of the liberal period produced faultless work that need not be superseded. But the vital question is *how* it shall be superseded. Are we to adopt the attitude of those Catholic theologians who think that the only thing to do in philosophy is return to Thomas Aquinas, paying no heed to Descartes, Kant and Heidegger? The exegetes of today run just such a risk. A craving for *theological security* that is in turn based on an *unconscious philosophical security* leads most researchers to abjure the critical position of their predecessors rather than strike out beyond it; whereas 'the critical work of earlier generations must not simply be allowed to fade away, it must be taken up again in a positive spirit' (KM I, p. 24).[26]

---

26. Let us give one final example of the danger we are warning against. It is by no means uncommon to meet young Protestant exegetes who profess the utmost contempt for the theory known as that of the two sources, which they consider 'has had its day'. Some of them thought very highly of L. Vaganay's book *Le problème synoptique* (1954), without sufficiently reflecting whether its scientific approach was not more or less dictated by the philosophical and theological assumptions of Catholicism or, at a deeper level, by a certain need for dogmatic security. Bultmann is not alone in his opinion that the book 'fails to carry conviction' (GST, *Ergänzungsheft* [1958], p. 5). Some of the best Catholic exegetes

The *purpose* of conservative exegetes is sound: they aim to safeguard the originality and transcendence of the New Testament. But setting revelation as they do on the plane of supra-objectivity—which is only the philosophy of natural man touched up for the occasion—they are forced to do history violence of one sort or another. Hence the disquiet which their exegesis leaves in the mind of all who regard *absolute honesty* as one of the first things God demands.

In 1927 Bultmann wrote with reference to criticisms of his book *Jesus*: 'People wonder why I have not yet been burnt at the stake. Men of the sagacity of Althaus and Traub have even disclosed that Barth and Gogarten would save me from my [critical] scepticism. They must forgive me, but I find their sagacity a source of merriment. I have never yet felt ill at ease about my critical radicalism; on the contrary, my mind is perfectly at ease. On the other hand it often seems to me that my conservative New Testament brethren feel very ill at ease, for I always find them busied with salvage operations. For my own part, I watch the blaze with equanimity; for I see that what is going up in flames is only the χριστὸς κατὰ σάρκα' (GV 1, pp. 100–1).

In a text of 1931 Bultmann writes that the New Testament has been subjected to criticism, that as a result our knowledge of this historical Jesus has become 'problematic' (GV 2, p. 16), and that Christianity seen thus in the context of the history of religions seems to be one relative thing among a host of others. But the aim of Christian preaching, he goes on, is not to inform its hearers about a 'scrap of the past' as an object of science, that we might reject or accept on grounds of historical criticism. Faith tells us that God was at work in what happened then, 'however it happened' (*ibid.*). Now 'historical science can in no way control this affirmation, either to confirm it or invalidate it. For the fact that this word [of God's judgment and his forgiveness] and the proclamation of it are the doing of God, lies beyond the reach of historical observation' (*ibid.*).

Accordingly we can understand why there has been and always will be a conservative exegesis: it is a datum of the human mind just like the natural metaphysics of that mind, on which it relies. So long as the incarnation of God in Jesus is thought of as an historical-suprahistorical reality, so long as the virgin birth, the theophanies of the baptism and

---

agree. Thus Père Levie, subjecting Vaganay's work to minute critical examination, defends the theory of the two sources (at least so far as is compatible with the decrees of the Pontifical Biblical Commission) and concludes with these words: 'We feel that it would be a mistake to give up the findings accumulated by so many earlier labours, on the strength of Monsieur Vaganay's book' (J. Levie, 'L'évangile araméen de S. Matthieu est-il la source de l'évangile de S. Marc?' in *Nouvelle Revue Théologique* 76 (1954) 843.

transfiguration, the apparitions of the risen Christ, the ascension and the parousia are believed in as objective-supraobjective events—in a word, so long as the New Testament is understood in terms of categories that thwart its real purpose—history will never be done justice. Moreover, one may incur the gravest responsibility by causing others to lose the very faith one means to defend. We have already recalled Bultmann's saying that he and his friends would have led a wretched life at any of the orthodox universities (pp. 62–3, above).

Bultmann has always said that one of the great virtues of liberalism was its absolute critical honesty (GV I, pp. 2–3). But basically liberal theology was vitiated by the same weakness as orthodoxy—that of sticking on the plane of the *Was*, though in a different way. In order to save the faith, orthodox critics more or less outrage history by attributing to Jesus himself the later ideas which Christians formed about Jesus. Liberal critics and critics belonging to the history-of-religions school respect history, by recognizing, for example, that Hellenistic Christianity was radically different from Palestinian Christianity. But they fail to see the *oneness* of the two Christianities because, as we have explained (§1, above), the eschatological dimension of the *Dass* is missing from their thought.

'When the primitive community calls [Jesus] the Messiah, it is saying in its own way that it has understood him. This insight, that what really matters is the *Dass* of preaching, solves the great riddle of New Testament theology, which is to know how the herald became the heralded, why the community did not simply proclaim the ideas of Jesus's preaching, and moreover why Paul and John almost entirely disregard the content of that preaching. The "riddle" arises because what people look at is the "religious and moral" ideas, the conceptual content, instead of the event. Then they discover a twofold gospel— two preachings, each with its own type of thought—and to account for it construct an evolution of ideas that is either spontaneous or the effect of outside causes. This is fair enough so far as ideas themselves are concerned, but it is missing the main point' (GV I, p. 266)—the main point being that Jesus is a *Dass*.

If liberal critics and those belonging to the history-of-religions school perceived that Hellenistic Christianity borrowed many of its categories from the pagan syncretism of that day, they nevertheless did not realize that these images were 'means of expressing the significance of Jesus's person as the decisive eschatological action of God' (GV I, p. 267). So it is the business of historical science to determine what concepts Palestinian and Hellenistic Christianity used in order to confess that Jesus was the Word of God. And by that very fact the critics 'show that each age and culture must necessarily say the decisive thing [that Christ is the salvific event of God] in categories of its own' (GV I, p. 266). In short, the proper field of exegesis is *Historie*, the sphere which man controls and can know scientifically. In so saying we establish both the importance of exegesis (which orthodoxy does not sufficiently recognize) and its limitations (which liberalism does not sufficiently recognize).[27]

27. Here let us point out once for all that as this book cannot be expanded we shall be unable to set forth a major aspect of Bultmann's work. We refer to the scientific grounds for his statements in the matter of New Testament criticism. Time and again we have said, and shall say, that this account is legendary, that that verse or section of the synoptic gospels or of John is an interpolation, that such and such miracles were invented in order to illustrate some saying of Jesus, and the like. Now all we can do is say these things; we cannot prove them. To recapitulate a critical study is inevitably to destroy it. Thus in the matter of Jesus's messianic consciousness we were only able to touch upon the historical basis for Bultmann's position. A careful examination of his own books is the only answer here. Let us say no more than this: we are sure that minds which insist on complete scientific honesty and unshakable scientific proof will find those books *an answer to prayer*, as Karl Jaspers very aptly observed in his opinion of Bultmann as an historian (p. 191, above). To read them after soaking for years in Catholic or conservative Protestant exegesis is deliverance for good and all from the endless compromises of orthodoxy, which are bound to distress anyone in love with intellectual exactitude. As for the contemporary scholars who claim to strike out beyond *Formgeschichte*, dip into their work and you find that as often as not their strides forward are strides backward. Obviously *Formgeschichte* must be superseded, like everything else in this world; but to confuse the search for truth with the search for security is not an advance, it is a retreat.

CHAPTER TEN

Tradition, Church, Sacrament

The Church, as an eschatological society, is only another name for God and Christ. God is present and at work in it through preaching and sacrament—if these are interpreted in a demythologized sense, of course; if we realize that through preaching and sacrament the salvific event summons us to answer. Thus the Church is the *Verstehen* of the Christian community, its *eschatological* mode of being. We shall show that this is the case by first explaining what Bultmann understands by tradition.

I

TRADITION

The concepts of otherness and tradition are inextricably bound up together. Science does not raise the question of tradition; for it concerns itself with the world of objects, of which I have at least a rudimentary knowledge. When I am taught that Caesar conquered Gaul, or that there are so many kinds of mushroom, the tradition or handing on of that knowledge is *accidental* to it: what I am being taught I can find out for myself. We have seen that rational knowledge does not require a man to destroy his in-sistence. With ec-sistentiell knowledge the case is different: it gives me a true future. Here communication of the knowledge is part of its very *nature*.

When someone offers me his friendship, his communicating it to me is an essential part of it: by myself I cannot create the ec-sistentiell possibility of friendship: it is a gift of the other. The communication of what is communicated is what is communicated. I cannot possibly teach myself that my wife or my children love me. I do not know that they do until they have admitted the fact to me by their outward and inward attitude. And their outward and inward attitude towards me are their very love, which is essentially a relation to me. Their love coincides with the 'tradition' of it to me. Evidently I cannot transmit it to myself; I cannot determine myself by it, which would simply be determining myself by myself. In this respect I entirely depend on them; it is for them and them alone to give me this new being which is sheer gratuity. Thus the idea of otherness necessarily involves the idea of tradition.

By definition, otherness must be given, transmitted; to give it, transmit it, to oneself would be to destroy it. So the giving and transmitting of otherness is part of otherness. If an event is really an event, it must be 'delivered' (*traditum*). If I find it by myself, then it is only an object that I control. 'Tradition is part of event itself' (GV I, p. 160), a 'co-constituent' of it (*ibid.*, p. 332).

When we turn to salvific event, which is the very otherness of *God*, the idea of tradition takes on crucial importance. Man cannot discover it for himself. Of course he can know by himself that there once lived a certain Jesus of Nazareth who claimed to be the Word of God, he can have a scientific and objective knowledge of Christianity; but he can only become a Christian if he is encountered by the eschatological *Dass*—which is to say, if this God is delivered to him by an authentic tradition. Christ being the grace of God in person, we cannot reach him in our own way, where we please and when we please. We can only find him if he first finds us. Now it is in the Church of word and sacrament that he finds men. If the event of salvation were only an objective event that went on between the years 1 and 30 there would be no need of tradition. But because a transcendent dimension makes it what it is, it still endures, still lives and ceaselessly delivers itself to us in its salvific otherness—that is, in the Church. The Church is that event itself, ever present and ever at work: as an eschatological reality the Church is none other than Christ himself constantly summoning men in order to save them—is the very *Anrede* of God.

Bultmann holds that 'the word of Jesus constitutes the whole of his person' (GV I, p. 264). He has often been accused of diminishing Christ by thus reducing him to the kerygma. This happens simply because people think of person and word in terms of naturalist categories; they think of the person as a subject of which the word is an attribute, and of course on that basis to reduce the person to the word is to evaporate the person. But when Bultmann says, with John, that Jesus is the word and only the word, he means to stress the fact that the historical personality of Jesus is not his real *being*. What he was as an earthly phenomenon, his human traits, his piety, and the rest—all that is Christ known κατὰ σάρκα, with which Paul and John will have nothing to do. The true Christ is the Christ who is the Word of God—the Christ of the kerygma. Christ as the *Deus revelatus* has no connection with Christ according to the flesh. Otherwise we would only be dealing with the founder of a new religion.

When Bultmann keeps saying that Christ exists only in preaching, he does not mean that Christ is preaching—he means that preaching is

Christ. In it 'the event of Christ ceaselessly happens' (GV 1, p. 289), 'is continued' (*ibid.*), so that Christians of today have no reason to envy those of long ago who saw and touched Jesus; for in so doing, the first Christians did not see or touch the Word itself; just like us, they could only *believe* in it. Saying that Jesus is the kerygma is only another way of stressing his otherness—that is, his real *being*, which is not of this world although it meets us in this world. The kerygma is the prolongation of the *logos* made flesh, so that in the eyes of faith there is no favoured era. Paul is so far from regretting that he never knew the historical Jesus that he says he has no wish to know him (2 Cor 5:16).[1] Christ known according to the flesh may easily create the false impression that the divine in him is an objective reality; whereas being the revelation of God, he is the *Thou* which summons me and which I do not know until I have made it my *Verständnis*.

Hence it comes about that Paul and John do not dwell on the historical Jesus but on the Christ of the word, who is God himself as judging and pardoning us. Paul knows that the word he proclaims *is* Christ himself and that the hearer is summoned by Christ himself: 'We are ambassadors for[2] Christ, God making his appeal through us. We beseech you on behalf of [or in the place of] Christ, be reconciled to God' (2 Cor 5:18-19). The fact that Christian preaching brings death and life (2 Cor 2:15-16) is proof enough that Christ judges and saves in it. (Such is the whole burden of 2 Cor 2:14 to 6:10.) Just as Christ is 'the power of God' (1 Cor 1:24), so the preaching is 'the power of God for salvation to every one who has faith' (Rom 1:16). The 'now' of the preaching is the 'now' of Christ and salvation (2 Cor 6:1-2). The fact of salvation is contained in the preaching (Rom 10:13-17). 'Faith comes from what is heard, and what is heard comes by the preaching of Christ' (verse 17). We have seen, indeed, how John reduces Christ to the word (ch. 8, §IV and ch. 9, §III d, above). Thus 'Christ is present is the word [of preaching]' (GV 1, p. 260). Preaching is the *tradition* (in the active sense) of Christ: it 'delivers' him to us. Or more accurately, he delivers himself in it.

In short the idea of tradition is rooted in the transcendence of God, whom man can never control and who therefore can only be

---

1. Does the κατὰ σάρκα of 2 Cor 5:16 refer to the objects ('no one' and 'Christ') or to the verbs? The grammatical answer in no way affects the sense. For to know Christ according to the flesh (assuming, as is more probable, that κατὰ σάρκα refers to the verb) is simply to know him insofar as he is a being of this world and fail to recognize him as the Word of God. Accordingly a Christ known κατὰ σάρκα is a Χριστὸς κατὰ σάρκα (TNT, pp. 238-9).

2. Bultmann thinks that perhaps we should even translate this word 'in place of' (GV 3, p. 19).

'delivered'. He delivers himself in Christ, who is his word. The word
lives on in the apostolic message, in scripture which gave it set form,
and in the preaching of the Church. In the Church the incarnation is
continued: 'A man such as I am myself preaches the Word of God to
me; God's *Logos* becomes incarnate in him' (KM 2, p. 206, note 1). It
is not something in the past, 'it is always event in the event of its proclamation' (*ibid.*). Sacrament is another form of the tradition of Christ,
as we shall see in the next section.[3]

II

THE PRIMITIVE COMMUNITY AS AN ESCHATOLOGICAL COMMUNITY

(1) We have said that Jesus is the advent of God. As a preacher of the
Word he gathered together a certain number of men, taking them
away from their homes and their work, and they bore him company
on his wanderings (Mk 1:16–20; 2:14). But by so doing he did not
found an order or sect, nor a 'church' in the sense of a visible religious
society; for he summoned everyone to a decision that was *eschatological*
in nature.

Against all the recent attempts to show otherwise (notably that of
Cullmann), Bultmann bluntly declares that the words of Mt 16:17–19
were put into Jesus's mouth by the Palestinian community.[4] This does
not mean, of course, that they represent an error, much less a hallucination. Quite the contrary, they express the consciousness which the first
disciples had of being the *eschatological* community. They show that the
disciples had discerned the Word of God in Jesus and that in turn they
looked on themselves as the community of those who are no longer
of this world. The text we are speaking of calls them the community
whose leaders hold the keys of the kingdom of heaven, the community
which is a sort of entrance-hall to the kingdom. Against it the forces
of hell will be powerless. It is the 'little flock' to which God has given
the kingdom (Lk 12:32).

The theme of the 'Twelve' is also of eschatological significance. The
saying that they will judge the tribes of Israel when the kingdom of
God has appeared (Mt 19:28; Lk 22:29–30) must by no means be
attributed to Jesus himself (GST, pp. 65, 170f, 176). But again this does

3. It will be obvious why Bultmann does not accept the Roman idea of tradition,
which is largely set on the plane of the *Was*—that is, in Catholic terms, on the
visible and institutional plane. Hence the weight attached to apostolic succession,
the papacy, doctrinal tradition, the magisterium, institution of the sacraments by
the historical Jesus, and so forth. Here again Bultmann 'derationalizes'.

4. Critical discussion in GST, pp. 147–50, 277f, and in *Theol. Blätter* 20 (1941)
265–79.

not mean that its content is false. In it the Twelve are envisaged not as an ecclesiastical hierarchy but as eschatological symbols. They are a certain number of men who preached the Word and were less an institution than an embodiment of the community insofar as it considers itself the true Israel. So this theme is only another way in which the community testified to its consciousness of being something more than earthly.

The same must be said of the term ἐκκλησία (Mt 16:18 and elsewhere). What Aramaic word does it represent? Almost certainly the word which in Hebrew was *qahal*. In Judaism *qahal* had taken on an intensely eschatological meaning, for at that period the people of God were scattered, weakened and enslaved. That is why Judaism expected from God's future alone the gathering-in of the people, the 'manifestation' on the last day of the 'true Israel', the 'community of the saints'. The existing community was only that of the 'poor', the 'godly', who looked forward to the eschatological event with a longing that is well known. By calling themselves God's *ecclesia*, the disciples of Jesus plainly showed that the community they formed was the one which fulfilled that expectation and all the hopes of apocalyptic literature. And therefore its members bore the eschatological titles of the 'elect' and the 'saints'. (These expressions are attested in Paul but go back to the primitive community.) Henceforth God's *qahal* was a fact, no longer a mere hope; but of course an eschatological fact which was the determination by God of the lives of believers.

(2) We have seen that Jesus never instituted any sacrament. The legendary narrative in Mt 28:19 about baptism simply reflects the practice of the Hellenistic community. But there was nothing to prevent the Palestinian disciples from reviving the baptism of John and making it a rite of initiation into the eschatological community; for that was only saying in another way that Jesus was God's grace bestowed on the world.

It is a delusion to suppose that one can only regard sacrament as one of the forms of God's action (the other being preaching, as we have said) by tracing its 'institution' back to Christ according to the flesh, which inevitably means sacrificing historical truth. To be sure, conservative exegetes claim that that institution *is* the historical truth; but alongside the arguments which they think valid there is always the philosophico-theological assumption (whether avowed or not) that the divine is merely a higher sort of *Was*. Hence the effort to connect the sacraments with Jesus on the plane of visible things, of data.

By contrast, liberal exegetes are honest as the day is long; but the eschatological significance of a sacrament does not come home to them. In fact a sacrament is a means of saying that man does not control grace. Christ is not an historical phenomenon of the past, he is the very manifestation of God, which therefore must be handed on or handed over (be the object of a *tradition* in the active sense of the word). The Church is this tradition of Christ, which it effects through preaching and sacrament. Or more precisely, the Church is Christ himself delivering himself to us in preaching and sacrament, so that 'the sacraments stand beside the Word as a *verbum visibile*; for they do nothing else but what the Word does: like it, they make present the fact of salvation . . .; like it, they contain both the possibility of bestowing life and the possibility of wreaking judgment (1 Cor 11:29)' (GV I, pp. 180–81). Thus it is the χριστὸς κατὰ πνεῦμα who 'instituted' the sacraments. In other words, they do not stand on the plane of the *Was* but on the plane of the *Dass*.

The orthodox outdo themselves to trace the sacraments back to the earthly Jesus because they regard the event of salvation as an historical-suprahistorical reality, something 'supra-intra-mundane'. Here again they fall victim to the objectifying idea of the incarnation which we never weary of condemning. The liberals are models of scientific honesty, or at least have ample scope for being such; but they do not know what to make of sacrament, theologically speaking, and to all intents and purposes leave it unexplained. At best they take it for a symbol, which is to stall on the level of psychology and sociology. They do not really see that a sacrament is the very *Anrede* of Christ in person.

(3) The eschatological character of the primitive community also finds expression in the common meals (the 'breaking of bread'), where, the obviously revised tradition of Acts 2:42–47 informs us, ἀγαλλίασις prevailed—that is, a mood of eschatological joy. Chapters 9 and 10 of the *Didache* give us some idea of these celebrations, although it is impossible to tell whether, or to what extent, the prayers used go back to the primitive community. They bear witness to the eschatological spirit which filled the hearts of those Christians. Hellenistic Christians looked on Jesus as the author of a sacramental meal, just as they believed him the author of sacramental baptism. The words of Mk 14:22–24 are taken from the eucharistic liturgy of the Hellenistic community, which thus recast the account of Jesus's last meal with his disciples. Only fragments of that account survive, notably in Lk 22:15–18 (we have put the later additions into brackets):

> I have earnestly desired
> to eat this passover with you
> [before I suffer];
> for I tell you

I shall not eat it until it is fulfilled
in the kingdom of God.
[And he took a cup, and said:
Take this, and divide it among yourselves;]
For I tell you
that from now on I shall not drink
of the fruit of the vine
until the kingdom of God comes.

Even this text has been coloured by legend; but possibly it overlies an old saying in which Jesus expressed his certainty of eating the next (paschal?) meal with his disciples in the kingdom of God (JS, pp. 29, 130, 179; GST, pp. 285–7).

Here again the Hellenistic Church was not 'innovating' when it turned Jesus's last meal into a sacrament. At most it was mythologizing. The Eucharist is indeed the *Anrede* of Christ himself or, if you prefer, is Christ himself as an *Anrede*. On the level of meaning and the *Dass*, the last meal of Jesus and the Hellenistic sacrament are absolutely identical. Liberal theologians and orthodox theologians make the same blunders about this sacrament that they do about baptism.

(4) The community received the Spirit—that is, the supreme eschatological gift. Jesus thought that when devils fled before the Spirit that was at work in him, the kingdom of God must have come (Mk 3:28f; Mt 12:28 ?; see Lk 11:20). Likewise the primitive community knows that it has been given the Spirit, which Judaism held to have withdrawn from Israel with the last of the prophets but which is promised at the last day. Moved by the Spirit, prophets arise once more, as we see in Acts 11:28 and 21:9ff. Paul (and the *Didache* as well) takes it for granted that there are prophets in the Church. Miracles are worked by the power of the Spirit (Mt 10:8; Mk 6:13; Acts 11:28; 21:20f)—which Paul also considers to be obvious (1 Cor 12:9, 28f).

In times of persecution the Spirit inspires Christians with what to say when they stand before the judge (Mt 10:19f or Mk 13:11). It is hard to say whether the manifestations of the Spirit in ecstasy and speaking with tongues, which loomed so large in the Hellenistic communities (1 Cor 14), had already been familiar in the primitive community. A phenomenon of that nature seems to underlie the legendary account of Pentecost (Acts 2:1–13), as can be gathered from verse 13.[5]

---

5. Here again it should hardly be necessary to point out that this account is legendary in respect of the mythological language used and the historical setting chosen for the gift of the Spirit; but that the reality of the Spirit and its sending to the Church are so far from being legendary as to constitute revelation itself.

(5) Inevitably the primitive community was organized on an eschatological basis. As we have observed, the title *the Twelve* was chosen less because they were the leaders of the community than because of its eschatological import. In fact, the 'Twelve' were not 'ecclesiastical authorities' but preachers of the Word in the Church and outside the Church. (Here Peter played the leading part, as Paul and the synoptic tradition make abundantly clear. The three 'pillars' were Peter, John the son of Zebedee, and James the brother of the Lord— Gal 2:9; see 1:18f.) For the only institution compatible with an eschatological community is that of the Word. Along with his reconciliation, God established the 'ministry of reconciliation', the 'message of reconciliation' (2 Cor 5:18f).

In the Christian community this ministry and message were the business of the Twelve, who at the same time were the custodians of tradition. Tradition, as we have said, is essential to a community which is not a human association but a thing other with the otherness of God himself. In it the undergirding eschatological event is preserved and made present, as the legendary account of the election of Matthias very well shows (Acts 1:21–22). Evidence that the tradition of the salvific event is hardening into a set kerygma is offered by 1 Cor 11:23 and 15:37.

Tradition demands continuity and therefore succession, but not in the institutional and earthly sense of those words. In Paul (see 1 Cor 12:28) and also in Eph 4:11f the succession is 'free'—left, that is, to the guidance of the Spirit. The apostle receives his vocation from his vision of the Lord and is then vindicated by his ἔργον, his missionary work (1 Cor 9:1). This means that 'all patience, signs and wonders and mighty works' are 'the signs of a true apostle' (2 Cor 12:12; see 1 Thess 1:5; 1 Cor 2:4f; Rom 15:9; Heb 2:4). Only in the pastoral epistles does the succession become an institution, do we come upon ordination by the laying on of hands.

In short, if the eschatological organization is still embryonic, if it is only an attempt at giving the community an outward look that will befit its transcendent nature, Christians 'still avoid the pitfall of considering the Church a religious institution that mediates salvation through its established order and its sacraments' (TNT, p. 66). To put it another way, they still avoid the danger of a mythologized, rationalized Church.

III

PAUL'S VIEW OF THE CHURCH

(1) We know what weight Paul attaches to preaching. Preaching is the presence and the action of God himself. Of course, like any word, it has a visible and earthly aspect. It can be looked at simply from the outside. An unbeliever sees nothing more in preaching than a phenomenon of the history of religions, just as he sees nothing more in Jesus than such a phenomenon. But to the believer, preaching is the Word of God; that is, Christ himself (ch. 9, §III c 5, above). It is the word that gives birth to the Church. It is the word that calls men and assembles them as an ἐκκλησία, making them the community of the κλητοί and the ἅγιοι. The Church is actually part of the eschatological event, being its presence. Just as the Word brings it into being, so it in turn brings the Word into being.

Only in the Church is an authoritative preaching to be found—that is, the 'ministry of reconciliation' and the 'ministry of a new covenant' (2 Cor 3:6ff); which means that apostolic preaching exists only within the framework of redemptive history, whose subject is the people of God. The apostles, to whose missionary labours the communities owe their existence, belong to the Church. Were Paul not certain that his work enjoys the approval of the primitive community—that of Jerusalem—he would consider that he 'had run in vain' (Gal 2:2).

The Church presents two aspects, one earthly and one eschatological, one historical and one 'historical', as is made quite clear by the fact that the word ἐκκλησία sometimes means the Church and sometimes the churches. On the one hand the Church is not a phenomenon of this world but belongs to the new aeon. On the other hand this eschatological community which is invisible as such, takes visible form in the individual communities. It finds its purest eschatological embodiment in the meetings for worship, where believers confess Christ as the Lord (1 Cor 12:3; Phil 2:11). In their 'assembly as a Church' (1 Cor 11:18) he is present and manifests himself by the workings of the πνεῦμα in the various χαρίσματα (1 Cor 14). Indeed God himself is present, 'inspiring them all in every one' (1 Cor 12:6); so that if an outsider is there as a guest and is called to account by the prophetic word, he will admit that 'God is really among you' (1 Cor 14:25).

The eschatological holiness that is manifested at worship determines the whole structure and life of the Church. Since the community is something more than earthly, all earthly differences have become meaningless there:

There is neither Jew nor Greek,
there is neither slave nor free,
there is neither male nor female;
for you are all one in Christ Jesus.
(Gal 3:28; see 1 Cor 12:13)

Paul means the same thing when he says that everyone is to remain in the state of life in which God's call found him (1 Cor 7:17–24). So the abolition of all earthly distinctions is not a social ideal or policy: it applies only within the eschatological community. As the temple of God (1 Cor 3:16f), the Church is set apart from the world round about it—that is, from those who are 'outside' (1 Cor 5:12f; 1 Thess 4:2) and who are ἄδικοι (1 Cor 6:1). Believers must be 'children of God without blemish in the midst of a crooked and perverse generation', shining 'as lights in the world' (Phil 2:15). It is taken for granted that they shun the worship of pagans (1 Cor 10:1–22), whereas the adherents of the mystery religions were allowed to participate in other cults (p. 52, above). Nor may Christians go to law in the pagan courts (1 Cor 6:1–8), although they must conscientiously do their duty towards civil rulers (Rom 13:1–7). They are not forbidden to have any dealings with 'unbelievers' (1 Cor 5:9f; 10:27).

The eschatological character of the community is not manifested in worship alone but radiates thence in an ordinary life that Christians lead together, as we gather from the texts referring to mutual duties and good offices such as 'help', 'administration', 'presiding', 'labour', 'service', all in a variety of forms (1 Cor 12:28; 16:15f; Rom 12:7f; 1 Thess 5:12).

When he proposes to demonstrate the transcendence of the Church, Paul may turn first of all to the categories of redemptive history, which were much used before him in the Christian community. Thus the Church is the 'new covenant' (2 Cor 3:6ff; 1 Cor 11:25), the 'Israel of God' (Gal 6:16). Abraham is the father of all believers (Rom 9:7ff; Gal 4:22ff). The Church is the end of redemptive history, because in it all the promises are fulfilled (Rom 15:4; 1 Cor 10:11). But he may also turn to Gnostic themes, as when he speaks of the σῶμα Χριστοῦ (1 Cor 12:27) or the σῶμα ἐν Χριστῷ (Rom 12:5; ch. 9, §III c 2, above). Here he is expressing two things: the oneness of the Church, and the fact that its origin lies beyond the will and doings of human persons.

The ἐκκλησία is not a society which unites people of the same *Weltanschauung*; although, seen from outside, it appears to be just that. Nor is it a gathering of pneumatic individuals, the pneumatic individual being such through his personal relationship with Christ. Paul combats this notion, which was taking root at Corinth (1 Cor 12:12–30). By rejecting it he does not mean to put forward instead the notion that the Church is a kind of organic σῶμα. Though he does use the metaphor of an organism, that is only incidental. His main idea is something else: it is not as differentiated individuals that the members make up the whole, not because his own singularity is irreplaceable that each member is as important as the next; rather they are all equal because they belong to Christ and therefore the differences among them do not matter (verse 12). The body is not constituted by its members but by Christ (thus too in Rom 12:5).

(2) (a) Baptism brings the individual into the body of Christ: εἰς ἓν σῶμα ἐβαπτίσθημεν (1 Cor 12:13); or to put it more simply, one is baptized εἰς Χριστόν (Gal 3:27; 2 Cor 1:21), so that Christian life is an εἶναι ἐν Χριστῷ (Gal 3:28). To belong to the Church is to be ἐν Χριστῷ (ἐν κυρίῳ) (Rom 16:7, 11; 1 Cor 1:30) and defined by the ἐν Χριστῷ (Gal 1:22; 1 Thess 2:14). So the formula 'in Christ' is not by any means a mystical formula—one which would refer to an individual relationship with Christ—but rather an ecclesiological one: it designates entry by baptism into the body of Christ, although there is not invariably a direct reference to baptism (for example see Rom 8:1; 2 Cor 5:17; Gal 2:17) and although the formula acquired the more general sense of the determination of man's life by Christ (standing in for the adjective 'Christian' when that word did not yet exist). Since the community which baptism ushers one into is something eschatological, the 'in Christ' obviously has an eschatological sense: 'If any one is in Christ, he is a new creation' (2 Cor 5:17). This meaning also emerges from the fact that ἐν Χριστῷ and ἐν Πνεύματι are interchangeable (Rom 8:9; 14:17). But baptism also bestows the Spirit (1 Cor 12:13; 2 Cor 1:22), so that the ἐν Πνεύματι is likewise an ecclesiological formula, though it is used in a wider sense.

We have spoken of the importance which Paul attached to preaching. The Word constitutes the Church. In the kerygma the event of salvation 'still goes on' (TNT, p. 312) and by believing in the Word that is preached one becomes a Christian. Now what connection is there between preaching and baptism? Does the one work the same way the other does, or must we speak of an *ex opere operato* (as in the mystery religions and, in a different sense, in Catholicism)?

Certainly Paul found that the Hellenistic Church interpreted Christian baptism as the mystery religions interpreted their own baptism. But he did his best to demythologize it ('denaturalize' it) by making it an *imperative* as well as an indicative. To be sure, one can hardly say that he quite succeeded. A baptism for the dead is mentioned in 1 Cor 15:29. (The Corinthians had themselves baptized for their dead, thinking that this baptism by proxy enabled the supernatural energies contained in the sacrament to become efficacious for the dead.) Now Paul, who of course did not himself introduce this custom, speaks of it without any censure; because the kind of idea it implied was familiar to him, as it was to all religious minds of that day. But it must be observed that he does not credit baptism with unconditional efficacity (of a magic sort), as though it guaranteed anyone's salvation. Just as the generation in the wilderness who received the prototypes of the Christian sacraments were not saved from destruction, so the warning 'Let anyone who thinks that he stands take heed lest he fall' is addressed to baptized Christians.

Moreover when Paul declares with all the solemnity befitting the occasion, 'Christ did not send me to baptize but to preach the gospel' (1 Cor 1:17), baptism is evidently very much subordinate to the Word. He who baptizes is not, as in the mystery religions, invested with a priestly character and the sacrament creates no mysterious bond between him and the person baptized, as was often the case in those religions.

Neither is the sacrament a bare symbol of what happens in the subject. Paul never gives the experiences of the baptized a thought. Baptism makes the eschatological event of salvation *present*, as the Word does. The only difference is that baptism does so for a particular individual. The saving event which is present in baptism must be personally *appropriated* just as in the case of preaching. We have evidence enough of the fact in Rom 10:9: 'If you confess with your lips that Jesus is Lord and believe in your heart that God raised him from the dead', which is almost unquestionably a confession that was made during baptism. So on the part of the baptized, baptism is a public confession of faith. Just as acceptance of the Word consists in a free acknowledgment of the Lord who summons me in it, so baptism subjects a man to the dominion of Christ. The ἐν Χριστῷ is at the same time a Χριστοῦ εἶναι—that is, a belonging to Christ (compare Gal 3:29 with 3:27f; 5:24; 2 Cor 10:7; Rom 8:9; 14:8).

If accepting the 'word of the cross' is nothing else but the readiness to let it become our *Verstehen* (our life), baptism likewise means being crucified with Christ (Rom 6:6), so that the indicative of death and resurrection with Christ through baptism becomes the grounds for the imperative 'Yield yourselves to God as men who have been brought from death to life' (Rom 6:13). Similarly the imperative of Rom 13:14, 'Put on the Lord Jesus Christ', corresponds to the indicative of Gal 3:27, 'As many of you as were baptized into Christ have put on Christ'. Thus when all is said and done baptism works no differently from the Word.

(b) Exactly like baptism, the Eucharist was also a sacrament of the kind found in the mystery religions: receiving the bread and wine automatically put one into communion with the crucified and risen Christ (TNT, pp. 146–53). Here again Paul did not altogether break away from the naturalist idea. Two facts show us that this is so. On the one hand he holds the effect of the Eucharist to be much like the effect of the pagan sacrament: the initiate become κοινωνοὶ τῶν δαιμονίων and Christians receive κοινωνία with the κύριος (1 Cor 10:20f). Moreover communicating unworthily causes bodily injury and even physical death (1 Cor 11:29f). But the substance of his thought is something else.

When Paul says in 1 Cor 10:16f that Communion makes all who partake of it into a single body, there can be no doubt that his idea of the body of Christ (which is 'historical', as we have seen) determines his idea of the Eucharist, ridding it of any trace of magic. And when he declares that the Lord's Supper makes Christ's death present as by a καταγγέλειν (a proclamation; 1 Cor 11:26), thus using the same word which he elsewhere applies to preaching (Rom 1:8; 1 Cor 2:1; 9:14; Phil 1:17f), it becomes evident that the Eucharist, like baptism, is ordered to the preaching of the Word, 'of which it is in the last analysis only a particular form' (TNT, p. 314). The particular feature of the Eucharist is that, like baptism, it applies the event of salvation to those who celebrate it and moreover creates an intimate bond among them (1 Cor 10:16f). (This latter effect is also the effect of preaching and baptism, but Paul does not dwell upon the fact.)

Thus in Paul's eyes the efficacy of the sacrament—notwithstanding the influence of the mystery religions—does not arise from the 'elements', from the eating and drinking, but from the sacramental action insofar as it is a καταγγέλειν. At any rate he does not, like Ignatius of Antioch, regard the Eucharist as a φάρμακον ἀθανασίας, receiving which guarantees one immortality. The warning in 1 Cor 10:1–12 against any complacency applies quite as much to the Lord's Supper as to baptism. To take part in the κυριακὸν δεῖπνον is to submit to the lordship of Christ.

IV

JOHN'S VIEW OF THE CHURCH

(1) We have seen that the 'facts of salvation', understood in the traditional sense, do not figure in the fourth Gospel and that the incarnation, death and resurrection of Jesus, Pentecost and the parousia are all reduced to a single, thoroughly demythologized event: the revelation

(or action) of God in the man Jesus of Nazareth. That is why nothing is heard of the sacraments either.

True, John is presupposing the ecclesiastical practice of baptism when he says in 3:22 that Jesus baptized disciples, although the correction in 4:2 (is this an ancient gloss?) explains that it was not he himself who baptized. At any rate the ὕδατος καὶ of the familiar text 3:5, 'Unless one is born of water and the Spirit, he cannot enter the kingdom of God', is obviously an ecclesiastical interpolation; for what follows has to do solely with being born again of the Spirit—there is no more talk of baptism. Moreover, if the Spirit were tied to the water of baptism that would contradict verse 8, which lays down that the Spirit is like the wind that blows wherever it will and whenever it will.

The washing of the feet is often considered to be a figure of baptism, but wrongly so. That episode illustrates the 'service' of Jesus in general, which makes the disciples clean. Now according to 15:3 they are made clean by the word he has spoken to them. In Jn 19. the ecclesiastical editor has also added a gloss (verses 34b and 35) on the piercing of Jesus's side. The 'anointing' which 1 Jn 2:20, 27 says the community has received, means the 'Spirit of truth', although one may wonder whether the word 'anointing' does not imply that this Spirit is bestowed by baptism.

A much mythologized version of the sacrament of the Eucharist has been interpolated into the Gospel of John by the ecclesiastical editors, not only in 19:34b but also in 6:51b–58. The 'living bread' to which there is reference in the text preceding verses 51b–58 is not the sacramental meal at all but (just like the 'living water' and the 'light') Jesus himself as the one who brings men life (11:25; 14:6). What is more, the idea of the φάρμακον ἀθανασίας, found in 6:51b–58, contradicts the whole Gospel of John, which, as we have stressed again and again, is the very antithesis of Gnostic mythology and naturalism. And finally the offence which the 'Jews' take (verse 52) at Jesus's offering them his flesh and his blood is not in the least the true Johannine scandal (which we have adverted to) of the Word made flesh.

It will be recalled that John says nothing about the institution of the sacramental Eucharist in his account of Jesus's last supper. To suggest that he is silent on the subject so as not to repeat the Synoptics, is naive or arbitrary. In fact he demythologizes the Eucharist by putting the high-priestly prayer in its place. As early as chapter 6 he sets aside the prevailing Christian idea (taken up again by the ecclesiastical editor and inserted in 6:51b–58), which made the gift of life depend on the sacrament, in favour of a concept that connects it with faith in Jesus as the revealer of God.

In the high-priestly prayer and the appended discourse we find the characteristic themes of the Lord's Supper: the community, grounded in Jesus's sacrificial death for his own, is united with him by partaking of his flesh and blood and thus becomes the 'new covenant' (1 Cor 11:23–34). But they are demythologized. It is as the hour of glorification that Jesus's death establishes the fellowship of believers with him and with each other. This is the sense in which he 'consecrates' himself for them (Jn 17:19). And it is not by the sacrament but by knowledge, faith and love that the disciples are united with him and with each other. The καινὴ ἐντολή displaces the καινὴ διαθήκη of the traditional narrative (1 Cor 11:25).

Thus John accepts the ecclesiastical sacrament but only in its eschatological meaning; the sacramental action as such is of no interest to him (EJ, pp. 370–71). In short, it is fair to conclude that he 'does not directly attack the sacraments but that his attitude towards them is critical and guarded, to say the least of it' (TNT, p. 412).

(2) Does all this mean that there is no Church in John's scheme of things? Quite the contrary. If unlike Paul he does not treat the Church as a separate theme, that is because the Church is in a sense his only theme.

(a) The life of believers is an eschatological ec-sistence delivered from the *world* and from *sin*. If the believer is in the world, he does not live by the world. He is in it without being of it (17:11, 14, 16). He is already beyond the reach of judgment, has already entered into life (3:18; 5:24f). Henceforth death lies behind him (8:51; 11:25f); henceforth he has life (3:36; 6:47; 1 Jn 5:12). Just as Jesus is a stranger to the world because of his 'glory', so are those who believe in him; for at his departure he gave it to them: 'The glory which thou hast given me I have given to them' (17:22).

What exactly is this glory which has become the believer's own? It is the *knowledge* that is vouchsafed to those who believe. That Jesus gives his disciples glory means that he gives them eternal life (17:2). But what is eternal life? 'This is eternal life, that they know thee the only true God, and Jesus Christ whom thou hast sent' (17:3). Now this twofold knowledge—which is really one, because God is known only in Jesus the revealer and the revealer is known only when God is known in him—is identical with the knowledge of the truth which is promised to those who believe (8:32), with the knowledge which sees God as the one reality and the world as a mere shadow. Of course, this knowledge of God is not an objective knowledge; it is a *Selbstverständnis*, a determination of the knower by the known, a mode of being. That is why man's relation to God and Christ is described as an εἶναι ἐν (15:3ff; 17:21).

Therefore knowledge is simultaneously *freedom*. The believer is independent of the world. Just as Jesus has vanquished the ruler of this world, who has no power over him (12:31; 14:30), so believers too have overcome the evil one (1 Jn 2:13f). To be delivered from the world is to be delivered from sin (8:31–36). Those who have accepted the service of Jesus (symbolized by the washing of the feet) are clean (13:10). What makes them so is the word he has spoken to them (15:3). He has 'consecrated' himself for them, so that they may also be consecrated in truth (17:19) and he prays to the Father: 'Sanctify them in the truth; thy word is truth' (17:17).

This prayer (and the one in 17:15: 'That thou shouldst keep them from the evil one') shows the real meaning of the indicatives we have set forth. John stands firm on the plane of 'historicity'. Deliverance from sin does not consist in the believer's being given a new, stainless $\phi\acute{v}\sigma\iota s$ for his own, so that like the Gnostic and the initiate in the mystery religions he can never sin again. Faith is not a state attained once and for all but a victory that must be won again and again over the world.

Texts which say that faith has overcome the world and that the believer can no longer sin (1 Jn 3:9) are, as the context shows, imperatives: they set before those who have been summoned by God the true nature of the faith for which their decision was made. The 'He cannot sin' of 1 Jn 3:9 does not describe the empirical state of the believer (as happens in Gnosis) but explains the import of faith. On the one hand a Christian does not sin (1 Jn 3:9; 5:18), and yet 'If we say we have no sin, we deceive ourselves, and the truth is not in us' (1 Jn 1:8). This paradoxical combination of 'walking in the light' and confessing one's sins is thrown into bold relief by 1 Jn 5:10. So the 'He cannot sin' does not give rise to a false sense of security but rather deepens the believer's consciousness of being a sinner: knowing his constant need of forgiveness, he also knows that he can always rely on grace if he lets Jesus Christ determine his relation to God: 'If anyone does sin, we have an advocate with the Father' (1 Jn 2:1).

(b) Delivered from the world and from sin, believers are able to observe the 'new commandment' which is the commandment of love. On the negative side, it forbids one to love the world or the things that are in the world (1 Jn 2:15)—which concretely means that one must shake off the bondage of $\epsilon\pi\iota\theta\upsilon\mu\acute{\iota}\alpha$ (1 Jn 2:16). On the positive side it requires one to do what is pleasing to God (1 Jn 3:22)—that is, to love one's brother (1 Jn 2:9–11). Loving one another is the real content of 'the commandments' or 'the commandment' (Jn 15:2; 1 Jn 3:23; 4:21). Here we once more find the dialectic of indicative and imperative: from the love that we have received there arises the obligation to love.

'A new commandment I give to you, that you love one another; even as (καθὼς) I have loved you, that you also love one another' (13:34). In this text καθὼς not only describes the nature of love but at the same time points to its foundation: 'If God so loved us, we also ought to love one another' (1 Jn 4:11). Precisely this eschatological indicative is what makes Jesus's commandment something new. On the plane of the *Was* the commandment of love has always been known, as 1 Jn 2:7 plainly declares by calling it an 'old commandment'. What makes it new, and perpetually new, is its being carried out now in eschatological existence.

In order to love efficaciously one must be free of the world, of sin and of oneself. Now only Jesus has given us that freedom. So what is new is love as an event: 'It is a new commandment . . . because the darkness is passing away and the true light is already shining' (1 Jn 2:8). 'We know that we have passed out of death into life, because we love the brethren' (1 Jn 3:14). These brethren are not Christians alone; for the eschatological community must bear witness (Jn 15:27) so that the circle of those who must be loved is constantly widening. Besides, the brotherly love described in the first Letter of John does not by any means seem limited to Christians (see 1 Jn 3:17).[6]

(c) Eschatological life is present as a 'life-in-the-revealer' or as 'the life-of-the-revealer-in-believers', so that they are one with each other and with him in a unity whereby they are also one with the Father, the Son being in the Father and the Father in the Son. Unity is both an ideal to be striven for and a promise: 'Abide in me, and I in you' (15:4) or a pure promise: 'In that day you will know that I am in my Father, and you in me, and I in you' (14:20). In his farewell prayer Christ says:

> The glory which thou hast given me
> I have given to them,
> that they may be one even as we are one,
> I in them and thou in me,
> that they may become perfectly one.
>
> (17:22f)

John may express unity in mystical language, in the texts that speak of a mutual 'knowledge' (10:2f, 14f, 27); or in apocalyptic language, in the promise that Jesus will return (14:18f, 28; 16:16f; and especially 14:23—'If a man loves me, he will keep my word, and my Father will love him, and we will come to him and make our home with him').

---

6. We shall devote a chapter to Christian love (ch. 12).

The former words no more refer to a mystical bond between Jesus and his disciples (see ch. 8, §IV 3, above) than the latter refer to an objective parousia. Eschatological existence is an existence in faith; it is not a natural affinity with Jesus or God and therefore not a direct contact with either; always it must cope with the scandal of the Word made flesh.

The disciples have no relationship with the glorified Christ which would dispense them from believing, at any rate until he has come for them (14:3) and shown them his glory (17:24). So long as they are 'in the world', the direct sight of him is denied them. 'Yet a little while I am with you. You will seek me, and as I said to the Jews so now I say to you, "Where I am going you cannot come" ' (13:33). They must rejoice at his departure, for unless he goes he cannot send them the Spirit (16:7). It is precisely in the Spirit that his return will take place. The old apocalyptic idea of a visible parousia, which was that of primitive Christianity, is now abandoned: the world will notice nothing at all when Jesus returns (14:21–23; see ch. 9, §III d 8, above).[7]

(d) Having the Spirit is really the final criterion of eschatological existence. 'By this we know that he abides in us, by the Spirit which he has given us' (1 Jn 3:24); or 'By this we know that we abide in him and he in us, because he has given us of his own Spirit' (1 Jn 4:13). In the farewell discourse the Spirit is called the Counsellor whom Jesus promises to his disciples (14:16f; 15:26; 16:13). Evidently the Spirit and the Counsellor are identical, since the latter is called the 'Spirit of truth' (14:17; 15:26; 16:13) or the Holy Spirit (14:26). So in the eyes of John, as of the primitive community, the Spirit is the eschatological gift. But he is no longer a power that works *Mirakel* and extraordinary phenomena (§II 4, above). He is thoroughly demythologized: he is the power in the Church whereby the Word is known and proclaimed.

First of all he makes the Word known. He is the 'Spirit of truth' who 'teaches all things' (Jn 14:26) and 'guides into all the truth' (16:13), so that those who have him 'know everything' (1 Jn 2:20f), without needing anyone to teach them (2:27). Of course the truth that he imparts is not a sum of information, an appendix to what Jesus has taught. The Spirit will only 'bring to remembrance' what Jesus has said (14:26). He will not speak 'on his own authority', he will declare 'whatever he hears' (14:26), because he only takes 'what is mine' (16:13f). He will only 'bear witness to me' (15:26). Thus he will not teach anything new on the plane of the *Was* but shed new light instead

---

7. If 1 Jn 2:28; 3:2; 4:17 are not interpolations by an ecclesiastical editor (and Jn 5:28–29 certainly is), then they must be interpreted according to the farewell discourse, notably 14:3.

on all that Jesus has said and done. He will fulfil the promise made to
Peter: 'What I am doing you do not know now, but afterward you
will understand' (13:7).

When Jesus says at his departure, 'I have yet many things to say to
you, but you cannot bear them now' (16:12), what he has in mind is
not a complement of dóctrine but a complement of meaning. For he
has said everything: 'All that I have heard from my Father I have made
known to you' (15:15). 'I have manifested thy name to men' (17:6).
'I have made known to them thy name' (17:26). But our text goes on
to say: 'And I will make it known'. The contrast of tense plainly
shows that the revelation made by Jesus is neither a sum of doctrine nor
a deed in the past but a thing that is ever new, a perpetual *Dass*. What
the Holy Spirit does is precisely to make the event of revelation ever
present.

We have seen that Jesus brought men no 'teaching' that can be set
down in propositions: he himself is the Word (pp. 130, 150–54, above).
But what he is, what his coming and departure mean—that is, the
κρίσις τοῦ κόσμου—must be constantly perceived more clearly and anew
at every moment in history. The Spirit 'bears witness' and 'calls to
remembrance' what Jesus has said, by making possible this eternally
new understanding of Jesus's word, which itself never changes. It
remains the same precisely because it is always new with its own
perpetual and eschatological newness. This is how the Spirit 'glorifies'
Jesus (16:14).

John seems to entertain a mythological (metaphysical) notion of the
Spirit when he calls him 'another Counsellor', as though the Spirit
were a duplicate of Jesus. In fact it is Jesus himself who comes to his
disciples in the Spirit, as we see from the very parallelism between the
promises which refer to the sending of the Spirit (14:16f; 16:12–15)
and those which refer to the return of Jesus (14:18–21; 16:16–24;
pp. 180–82, above). Hence we are told exactly the same things about
the Spirit as about Jesus: the Counsellor will not be merely 'with'
believers and 'dwell with' them (14:16f), he will also be 'in' them and
abide 'in' them (14:17; 1 Jn 2:27). Just as the world has not known
Jesus (8:19; 17:26), neither does it know the Spirit (14:17). Just as the
word of Jesus is 'heard' only by one who is 'of God' or 'of the truth'
(8:47; 18:37), so it is with the preaching of the Church (1 Jn 4:6).
Accordingly the Spirit is not a substitute for Jesus but his way of being
present to men.

He not only makes his word known, he proclaims it and has it proclaimed. We are told in 15:26 that the Counsellor bears witness to
Jesus, and the text goes on to say: 'You also bear witness'. Thus the
knowledge bestowed by the Spirit must be alive in the preaching that

makes the *Dass* of revelation present. This point is driven home by the ἐλέγχειν ('convincing') which the Spirit will do (16:7–11): 'He will convince the world of sin and of righteousness and of judgment', which means that in its preaching the Church must show the world what sin is—nothing else but rejecting revelation and faith—what righteousness is—Jesus's victory over the world—and what judgment is—the condemnation of the unbelieving world, for 'he who does not believe is condemned already' (3:18; 12:48). In other words, the eschatological event which took place with the coming and the departure of Jesus 'goes on' in preaching (TNT, p. 442). 'The operation of the Spirit in preaching is that eschatological event' (*ibid.*).

Brotherly love likewise manifests the same event (being itself an eschatological thing, as we have seen). The mission which believers have received, and the discharge of which gives meaning to the life of the community in the world, is this: seeing to it that the Church shall exist as an eschatological thing, as an 'envoy' just like Jesus the first 'envoy' (17:18); that, set apart from the world as the community of the 'consecrated' (17:17, 19), giving the world perpetual scandal and suffering its persecutions (15:18–16:4), and in union with the Father and the Son, it shall present the world with the constant opportunity to believe (17:20–23). 'Since it is Jesus himself who speaks in the word of the Church' (TNT, p. 443), wherever that word rings out 'the hour is coming, and now is, when the dead will hear the voice of the Son of God, and those who hear will live' (5:25). 'The Gospel of John, by accepting tradition and completely transforming it, shows how that word must ring out ever the same, yet ever in a new form' (*ibid.*).

(e) Such in substance is John's idea of the Church, which he does not treat as a separate theme. Never once mentioning it, he speaks of nothing else. The term ἐκκλησία is nowhere to be found in his writing, except for 3 Jn 6:9f where it simply refers to a local community. He shows no sign of interest in ecclesiology as such; he entirely disregards worship and Church organization. Indeed the third Letter hints that he is opposed to the ecclesiastical institution now taking shape. But he has, as we have seen, a keen sense of the eschatological community. True, he does not speak of it in the categories of redemptive history. In the tradition of the Old Testament and Jewish Christianity, the Church is the people of the last day in whom sacred history has reached fulfilment (p. 207, above).

John looks rather to the Gnostic vision, according to which the pneumatic form a potential whole that is activated when the redeemer gathers in the captive selves from their dispersion and unites them with himself (p. 53, above). Paul, as we have seen, used this idea. So does the fourth evangelist. But remarkably enough the theme of the σῶμα χριστοῦ, so prominent in the Pauline and deutero-Pauline writings, is not found in John and he has no word that means Church in the singular—only plural words. Those who have been gathered into the Church are called the μαθηταί of Jesus (see 13:35; 15:8), his φίλοι (15:33ff), or 'his own' (13:1; see 10:3f). We know that the latter concept is specifically Gnostic. This wholly plural usage serves to convey the thought that the Church is a community made up of individuals who have become Jesus's disciples by a decision of their own faith (see especially 6:60–71).

In one sense John envisages the Church as an 'invisible Church', to the extent that those who 'are of the truth' already belong to Jesus even though they have not yet heard his voice (18:37; 10:3). They become his own when they follow him in response to his call (10:1–6). Consequently their unity as the one flock is something that lies in the future (10:16; 17:20f) and it is incumbent on those who already believe to work for that end (17:18). Now scattered through the world, his own must become entirely one with him (17:21f). But this process of unification has begun with Jesus, so that little by little the invisible Church becomes the visible Church of his disciples.

To sum up, the Church is something we define negatively by its separation from the world, which hates it. In positive terms, it is the eschatological community, delivered from the world and from sin by its faith that is grounded in Jesus the shepherd and the vine. By that very fact it is the assembly of those who love one another. It does not perfect its transcendent character by holding aloof from the world, by ascetical practices or a sacramental worship. Being the Church of the Word, it lives by the Word which is also its business in the world. Its life is ruled by the Spirit, present within it as the power which causes it to know and proclaim the Word.

V

OBJECTIFYING THE CHURCH

(1) Even in certain of the New Testament books we find the beginnings of a rationalizing process that will end in ancient Catholicism. The transcendence of the Church is seen less in its perpetual future than in its present, as an institution. Slipping from the plane of the *Dass* to that of the *Was*, it tends to become a reality in itself, a religious institution which claims to mediate salvation through the sacraments and the priesthood. It is in this sense that Ignatius speaks of the 'catholic Church' (Smyrnians 8, 2), a sort of objectified duplicate of Christ which therefore loses its ec-sistential and 'historical' character. Instead

of being sheer relation to God and thus allowing him to be the Lord, it tends to control him. The Pauline and Johannine dialectic between the present and the future slackens; the Church becomes an intermediary between God and men, its transcendence the transcendence of a supernature. Instead of a community of salvation it becomes an organism of salvation. The Spirit is no longer the sovereign *Anrede* ceaselessly calling the Church in question: it sinks to the status of a power at the Church's beck and call as dwelling in the Church's institutions, especially in the sacraments.

This rationalization of the Church necessarily goes hand in hand with a new conception of the sacraments, already found in the vicarious baptism to which 1 Cor 15:29 alludes. Now baptism is not simply a form of the Word—that is, an *Anrede* which demands the decision of faith—now *of itself* it bestows divine life, that life being understood as a supernatural *attribute*. We have an example in 2 Tim 2:11 (which relates to baptism): 'If we have died with him we shall also live with him'; in Hermas: 'They had to rise . . . through water to receive life, for they could not enter the kingdom of God without having put off the mortality of their first life' (*Sim.* IX, 16, 2), or again: 'Your life was and will be saved by water' (*Vis.* III, 3, 5). By weakening the dialectic of indicative and imperative, Christians come perilously close to the pagan sacraments. The Lord's Supper becomes a φάρμακον ἀθανασίας (as is perfectly clear from the interpolation of Jn 6:51b–58) which leaves no room for decision, because the life received from Jesus is thought of as a φύσις. All that is necessary for salvation is to eat his flesh and drink his blood.

This view reaches its climax in Ignatius, particularly in Ephesians 20, 2, which defines the eucharistic bread as a φάρμακον ἀθανασίας, an 'antidote to death'. In the same vein Justin says that by the prayer comprising Christ's words the eucharistic elements become his flesh and blood and that by this food 'our blood and our flesh are nourished κατὰ μεταβολήν'—in other words, are transformed into a supernatural essence (*Apol.* 66, 2).

'No such thing as a Christian "priest" is known to the New Testament' (GV 1, p. 167). But the degeneration of the Church into a religious organism gave rise to a priesthood in the strict sense. Henceforth the Spirit had its *dwelling* in the institutions of the Church, in the sacraments and in certain individuals who were armed with supernatural powers. He became the official possession of official personages who were thereby turned into priests, and no longer operated in laymen except indirectly, through the mediation of priests (detailed analysis of the texts in TNT, pp. 453–63; compare GV 3, p. 46).

(2) Small wonder, in these circumstances, if the eschatological tension

slackened. There was still hope, of course, but any fulfilment of it was indefinitely postponed. No longer was the future already there, as in Jesus, Paul and John. Certain texts (2 Pet 3:1–10, for example) reveal that there were even Christian circles where expectation of the future had disappeared or was disappearing. 1 Clement 23:3–5 and 2 Clement 11 and 12 contend with the same scepticism. Exhortations to patience likewise show that eschatological faith was in danger of dying out (Jas 5:7–11; Heb 10–36; 2 Clement 12:1; Hermas *Vis.* III, 8, 9). Late texts in the synoptics which exhort Christians to be vigilant (Mk 13: 33–37; Lk 12:35–38; Mt 24:43–51) reveal the existence of the same danger. In times of stress (during persecutions, for instance) awareness of the other world would revive, as we see from the Apocalypse and the first Letter of Peter. But such books as Acts and the Pastoral Epistles show that the Church was settling down for a lengthy sojourn in the world and that faith, as it lost its eschatological tension, 'was becoming an earthly Christian piety' (TNT, p. 467) of which we have a perfect example in the paraenesis of the Pastoral Epistles.

Small wonder, therefore, if Christianity thought of itself as a *new religion*, on a level with Judaism and paganism. We find this idea throughout the Acts of the Apostles, particularly in the passages which have to do with the 'Way'. Saul goes to Damascus in hopes that there he will find people 'belonging to the Way' (9:2), and later he describes himself as the man who persecuted this Way to the death (22:4). At Ephesus the Jews speak ill of the Way (19:9) and no little stir arises there concerning the Way (19:23). The Roman governor has a rather accurate knowledge of the Way (24:22). The Way is Christianity turned into a religion. Later, Christians will regard themselves, in the same sense, as the 'third race', alongside the Gentiles and the Jews.

This objectification of faith continued, matters going from bad to worse down the ages; and it should come as no surprise to find Bultmann saying that the Church only recovered the fullness of its eschatological meaning with Luther.

CHAPTER ELEVEN

Sin, Grace, Predestination

I

SIN AND GRACE

As we know, for man to be is to ec-sist, which is possible only when there is a *Thou* to tear him away from himself and make him what he is not. It is his true nature not to be a nature but always to be ahead of himself. How can he do this, left to his own resources?

By definition, man cannot give himself what he is not, and yet his salvation and his happiness are only to be found in what he is not. This amounts to saying that he must *receive* his true being as a gift. The *I* only exists by the grace of the *Thou*, which is why the highest form of human relations can only be love. But only Christian revelation is the revelation of love. It is not just any *Thou* that can make man ec-sist and give him true life. Only from a radical otherness—that is, from God—can he receive the being that will bring him salvation, peace and joy, because it will be an *absolute* future, the very future of God. Being a creature, man can only find his life in his Creator.

Sin, therefore, can consist in nothing else but refusal to accept true being from God; that is, in *unbelief*. Contrary to what people often imagine, sin is not so much a matter of transgressing God's laws as of trying to observe them out of one's own strength. Transgressing a commandment at least has the salutary effect of restoring one to humility and helping one despair of oneself. But trying to observe the commandment in sole reliance on one's own resources, and succeeding, is the epitome of sin. The real sinners are not those whom the religious man looks on as such (publicans and harlots . . .); the real sinner is the religious man himself, the pharisee. The pharisee has lost all sense of grace. He rushes to his own destruction. To be more precise, his success is his failure, his glory is his ruin, simply because, never for an instant having given up himself, he does not find God. Hell is nothing else but self-righteousness, which is the categorical denial of God. The religious man does not deny God directly: he makes God the means to his aseity.

(1) Even in the Old Testament we find this idea that sin is less a matter of transgressing the commandments than of observing them by

one's own strength. The Old Testament regards man as God's creature. Therefore he cannot be his own creature—which is to say, he cannot save himself by himself. But such is his craving for in-sistence that he thinks he can and claims he can. This is what is meant by the story of the Fall, which simply conveys man's everlasting attempt to be in-dependent, his refusal to be a relation to God. All through the Bible sin is presented as this will to autonomy, which God constantly condemns:

> For the Lord of hosts has a day
>   against all that is proud and lofty,
>   against all that is lifted up and high;
> against all the cedars of Lebanon,
>   lofty and lifted up;
>   and against all the oaks of Bashan;
> against all the high mountains,
>   and against all the lofty hills;
> against every high tower,
>   and against every fortified wall;
> against all the ships of Tarshish,
>   and against all the beautiful craft.
> And the haughtiness of man shall be humbled,
>   and the pride of men shall be brought low;
>   and the Lord alone will be exalted in that day.
>   (Is 2:12–17)

The king of Assyria thinks exultantly, 'By the strength of my hand I have done it, and by my wisdom, for I have understanding'. And yet:

> Shall the axe vaunt itself over him who hews with it,
> or the saw magnify itself against him who wields it?
>   (Is 10:13–15)

And again:

> Let not the wise man glory in his wisdom,
> nor let the mighty man glory in his might.
>   (Jer 9:23)

Yahweh is a jealous God. Among the Greeks too there is talk of the gods' being jealous, but their jealousy is only provoked when mortals are *too* happy. Greek gods only strike down the excesses of men. This rather benign sort of jealousy is unknown to the Old Testament, which contains nothing comparable with the *Ring of Polycrates.* What Yahweh condemns is *any* confidence in oneself. It never occurs to the

Greek to thank God for the mere fact of existence. But the Bible says that man is sheer dependence on God and that therefore the slightest inclination to be autonomous is sin.

(2) Compared with the radicalism of the Old Testament, Judaism is a step backwards caused by a certain rationalization of God and man. God is no longer he who totally determines the existence of man, and man is no longer he whose existence is totally determined by God. It is later—on the last day—that God will *actually* be the Lord. In other words, though he is the judge even now, his sentence is not final, because man can hope to alter it by his good works. Likewise God shows his mercy even now, but it is only on the day of judgment that he will definitively pardon those who have proved themselves worthy of his pardon. Accordingly the question arises: Who will be among the damned and who among the elect? Since the matter is not yet settled, man can tip the balance one way or the other by his works, be they good or evil. At the very least, he can always admit his sins even if he is unable to do good deeds. Hence the confession of sins, the prayers of repentance, the displays of humility which are so characteristic of Judaism and which the devout use as a means of laying hold on the grace of God (4 Ezra 8:31–36, 47–49). Obviously the absolute character of sin is no longer grasped, since good works are considered possible, or at least the confession of one's sins can give one a *right* to God's favour. On the day of judgment God will give his decisions according to the good or evil deeds of men.

Jesus's preaching about God will be recalled (pp. 101–12, above). It involves a radical view of sin. In each of his decisions man is totally good or totally bad according as he allows himself to be determined by God or by the world. Sin is not the adulteration of a nature which is otherwise good, an unfortunate halt in the course of a man's spiritual development, an accident that can be put right, a false step that can be retraced, a leak that can be plugged and need not sink the ship. No, in the decision of the 'moment' which he takes against God, man is sin and nothing but sin. Sin is by its nature absolute; it is the *Verstehen* of a man who has decided against God. So it is futile for him to expect his sin to be wiped away by future good deeds. He cannot do good deeds, because he is wicked to the core. Sin is his ec-sistentiell determination. That is why grace alone can wipe it away. Not even the humble confession of his faults can draw down pardon upon him, for pardon must be wholly gratuitous.

Judaism supposed that until the day of judgment came, God turned a blind eye to the faults of the righteous so as to give them a chance of conversion, his mercy as it were forestalling his justice. So grace was not really grace. It was in view of the good works of a lifetime that

God would utter a man's absolution on the day of judgment. Ultimately a man saved himself. And therefore he never left the realm of damnation.

Such is not the mind of Jesus. God does not close his eyes to sin; he absolutely condemns it; which is to say that he can only pardon it. His very judgment is his grace. Because every inch of a man is judged, every inch of him is pardoned. Only where there is utter sin is there utter grace. God's judgment is his grace and his grace is his judgment.

Sin in this view has nothing to do with 'original sin', at least if the latter is taken to be an inheritance that is passed on and received. Not a trace of that idea can be found in Jesus's preaching, and for good reason: it would contradict his preaching. For the idea of an inherited sin presupposes the existence of a human nature which that inheritance affects. Sin would no longer be a mode of being of man who is freedom; it would be one attribute of a timeless essence. The theory of original sin arises from a naturalist view of God, man and grace which is altogether foreign to Jesus's mind.

In the parable of the pharisee and the publican (Lk 18:10–14) Jesus stresses the utter sinfulness of man, his inability to say *anything* for himself before God. The story is not meant to show, or even hint, that the pharisee is lying when he praises himself. He certainly does all that he says he does. But the way he speaks shows that he has no inkling of what grace is. Grace is possible only when a man holds his tongue about himself, only when he realizes that absolutely nothing in himself is of any avail before God. Doing what God's commandments require gives him no standing: 'When you have done all that is commanded you, say, "We are unworthy servants; we have only done what was our duty" ' (Lk 17:10). So sin can only be *pardoned*. But pardon condemns a man to his very depths: a man is only pardoned when he can say nothing in his own defence, when he is quite powerless to free himself, when he is utterly dependent on the other.

When I have been guilty of an offence against my friend, only his forgiveness can restore the bond between us, for it has been destroyed by my offence. The attributes that I still have (be they as noble as you like) cannot make up for it, cannot make it one whit less real. It will be there forever unless my friend forgives me. I myself can do nothing to blot it out. I am altogether at the mercy of the other man. The most moving appeals I can make to him only prove my utter dependence on him. The more I beg him to be lenient, the plainer I make my helplessness. His forgiveness can only be *event*. I can only ask him for it. Of themselves my most heroic deeds can do nothing about my offence, of which only a free decision on his part can ever absolve me. That decision is at once a judgment on me and a grace: a judgment because it proves that I can do nothing of myself; a grace because through it I recover my lost friendship for no merits of my own.

With stronger reason matters stand so between God and man. God's forgiveness is sheer grace, and therefore at the same time utter condemnation. It is a great mistake to imagine that Jesus did not preach the God of anger and judgment. Indeed no one ever preached him as Jesus did, less by direct threats of divine wrath than by speaking of grace in the radical way we well know. To proclaim the forgiveness of sins is to declare that God pronounces judgment on men from which there is no appeal, because he finds nothing in them to spare them his forgiveness. Accordingly we understand why Jesus spoke chiefly to the 'poor', why he said that the kingdom of God is theirs (Lk 6:20), and why men said of him 'Behold, a glutton and a drunkard, a friend of tax collectors and sinners!' (Mt 11:19; see Mk 2:16). The poor man, the publican and the sinner understand God's *Anspruch* upon man better than the righteous do, and are therefore readier to receive God as grace itself.

A series of figures and parables drive home this point: the parable of the two sons (Mt 21:28–31), which ends by saying that 'the tax collectors and the harlots go into the kingdom of God before you'; that of the lost sheep and the lost coin (Lk 15:4–10), where we are told that God rejoices more over one sinner who repents than over ninety-nine righteous men; that of the prodigal son (Lk 15:11–32), where a comparison between the two brothers shows that only the younger one has understood what grace is. All these parables are aimed at those who will not admit that man can only receive his salvation as a pure gift and that therefore the sinner alone knows what God's grace is. For the same reason Jesus sets his disciples the example of children (Mk 10:13–16): a child knows nothing of his 'rights', his 'works' and his 'claims'; he is prepared not to owe everything to himself. 'Truly, I say to you, whoever does not receive the kingdom of God like a child shall not enter it.'

If grace is a *Dass*, one can readily see why asceticism and mysticism are religious phenomena absolutely alien to Jesus's way of thinking. Asceticism and mysticism ignore the true nature of sin and grace. They make sense only within the framework of a basic analogy between God and man—that is, within the thinking of *homo religiosus*, as we have shown when discussing Gnosis. In Jesus's eyes God is not that spiritual and infinite being to which all that is noblest and best in us is akin, so that the ascetical effort we make to rise above our baser instincts enables us to approach him and even reach him in ecstasy and mystical union. The religion of spiritual experience, mystical states, piety based on the soul's contact with God, have no place in his preaching. He knows God only as sheer encounter, as the *Thou* that reveals itself to the human *I* by delivering the sinner from his sin through pardon and giving him a new being which he did *not* have '*in potentia*' before. Of course Jesus admits as perfectly obvious that man knows what salvation is and desires it, that he understands what is meant when one speaks to him about God and 'life' (because he has a precomprehension of all these things); but God himself, salvation itself, and life itself can only be a pure gift.

(3) (a) The formal study we made of the concepts σάρξ, κόσμος and πνεῦμα in Paul has already shown us what sin and grace meant to him —exactly what they meant to Jesus, of course. Sin is man's effort to save himself without God. We know that σάρξ does not mean what the Greeks meant by it, an objective reality (the material principle in man as contrasted with the spirit), and that it does not chiefly mean immorality either (the 'sins of the flesh'), but rather the world of man, 'this world', the realm of earthly and mortal things (ch. 3, §5, above). Thus the word signifies a contrast with the 'world of God', a contrast always latent when not declared outright, as it often is. Sin has its roots in the flesh thus understood, sin which consists in a man's making the world the standard of his life and his deeds, looking for his security, his happiness, his true being in this world as if it were no longer God's creation. Sin is man's extermination of otherness (God's and the world's as the creation of God), making himself the ground-work of all things, dismissing the ὡς μή (1 Cor 7:29ff). To live according to the flesh, then, is to live according to the natural man, referring all things to oneself or owing all things to oneself.

The passions and desires of the flesh which Gal 5:24 says the Christian has crucified include sensuality in the strict sense but also the many forms of self-seeking and rejection of others that are listed in 5:19–21 as 'works of the flesh'. When Paul warns us in 5:13 not to make Christian freedom an opportunity for gratifying the flesh, here again, as verses 14–15 plainly declare, the 'flesh' is self-seeking and rejection of others.

The 'sinful passions' of Rom 7:5 that were at work in our members 'while we were living in the flesh' also mean the attitude of natural man; so, no doubt, do the 'deeds of the body' which make up life according to the flesh (Rom 8:13). The Corinthians are still 'of the flesh' (1 Cor 3:3) because there is jealousy and strife among them. When Paul's adversaries accuse him of being guided by 'fleshly wisdom' (2 Cor 1:12, Greek text) and of 'walking according to the flesh' (2 Cor 10:2, Greek text), they are charging him, as the whole second Letter to the Corinthians shows, with insincerity, pride, lust for power, and untrustworthiness.

But first and foremost, to live according to the flesh means zealously observing the law in the hope (conscious or unconscious, avowed or unavowed) of thereby acquiring some kind of worth before God and being saved according to the zeal with which one has obeyed him. Paul rounds on the Christians of Galatia who would adopt the law and be circumcised: 'Having begun with the Spirit, are you now ending with the flesh?' The flesh is not carnal passions but the law (Gal 3:3). To pride oneself on all the privileges and rights of the devout Jew is the epitome of fleshly behaviour. The law, the prerogatives and the dignity of Israel are all flesh because they are all of this world, representing only human confidence (Phil 3:3–7). This text is admirable proof that the man who lives according to the flesh is the man whose confidence is in himself, who relies on his worth, his rightful claims, his works.

The Christian attitude is described in 3:9: it is giving up all righteousness of one's own. Rom 10:3 says that the great sin of the Jews is cleaving to their own righteousness. Consequently we see why the 'letter' (the law of Moses) is opposed to the Spirit, why it belongs to the realm of the flesh (Rom 2:29; 7:6; 2 Cor 3:6), for a man uses it as a means to attain 'righteousness' and 'life' by his own strength. The law is the 'letter' in that it is a code of rules that can be observed by corresponding works.[1]

If the sin of the Jew is doing the works of the law, the sin of the 'Greek' is his quest for wisdom and the pride he takes in knowledge and spiritual gifts. The 'wise according to the flesh' of 1 Cor 1:26 (Greek text) are those who rely entirely on themselves and will not recognize their wisdom as nothingness before God. Paul's adversaries of 2 Cor 10–13 who boast 'according to the flesh' (11:18, Greek text) and do battle with 'fleshly weapons' (10:4, Greek text), are people who

---

1. People often suppose that the law was an occasion of sin to the Jews because they were unable to keep its commandments. That is a piece of Christian nonsense which Jewish scholars have rightly denounced again and again. For anyone born and bred in Judaism the law is no burden but a joy, a security, a deliverance, a native country. The Jew knows of course that he is a sinner, but that only intensifies his zeal for the law. He is sorry for his sins and confident that new efforts will enable him to attain the perfection required. Paul never felt unable to observe the law. He says the direct opposite: so far as observance of the law was concerned, he led a blameless life (Phil 3:6f; Gal 1:14). As to Rom 7:14ff, it does not describe Paul's subjective state before his conversion but the *objective* conflict there is in every Jew (in natural man) between will and deed, *which only the Christian can see*. Only the Christian knows that the Jew, despite his actual observance of the law—nay, *because* of that observance—will not be saved (see GV 2, pp. 44f). Paul holds that perfect observance of the law is the sin of sins, because it is the most pernicious way of repudiating grace: anyone who does not see that this is so has not an inkling of Paul's thought.

proudly compare themselves with others and measure themselves only by their own yardstick (10:12–18), boasting of their 'visions' and 'revelations' (12:1). By demanding 'proof' from Paul (13:3) they automatically admit that so far as they are concerned only a visible work is evidence of possessing the Spirit—which is equivalent to denying him.

In short, whether by giving himself up to the enticements of this world or by being zealous for the law and religious matters, man refuses to forsake himself. He forgets that all human wisdom, power and nobility are foolishness before God (1 Cor 1:26–31).

Then Paul goes on to describe this human 'insistence' in terms of four themes that are very much his own—the themes of covetousness (ἐπιθυμεῖν), anxiety (μεριμνᾶν), boasting (καυχᾶσθαι) and trust (πεποιθέναι). 'Thou shalt not covet', says God's commandment; but by saying so it arouses covetousness (Rom 7:7f). Now covetousness has its seat in the flesh, so that Paul can describe the flesh as its subject (Gal 5:16f, 24; Rom 6:12; see Rom 13:14). The 'desires of the flesh' are the desires of those who have worshipped the creature (Rom 1:24) and the dishonourable passions to which they have given themselves up are none other than the works of the flesh of Gal 5:19ff. Thus life according to the flesh is a life of coveting—that is, a life whereby a man relies only on himself, on his own resources, his own designs for getting hold of things. It consists in making the world one's own country.

Anxiety is likewise the desire to control the world. More precisely, it is the attempt man makes to encroach on his future; it is helping oneself to the future, or (what amounts to the same thing) trying to perpetuate the present. At bottom, μεριμνᾶν is the antithesis of faith, whereby a man constantly allows himself to be torn from the past so as to receive whatever God is pleased to send him. 'Anxiety about worldly affairs' (1 Cor 7:32ff) springs from the illusion that one's existence can be anchored in visible and controllable things. Paul contrasts it with 'anxiety about the affairs of the Lord', which is precisely an ἀμέριμνος εἶναι (1 Cor 7:32), a μηδέν μεριμνᾶν (Phil 4:6).

But man's most significant attitude issues in 'boasting'. Καυχᾶσθαι is the sin of sins—in the Jew who boasts of God and the law (Rom 2:17, 23) and in the Greek who boasts of his wisdom (1 Cor 1:19–31): it is a natural instinct of man to compare himself favourably with others and to boast of the comparison (Gal 6:4). In Rom 3:27 Paul shows how characteristic καυχᾶσθαι is of the Jew. Having proclaimed justification by faith without works, he explains what he means by asking 'Then what becomes of our καυχᾶσθαι? It is excluded'; and he cites the example of Abraham, who as a believer had no καύχημα (4:2). To boast is to forget one's position as a creature: 'What have you that you did not receive? If then you received it, why do you boast as if it were not a gift?' (1 Cor 4:7). What God means to do is shatter all human standards of greatness, 'so that no human being may boast in the presence of God' (1 Cor 1:29).

Only one kind of boasting is in order: 'Let him who boasts, boast of the Lord' (1 Cor 1:31; 2 Cor 10:17). Therefore the Christian must not boast in the sense of thinking himself better than others (Gal 6:4; Rom 11:17f). When Paul boasts, he knows—and says several times over—that it is folly (2 Cor 11 and 12). And even while doing so, he contrives to insist that he is boasting of his weakness (11:30; 12:9; see Rom 5:2). Thus he exclaims: 'Far be it from me to glory except in the cross of our Lord Jesus Christ' (Gal 6:14; see Rom 5:11).

To boast according to the flesh is also to 'put confidence (πεποιθέναι) in the flesh', as Phil 3:3 shows. Here 'putting confidence in the flesh' is the opposite of 'glorying in Christ Jesus' (and compare 2 Cor 1:12 with 3:4). If 'glorying in Christ' is counting all honours, all dignities and all works 'loss' and 'refuse' (Phil 3:4–8), if it is giving up one's own righteousness (3:9), then contrariwise to 'put confidence in the flesh' is to seek one's safety and salvation in visible, controllable things, in what a man can do for and of himself. It is the pride of the Jew which issues in his boasting about the law (Rom 2:23) and makes him sure (πεποιθέναι) he is a guide to the blind, a light to those who are in darkness, a teacher of children, and so forth (Rom 2:19ff). Trust in the flesh, with Paul, is a man's trust in himself, the antithesis of trust in God. He puts it this way: '[We had to learn] to rely not on ourselves but on God who raises the dead' (2 Cor 1:9).

Man's sin, then, is trying to dispense with God by appropriating him. But in trying to be his own master man becomes a slave. He supposed he was mastering all transcendence and lo, he 'sets up' over himself the flesh, sin and the world as dreadful, tyrannical othernesses. This enslavement is not only to what Paul, using a Gnostic expression, calls 'the elemental spirits of the universe'—the powers which rule it represented for the Jews by the law and for the Gentiles by 'beings that are by nature no gods' (Gal 4:1–10). Above all it is enslavement to the flesh and to sin. The man of ἐπιθυμεῖν, of μεριμνᾶν, of καυχᾶσθαι and of πεποιθέναι falls under the sway of that which he thought to control. Hence the sharp reminder to the Galatians, who, as we have seen, sought to achieve righteousness through the law: 'For freedom Christ has set us free; stand fast therefore, and do not submit again to a yoke of slavery' (Gal 5:1). To the Corinthians, who were proud of their wisdom, Paul says: 'All things are yours' (1 Cor 3:21f); that is, do not fall back under the tyranny of human authorities, of 'flesh and blood'.

Anyone who thinks he ought to live by the standards of the world must be reminded that he is rushing into bondage: 'You were bought with a price; do not become slaves of men' (1 Cor 7:23). And those who confuse Christian freedom with complete sexual licence must also be told: 'You are not your own; you were bought with a price' (1 Cor 6:19–20). This text makes it as plain as day that a man who seems to be his own master is really his own slave. Certainly man was liberated by Christ; but not so as to belong to himself, which would be the worst of servitudes. Paul has no interest at all in freedom for freedom's sake. Only a man who belongs to God (the Lord) is free of the flesh and of sin (Rom 6:15ff; 7:5f). Indeed to live according to the flesh is to make it one's god (Rom 16:18; Phil 3:19).

Paul strikingly conveys the fact that the flesh and sin can become powers which enslave a man when he speaks of them as though they were actually persons. A man becomes a 'debtor' to the flesh (Rom 8:12). The flesh can have cravings (Gal 5:17). It can have thoughts (Rom 8:6), passions and desires (Gal 5:24), and do works (5:19). The world too may be personified: it has a wisdom of its own (1 Cor 1:20f). But above all it is sin (ἁμαρτία) that figures as a personal being. It 'came into the world' (Rom 5:12). It 'reigned' (Rom 5:21). Man is its slave (Rom 6:6, 17ff), has sold himself to it (Rom 7:14), or has paid it wages (Rom 6:23). It 'revived' (Rom 7:9); it dwells within man and operates within him (Rom 7:17–20).

Unlike the Gnostics, as we have already seen, Paul does not look on these personified powers as objective realities pressing upon man from outside him, like some fate for which he has no responsibility. The flesh and sin are a *Verständnis* of man's; it is he who 'sets them up'. Not indeed as though they were mere physical phenomena, but just the opposite—because he becomes their slave by ec-sisting towards them. In Gnosticism (and in mythologized Christianity as well) the powers are not dangerous: being objective things which attack man only from without, they cannot prejudice his freedom. But so far as Paul is concerned they can become a man's self-determination (his *Wie*), and that is why they are dangerous—when he uses his freedom to set them up over himself. It is man who 'allows them to exist' in their otherness and their tyrannizing transcendence. Then he becomes a being divided against himself. He meant to safeguard his security and his life with the help of the world, of visible and earthly things, and now he is losing them instead.

Paul personifies sin in order to drive home the fact that a man tears himself apart when he tries to save himself by his own resources (by and in the world): 'I am carnal, sold under sin' (Rom 7:14). 'I know that nothing good dwells in me, that is, in my flesh' (Rom 7:18). According to the latter text the flesh is part of the *I* (*my* flesh), which in effect is torn in two. It is at once the I-which-desires-the-good and the I-flesh which does not do the good. Similarly the self which in Rom 7:17-20 distinguishes itself from sin dwelling within it is also the self described in verse 14 as out-and-out carnal and sold under sin; and in verses 14-24 we are still dealing with the first person, both as to the will and as to the deed. Thus sin is a power that has a hold over man's freedom. By his very essence, man under sin is a divided, unhappy being—in short he is already dead.

Although Paul does accept the traditional idea of death as the penalty of sin (Rom 1:32 and elsewhere), he rises above that juridical view. Since sin consists in living according to the flesh—that is, seeking one's salvation in the fleeting and failing things of this world—by an iron law it leads straight to death: death is its fruit. 'If you live according to the flesh you will die' (Rom 8:13). Whoever makes the world his *Verständnis* will have death as his inheritance from it. 'He who sows to his own flesh will from the flesh reap corruption' (Gal 6:8). He who 'is anxious about the affairs of the world' enslaves himself to the world, of which 'the form is passing away' (1 Cor 7:31).

Worldly grief produces death (2 Cor 7:10), because it attaches itself to what must die. So we can say that death issues organically, as its fruit, from life according to the flesh (Rom 7:5). It is the term of sin (Rom 6:21). But let us bear in mind that we are dealing with more than sin as a transgression: sin here is also, and primarily, the attempt to observe the law by one's own strength. When Paul says in 2 Cor 3:6 that 'the written code kills, but the Spirit gives life', he is not thinking of offences against the law but of the supreme reverence which Jews had for the law: they considered it eternal and 'radiant with splendour'. Against this pride, which had been his own, Paul says that the Mosaic ministry was a 'dispensation of death' and that its splendour has 'faded away' (verses 7 and 11). As we have seen (p. 227, above), the law belongs to the realm of the flesh. Therefore observance of it leads to death as surely as transgression of it. By trying to owe his life to himself, a man meets with death (Rom 7:9f).

The power of sin is universal, it extends to all men without exception: 'All have sinned' (Rom 3:23; see 3:9, 19), and 'scripture consigned all things to sin' (Gal 3:22). Is this universality of sin a fate or a challenge? When Paul grounds his thesis of justification by faith without works on the universality of sin (Rom 1:18-2:20), he speaks of that universality as a challenge and responsibility. Only in Rom 5:12-19, in tracing the sin of all men back to Adam, does he have recourse to the Gnostic myth of fate. But he makes a clean break from it by turning Adam's sin into a free act.

Are Adam's descendants also to blame? Verse 19 suggests that they are not, and here again one may wonder whether Paul has quite got away from Gnostic naturalism. However that may be, a close analysis of his thought (TNT, pp. 251–4) shows that his real purpose is to stress that men have *always* sinned (freely) since Adam delved and Eve span; that each individual is born into a human race which from its earliest days has (freely) separated itself from God. This is what the idea of an hereditary sin really means.

(b) We have already dealt with Paul's christology. With regard to our special concern at the moment, which is the relation of grace to individuals, it must be said that Christ is first and foremost the abolition of man. Jews and Gentiles alike are sinners: Gentiles by transgressing the law of God, Jews by keeping it. Therefore grace is the utter condemnation of man.

Like Jesus, Paul stoutly dwells on the anger of God. 'For the wrath of God is revealed from heaven against all ungodliness and wickedness of men' (Rom 1:18). The sinner stores up wrath for himself (Rom 2:5, 8). It is part of God's faithfulness, truth and justice for him to be anger as well (Rom 3:3–6). Anger is not an attribute, an emotion that affects God, but an event. The 'revealing' of his anger (Rom 1:18) is not a doctrinal communication about the nature of God but the actual manifestation of his wrath. God's wrath as described throughout this passage (Rom 1:18–32) is the concrete position of the Gentiles which it has created: God has given them up to the lusts of their hearts (verse 24), to their dishonourable passions (verse 26), to their base mind (verse 28).

The day of wrath is the event of judgment (Rom 2:5), the same thing as the day of eternal life (Rom 2:7f) and the day of salvation (1 Thess 5:9). The judgment is not merely to come, it is here and now (as in Rom 1:18–32; 13:4f). It is going on all the time (Rom 4:15; 12:19). God's grace is his judgment and that is precisely why it is grace. Judgment does not come first and then grace afterwards. It is as our judge that God is grace. We must not suppose that the past of his anger yields to the present of his grace. Christ is our saviour in his very capacity as our judge, and he is our judge in his very capacity as our saviour.

If grace is the utter judgment of man, then evidently it cannot be an attribute inhering in the justified man, some supernature that he possesses. Though it is certainly his being, one could say that he is that being by the mode of non-being—that is, of freedom: grace ceaselessly calls him to ec-sistence, to self-surrender, to the love of God and neighbour. In other words it is an indicative at the same time as it is an imperative. It is his *Verständnis*, his ontic determination. In Gnosis it was a new nature. The Gnostic was pardoned as a stone is a stone, which means that he was not really pardoned. The Christian is pardoned as a being whose ontological structure is freedom, who is called on to be forever ahead of himself, and who therefore must be constantly torn from his sinful past so as to be open to a genuine future.

Grace is that otherness which ceaselessly invites us to obey. And so when all is said and done man has only exchanged one bondage for another (Rom 7:6): he has become the slave of the living God (1 Thess 1:9), the slave of Christ (Rom 14:18), the slave of righteousness (Rom 6:16–18). Yet this bondage is true freedom. The slave of Christ is a 'freedom of the Lord' (1 Cor 7:22); because in becoming that man's *Selbstverständnis* Christ brings him the salvation of which he only had a *Vorverständnis*. Such salvation is supernatural power, engrafted upon human nature, to do good henceforth: it is an opportunity for ec-sistence which must be constantly seized anew, for the 'tempter' is forever trying to rob the Christian of his freedom (1 Thess 3:5; 1 Cor 7:5; 2 Cor 2:11). Humanism's 'Become what you are' is shifted from the plane of nature to the plane of 'historicity'. There is no question of developing some spiritual life which exists in embyro within us and needs to be drawn from potency into act.

When a believer responds to the *Anrede* of grace that is constantly addressed to him, he becomes what he is not by any manner of means. The Spirit bestowed in baptism is the eschatological gift which is simultaneously the eschatological imperative. The whole argument of Gal 5:12–26 underlines the fact that the Spirit does not exist in the mode of a spiritual substance but in the mode of 'historicity', and that it is forever making new demands. A lapidary paradox concludes the passage: 'If we live by the Spirit, let us also walk by the Spirit' (verse 25). In the first clause of the sentence the Spirit is the power that delivers man, is man's new indicative. In the second clause, the Spirit is the norm that man must follow. So our 'being Christian' is not something we 'are' in the ordinary sense of the word, but a being that is ahead of us and that we are by way of not being it. It is always 'forensic', always received.

Christians are saints (Rom 8:27; 1 Cor 6:2) and sanctified (1 Cor 1:2; 6:11). But from this indicative of holiness there arises the duty to be holy (1 Thess 4:3; Rom 6:19–22); and to disregard that duty is to disregard God himself, who has given us his Holy Spirit (1 Thess 4:8). On the one hand our body is the temple of the Spirit, but on the other hand we must keep it pure (1 Cor 6:19). The indicative 'You have put on Christ' (Gal 3:27) gives rise to the imperative 'Put on the Lord Jesus Christ' (Rom 13:14).

All the same it is certain that now and then, for want of due reflection, Paul falls in with the popular mythology which objectifies and, as it were, 'reifies' the Spirit. Instead of being a man's *Verständnis*, the true *Thou* which determines his ec-sistence, the Spirit becomes a supernatural substance, a sort of divine fluid that inhabits him and acts in his place. This naturalist idea underlies all the passages where Paul speaks of the Spirit as something that is 'given' to man or 'poured' into him (Rom 5:5; 2 Cor 1:22; 5:5; 1 Thess 4:8). But while keeping to mythological language he profoundly changes its content in the way we have mentioned: the Spirit is an indicative and at the same time an imperative.

(4) A study of sin and grace in John would show that he too shifted these ideas to the plane of 'historicity'. But as we have already explained the substance of his thought (pp. 57–9 and 210–18, above), it will be of more interest to see how largely, outside Paul and John, this living dialectic of indicative and imperative yielded once more to objectivism and legalism. Bultmann has traced the development in a lengthy study of extra-Pauline and extra-Johannine Christian literature. Here let us merely sketch the outlines of this relapse, which of course was not a complete breakdown but rather a general weakening, hardly noticeable in some writings and a good deal more serious in others.

Paul and John, as we know, hold that grace does not give man a new nature which he must then use in an attempt to gain his salvation by works. If that were what the gospel taught, it would only be a Christian Judaism. No, my old sinful nature is not destroyed by baptism and replaced by another that enables me to do good deeds in view of which God will save me at the last day. The truth is that grace is always 'forensic'. It is an indicative-imperative. It does not save me as it would a tree or a stone: I never am 'saved'; I have to keep being saved from moment to moment.

The things I do are not 'works', deeds done on my own initiative by my own strength that give me any standing before God. They are a response to the eschatological imperative, and therefore they merit nothing. My last judgment takes place at every moment (as John declares with such force), and *it is not for me to make my present life, by the help of grace, a meritorious preparation for the life to come*. Grace is not a supernatural in-sistence; that would be worse than the natural in-sistence of the unbeliever, for it would amount to using God in order to dispense with God. It would be self-justification by grace. Grace would only be 'a new chance for man to exert himself in view of his future salvation' (TNT, p. 548). It would be what enables him to do works that will ensure him a favourable sentence at the moment of the last judgment.

This Christian Judaism is exactly what the extra-Pauline and extra-Johannine writings lapsed into to one degree or another. We have a real breakdown not only in the *Didache* and the first Letter of Clement but also in the Letter of James and the Apocalypse (both of which Luther so rightly castigated), in the Gospel of Luke (insofar as it is the evangelist's own work), and in the Acts of the Apostles. The literature influenced by Pauline thought, of course, is that which shows least sign of the relapse. This salutary influence which Paul had is most potent in Ignatius of Antioch, less so in the Letters to the Colossians and the Ephesians[2] and in the first Letter of Peter, and feeblest of all in the Pastoral Epistles, which in many respects represent a Christian Judaism.

Let us delve somewhat into the Letter of James, for it is typical. Obviously it holds that a Christian is subject to the law, whose authority is grounded on the epithets 'perfect' (1:25) and 'royal' (2:8). Good behaviour is demanded as a work (3:13) and 'a doer that acts' (1:25), we are told, 'shall be blessed in his doing'—that is, in keeping the law (*ibid.*). In 2:14–16 the author attacks those who attribute salvation to faith without works. Very likely he is aiming at Paul or a group who appeal to Paul's authority, for he denies that Abraham was justified by faith alone. At any rate the Pauline idea of faith is completely disregarded here.

Needless to say, Paul would have admitted that a faith without works is a dead faith (2:17–26); but he would not on any account have accepted the thesis that 'faith is active (συνήργει) along with works' (2:22). To his mind faith is the source of works, because, not being an attribute, it is always ahead of a man, ceaselessly calling on him to act. Therefore it cannot possibly co-operate with works. But the faith James speaks of is an *attribute* which man has received from God and uses according to his own good pleasure. That is why it can be put on the same level as works. We are told bluntly enough that such is the case by the celebrated text on the faith which devils have (verse 19). Obviously a statement of this kind would be quite unintelligible to Paul, because he regards faith as a transformation of man, a relation to God, a new life, an opportunity for ec-sistence, a *Verstehen*—so the text of James would mean that the devils love God, are 'elect', 'saints', 'Christians'! On the other hand if one envisages faith as James does, as an *abstract* persuasion that God exists, then the devils can believe without ceasing to be devils. Objective knowledge, as we have seen, exists without man's forsaking himself in order to become what he knows. The Letter, then, is steeped in the moralism of the synagogue.

Turning grace into a *Was* ultimately meant turning Christian faith

2. The only Pauline writings of unquestionable authenticity are Romans, 1 and 2 Corinthians, Galatians, Philippians, 1 Thessalonians and Philemon.

into an *ethic* of perfection and sanctity, both conceived of along the lines of the Greek ideal. Since in baptism the Christian has received grace as a divine attribute, he must draw it out from potency into act by shunning vice and practising virtue. God's commandment is no longer regarded as an imperative which demands the gift of oneself to God and one's neighbour, but as a means to personal perfection which enables us to advance along the road of salvation. This view of things is to be found far and wide but becomes particularly crude in Hermas (see *Mand.* II, 4–6; *Sim.* I; V, 3, 7f). It quite naturally led to the preoccupation with asceticism which is so typical of *homo religiosus*.

Ascetical trends early put in an appearance. 1 Tim 4:3 inveighs against those who forbid marriage and the eating of certain foods (see 2:15; 5:23; Titus 1:14f). A document like the second Letter of Clement, which urges Christians to 'keep their flesh pure' (8:4; 14:3) and extols celibacy (12:5) shows clearly enough which way the wind is blowing. Possibly the 'chaste men' of Apoc 14:4 'who have not defiled themselves with women' are ascetics. At any rate a passage in Hermas (*Sim.* IX, 11) gives us the most vivid picture of the persistence of that 'spiritual' marriage in which ascetics and virgins lived together. The practice existed, of course, even in Paul's day (1 Cor 7:25, 36f).[3]

The ascetic ideal gave rise to a distinction between two levels of Christian morality and Christian life, as we see by the admonitions that an ascetic is not to be puffed up (1 Clem 38:2; 48:6; Ignatius, Epistle to Polycarp 5:2). The perfectionist ideal had a similar effect, for it very soon became clear that not all were able to satisfy the demands of ἐγκράτεια, interpreted as permanent renunciation of the necessaries of life, of the preoccupations and pleasures of this world. Witness the Pastoral Epistles on the one hand and Hermas on the other.

Hence the concept of perfection (τελειότης, τέλειον) takes on a new meaning. In Mt 5:48 ('You, therefore, must be perfect, as your heavenly Father is perfect'), τέλειος seems still to bear the mystical sense and mean what is entire, whole, free of any break or division (p. 246, below). But in Mt 19:21 the word refers to the ideal of perfection: 'If you would be perfect, go, sell what you possess . . .' ('If you would be perfect' is missing in Mk 10:21). The same is found in the *Didache*, 1, 4 and 6, 2; the latter passage clearly differentiates between the two levels of holiness: 'If you are ready to bear the Lord's yoke whole and entire, you will be perfect; if not, then do whatever you are able.'

It is true that Paul himself used the word τέλειος in the Greek sense (1 Cor 14:20; Phil 3:15), but the reference was to adulthood; he was

3. Although it has been suggested that 1 Cor 8:36–38 refers to people who are engaged (W. G. Kummel, *Neutestamentliche Studien für R. Bultmann*, 1957).

not preaching the ideal of perfection. The same must be said of Heb 6:11. In Ignatius, τέλειος means perfection (Ephesians 1:1; 15:2; Smyrnians 11:2f), the acme of which is martyrdom because there we have the utmost effort of man to detach himself from the world. Hermas too distinguishes several degrees of morality. He does not merely differentiate between the justified and those who are in need of repentance, but also speaks of the works of supererogation whereby one merits greater glory in heaven (*Sim.* V, 2, 4–11; 3, 3–9).

II

PREDESTINATION

The foregoing section—and indeed everything we have said from the beginning of this book about the relations between the (human) *I* and the (divine) *Thou*—indicates a solution to the eternal problem of how grace and freedom can be reconciled. We shall now explain what the solution is. As we have seen, Bultmann invests the *Dass* with an absolute primacy. It is always the other that tears me away from my past and gives me my future. In Pauline language, 'God is at work . . . both to will and to work' (Phil 2:13). How then can there be any question of *Entscheidung* (decision) by man? If he is justified by faith without works (Rom 3:28), what room is there for any activity on his side?

Let us begin by considering what Paul means by 'works'. Rom 3:27–28 makes the matter perfectly clear. Having said that all men are gratuitously justified by grace, he asks: 'Then what becomes of our καύχησις (the right to boast, to glorify oneself)?' And he answers: 'It is excluded. On what principle? On the principle of works? No, but on the principle of faith'. And he goes on: 'We hold that a man is justified by faith apart from works of law'. Therefore self-glorification and justification by works go hand in hand. In ruling out the one, Paul rules out the other. The attitude of the man who would be justified by works is the same as the attitude of the man who would glorify himself. For this reason we are told a little later: 'If Abraham was justified by works, he has something to boast about, but not before God' (4:2).

What exactly is the desire to glorify oneself? When he boasts of his works, what the Jew is after is his own righteousness, none other than the righteousness that is bestowed on him by the judgment of *God*, the right that is granted him by *God*, the honour and standing that *God* acknowledges he has; but God bestows and acknowledges all this (so the Jew thinks) *in view of his works*. For the devout Jew, to attain to righteousness by works is to attain to a certain standing before

God. Because of his works God will not (he thinks) deprive him of that standing. In modern parlance, this human need of καύχησις would be called the need for status—something which is found even in children and can manifest itself in a thousand different guises. But the specific form which *homo religiosus* gives it is that of using God's command-ment in order to gain some standing before him, as Jesus showed in the parable of the pharisee and the publican.

The 'Jew' uses the law to lay an *Anspruch* upon God. Consequently his obedience is the direct opposite of true obedience. With God's help he makes himself independent of God. What he is after is aseity. First he means to achieve it with regard to men, carving out a status for himself in their eyes through his abilities, his talents, his achieve-ments. But being aware that no human judgment, however flattering, can give him any permanent security, he seeks that security before the highest tribunal of all (perhaps not calling it by name). This man—who is natural man—is the one Paul has in mind as he sets forth his doctrine on justification by faith.

Faith is the attitude diametrically opposed to καύχησις; faith alto-gether renounces boasting and the desire to push oneself forward on the strength of one's own accomplishments. It acknowledges that the standing which is my whole security can only be *received*. Faith it is that says: 'What have you that you did not receive? If then you received it, why do you boast as if it were not a gift?' (1 Cor 4:7.) The believer receives his righteousness, honour and worth from God. Paul is aware that man absolutely needs standing in order to exist, that he simply must have the recognition of others, that he cannot live without certainty, peace of mind, and confidence. In this sense there is nothing blameworthy about the need for standing (status). Since man must live in the presence and in the company of other men, he must be acknowledged in his rights and dignity. His mistake, however, is trying to base his rights and dignity on himself.

Even in the sphere of human relations a person with a keen sense of his own worth is unbearable and instead of the good opinion of others, which he so much desires, earns himself the contrary. The worth that we recognize in others we wish to admit *of our own accord*; we dislike people's trying to compel recognition by flashing their merits at us, even though their merits may be undeniable. Certainly it is by a man's deeds that we perceive his worth, but all the same he must not try to make us respect and like him on the strength of his deeds. Whether we respect and like him is for us to decide, not for him. If the tree is known by its fruits, it still has no business forcing its fruits on our attention. On the contrary, to the extent that a man refrains from boasting he is really acknowledged by others.

This is all the truer on the plane of the relations between God and man. I cannot assert myself before God on the strength of my good deeds, my efforts, my sacrifices. Whatever worth I have can only be a a pure gift from him. Until a man accepts that fact he must be a constant prey to fits of pride and despair. Giving up all claim to a worth of one's·own, unconditionally surrendering to grace—that is faith. And the grace of God is nothing else but the kindness with which God takes man as he is and transforms him. It does not require man to make the first move, to begin by pulling himself together; it seeks him out where he is, in his wretchedness, and starting from there it enriches him.

Nevertheless Paul says that faith is an obedience (Rom 1:5; 10:16; 15:18; Gal 5:7; 2 Cor 9:13; 10:5f). Therefore it is something a man *does.* Well then, must it not be a work? How can it be both an utter renunciation of self and an obedience? It is obedience because faith breaks a man's pride. To find his *true* being is of all things most difficult for natural man. He is not disposed to give up his own worth; it has become part of him; it is himself. He feels he will lose himself in losing what he has acquired by himself. He cannot admit that that is just what he must do—lose himself in order to find himself.

Paul sets forth this 'reversal of values' in language that has never been equalled: 'If any other man thinks he has reason for confidence, I have more: circumcised on the eighth day, of the people of Israel, of the tribe of Benjamin, a Hebrew born of Hebrews; as to the law a Pharisee, as to zeal a persecutor of the Church, as to righteousness under the law blameless. But whatever gain I had, I counted as loss for the sake of Christ. Indeed I count everything as loss because of the surpassing worth of knowing Christ Jesus my Lord. For his sake I have suffered the loss of all things, and count them as refuse, in order that I may gain Christ and be found in him, not having a righteousness of my own, based on law, but that which is through faith, the righteousness from God that depends on faith' (Phil 3:4–9).

Paul's conversion was not at all a matter of repentance and reparation for a life of sin in the ordinary sense of the word; it was the sacrifice of everything that he had been *proud of.* We know how difficult giving is on the plane of human relations. Many people who long for friendship and love—and therefore long to give themselves— nevertheless prove incapable of it. If so many friendships, loves and marriages are partial or total failures, that is because a man always tries to keep some foothold, some security for himself. Now the same danger threatens the relations of man with God. Faith is a trust that asks for no guarantees, because it places a man in the hands of him 'who gives life to the dead and calls into existence the things that do not exist' (Rom 4:17).

Thus obedience and trust are one and the same thing. Therefore obedience is not a work. It is not an expression of our strength but the sacrifice of all strength, a readiness to receive our strength from God alone. It is not a general, abstract trust in God, an ability, an attribute, an initiative of man's own. On the contrary, it is something called forth by God. It is a *Verständnis*; that is, a response to our having first been understood. Were we to confuse it with trust as a general disposition of the soul, like piety, then we would be lapsing into works. Paul made any such misunderstanding impossible by never using πιστεύειν in the ordinary sense of the devout man's trust in God. Thus he never has this verb in a dative construction (such as very commonly occurs in the Septuagint and also in the rest of the New Testament) except for the Old Testament quotations of Gal 3:6 and Rom 4:3 which deal with the faith of Abraham. He uses πιστεύειν with ὅτι, εἰς, ἐν, πρός and ἐπί to underline the primacy of the divine *Dass*, which Luther has perspicaciously rendered in the text already quoted: *Semper ita fit, ut opus nostrum intelligamus, antequam fiat, Dei autem opus non intelligimus, donec factum fuerit.* Evidently obedience and trust thus interpreted are man's *Entscheidung* against himself and for God. As that decision, therefore, faith is an act (*Tat*).

It is an *act* (*Tat*) but not a *work* (*Werk*). The difference between the two will now be understood. To do a work is to operate of and for oneself, remaining in one's in-sistence, doing a thing which has no intentionality because it is not called forth by the summons of a *Dass*. The devout Jew did not forsake himself, he used God's commandment to perfect himself; he tried to owe his salvation to himself; he used God while imagining that he was serving him. Doing an act (*Tat*) is responding *to* something, forsaking oneself by listening to the *Anrede* of the other. By an act one obeys the *Thou*; by a work one obeys oneself.

Our friendships are often mere works because we seek ourselves in them, loving the other only from our own point of view. It also happens that Christians love their neighbour for the sake of their own perfection, so as to boast before God that they have kept the commandment of love. Genuine faith is the act whereby one renounces works, knowing that grace will be received only in that renunciation—grace which Karl Immermann sees embodied in the holy grail. The door of its shrine bears the following inscription:

> *Ich habe mich nach eignem Recht gegründet,*
> *Vergebens sucht ihr mich.*
> *Der Wandrer, welcher meinen Tempel findet,*
> *Den suchte ich.*[4]

4. 'I am set up by my own sovereign law,
   To seek me is in vain.

And here is his confession:

> *Was wär' das Heil'ge, ständ es zu erringen?*
> *Unendliches, was wär' es, wenn das Endliche*
> *Zu ihm gelangte mit der Sehnsucht Schwingen?*
> *Nein, mich umfängt das Unabwendliche!*
> *Es fassen mich die Ketten, die Gestählten!*
> *Des Menschen Tat, die einzig kenntliche,*
> *Ist: Fühlen sich im Stande der Erwählten.*[5]

We seem to have strayed far off from our problem. And yet we may have solved it already. Faith as an act of decision is surrender to grace in the profoundest sense of the word: it cannot gaze at itself, account for itself, boast of itself. Though it is the condition for receiving grace, there is no question of the believer's being able to lay any *Anspruch* upon God on the grounds that that condition is fulfilled. Faith is an act in the sense that by it a man realizes there is nothing to be said for him. The Christian knows that God has found him. And there is the difficulty: faith is a free act and yet it is an election on the part of God. How can that be?

First of all, who is asking the question? Someone who is trying to look at the act of faith from outside and put his finger on it to make sure it exists. But that is entangling oneself in hopeless difficulties. Faith simply cannot be thought of as both a free act and a 'being-chosen' unless the being-chosen is understood as a sheer avowal (itself a confession of faith, if one chooses to speculate about God's election in terms of a theory of predestination). If my decision is not a free act, if God has laid down from all eternity that it shall be an act of belief or of unbelief—in a word, if it is predestined—then it ceases to be a decision and we can no longer talk seriously of belief or unbelief.

Faith is faith only if it is a decision and it is a decision only if it is free. Even Paul, it is true, seems to involve himself in predestinationism when he says that God has mercy upon whomever he wills and hardens the heart of whomever he wills (Rom 9:18) and when he compares man to the clay that the potter moulds whichever way he has

---

> The traveller who stumbles on my temple
> I have myself sought out.'

5. 'What were the Sacred, could one conquer it?
   What were the Infinite if finite man
   Could reach it on the wings of his own longing?
   No, a fatality holds me in thrall.
   Its stout fetters bind me hand and foot.
   The only act of man that is perceptible
   Is feeling he is one of the elect.'

a mind (verse 20). But evidently Paul does not mean to excuse man from the decision he must take with regard to grace. For we have seen that he holds faith to be an act of obedience. By speaking in terms of predestination, he only means to stress the absolute freedom of God, who is not bound by the dignity, merits or claims of any man.

Man's freedom and God's action are not mutually exclusive, because it is God's action that makes man free. Before God has chosen him, man is the slave of his in-sistence. All that he can do is works. Once delivered by grace, he is free for obedience—which means that now he can do acts instead of works. Grace has delivered him from himself for God. That is why he cannot know God's action *donec factum fuerit*, as Luther says, or speculate about how grace and freedom are reconcilable: he is only free in the moment when God finds him, because it is just this encounter, and it alone, that makes him free. To it he owes his freedom to decide for or against God. So there is freedom only where there is grace. The victory of grace is its bestowing on me the power to accept it or reject it. In other words it *pardons* me and thereby delivers me from the works to which I was condemned. God's antecedent election of me creates my freedom, from which henceforth free decisions can issue.

At this point it will be evident where the classical theory of predestination goes wrong. By saying that from all eternity God has predestined each individual to belief or unbelief, one entangles oneself in insoluble difficulties. All these come of making freedom an *attribute* of man which he possesses *before* grace encounters him, so that God's election finds a partner in a freedom already present. Thus freedom exists independent of grace, and inevitably the more we give to grace, the less is left for freedom, and the more we give to freedom, the less is left for grace. On the other hand if man is not a *nature* with freedom as one of its *attributes*, but rather an *ec-sistent*, and if ec-sistence is such only thanks to the *Thou*, then there is no freedom *antecedent* to God's call. Divine election draws it out from in-sistence into ec-sistence. No freedom constituted independent of him acts as God's partner, but rather a being which is not yet freedom and which will only be freedom through him. On the ontological plane, of course, man is a freedom (he is never a stone); but not on the ontic plane. The election that is made of him gives him his *ec-sistentiell* freedom and enables him to do an act (*Tat*)—that is, to decide for or against his new freedom.

Homo religiosus (be he Jew or Christian) thinks that his deeds are proof of his freedom and that he can obey God of himself by keeping the divine law. This is just where he is wrong. He does not see that his actions are only *works* which bring him no real future because he is not free to break out of his bondage. He imagines that he is serving God by keeping God's laws, perhaps at heroic sacrifice; but since he does it of himself he is obeying no one but himself, even though he should lay down his life: 'If I deliver my σῶμα [=if I deliver myself] to be burned, but have not love, I gain nothing' (1 Cor 13:3), because I am only doing a *work*. I cannot obey God until by his grace he has set me free to obey him.

Here once more the analogy of human affairs is enlightening. Friendship simply cannot be a *work*. I am not capable of it by reason of my good points, even though they may be admirable. My friend may indeed love me for my merits, but before he loves me I cannot assert any right to his friendship on the strength of them. Here there is nothing at all that I can do: nothing about myself will ever enable me to demand his love. In this matter I enjoy no freedom at all; I am the other's bondman. Only when he has *chosen* me shall I be free to accept his choice or refuse it, to love or not to love. Only the other as the other makes me free for himself.[6] In that respect my freedom utterly depends on him. The choice he makes of me, far from prejudicing my freedom, creates it and makes possible the decision whereby I receive the gift of a new being—that of friendship.

Of course human friendship gives me only a comparative freedom. Nothing less than the Wholly Other is my complete deliverance from myself and the world. Nothing less than the saving deed of God in Jesus Christ brings me an absolute future, which is the very future of God. Such is the power of God's election that it makes me free with respect to all things:

> Let those who have wives live as though they had none,
> and those who mourn as though they were not mourning,
> and those who rejoice as though they were not rejoicing,
> and those who buy as though they had no goods,
> and those who deal with the world as though they had
> no dealings with it.
>
> (1 Cor 7:29-31)

6. Before I am chosen by the other, of course I am free as to everything else (my work, my other relationships, and so forth), but I am not free *with respect to him*. I have no power to accept or reject the friendship of one who has not made choice of me; I am entirely servile as to my being ec-sistentielly determined by *his* friendship.

CHAPTER TWELVE

The Commandment of Love

Catholic critics have found fault with Bultmann for giving love no place in his theology. But we have spoken constantly of love from the very beginning of this book. Ec-sistential theology is a theology of otherness and therefore a theology of love. With Bultmann everything —be it God, Christ, Church or man—is centred on the theme of encounter, relation and gift. To demythologize is to discard the rationalism of in-sistence—that is, selfishness, inward-looking, hatred, smugness, the ingrained desire to control others. Bultmann's work is to destroy natural man.

Love is often thought of in terms of objective morality. Obviously we all agreee that moral behaviour is essential. But the 'thou shalt' can be looked at in two ways. It may be a goal to be attained, an ideal to be lived up to. Then moral behaviour means acting in a way consistent with that goal and ideal. By so living a man will gradually shorten the distance that separates him from the perfection he has in view, which is a state and not an act. Evidently this conception leaves no room for the *Thou*. I do not make my decisions at the command of a *Dass* nor for love of it, but only in view of an end to be gained.

The archetype of this sort of ethic is the Greek ethic. It assumes that there is an Idea of man which it is the business of morality to embody bit by bit. Moral activity is analogous to objective and 'technical' activity. A man who wants to build a house first conceives the 'idea' of it, which all that he then does helps to carry out. The matter must be 'formed' until the house stands there, a harmonious blend of matter and form.

With a work of art the case is the same: a statue is a lump of matter 'formed' according to a particular ideal of it which the artist had in mind. Likewise there is a human ideal (of the individual and of society) that exists as a mere potency in each individual and each group. To live morally is to achieve this τέλος bit by bit. The individual ideal is καλοκἀγαθία or δικαιοσύνη; the ideal of the city is κοσμοπολιτεία. Virtue (ἀρετή) is nothing else but fitness to attain the set end, the means proportionate to the end, ability to carry out the work as planned. Thus man constructs himself and constructs human society just as he builds a house or sculpts a statue.

244

We have already had occasion to observe that the moral language of the Greeks is entirely borrowed from the 'technical' field (pp. 24–5, above). Plato says that man is at once stronger and weaker than himself (*Republic* 430 e–f). Weaker because he is a matter to be formed; stronger because he is the 'technician' able to form the matter thanks to having the appropriate virtues. Obviously the *Thou* does not figure at all in individual morality: my imperative is my ideal being—that is to say, myself. But neither has the *Thou* any place in the morality of the city. For the other is not my neighbour, who is no less subject to the demands of the Idea than I am myself. Accordingly we must help each other to realize the ideal of individual and society alike—to 'form' each other.

Human relations are envisaged from the point of view of παιδεία, of mutual training and education. My business is not submitting to the *Thou* as such but rather to *what we have in common*, which is καλοκἀγαθία and κοσμοπολιτεία. There is no fundamental difference between the *I* and the *Thou*, and perfection consists in removing what difference there is. Being human means ceasing to exist as an individual.

The moral imperative can also be thought of in quite another way, no longer as a work to be done and a goal to be attained but as obedience to a *Thou*. The Greek ethic is rationalist: man knows where he is heading; he is master of his own acts; he is not concerned to trust in the other; he carries out a clear-cut, intelligent design, which is to achieve his own nature and that of the city. Contrariwise a morality based on the *Thou* demands that one renounce the *I*, its desires and its own ends. My business is no longer achieving myself by seeking my perfection but rather submitting to the other. Here the moral act is such not by its upshot but by its very doing. Of course there is an upshot too, but not one that constitutes the imperative.

What matters to the Greek is the end to be gained and a man is good only insofar as he gains it. In a morality of the *Thou,* what makes me good is my response to the demand of the *Thou.* Consequently every one of my acts involves my whole being. The Greek works towards his perfection step by step, because his perfection is an ideal to be realized and that cannot be done all at once (any more than a house or a statue comes into being all at once). The Christian—for the morality of the *Thou* is Christian morality—takes on his *whole* character with every one of his acts, because God does not ask him to make a work but to *obey*. Now obedience either is or it is not. Either a man obeys the commandment of God or he refuses to obey it. In each case he takes on his character absolutely.

Moreover, since it is a work to be achieved, the Greek imperative must by nature expire. To the extent that it is realized it becomes an indicative (a state). Thus man transforms himself into a perfect nature.

He has no more 'history': what is perfect is what is finished. On the other hand the Christian imperative endures valid for ever. The believer is constantly exposed to God's demands, perfection never becomes an attribute of the believer, the *I* never melts into the *Thou*.

This is how we must interpret the text 'You, therefore, must be perfect, as your heavenly Father is perfect' (Mt 5:48). Here we almost certainly have an authentic saying of Jesus which was uttered in Aramaic. It must not be interpreted in the sense of the Greek τέλειον, as referring to an ideal that man realizes bit by bit, that does not stamp him all at once, being the term of a process at each stage of which a man is less bad without having become entirely good. Such a notion fits in neither with Jesus's view of God and man nor with the Semitic concept of perfection, which is an 'absolute' concept. To the mind of the Bible a thing is perfect when it is whole, unimpaired, neither divided nor under strain. Jesus's saying means that a man is wholly on one side or wholly on the other, unreservedly for God or against him; that each one of his acts involves him completely, is an either-or which makes him an utter sinner or an utter saint.[1] Each one of his acts is a matter of his damnation or his salvation.

If a moral act consists in its doing and not in its upshot, in obedience to a demand and not in a work that results from it, we must perforce assume that there is some primal bond between the *I* and the *Thou*. I need not search for my neighbour, he being by definition the one who is already there. Man is not set in this world all by himself, needing to discover another individual so as *then* to have dealings with him.

Otherness is always there from the start, and precisely for that reason man is a being who ec-sists, not a being who 'exists'; a freedom, not a nature. 'Being-with' others makes man man. The business of being human is a *Miteinandersein* (a being-with-the-other). In a sense, to ask the question 'Who is my neighbour?' or 'What must I do for him?' is already a withdrawal into my ivory tower, a severing of my primal bond with him, a yielding to the devil of mistrust and hatred. I misconstrue the true nature of the *I* by supposing that it can exist without the *Thou*, and the true nature of the *Thou* by making it an object which I can directly observe and manipulate. And finally I turn the relation between the *I* and the *Thou* upside down by making it a relation which has to be created after my discovery of the other, whereas in fact it is there beforehand—*Miteinandersein* comes first.

---

1. Naturally what we say must not be taken in a psychological sense. On the psychological plane a man is often neither 'cold' nor 'hot' but 'lukewarm' (see Apoc 3:15–16). But a 'lukewarm' act stamps me *absolutely*, just li e any other act. It is my *Selbstverständnis* at the moment when I do it.

Such is the importance of *Miteinandersein* that even the Greeks found it was beyond them to construct a morality altogether within the confines of in-sistence. Had their ethic lost all sense of 'being-with' the other, then it could not have been an ethic. Wherever we are dealing with moral acts, imperatives come into the picture which presuppose the primal bond between the *I* and the *Thou*, though later they may become warped by being thrust into a wrong-headed framework.

Thus justice, truthfulness and loyalty (known to the Greeks as they are to the men of every culture) require no more than their own observance; there is no reason at all why they must imply an ideal perfection to be attained, a work to be done. Obviously, their original meaning is not that I must acquire the personal attributes of justice, truthfulness and loyalty (though this is more or less what the Greeks twisted them into meaning), but rather that I must act towards others with justice, truthfulness and loyalty. They really mean that the *Thou* is not matter for the *I* to form, nor a means to my personal perfection, but an absolute that I have no right whatever to control. On the contrary, I must serve it. In short, there can be no question of a moral act except where my behaviour is determined by the demands arising from the *Thou*. For example, when justice, truthfulness and loyalty are not respected, being-with-others is destroyed, the *I* seeks itself, and morality has taken its departure.

Evidently concepts such as those we have been speaking of (justice, loyalty, truthfulness) designate only the *formal* structure of a moral act; they do not tell us what must be done, any more than logic tells us what the object of thought is. Morality has no business calling for concrete acts, or it lapses into objectivism and the imperative is reduced to an indicative. Its only business is to indicate the form of moral acts. So it cannot be a material ethics. It would be its own negation if it tried to answer the question 'How must one act?' It can only set forth the formal structure of the moral agent, showing that he is a freedom rooted in *Miteinandersein*. In other words, its business is to set forth the ec-sistential nature of moral conduct but not its ec-sistentiell aspect; to show that only I can and may answer the question 'What must I do?', and that there are no general principles from which I can work out what to do here and now.

Moral demands arise from a *Thou* which I do not control, and nothing can excuse me from decision. Any ethic that lays down what must be done misjudges the nature of the imperative, seeing it in the *I* instead of the *Thou* and denying the primal bond between them. This is what Greek morality did, as we have seen, when it envisaged the 'thou shalt' as an ideal self to which the empirical self must be moulded. But all objective moralities do the same; particularly the modern ethics of good and value [*Güterethik* and *Wertethik*], which likewise consider that the meaning of moral acts lies not in their very doing but in the results they produce, thereby failing to recognize the 'historical' and temporal structure of man. They are essentialisms.

How, then, shall we interpret the Christian commandment to love our neighbour? Does it answer the question 'What am I to do?' Yes and no. No, in the sense that it does not have reference to the results of my act or to a goal I must reach, an ideal I must achieve, as in the moral systems we have just criticized. It has to do not with the *Was* but with the *Wie* of my act. It does not tell me what (*Was*) I must do, but how (*Wie*) I must do it. It defines a mode of being.

Love's *Wie* is of such a nature that in telling me how to act it reveals to me what I must do. Love is not a purely formal commandment like the commandments of justice and loyalty which we have considered above. It does not reveal the structure of moral acts *in general*. It does not define the relation between the *I* and the *Thou* on the ec-sistential plane, as do justice, truthfulness or loyalty, which are meant to show us that no ethic is possible where there is not a *Miteinandersein*. But neither is it a material rule. It says nothing about any goal to be reached, any ideal to be achieved. Nor is it a principle from which I could deduce what I ought to do, as a psychologist or psychiatrist can deduce what his patient ought to do.

Suppose that we turn to the commandment of love as it is enunciated in the sermon on the mount or to the description of ἀγάπη in 1 Cor 13: nowhere do we find a hint of the act's *Was*. Love is not a value to which effect must be given. At the same time—and in this respect it differs from the commandment of justice or truthfulness—neither is it a general expression of *Miteinandersein*. It is not meant to disclose that relationship in general but rather my own relationship with my neighbour in the situation of the 'moment'. It does not disclose the *concept* of my neighbour but my neighbour himself and thereby enables me to see what I must do; whereas the requirements of justice, say, and loyalty only reveal that a neighbour is necessary. They show that in general no moral act is possible apart from *Miteinandersein*. Love reveals the concrete *Thou* to me and ipso facto enables me to see what I must do.

Since the bond between the *I* and the *Thou* is there from the start, the love that is a particular *Verstehen* of it cannot be a thing Christianity has invented. Man has always been a being-with-the-other. And so he has always had a neighbour. Just as sin was not able to destroy *Miteinandersein*, only to warp it, so it was not able to destroy love either. In fact there is nothing very new about the Christian commandment. Remarkably enough, it is mentioned only twice (Mt 5:43–48 and Mk

12:28–34) in the course of Jesus's preaching, which shows that he and his disciples did not mean to say anything startling on the subject. 'You shall love your neighbour as yourself' is not by any means a rule peculiar to Jewish literature, and the very language in which it is couched assumes that everyone knows what love is and who his neighbour is.

The commandment to love one's enemies is known to the pagans: Seneca says one must not weary of helping one's enemy. His answer to the objection that rendering evil for evil comforts a man is that whereas it is glorious to get the better of one who does us good by doing him still more good, it is shameful to get the better of one who does us harm by doing him still more harm.[2] But there is a tremendous difference between the pagan idea of love and the Christian one. As we have seen, the Greeks tend to make justice, loyalty, truthfulness, and the rest mere attributes (*works*, in the Pauline and Lutheran sense of the word); and just so the best of the pagans quite mistake the nature of love. Why, in the texts to which we have referred, does Seneca say that hatred must not be returned for hatred? Out of reverence for the *Thou*? No, out of concern for one's personal dignity. It is part of the human ideal not to let the harmony of one's soul be upset by insult or injury. A man must be strong enough to keep his anger and resentment in hand. Has someone struck him? Let him feel as though some animal had done so. Can one be vexed with an animal? Has someone spat in my face? I will consider that the sea has spattered me with its scum. Why be vexed with the sea?

In this view of things, obviously the *Thou* is of no account. Love of the other is only an occasion for living up to the human ideal, for building the nobler self. This is the morality of works, and of the rankest kind. Love is a virtue, a means of perfecting oneself. Elsewhere Seneca sets forth the same principle (in slightly different form) with his elegant phrase *Homo res sacra homini*.[3] Man must be loved because he is something sacred. I do not love him purely and simply because he is my neighbour, but because he has the same fundamental worth as I have. It is human nature (the noblest of all natures) that I love: 'human dignity'. My love is motivated by my kinship with the other, by our common membership of the human race. So it is a love of my kindred —in short, philanthropy.

Christian love is altogether different. It is not a virtue that forms part of man's perfection. It is not an attribute, like self-control or bravery. It is not something in my personality, a feature of my character. It is the gift of myself to the other, the renunciation of all that I

2. *De otio* I, 4; *de ira* II, 32, 1–3; see Plato, *Criton* 49b–e and *Gorgias* 508d–e.
3. *Letter* 95, 33.

am. 'The virtue of love cannot be kept for yourself, because through love and in it you exist only for the other' (Kierkegaard, quoted by Bultmann). Nor is it an emotion, an affection. Its basis is not choice, kinship or fellow-feeling. All that is mere self-love, its criterion being the self. Why have I decided to love this person if not because he satisfies the aspirations and needs that I feel or has attributes that I like? Such a love does not deliver me from myself, because what I meet with in it is myself. I find in it what answers to my desires and my tastes— or at least, and more generally, that human dignity which is also mine (Seneca).

This is the case with all natural loves (notably with friendship, and love between the sexes), which as such are neither good nor evil. They are evil if the will of the man concerned is evil, and good if they are lived in faith. But to regard them as the embodiment of Christian love would be to confound Christian love with love of self.

My neighbour is not this man or that to whom I am drawn by liking or some natural kinship. My neighbour is every man, not all man in general but the concrete man whom I actually meet with. That is why Christian love is a commandment. It summons the will because *God* puts me into a given situation, because *he* calls me through my neighbour and confronts me with the either-or. If love were a mere emotion or choice, if it were grounded on some sort of kinship or on human nature, then making it obligatory would be nonsense. But the fact that it is an imperative shows that it has to do with the will and that therefore it is an absolute which demands the sacrifice of my instincts, tastes, desires, sympathies (my dislikes, antipathies, hatreds), of all that I have and all that I am.

Thus Christian ἀγάπη is not an enrichment of the subject. Here it is differentiated from the ancient ἔρως, the offspring of πενία. Ἔρως is not primarily a mark of *Miteinandersein*. It is a form of in-sistence. It embodies the effort to achieve a higher, more perfect life; it is ἐπιθυμία— that is to say, the antithesis of ἀγάπη, which covets nothing but gives instead. Therefore ἀγάπη is no less opposed to mystical love, which is the expression of the soul's deepest instinct—the ardent longing it has to be re-united with its origin, to enjoy the plenitude for which it was created. The fact that mystical love is mingled with feelings of humility and that the life it aspires to is the life of God, does not alter matters in the least. All that is no less true of ἔρως. The only difference between mystical love and ἔρως is that ἔρως has an intentional character, is bent on 'giving birth into the beautiful' (Plato), whereas mystical love does not issue in an ἔργον but is an emotion imprisoned within itself. The eternal pattern of mysticism is that of the imprisoned soul panting to be freed. 'Man's faith in himself—that is, the opposite of faith in God—

always remains the dominant theme of mysticism' (GV 2, p. 17).

Christian love is the ultimate in opposition to natural man, who tries with might and main to separate the *I* from the *Thou* so that he may control the *Thou*. Love demands that the *I* be vanquished, for my neighbour is discovered as my neighbour only in the very act of loving. So long as I do not love, I am living in in-sistence and therefore neither see the other nor what he requires of me. It is nonsensical to ask 'What must I do in order to love?' since it is only in loving that I shall know what I must do. This is the deepest meaning of the commandment 'You shall love your neighbour as yourself', which is a mere rule of thumb, but precisely as such puts a man to shame when he asks 'What must I do in order to love?' In reply he is referred to the workings of natural love.

By the very fact of loving himself, natural man knows without ado how he would like others to love him; he knows, not thanks to abstract principles but simply because he loves himself, what they ought to do for him. Conversely, if I really love I shall perceive who my neighbour is and guess what he expects of me. This truth is strikingly illustrated by the parable of the good Samaritan (Lk 10:30–36). Because they live in in-sistence, the priest and the levite do not see who their neighbour is and they do nothing for him. Because he loves, the Samaritan discovers his neighbour and sees what must be done for him. Such is the meaning of 'as yourself'.

'This commandment ["You shall love your neighbour as yourself"] picks the lock of self-love, strips a man of self-love. Were the commandment to love our neighbour expressed in any other way than by the little phrase *as yourself*, which is so easy to handle and yet is as hard and sharp as eternity, the commandment could not get the better of self-love. That "as yourself" can neither be twisted nor explained away. With the keen blade of eternity it pierces to that inmost den where a man loves himself. It leaves self-love without a leg to stand on, allows it not the faintest subterfuge. How curious! One could discourse long and searchingly about the way a man must love his neighbour, and yet self-love would still contrive to put forward excuses and evasions: protesting that the last word on the subject had not quite been said, that such and such a case had been passed over, such and such a point not made with all due exactitude and force. But that *as yourself* . . . No, not a wrestler in this world can lock his opponent in the iron grip in which this commandment locks and crushes self-love' (Kierkegaard, quoted by Bultmann).

Christian love, then, is not a principle which we possess, from which we can deduce what we must do in order to achieve a personal or a social ideal. Humanist love is of that sort. The evangelic commandment requires that we love enough to recognize our neighbour in this, that, and the other concrete situation and to perceive what we must do for him. Man's ec-sistential structure enables him to hear the call of the other and to love it ec-sistentielly by making it his *Sichverstehen*. Evidently there is no such thing as a Christian ethics, a moral theory which lays down in advance what the Christian must do and refrain from doing. The commandment of love is not addressed to a timeless man but to an 'historical' and temporal man whose ec-sistence is at stake day in day out because day in day out he has to decide on the spur of the moment whether he will love or not.

Since love exists only in the act of loving, it is always something hidden from the eyes of the observer. It can never be demonstrated, because it is neither an ἔργον nor a κτῆμα. Not even he who loves can prove to himself that he loves. In order to do so he would have to stand outside love. One who loves is absolutely unsure of his temporal ec-sistence, and there is no reassurance for him in looking at the things he has already done. In other words the commandment of love is never obeyed once and for all. Its demands are endless: the duty to love one another never ceases (Rom 13:8). 'Once love trusts in itself it is a fish out of water . . . When it makes itself its own object, it is no longer an endless task but a finite state' (Kierkegaard, quoted by Bultmann). Love has no time to study itself in the looking-glass.

Accordingly love is forgetfulness of self. First and foremost it is renouncing one's personal perfection and any arbitrary ethics which would show me what I must do to become perfect by loving my neighbour. Genuine selfishness (if we may be allowed the expression) must not be confused with common or 'garden' selfishness, which rather is a matter of being lazy, of preferring one's own comfort and enjoyments. The dyed-in-the-wool egotist is the man with a vision of the world, a well-established hierarchy of values and duties, to which he conforms his whole life, often at heroic sacrifice. In fact his obedience is only obedience to himself, to the ideal of man and society that he has set up for himself. Christian love is essentially the rejection of any such ethics, of *all* ethics, because all such is the work of man's hands. Through ethics *we* tell ourselves how to love our neighbour, whereas it is his business to tell us. Christian love is hearkening to sheer otherness, to God *as* God and our neighbour *as* our neighbour, who are always shattering our categories, our moralities, all our systems.

If love turns natural man absolutely inside out, the question arises whether he can do it for himself; and Christian faith replies with a blunt no. That is why Jesus establishes such a close connection between the love of God and the love of our neighbour (Mk 12:28–34). When this connection is examined in the light of Jesus's preaching about God, it becomes clear that the connection does not mean that loving our neighbour is the same thing as loving God—as though one could say: Since it is impossible to love God, let us love our neighbour and then we will be loving God. Such a train of thought assumes that man of himself has a sacred dignity, so that in loving him we love God as it were by proxy. That is to interpret love in the philanthropic sense, which we have already rejected, and substitute a bond with man for the bond with God.

Jesus is not in the slightest doubt that the first commandment is to love God—that is, to give up one's own will by an unconditional surrender. And obedience to God is what gives the second commandment its meaning: my attitude towards my neighbour must be determined by the attitude I take up towards God. It is as one who has utterly renounced self-will before God that I stand before my neighbour. Just as I am ready to sacrifice myself for God, I am ready to do so for my neighbour. Conversely it is the second commandment which invests the first commandment with its meaning. By loving my neighbour I show that I am obedient to God. There is no obeying God 'in mid-air', apart from the concrete situations where I am a man among men; I cannot obey God directly and in himself. What I do for my neighbour in the most various ways is not something I would do for God, but something I really do for my neighbour. He is not a means of loving God. I must not love others as it were while glancing sidelong at God. On the contrary, by delivering me from myself my love for God enables me to love my neighbour for his own sake.

In loving God I am delivered from my selfishness, my pride, my sloth—in a word, from my sin. I am now free to love others. Far from making my neighbour a go-between, my love for God (and it alone) enables me to love my neighbour for his own sake. And the other way round, it is only by loving my neighbour in this way, for his own sake, that I love God; for such a love of others is the sure sign that I have given myself to God without reserve—that I have let him purify me as far as was necessary to enable me to love others purely. 'If any one says, "I love God", and hates his brother, he is a liar; for he who does not love his brother whom he has seen, cannot love God whom he has not seen' (1 Jn 4:20).

Thus so long as I do not love my neighbour for his own sake, neither do I love God for his own sake, and so long as I do not love God for his own sake I do not love my neighbour for his own sake. Before he can love his neighbour, a man must be delivered from himself, snatched from egotism and hatred. But who can open him to love in this way except a being who himself is love? A relative and finite love could not utterly liberate a man. Only God can turn a sinner inside out by pardoning him. Man cannot tear himself away from his in-sistence; he can only *receive* his freedom. And no one can pardon man but the One who himself needs no pardon because he is infinite love.

The forgiving love of God is Christ. It is Christ alone, because he is God's saving deed and delivers man from his sin. God's love for us in Christ is not an emotion but an act, so that we are really transformed and thenceforth are able to love. When Rom 5:8 says 'God shows his love for us in that while we were yet sinners Christ died for us', the love in question is indeed an act, since God 'shows' (proves) it by having Christ die for us. This is the sense in which we must read verse 5: 'God's love [subjective genitive] has been poured into our hearts through the Holy Spirit which has been given to us'; it is through the Spirit that the act of God's love (described in verses 6 and 7 as an act of Christ) becomes efficacious for us. The question in Rom 8:35, 'Who shall separate us from the love of Christ?' casts back to the salvific event of Christ's death and resurrection in verse 34.

If Christ is the one who has loved us, that is because he gave himself up to death for us (Rom 8:35; Gal 2:20). The abundantly efficacious oneness of God's love and Christ's shines forth in the declaration that nothing can separate us from 'the love of God in Christ Jesus our Lord' (Rom 8:39)—that is, from the salvation which God has wrought through Jesus Christ. When 2 Cor 5:14 says that 'the love of Christ [subjective genitive] controls us', we must take this to mean the fact that Christ died for all, as the following verses clearly show. God's love is synonymous with his grace (2 Cor 13:11; 13:13); and therefore, like his grace, means everything that God has *done* for the salvation of men.

John dwells as firmly as Paul on the primacy of God's forgiving love, without which love of our neighbour would be impossible. 'In this is love, not that we loved God but that he loved us and sent his Son to be the expiation for our sins' (1 Jn 4:10). Only thanks to Christ does love become an opportunity for ec-sistence. Just as faith in God is only possible through him, so is Christian love, which does not arise from this world but is eschatological in nature. In this sense the command-ment of love can be called a new commandment (Jn 13:34; 15:12): love has become possible only through God's acts in Christ. It is also an old commandment (1 Jn 2:7), as old as *Miteinandersein*, to be found (more or less warped) in every religion and every moral system. But love is a reality (and therefore something new, for the sole genuine newness is the newness of event) only in Christ, apart from whom men have only a *Vorverständnis* of love. At best they manage to rough-hew acts of love, because before one can really love one must be stripped bare of in-sistence by God's forgiveness—that is, by the deed which God has done for us in Christ. God must first love us before we can love our brethren. Now God's act of love for us is Christ.

Once delivered by him, the believer can love men. And this love will attest his belief in God, for the only genuine faith is that which works through love (Gal 5:6). A man who does not love his brethren does not believe in God. For if he does not love his brethren it is because he has not been delivered from his sin and therefore does not have faith. But if he has faith he is subject to the law of Christ (1 Cor 9:21), which is the law of love (Gal 6:2) and commands us to be the servants of one another, not to seek our own good but the good of others (1 Cor 10:24; 13:5)—in a word, to sacrifice ourselves in the way 1 Cor 9:19-23 and 13:4-7 describe. He who loves is he who makes himself 'all things to all men'. So we can understand why love is such a noble thing, the first fruit of the Spirit (Gal 5:22). It is not simply one gift among many: 1 Cor 13 presents it as 'a still more excellent way', as the gift which excels all other gifts and without which all the rest would be nothing. They will all vanish when perfection has come, whereas love will abide, along with faith and hope. But there is more to be said: love must also be exalted above faith and hope. Why? Because in love the possibility of ec-sistence which faith and hope have created becomes a reality. Faith and hope bind me to God and free me for love, but only in love do I actually use this freedom of mine to live for God and my neighbour.

Love of our neighbour finds one of its purest expressions (indeed the purest of all) in readiness to forgive, which presupposes the utter death of natural man, utter forgetfulness of self, of one's own dignity and worth. To give up vengeance, to do good to him who has harmed us, to pray for our enemies—all that is fairly easy. But to *forgive* is something else again. To think so ill of oneself as to scorn one's most unquestionable rights, the cruellest wounds (because they are the most unfair)—that is beyond natural man. So the gospel is in deadly earnest when it demands forgiveness: 'Lord, how often shall my brother sin against me, and I forgive him? As many as seven times?'—'I do not say to you seven times, but seventy times seven' (Mt 18:21–22). The duty to forgive knows no limits, it is the ultimate consequence of the Christian attitude towards one's neighbour, which consists in the renunciation of every *Anspruch*.

In short, 'the Christian commandment of love is not a programme, an ethical theory, a principle from which one can deduce particular moral precepts of universal validity. Quite the contrary, such an undertaking would only obscure the real issue. The Christian commandment of love sends me to my *moment*, bidding me love so as thereby to understand the *Anspruch* of the *Thou* that encounters me—love so that I may discover what it is I have to do. If anyone's heart is set on having a rule, then let him go to the ten commandments, for Paul tells us (Rom 13 :9) that all they say is summed up in one sentence: You shall love your neighbour as yourself. If a man wanted something more, something nobler, he should be reminded of the dialogue between father and son in Dostoievski's book *The Youth*. In connection with an alarming prediction of some world catastrophe to come, the son asks:

'Yes, but what is to be done?'

'Heavens above, don't be in such a hurry; it is not going to happen tomorrow. But speaking in general, there is nothing to be done except one's best. Then at least one will have an easy conscience and can say that one has not had a hand in any mischief.'

'No, wait. Stick to the point. I want to know what I must really do and how I must live.'

'What you must do, my dear boy? Be decent, do not tell lies, do not lay hands on your neighbour's goods. In other words read the ten commandments, where it is all put down for ever.'

'Stop, stop! All that is old stuff, and besides it is just words and what we need now is action.'

'Well then, if boredom is getting too much for you, try taking a fancy to somebody or something, or just set your heart on something.'

'You are only making fun of me! Anyway, how am I supposed to start, with nothing but your old ten commandments?'

'Just keep them, in spite of all your questioning and all your doubts, and you will be a grown man.'

(GV 2, pp. 18–19)

CHAPTER THIRTEEN

The Old Testament and the New

I

(1) Traditionally the relation between the two testaments has been defined as that between the law and the gospel. In the Old Testament God merely made demands, whereas in the New Testament he revealed his forgiveness and his grace. Now is this antithesis perfectly sound? Is it true that the Old Testament knows only of being-under-the-law?

The answer is no. Even the Old Testament regards being-under-the-law as being-under-grace. For the grace of God brought Israel into being and gave it a law *which keeps it alive* and which, as such, is an earnest of God's goodwill. The law is at once a demand and a favour, since its aim is the salvation of those on whom it is laid. God's grace is seen in the birth of the nation, in the covenant he made with it, and in his choice of its fathers, leaders and prophets . . . God has given it a history which is a history of salvation. So there is really no dialectic between law and grace in the Old Testament. It is not mere obedience to the law which makes Israel a nation, but primarily the grace of God: grace takes the initiative, grace chooses, so that the law is kept only by faith in the God who finds man. Grace creates the bond he has with God and grace is the ground of his obedience. Always, being-under-the-law is understood as a simultaneous being-under-grace.

There is more. Grace is not only a gift but also forgiveness. The people often abjure the faith God promises, but it is his good pleasure to spare them. Man's faithlessness is answered by the faithfulness of God. God is at once the wrath that punishes transgressors and the grace that has compassion. It is not the New Testament alone which knows that God is 'slow to anger and abounding in steadfast love', pitying his own 'as a father pities his children' (Ps 103:8–13). (That is why the Christian Church has again and again adopted those words of the psalmists and prophets which beg God's forgiveness and promise his grace.)

Insofar as the gospel is God's grace for sinners, no one can say that it is missing from the Old Testament. Of course one can point out it is there in a limited form: the Old Testament does not always plumb the depths of sin and grace. In Psalm 103 itself, for example, man invokes his status as a creature when appealing to God: 'For he knows our frame; he remembers that we are dust' (verse 14). Certainly it is true that so long as man tries to base his appeal to God on anything, even his own frailty or nothingness, he has not yet perceived what grace is. But the Old Testament also contains a text which puts down the annihilation of creatures to the anger of God: 'We are consumed by thy anger; by thy wrath we are overwhelmed' (Ps 90:7), so that there remains no reason at all for God to forgive. God heals the broken-hearted (Ps 147:3; see Is 57:15), and the tones of utter humility and sheer trust that we find in Ps 51 (notably verses 3–6, 12–13, 18–19) and Ps 130 are familiar enough.

This conception of grace is paralleled by a no less profound conception of sin and faith. Rather than a moral transgression, sin is primarily an injury done to God's honour, a lack of trust in him, and therefore a token of human self-reliance (in-sistence). In a word, it is unbelief. For what God demands of man is an absolute renunciation of self—that is, faith:

> His delight is not in the strength of the horse,
>   nor his pleasure in the legs of a man;
> but the Lord takes pleasure in those who fear him,
>   in those who hope in his steadfast love.
>   (Ps 147:10–11)

> Only in the Lord are righteousness and strength.
>   (Is 45:24)

> Let not the wise man glory in his wisdom,
> let not the mighty man glory in his might.
>   (Jer 9:23; Is 7:9; 28:16; 30:15)

The Old Testament believer does not always experience the grace of God. But when grace seems to be denied him he goes on hoping. Then it is that eschatology comes into being.

Eschatological hope springs forth, in the prophets, from a deep consciousness of the people's sin: they have deserved nothing but God's annihilating judgment and can put forward no shadow of a right to his grace. So if there is a future for them it can only be sheer pardon, a sheer gift: 'For my own sake, for my own sake, I do it', God says (Is 48:11; see Ez 36:22f). Humanly speaking there is no continuity between the present and the future: Israel is dead, God's judgment has done away with it. Yet his Spirit is able to raise the dead, and will do so (Ez 37:1–14). It will regenerate the people (Ez 36:26f: 'A new heart I will give you . . .') and make a new covenant with them (Jer 31:33f: 'I will put my law within them . . .').

Thus insofar as Israel worked out a radical idea of God from an equally radical idea of grace and sin, Old Testament faith is an eschatological hope which the New Testament fulfils. The heart of the gospel is this: that in Jesus Christ God has made a reality what was only expectation for the Old Testament. In Christ he has forgiven sin, founded the new Israel, and bestowed his Spirit. That is what the New Testament means when it makes man's relations with God depend on the person of Jesus. As we have seen at considerable length, Christ is the salvific deed of God reconciling the world to himself (2 Cor 5:19).

But what bearing has all this on the connection between the two testaments? To say that Christ is an eschatological deed is to say that he alone is grace—grace which cannot be an earthly gift, because it is the condemnation of the old aeon, the stark cross, the abolition of the world. Jesus Christ is God's judgment upon history, and he brings history to an end. Therefore the grace of the New Testament—Christ —differs fundamentally from that of the Old Testament. For the grace of the Old Testament belongs to one concrete people and has been given for that people. The dialectic of law and grace which we have described operated exclusively within the particular history of one particular nation, to whom God assigned a destiny in *this* world, not in a world to come. He revealed his grace by creating an historical people (not an eschatological one), delivering them from Egypt, causing them to pass through the Red Sea dryshod, granting them the law on Sinai, bringing them into the promised land, constantly intervening in their affairs.

When the prophets want to describe God's grace they recall *events* (Amos 2:9–13; Is 43:1, etc.). The Psalms praise God as the ruler who directs the nation's destinies (Ps 105; 135; 136). What he has given them, both as a nation and as individuals, is a *history*: individuals are pardoned in the sense that they enjoy the favours that God formerly bestowed on the people. In and through tradition the past is made present and efficacious for them. (The Jewish liturgy of the Passover is a splendid example: for those who take part in it it actualizes the past history of the nation.) Accordingly God's grace in the Old Testament is not the radical grace of the New Testament, where we are no longer dealing with the condition of a visible people but with the eschatological community of the last aeon. God's deeds in Christ are not of an historical, earthly nature, as though the link with past generations enabled the present generation to benefit by what Jesus did long ago.

The grace of the New Testament is not the gift of a past history made present by tradition for the benefit of men now living: it is the *abolition* of history. For the Church is not an historical thing, it stands 'outside and above' history (GV 1, p. 293) because it is not of this world, and for that reason it is absolute grace. In Israel the grace of God lived on in the leaders God sent (Moses, the prophets). But one cannot speak of the Fathers of the Christian Church (such as Augustine and Luther) as one does of Christ; because he is God's *eschatological* deed, whereas obviously Peter is not, nor John, nor Paul, nor Augustine, nor Luther. No doubt, as we have seen, the Old Testament did get as far as eschatological expectation. The prophets announced the nation that was to come; they understood that nothing was to be expected from this world; they spoke of an absolute death and resurrection; they entertained a radical idea of sin and grace. But it was all thinking and hoping; they only had a *Vorverständnis* of these things. With them the eschatological Israel is only an ideal, whereas in the Christian Church it is a reality.

It follows that 'for Christian believers the Old Testament is no longer revelation, as it was and still is for the Jews' (GV 1, p. 333). For a man who lives in the Church, the history of Israel is over and done with. Christian preachers cannot and must not remind Christian people that God brought their ancestors out of Egypt, led them into the promised land, rebuilt Jerusalem and the temple, and the rest. The history of Israel, which was a history of this world, is not ours: our history is not of this world. Insofar as God's grace was formerly identified with the people of the old covenant, it is not ours. Events which for the Old Testament were the utterances of God, are no longer that for us. Of course they still mean something to us on the purely human plane. The biblical past, like the Greek past and the Roman past, is part of our inheritance as twentieth-century men of the West. From this point of view the exodus from Egypt, the settlement of Canaan, and the work of the prophets are elements of our present; but they are such on the same basis as all other events in world history. 'In this sense Jerusalem is no holier a city than Athens or Rome' (GV 1, p. 334).

Insofar as the doings and achievements of Israel embodied God's grace for them, those things are no longer God's grace for us, because that grace was the grace of the old aeon, whereas we are living in the new aeon that Christ and his Church have ushered in. The long and short of it is that we must go back to Paul and Luther: the Old Testament is nothing more than promise. If it was law and grace for the Jews, it is nothing of the kind for us. The New Testament alone is grace pure and simple. The Old Testament is only the *Vorverständnis* of grace.

(2) Precisely as the *Vorverständnis* of grace the Old Testament retains a certain validity for us. Insofar as it is not the mere private history of Israel it still *can* be revelation to a Christian believer. It can be to the extent that one interprets it in the light of Christ—that is, to the extent that it heralds the Christian *Verständnis*. Now in what sense does it herald the Christian *Verständnis*?

The New Testament itself and primitive Christianity often draw on the Old Testament for 'scriptural proof'. They claim that the Old Testament prophesies the truth of the Christian faith, the necessity and salvific meaning of Jesus's fate. Will that argument bear examination? Our answer must be no. In fact that sort of 'scriptural proof' is impossible. First of all the alleged prophecies are not prophecies in the strict sense of the word—the sense in which the New Testament understands them—that is, predictions that come true before our very eyes. And on the other hand they have no bearing whatever on Jesus and the Christian community but are mere images of the future which the Jews and Judaism looked forward to. In order to make real prophecies of them, the New Testament has to read a meaning into them that goes dead against their real meaning, by recourse to the allegorical method; which shows, of course, that Christian faith existed without them since it discovered them later on.

Such proofs, therefore, are worthless and by rights *must* be worthless, because a faith which relied on them would only be a 'work'. No, the New Testament 'scriptural proofs' must be abandoned, not on grounds of historical criticism alone but because they can only obscure the true nature of faith. The requirements of controversy produced them, first in order to refute the Jews and then to make those features of the gospel which particularly scandalized the Gentiles more acceptable to them by showing that they were all predetermined and foretold. This sort of reasoning leaves us cold nowadays but had a powerful effect on ancient man. In fact what we have here is a mythologization (a naive rationalization) of faith.[1]

If that is the position, how can the Old Testament still be the Word of God for us? It can be in the sense of preparing the way for the Christian *Verständnis*. In the chapter where we examined biblical thought we began with the Old Testament, which teaches us that man is not reason but will, ec-sistence and relation to God. In the chapter on God we said that Jesus only takes up and deepens the Old Testament idea of God. In the chapter devoted to history we stressed

---

1. In GV 2, pp. 162–8, Bultmann has shown, by the very examples which the New Testament writers give us, that scriptural proof as they understand it is critically and theologically impossible.

the Old Testament origins from which the ec-sistential idea of historical fact derives. And finally, in the present chapter we have seen that the Old Testament takes a radical view of sin and grace, law and promise. Thus it foretokens the Christian *Verständnis* and on that basis can still be the Word of God for us; but only a *mediate* word, for Jesus Christ suffices unto himself—he alone is the Word. For the Christian, the Old Testament is valid only as a type (1 Cor 10:11, Greek text; see Rom 15:4), to the extent that 'it clearly embodies the *Verständnis* of man as a creature who in his "historicity" always remains subject to the demands of God' (GV 1, p. 336).

What this means is that the Christian *may* have recourse to the idea which the Old Testament gives us of God, sin, grace and the rest, but need not do so, because God has given us everything by giving us his son. It is a remarkable fact that the Gospels, certain Letters of Paul and the first Letter of John pay the Old Testament little heed or none. At any rate if the Church's preachers go back to it as to the Word of God they can do so only on condition: (a) that they interpret it according to its real meaning—that is, without bringing in allegory— and (b) that they eliminate its reference to the Jewish people and their particular history. The Old Testament may only be used insofar as it is really promise—that is, insofar as it paves the way for the Christian *Verständnis* of God, man, sin and grace.

II

The burden of the foregoing section—that Jesus Christ (the New Testament) is the *Dass* of which the Old Testament is mere expectation—can be put in a slightly different way if we turn to an idea given currency towards the mid-nineteenth century by Johann Christian Konrad Hofmann, an idea that made a great impression on people. Instead of looking on the *words* of the Old Testament as prophecies of the New, Hofmann thought that the very *history* of Israel is fulfilled in the history of Christ and his Church. History in general is prophecy, because it moves towards a goal that is carried within it in the form of promise. In the light of its fulfilment it is understood to be prophecy, because only when it has been fulfilled can men see where it was heading. Since Christ, in Hofmann's eyes, is the end of history, history is prophecy of Christ.

Evidently Hofmann was influenced by the philosophy of Hegel. He is right in saying that it is not the isolated words of the Old Testament that herald Christ but the very history of Israel as related in the Bible. He is also right to interpret that history in the light of its end—that is, of Christ. But does he not go astray in thinking that history is a process whereby trends which are active from the beginning reach their fulfilment, so that the term of historical evolution only realizes its original potentialities? Is Christ immanent in the Old Testament, even in the most rarefied form, or is he something utterly new? That we shall discover by examining the three major categories which are the covenant, the kingdom of God, and the people of God.

A

THE COVENANT

The theme of the covenant sets forth the specific relationship obtaining between God and Israel. It is not a figurative description of that relationship, but actually constitutes it. Of course the people and God are not equal partners, but each partner does have his obligations to the other. God demands the faithfulness of men and men count on the faithfulness of God. The chosen people are an earthly, concrete, historical nation. For that reason the covenant is set up, preserved and if need be restored by ritual sacrifice—that is, by an objective act whose validity does not depend on the personal holiness of the nation's members.

Under the influence of the prophets it takes on another aspect. The prophets protest against the view that the covenant is indestructible if only the people are punctilious in observing ritual. They inveigh against the mistaken idea that God is tied down to the land in which Israel has made its home. They denounce the false assurance that the validity of the covenant does not depend on the behaviour of individuals because it is based on the people's existence as a people. They preach that the covenant depends on obedience, the doing of justice and righteousness. There it is not indestructible: God can perfectly well reject the nation he has chosen for himself. Israel has no claim to God's preference as against other nations (Amos 3:2). But Israel must beware of thinking that God's election is its due or its unquestionable possession, and remember that faithlessness to God's requirements will break off the covenant.

Now here a difficulty arises. Since the covenant is made with an historical people, it can only be made contingent on conditions which that people are able to fulfil as an *historical* people—that is, on the celebration of the official rites and (in Judaism) on the observance of a certain manner of life. A covenant with an earthly people which was made to depend on their living up to moral standards would be utopian: in this world, where sin is a fact, such standards are never observed by the people as a people. A concrete community can be required to discharge ritual duties or keep to a certain form of life, but it cannot be required to be holy in the true sense of the word. So when the prophets protest against the popular view that the individual is holy by the mere fact of belonging to the nation, when John the Baptist takes up the same theme (in Mt 3:9: 'Do not presume to say to yourselves, "We have Abraham as our father" '), they are raising the covenant from the concrete plane to the eschatological plane, for only in the new aeon will it be possible for the covenant to rest upon the holiness of individuals. They are destroying any idea of a covenant with an earthly nation. Jesus himself makes this plain as day in Mt 8: 11–12: 'I tell you, many will come from east and west and sit at table with Abraham, Isaac and Jacob in the kingdom of heaven, while the sons of the kingdom will be thrown into the outer darkness'. Thus the covenant with a people whose individual members obey God's law can only be eschatological.

Evidently the prophets attached an otherworldly meaning to the idea of the covenant. Since the old covenant was broken by sin, God will establish a new one in the age of salvation that is to come. It will be miraculous in character—that is, it will not be the work of men. Such is the vision we find in Jer 31:31–34 and Ez 37:26–28. It must be added, however, that the two prophets have not really thought out their eschatology, since they still foresee an earthly grandeur for the Israel that is to come.

For its part, the New Testament envisages the new covenant in purely eschatological terms, declaring that the prophecy of Jeremiah has now been fulfilled in the Christian community (Heb 8:8–12; 10:16f). The Church is not of this world; as we have seen, it comes from above. And the event which sets it up is not an historical fact but the eschatological *Dass*: it is born of Christ. The appearance of Jesus cannot be compared with the event of the institution on Sinai, which was a phenomenon of this world and moreover constituted only one incident in the total history of Israel. The event of Christ is transcendent and peerless. And so 'Jesus suffered outside the gate in order to sanctify the people through his own blood. Therefore let us go forth to him outside the camp, bearing abuse for him' (Heb 13:12f).

Christian worship is no longer a national concern, like the Jewish Passover: the paschal lamb has yielded to Christ, who was sacrificed 'as our passover' (1 Cor 5:7, Greek text). This abolition of the old covenant is driven home to us by the synoptic tradition when it has Jesus's last supper (during which the Eucharist was supposedly instituted) take place on the eve of the Passover, and by John when he has Jesus die on the day of the Passover. Paul sees the two covenants at variance as the written code (the Jewish law) and the Spirit (2 Cor 3:18).

The new covenant, which 'is permanent' (verse 11), being the dispensation of the 'Spirit' and of 'righteousness', outdoes the old in 'splendour'. But that splendour cannot be seen; it is not bestowed on a concrete nation, as in Deutero-Isaiah (see 60:19f), but only on those who turn to the Lord (2 Cor 3:16). Moreover they have this treasure in earthen vessels (2 Cor 4:7ff), which means that all one can see in them is frailty and death; this is how the 'life of Jesus' looks to the eyes of the world.

Obviously the new covenant must be an absolutely eschatological thing. For that reason circumcision, the visible sign of the old covenant, has now been done away with. True circumcision is 'a matter of the heart, spiritual and not literal' (Rom 2:29; see 1 Cor 7:19; Gal 5:6; 6:15). And the new covenant must be transcendent because 'there is no distinction between Jew and Greek; the same Lord is Lord of all' (Rom 10:12). There is neither slave nor free, neither male nor female (Gal 3:28; see 1 Cor 12:12f).

B

THE KINGDOM OF GOD

Like other Semitic peoples, Israel pictured its God as a king. Scholars do not agree as to the time when this happened. The image stands forth plainly enough in Is 6:5, but there is good reason to believe that it goes back to an earlier period. Yahweh's being king means that he is Lord of the people, that his will rules them through his ordinances (*chuqqim*) and commandments (*miswôth*). Acting as judge, he settles disputes, thus showing himself to be the pillar of justice within the nation. Without, he is that pillar by directing Israel's wars and giving them the victory. His kingship is thought of in such realist terms that he appears as the (victorious) rival of the princes of this world. As a ceremony ushering in the New Year there seems to have been a feast of Yahweh's coronation (or rather enthronement), where he was praised as set above all the other gods and lords of earth. 'The Lord reigns' was the watchword at this celebration (Ps 37; 93; 96; 97; 99).

And then, by a process which we are familiar with already, his kingdom was gradually shifted to the eschatological plane. At the period of the exile, when God has forsaken his people, the restoration of his power is set in the *future*. Deutero-Isaiah identifies that future, which will bring salvation, with the end of the exile. The messenger whom he sees in spirit announces: 'Your Saviour is coming, your God reigns' (Is 52:7).

In the post-exilic period, affirmations about the present and the future character of God's kingdom go hand in hand. But there is a strong conviction that the kingdom does not yet exist. Nothing can be seen of it, because foreign nations rule the whole earth, even God's own land. When the idea of Satan as the prince of this world becomes established in Judaism, the eschatological nature of the divine kingdom is thrown into bolder relief than ever: there can be nothing in common between Satan and God, and God can only be an absolute future. Consequently in apocalyptic literature the judgment no longer takes place, as with the prophets, in concrete history but becomes a totally 'forensic' act: the whole world as such will be judged and annihilated. God's kingdom is really a new aeon.

Here again Jesus takes a decisive step forward. To his mind the kingdom of God is no longer the theocracy of which the Old Testament dreamed. It is not a country delivered from its enemies, where God rules over a people enjoying the height of power and well-being and a heavenly peace amid their fields, their fig trees and their vineyards. No imagery of this sort will be found in Jesus's preaching. All that can be found is the expression 'kingdom of God' and the idea of a kingdom where his name will be honoured and his will done. The saying we have quoted from Mt 8:11f shows plainly enough that the kingdom stands outside the framework of history. So does the parable in Lk 10:30–37. Again, the demands of the sermon on the mount and the commandment of love (Mt 25:31–46), which make mincemeat of all tidy rules and laws, prove that Jesus does not consider the kingdom to be a thing of this world.

Obviously the kingdom of God cannot be realized here on earth, not even in a millenarian future. It is absolutely and utterly eschatological, a fact which the New Testament conveys by representing the Church as the kingdom. For the Church is not, we must repeat, an historical thing; it transcends the world. Its king is the risen Christ (risen in the demythologized sense which we have explained). Though the Hellenistic community borrowed from a pagan religious environment the title Kyrios, which they applied to Jesus, Paul, there can be no doubt, gave that title an altogether transcendent meaning by 'historicizing' it: for him Jesus is absolute Lord. The age of the Church and the age of salvation are the age of Christ's reign (1 Cor 15:23–28; 2 Cor 6:2), the 'splendour' of which dwells in those who believe in him and thereby spread death and life (2 Cor 2:14–16).

Thus the kingdom of God is something quite different from what the Old Testament prophets looked forward to: it is 'eschatological and supraterrestrial' (GV 2, p. 179), so that the Christian no longer lives 'according to the flesh [= according to the world]' even though he does still live 'in the flesh [= in this world]' (2 Cor 10:3; ch. 3, §5, above). As we know, John conceived of it still more eschatologically.

In Paul the new aeon is made up of two consecutive periods: God does not yet reign unchallenged (1 Cor 15:23–28). But with John the kingdom is totally present here and now. 'My kingdom is not of this world' (Jn 18:36)—in other words, it is the utter judgment of this world. The judgment is not, as with Paul, an event which belongs in part to the future: it has already taken place. Light has come into the world and for every man its coming means the choice of eternal life or eternal death. The parousia is 'there'. He who believes in Christ has already risen, has passed from death to life (3:16–19; 5:24f; 8:51; 11:25f; 12:31; 14:6). Jesus has overcome the world (16:33) and his victory is also the victory of the Church (1 Jn 5:4).

C

THE PEOPLE OF GOD

God's kingship and earthly kingship cannot co-exist. In Judg 8:32 Gideon says to the Israelites: 'I will not rule over you, and my son will not rule over you; the Lord will rule over you'. According to Hos 9:15 the sin of Israel began at Gilgal, where Saul was anointed king (1 Sam 11:14f). When David had made it popular, perhaps the prophets no longer launched open attacks upon the monarchy. Nonetheless the conflict which necessarily exists between the idea of the people of *God* and the idea of government by a man, made itself felt. For earthly kingship inevitably settles into the world and organizes itself: it needs officials, an army, taxes, and so forth (1 Sam 8:10–18). It must have a foreign policy, make treaties with pagan states or wage war on them. All these activities have nothing to do with the life of a people who are the people of *God*; the prophets, well aware of the fact, fiercely resisted them. The text of Samuel that we have just cited is but one proof among many. They feel that justice and righteousness cannot prevail in a nation which is organized as a state. Well then, what do they advocate? A return to the old patriarchal system where there was no state! When they suggest a new constitution they lose touch with reality, producing the utopian ideal of Deuteronomy, the utopian ideal of the 'Priestly' source—ideals, that is, which are unworkable given the concrete demands of a nation's life in this world.

After the exile we have a recrudescence of theocratic dreaming, but Israel is no longer a state. It lives under foreign rule and at heart acknowledges that this must be so, that it must give up political power if it would be the people of God. Accordingly the 'devout' withhold their support from the Hasmonaean dynasty when it has rid the country of the Syrians and restored an organized state along with the institutions that a state involves. It will likewise be recalled that they readily submit to Roman rule when Pompey makes his entry into Jerusalem. Thus the Jews recognize that if they wish to exist as the people of God they cannot do so in the form of a state but only in the form of a religious community—a kind of church.

Does the Jewish 'church' of Persian and Roman days really represent the people of God? A community shorn of national structures it certainly is, being ruled by cultic and ritual laws which have nothing to do with the institutions a state requires for its existence, nor with the old religions of the pagan city, and which as time goes on become more and more irrelevant to the business of life in this world. On the other hand this community is transcendent only in a very qualified sense, because it remains peculiar to one given people, the Jewish people. Moreover that in it which excludes other nations is precisely its 'eschatological' feature: its worship and ritual, which instead of making for universality make for particularism. It is only at this period that the sabbath and circumcision take on their well-known historical significance. Thus Judaism is a thing at war with itself.

Contradictory too is the future which Judaism awaits and expects as of right:

> Sound the trumpet for our deliverance
> and raise the standard to gather in our exiles.
> Bring back our judges as before
> and our counsellors as at the beginning.
> Yahweh our God, take pity on Jerusalem, thy city,
> and on Zion, the place where thy glory dwelleth,
> and on the kingdom of the house of David,
> and on the Messiah of thy righteousness.
> —*Shemoneh Esreh* (the liturgical
> prayer of eighteen petitions)

Judaism seeks the re-establishment of an independent nation in the form of a state and curses Roman rule, yet it is far from thinking to win freedom by political means—war, to be precise. It looks for a miraculous intervention on the part of God. There is to be a Jewish kingdom of this world but not in the form of a real state.

And finally the Messiah too is a contradictory figure. The king who reigns in the age of salvation must be of David's stock—that is, he must be both concrete and eschatological, from below and from above. Consequently he has to be made a sort of phantom so that he shall not usurp the place of God, the only real king. In theory the Messiah competes with the sovereignty of God and in practice with the sovereignty of the Jewish priesthood, which latter is the only actual form that theocracy can take. These contradictions explain why the Messiah is missing from a good many visions of the future and why he faded at last into insignificance. The Davidic Messiah was thrust into the background by the mythological figure of the son of man and the messianic age became a mere prelude to the real age of salvation.

This evolution which we have sketched underlines the inevitable contradiction there will be between any people of God and all concrete peoples, for concrete peoples must be organized as states if they choose to remain an earthly reality at all. God cannot be the king of a nation. The error of Judaism was its attempt to identify the next world with this world. On the one hand it had to give the concrete Jewish people the form of an ecclesiastical state, and on the other hand it had to put off the realization of God's kingdom until the messianic age.

The New Testament sheds entirely fresh light on the problem by declaring that the new aeon has begun with Christ. The eschatological kingdom is the kingdom of God's Word and the true Israel is the Church. No longer is the people of God something concrete and historical. It does not exist as a nation which must have some historical framework. That is why the state remains free in its own sphere, the sphere of law (Rom 13). It need not trouble itself about the specific interests of the eschatological community (see 1 Cor 6:1ff). Thus the Christian faces a special problem because he finds himself the subject of state and Church alike, and the Church is the true people of God. As an eschatological thing it is no less present in each separate community than in the sum of the churches. One does not become a member of it by right of birth but when one hears the call of the gospel, is torn away from the world, and sanctified by baptism, which incorporates believers into one body. The members of God's people are the 'called', the 'elect', the 'saints', they are 'Christ's', they are 'in Christ'. They constitute the 'Israel of God'. Theirs are the 'fathers' and the promises, and the Jews are only 'the synagogue of Satan' (Apoc 2:9).

D

CONCLUSION

We asked at the outset how far the history of the Old Testament and of Judaism foretoken what has been realized in the Christian Church. Now we are in a position to answer that it does so 'in its essential contradiction, in its failure' (GV 2, p. 183). The antinomy we have laid bare runs throughout the entire consciousness and hope of Israel. The people of God refuse to consider themselves as something of this world pure and simple. They will not interpret their history as the mere work of human wills, nor yet as a fate. It is an exploit of God's. Thus Israel's whole mind is bent on the supraterrestrial God and his doings. The contradiction arises because God and his doings are not understood 'in their utterly transcendent and eschatological meaning' (*ibid.*, p. 184).

God's work is expected to coincide, as it were, with the earthly history of the Jewish people. But God's *covenant* with a people proves to be impossible in this world and therefore becomes an eschatological concept. The *kingdom of God*, likewise, proves to be impossible of realization in this world and hardens into the 'grotesque image' (*ibid.*) of Jewish theocracy, compounded of priesthood and legalism. And finally the *people of God* is only a dream, because the Jews try to identify it with a nation which, to exist, must be a state, must have institutions, civil servants, armed forces, and the rest. So to speak of an historical people as being the people of God is a contradiction in terms.

The Old Testament breaks down, and precisely therein lies its promise. Nothing else can hold out promise to man but the thwarting of all his ways, the clear perception that his earthly history will never enable him to reach God. Of course defeat is seen as promise only when its promise has been fulfilled—in encounter with grace, which reveals itself to no man until he knows full well that his situation is desperate. That knowledge must arise from an historical evolution. Everything would have been finished had God not produced a new beginning in Christ which is not in the least the dawn of a new history but rather a 'new creation'.

Eschatology is always waiting for men who discover that the road they were travelling, which they hoped would show them in this world the meaning of their life, can only lead them to disaster. When grace finds a man it reveals to him that God's action must be eschatological, and it enables him to live eschatologically. If we look at the matter from this point of view, then we are right to consider the Old Testament a promise, and the contradiction which runs through it from one end to the other reveals its fundamental meaning. It is not a human contradiction that exists between sin and grace: man, the work of God's hands, dreams of finding him in this world and rejects the folly of the Cross.

Here we are back at the Pauline interpretation of law, our theme in the first part of this chapter. If law is our παιδαγωγὸς εἰς χριτόν (Gal 3 : 24),[2] it is so in that it leads man to failure. 'But the Scripture consigned

2. To translate παιδαγωγός as 'pedagogue' is nonsensical. Law does not lead a man to Christ by helping him achieve the 'Become what you are' but by leading him to utter failure (TNT, p. 267). The 'pedagogue' of ancient times, whom Paul refers to, is the master that rules with a rod of iron. The law was a prison (Gal 3:2), and *as* a prison it was a παιδαγωγός. (See also GV 3, p. 159).

all things to sin, that what was promised to faith in Jesus Christ might be given to those who believe. Now before faith came, we were confined under the law, kept under restraint until faith should be revealed' (Gal 3:22f). 'For God has consigned all men to disobedience, that he may have mercy upon all' (Rom 11:32). Insofar as it is the law of *Moses*, the law is the road of failure in sin, and Christ is its end (Rom 10:4). Insofar as it is the law of *God*, it is good and holy (Rom 7:12). This means that it could not be observed under the old dispensation—that is, within the framework of this world. The observance of it can only be eschatological. It can only be obeyed 'in Christ'; man can perfectly carry out God's will only to the extent that he is determined by God—that is, by what is Wholly Other than this world.

We must not regard the connection between the two testaments as a mere theory, or a religious philosophy of history, or an interesting line of inquiry, or an 'historical question to be cleared up'. The dialectical relation we have described has a theological meaning which always remains pertinent. We must always be experiencing it, just as we must always be experiencing the relation between law and grace. Only he can understand what grace is who is constantly experiencing law. At every moment we are tempted to 'works', or our own righteousness, and faith is none other than the constant annihilation of that desire.

When Paul sets forth his doctrine on law and faith he is not giving us an interesting lecture on an historical subject; he is describing the eternal drama of man, who forever tries to win salvation by himself, to achieve perfection by his own resources; he is teaching us that we shall never know what grace is until the day comes when we despair of ourselves. Similarly the Christian needs to contemplate the Old Testament again and again as a history of failure, so as to understand that 'the state of a justified man is rooted in nothing else but defeat' (GV 2, p. 186). Just as faith must be a constant victory over law if it is really to be faith in grace, so it must constantly overcome the temptation to turn the eschatological event into a thing of this world.

CHAPTER FOURTEEN

Christianity and Humanism

Over and over again we have contrasted natural man and his philosophy with the believer and revelation. Are Christianity and humanism then absolutely incompatible? Or are there points of agreement between them in spite of everything?

I

(1) What we call humanism has its roots in the Graeco-Roman tradition. It may be called a belief in the spirit—that is, in all that is noblest and best. Humanism holds that man is essentially spirit, which constitutes the world of the true, the good and the beautiful. That world is also the world of the divine, for the divine reveals itself in and by spiritual things. Spiritual things are invisible and eternal, as contrasted with visible and transitory things. In man it is body and soul which express this contrast. But the dualism of things visible and invisible is not such as to prevent the invisible from manifesting itself in things visible as the power that is able to create the latter. Thus visible things are data open to the working of spirit. The universe is an intelligible whole governed by set laws.

For its part, the human community must try to realize the ideal of justice and righteousness on which it is grounded, while the individual must develop his spiritual personality to the utmost by leading a cultural and moral life that becomes him. So the life of the individual, like history itself, is a struggle between spirit and matter, with matter always trying to subdue the spirit to its own will. Man does not become a person by repressing his instincts and passions but by mastering and spiritualizing all his lower nature. Humanism holds that it is an error to see the meaning of life in the organization of life on earth and in technology. The only end worthy of man is man, and in man the only end worthy of him is the spirit. In other words, the shaping of personality should be the purpose of all education. Society is not an end in itself. All factors that go to make it up—law, economics, politics, and the rest—must serve man. The spirit, which sets the whole tone of humanism, manifests itself in the true, the good and the beautiful. Thought and knowledge are propelled by the idea of truth. Knowledge sheds light; it helps us understand the world through science and transform it through technology, so that it becomes more and more a human universe.

Morality is grounded in the idea of good. It enables the individual to control his lower instincts, to live by a high ideal, and to acquire the dignity of a person. It begets law and justice in society, being the absolute without which no real human community can exist. The idea of the beautiful is the source of art, and art creates a world where our eyes are opened to the invisible forces that lie hidden in visible things. Thus, in a sense, mystery becomes accessible to esthetic contemplation. In short, knowledge, law and art, issuing from the true, the good and the beautiful, make up the native country of man. The world, man and the divine comprise one whole, which is the whole of the spirit.

> *Alle Tag' und alle Nächte*
> *Rühm' ich so des Menschen Los.*
> *Denk er ewig sich ins Rechte,*
> *Ist er ewig schön und gross.*[1]

(2) What shall we say of Christianity as it compares with humanism? Gathering up in one sheaf all that has been said of Christian faith through the foregoing chapters, we immediately perceive that it conflicts with humanism. Though the world should become completely spiritualized, faith will never look on it as man's true country. No doubt there is an order in the universe, a determinism in nature, there are laws that govern the course of history; above all there is the human spirit that tries to make the world the world-of-man; but that world is not the world of faith. Christianity says that true life is not the life of the spirit. The God that Christianity preaches is not the sort of quintessence of spirit which humanism talks about, but the Wholly Other. Man cannot find him by pursuing the true, the good and the beautiful but only by a willingness to die to all that is human in the best and noblest sense of the word. Faith is an utter *Entweltlichung* (deterrestrification) on the three planes of the true, the good and the beautiful. The Christian is crucified to the world and the world is crucified to him (Gal 6:14).

What meaning has the idea of truth in Christianity? The truth that humanism talks of is first of all the truth of nature as discovered by science. And then it is the truth of the spiritual world. Knowing the

---

1. 'Day and night
   I celebrate man's lot.
   Let his thoughts but ever run on right,
   And ever he is beautiful and great.'

truth, therefore, is knowing the laws that make the universe one and knowing the moral law, the justice and righteousness that enable the individual to become a person and the sum of individuals to become a community. The truth and knowledge which Christianity speaks of are the truth and knowledge of *God*. He is not a God who is in any way perceived, felt, experienced—that is, known—in earthly, human terms. Christianity has to do with a God who *encounters* man, with ec-sistentiell knowledge of the moment, in which God's judgment and grace are offered to me as events. Christian truth is a truth that man does not possess in any way, that is always astonishing because it is an absolute otherness: I never know beforehand what God is going to tell me. So it is not a knowledge. The believer is crucified because he never controls the truth, it controls him instead.

Goodness, in the eyes of Christian faith, is not an ideal (for man or society) to live up to. God's commandment is not the categorical imperative; it is not equivalent to the individual's moral and spiritual life, nor to the demands of that justice which must preside over human relations. Even the loftiest ideas fail to convey what it is. There is no Christian morality (either individual or social). God's will can only *encounter* man; for him it is always a fresh *Anrede*. The knowledge he has of it is never his possession. He cannot tie it down to principles, much less to any system of ethics. He can only listen when it suddenly speaks to him in this or that concrete situation. What God demands is what love demands, and love is a relation with the other man based not on my spiritual kinship with him but on the fact that he is my neighbour. Here again the Christian is completely deterrestrified. He must give up any kind of *Weltanschauung*—that is, give up loving according to his own notions. He must be utter listening and utter gift. Goodness is always a *Dass* that faces him with an absolute decision to be made in absolute solitude, because he cannot base it on anything outside the call he hears. That decision, of course, is a lucid act; but the light that illuminates it does not come from the believer's reason, it is received.

So Christianity 'dehumanizes' the true and the good by regarding them as a *Dass* which man cannot control. They can only be a *Verstehen*. But can the beautiful be thus deterrestrified? Can it be a *Dass*? Is not art essentially a transfiguration of the world? And therefore can faith judge art to be anything else but an attempt to distract us from what cannot be transfigured? After all, does not transfiguring a thing mean dominating it? If we regard the beautiful as an illumination whereby the enigmatic, unfathomable flux of life is perceived and brought under control—if esthetic contemplation is a way of laying hold on things—then Christian faith must say that art is shut out from the depths of reality; because those depths cannot be 'seen', they can only be 'undergone'. The answer to the riddle of fate can never be objectified in a work of art; it is only to be found *im Leiden* (GV 2, p. 137). So faith understands the beautiful as something always beyond us which it is the business of *Entscheidung* to disclose.

Christian life is a perpetual ec-sisting under the impulse of the καιρός God sends us. Therefore it is an utter rejection of 'works'. It is sheer faith. The spirit that humanism talks of is known by its fruits: by the 'shaping' and transfiguration of the world, by the organization of society, by works of art, and above all by education, which seeks to turn individuals into persons. Not so the Holy Spirit: it is in no sense the principle of growth and spiritual balance in man, society and the world. God is always an absolute future. Christian faith has no political programme and no social programme.

'There is no such thing as Christian art, Christian education, Christian pedagogy or "Christian humanism". To be sure, they all exist in the sense that Christians are busied with them and insofar as science and art, for instance, draw their subject-matter from the world of Christian thought and Christian history. But even so it would be a mistake to speak of "Christian" science or "Christian" art, for there is no "Christian" method which can be used in those fields of intellectual life. There are Christian cobblers but there is no Christian cobbling' (GV 2, pp. 137–8). Humanism believes that the human mind can see an image of eternity in transitory things, a reflection of the invisible in things visible. It holds that the things of this world can be 'spiritualized' (divinized).

Faith takes a radical view of God's eternity: it looks on God as the being who is always hidden. His transcendence is not his spiritual nature but his perpetual future—in other words, his lordship. To know him one must be ready to plunge into darkness, as Luther has said so often and so well: 'Here we need the utmost wisdom, which does not consist in being wise about what is seen (for we must despair of visible things), but about the future, the unknown, the invisible.' 'Hope bears on what is hoped for, but what is hoped for is not part of the visible world. Thus hope turns its gaze upon what is unknown, what is hidden, upon pitch darkness. It does not know what it hopes for, although it knows what it does not hope for.' 'It is indeed a harsh beginning, one that violently rends a man. The soul must make no move to understand or to will, which means that it enters upon darkness, upon a kind of withering and annihilation from which every fibre of its being shrinks in horror' (Luther, quoted in GV 2, pp. 138–9).

Nevertheless it is certain that humanism too has a real sense of otherness. The life of the spirit which it advocates is a constant outdoing of oneself; a constant rejection of facts as given; an endless battle against accepted ideas, manners and institutions, against smugness, mental sloth and selfishness in all its forms; a marching on towards the infinite, a movement that would 'give birth into beauty' (Plato), a life that consists in victory after victory over self, its watchword '*Stirb und werde*' (Die and become). Where is the difference between this and Christian faith?

The humanist, as it were, holds his life in his hands. He evolves; that is, he becomes more and more what he is already. Now the believer does not advance from an embryonic faith towards the ideal of a perfect faith: he is subject to the either-or. Certainly, his life is made up of a series of decisions so interwoven, to the naked eye of man, that it can be described as the evolution of a spiritual personality. But faith thinks differently. All those decisions are not so many steps forward, for in each one of them *everything* is at stake: his damnation or his salvation. 'Whoever is not with me is against me' applies to each one of them. Every call of God is an absolute that utterly judges the believer or utterly pardons him. There is no middle ground: either his sin is forgiven or it is not. The Christian is the man of the either-or.

Humanism also seeks to deliver a man from his past, but precisely here the difference between it and Christianity shines forth: in the attitude towards the past. Humanism is well aware that man is never what he should be, that he always tends to rest on his oars, that that is his sin, and that he must constantly do battle with himself in order to achieve the pure ideal which he has of his future. But since the idea of education and growth inspires the humanist effort, sin is always a negative thing: it is a mere lack, an absence, a 'not yet'. A man leaves his past behind him as a mere stage which does not prevent his advancing step by step towards his ideal and does not stamp that ideal. All that stamps it is his advance towards it.

Contrariwise Christian faith says that a man cannot be delivered from his past by his own strength; he sticks root-fast in his in-sistence, which dogs him everywhere in his present and prevents his having a future that is a real future. For the significance of the past is not purely negative, as in humanism. It is a positive thing, an evil, a rebellion against God, a *sin*. Because his past is a sin man must drag it about everywhere with him. Only an intervention from outside—God's intervention— can deliver him from it. In short, he can only be *forgiven*. His future cannot be a stage along his spiritual journey, it must be sheer grace. That is what 'Die and become' means in Christianity. Christ's cross is the utter condemnation of what the humanist considers his greatest glory: constantly outdoing himself, by his own strength, in a reaching towards the values of the spirit. In the eyes of faith, humanism is the quintessence of 'works'.

(3) (a) Is this to say that our problem can be disposed of by the brutal divorce we have just made? Humanism will exist so long as there are men endowed with the use of reason who believe in the nobility of spiritual living. It is the exemplary triumph over barbarism. But is Christianity bound up with barbarism? Does it necessarily demand that we jettison knowledge, law and art? There have always been Christians who rejected culture and there always will be. But do they not realize that they embrace the very danger they seek to avoid (making the gospel dependent on a given style of life, in this case a primitive one)? Does being crucified to the world mean that one must live outside the world? On the scientific plane, for example, does not applying the historical method to the Bible allow revelation to *be itself* in all its purity, to be the naked scandal it is, better enabling us to sift out what is only human? Is theology possible without culture? Can there be a human world—for that is where faith must work through love (Gal 5:6)—without laws and without a state? And is art no more than a sinful metamorphosis of this world masking the next world? May it not also reflect transcendence?

The gospel does not need to be completed by humanism or the grace of God by civilization. Christianity does not need them; but the Christian does, the Christian who must proclaim his faith by subjecting the world to God and not by running away from the world. That is the necessity for humanism. Science and technology master nature. Law helps to civilize men and makes life in society possible. Art and culture sharpen men's wits, inspire their souls, ennoble their minds and hearts. All this, as such, is not a Christian task; but the Christian does have a duty to humanize the world in obedience to the Creator. In short, if it is nonsense to bind Christianity up with humanism it is also nonsense to demand that faith reject humanism. Here the golden rule is still Paul's ὡς μή.

For its part, humanism would be wrong to have no dealings with the world of faith. After all, Christianity has left its mark on man. It has revealed new depths in the human condition, setting in a new light all the problems which the ancients discovered. It has let loose an intellectual power unknown to antiquity. Science, letters, history, philosophy, art—all are much in Christianity's debt. Modern humanism would not be what it is without Christianity, whether one rejects the latter or accepts it. Moreover, has faith not rendered humanism the most valuable of services by constantly querying it? In trying to make the world man's own country through science, law and art does humanism not risk persuading man that he is the lord of the earth and the master of life? Does it not overlook, at its peril, the changeless sovereign power of fate, suffering and death?

Humanism solves only some of man's problems. Is it solving them all to make man at home in the universe and in society? Faith warns against that misguided policy, reminding us that science, law and art cannot satisfy the deepest needs of a being created by and for God. Humanism cannot be the ultimate meaning of life. It must realize that to save itself it needs the message of the cross, of grace and of love.

(b) But apart from these general considerations, there are two special reasons today for an alliance between Christianity and humanism. The first reason is the struggle against the nineteenth- and twentieth-century relativism (at least in the West) which we have spoken of before (p.70, above). The child of Romanticism, it denies that there exist a universal human reason and universal truths that reason can ascertain. Neither is there any moral absolute or any natural law. Thought is wholly subject to the dictates of history, so that no certitude has more than a relative validity (the word 'relative' here meaning the *negation* of the absolute, not its temporalization).[2] Truth being nothing but the product of circumstances, there can be no such thing as the problem of truth. The mind does not determine the course of history; rather history determines the fate of the mind—insofar as one can still speak of the mind. The world, nature, being, God, are seen only in relation to man, because it is always a question whether they are not a function of our point of view. Thus subjectivism leads on to nihilism: things only exist if we human beings decide that they do. Nothingness yawns at our feet until we adhere to this *Weltanschauung* or that.

Some have laid the responsibility for this state of affairs at the door of humanism, but that is a crying injustice. Humanism, based on the sovereign norms of the true, the good and the beautiful, is thereby the very antithesis of subjectivism and relativism. Of course from the Christian point of view it is not the real absolute (as we have insisted throughout this book); but as contrasted with nihilism, the Greeks (the fathers of western humanism) must be admitted to have had a sense of the eternal. With them, the world and man are bound together. The same divine law governs both. Only as a member of the cosmos does the individual achieve his perfection. The *logos* is a supreme reality of which the human mind represents a participation and which it must obey.

Western humanism continued the tradition of the mind's absolute

---

2. Of course we must carefully distinguish between the 'historicized' absolute and relativism, according to which man is the measure of all things: pp. 23, 72-4, above, and 327, below.

primacy, and for that reason it is Christianity's natural ally in the struggle against subjectivism. So far is Christianity from denying that the true, the good and the beautiful are absolute values, that it declares man incapable of attaining them by his own resources; humanism thinks otherwise, and there is its error. Only in *this* sense is Christ the end of the law (Rom 10:4). Sin enters the picture when man tries to make the law a means to his perfection, treats observance of the law as a work that will bring him salvation. But in itself the law is good, just and holy (Rom 7:12). It is God's *eternal* demand, so that love, the great commandment, only fulfils the law (Rom 13:8–10; Gal 5:14). So Christianity and humanism can and must join forces in their struggle against relativism and nihilism.

(c) There is also another sphere where they can back each other up. Adherents of the humanist tradition, who think that man is a person, not an object, and who make their watchword *homo homini res sacra*, have often warned us against the dangers of modern science and technology. Bultmann in his turn warns against the dangers of 'organization' in all its forms (planning, technocracy, bureaucracy, and so forth), of everything in our world today that would reduce man to a cog. He does this subtly, well aware how complex the problems are. For example, he thinks that the state cannot refrain from all intervention whatever in economic life; for if in some cases that intervention will prejudice liberty, in others it alone can protect the rights of the individual. But technology must remain the servant of man, and here the role of humanism is primary and indispensable.

In humanism 'man is not regarded, and does not regard himself, as captive to, enslaved by, the purposes of down-to-earth life in material nature, of economics or politics, but as a person—as a being, that is, who exists for his own sake, bears within himself his meaning and validity, exists independent of his usefulness for the purposes of practical life' (GV 2, p. 147). Humanism proclaims and upholds the 'dignity of the human person'. In this respect it is the ally of Christianity: humanism and Christianity 'constantly recall man to awareness of himself as a person' (*ibid.*, p. 148). If we dwell no further on these views of Bultmann that is not because he attaches little importance to them but because they are shared by all Christian and humanist minds of our day.

II

A study on 'the forms of human society' takes another approach to the theme we have just examined and puts us in a position to consider what can be called, for brevity's sake, the question of existentialist humanism.

(1) The first of human societies is based on nature. From nature issue the family, the tribe, the nation, bound together by 'blood' and 'soil'. Though Nazi Germany went on and on about the bonds of blood and soil, it completely ignored their meaning because it drained them of any human content. Bultmann illustrates the point by a comparison with *Romeo and Juliet*. Recalling that Shakespeare's tragedy is one of the purest examples of eros, he shows how National Socialism degraded the community between man and woman to the level of mere reproduction and made education a matter of producing handsome human animals. The natural activity was perverted, first by being shorn of those higher values that alone give it its meaning, and then by being made to serve political ends. Evidently the community of blood and soil needs something else besides in order to be itself: it must at the same time be a community of *persons*. In particular, the love between man and woman only becomes itself when it is a gift of each to each, experienced in nobility of heart.

How difficult this is to achieve, Goethe conveys by the bitter question he addresses to fate in the poem for Frau von Stein:

> Why did you look deep at us in such a way
> that it should flash upon us then what was to come,
> and so the sweet illusion never should be ours
> of trusting in our love, our happiness on earth?
> Why, O Fate, did you let each of us make out
> the writing at the bottom of the other's heart,
> finding our way through all those shadowed labyrinths
> to gaze upon the true bonds that unite us two?
>
> Ah, what multitudes of men wander bemused
> with scarce an inkling what their own heart is,
> drifting flotsam-like hither and thither, ever
> and anon ensnared in evils unforeseen.
> But they can rejoice exceedingly at the
> unhoped-for dawn of joys that will not stay an hour.
> Only we of all who love, poor wretches, are
> destined not to know the simple happiness
> of loving without understanding one another,
> each seeing in the other what he never was;
> of questing, on fire, a happiness that is a dream
> and shuddering at perils that are dreams as well.
>
> Blessed is he whose mind is bent upon a dream,
> and he who for a phantom thing lives in foreboding.

In us, alas, each meeting and each glance exchanged
prove all too sound both our foreboding and our dream.
Tell me what it is fate has in store for us.
Why has it so harshly bound us two together?

(2) The second form of society is based on history—that is, on common
living and working together, on common experiences, traditions,
habits and manners. Thus we have comradeship among students,
solidarity among workers, national society and, it is to be hoped
(Bultmann adds), the society of nations. Here again historical society is
really itself only if it is something more than itself—that is, a community of persons. The dangers which threaten it are convention,
organization, cliquishness and class feeling, chauvinism and totalitarianism. Its most formidable enemy is, to use Heideggerian language, the
omnipotence of the 'they' [*man* in German, *on* in French], which
blights initiative, crushes freedom, and destroys personality. Rilke has
well described how the world of men loses all its authenticity and
realness once the *I* is gone:

Big cities are not honest, they deceive
the day, the night, and animals, and children:
they lie with silence and they lie with noises;
they lie with things, for things are pliable.
None of the tremendous, honest doings
that are always throbbing round about you,
O evolving man, is done in them . . .

Cities love only what is of themselves,
and make away with all they come upon.
Animals they crush like so much brushwood,
and many are the nations they devour.
And men who dwell within them are the slaves
that labour for civilization's good,
and call their poor slug's progress betterment,
and diddle quick instead of diddling slow,
and smell of scent and flirt like prostitutes,
making endless din with glass and metal.
Always some delusion seems to hoax them:
they have forgotten how to be themselves.

(3) Art and science underlie a third kind of society. Art establishes a
deep communion among men, one of the noblest there can be. But it
has its dangers. It may harden into convention and become an in-

strument of real exploitation. For his part, the artist is tempted to cut himself off from the public and also from his fellow-artists:

> So as to create and then perfect
> creation, artist, often be alone.
> So as to enjoy your work, go forth
> to mingle with the rest, and there, entire,
> you will behold the course of your own life.
> Your fellow-artist will reveal to you
> what you have been about this many a year.
> The tools you use must make no difference:
> be you his brother and let him be yours,
> and let the fire and smoke of sacrifice
> rise from the altar in pure harmony.[3]

Goethe himself gave us a biographical illustration of these lines by leaving the Weimar circle, taking refuge in Italy to seek and find himself, and then returning to Weimar. Isolation does not present a danger to the artist alone but also to the cultured public who have made art their own heart's country; for they are tempted to withdraw altogether into art, forgetting the suffering and grief of the world. Then, instead of helping to build human society, art becomes a barrier cutting men off from each other. Here again Goethe has well brought out the ambivalence: 'There is no surer escape from the world than art, and no surer involvement in the world than art.'

The same must be said of science. Is the scientific brotherhood a real community of persons or a mere aggregation such as, say, a congress is? Technology, growing by leaps and bounds, has aggravated the danger for men of science; it too provides the basis for various associations, but are they really associations of persons? Let us consider not only the relations of technologists among themselves but also the state of mind produced in those who use the various techniques—for example, the attitude common to motoring enthusiasts, fliers, and so forth. Thus 'worlds' arise which unite all the zealous adherents of a particular science or a particular sport. But if people communicate something on this level, must we not say that they do not communicate themselves?

Knowledge, like art, can raise barriers which cut men off from each other. It can as easily be a weapon as a means of communication. Dogmatism is a temptation to every school of thought and always leads to futile polemics. Bultmann finely observes that 'orthodoxy has

3. Goethe, quoted by Bultmann.

no sense of humour' (GV 2, p. 269). And he quotes Goethe: 'If a man appears with something new, something that contradicts the credo we have droned through for years and handed on to others in our turn, something likely to capsize it, then every passion is whipped up against that man, we move heaven and earth to crush him. We set up our bristles as best we can, we feign not to hear or not to understand, we speak scornfully of the new thing . . . Thus it may be a good long time before a new truth makes any headway.'

(4) Only where there are men who are persons shall we find any real human society. Now being a person means first of all bursting the bonds of nature by a flight forward. Man is that being who never possesses his being, who is always ready to abandon what he has and what he is:

> *Und solang du das nicht hast,*
> *Dieses: stirb und werde!*
> *Bist du nur ein trüber Gast*
> *Auf der dunklen Erde.*[4]

Such is the paradox: one must first die to the world and men before one can give oneself to the world and men. Christian faith brings this paradox to its climax. First of all it is a complete break with all human society: 'If anyone comes to me and does not hate his own father and mother and wife and children and brothers and sisters, and even his own life, he cannot be my disciple' (Lk 14:26). As we have said often enough, Christianity is an utter deterrestrification. He who would find God 'must be dead to all things—to good and to evil, to death and to life, to hell and to heaven—and must confess from the heart that he can do nothing by his own powers' (Luther, quoted in GV 2, p. 271).

Now it happens that modern non-Christian thinkers also admit, in their own way, the inadequacy of natural, earthly data and call on man to despair of himself, to reach beyond himself towards a future where alone he will find his true being. Thus Nietzsche, for whom man is beyond man and has not yet existed. A kind of fierce eschatology makes Nietzsche yearn for the utter transmutation of all that has made up human nature until now. Thus Heidegger: every word he has written is an onslaught on humanism and a preoccupation with the grace of being. Thus Sartre, who declares that for himself 'human life begins on the far side of despair'. Sartre is by no means the nihilist

4. 'Till you learn to die the death
   that brings man to birth,
   you will be but a sorry guest
   on the sunless earth.'

people often make him out to be. He thinks that man can find his being only by a perpetual reaching beyond himself and all data. Obviously Jaspers is of the same mind. And finally there is T. S. Eliot, for whom 'in my end is my beginning'. All these thinkers believe that a man must die to what he has and what he is in order to find himself.

This conviction provides the basis for a last kind of society, society in transcendence. Here we are on the very verge of Christianity, and Bultmann asks whether these philosophies of freedom represent the acme of hubris or an act of humility. In fact, he says, they have clearly perceived that man cannot rely on any ready-made truth or ethics or meaning of life. There is no general anthropology, no science of human nature. Man is freedom. It is for himself to decide whether he thinks he can create his being by his own powers or can only receive it as of grace. Therefore his awareness of not being a thing ready-made may either be the height of arrogance (which Bultmann thinks is the case with Nietzsche) or else 'openness to the Beyond that meets and masters us, and that one can only recognize by despairing of oneself' (GV 2, p. 291). Perhaps then we may apply to atheist existentialism these words of Luther's: 'I make bold to say one thing outright: no one is closer to God in this life than those who hate and outrage him; of all his children these are most pleasing to him and dearest to his heart' (quoted in GV 2, p. 291).

Be that as it may, true society is grounded in God alone. It can only be made up of persons who really love one another, which is impossible without faith. God alone utterly delivers man from his selfishness. I can only love if I am freed of myself—that is, pardoned by God's deed in Jesus Christ. The Church is not the society of those who seek God but the society of those whom God has sought. The first sin and the ultimate sin is trying to find oneself, others and God by one's own strength. That is why the various kinds of human society are always imperfect. Of course the Church too is constantly tempted to manipulate others and God, and often yields to the temptation, confirming in the unhappiest and most dramatic way that *corruptio optimi pessima*. The Church can become an organization. And its gravest temptation is 'orthodoxy, which turns the confession [of faith] into a dogma' (GV 2, p. 272), controlling God instead of being controlled by him. But when the Church is the eschatological thing we have spoken of, it establishes the only real society—that of love.

Christian love, as we know, is not a love of humanity in general. Natural man is not unaware that he should love his neighbour and he may even do so to a certain degree, but without grace there is no utter love. And therefore only the society that is grounded in God 'answers to the purpose and meaning of every human society' (GV 2, p. 273). In other words, true humanism is not to be found outside Christian faith; and obviously the existentialism we have spoken of, insofar as it really tries to dispense with God and nevertheless secure man a perpetual ec-sistence beyond himself, does represent the height (and bankruptcy) of arrogance.

In an article entitled *Humanismus und Christentum* (1953; GV 3, pp. 61–71), Bultmann takes up the theme we have been considering. He adds nothing new; but we must note that he defends humanism more stoutly than ever against its modern Christian detractors, who would lay at its door the blame for two global wars and, more generally, the plague of technology and organization which threatens to destroy our present world. He shows that contrariwise our abandonment of humanism has led to this contempt for and even denial of the human person.

CHAPTER FIFTEEN

Christianity and Other Religions

I

If one considers Christianity, as liberal theology does, to be a manifestation of religion in general, the latter being itself an expression of the life of the spirit, then one will distinguish Christianity from other religions by simply saying that it is the loftiest form of religion. Then the connection between Christianity and those others will be self-explanatory, since we are dealing with a progression from the less perfect to the more perfect.

History seems to uphold this view, for the observer can certainly look on the pagan religions as a first stage of the Christian religion or as phenomena which run parallel to it. He can show that Christianity completes what remained rudimentary elsewhere because its growth had been cut short or crippled in one way or another. Christianity exhibits the normal features of religious life no less than other religions do, which proves that there is a basic kinship between them. In every case we are dealing with a society which has cultic celebrations and sacramental acts, its own discipline, its priesthood and its tradition. In the higher religions we find a sacred scripture, a system of dogma, an ethics, and often a mysticism. From this point of view the link between the Christian faith and pagan religions raises no issue of principle but only practical problems. The Christian missionary must start with the forms and content of other religions so as to purify and complete them. Whether we have to do with God, or ceremonies, or morals, or other matters, the missionary's task is to show pagans that it all finds its true meaning and its fullness only in the faith he brings them. The only problem is a concrete problem: how shall this be done?

But it is possible to take another view. One can consider that faith is not an instance of the life of the spirit or of religion at large, but the response to a particular revelation of God; not the term of an evolution or a flower from the garden of the human spirit, but an exotic plant brought into this world from the next world. In that case there is obviously no continuity between it and the non-Christian religions. We must speak not of resemblance but of contrast. All ideas of God other than the idea Christianity gives us are faulty and misguided.

Religions (religion in general) must be judged a contrivance of man whereby he attempts to make the burdens and riddles and terrors of this life bearable. To reassure himself man attaches a name and a face to what crushes him. This mysterious and dreadful power that rules his fate he calls God, thinking thereby to establish relations with it, speak to it, pray to it, move it—in short, to neutralize it. Rather than rebel against it, taking on an unequal struggle in desperate solitude, he prefers to submit in the safety of dialogue and the sweetness of prayer. There is the God of religion: a God believed in in terms of the world and oneself—that is, a God designed to make this world man's own country. History upholds this judgment of ours. Primitive mankind needed religion in order to endure the strangeness and hostility of the universe. Today we cope with the forces of nature through science and technology, which explains the steady dwindling of all religions.

If Christian faith is only the loftiest embodiment of religion in general, then the decline of religion must mean the decline of that faith. But such is not the case. Christian faith is the response to God's revelation in Jesus Christ, not a way of facing the riddle of the world and life. Accordingly the theology of recent years ('dialectical theology') has answered with a firm *no* the question whether there may not be a connection between Christianity and pagan religions. We can and must say that they are completely opposed to each other. Well then, are pagan religions to be combated as so many wicked errors? Must we go back to the attitude of the old missionaries who thought paganism was an abomination to be done away with, root and branch? Is there no good in it at all? Was that attitude not based on scanty knowledge and an unacceptable fanaticism? But if one agrees that it was, is one not undermining the absolute and therefore the exclusive nature of the revelation one is charged to make known? What escape is there from this dilemma?

II

(1) It is certain that God's action finds no *Anknüpfung* (point of contact) in man—not even in the noblest part of him: the spirit. To make him live, it makes him die; to raise him from the dead, it crucifies him. So God is utter opposition to man, above all to man who tries through religion to ease his anguish and protect himself from the juggernaut of the world, fate and death. God's grace is understood only by one who utterly strips himself of himself, allows himself to sink into the bottomless gulf, seeking nothing to cling to. The only genuine Christian preaching is that which roundly declares the utter opposition between God and man.

Precisely this opposition creates the *Anknüpfung*: opposition is only possible where there is some further contact. I cannot really oppose a tree, only another freedom. Nor can God oppose a tree, a thing that has no senses, but only a being which he has created in his own image and likeness. This means that the man he condemns is a being who has damned himself; hence God's opposition, paradoxically, is an appeal which calls upon man to recover his authenticity (to become once more the image and likeness of God). In other words, God's opposition takes the form of a lack, an emptiness, a distress in man—a straying, if you will. It is not the opposition that we find between two objects, but an opposition between two beings one of which (man) has his existence determined by the other (God). The stray is defined in terms of the road. The tree planted alongside the road has no intrinsic relations to the latter; it might quite as well be somewhere else as be here; it is neutral towards this road. But man is a stray, which means that even in the midst of his opposition to God he is determined by God, as the stray is by the road he must get back to, as the sinner is by the grace he must recover.

A man in enmity with God has not lost his authentic self (his relation to God) as one loses an object. The object exists outside the person who owns it and can be lost without any change occurring in the owner's basic nature. But a man's relation to God, strictly speaking, cannot be lost. Though 'lost', it goes on affecting his life whether he be conscious of the fact or not, because he cannot dispense at will with his real being (God), which is always there in him as an absence, a lack, a wistfulness, a desire: *Tu nos fecisti ad te, Domine, et inquietum est cor nostrum, donec requiescat in te.* What sets man against God is ill-will. So between them there is not that substantialist dualism which separates objects but the 'historical' dualism which exists between two freedoms when one of them breaks away from the other—which is not an event outside him but a mutilation of himself, so that a man is wholly defined by his lost relation to God.

Thus we arrive at the paradoxical conclusion that sin is the bridge-head of grace, that the opposition there is between God and man provides their meeting-ground. 'Man's sin is the *Anknüpfung* for the contradictory word of grace' (GV 2, p. 120). It is obviously not this or that part of the human being, supposedly undamaged or more noble (the spirit, the heart, or such) that offers grace an *Anknüpfung*: man is totally wicked, and his being-a-sinner is an intaglio of grace. It is perfectly true that man has no 'religious organ' endowed with a special receptivity to the Word of God. There is in him nothing positive of this kind, nothing which escapes absolute condemnation by the divine judge. He is altogether a sinner, even—indeed especially—in what the mystics call the apex of the soul or of the spirit. What is best and most religious in man is precisely what most sets him against God and must be crucified. Only as a sinner does he afford grace an *Anknüpfung*.

(2) Christian preaching must always bring out the absolute opposition between God and man. Does it follow that insofar as that preaching is human language (which it cannot help being), it must always be obviously remote from and hostile to immanence—that is, the concrete situation of those to whom it is directed? Not at all. The preacher must always speak from the point of view of his audience, allow for the age and the culture they belong to, for their cast of mind and habits of life, their troubles and their needs. He must speak the language of those he is attempting to evangelize, by which we mean that he must speak to their ec-sistentiell condition, their *Verständnis*. Each era in history is a 'world' made up of particular forms of religion, philosophy, law, art and economics. Christian faith must take the fullest account not only of this worldwide position but also of the special position in each particular country, each social group, even — ideally—in each individual.

Preaching reaches people of all sorts and conditions, of every occupation and every character. Some seem blind to the problem of religion, as if they had settled in for good on earth. Others are full of a gnawing unease. Each and every one has a set *Weltanschauung*. The apostle cannot ignore this extraordinary diversity, which offers the scandal of the gospel its *Anknüpfung*. In other words, he must start with the ruling sin of each age and each man. Sin is always sin but it does not always wear the same countenance. The 'in-sistence' of modern man looks quite different from that which was familiar to ancient man. Preaching must always be given 'in context', so as to make known the paradox of faith in all its purity.

III

The New Testament gives us a perfect example of *Anknüpfung* and *Widerspruch* (bridgehead and opposition). It stoutly denies that there can be any foothold in man for the Word of God, which presents itself in Christian preaching as a scandal, an opposition between God and man so categorical that even the best of human deeds are only sin. All men are equally guilty before God, and therefore whatever differentiates them on the human plane is totally unimportant. In this context there is no reason to distinguish between the learned man and the ignorant, the rich and the poor, the foolish and the clever, the kindly and the vicious, the wicked and the good, the rake and the ascetic: all are under the wrath of God. The world as a whole is a *massa perditionis* and almost without exception its alienation from God is understood as a fall into evil and death. All the more remarkable, then, that here and there the New Testament bases itself on the thought of the pagan world, as three examples will show.

(1) Anknüpfung *established by the popular philosophy of Hellenism, especially by Stoic natural theology*—Paul's very language is coloured by the popular philosophy of Hellenism. From it derive certain of his rhetorical devices, and notably his liking for antithesis and paradox. To it he is indebted for the catalogue of virtues and vices that figures in his epistles. In a sense the doctrine of the Cynics and Stoics summoned man to conversion and claimed to deliver him from the passions and vices in which he was sunk. It taught what we would call nowadays a reversal of values. It showed how man labours under a false conception of happiness and suffering, freedom and slavery, life and death, and tried to instil the true conception of them.

Paul adopts this morality and in so doing borrows ideas from the philosophic tradition which are either alien to the Old Testament or but dimly represented there: συνείδησις, καθῆκον, ἀρετή, ἐλευθερία and even φύσις. He entertains not the slightest doubt that the moral demands which pagans acknowledge are the demands of God. In Phil 4:8 he *implies* that they are ('Whatever is true, whatever is honourable, whatever is just, whatever is pure, whatever is lovely, whatever is gracious, if there is any excellence, if there is anything worthy of praise, think about these things') and in Rom 2:14f he says so *outright*: 'When Gentiles who have not the law do by nature what the law requires, they are a law to themselves, even though they do not have the law. They show that what the law requires is written on their hearts, while their conscience also bears witness and their conflicting thoughts accuse or perhaps excuse them.'[1]

These words, and the context in which they appear, represent both a linkage and an opposition: a linkage because conscience makes known the law of God, and therefore is something good. But at the same time it is through conscience that pagans come under the wrath and judgment of God. Here we have the opposition: knowing the law, they have not kept it. Therefore they are subject to condemnation and death. In fact they have never perceived God through conscience; they *should* have perceived him, obeying and loving him as their Lord, but they have not done so. They have not allowed their conscience to be the word of God for them. When they let conscience guide them they

---

1. Νόμος must be translated 'the law'. Paul means the Jewish law.

were never, in fact, letting God guide them. They never forsook their natural *Selbstverständnis*.

Paul's idea of freedom furnishes us with another example of the dialectic between *Anknüpfung* and *Widerspruch*. It comes remarkably close to the idea of freedom which the Stoics had. Like the latter, Paul does not take an outward and sociological view of freedom but an inward and spiritual one. When speaking of it he means emancipation from judgments of the world and the values which men accept ('Do not become slaves of men': 1 Cor 7:23), from the flesh (Gal 5:13), from all that is alien to our true self, from the 'world'. All this is Stoic. Equally Stoic is the dialectic of the '"All things are lawful for me", but I will not be enslaved by anything' (1 Cor 6:12). But while he uses this idea of freedom as his starting-point, Paul also impugns it.

The Stoic is right to regard freedom as an inward detachment from things. But he assumes that man is able to detach himself from things by his own powers; that man is master of his own inner world. For Paul the real problem of freedom begins at the point where the Stoic thinks it ends. A believer knows he is incapable of conquering freedom by his own resources, because in so doing he would not be forsaking himself, and therefore looks on the Stoic as the slave of slaves in the midst of what he imagines to be freedom. The Christian is free only because he has given up the pride and joy of the philosopher—a freedom conquered in doughty battle. Now if a man has really achieved that freedom, then there is the proof that he is stuck in his old *I*, the prisoner of himself, of what he is and what he does. The self that is really free can only be a self which has been received, and received from God. Only when Christ has become a man's new *I* (Gal 2:19f) can there be any talk of freedom.

Paul also uses the 'natural theology' of Stoicism when he says in Rom 1:18f: 'What can be known about God is plain to them [the pagans], because God has shown it to them. Ever since the creation of the world his invisible nature, namely, his eternal power and deity, has been clearly perceived in the things that have been made.' In form and content alike, this text merely reproduces the Hellenistic proofs for the existence of God. But there is more: Paul also agrees with the Greeks in holding that the knowledge of God derived from contemplation of the universe is not abstract; it is a knowledge in which man finds his true being, a being constituted by his relation to the godhead and by his obedience to immutable law.

In what context and to what end does Paul bring in this natural theology? Does he mean to insist on the positive fact that pagans can know God? Quite the contrary, he means to demonstrate that they are under wrath, for their knowledge of the Creator has not moved them to give him thanks and serve him but rather to deny him by their whole life. So—like their moral consciousness, as we have seen above—it only ensures their guilt and condemnation. Nonetheless this ineffective knowledge of God is an *Anknüpfung* because their sin gives pagans an opportunity to listen to the gospel: in becoming aware of his sin a man becomes aware of grace.

The discourse which Acts puts into Paul's mouth (Acts 17:16ff) quite deliberately ties up with natural theology. Paul begins with an inscription he has read on an altar: 'To an unknown god'.[2] Therefore he assumes that his pagan hearers have an intuition of the true God which only needs to be actualized, so to speak: 'What you worship as unknown, this I proclaim to you' (verse 23). This very Hellenistic theology also forms the burden of his speech. True, verse 24 casts back to the Old Testament, speaking of the one God, who as the Creator of heaven and earth needs no temple to be honoured in. But then the Hellenistic style returns (verse 25) and Paul embarks on the theme, so characteristic of Stoicism, that God has no need of anything. This theme is entirely absent from the Old Testament, which nowhere attempts to deduce God's attributes by the *via negationis*. Next follows a no less Hellenistic consideration of the decrees which God has laid upon men: 'He made from one every nation of men to live on all the face of the earth, having determined allotted periods and the boundaries of their habitation'. This he did so 'that they should seek God, in the hope that they might feel after him and find him. Yet he is not far from each one of us' (verse 27).

In this text the search for God is not, as in the Old Testament, a matter of the will and of faith, but is conceived of in the Greek way, as an investigation: by looking for God one can find him. The Hellenism of this discourse reaches a climax in the following verses:

> 'In him we live and move and have our being';
> as even some of your poets have said,
> 'For we are indeed his offspring.'

'Being then God's offspring, we ought not to think that the Deity is like gold, or silver, or stone, a representation by the art and imagination of man' (verses 28–29). Here is the central theme of Greek thought: the basic kinship existing between God and man, which calls for a right knowledge of and a pious reverence for the Deity.

Of course, this speech in Acts is not Paul's. It contains no trace of his idiosyncratic doctrine on the Gentiles—that their knowledge of God

2. Ch. 4, p. 47, above.

makes them all sinners. Moreover the idea that God and man share a common nature is quite alien to him. No, what we have here is a literary composition by the author of Acts, who dwells (in a way not at all characteristic of the New Testament) on Hellenistic theology as an introduction to Christian faith. Nevertheless the antagonism between the gospel message and the religious message of paganism does not go unheeded. It comes in at the end of the speech, with the summons to repentance (verse 30), the announcement of the judgment which God will execute through Jesus Christ, and especially the assertion that God has raised Jesus from the dead (verse 31)—which calls forth the mirth and unbelief of Paul's hearers. The author of Acts knows well enough that faith is a scandal to natural man, though he does not get below the surface of the dialectic between sin and grace, or see that the *Widerspruch*, paradoxically, is just what establishes the *Anknüpfung*.

(2) Anknüpfung *established through the mystery religions*—We have had frequent occasion to note the similarities and differences between the Christian faith and the pagan mysteries. Though baptism and the Lord's Supper, as we have seen, certainly go back to the tradition of the primitive community, it is no less certain that in Hellenistic Christianity the two sacraments took on a form and meaning very like the form and meaning of the pagan sacraments. Just as in the mystery religions a cultic act causes the initiate to share the fate of the deity— that is, his death and his return to life—so Christian baptism makes a man die and rise again with Christ.

This resemblance on the sacramental plane entails another one on the anthropological plane. We have seen that the mysteries are a deterrestrification. A man who belongs to these religions is convinced that he can no longer find his true country in this world, in the cosmos and the city. He believes that this world cannot assuage his sufferings or the distress of his heart. He quakes at the thought of death, knowing he has no control over it. The god who is the city's providence, even the *logos* which is the law of the universe, does not satisfy him. What he needs is something that lies beyond them: he takes refuge with this transcendent god, hoping for his grace, looking for his salvation.

In the mystery religions the initiate gives up his old worldly self, which is delivered to death, so as to receive a new being over which fate has no power, which will have beatitude and immortality for its lot once this fleeting life is over. That is why all differences of social standing, nationality and race are ignored in these religious communities (with the exception of Mithraism). Obviously, then, Christianity found the mystery religions an invaluable 'accomplice'. The demand for repentance and conversion, the gathering in supraterrestrial communities, the sacraments whose power made a new creature of the initiate and caused him to share the fate of the god—all these things were bound to commend Christianity in the eyes of all pagans who responded to the message of the mysteries.

But there is also an antagonism. As we have said time and time again, the mystery religions remain the prisoners of naturalism. They have no true sense of sin and grace. The plane of historicity—the plane on which Christian faith operates—remains a closed book to them. With regard to sacrament in particular, Paul will not accept that it is an automatic guarantee of salvation, independent of faith. Israel too received a baptism and shared a sacred meal in the wilderness, and nonetheless still incurred the judgment of God. 'Therefore let anyone who thinks that he stands take heed lest he fall' (1 Cor 10:12). The Lord's Supper does not act *ex opere operato* but only when it is worthily received (1 Cor 11:27–29).

After all, what does a sacrament mean? Baptism ushers one into the death of the Lord and the Eucharist proclaims it. Do not the mystery religions tell men the same thing? Yes indeed, but Paul's interpretation is very different. Death in the mystery religions is not a death: what a man sheds is what is corruptible in him, so that the old self goes on living, merely disencumbered of sickness, every kind of danger and death. Here the will to live is set free, whereas in Christianity it is crucified. The 'mystic' initiate does not renounce himself. Quite the contrary, the sacrament ensures immortality for what he has and what he is—it consecrates and perfects the natural man. Now Paul says that the natural man must be annihilated: that is the meaning of the cross. The business of the pagan god is to guarantee natural life by immortalizing it. He is the servant of the initiate and of the initiate's will to live. But to Paul the sacrament means an utter renunciation of sin and a total gift of oneself to God: 'You must consider yourselves dead to sin and alive to God in Jesus Christ' (Rom 6:11).

Accordingly the Christian communities differ from the 'mystic' communities in being exclusive: the event of Christ's death and resurrection is an absolute which forbids any recourse to other gods with a view to bracing the salvation one has already received in one's own religion. (It will be recalled that pagans would join several different cults so as to be on the safe side.) Moreover the Christian communities are not isolated: the whole Church is present in each one of them. This means that they absolutely transcend the world, forming an eschatological entity within which all historical and earthly differences pass out of sight.

(3) Anknüpfung *through Gnosis*—As we are aware, Gnosis is marked by a keen sense of man's transcendence. It looks on him as a being totally foreign to earth. The Old Testament declared the world to be

God's creation and earthly events so many witnesses to his grace and his might. Far from situating man's true self in eternity, it hardly knows of any life at all after death. True life is life on this earth when acknowledged as a gift of God and lived in his presence and in obedience to his laws (as we have seen in the chapter on the connection between the two testaments).

The Greek thinks that the same *logos* rules the godhead, the world and man: there is no real transcendence. The Gnostic takes yet another view. He believes that his being is alien to the universe: there he finds himself in solitary confinement, there he suffocates, there he dies of fear and anguish. Moreover he himself is a source of his own fear and anguish, for he is conscious of impulses and cravings within him that enslave him to the charms and enticements of the world, addle and intoxicate him. When he awakens from this drunken state he is horrified at himself—that is, at the powers fermenting in the depths of his being. His true *I* (the *pneuma*, for Greek-speaking Gnostics) is chained to his soul, the second self that he cannot shake off.

By the fall of the first man (Gnostic anthropology is couched in this mythological, objectifying language) he has become a prisoner of the powers of darkness. Of himself he cannot escape from them: he can only receive his freedom from elsewhere—that is, from the Son of God, who leaves the world of heavenly light, assumes a human form, and is pleased to live the life of this world with all its attendant sufferings and wretchedness. He reveals to men their true nature and their fallen state—in short, he informs them of their situation. Then he clears the way for them to their own country on high by doing battle with the demoniac powers, worsting them, and ascending once more to heaven. After their death, men (their true self) can also travel the road he has opened to them and, in company with the heavenly host, forever sing hymns of praise and thanksgiving to God. So long as the Gnostic lives on earth, he must completely detach himself from the world by ascetic practices and mysticism. Not by thought and meditation alone does he become aware of his divine *I* but also by ecstasy, in which he has a foretaste of shedding his earthly husk and entering into the world of light.

Evidently Christian preaching found in Gnosticism much that was congenial and helpful. Paul adopted many Gnostic ideas and the author of the fourth Gospel still more, making this myth the framework of his book. John fits the preaching of Jesus into the Gnostic dualism of light and darkness, truth and lies. It is Gnostic language he puts into Jesus's mouth in those great utterances: 'I am the light of the world', 'I am the bread of life', 'I am the true vine', 'I am the resurrection and the life', 'I am the way, and the truth, and the life'. Thus he recognizes that Gnosticism has correctly stated the fundamental problem of human life, to which he means to give the only real answer in Jesus's *I am*.

But *Anknüpfung* cannot be disentangled from conflict. As against the Old Testament and Judaism, Christianity and Gnosis alike hold that the world as it is does not reveal a God of grace. If it is a created thing (Gnosis goes on), its Creator can only be a power inimical to man. For its part, Christian preaching also declares that God and man are enemies (Rom 5:10; see 8:7 and 2 Cor 5:9), that man is under the wrath of God (Rom 1:18ff). But for the substantialist dualism of Gnosis, Christianity substitutes the 'historical' dualism of decision, affirming that the world is the work of Jesus Christ's Father, that the Creator and the Redeemer are one and the same God, that the enmity between God and 'this world' does not arise because the world was created by a demoniac being as something evil, but because man's will is perverse, so that creation must now face him as a hostile power.

In regarding salvation as a complete deliverance from the cosmos, the New Testament likewise stands closer to Gnosis than to the Old Testament, for the Gnostic is an exile who cannot bear the separation from his heavenly country. But there is a difference: Gnosis puts down man's captivity, and therefore his suffering and anguish, to a fate outside him, not to his own sin. His fallenness is not the consequence of a rebellion, it is decreed by fate. Therefore his redemption is a simple and natural business which leaves him intact and dispenses with the cross. In his exile the Gnostic is already what he will be in his own country: he need only be freed of his earthly husk. So there is no true death and no true resurrection.

Christian faith will have none of this bargain-basement salvation. No doubt, even in this world, sin is forgiven and the believer already has eternal life. But he still must live in the world, on the dialectic basis of the ὡς μή (1 Cor 7:29–31). He walks by faith, not by sight (2 Cor 5:7), he finds himself between the 'no longer' and the 'not yet': 'Not that I have already obtained [the prize] or am already perfect; but I press on to make it my own, because Christ Jesus has made me his own' (Phil 3:12). Here there is no question of possessing God in ecstasy; he who would see God is referred to the Word made flesh: 'He who has seen me has seen the Father' (Jn 14:9).

PART THREE

Theology and Ontology

THE PROBLEM STATED

Bultmann's work has called forth a sizable literature which there can be no question of our considering in detail. Some of his critics have taken a niggling approach and most have misunderstood his thought. But there is a weightier consideration. Skim through these contributions from the most diverse minds and you soon see that they all busy themselves with one and the same problem: that of the relation between philosophy and theology. Even when their authors are unconscious or but dimly aware of the question, it is what links together this whole body of writing, at first glance so heterogeneous; and by making it the theme of Part Three we hope to offer at least a sound definition of the great quarrel over demythologization, if not to settle it.

Inevitably we begin by clarifying Bultmann's connection with Heidegger, after which some thought devoted to his passages at arms with Jaspers the philosopher and Barth the theologian will shed light upon the necessary bond between theology and ontology. By listening in this way to Heidegger, Jaspers and Barth, we shall be listening to all who have written about Bultmann.

CHAPTER SIXTEEN

Bultmann and Heidegger

I

WHY ONTOLOGY IS NECESSARY (THE DIRECT PROOF)

It will be recalled that Bultmann distinguishes between the ontic plane and the ontological plane. The former is the plane of things (God, man, the world, life, death, salvation, and so forth). It is the plane of the *Dass*. The latter is the plane of the significance which these different phenomena have. For example, the ontology of man is not the ontology of stone. What man and stone have in common is that both exist (ontic plane), but they do not exist in the same way (ontological plane). Phenomenological analysis reveals that the existence of the one has a different significance from the existence of the other: stone exhibits the structure of *Vorhandenheit*, and man the structure of freedom (ec-sistence). Thus ontology has to do with the formal plane, with the world of each being's own particular manifestation: ideas are not manifested as time is, nor time as the atom is, nor the atom as quality is, nor quality as a tree is, nor a tree as God is, and so on. There are regions of being, each with its own ontological structure. In classical terms, each being has its 'essence'.

Bultmann has often made known his conviction that revelation, faith and theology need what he calls '*die sachgemässe Begrifflichkeit*' (GV 2, p. 234) or again '*die "richtige" Philosophie*' (KM 2, p. 192). A being's *Begrifflichkeit* (conceptuality) is its ontological or formal structure, its *Was*, or, we may say, its *Vorverständnis*. The precomprehension of love is the idea or the essence of love. As to the phrase '*die "richtige" Philosophie*' ('the "right" philosophy'), the word 'philosophy' in it must on no account be taken to mean what it ordinarily means— that is, a particular view (a *Verständnis*) of God, man and the world. Here *Philosophie* is strictly synonymous with *Begrifflichkeit*. We are not dealing with a scheme of God, man and the world but with the disclosure of their being.

Thus when we say that revelation cannot do without ontology, we do not mean that it needs philosophy in the ordinary sense of a set attitude towards beings (notably God, man and the world). Revelation peremptorily rules out all philosophy, whatever its content (materialist, positivist, rationalist or spiritualist; realist or idealist; essentialist or existentialist; atheist, theist or pantheist), whatever its form (popular or learned, systematic or anti-systematic), whatever the age (ancient or modern) and country (eastern or western) it may spring from. Every philosophy, because it is a *Weltanschauung*, contradicts faith. We do not mean such a philosophy but the science of formal structures. Not beings are at issue, but the significance of their being.

'Theology is certainly irreconcilable with philosophy if philosophy be taken as a system of all truth, as the science of beings. For theology cannot agree to be allotted either its object or the method of dealing with its object. But if philosophy be taken as the critical science of being—in other words, as the science that must control all the positive sciences (which deal with beings) by judging their concepts of being— then indeed philosophy does theology a vital service.'[1]

Revelation, after all, is not addressed to stones but to a thinking creature. It is not as though man were an object, which God must first turn into a rational being to whom he can reveal himself. God summons a partner who is able to understand him—that is, who has a pre-comprehension of all that God says to him. If man, say, had no antecedent notion of sin in general, then all that the Bible teaches him about sin would have no more meaning to him than to a stone. When the Bible speaks to him of sin it does not invent the concept. It addresses a being who has wits enough to know that sin is not virtue or grace. Consequently even the unbeliever does not confuse these things. He understands what is meant when one speaks to him of guilt. He knows well enough that the believer, at that moment, is not talking about some theory in microphysics but about a thing that they can discuss. They will not agree about it, of course; but how could they disagree about it unless there were a tacit, fundamental agreement between them as to what concept is at issue?

Similarly when revelation makes known to a man the event of salvation in Jesus Christ, it assumes that he has a *Vorverständnis* of salvation in general, without which salvation in Christ would be as meaningless to him as it is to a tree. God's Word does not create this concept in him, which even the unbeliever does not identify with the concept of damnation, knowing perfectly well, by the *lumen naturale*, what salvation is in general: if he does not accept Christian salvation, that is precisely because he thinks it a spurious salvation; behind the disagreement there lies common ground. Nor is the idea of God an

---

1. R. Bultmann, 'Vom Begriff der religiösen Gemeinschaft' in *Th. Bl.*, 1927, col. 73.

infused idea. The Bible speaks of God to people to whom the concept has a meaning before there is any question of revelation, people who will not confuse God with a shooting star or the chemical industry. Precisely because the word *God* has a meaning for them, they can understand (and then accept or reject) what faith says about him (whereas a stone can be neither a believer nor an unbeliever). An atheist or a man indifferent to religion can reject the gospel only because the word *God* means something to him—that is, because he has a *Vorverständnis* of God. Thanks to this precomprehension of God in general, he does not confuse God with other absolute values which he may have chosen instead (wealth, power, art, or the like).

Thus man is that being who, unlike minerals, vegetables and animals, has been endowed by nature with a precomprehension of all things. He *is* all things in a certain sense—that is, by way of absence and lack, or again by way of images and concepts: to have a mental picture or a concept of a thing is not to have the thing itself. He is a being perpetually in search of his being (of happiness, power, virtue, love, God). Since he is never satisfied, he is always ahead of himself. And that is why the connection between revelation and philosophy presents a problem. Because God's Word is addressed to a being who has a *Vorverständnis* of all things, it does not bring him the *idea* of salvation (ontological salvation) but the *reality* of salvation (ontic salvation), not the *idea* of God (the ontological God) but the *reality* of God (the ontic God). No doubt it corrects, explicitates and enriches the concepts of God and salvation, but it does not create them in the man whom it summons.

If man, unlike things, has the power to understand (and then accept or reject) God and God's salvation, that is because he has a *Vorverständnis* of them by virtue of his nature as a rational being (by virtue of the *lumen naturale*). To be human and to have a precomprehension of all that exists, is one and the same thing. Of course as a rule the *Vorverständnis* is somewhat vague and incomplete, more a capacity, an aptitude. To be at least that capacity and aptitude is to be a man; not to be it is to be a thing.

It is important to have an *exact* precomprehension of sin, grace, judgment, death, life and love before we embark on the revelation which tells about those things. If warped categories carry us beyond what revelation says, then we shall inevitably misinterpret it. How did the ancient Church come to think of Christ in terms of the concept of 'nature', the liberals in terms of 'spirit', and the contemporary orthodox who oppose Bultmann in terms of 'supra-history'? How do classical theologians come to look on redemption as a juridical act or a sacrifice, and liberal theologians as a mystical experience? Why does traditional

Catholicism envisage faith as an infused supernatural virtue, and most of Protestantism envisage it as an act? Why is sin set now on the plane of magic, now on the plane of ethics, and now on the plane of religion? Why else than because underlying these different interpretations there are as many precomprehensions of Christ, redemption, faith and sin?

Every reader dips into the Bible with an antecedent idea (drawn from his temperament, his education, his culture and his freedom) of God, of salvation, of redemption, of guilt; and interprets scripture according to this precomprehension. Therefore it behooves us to take a careful look at the *Begrifflichkeit* through which we become aware of the biblical message, and ask ourselves how far it is suited to that purpose.

First of all, theology must be distinguished from philosophy. Theology stands on the ontic, ec-sistentiell plane. Faith presupposes a particular view of God, man and the world. It is a scheme of things which excludes every other, above all every religion and philosophy properly so-called, which it regards as mere variations on the 'thought of natural man'. But it has no objection to ontological philosophy, which studies the formal structures of being. Indeed it needs this philosophy. It tells us about God and his deeds, about salvation, about sin. But what do all these words mean? A man who does not understand them on the ontological plane will never understand them on the ontic (Christian) plane. For faith, though it has not created them, uses them in their right signification, their strict sense, which it is the business of ontology to work out. Phenomenology does not tell me about any concrete revelation (God's revelation in Jesus Christ or Mohammed), any concrete salvation (salvation through Jesus Christ or through Buddhism), but it tells me what revelation and salvation mean in general; it discloses, explicitates, and where necessary corrects the precomprehension I have of them.

The New Testament declares that Jesus is the Word of God. That is a particular message, one that stands on the ontic plane. What does the term 'word' mean? Must we look on Christ as the ancient Church did? Must we accept Calvin's stricture upon Arius and the Fathers: *Utrinque erratum est* (§11, 3a, below)? On the ontic plane Arius, the Fathers and Calvin all agree: for all of them Jesus Christ is the Word of God. But they differ on the ontological plane, because they do not attach the same meaning to the term 'word'. Here we see how necessary a phenomenology of word is, which will not be concerned to show that Jesus of Nazareth is or is not the Word of God (that problem is one of ontic decision) but to define what word is in general, so that we can then correctly understand the New Testament when it says that Jesus Christ is the Word of God.

Phenomenology does not have to do with decision, the giving of myself to (or withholding of myself from) otherness when it summons me; it has to do with the meaning of what otherness says to me. Since revelation does not invent concepts but uses those already familiar to men, and since men—even without revelation—have always known that salvation is not damnation, virtue is not vice, and so forth, having these concepts within them by the *lumen naturale*, it behooves us to examine their ontological structure by phenomenological analysis, thus putting ourselves in a position to understand the ontic message which the New Testament bears.

To take one instance, it was because he had a more accurate idea of what *word* is in general that Calvin understood better than the Fathers and Arius what is meant by the affirmation: Jesus Christ is the Word of God. Or take an example of wider extension: what separates Protestants and Catholics is obviously nothing on the ontic plane— both alike believe in Jesus Christ. There is a difference of *Begrifflichkeit*. Both sides admit the reality (the *Dass*) of Christ, but they have different conceptions of it; words like sin, grace, salvation, nature and person do not mean the same thing to each. Failing any phenomenological criterion, a man is bound to interpret revelation in accordance with the meaning which is attached to these human terms by tradition, common sense or philosophic reflection, since revelation speaks in these terms.

Let us sum up. (a) God's revelation is not a revelation of concepts which hitherto were unknown to man. There is nothing in the Bible that a human being cannot grasp. Unbelievers can understand it. Whether their understanding of it is more or less incorrect matters little on the plane where we are thinking at the moment. To be able to misunderstand is still to be able to understand (a plank cannot misunderstand anything). The atheist or agnostic does not behave towards the Bible like an animal but like an intelligent, responsible being, which implies that in one way or another he is able to under-stand the very thing he rejects.

Thus man has a *Vorverständnis* of revelation—by which we mean primarily an ability (not enjoyed by things) to read the Bible. God does not speak to a creature which must first be miraculously transformed into a partner capable of understanding him; he speaks to a creature whose ideas and parlance he uses. Scripture is not made up of angelic ideas and words, only of human ideas and words; which implies (and proves) that man has a precomprehension of all it says to him, that he knows the *general* meaning of the *Begrifflichkeit* scripture uses to speak to him.

(b) It is certain that God uses human language in its true meaning. With its own ontology it tells us about God and about other things:

the world, sin, grace, the Church, the sacraments, love, judgment, eternal life. All these are so many phenomena one must understand according to the true mode of their manifestation (according to the truth of their 'essence'), or else one will not make head or tail of biblical thought.

If I envisage man according to the warped ontology of common sense I shall misinterpret the Pauline notions of 'body', 'spirit', 'conscience', 'heart', and more besides. If I take a magical or juridical or ethical or religious view of sin, I shall fail to grasp the Christian view of sin. If I envisage love as humanism does, I shall fail to grasp what Christian love is. If I envisage salvation as Gnosis does, I shall fail to grasp what Christian salvation is. Only if I have a sound *Vorverständnis*, an accurate *Begrifflichkeit* of all these things, shall I be able to understand what the Bible says to me through them.

(c) Here a vital question arises. As we have just said, revelation uses a possession of man's which is peculiarly his own—his concepts and his words—in accordance with its ontological truth. Now, through sin man has more or less perverted all *Begrifflichkeit*, rationalizing it; in other words, using it to express what he has made of the Creator and creation—his thing. Faith he has turned into religion or philosophy, and creation he has turned into the world as the world. Well then, can he rediscover the real significance of beings, the purity of their essence and of the concepts which embody their essence, through phenomenological analysis—that is, by his own resources? Can he win through, of himself, to the accurate *Vorverständnis* of what God is saying to him? Before examining this problem we must set forth the indirect proof for the necessity of a sound *Begrifflichkeit*.

II

WHY ONTOLOGY IS NECESSARY (THE INDIRECT PROOF)

Here we need only synthesize the points regarding *Begrifflichkeit* which have already been established.

(1) *The false ontology of myth*

We know the genuine meaning of myth, which sets out to speak of a power lying beyond the world and man. That *beyond* is not spatial and objective, for if it were, it would still be part of the world and man. Myth deals with a transcendence which demands to be acknowledged and obeyed. It has sometimes been called 'primitive science'. We shall presently see how far the description is acceptable, but in fact myth is much more than a primitive science. 'Myths speak of gods and devils as powers on which man knows he is dependent, whose favour he needs, whose anger he fears. Myths convey the idea that man is not master of the world and of his life, that the world he lives in is full of riddles and mysteries' (JCM, p. 19). Myth 'holds that the world and human life are sustained and hemmed in by a power lying beyond all that is subject to our reckoning and control' (*ibid.*).

But a misguided *Begrifflichkeit*, spawned by the *logos* of natural man, comes along to thwart the purpose of myth, which then, indeed, sinks to the status of a 'primitive science'. We have an example in the 'aetiological myths, which attempt to explain curious, startling or horrendous natural phenomena like eclipses of the sun and moon or the different positions taken by Orion's legs' (KM 2, p. 182). Primitive man uses myth as a tool for getting the better of the world.

With the pattern of cause and effect we have the emergence of the scientific attitude, which man applies to myth, thus rationalizing it. He speaks of the godhead 'in unworthy terms when he represents the beyond as a reality that is far off in space, as a heaven set above the earth, a hell set beneath it. He speaks in unworthy terms of the powers of the beyond when he represents them as comparable with the powers of this world, superior to them only as being unpredictable and mightier. Witness the mythical notion of *Wunder* and *Mirakel*. Here the action of the power beyond (the action of God) is represented as an event which disrupts the natural or psychological course of events and yet connects with it. Transcendent causality is thrust into the chain of earthly events, and a power which works miracles of this order is willy-nilly thought of as an earthly force and shifted to the plane of earthly events. Myth speaks of gods as if they were men, of their acts as human acts, except in the particular that the gods concerned are armed with superhuman might and that their unforeseeable acts can upset the natural course of things. It makes the gods (or God) ultra-powerful men, and that even when it speaks of God's omnipotence or omniscience, because it does not distinguish them *qualitatively* from the power and knowledge of man, only *quantitatively*' (KM 2, pp. 183–4).

We have seen how two noble forms of religion—Gnosis and the mystery religions—with their astonishing transcendent purpose, mark the climax of the history of religions, and yet are spoilt by an inadequate ontology borrowed from the objectifying philosophy of natural man, and more or less reduced to the level of that philosophy. The god who dies and rises again in the mystery religions is devoid of real transcendence, for he is of the same nature as those whom he is supposed to save. All he has to do is deliver beings (men) who are only the prisoners of fate, of an arbitrary ordering of events. The salvation they receive does not transform them, brings them nothing utterly new; it only unbinds their old will to live. Properly speaking, there is no sin and no grace, because the mysteries use the language of the naturalist ontology man has invented to designate the cares and prosaic realities of his daily life in this world. This ontology expresses man's desire to be his own master and the master of things. Therefore it is unfit to express true transcendence, as we also see by the 'mystic' community's image of itself. A man could be initiated into several mystery religions and also take part in the city's official worship, which would have been unthinkable had initiates felt they were totally determined by the god in whom they believed.

Gnosis is the prisoner of the same objectifying ontology. The fall of man is no fault of his own, it is a fate which smites him from outside, leaving intact his essential self, which is divine. Just as in the mystery religions, man's salvation is a deliverance in the purely outward sense of the word. Once saved, man is what he was when damned; and damned, he is already what he will be once he is saved. It is suicidal for a theology of redemption—and first and foremost Gnosis is such a theology—to try to express itself in the ontology of natural man: that ontology rejects out of hand any redemption which is not self-redemption. All its concepts and all its language are born of a yearning for independence. Applied to a redemptive religion, they necessarily subvert it, leaving no room for a correct idea of sin or grace. Only categories drawn from the sphere of ec-sistence are able to express the relation between God the Saviour and sinful man. Gnosis can see it only in terms of ascesis and ecstasy, and they are part of the same substantialist ontology that turns redemption into a 'work'.

As we have seen, the New Testament itself is not uncoloured by a certain mythologization: here and there it uses a *Begrifflichkeit* which is that of *homo religiosus*. In the first place this unsuitable ontology is applied to God, who is pictured as dwelling in a space set above the earth (heaven). He has a son, a pre-existent being whom God sends to earth in human form and who, once his mission is accomplished, will return victorious 'to God's right hand'. The judgment is a cosmic event: the son of man will come on the 'clouds of heaven' and believers will be taken up into the air to meet him (I Thess 4:15ff). The devils live in hell, an underground place into which the Redeemer 'descends'. The stars are living, demoniac beings whose malice is the root of the evils afflicting man, and at times man himself seems to be more a substance than a responsible freedom. He is the passive object of assaults by the devils, who attack him in his body and in his soul without his will being in any way involved (sickness, diabolic possession, and so forth). God's intervention on man's behalf is more often a *Mirakel* than a *Wunder*—that is, the divine action is pictured as mere natural causality lifted one storey higher. God acts like an ultra-powerful man. He does not abolish nature's determinism, he only competes with it.

Most New Testament miracles are of this super-natural type. Sometimes the Holy Spirit is a fluid 'poured forth' or 'poured into' believers. The sacraments may operate magically: Christians are baptized for the dead (1 Cor 15:29), and unworthy reception of the Eucharist may be the cause of fatal illness (1 Cor 11:30). Even the event of salvation itself is expressed in an inadequate ontology borrowed now from Judaism, now from Gnosis. Christ's death is a sacrifice of expiation, of atonement. Evidently these juridical and ritual categories of themselves rationalize God's action. They imply that sin is something outside the sinner and that he can be saved by a redeemer with a metaphysical essence, who is sent from heaven and returns thither according to the pattern of the mystery religions and Gnosis: the pre-existent Son assumes a human form, dies a sanguinary death, rises again, and ascends to heaven to sit once more beside the Father.

But we know that alongside this objective *Begrifflichkeit*, a remnant of the thought of natural man, the New Testament exhibits another ontology. Revelation has disclosed the real *meaning* of God, man, the world, freedom, responsibility, sin, grace, obedience, love, encounter. We have seen in a number of foregoing chapters that the New Testament speaks of God, of his word and his deeds, of Jesus Christ, of the Church, of the sacraments, of love, of sin, of grace, in a demythologized *Begrifflichkeit*. God is not a metaphysical being but the Lord who determines man's existence. The mythological concepts which convey the event of salvation—the concepts of pre-existence, incarnation, expiatory death, resurrection, ascension, parousia—have been purified. The Son of God does not pre-exist in the sense of being a second divine person alongside the first: the category of pre-existence merely underlines the fact that in Jesus of Nazareth God himself encounters men.

Paul and John know nothing, or rather choose to know nothing, of any miraculous conception or virgin birth: so far as they are concerned, the Word has really become flesh. Jesus's death is not essentially (Paul) or not at all (John) an expiatory sacrifice but rather his victory over the world. No more are the resurrection, ascension and parousia (at least in John) 'supra-intra-terrestrial' things: they constitute an event—the eschatological event which annihilates the world and ushers in the kingdom of God.

In one page of *Jesus Christus und die Mythologie* Bultmann has summed up the way Paul and John displace the mythological categories with the ontology which is suited to revelation. 'Very early the process of demythologizing [eschatology] began, going half-way with Paul and all the way with John. The vital step was taken when Paul declared that the decisive moment [of transition] from the old world to the new did not lie somewhere in the future but had already occurred in the coming of Jesus Christ. "When the time had fully come, God sent forth his Son" (Gal 4:4). No doubt Paul still expects the end of the world to be a cosmic drama; he awaits the parousia of Christ on the clouds of heaven, the resurrection of the dead, the last judgment; but with Christ's resurrection the decisive event has already happened. The Church is the eschatological community of the elect, of the saints, who are already justified and live because they are in Christ—in Christ who as the second Adam has destroyed death and caused life and immortality to shine forth through the Gospel (Rom 5:12–14; 2 Tim 1:10). "Death is swallowed up in victory" (1 Cor 15:54). Consequently Paul is able to say that the hopes and promises of the prophets of old are fulfilled when the gospel is proclaimed: "Now is the acceptable time; behold, now is the day of salvation" (2 Cor 6:2). The Holy Spirit, who was awaited as a gift to be given on the day of blessings, has already been given. In this way the future is anticipated.

'This demythologization can be studied in a particular instance. In the hopes of Jewish apocalyptic literature, expectation of the messianic kingdom loomed large. That kingdom is, as it were, an interregnum between the age of the old world ($o\tilde{v}\tau os$ $\acute{o}$ $a\dot{\iota}\acute{\omega}\nu$) and the new age ($\acute{o}$ $\mu\acute{\epsilon}\lambda\lambda\omega\nu$ $a\dot{\iota}\acute{\omega}\nu$). This apocalyptic and mythological idea of an inter-regnum, at the close of which Christ will deliver the kingdom to God the Father, Paul interprets as the present age, stretching from Christ's resurrection to his eventual parousia (1 Cor 15:24). In other words the present age, in which the gospel is preached, is really the age formerly awaited as the messianic kingdom. Jesus is now the Messiah, the Lord.

'After Paul's day, John thoroughly demythologized eschatology. In his eyes the coming and the departure of Jesus is the eschatological event. "And this is the judgment, that the light has come into the world, and men loved darkness rather than light, because their deeds were evil" (3:19). "Now is the judgment of this world, now shall the ruler of this world be cast out" (Jn 12:31). For John the resurrection of Jesus, Pentecost and the parousia are one and the same event, and those who believe already have eternal life [quotations from Jn 3:18; 3:36; 5:25; 11:25f].

'As in Paul, so likewise in John demythologization can be studied in a particular instance. In the expectations of Jewish eschatology we see that the figure of Antichrist, as depicted for example by 2 Thess 2:7–12, is an eminently mythological one. In John (1 Jn 2:18–23) the false preachers fill the role of that mythological figure. Mythology has been transposed into history.[2] These examples, it seems to me, show that demythologization was set afoot in the New Testament itself and that therefore our undertaking is vindicated' (JCM, pp. 32–4).

If the New Testament has been essentially demythologized—that is, speaks in a *Begrifflichkeit* suited to the mystery of God—the fact remains, as we have seen, that the biblical writers are more or less prisoners of the ontology of the object. That is why we have a duty to subject even the books of the New Testament to 'a *Sachkritik* such as Luther made of the Letter of James or the Apocalypse of John' (TNT, p. 587; on Luther, see pp. 83–4, above).

(2) The false ontology of history

As we have seen, history can be interpreted in one of two *Begrifflichkeiten*. One may look on historical event as something over and done with—that is, as an objective fact. The science which studies it in this aspect is basically of the same nature as other sciences. It tries to discover 'how things really happened', by recourse to literary evidence (public records, private papers, memoirs), epigraphy, archaeology, and so forth. Thus one assembles, as far as may be, an *objective* restoration of the past. But this implies a whole philosophy: historical fact is assumed to be something tangible. It is assumed that man can master the past, as the natural sciences master the world in theory and technology masters it in practice. Thus the function of history is to provide us with 'instruction' or 'lessons', which enable us to control the present and even the future so far as that is possible.

We have seen that scripture cannot be reconciled with this rational ontology. Of course the Bible is an objective phenomenon to the extent that a series of facts and documents make it up; but as the Word of God it is no longer a history which man can control through knowledge. True, the temptation for the biblical authors to regard revelation as an objective thing, there for man to lay hold on, sometimes proved too much for them, so that they turned revelation into a *Mirakel* whereby the divine can be verified. We also know that the idea of history which conservative exegetes have is dominated by the philosophical assumption (generally unconscious) that the Word of God is something 'supra-objective' and 'supra-historical'. But in reality this false ontology betrays the *geschichtlich* nature of revelation, which is *Anrede*, which summons man to ec-sistence (to faith, obedience and death to all he has and all he is), which demands to be the determination of his life and therefore cannot be an objective fact but must be a fact that calls him in question.

2. Of course in the sense of 'history'.

We have seen how the Yahwist, Elohist and Priestly sources present history as God's *Anrede*; how Jesus believes he is the Word of God summoning men to decision; how the New Testament looks on him as the one in whom and through whom God reveals himself as life and death, the abolition and the resurrection of man. Thus to look at revelation through the ontology of the object is to turn it into a *Historie*, whereas by definition it is a *Geschichte*.

(3) *False ontologies drawn from the various philosophies*

Philosophy properly speaking, as we have remarked, stands on the ontic plane; it is the taking up of an attitude. Ontology, on the other hand, has to do with the 'essence' of things. Evidently each philosophy has its own ontology. If I adopt Greek philosophy, I look on the being that is man as if he were an object, a composite of matter and form. Greek philosophy, which is a scheme of God, man and the world, in its own way reveals the essence of each of those three. Each philosophy conveys its particular *Begrifflichkeit*. Down the ages Christian faith has always tried to express itself in the *Begrifflichkeit* of the philosophy which happened to prevail at the time. The failure of these attempts drives home to us once more the necessity of a *sound* ontology.

(a) The ancient Church borrowed its major dogmatic and ethical categories from Greek philosophy and these were hallowed by the great councils (particularly Nicaea and Chalcedon). Basically, the Christian mystery was expressed in terms of nature and person. The Trinity became the mystery of a *physis* in three *hypostases* and christology the mystery of one *hypostasis* in two *physeis*. No doubt this formulation safeguards the underlying purpose of faith; but the concepts chosen are unsuitable, because they derive from a philosophy which was constructed solely to express the things of this world, the sphere of things that man can lay hold on. The very term *hypostasis* reveals plainly enough that what it designates is thought of as the ultimate principle in which all the elements constituting a thing are rooted—that is, as a thing *in se*. All the Greek categories adopted by ecclesiastical tradition (ὑπόστασις, οὐσία, φύσις, *substantia*, *natura*, *persona*) derive from what we have called the philosophy of in-sistence. When applied to God, Christ and man, these categories turn them into so many metaphysical beings. Even the idea of relation is quite inconsistent with freedom.[3] If the Middle Ages were more creative than people often suppose, they never ventured beyond the framework of ancient thought.[4] In patristic, conciliar and medieval theology the

3. See A. Malet, *Personne et amour dans la théologie trinitaire de S. Thomas d'Aquin* (1956), pp. 11–21.
4 *Ibid.*, pp. 71–161.

divine persons, Christ and man are seen through an objectifying *Begrifflichkeit* which is not that of the New Testament.

New Testament *Begrifflichkeit* is steeped in the idea of revelation. Jesus is not a metaphysical being made up of two natures, but God's mode of being towards us. He is God himself manifesting himself to men and determining their being and their life. Only on this footing are the otherness, transcendence and lordship of God in Jesus Christ respected and confessed. They are automatically rationalized by any *Begrifflichkeit* of the metaphysical sort. 'As we know, in the ancient Church men dwelt on the φύσις, the nature of Christ. That is understandable enough when one takes into account the tradition of Greek thought . . . But I think that in the New Testament, at least for the most part, the affirmations of Jesus's divinity or godhead are not really meant to express its nature but its import; they are affirmations confessing that what he is and what he does does not arise from this world, from the human thoughts and the events of this world, but is the medium through which God speaks to us, acts upon us and in our behalf. Christ is the power and the wisdom of God; God has made him our righteousness and sanctification and redemption (1 Cor 1:30)' (GV 2, pp. 252–3).

Likewise in John 'all the statements that the Son does what the Father does, that he obeys the Father's will, keeps his commandments, carries out his work, acts by the Father's authority (Jn 5:27; 17:2), that those who are his are the Father's and vice versa (17:10), that he declares God's word or whatever he has seen and heard with the Father, that anyone who has seen him has seen the Father (14:9), that he and the Father are one, he in the Father and the Father in him, that the Father in him does his works (14:10)—all these statements announce the same thing that the καὶ θεός ἦν ὁ λόγος announces: that Father and Son cannot be considered two separate persons, as though the action of one completed the action of the other . . . or as though they were united by a common intent of the will. What we are told is that the operation of Father and Son is identical' (EJ, p. 188).

As Calvin well observed with regard to Jn 5:23: *Deum non ita in Christi persona regnare, quasi ipse, ut solent ignavi reges, quiescat in caelo, sed quia in Christi persona potentiam suam declaret seque praesentem exhibeat* (quoted in EJ, p. 188, note 12). Commenting on Jn 5:19 ('the son can do nothing of his own accord'), Calvin lays bare the wrongness of the metaphysical categories used by the ancient Church: *Arius minorem Patre Filium inde colligebat, quia ex se nihil possit: excipiebant Patres, notari tantum his verbis personae distinctionem, ut sciretur Christum a Patre esse, non tamen intrinseca agendi virtute eum privari. Atque utrinque erratum est. Neque enim de nuda Christi divinitate habetur concio, et quae mox videbimus, in aeternum Dei sermomen per se et simpliciter minime competunt, sed tantum quadrant Filio Dei quatenus in carne manifestus est. Sit nobis ante oculos Christus, ut a Patre missus est mundo redemptor* (quoted in EJ, p. 186). This search for a new ontology, which the Reformers began, must be carried on: 'Christology should at last be completely freed from the clutches of an objectifying ontology and set forth in a new ontological *Begrifflichkeit*' (KM 2, p. 206, note 1); and we must apply this dictum of Bultmann's to the whole of theology.

(b) The *Begrifflichkeit* of modern philosophy is no more fit to express revelation than that of ancient philosophy. We have seen how the liberals, by attempting to use it, undermined the transcendence of Christianity, turning it into a religious humanism. Those theologians generally had recourse to idealism. Now idealism is a philosophy of immanence (pp. 29–31, above, and 321–3, below). 'In the idealist scheme of things, man's being is constituted by the *logos*, reason, the eternal and the absolute. An idealist theologian thinks he is talking simultaneously about God and about man because, following in the footsteps of the old classical tradition, he is used to bracketing God and the absolute. In fact he is only talking about man' (GV 1, p. 118).

(c) Liberalism, the child of idealism, was succeeded by the 'history of religion school'. Bousset's conception has already been set forth (ch. 9, §II, above). Plainly enough it presupposes a *Begrifflichkeit* that is unable to express the transcendence of Christian faith. Bousset does mark a considerable advance beyond liberalism in recognizing that Christianity is not a religious idealism, but a thing beyond this world and beyond the man of this world. Nevertheless he thinks of it in categories (such as piety, mysticism and ecstasy) which are still drawn from the thought of *homo religiosus*.

With Bultmann himself, let us examine a precise example of this inappropriate *Begrifflichkeit*. Bousset embarks on a study of Paul with a substantialist anthropology in his mind, and therefore interprets the ἄνθρωπος πνευματικός as 'a being of a different and higher order than ordinary man' (Bousset quoted by Bultmann, GV 1, p. 131). Thus Paul is supposed to regard the Christian as a supernatural being which has lost its former identity. So strong is Paul's supernaturalism, says Bousset, that 'it threatens to dissolve the oneness and continuity of the human *I*. Like the ecstatics, the Pauline Christian has lost his self, not for the moment but permanently. Man's self is nothing; the powers which determine that self, whether the Spirit or the flesh, are everything' (Bousset, quoted *ibid.*). Bousset fails to perceive that in Paul's eyes man is a dialectical being, at once past and future—an aptitude for ec-sistence. While becoming utterly new, he never loses his identity.

He is a freedom, which is why he can be *simul peccator simul justus*, determined both by the world and by God.

(d) We have seen how contemporary orthodox theologians are also the victims of a false *Begrifflichkeit*, itself the spawn of a false philosophy. They imagine they have left the metaphysical dogmatics of the ancient Church behind them. They even claim to repudiate all philosophy, ancient or modern, talking in terms of event and history, centring everything on the 'facts of salvation', which are supposedly both historical and supra-historical. Yet we know that this ontology derives from a definite philosophy and is unfit to express the message of revelation (ch. 9, §IV above).

(4) *The false ontology of science*

Because Bultmann has criticized New Testament mythology in the name of modern man bred to scientific thought, people have supposed that he meant to interpret revelation with the help of scientific ontology. Assuredly the science of today renders theology a very valuable service—but precisely by showing it that it cannot use the categories of science. God's Word dismisses both mythology and science as unsuited. Mythology objectifies the Word by turning it into a thing for man to manipulate. Science is an instrument with which man conquers the world: it is 'the logical and systematic development of a kind of thought which strives to master the world' (KM 2, p. 189), supposing the world to be ruled by laws. Its fundamental premise is the determinism of nature. Accordingly the *Begrifflichkeit* of myth and the *Begrifflichkeit* of science both derive from the thought of natural man. And when the ec-sistential interpretation sets out to rid scripture of mythological categories it is 'obviously not so as to hand it over to the *Begrifflichkeit* of objectifying, scientific thought. On the contrary, we demythologize so as to achieve an understanding of scripture innocent of any earthly image produced by objectifying thought, whether it be that of myth or that of science. The complaint that demythologization would "make science" of scripture—meaning by science the objectifying thought of science—is stuff and nonsense. Scripture has no need to defend its affirmations at the judgment-seat of an objectifying science' (KM 2, p. 187).

Modern man, bred in science from the cradle, is well aware of the fact. He does not admit—and here, without having the faith, he is much closer to faith than many who think they have it—that God can intervene in the world as a sort of 'higher-grade technician', that God's action can take the form of *Mirakel*. We have seen how the theology of *Mirakel* rationalizes revelation, reducing it literally to the status of an object for science to study. Here God becomes a mere successful competitor of natural forces. Modern man is right to reject this false God. He must be offered the gospel, which has nothing to do with scientific concepts and scientific language; he must be faced with the 'real scandal' (KM 2, p. 188) of God's Word, so that he can assume full responsibility for accepting or rejecting it. This means that we have absolutely no right to deck out the gospel in the trappings of science.

In fact people's 'distress at demythologization may spring in part from their fixed belief that the only possible choice is between mythology and science, so that science must inevitably be the science which objectifies existence into an earthly thing.[5] But is there no other language at all apart from the language of science and of myth? Are utterances like "I love you" and "I beg you to forgive me" couched in scientific language? And if not, then are they couched in mythological language? Well then, there is a language which naively expresses existence, and corresponding to it a science which speaks of existence without objectifying it into an earthly thing' (KM 2, p. 187). It is this science of ec-sistence which we have been setting forth throughout the present book. As we have repeatedly seen, it rules out mythology and science alike, because both are expressions of 'natural man'.

III

FAITH AND ONTOLOGY

An accurate ontology, therefore, is necessary if one is to have an accurate understanding of revelation. But if man, by his very nature as a thinking being, has a *Vorverständnis* of all things, including God, can he have an accurate *Verständnis* of them? Can he work out an accurate phenomenology of God, himself and the world? Is faith not necessary for this accurate *Begrifflichkeit*? Historically speaking, it certainly is. We have declared and established over and over again that the Bible reveals the true import of God, man and the world. Moreover modern thought, which sheds such a vivid light upon the 'historicity' and temporality of man, has been deeply influenced by Christianity. 'There would be no modern philosophy but for the New Testament, Luther and Kierkegaard' (KM 1, p. 35). But are temporality and 'historicity' *as such* part of the faith? No, because unbelieving philosophers have been able to adopt this *Begrifflichkeit*, deepen and enrich it. While rejecting the ontic Christian scheme of things, they use for their own purposes the ontological structures which Christianity

---

5. That is, a thing like the things that the sciences concern themselves with.

lays bare. Thus it comes about that the accurate idea of man as ec-sistence has been secularized not only in Heidegger but also in Dilthey, Jaspers and Sartre.

Philosophers know that man is freedom and faith (Jaspers), a 'being-forever-ahead-of-oneself' (Heidegger). Moreover among the concepts they admit is the concept of a fall. Man is damned in the 'they' [German *man*, French *on*] (Heidegger); he is a 'dirty dog' (Sartre); a *Dasein* (Jaspers). They also declare that his salvation is to be found in a constant reaching beyond himself, in a perpetual future. Conversely, as we have seen, the Christian scheme of things can co-exist with an ontology which does not suit it. There can be no doubt that Christians in the ancient Church, in the Middle Ages, Christians who adhered to classical orthodoxy and classical liberalism, lived by the gospel; their ec-sistentiell scheme of things was the Christian one, but they had not an accurate *Begrifflichkeit* of this scheme of God, man and the world, influenced as they were by one prevalent philosophy or another. Moreover modern phenomenology has perfected the ontology of the Bible. Scripture does not directly concern itself with ontology, which it rather takes for granted than expounds.

What chiefly interests revelation lies on the ontic plane; it is not a *Was* but a *Dass*. Paul, for instance, is not primarily concerned to give us an accurate idea of the body, the spirit, the heart, and all those notions in his writings whose ontological structure we have analysed. His great concern is the Christian scheme of things, not the *Begriff-lichkeit* implicit in it. But phenomenology concerns itself exclusively with the ontological plane. Consequently the formal analysis of the human being in Kierkegaard is more scientific than that in the New Testament, and in Jaspers and Heidegger is more scientific than in Kierkegaard (see GV I, p. 308).

Modern thinkers disclose the 'phenomenon of man' better than the Bible does. The fact that phenomenologists can adopt the ontology of man as revealed by the New Testament without thereby accepting the Christian scheme of things, shows that the connection is only a de facto one and that their idea of man 'is not actually grounded in its historical origin' (KM I, p. 35). How could the case be otherwise? If man is really freedom and temporality, how can he help discovering his own significance—how can he fail to see, at least in general and provided he keeps mulling over the facts, that he is not a stone and not an animal?

Obviously the ontic plane and the ontological plane are closely interwoven, as witness what we have just said. We observed at the outset (p. 13, above) that the ontological structure never exists in isolation. My ability to be something is always concrete; I am always involved in an ec-sistentiell scheme of things, if only in the multifarious business of everyday life. Conversely, the ontic scheme of things always presupposes the ontological structure thanks to which I am a being capable of entering into schemes. So revelation, which is a *Verständnis*, the determination of a man by his Lord, necessarily implies that the human being (unlike mineral objects, for instance) can be determined by God—that is, that he has an ec-sistential ontological structure. Revelation is an ontic aptitude grounded on an ontological aptitude. Faith is a divine phenomenon and at the same time a human one, because it does not destroy man's ontological structure to make him either a beast or an angel.

This interplay of the ontic and the ontological (I know my ec-sistential structure as a human being only through my concrete scheme of things: it is in my 'being-middle-class', my 'being-a-bachelor', and so forth, that I grasp my 'being-human' in general) might be invoked as an argument against the validity of pure ec-sistential analysis; notably to affirm that the true ontology of man can only be revealed in terms of the Christian scheme of things. Certainly it *can* be deduced from Christian faith; the New Testament is ample evidence of the fact. But it can likewise be deduced from any profane scheme of things, because all man's ontic aptitudes necessarily imply his ec-sistential structure. Whichever I may have chosen (this or that idea of life, belief or unbelief, marriage or the single state, and so forth), they all refer me to my ec-sistential structure: those schemes are only possible because I am a capacity-for-being-something, which I become aware of through them. All of them necessarily imply that I am not an object— even the scheme whereby I reduce myself to being an object!

Thus the philosophy of being (that philosophy which studies the significance of beings) does not need Christian faith in order to discover the true ontological structure of man: it only 'elaborates in a suitable *Begrifflichkeit* the understanding of existence that is innate in human existence' (KM 2, p. 192). The ontology it reveals is implicit in every scheme of things whatever, in every one of the decisions that fill my life from dawn to dusk, from the cradle to the grave. Whatever the ontic aptitude from which I start, it always sends me to my ontological aptitude, without which it could not exist.

Thus it is clear that if 'the ontological plunges its roots into the ontic' (GV 1, p. 312), it does not do so 'in the sense that a given *Weltanschauung* enables one to map out a corresponding ontology. On the contrary, the mapping out of *Weltanschauungen* in general displays the *Daseins-verständnis* in which ontology is rooted. When *Dasein* ontologically understands itself in a philosophy, it does so against the background of the primal *Seinsverständnis* in which it takes shape. Since there is no other *Dasein* than the one which takes shape in its freedom, the formal

structures of *Dasein* which ontological analysis reveals are "neutral"—
that is, valid in the case of any *Dasein*. They are also valid, then, for the
Dasein that preaching addresses, for the unbelieving *Dasein* as well as
the believing one, which can only believe by constantly worsting
unbelief' (*ibid.*).

In other words, every ec-sistentiell scheme of things necessarily
presupposes the ec-sistential structure of man. Consequently the latter
is neutral and does not derive from faith. Of course this 'atheism' has
nothing to do with unbelief, which is rejection of God. Rejection of
God occurs on the ontic, not on the ontological plane. Accepting God
or refusing him are two ec-sistentiell schemes each of which implies
that man is a being capable of accepting and refusing this or that—that
is, that he has an ec-sistential structure which is 'undifferentiated' from
the ontic point of view.

'The philosopher abstracts altogether [from the question of] whether
such a thing as faith or unbelief can occur in *Dasein*. Were he to reflect
on these phenomena, he could only say that his analysis shows man to
be capable of behaving as a believer or as an unbeliever. The "atheism"
of philosophy is not the same thing as the theological concept of
unbelief . . . Since faith and unbelief are responses to a concrete,
contingent preaching which always addresses a concrete *Dasein*, it
would be as absurd for philosophers to reflect explicitly on faith and
unbelief as to consider whether in a concrete case a declaration of love
should be accepted or rejected. True as it may be that philosophic
analysis of *Dasein* must make clear the conditions under which such
a thing as a declaration of love, and its acceptance or refusal, can occur
in *Dasein*, it simply cannot examine a concrete declaration of love.
Neither can the philosopher examine Christian preaching . . . and yet
philosophy alone enables us to understand conceptually (*begrifflich*)
what such things as "preaching", a "word", an "*Anrede*", a "hearkening" are—without ever teaching us to understand a concrete
preaching.'[6]

Evidently 'philosophy' in the sense of phenomenology in no way
threatens the independence of theology, as Bultmann explained to
G. Kuhlmann in the same article: 'If theology as a positive science
speaks of a particular thing, then the significance of the thing concerned
must be a particular significance—in other words it must also be an
"originated"[7] significance and philosophy must sit in judgment on that

6. R. Bultmann, 'Die Geschichtlichkeit des Daseins und der Glaube' in *Zeitschrift
für Theologie und Kirche* 11 (1930) 340–41.

7. The term is Kuhlmann's. He thought that it was a matter of deducing the thing
(theology) from being (philosophy). In fact what derives from being is only the

"origin" without the slightest prejudice to the independence of theology. No more is the independence of esthetics prejudiced, no more are works of art treated as the fruits of philosophy, when philosophy inquires what conception of being it is that guides esthetics, what mode of being is that of a work of art, and how this particular import "originates" in a bond with import in general. If all the positive sciences, which have an area of things for their object, are guided by a particular pre-ontological view of being—which fact is precisely what makes philosophic ontology possible—it is no less true that this view of being is not the special concern of the positive sciences but rather of philosophy. When the root concepts of a positive science are shaken and come under attack, that science may ask philosophy to clarify them. But philosophy works on the basis that the positive sciences, and the matters which occupy them, are independent.'[8]

The very nature of faith demands that the phenomenology of the human being, in particular, shall be 'atheist'. Faith is a *Verständnis*, or rather it is the eschatological *Verständnis*—in other words, sheer grace. It springs from the initiative of God, who decides to reveal himself to man and save him; whence it follows that man cannot find God by ontological analysis of himself. If phenomenological philosophy does not find God when it tries to lay bare the 'phenomenon of man', that is simply because God is the Wholly Other, because man is empty of God. No doubt he raises the question of God, he has an idea of God; but that means precisely that he is the lack and the absence of God. If phenomenological analysis of *Dasein* discovered God there, then revelation would no longer be necessary. So in that analysis, 'eliminating man's relation to God is an expression of the personal knowledge I have about myself, an admission that I cannot find God by looking at myself or into myself. My personal relation to God can only be created by God, by the doing of God when he encounters me in his word' (JCM, p. 59).

Now we see why revelation does not depend on any philosophy properly-so-called, whatever may be its content (whether the thinking of common sense, or realism, or criticism, or idealism, or positivism or some type of existentialism, or what-have-you) or whatever its form (popular or learned, literary or technical, systematic or anti-systematic); but also why it cannot dispense with an examination of formal

---

significance of the thing (its *Begrifflichkeit*, not its *Dass*). Obviously the particular significance of theology traces back to significance, import, in general. But the thing 'itself' (theology in this case) is entirely independent.

8. R. Bultmann, *ibid.*, p. 340, note 3.

structures, because God reveals himself through human concepts and addresses a being (man) whose structure is *Verstehen*. It is the business of the *lumen naturale* to work out this *Begrifflichkeit*, because the direct purpose of revelation is not to *teach* us the *idea* of God and salvation but to *give* us the *reality* of God and salvation.

Phenomenological analysis of 'human reality' has a special importance. When God's Word addresses man it demands that he receive it according to his true nature as man, which nature is not to be a thing or an animal but a capacity for being. All that we have been saying can be summed up in these few words: in order to perceive revelation and then accept or reject it, a man must really be a man. 'Without the will to be a man, to be a person who accepts his being in responsible fashion, no man can understand a single word of scripture' (KM 2, p. 193).[9]

---

9. Let us say at once and subject to the reservations which will be made in the following paragraph that Heidegger envisages the relation between theology and philosophy just as Bultmann does. An excellent account of his position will be found in H. Birault's article, 'La foi et la pensée d'après Heidegger' in *Recherches et Débats* 10 (1955) pp. 108–32. From it we extract the following passage, a synopsis of what we have just said about Bultmann:

'It is the peculiarity of Christian existence to present itself not, indeed, as reminiscence but as "rebirth". Faith overcomes unbelieving existence and at the same time reveals it for what it is—sin. In other words that existence is not simply abandoned, it is at once retained and superseded . . . And so all theological concepts necessarily have . . . a vital bearing on unbelieving existence . . . The existentiell or ontic meaning of that unbelieving existence undergoes an essential change or transposition when a man believes; thus the pre-Christian meaning of non-Christian existence will be "existentielly impotent" or "ontically overcome". Nevertheless that fact in no way hinders the existential meaning or ontological content of one's non-Christian existence from remaining active within theological concepts themselves. And so theology always and necessarily conveys a certain view of man's being in general—an ontological or philosophic view which is not at all the proper concern of theology but helps to shape the meaning of theology's root notions all the same . . .

'In order to illustrate the relation which may thus be established between philosophy and theology, Heidegger briefly considers the concept of sin. Sin is the "antagonistic force" corresponding to faith. For faith is what delivers us, absolves us, from sin. The Son is the Lamb of God who takes away the sins of the world. But sin is not "taken away" as though it were simply blotted out . . . Sin, which always remains sin before God, is so far from having been swallowed up in faith that it rather stands out there for the first time in all its starkness: just as though by delivering us from sin, Christ had unbound sin itself to be seen for what it is. Faith is victory over sin, but a victory which entails a battle and that battle is as it were the well-spring and homeland of both faith and sin; so that both intertwine in a specific unity. The instant theology tries to set down what this existentiell phenomenon means in conceptual terms, it is driven to the "existential" or "ontological" concept of guilt (*Schuld*); not as though sin could be "deduced" from guilt or even be considered a particular fruit of guilt, but because guilt as Heidegger envisages it in *Sein and Zeit* is a formal structure of man's being which alone makes *possible* the *possibility* of sin in pre-Christian existence. So the guidance that philosophy can give is indeed only formal guidance. Theology never studies the ontological concept of guilt as such, which therefore is not a real

IV

HEIDEGGER'S ONTOLOGY

Heidegger's 'philosophy' is not a philosophy. It does not deal with things (God, man, animals, nature, history, science, and so forth) but with the *Being* of things. Let us illustrate this point by means of the first few pages of *Sein und Zeit*.[10] At the outset, Heidegger says, all sciences form a pre-scientific idea of their object. Then for a certain period they work along without querying that first crude idea, which continues, more or less happily, to guide their development. Biology, for example, is built up round a central phenomenon not scientifically defined: life.

Little by little the successes that are achieved and the difficulties that are encountered draw attention to the idea on which everything rests, and we have a 'foundational crisis'. Heidegger thinks that the calibre of a science can be gauged by its ability to weather a foundational crisis. Mathematics, physics, biology and theology, he holds, have reached the crucial stage in their growth. Their foundations must therefore be laid bare. This task is not the business of science. It is a matter of defining, strictly this time, a particular structure of being which in turn refers the investigator to being in general. Thus to study the Being of a thing is to study the thing's foundation. Here we come to the celebrated 'ontological difference', the difference between a thing and the Being of the thing, which forms the heart of Heidegger's thought.

Someone may object that philosophy has long concerned itself with the Being of things. Does not the εἶδος loom large in Plato, the οὐσία in Aristotle, the *essentia* in the Schoolmen? Is not the εἶδος the Being of the ὄν, the οὐσία of the τὸ τί, the *essentia* of the *ens*? Are the ancients and the medieval thinkers not familiar with the ontological difference? Did they not pass beyond the limits of the ontic and reach the ontological? Did they not explicitly deal not only with the particular thing but also with the area of being to which it belongs? How can we accuse them, as Heidegger does, of having *forgotten* Being?

In his book *Platons Lehre von der Wahrheit* (1947) Heidegger explains why he considers Platonist metaphysics a metaphysics of subjectivity.

"foundation" of theology but nevertheless "formally determines it to the extent of indicating the ontological character of the area of being [*Seinsregion*] within which the concept of sin, as an existentiell concept, must inevitably confine itself".'

10. English translation, *Being and Time*, by J. Macquarrie and E. Robinson, London, SCM Press, 1962.

The Platonist *eidos* is something which relates to man. Of course, the idea of essence supposedly designates absolute essence—in other words, that which is essential to Being. But it does nothing of the kind: in the philosophy of essences, Being is buried behind the essences themselves. The essential is what seems such to the eyes of the mind. The concept of essence is bound up as tightly as can be with the concept of reason, and therefore with a human faculty. How essence relates to Being in its openness becomes a secondary question; the primary question is how it relates to one of *man's* major capabilities. Reason is the locus where essence becomes visible and essence is defined in its essentiality as what is rational. Thus a thing is envisaged in terms of the mind, since it is in terms of essence that the mind perceives a thing and conceives of it.

The mind becomes the measure of a thing's truth. There is no longer any attempt to know a thing, and therefore man, through their source and ground in Being and the truth of Being; instead a thing must undergo the judgment of reason, give an account of itself to the mind. Man assumes the central position in philosophy, and Being is forgotten.[11] This oblivion emerges in another way as well. Every intuitionist theory of essences ignores the Being which soaks and determines every thing, making it real; because an essence only unites things of the same species or genus. The essence is not the *logos* in them as a fundamental force gathering them into one, but as the locus of the species. While unifying in one way, the essence excludes in another. No doubt it is more universal than the thing, but as a 'species' it is always 'special' and therefore refers us to the κοινωνία τῶν εἰδῶν. It is only an intermediary between the thing and Being; to behold it is not to experience Being itself, and beholding the one can never do duty for experiencing the other.

Heidegger has also shown that in medieval philosophy, particularly the philosophy of Thomas Aquinas, the *lumen naturale* (which is the light of Being itself and without which there can be no talk either of things or of essences) is not defined in its own nature but merely described in its operations. Thus the *lumen*, and therefore Being, is still envisaged in relation to man. On the other hand man is never candidly considered in terms of what the *lumen* and Being are in themselves, though it is through his participation in them that man 'takes possession of' himself. In short, we may say that the ancient and medieval philosophers established a difference between essence and thing which is a beginning, or rather the residuum, of the ontological

11. In ch. 2 we brought out the anthropocentrism of Greek philosophy in a different way (by a comparison with the Bible).

difference—that is to their credit—but altogether neglected Being it-self—and that is their discredit.

This neglect is much aggravated in idealism, where subjectivity (empirical or transcendental) rules supreme. If Plato made philosophy a metaphysics of subjectivity, Kant makes it a metaphysics of *finite* subjectivity. Plato recognized that we turn a sort of gaze upon essence as the absolute measure of things. St Thomas said that knowledge is possible thanks only to the intuition of Being—which he calls 'the first object known and the object best known'. Kant denies man any *intellectus archetypus* and any intuition of essences.

If the Platonic essence, to Heidegger's way of thinking, is something relative to man, to Kant's way of thinking it is something in itself. With Kant essence is no longer validated by its role as an absolute standard. Nor does the relation of essence to Being give essence its significance, as in St Thomas. Essences are justified solely by man's need for them. They are the tools with which he knows things and does things. It is from this point of view that we must approach tran-scendental deduction. Since we cannot see essences as God does, Kant attempts a coherent deduction of categories on the basis of their necessity to thought.

Though the transcendental method certainly attempts to reach beyond the thing as a datum of objectivity, it does not reach towards Being but towards the conditions which enable the thing to become an ob-ject. According to idealism, essence is an *interna possibilitas* of the object as such with regard to the subject. Kant calls these conditions of possibility 'categories' and 'ideas'. For the words 'being' and 'essence' he substitutes the words 'category', 'idea' and 'objectivity' (in the etymological sense: *Gegenständlichkeit*). Since Being and essence have ceased to be absolutes, they are replaced by words which apply to the correlation between subject and object.

Post-Kantian idealism gives pride of place to the absolute and to 'transcendental' act. But what is this absolute, and what constitutes this act? The absolute is the '*Deus in nobis*' and the specific act of man con-sists in reaching his own infinity and godhead: Being becomes our own nature. God dwells, and the infinite opens out, in human subjec-tivity. Being becomes identified with our inmost frame of mind. It is not the a priori synthesis of subject and object, the sort of elbow-room prerequisite for the existence of subjectivity and objectivity alike. On the contrary, the subject is the locus of possibility for the absolute, for what lies beyond essences and Being. The repulsion between subject and object is abolished in favour of one of its poles—subjectivity. Being becomes the nature and essence of subjectivity; it loses its tran-scendence with respect to essence, loses its own dimension; it ceases to be 'itself'. The absolute subject usurps the throne of Being, now become the boundlessness of the mind.

Thus from Plato down to Hegel philosophy made shipwreck of Being. All that philosophy is rank anthropocentrism. Again and again it loses sight of the ontological difference. The same must be said of the neo-Kantians, of Nietzsche (whom Heidegger considers the last and most extravagant of the Platonists), and of contemporary existentialism —the existentialism of Jaspers and Sartre, with whom Heidegger repudiates any connection, as we shall see presently. As to Husserl, since we cannot enlarge on the subject let us merely recall Heidegger's judgment that his thought is a phenomenological idealism. For Husserl, Being is absolute life. Fundamentally, what set Kierkegaard against Hegel now sets Heidegger against Husserl, though on a very different methodological plane and under completely different circumstances. The recurrence is possible because on the one hand Being is represented from the outset and a priori as the absolute subject (Hegel) or as absolute life, that is, as constitutive consciousness (Husserl), whereas on the other hand it is a demand and a word. In Kierkegaard it is the summons of the transcendent God which makes a person of the man summoned. In Heidegger it is a Being which by disclosing itself makes a *Da-sein* of a man. An explicitation of this latter point will introduce us to the positive aspect of Heideggerian thought.

What exactly is the ontological difference which, as we have seen, the long tradition of Greek and Western thought more or less ignores? What is Being? It is not a thing (an inanimate object, a person, God), it is that in which a thing is rooted and grounded. For the sake of clarity, let us first give some thought to the connection between essence and an existent being. Essence is neither a mere concept nor an existent being. It does not exist in the ontic way. It grounds a being and in the process transforms itself into what it grounds. It 'is'[12] the *principiare* of the *principiatum*: it 'is' its own advanced post, its own thrust into the being whose essence it constitutes. Thus it has no static existence, it is perpetually grounding and founding; it does not stand alongside a being, it differs from it by a difference that wipes out difference. This difference is there and at the same time is not there (and the pro-cess goes on as long as the thing is this essence). Being, likewise, does not subsist apart from essence but is always embodied in an essence, as an essence is always embodied in a being. Being is what knits together and sustains all reality; it is 'real' but not in the way a being is real. It alone determines what can be an essence, what can be essential in a being. It

12. We put the word into inverted commas because it ordinarily designates an objectified thing.

is the ground of all essentiality, just as essence is the inner capacity of a being, of ontic reality. It is act, that transcendental act that can only be found in an essence, which in turn can only be found in a being.

The ontological difference, therefore, does not mean that on the one hand there is a *being*, and on the other hand *Being*. Being 'is' itself the difference from a being, it does not 'have' the difference. The basis of something does not stand apart from what is based, and therefore can have no relation to it: the basis is identical with what is based, and yet remains different.

Representational thought (which is to say, modern thought par excellence) finds it difficult to grasp this point; because it cannot get beyond objective reality, and ontological reality does not exist in the objective mode. In representational thought, Being no sooner appears on the scene than it is foundering. That kind of thought invariably levels down the ontological difference in favour of objects. In order to find Being one must cut across the normal bent of the mind, which tends to envisage everything in relation to itself, as we found in our brief scrutiny of Greek and Western thought. Idealism in particular strips a thing of its ontological ground, reducing it to the level of an object. This mastery of man over things leads on to pragmatism. Truth, no longer conceived of as the openness of Being and the openness of things to the light of Being, yields to a confident technological manipulation of things. Technology is born of the tendency to objectify everything, which in turn is born of the neglect of Being. It is the inevitable lot of any age that neglects Being.[13]

The otherness of Being is such that it can only be conveyed in terms of nothingness. Heidegger's theory of nothingness is a mere device for driving home the ontological difference. Our outlook is shaped by and for beings as they relate to man. By the natural bent of our mind, we objectify Being and beings, and our language has been coined so as to express the ontic, objective world. The verb 'to be' is the backbone of everyday parlance. So if we are to use this language, we must say that Being is nothingness, nothingness as contrasted with objectified beings —beings as they are defined by and for man. Though beings are grounded in Being and sustained by it, they do not reveal what grounds and sustains them. Being is hidden away; and even when it discloses itself to us it seems to be nothingness, because it is neither a being nor the attribute of a being. One cannot imagine or manufacture Being, Heidegger tells us, as one imagines or manufactures a being that is an object. Quite as different from any thing is that which is no-thing,

13. This does not mean that there is any going back to the pre-technological age. See M. Heidegger, 'Die Frage nach der Technik' in *Vorträge und Aufsätze* (1954).

nothingness. But this nothingness 'is' infinitely more than any thing, being the foundation of every thing.

To shed light on the matter, Heidegger chooses the old German verb *wesen* [= Old English *wesan*, to remain, be; it survives in the form 'was', used as the past tense of 'be'], which conveys manifestation, advent, the presence of something, and stresses the fact that Being does not exist in the same way as a being does. Thus nothingness 'exists' (*west*): it is the foundation of any being, the *principiare* of the *principiatum*. The advent of a being compels us to detach ourselves from objectified, everyday things as 'natural' man understands them. And by so doing it plunges us into anguish [*Angst*]. This anguish, which is dispossession of ourselves (*ent-setzen* and *ent-setzt werden*), is the first advent of Being, an intimation of it as wholly different from any objectified thing, is a hearkening to its summons. So much for Heidegger's alleged 'nihilism'. It is a nihilism which is nothing else but the affirmation of Being—in other words, the beginning of true thought and true manhood.

If man must be ever breaking with the world of the 'they' and of *Alltäglichkeit*, it is so as to find Being. In nothingness, Being discloses itself; and in Being, a being discloses itself for what it is—that which is grounded in Being, not in man the subject. Thus my breaking with things also establishes a new relation between them and myself. All I reject is adulterated things, things cut off from Being and enslaved to man which yet by a fatal twist enslave him. A man who would make a thing his own possession, mastering it through knowledge and technology, soon finds himself its slave; and there, Heidegger thinks, we have the tragedy of the modern world. Therefore to flee objectified things is to meet true Being half-way; to make possible a new relation, which is genuine humanism. Man's business is to let the advent of Being happen, to set his encounters with things not in that horizon which is 'human, all-too-human' and transforms them into objects, but in the horizon of Being itself, which is there in things and is the source of things. Thus the underlying purpose of Heidegger's ontology is to drive home the otherness of things.[14] In that respect it is anti-humanist

14. This does not mean that Being is a *Dass*: it is the foundation of the *Dass*. Its otherness is a grounding, not a grounded, otherness. Hence it stands on the plane of the *Was*, but not at all as in the philosophies of the 'Platonic age'. The realisms, the idealisms, and no less the existentialisms, define essence in terms of man and for him instead of defining man in terms of essence and for it. In those systems essence is no longer the genuineness of a thing and Being the *Sein* of the *Seiendes*, a manifestation, a *Wesen* in the old sense which we have given the word. By objectifying things, the classical philosophers ignore the Being of things. In Heideggerian philosophy the quiddity of a tree, for example, is just what it is in pre-Heideggerian philosophies, but Heidegger tries to lay the foundations of essence by searching out its genuineness in Being. Both essence and Being, therefore, are a *Was*, always provided that word is associated with the word *Wesen*.

to the core, but in the interests of rescuing true humanism. Heidegger's thought is marked by reverence and humility towards Being, by receptivity, heedfulness and obedience to Being.

What we have been saying lays bare the error of those readers and commentators who in the past identified Being with God. 'Being is not God'.[15] If God exists he is part of the ontic sphere, he is the supreme 'thing', the creator of all other things, whereas Being exists only in what it makes possible and in the act that makes those things possible. The ontological difference is not the theological difference. Being does not exist in itself, it exists as the possibility that makes everything possible. But if it is not God, it is, so to speak, God's potential country and dwelling-place. In other words, God must be thought of according to the ontological difference, otherwise he is no longer man's Lord but his possession.

Heidegger accuses Christian theologians of making too many concessions to metaphysics. He asks them whether they have really taken to heart the saying of Paul's that God has made the wisdom of the world foolishness. We have seen the havoc wrought in theology by the Greek metaphysics of the ancient Church and by the Catholic and Protestant orthodoxies, by the idealist metaphysics of Catholic modernism and Protestant liberalism. Theology has been an onto-theology: in other words, a humanism. God has been thought of in terms of the categories of the hoary philosophic tradition which stretches from Greek antiquity down to our own day—thought of, that is, in relation to man. In order to acknowledge and safeguard the transcendence of the Creator, we must think of him according to the ontological difference, which 'allows' things to be 'themselves'. To think of God according to the ontological difference is to admit that man is not the source and ground of God.

It now becomes evident in what sense Heidegger is an 'atheist'. Since Being is not a thing and God is the supreme 'thing', the philosophy of Being does not lead one to God—but not as though it were indifferent to the divine, to God: we have just seen that it is not. It tears man from himself; from his 'wisdom', which is the 'foolishness' of trying to rule all things; it teaches him to become a listening, a receptivity, an openness to all things and thereby to the *possible* revelation of the Lord of all things. 'Only in terms of the genuineness of Being is the essence of the sacred thinkable. Only in terms of the essence of the sacred is the essence of the godhead thinkable. Only in terms of the essence of the godhead can we think and utter what the word "God" should mean'.[16]

15. M. Heidegger, *Ueber den Humanismus*, p. 24.
16. *Ibid.*, p. 50.

But heedfulness of Being can never of itself be one day trans-formed into the presence of God—that is, what the *word* 'God' means does not lead to *God*. God 'himself' can only be revealed by God, and only faith can find him.

What has just been said about Being, following the later Heidegger, enables us to understand what the earlier Heidegger said about man, and keeps us clear of the pitfall of treating his *Sein und Zeit* as an anthropology—a pitfall so many have stumbled into despite the author's forceful warning at the commencement of his splendid book. Thus we spare ourselves the delusion that there are two Heideggers, one the man of *Sein und Zeit* and the other the man of the more recent works.[17]

To assert that the philosophic tradition which stretches from Greek antiquity down to our own day has more or less ignored Being, is to say that it has misinterpreted the real nature of man to the same extent. The philosophy of the 'Platonic age' (the age, that is, which reaches from Plato to Nietzsche) envisaged things and Being in relation to man. By thus referring Being to himself, man interpreted himself as an in-sistence. He remained in himself; he thought of himself as the *logos*—as that which gathers everything into one, as τόπος τῶν εἰδῶν.

This representational philosophy, and the idea of man as an in-sistence, culminate in Descartes. Descartes uses the same word (*sub-stantia*) to designate God, man and the world. True, he explains that God exists *a se*, whereas man and the world only exist *in se*; and he is forever saying that an infinite distance separates the *res cogitans* from the *res corporea*. But in that case it is idle to pretend that substantiality is an adequate description for things so disparate. The Schoolmen were well aware of the fact and therefore worked out a theory of the analogy of being. Not one of the substances Descartes talks about has a shred of ontological standing—least of all, alas, the *sum* of the *cogito*. He does not define 'the mode of Being of the *res cogitans* or rather the onto-logical meaning of the *sum*'.[18] In this respect he lags far behind the Schoolmen.[19]

17. Barth himself is entangled in this error, as we shall see in the chapter devoted to him. Small wonder then that he accuses Bultmann of sticking to the anthro-pology of *Sein und Zeit* and ignoring recent developments in the philosophy of Being. In fact there is no justification at all for the charge (also brought by H. Ott, *Geschichte und Heilsgeschichte in der Theologie R. Bultmanns* [1957], p. 173), since *Sein und Zeit* was never an anthropology but rather an ontology. Bultmann thoroughly understands Heideggerian thought. In a letter of 30 November 1954 Heidegger approves unreservedly of using his analysis of existence for interpreting the New Testament and states that Bultmann has 'made no mistake whatever' about his thought (Heidegger quoted by Ittel, 'Der Einfluss der Philosophie M. Heideggers auf die Theologie R. Bultmanns' in *Kerygma und Dogma* 2 [1956] p. 92).

18. *Sein und Zeit*, p. 24.   19. *Ibid.*, p.93.

Heidegger takes up these criticisms anew in one of the studies, 'Die Zeit des Weltbildes', in his *Holzwege*. He shows how Descartes's man is no longer the being who opens himself to a Presence that summons him, no longer a '*Sich-entbergen für* . . .' but an '*Ergreifen und Begreifen von* . . .'[20] Representational thought is an attack. This aggressive attitude indicates that 'man's essence is turned into the essence of a subject'.[21] We must confront this man of in-sistence with the man of ec-sistence, who is ex-posure to Being. In his real essence, man can only be openness to and for Being; he does not exist in himself but in Being itself. He is not a subject which bears within it the infinite and absolute *in potentia* and thereby, so to speak, contains Being, or at any rate hems Being in, by itself becoming the infinite and absolute. No, man is 'ec-static', 'ec-centric'.[22] He is not the *logos* that gathers all things into one, but the *logos* that permeates the unified whole and joins with it. He is not the lord and master, Heidegger says, but the 'watchful servant', the 'shepherd' of Being, which he holds in trust although it is infinitely above him. By thus surrendering itself to man Being gives him a share in its transcendence.

Man is merely the presence and locus (the *Da*) of Being (*Sein*): he is *Da-sein*. Therefore he has no nature and no shape of his own. He does not have his being within himself. That which has its being within itself is known, in the Western tradition, as a substance. Man's real essence is his utter incomprehensibility in terms of substance. To quote the celebrated dictum of *Sein und Zeit*, 'the "essence" of man is his existence'.[23] Heidegger puts the word essence (*Wesen*) into inverted commas because it is to be understood in relation to the old German verb we have mentioned: we are dealing with essence in terms of Being, no longer in terms of man-the-subject as realist, idealist or existentialist philosophies all do—with an essence grounded in Being, not with the classical *essentia*. Man is himself only when he is the presence, the disclosure of Being (of beings insofar as they are grounded in Being) in the act of ec-sisting. He does subsist, of course, but not with the autonomous subsistence of an object; he subsists through and in his ex-posure to Being. He *receives* his being from Being.

The summons which Being directs to him is always new, because Being itself is historical. Ontic history plunges its roots into an onto-logical history. Being is itself historicity; it is the historicity of history. If it is historical, that is not because fluid, finite reality captures it.

20. *Holzwege*, p. 83.
21. *Ibid.*, p. 81.
22. *Vom Wesen des Grundes*, p. 94, note 1, in the French translation by H. Corbin.
23. *Sein und Zeit*, p. 42.

Time does not lay hold on a being outside time; rather Being itself temporalizes itself (*zeitigt sich*), 'is' (*west*) its own coming. Thus we must not picture some sort of ready-made being that reveals itself, now in this light, now in that, according to the age concerned. Let us remember that Being never exists apart from things. At any given moment it is only its disclosure in things, and at the same time it is more than that disclosure. The Being which temporalizes truth is that truth and more than that truth. Its truth at one moment hides what it will be as the truth of another moment. It is its own step towards disclosure; and the disclosure of it, once made in a thing, will once more hide Being.

Therefore it is Being that produces the brilliant eras and the turning-points of history. It is on Being that the καιρός depends. One can never manipulate it as one does a timeless essence or an infinite *in actu*. In its καιρός it is always unforeseeable, always new, always startling. It is forever putting us off course. Our business is to keep watch for Being, to be at its beck and call. Man's vocation is this heedfulness, this openness to what transcends him and every thing. Freedom, for Heidegger, is this ec-sisting towards Being, a deciding in favour of obedience. Man finds his happiness and his perfection in this surrender to Being. Does not the very word *Da-sein* signify a presence, a deed well done, a safe arrival, a fullness?

Such is the ontological structure of man, the very one we described in our first chapter (though without laying bare its foundations) as an aptitude for Being, decision, freedom, 'historicity', temporality. Obviously, Heidegger never leaves the plane of the meaning of Being. He merely shows that man is not an object. Like the search for Being, the search for the ontological structure of man is 'a-theist', because it goes on in the sphere of *Begrifflichkeit*. Belief and unbelief stand on the ontic plane, according as man decides for or against God. That is what Heidegger has had it at heart to show: in virtue of it, man is not the 'goose' of Luther's dictum. And to know it faith is not necessary *per se*, as we have seen.

People often object that Heidegger does not respect the 'neutrality' of the phenomenological analysis of man, because he bluntly condemns one kind of life and enjoins another, thereby encroaching (they say) upon the ontic, ec-sistentiell plane.[24] It is perfectly true that Heidegger describes and censures existence in the 'they' and *Alltäglichkeit*, that he points the way to authenticity through decision or backbone (*Entschlossenheit*). But in so doing he is only saying to man: You must exist in

24. This objection is raised by certain commentators on Heidegger (K. Lehmann, K. Löwith, G. Gurvitch, de Waelhens, and others) and by many of the theologians who look askance at Bultmann.

conformity with your nature, which nature is precisely not being a nature; if you exist like an object, you are in a state of fallenness and guilt; therefore you must exist as a man by chalking out your capacities for ec-sistence.

Heidegger does not lay down any concrete, ec-sistentiell scheme of things. Shall Jack be a bricklayer or a chemist, get married or not, become a Catholic or a Protestant or an atheist, do this or that in given circumstances—all these are decisions that he alone can and must make. Heidegger tells him: Whatever you do, do it like a man. But he does not tell him *what* to do.

'What does *Dasein* settle on doing by an act of decision? What must it settle on doing? The answer can only be given by the act of decision. To suppose that decision is merely accepting the alternatives which are put and commended to one would be to misconceive the phenomenon altogether. The act of decision is first and foremost an incipient scheme, the settling on a concrete alternative at the moment. A necessary element of decision is that indeterminateness which stamps all *Dasein's* concrete aptitudes for being. Only in the act of deciding is decision sure of itself. Nevertheless the existentiell indeterminateness of decision—which indeterminateness is only determined by and in the act of decision—has its existential determination'.[25] Obviously the notion of authenticity and inauthenticity stands not on the ontic plane but on the ontological plane, whence it follows that ec-sistential analysis observes a strict neutrality.

As we have remarked, it is not the direct purpose of the Bible to make known man's ontological structure. In scripture the supreme being, God the Creator, summons another being, man, so as to reveal himself to him. Everything occurs on the ontic plane. But since God is speaking to man, not to plants or animals, revelation necessarily assumes that a man is a man—that it is addressing man as seen in his true ontology, which is ec-sistential,[26] and by so doing it indirectly reveals that ontology (see §π, above). We have seen how the Bible automatically treats man as 'historicity'. It is hardly surprising that Heidegger has minutely examined the revealed message and the tradition of Christianity—especially in those of its representatives who have (indirectly) shed most light on the ec-sistential structure of the human being—from this ontological point of view (but not from the ontic point of view), in order to lay bare the 'phenomenon of man'. He has a

25. *Sein und Zeit*, p. 298.

26. As anyone can see with half an eye, it does not address man in his ontic truth. On that plane, quite the contrary, it summons a being who has hopelessly damned himself by rebelling against God.

profounder knowledge of the New Testament than do many exegetes and theologians. He has meditated on Augustine, Luther and Kierkegaard. One of his students, Karl Löwith, [27] relates that 'Heidegger was especially drawn to the younger Luther, and better read in his complete works than many a professional theologian'.[28]

For his part Bultmann, whose close friendship with Heidegger is well known, wrote that the latter 'has always admitted to being influenced by the New Testament, notably Paul, by Augustine, and most of all by Luther'.[29] Bultmann goes on to observe: 'The existential analysis of *Dasein* in Heidegger seems to be a mere profane philosophical exposition of the New Testament concept of *Dasein*. Historically existing in anxiety about himself against a background of anguish, at the moment of decision man always finds himself hovering between the past and the future. Shall he damn himself in the world of data, of the "they", or shall he achieve his authenticity by giving up all self-reliance—unconditionally—to the future?' (KM I, p. 33). Such is Heideggerian *Dasein*. But, Bultmann asks, 'Is this not just what the New Testament means by man?' (*ibid.*)[30]

Let us cite one more highly significant example of Heidegger's bond with the New Testament and Christian tradition. The prominent part which the 'world' plays in his thought is well known. To say that *Dasein* ec-sists is to define it as *In-der-Welt-sein*. To lay bare the phenomenon of man is automatically to lay bare the phenomenon of the world. In his *Vom Wesen des Grundes* Heidegger gives us crucial particulars about his idea of the world. Now he does so by turning not only to the pre-Socratics [31] and Kant but also to the New Testament (Paul and John), Augustine and Thomas Aquinas. He emphasizes the fact that Paul's word κόσμος designates one of *Dasein's* modes of being.

---

27. Löwith, it is true, misunderstands the thought of his former teacher in important particulars, for example in his article 'Phänomenologische Ontologie und protestantische Theologie' in *Zeitschrift für Theologie und Kirche* 11 (1930) where he deals with *Eigentlichkeit* on the ontic plane.

28. K. Löwith, 'Les implications politiques de la philosophie de l'existence chez Heidegger' in *Les temps modernes* 2 (1946) p. 348.

29. Letter of Bultmann, 13 May 1955, quoted by Ittel, 'Der Einfluss der Philosophie M. Heideggers auf die Theologie R. Bultmanns' in *Kerygma und Dogma* 2 (1956) p. 92.—Ittel adopts the Barthian solution to the problem of the relation between philosophy and theology, not perceiving the real bond which links Bultmann's thought with Heidegger's.

30. We are dealing here, of course, with the ontological structure of man, not with his ontic determination, as Bultmann is often at pains to point out, for instance in JCM, p. 55.

31. We are not trying to belittle the importance of the Greeks, of the pre-Socratics in particular, for Heidegger; but neither must it be magnified at the expense of the Christian sources, as commonly happens in France.

The Pauline expression 'this world', he remarks, 'does not mean exclusively or even primarily a "cosmic" state of affairs, but the state and circumstances of the human being, the attitude he takes up *towards* the cosmos, the estimation he forms of its goods. Κόσμος is the being of man as modified by the alienation of his mind and heart from God . . . Κόσμος οὗτος means the being of *Dasein* in a set "historical" ec-sistence, as contrasted with another that is already dawning.'[32]

Heidegger has also observed the major role which the concept of the cosmos plays in John, how with him 'the world means the form of being peculiar to a *Dasein* which is utterly alienated from God; it is man's mode of being, pure and simple'.[33] If *mundus* in Augustine means the totality of created things, 'nevertheless it often stands for "*habitatores mundi*". And alternatively the term bears the specifically existentiell meaning of "*dilectores mundi, impii, carnales*". *Mundus non dicuntur justi, quia, licet carne in eo habitent, corde cum deo sunt*. In creating this notion of the world . . . Augustine was inspired by Paul no less than by the Gospel of John'.[34] 'Thus the "world" means things as a whole, and also means the hallmark stamped upon *Dasein* as it confronts things and holds its ground in their presence'.[35] Thomas Aquinas too is familiar with this latter sense of the word: *Mundi nomine amatores mundi significantur*.[36]

We can now understand why Bultmann finds the 'philosophy' of Heidegger best adapted to his own use. Since revelation is addressed to man, not to stones, it presupposes that he is really a man in the onto-logical sense, deep as he may be sunk in ontic degradation—and we know how deep he is. If a hearer of God's Word approaches it with a wrong ontology of *Dasein*, then he is doomed to misunderstand it. Twenty centuries' experience of Christianity shows that in fact revel-ation has been inaccurately understood whenever it was interpreted through a false *Begrifflichkeit*—that is, through an ontology which more or less pictures God and man as a *Vorhandenheit*. At all costs, then, the Bible must be read with a sound *Begrifflichkeit*. Indirectly, of course (its direct object standing on the ontic plane), revelation presents us with the true ontology of man. But as we know, that enlightenment was beclouded by mythological elements which are still there in scripture,

32. *Vom Wesen des Grundes*, p. 71 in the French translation by H. Corbin.
33. *Ibid.*, p. 71.
34. *Ibid.*, p. 72.
35. *Ibid.*, p. 73.
36. Quoted by Heidegger, *ibid.*, p. 73.

and has often been warped or ignored by Christian tradition under the influence of one prevailing philosophy or another.

As a New Testament exegete and theologian Bultmann has denounced these changes, and to let revelation itself (which stands on the ontic plane) shine forth in all its purity, he has striven to clarify the 'historical' ontology which it uses and therefore indirectly reveals. Thus his own ontological path (not his ontic one, of course) intersects Heidegger's. He has been delighted to find in the latter, at a very advanced scientific stage, what he himself had discovered and was discovering more and more, in the New Testament and Protestant tradition, thanks to his researches as an exegete and theologian. Bultmann has been able to adopt Heidegger's analysis because on the ontological plane Heidegger is more faithful to the New Testament than many a professional exegete and theologian. 'That', he says, 'is what must be taken into account if people would understand Heidegger's influence on my theology'.[37] And again, he says, that is why 'I think people should be somewhat alarmed at philosophy's discovering for itself what the New Testament says' (KM I, p. 33). In other words, theologians should be ashamed to go on interpreting the New Testament through the false ontology of liberalism and orthodoxy, letting the philosophers outrun them.

While using Heidegger, Bultmann does not depend on him in the slightest, since on the one hand Heidegger has only rediscovered New Testament ontology, and on the other hand ontological analysis does not take into consideration man's concrete footing with God: 'The New Testament does not differ from it [ontological analysis] at all by a different sense of what ec-sistence in general means, but only by ec-sistentiell decision.'[38]

Since Heidegger never set about constructing a philosophy, a *Weltanschauung*—that is a task belonging to the ontic plane—but simply lays bare the meaning of the human phenomenon, it is quite possible that others, today or tomorrow, may perfect his work. The formal analysis of existence is never complete, any more than any science is ever complete. In this field, as in every other, an exchange of views can be fruitful (KM 2, p. 194).

Friedrich Gogarten wrote a book to defend Bultmann against the attacks of the Lutheran orthodox. Having stated that Heidegger can teach us how theology is imprisoned in a false traditional ontology, he explains: 'Obviously enough, no one is compelled to learn that lesson from Heidegger himself. If a man thinks he can learn it better elsewhere,

37. Letter of Bultmann, 13 May 1955, quoted by Ittel, *ibid.,* p. 92.
38. *Ibid.,* p. 107.

then well and good. But one way or another the lesson must be learnt'.[39]
In expressing his gratitude to Gogarten, Bultmann singles out this
passage for unqualified approval (KM 3, p. 50). It is evident that
Bultmann does not make theology dependent in any way on Heideggerian philosophy. By the very fact that it is addressed to a being who
is man, revelation presupposes not a philosophy but the genuine
meaning of *Dasein*, and Heidegger merely happens to be the one who
has laid bare that ontological structure better than others.'In fact I base
no theology on Heidegger's philosophy';[40] in confirmation Heidegger
himself declares: 'Bultmann builds no theology upon my philosophy'.[41]

Bultmann says that there is a 'criminal streak' (*das Frevelhafte*) in philosophy at large (KM 1, p. 37) because it assumes that man can save
himself by his own efforts. This judgment is intelligible enough considering all that we have said of the different philosophies and the havoc
they have wrought in faith by turning it into a work. But one is taken
aback to find Bultmann pronouncing the same judgment, almost
unmitigated, upon Heidegger as well, whose thought is not a philosophy but a probing into formal structures and therefore in no sense
claims that man can save himself by his own efforts (since that affirmation—or its contrary—stands on the ontic plane).

Why this rigour, then? Because 'it is clear that if man subsumes
abandonment into the decision of death, he is very much controlling
himself' (KM 1, p. 37). We know that Heidegger defines *Dasein* as
'being-unto-death' or 'being-unto-the-end'. What does that mean?
In conformity with his general scheme, he does not propose to make an
ontic study of death, a 'metaphysics of death'.[42] He has no mind to
work out 'a biology, a psychology, a theodicy, or a theology' but
simply an ontological analysis of death.[43] From this point of view,
being-unto-death is only another name for *Dasein*. Man is *Da-sein*: in
other words, a particular, absolutely unique locus (*Da*) where a particular, absolutely unique disclosure of Being (*Sein*) takes place. Death
alone permits him to *be*.

Of all man's alternatives death is the one most proper to him, the
one in which his being-in-the-world is at stake. Death is the possibility
of no longer being the presence of Being; or again, 'death is the
possibility of the utter impossibility of existence'.[44] Through death man

39. *Entmythologisierung und Kirche* 2 (1954) p. 56, note 2.
40. Letter of Bultmann, 11 November 1954, quoted by Ittel, *ibid.*, p. 91.
41. Letter of Heidegger, 6 November 1954, quoted by Ittel, *ibid.*, p. 91.
42. Heidegger, *Sein und Zeit*, p. 248.
43. *Ibid.*
44. *Ibid.*, p. 250.

is 'isolated', 'unified', 'completed', 'fixed in selfhood'. This possibility
roots him forever in his absolutely proper being, which truly makes
him the *Da* of Being and thereby makes him utterly 'himself'. For this
reason death is relationless (*unbezüglich*). Being the end of man as a
scheme, death eliminates all bearing on any other possibility. Thus it is
also a possibility which cannot be outdone (*unüberholbar*): 'As a capacity
for being, *Dasein* cannot outstrip the possibility of death'.[45] In short,
'death discloses itself as the absolutely peculiar, relationless, unsur-
passable possibility';[46] which means that it gives *Dasein* selfhood.

   This existential analysis demands an existential attitude, which in
turn is the foundation for an existentiell attitude. If death is so much
part of *Dasein* as to constitute it in its very selfhood, then man must
plan all the possibilities of *Dasein* as a '*Dasein* that is ever dying'. It is in
the light of the self-fixing possibility par excellence, and hand in hand
with it, that man must live every moment of his existence; otherwise
all schemes before his death will be inauthentic—no longer his, but the
impersonal schemes of the 'they'.

   What 'personalizes' my life is a death ever-present as the most
characteristic of my possibilities. It alone makes my life *my* life, it alone
makes my life authentic. Therefore it is what enables me to be not a
thing, a substance, but historicity and freedom. Unless death constantly
'personalizes' my life, I sink to the status of an object. That is why the
man in the street flees death by turning it into an objective phenomenon,
an accident: 'We talk of death as though it were something that
happens to others. The ordinary explanation of *Dasein* is that "people
die", because by so saying each individual can delude himself that it is
not *he* [who dies]: the "*they*" is nobody. "Dying" sinks to the level of an
event which forms part of existence indeed, but is not peculiarly
anybody's own.'[47]

   By refusing to live in the horizon of death, the average man dooms
himself to live as a *thing*. He does not perceive that death alone can
'isolate' him, thereby making all his other possibilities authentic. A
human being is only himself when he plans possibilities; but in their
turn those possibilities are only themselves when they hinge on the
most characteristic of *Dasein's* aptitudes for being, not on the 'they in
person'. So we must be emancipated by death, tearing ourselves away
from the inauthenticity of the 'they'.

   Once free for its end, *Dasein* is automatically free with respect to all
possibilities which precede the final possibility. Living at all times in

45. *Ibid.*
46. *Ibid.*
47. *Ibid.*, p. 253.

the horizon of death, man is no longer the slave of his other earthly schemes. By constantly anticipating death, '*Dasein* . . . escapes falling behind itself and the aptitude for Being which it has already grasped'.[48] Or again, Heidegger says quoting Nietzsche, it escapes 'growing too old for its victories';[49] it 'is snatched from damnation by the fortuitous jangling of possibilities' and 'makes short shrift of any stiffening by dashing it against the ec-sistence achieved each time'.[50] The real attitude to death, then, is that of freedom for death, of stout-hearted readiness.

Thus *Dasein* is perfected by its unflinching attitude towards death—that is, by its own efforts. And matters are altered precious little by Heidegger's saying that the ec-sistential analysis of death 'implies no ontic decision as to whether some other existence, higher or lower, is still possible "after death"; whether *Dasein* "goes on"; or even whether "outliving" itself, it is "immortal".'[51] For when all is said and done, my selfhood is all my own work. So even in Heidegger we find the attitude of natural man, that of philosophy in general, which assumes that 'the knowledge man has of his authenticity suffices to make him master of it' (KM I, p. 37). Bultmann says it is 'utterly controlling' oneself to subsume death into stout-hearted readiness.

In his own way, Heidegger too applies the principle 'You *should*, therefore you *can*'. In other words, he rejects eschatology; he does not recognize man's utter helplessness with respect to his own selfhood, which can only be God's sheer gift. The eschatological freedom of *Dasein*, 'where it is achieved ontically, not in faith and love, faith counts it anything but freedom. The decision to live authentically—where it is reached ontically because factitious *Dasein*, dashed to pieces against death, allows itself to be thrown back upon its *Da* and decides in the situation (of itself, therefore)—is a decision of despair. It is understood ontologically: in it *Dasein*, whose being is aptitude for Being, always sees a possibility for itself. Faith and theology declare, and show, that in this aptitude for being (indisputable as an ontological thing) there always lies a duty-to-be. In every factitious choice which strikes it as a possibility for real existence, *Dasein* always in fact chooses what it already is. Thus it is never cut off from its own past and never free. Neither, therefore, is it ever historical, insofar as historicity means the possibility of an event that is real—that is, new'.[52] Thus faith judges 'all

---

48. *Ibid.*, p. 264.

49. *Ibid.*

50. *Ibid.*

51. *Ibid.*, pp. 247–8.

52. R. Bultmann, 'Die Geschichtlichkeit des Daseins und der Glaube' in *Zeitschrift für Theologie und Kirche* 11 (1930) 360–61.

ontic decision, all the freedom and historicity of unbelieving *Dasein*, [to be] a chimera', because those things exist only in faith and love.

Unbelieving *Dasein* does not forsake itself. The decision of a man who has not faith can only consist in 'being what *Dasein* always was anyhow'.[53] If we be asked how the unbeliever can lay bare his ecsistential structure nonetheless, then we must answer that a decision of despair is still a decision, and that 'in the decision of despair *Dasein* understands what is meant by a stout heart, freedom and historicity'.[54] So man cannot really be authentic on the ontic plane or ultimately, indeed, on the ontological plane itself, until he has faith, though he can understand even in his earthly schemes what historicity and freedom are (see §III, above). From this point of view it does not matter at all whether Heidegger is a believer or an unbeliever.

In an article written in 1958 Bultmann stresses yet once more that 'the ruin of metaphysics' (GV 3, p. 212) achieved by Heidegger helps us to reject all 'self-reliance', teaching us to give up all attempt at owing our ground and justification to ourselves alone. For existence must now be thought of in terms of *being*, not of things. Now *being* is never one's own possession; it is an historical destiny that keeps meeting man in new ways, and therefore the existence that flows from being can never be its master. 'Needless to say', Bultmann writes, 'such a reflection cannot vindicate the Word of God which encounters us . . . But I rather think it can shed light on what a word means in general[55] which encounters [us] in the *hic et nunc* and which is the forthcoming *Anrede* of God' (GV 3, p. 212).

Bultmann's view of Heidegger is still the same: the philosophy of Being can be of great help to the theologian on the plan of *Begrifflichkeit*; by so doing it does not impair the independence of faith in the slightest; on the contrary it drives home the absolute necessity of *Entscheidung*.

53. *Ibid.*, p. 361.
54. *Ibid.*
55. That is, on the formal, ontological plane.

CHAPTER SEVENTEEN

Bultmann and Jaspers

I

Jaspers has devoted his whole philosophy to critizing Bultmann. There-fore we cannot understand the criticism until we have some familiarity with the philosophy. But a mere exposition of Jaspers' general ideas would be an unsuitable introduction to his particular ideas on Bultmann; for though it be true that one must study the latter in the light of the former, the former must also be arranged in view of the latter. Jaspers' philosophy fits in perfectly with what he has said about Bultmann, but of course only from a point of view determined by the position of Bultmann himself. What, then, shall we need to recall of Jaspers' general philosophy?

First, perhaps, with M. Dufrenne and P. Ricoeur[1] we should point out the importance he attaches to knowledge. His philosophy of exist-ence is by no means designed to throw the classical tradition over-board. It never forgets the lessons of rationalism and it does not yield to the charms of the ineffable. Jaspers manfully upholds the necessity of representational and objective thought. Nothing exists beyond the reach of human consciousness, which in this sense becomes the measure of being. A being which would lie beyond the reach of our conscious-ness would be as good as non-existent to us.

All being passes through human consciousness, perception, imagina-tion, memory, intuitive or discursive thought. In a sense everything is consciousness and every being is an object of representation. Such is the 'principle of immanence' (PH I, p. 49). That consciousness which is defined in terms of its representation, Jaspers calls consciousness in general. Though it does not wholly make up the subject, the fact remains that there can be no subject without it. It forms the 'uttermost point of the subject, the point of the formal, impersonal *I* which con-trasts with things—in other words, is their correlative' (PH 2, p. 8). Kant's *I think* epitomizes this consciousness. Being as a representation or *Gegenstand* corresponds to consciousness in general. 'That is objective, in the first place, which forms an object of representation and cor-

---

1. *Karl Jaspers et la philosophie de l'existence* (1947), pp. 25ff.

responds to an *I* insofar as that *I* is subjective' (PH 2, p. 338). Or again
'*Die Sache gegenübersteht, das heisst Gegenstand ist*' (PH 2, p. 8). But represented being overflows the representation, which as it were is only
a first step towards objectivity.

Nothing is really an object but what is thought of (*Gedachtsein und
Objektsein ist dasselbe*)—in other words, has universal validity. That is
objective which holds good (*das Gültige*), which commends itself by its
rational intelligibility. It is the rational working up of a representation
which gives it the status of an object. Being becomes an object by
passing from the representational footing to the universal. Consciousness in general, then, objectifies being. Whereas it was a *Gegenstand* it
becomes an *Objekt*; for the *Gegenstand* is merely represented being, but
the *Objekt* is a *Gegenstand* promoted to the rigour of universality and
the universality of rigour. This is what science and philosophy do for
earthly *Wirklichkeit*: '*Die in der Weltorientierung Objekt werdende Wirklichkeit*' (PH 1, p. 167).

Consciousness in general has to do with the necessary and universal
knowledge of objects. It seeks to dispel the fogginess of being; it will
not put up with knowledge that is less than certain. The essential
features of knowledge are constraint (*zwingendes Wissen*) and generality
(*Allgemeinheit*). In this respect knowledge is not the exclusive business
of consciousness in general, but also becomes the business of the understanding—with its categories—and of reason. The *understanding* differs
from consciousness in general only by accentuating the intellectual
aspect of the latter. It works out objectivity in categories, which give
knowledge its accuracy and validity. As to *reason* (of which Jaspers has
most to say in *Vernunft und Existenz*), it is the soul of understanding,
which it also overflows because without reason there would be neither
representation (*Gegenstand*) nor object (*Objekt*): it is the *sine qua non* of
all thinking and all *straight* thinking. Above all, the highest aim of
knowledge, which is unity and wholeness, can be achieved thanks only
to reason.[2]

Here we see, in very broad outline, how Jaspers preserves everything
that is worthwhile in the classical tradition. The philosophy of existence
is not a species of irrationalism; it is steeped in reason. Without what
Jaspers calls, in controversy with Bultmann, 'the cleavage between
subject and object', without objective knowledge carried to the point

---

2. Throughout Jaspers' work, reason 'is not that understanding which exists the
very same in all men, consciousness in general, but the flow of existence, moving
with all its thought towards totality, using every possible means of communication
and always completely open to whatever is real' (Paul Ricoeur, 'Philosophie et
religion chez K. Jaspers' in *Revue d'histoire et de philosophie religieuses* 37 [1957]
p. 218).

of utmost rigour and universality, there would be no philosophy of existence and indeed no existence: 'If I have not taken everything into consideration, if I have not weighed every possibility, if I have not plunged into never-ending trains of thought, then I take no decision; I am a blind impulse' (PH 2, p. 181).

The error of the *philosophia perennis* was that it never got beyond the realm of knowledge and objectivity. It reduced reality to representation and being to object. Here Kierkegaard and Nietzsche sounded the alarm. Their whole life and whole philosophy are one impassioned protest against objectivity: it is nothing but an idol, they declare, and true being must be sought beyond it. Kierkegaard denounced the bankruptcy of Hegelianism and of a Christianity arthritic with dogmatism; he upbraided the established churches and the easy conscience of Christians everywhere. He preached the absolutism of the cross, which is 'absurdity'. Transcendence is the absurdity of God's incarnation. Nietzsche proclaims that 'God is dead'. But the death of God to him, Jaspers says, is an immense emptiness, an abyss at the bottom of which the voice of Zarathustra rings out—the call of Superman, the proclamation of the everlasting return. Kierkegaard and Nietzsche are essentially prophets. The business of philosophy is to think out the experiences they have undergone—that is, to shed light on transcendence.

The first thing to be done is to show that being overflows objectivity, which conclusion we arrive at through a critique of science and of knowledge in general. For all their exactitude, mathematics and logic do not take cognizance of their own assumptions. The certitude they offer does not extend to their foundations. Euclidean geometry depends on the immediately evident, and non-Euclidean geometries depend on arbitrary postulates. Moreover, mathematics and logic have no real content: 'They do not lay hold on being' (PH 1, p. 90). The experimental, natural sciences are based on fact but 'any fact is itself a theory'. Interpretation plays a leading role in these sciences because the richness of reality baffles all logic. Scientific theories are always tentative affairs. There is a residue of the unknown (*ein Zugrundliegendes*) which prevents even the best established certainties—astronomical calculations, for instance—being more than extreme probabilities, equivalent to absolute certainty only for practical purposes. As to the human sciences, they are unable to embrace the whole of the mind. The mind participates in existence; it is an inexhaustible 'totality'. That is why psychology and history cannot sound its depths. Who has ever been able to claim that he thoroughly understood the mind of an age? Can its particular features and its wholeness be taken in at one and the same time?

Is philosophy in a better position than the natural and human sciences to search out a knowledge that will be strictly accurate? When it pontificates and claims to know the whole of being, it is making the same mistake that science does. For what philosophy apprehends is *in* the whole but is never the whole itself. Despite its battery of concepts, definitions, methods and arguments, it cannot pin down being. To suppose that it can was the error of classical philosophy.

We can easily see that what Jaspers finds fault with (and this point is crucial if we would understand his objections to Bultmann) is not science or philosophy as such, but scientism and scientist philosophy. Positivism and idealism alike he brushes aside, meaning by idealism the doctrine which, in the Hegelian manner, identifies being with the being of the mind. Idealism and positivism both assume that, *per se*, knowledge can scrutinize all being. The only difference between them is that positivism lays more stress on the natural sciences and idealism more on the human sciences; but both of them completely objectify being.

In criticizing idealism Jaspers censures any philosophy according to which being participates in idea to such an extent that that participation becomes the measure of being. With them, being only exists in an idea; it is wholly intelligible because it is nothing but the manifestation of mind; and thought becomes 'the essence of all being' (PH I, p. 223). Scientism and rationalism look on being as no more than totality par excellence, the inexhaustible, the bottomless chasm, transcendence inaccessible to mere knowledge, to be reached only by a leap (*Sprung*). Yet were they to heed precisely what they claim to defend, they would observe that thought itself bears within it a kind of openness to transcendence. Reason is a darting forth that tends to overshoot the limits of understanding and its categories. Only unauthentic reason (*unwahre Vernunft*) comes into collision with the thought that transcends. Authentic reason joins in the act of transcending. Zeal for clarity and wholeness draws it to all that is misty and fragmentary, so that reason becomes fully rational only when it subsumes the irrational. Far from clashing with the totality that is being, reason leads one to it. This is a major theme which Jaspers will cast back to in his controversy with Bultmann.

To put the object on trial is to do the same with the subject—that is, with consciousness in general. Just as the object must be transcended in a dart towards being, so general consciousness must be transcended in a dart towards absolute consciousness, which is the singular subject or existence: representation does not cover all consciousness. Consciousness has other modes of being, first and foremost that of absolute consciousness—which is not representational, because it is identical with freedom. Consciousness in general cannot make the whole of absolute consciousness an object of thought. In other words, the subject which

I am cannot be reduced to consciousness in general: 'Every time I make myself an object, I am simultaneously more than that object—that is, the being which can thus turn itself into an object' (*Vernunft und Existenz*, p. 47).

In his controversy with Bultmann, as elsewhere, Jaspers conveys the inexhaustibility of freedom by speaking of the 'totality that we are'. This totality is the freedom, the existence, which constitutes my deepest being. There are moments when 'my essential being lays hold on me, as it were bursts upon me (*überkommt mich mein Wesen*)—that being of mine which I do not know from Adam. Insofar as I am that capacity for freedom, knowledge and action, I am possible existence' (PH 1, p. 13). I do not 'know' my being because 'if existence understands itself, that is not an act like the understanding whereby some content or other is understood regardless of who the understanding subject may be; it is not a seeing something, but a primordial spurting forth which becomes itself in daylight. It is not a participation in something alien; it is the comprehension and the being of him who comprehends, fused into one (*in eins*). It is not an understanding at large but . . . an ungeneralized understanding, in the absolute present, in activity, in love, in all the forms of absolute consciousness. [Here we see] the difference between the idea I have of another man's love—which I can never really understand—and the idea I have of my own love, because I actually am this love' (*Vernunft und Existenz*, p. 38). In my free act I am no longer a consciousness in general but a source (*Ursprung*).

'Where I am the source of myself (*Ursprung meiner selbst*), matters are not all settled in advance according to general rules. There I am not only unable to tell what the decision will be—because of the innumerable circumstances which condition it—but on another plane I am that which itself decides what is . . . When I cease to study myself psychologically, when I act not in naive ignorance but in virtue of my positive impetus (*Aufschwung*), in the illumination of a certitude that really springs not from knowledge but rather from my very being, at that moment I decide what I am' (PH 1, pp. 14–16). I am aware of myself 'as having given birth to myself for myself' (*als mir selber durch mich geboren*; PH 2, p. 207. 'To decide and to be oneself are one and the same thing' (PH 2, p. 182). In free decision 'I make my own being' (*mein eigenes Wesen schaffe*) (PH 2, p. 110). I do not create myself in the absolute, atheist sense, since I would be nothing without the transcendence that gives myself to myself, as we shall see in due course. Let us say that although I do not create myself, I make myself. I am *Ursprung*—that is, not exactly my own creator but the one responsible for myself[3].

3. See M. Dufrenne and P. Ricoeur, *Karl Jaspers et la philosophie de l'existence* (1947), pp. 151–2.

A leap must be made in order to get from consciousness in general to the freedom that I am. At the same time, just as Jaspers does not mean to repudiate the objectivity of knowledge, so neither does he mean to repudiate the *I think* which conditions it and needs only to be transcended. Egged on by reason, knowledge itself strives to reach beyond itself. Consciousness in general, understanding, reason and freedom, it may be said, are not wholly cut off from each other. Kant admirably grasped this point, and for good reason his method is called transcendental. While declining to look for transcendence in any objective being, he showed that the *I think* is not itself an object. By making transcendence the *sine qua non* of all representation, he removed it beyond the reach of all representation; so that Jaspers credits him with 'transcending towards consciousness in general' (PH I, p. 44). When I lower myself to an impersonal state in order to think objectively, even that act, whereby I abdicate all personality, is still the act of a person, the decision of a freedom. Thus general consciousness is the mode of being of the subject when it thinks objective thoughts, and such thinking springs from possible existence as from its motive source; so that under the goad of existence, general consciousness also transcends. Representation is animated by a darting forth towards existence. How much more so must reason be, which is 'the unrest that will not let us accept anything as complete' (*Vernunft und Existenz*, p. 40) and the striving towards oneness—that is, towards being.

Here we have a favourite theme of Jaspers', which looms still larger in his exchanges with Bultmann: general consciousness, understanding and reason are only authentic when transcended towards the true and total subject, which is freedom and existence, *enlightened* freedom and existence. Thus reason must not be divorced from existence. It is the bond which unites all degrees of truth and enables us to set them in order. It unifies empirical consciousness, general consciousness, understanding and the mind, which are summed up and outstripped by the leap of freedom. Accordingly it is the side of existence which lends itself to clarity, explanation, and even to a certain systematization. 'Reason alone sheds light upon existence' (*Vernunft und Existenz*, p. 41).

Having transcended general consciousness towards existence and object towards being, it remains for us to take a third step. The movement whereby we transcend in this way may seem to lead us outside the world: existence may seem to be something foreign to the individual; and being, something foreign to the empirical world. Jaspers distinguishes three forms of absolute consciousness, or three modes of being for the subject—the empirical individual, the *I think*, and freedom or existence—to which correspond three forms of being—empirical being, objective being, and being in itself or transcendence.

Generally speaking, *Dasein* in Jaspers means all empirical reality,[4] whether the *Dasein* of the world, the *Dasein* of man, or the *Dasein* of spirit. 'What merely subsists or happens (*Was nur besteht oder geschieht*), is *Dasein* as contrasted with freedom' (PH 2, p. 177). *Weltdasein* is the world in whose midst the life of man goes on. 'The whole of *Dasein* is the world . . . The world is the *Dasein* that confronts me as the ever determinate being of objects, and that I myself am as an empirical *Dasein*' (PH 1, p. 28). I am an empirical being through my body, my temperament, my character, my consciousness in general, through everything in me that is objective. Consciousness in general, understanding, reason and spirit are part of *Dasein* because they make up the realm of objectivity—although, as we have said, reason has a bent towards transcendence. But only as 'appropriated' by existence can all these things become the mark of transcendence.

We must observe that transcending general consciousness towards existence and object towards being does not mean cutting oneself off from the empirical individual and empirical being. The distinctions we have drawn within consciousness and the world refer to modes of being of one and the same thing. Generally speaking, the *Tranzendieren* that is the heart and soul of Jaspers' philosophy does not consist in escaping from *Dasein*. There is no other world of the empirical individual and of empirical being into which the act of transcending could take us. Jaspers constantly speaks of an *Ueber die Welt hinaus* (PH 2, p. 145 and *passim*) which is not a *Jenseits der Welt*. There is no other world in the background (*Hinterwelt*), and there is no double world (*Weltverdoppelung*). It is art which best helps us understand that transcendence, though a wholly other, is not a 'beyond'. In Van Gogh, for example, Jaspers says, reality is illumined by a transcendence that is not something new but rather a different dimension or new mode of reality.

Kant had already seen that we must not only transcend empirical being but also take care not to interpret transcendence as meaning that there is some other world hidden behind the appearances of the sensible world. With Kant, the thing in itself is not an object. Just as he does not consider that the intelligible character of a thing is something different from its empirical character, so Jaspers, while making transcendence the wholly other, does not refer it to any other world than the empirical world; and existence, for its part, is not something new added to the empirical self.

---

4. Obviously Jaspers' *Dasein* has nothing to do with Heideggerian *Dasein*. What Jaspers calls *Dasein*, Heidegger and Bultmann call *Gegebenheit* or *Vorhandenheit*.

344 Theology and Ontology

In other words, existence will always be found 'in context', is always 'historical'. It neither can nor may be cut off from *Dasein*. 'Existence is a vista seen through a chink in *Weltdasein* . . . But this vista does not lead one outside the world, it ends within the world' (PH 2, p. 8). 'If existence tried to act freely in the absolute sense, without seizing upon *Dasein* as a means of manifesting itself, it would issue forth from this world and drop into the void' (PH 2, p. 123). It can neither drown itself in *Dasein*, for example 'chaining itself to sensible things as though they were actually its life' (*ibid.*), nor yet escape *Dasein*. It must live '*in Spannung*' (strung taut). On the one hand (here Jaspers sees eye to eye with Bultmann) *Dasein* must not be set up as an absolute, must not itself become a thing simply because it lives in things. In Heideggerian parlance, we must wash our hands of the 'they' and *Alltäglichkeit*, give up the life that is led by the man in the street. On this point Jaspers stands as foursquare as all philosophers who are worthy of the name, and his thought is nothing else but an urgent appeal to us to get out of the rut of hum-drum everyday life.

Escaping *Dasein*, living outside historicity, also means slumping into unauthenticity, for *Dasein* cannot be dispensed with as 'the expression or manifestation of existence'. 'Embraced by personal being', it takes on 'an absolute weight' (*absolutes Gewicht*), 'an infinite importance'; only 'in empirical being does man become possible existence' (PH 2, p. 2). 'By free appropriation' (*durch freie Aneignung*) existence melts into it [*Dasein*] (PH 2, p. 123). Historicity is the 'oneness of *Dasein* and existence' (PH 2, p. 122). What we must do, therefore, is 'concentrate the unconditionality [of existence] upon the historically concrete present' (PH 2, p. 124). Then 'the depth of being, properly speaking, will be irreplaceably present in temporal reality, which happens only once' (PH 2, p. 122). In other words, eternity presents itself within time and only thus is it eternity at all. Moreover it exists only where it has been temporally bodied forth. Through decision I get the better of time, 'not for the benefit of some abstract intemporality but in the sense that within time I hold myself aloof from time; above it, not outside it' (PH 1, p. 16). Eternity 'is indissolubly bound to that moment' (PH 2, p. 127).

Being is not identical with *Dasein*, but it only exists through my free appropriation of *Dasein*. This appropriation (*Aneignung*) of *Dasein* by freedom Jaspers calls historicity (*Geschichtlichkeit*), distinguishing it from *Historie*. Here we have a distinction that is already familiar to us. Like Heidegger and Bultmann, Jaspers considers *historisch* that 'theoretical' (PH 2, p. 120) or 'public' knowledge (PH 2, p. 119) which relates to the bare facts of empirical history. The *geschichtlich* begins when I find that facts 'are oriented towards me, summon me', and are capable of being 'assimilated, appropriated' (*angeeignet*). Then they become *beschichtlich* and I myself become *geschichtlich*: 'This oneness of myself with my *Dasein* as the manifestation [of my existence] is my historicity' (PH 2, p. 121). But from time to time this exactitude of Jaspers' flags and he takes historicity to mean everything that contrasts with the timeless, the abstract, the universal. The importance of freedom and appropriation seems to be belittled, almost forgotten. Anything concrete automatically becomes historical. As we shall see, he seems to take this view in the exchanges with Bultmann, and Bultmann scolds him accordingly.

The notion of historicity leads on to that of symbol [*Chiffre*]. By appropriating *Dasein*, existence discloses being-in-itself within *Dasein*. Nevertheless the transcendence which is the 'wholly other' than the world, exists only in the world. That is precisely what constitutes its historicity. Therefore the world becomes a symbol of transcendence. As such, it is no longer the trivial, groundless world (*ohne Grund*) of knowledge and technology but the echo of transcendence. The theory of the symbol merely states in another way that transcendence does not exist apart from *Dasein*: 'If there were no symbol, neither would there be any transcendence . . . After all, for the symbol to exist and for transcendence to exist amounts to the same thing so far as we are concerned . . . The symbol is the only form in which transcendence manifests itself to existentiell consciousness' (PH 2, pp. 205, 206). Jaspers thinks that 'everything should be capable of becoming a symbol' (PH 2, p. 168): a sunset, nature as a whole, man, history, consciousness in general . . . Thus the symbol has a body which is *Dasein*. Existence seizes upon it, 'appropriating' it by an act of decision and faith, and during this act transcendence reveals itself to existence— not, of course, as an object but as a 'fleeting'[5] light. It shines 'for the twinkling of an eye' (PH 2, pp. 154, 156 and *passim*), it is not steady but 'wavers' (PH 3, pp. 161, 162); that is, it remains dim and a will-o'-the-wisp even while manifesting itself (PH 3, pp. 152, 164 and *passim*).

Since transcendence is not an object, general consciousness cannot reach it. It reveals itself to freedom alone. Reaching transcendence is a 'leap' that goes to make up faith (*Glaube*), and faith is the degree of truth proper to existence, just as constraint and universality are the degree of truth proper to general consciousness. Transcendence is a *possibility* of existence. Jaspers often says that existence confronts, not transcendence *as such*, but its *own* transcendence. Nearly always, existence bears the label 'possible existence'. Thus it is up to each person whether he will see what the symbol betokens. Whereas

5. This expression crops up in countless passages.

empirical reality thrusts itself upon me, transcendence does no such thing: I can perfectly well turn a blind eye to the symbol, close myself against it; and if I open myself to it, another man's interpretation may be altogether different from mine: it has a double or even a multiple meaning, and therefore in order to experience transcendence one must 'contribute the personal being of possible existence' (PH 3, p. 150).

Jaspers groups his symbols under three headings. The first element of which freedom will make a symbol is experience in the ordinary sense of the word: perception, inductive and deductive reasoning, intuition, and so forth. This is the way in which I know nature, history, consciousness in general, the existence that I am. Then, 'on the foundation of all these common experiences, there rises metaphysical experience' (PH 3, p. 30), which discerns transcendence in them. This first language of being is the primordial, direct language, which does not owe its form to man.

There is, however, another language, that of myth and religion. It is a language in the second degree, because—unlike the primordial symbols we have just spoken of—myth and religion are works of man that 'mediatize' the direct language of being. Moreover myth and religion are not absolutely synonymous. Myth in the first degree remains closely interwoven with the world, as we see in Greek mythology. Only on the plane of the great religions does myth figure as a divorce between this world and the next. What perfectly constitutes religion is the idea of revelation. At that stage myth is an extraordinary story which recounts the invasion of this world by the other world. Finally we have a higher form of myth which partakes more of art than of religion: in a work of art transcendence makes its appearance. Art—particularly that art which no longer uses the ordinary language of myth, which for example balks at representing Apollo or Christ—takes us back to the primordial symbol. Reality is directly transfigured, as in Van Gogh, whose painting Jaspers considers to be an astonishing manifestation of transcendence.

The third language is 'speculation', by which we mean the systems of every age. Thus Jaspers brings back ontology, having harshly condemned it elsewhere. Classical philosophy, from Aristotle to Hegel, can also be a symbol of transcendence. With oneness for their aim and their marrow, the major theories of thought are the speculative expression of the totality of symbols, and witnesses to being.[6]

For all his keenness to shed light on existence and transcendence, Jaspers finally bows to the prestige of the ineffable. In his controversy

6. For a thorough disquisition on the three languages, see M. Dufrenne and Ricoeur, *Karl Jaspers et la philosophie de l'existence*, pp. 286–323.

with Bultmann he calls transcendence the incomprehensible (*das Unverständliche*), the infinitely illuminable (*ein ins Unendliche Erhellbares*) which nonetheless is never illuminated. If transcendence becomes an image (*Bild wird*), then it has ceased to be transcendence (PH 3, p. 23). 'If I try to lay hold on it [being], I lay hold on nothing. Unless I try to push on to the very source of being, I drop into the void' (PH 3, p. 3). I am swallowed up in 'an abyss which to reason seems emptiness' (*ibid.*). When it comes to transcendence, 'everything thinkable is brushed aside as irrelevant' (PH 3, p. 8). Being is often called unthinkableness, the unthinkable, non-thinking. In any case the theory of the symbol (and of border-line situations) sufficiently indicates that being always remains hidden.

Hence the philosophy of Jaspers adds up to failure. 'Here unknowing —the dark night of the understanding—is total: the world as failure, freedom as failure, speak to me only of the hidden godhead . . . God is hidden because I am in a border-line situation and a border-line situation is the germ or synopsis of all failures'.[7] Even ultimate failure, of course, still remains a symbol; 'but this time the symbol is no longer a language, and it can no longer be commented on in a mythical narrative or a philosophic discourse. The last failure of all is silence.'[8]

What we have been saying takes on its full significance when Jaspers is compared with Heidegger.[9] For the latter, as we have seen, being is light; the otherness of being is not its obscurity. Jaspers reaches beyond classical ontology into unknowing. His critique of science and scientific philosophy means nothing else but this. He might well make his own the dictum of Kant: 'I had to get rid of knowledge so as to make room for faith', despite his effort to 'appropriate' the great metaphysics by cutting them down into symbols. Jaspers' thought is a philosophic *faith*.

Heidegger's approach is altogether different. He charges the philosophy of the Platonic era with having been an anthropocentrism, an *Ergreifen von* . . . Therefore the tables must be turned, so that being may enjoy pride of place. Now being is light. Only instead of being that of which man is the source, this light is the source of *Dasein*. The

---

7. *Ibid.*, p. 321.

8. *Ibid.*, p. 322.

9. We would not presume to adopt the comparison drawn by M. Dufrenne and P. Ricoeur (*ibid.*, pp. 363–72) between Jaspers and Heidegger. If what we have just said about Heidegger, in the chapter devoted to him, be true, will it really do to speak of his thought as a 'fixed-focus' philosophy? Judging, at any rate, by the quotations they choose from it and base their opinion on, Dufrenne and Ricoeur would seem to have relied overmuch on de Waelhens' book which misses the pith of Heidegger.

primacy of being in no way entails a primacy of unknowing. Heidegger keeps to the traditional theory of truth, simply inverting its sense: man now emerges as the *Da* of being, instead of being's being the *Da* of man; man has ceased to be the lord of being, being has become the lord of man. With Jaspers, transcendence is obscurity, with Heidegger it is light. To be sure, Heidegger also declares that being is the 'obscure', but he only does so in order to underline its historicity (see p. 328, above): just as true being is nothingness, so true light is darkness. Man is ec-sistence, not towards the ineffable (as with Jaspers) but towards the *logos*.[10]

Jaspers, of course, fully realizes the issue which divides him from Heidegger. In his controversy with Bultmann, as we shall see, he accuses Heidegger of not sticking to the existentiell alone but yielding to the glamour of knowledge with his theory of the existentials, thus ending up with a philosophy that looks very like 'a fabric of steel' (KJRB, p. 12). Certainly he misunderstands the true nature of the Heideggerian existential, but that misunderstanding speaks volumes on his utter repudiation of ontology. When all is said and done, compared with the philosophy of Heidegger and despite certain disavowals on its author's part, Jaspers' philosophy emerges as the very epitome of irrationalism, the final stage in the vast movement of reaction against the Enlightenment. It is a form of existentialism because although it constantly dwells on being, it throws all ontology overboard. Heidegger's philosophy is not a form of existentialism because, as we have seen, it replaces the classical ontologies with the philosophy of being and not with a philosophic faith.

II

Having thus explained why knowledge is necessary and stressed the fact that objectivity must be transcended though not done away with (the theory of the symbol), we are now in a position to understand Jaspers' fundamental criticism of Bultmann. Bultmann never gets beyond the level of general consciousness and objective things. Instead of interpreting the Bible by the theory of the symbol, he has done so by a scientific philosophy. In accordance with the key idea of his philosophy, Jaspers constantly distinguishes between what he calls *Aufklärung* (which means authentic reason, or reason as an 'infinite flux open to transcendence') and *Aufkläricht* (which is reason pretending to omniscience). He uses the terms *Aufkläricht* and *Rationalismus* as

10. This, need we say, is not the *logos* seen from man's point of view, as in the philosophies of the Platonic era, but the *logos* which is being itself.

synonyms (KJRB, p. 41). Bultmann, he says, never sets foot beyond *Aufkläricht* and *Rationalismus*. Such is the general charge which we must subject to closer scrutiny, condensing Jaspers' rather wordy exposé into three themes.

(1) *Scientific ontology and philosophic ontology*

Bultmann starts with an erroneous idea of science and philosophy. Modern science exhibits a twofold character. On the one hand it has become universal and apodictic to a degree of which we find only hints in the mathematics and medicine, geography and astronomy of the Greeks. No science and no philosophy of the past ever used such strict method or yielded such accurate findings. As a result—and here we have the second feature of science in our time—it no longer claims to offer a representation of the world. The more accurate it becomes, the more readily it acknowledges its own limitations and the fact that reality as a whole eludes it. It 'realizes that it never knows being but only objects in the world' (KJRB, p. 10). Here we have one of Jaspers' favourite themes, for he rejoices at science's own avowal that it cannot and must not put forward a *Weltbild*. But many scientists (not to mention laymen) ignore the limitations of science and think that it can give us a total picture of the world. Bultmann is 'apparently' of their number (KJRB, p. 10). He is clinging to the Greek conception when he assumes that the problem of how the world began falls within the field of science, whereas in fact it is the business of philosophy. 'For the totality of being remains inaccessible to science' (KJRB, p. 11).

Bultmann proves to be as clumsy a hand at philosophy as at science. In philosophy he sits at no one's feet but Heidegger's. Now there are two contradictory aspects to *Sein und Zeit*. On the one hand the book is a summons to authenticity, and makes much of historicity, appropriation, the 'seriousness' of a life of 'commitment'. So we find there an existential philosophy in the spirit of Augustine, Luther and Kierkegaard. But on the other hand Heidegger objectifies his thought, turning it into a doctrine through his theory of the existential, which makes philosophy a science with the look of a fabric of steel. Its accuracy, therefore, has enabled it to be used in psychiatry with good results. Unfortunately, Bultmann considers only this scientific aspect of Heidegger's book, which he even accentuates, thereby cutting himself off from the real philosophy. He sticks fast in the quagmire of nineteenth-century academic philosophy: 'No breath of Kantian or Platonic thought seems to have affected him' (KJRB, p. 13). For according to Jaspers, it will be recalled, one of the great achievements of Kant (indeed of Plato) was to transcend objectivity (see p. 342, above).

With a touch of haughty contempt (and rather contradicting what he has just said), Jaspers professes not to know whether the distinction between existential and existentiell is there in Heidegger or is an invention of Bultmann's. At all events it is an unfortunate distinction, because it sets us talking about man from the standpoint of consciousness in general; we imagine that our knowledge is absolutely accurate, 'whereas everything depends on that ground which is never known, which since Kierkegaard we call existence' (KJRB, p. 14); we snap our fingers at the necessity for seriousness (*Ernst*), action, life, 'appropriation'; we take no account of concrete circumstances; in a word, we do not transcend thought towards existence. With Bultmann the thought of *Sein und Zeit* 'has been isolated as though it were a universal scientific knowledge of the human being' (KJRB, p. 14), whereas in fact there is no such thing as existential analysis. Distinguishing between existentiell and existential is trifling with the serious business of philosophy, because 'the existentials objectify what can only be intimated by signs' (KJRB, p. 13).

Jaspers contrasts his own idea of philosophy with Bultmann's idea. Philosophy cannot be scientific, it can only be transcendental—that is, it has nothing to do with the content of thought, only with the form of thought. It can only be an illumination of the modes of totality. Without the divorce between subject and object there can be neither thought, nor lucidity, nor language; but that divorce is a flame that must draw nourishment from the inexhaustible whole, it is the luminous crest of the wave that is sustained by the ocean depths. Where only subject and object come into the picture, we have nothing but the rustle of dead leaves, an empty husk of words. Philosophy attempts to understand all the modes of totality: *Dasein* in its *Umwelt*, general consciousness and its objects, the mind and its whole world of forms, existence and its transcendence. All these philosophical investigations have one feature in common: they try to pin down in a scientific way something that is not the object of science at all. They deal with what forms the foundation of objectivity and yet is not an object. For that reason, since Kant's day, they have been called transcendentals. They do not transcend ahead of objects, to reach something that lies beyond them; they transcend as it were behind all objective knowledge, towards the foundation that makes objective things possible. Hence the inadequacy of all that philosophy can say—though it must all be said and all abounds with meaning—because neither consciousness nor thought would exist but for the divorce between subject and object. Not that we may remain the prisoners of objectivity, we must scale its walls by being serious.

If totality were a mere object it would no longer be totality, and yet the mode of objectivity is what clarifies it. Its non-objectivity is present in the objectification of its modes. Totality manifests itself only in symbols—whether the symbol of *Dasein* or of consciousness at large or of myth. So objectivity is not to be sneezed at: without objectification nothing becomes clear. But we must attack false objectification. When philosophic speculation concerns itself with being, that object only yields up its meaning once the operation of thought has destroyed it as an object. Then what was conceived of as an object becomes a sign of possible existence. But if signs are made the existentials of a reality which we think of objectively, then they lose their true import. Thus we find ourselves still faced with the same problem: how to understand objectivity as at once necessary and halting, and how to distinguish it from false objectification?

It must be conceded that Bultmann has gone straight to the heart of the matter in setting his thought under the general head of *Glauben und Verstehen*. Of course a sound notion of faith and understanding, and of their interrelation, is also necessary. At some length Jaspers explains his mind on this point. We here give the substance of what he says. He distinguishes between 'original understanding' and 'understanding of what is understood'. Original understanding is a mode of being: 'Understanding is the mode of presence of the being that we are' (KJRB, p. 25); this understanding makes up our being itself. On the other hand the understanding of what has been understood by someone is not a mode of being; it is possible without my sharing in the reality of what I wish to understand, without my understanding of an original understanding being itself an original understanding, as happens in the human sciences. The religions of the past, for example, are a thing 'understood' (for their devotees they were an original understanding) which I can understand without their being my own original understanding. Understanding of what is understood can operate within the framework of the 'precise' and the 'imprecise', whereas original understanding—being choice and decision—makes value-judgments. As a mode of being, it decides (for myself and also absolutely) what is true or false, good or evil, beautiful or ugly.

Nevertheless—and this is a vital point—the distinction we have just made is not an adequate one, because the two sorts of understanding can never be separated. Understanding of what is understood always presupposes the capacity for original understanding and that capacity is itself a kind of sharing in the thing understood. Though I do not meddle with politics (do not have an original understanding of politics), I do have a certain insight into politics, which I owe to my capacity for original understanding. Thanks likewise to it, I can love art without being an artist, catch the drift of Christianity without being a Christian, and so forth. Similarly it is thanks to his capacity for original understanding that the historian can objectively bring back the past (understand what is understood). It is not scientific wits and scientific method alone that make a great historian, but first and foremost his capacity for an original understanding of the past.

The aforesaid distinction can hardly be news to Bultmann, but he divorces the two understandings, just as in Heidegger he divorced the existentiell from the existential. Existential interpretation is a false objectification, because it leaves out of account the historicity of myth and of ideas.[11] It does not treat them as symbols in which the incomprehensible manifests itself while yet remaining hidden. Bultmann honestly searches for the 'precise' in this respect and he is a great scholar; but locked up as he is in a mistaken idea of modern science and scientific philosophy, he never gets beyond consciousness in general. His writing lacks that certain something which testifies to appropriation (*Aneignung*). He speaks of biblical myth in a scientific vein, like one who thinks he can competently treat of this matter without faith and responsibility making any perceptible contribution. He envisages the appropriation of biblical myth as a sifting out of that in it which is scientifically impossible or scientifically unacceptable. Having isolated the theory of existentials in Heidegger, he makes it a tool for intellectually appropriating (*Werkzeug denkenden Aneignens*—KJRB, p. 14) the existentiell affirmations of scripture. He thinks he has discovered 'in his existential interpretation a new method for really appropriating faith' (KJRB, p. 49).

No breath of pneuma can be detected either in Bultmann's science or in his theology. And yet what else can theology base its understanding on than the Holy Spirit? Bultmann pays the meaning of totality no heed, his understanding of what is understood has no roots in an original understanding of that understood thing, and therefore, in him, necessary objectification becomes a false objectification. He separates subject from object, whereas the objectivity of what is said and the subjectivity of him who says it must be one (*in eins*) in totality. Seriousness flies out the window when the subject becomes a general consciousness and the object an abstraction. This truth will stand forth better in the study of myth and the idea of revelation upon which we now embark.

(2) *Myth and ontology*

Bultmann distinguishes between myth and science, holding that science has knocked myth into a cocked hat once and for all. Therefore,

11. With regard to speculation as a symbol, see p. 346, above.

he says, we must translate the content of myth into rational language.

This is stuff and nonsense, because in fact mythical thought must always have its legitimate place in human life. Myth is not general, either in form or in content: it is historical. It does not clothe a universal which would be better expressed in concepts and laws. By its very nature it balks all attempts to translate it into a language other than its own. It cannot be interpreted rationally, but only by new myths. Myths are explained by other myths. Thanks to science we know that the sun does not rise, since it is the earth that revolves round the sun. Must we therefore cease to look on sunrise as a bodily reality (*leib-haftige Wirklichkeit*) that is always new, that touches the heart and fills us with delight? We know that the manifestation of God on Sinai or in the burning bush was devoid of spatio-temporal realness (*Realität*), was only a human experience. Must we therefore say that that manifestation is no longer a gripping reality (*ergreifende Wirklichkeit*)? Well then, is it not blasphemous to talk of demythologization? Demythologization is not an *Aufklärung* but an *Aufkläricht*.

Nevertheless it must be granted that Bultmann's work conveys a 'half-truth' (KJRB, p. 19), embryonic in the distinction we have just drawn between *Realität* and *Wirklichkeit*. *Realität* is the equivalent of what Heidegger and Bultmann call *Gegebenheit* or *Vorhandenheit*—what common sense means by saying that a thing is real or objective. In every age myth has been thus degraded into a 'material reality' (*materielle Realität*) or something 'tangible '(*Handgreiflichkeit*). When Jaspers talks of bodiliness (*Leibhaftigkeit*) we must not picture it as anything that can be felt or seen.

Bultmann is absolutely right to deny that myth has any bodiliness comparable with that of objects which are in the world (*in Bezug auf Dinge in der Welt*). Jaspers cites an example to show what he means. The first Christians laboured under the delusion that a dead man can rise again, for 'a corpse cannot come back to life and walk out of the tomb. Sketchy historical accounts by witnesses who contradict each other do not suffice to establish an historical fact' (KJRB, p. 20). In a letter to Bultmann he declares once more that he can believe neither in the return of a corpse to life, nor in devils, nor in magic of any sort whatever (KJRB, p. 105). In short, the bodiliness of the mythical symbol cannot be a bodiliness 'that is guaranteed and that guarantees'. This objectification of myth happens in every age; it has even found its way into the New Testament and to that extent Bultmann's undertaking is legitimate: it is necessary 'to expose the wrongness of reification (*Verdinglichung*), of the opaque bodiliness of an alleged reality '(*Realität*; KJRB, p. 20).

But to repudiate *Realität* is not to repudiate *Wirklichkeit*. Neither the sunrise, nor the manifestation of God on Sinai, nor the resurrection of Jesus are *Realitäten* (objective facts). Nonetheless these myths are the language of the reality (*Wirklichkeit*) we existentially live with; and that is not the empirical reality (*empirische Realität*) in which our *Dasein* is always attempting to submerge, as though it were *Wirklichkeit* itself. The only man who has a right to demythologize is he who clings all the more doggedly to the real thing (*Wirklichkeit*) which lies there within the symbolic language of myth. But properly speaking that would no longer be demythologization. Our business is not to demythologize but to rediscover mythical thought in its purity; that is, in the certitude (*Vergewisserung*)[12] of the *Wirklichkeit* which it discloses. We must appropriate (*aneignen*) the mythical content which brings us near, though never quite to, 'the lofty . . . idea of God, imageless transcendence' (KJRB, p. 20). We are forbidden to objectify *Wirklichkeit* into *Realität*, by the biblical commandment 'You shall not make for yourself a graven image'. That is why 'there exists no such thing as devils, or effects produced by magic, or sorcery' (KJRB, p. 21).

When in the Old Testament three angels visit Abraham and Moses receives the tables of the law, when in the New Testament the risen Christ says *Noli me tangere*, when he departs into heaven, when the Holy Spirit lays hold upon believers, all these things are 'a gripping image that remains with us' (KJRB, p. 22). They have no objective reality: they are symbols. Only a mind enlightened by philosophy can distinguish the reality of bodiliness from the reality of a symbol. But those who are really devout without being philosophers, while they conceive of bodiliness as if it were also an empirical reality, still avoid the implications of their materialist view by a kind of instinct. On the other hand those whose piety is a sham look on the bodiliness of myth as a tangible reality (*Realität*) and, blind to its symbolic nature, lapse into superstition.

So much having been said, it is the inescapable duty of every man to fight 'for what he believes to be true' (KJRB, p. 22) in the matter of myth. But the struggle must be carried on within mythical thought, not from a rational standpoint.

Myth is an existentiell possibility of faith: one cannot judge it as an outsider. In order to be discriminating about the content of myth,

---

12. The certitude meant is the profound certitude of existence, which ranks far above that of empirical consciousness and general consciousness. See M. Dufrenne and P. Ricoeur, *K. Jaspers et la philosophie de l'existence*, who stress the ethical nature of certitude in Jaspers. In the text which we are examining here, what the philosopher repeats is precisely that myth is a symbol, and like every symbol conveys no general knowledge but only an existentiell certitude. Though not universal, indeed *because* it is not, this certitude is absolute

accepting some things and rejecting others, one must share in that content. I cannot fight one myth and defend another by means of objective science but only by means of my participation (*Teilnahme*) in the rival myths: 'The fight is fair and illuminating only when carried on between origin (*Ursprung*) and origin' (KJRB, p. 122). Approval or rejection must necessarily be existentiell. Thus the Bible offers a great many existentiell possibilities, some of which complement each other while others rule each other out. But we are not to shift them onto the plane of concepts and the universal (or existential); we must live in them and on that footing make our choice. Rejected possibilities, therefore, are obviously not beaten and done for. For that which we have rejected 'remains present to our mind as a rejected possibility' (KJRB, p. 23).

This fight that everyone must put up for certain things in the Bible and against certain other things in it, seems to lead Bultmann to a position which Jaspers declares himself unable to accept. The Old Testament hardly interests Bultmann at all. The synoptics do not much concern him, but he makes much of Paul and John. This is a pity, for Paul and John stress a saving event and justification by faith in that event—'an idea as alien as can be to our philosophizing' (KJRB, p. 24) because, as we shall see, it reifies transcendence. John's spiritualized Christ strikes one as a piece of fairy-tale magic set against a golden background, and although he says certain things that are beautiful or intriguing, his *Wirklichkeit* seems strangely inferior to that of the Jesus in the synoptics. Moreover the evangelist of love is the first to justify Christian antisemitism by means of myth, which sheds a flood of light upon the nature of his faith.

(3) *Revelation and ontology*

To say that appropriating biblical myth is the business of faith, not of science, is to say that it concerns the *Seelsorger*[13] rather than the theologian. 'Thanks to him, the language of myth goes to work. He welcomes the mythical world, makes it present, not by the theories of philosophers and theologians but by the original spurting forth of appropriation (*Ursprünglichkeit der Aneignung*), on the basis of the seizure [he feels] in the bosom of his own faith' (KJRB, pp. 35–6). Bultmann envisages the appropriation of biblical myth as a matter of eliminating whatever in it will not hold water scientifically. He does not realize that nobody can 'know', either by scientific exegesis or by

---

13. The *Seelsorger* is one who has the care of souls. Jaspers takes the term to mean a priest or minister or anyone, indeed, who gives spiritual guidance outside the churches.

existential analysis, what things in the Bible hold good for faith. That is a supremely personal and existentiell question. He gets bogged down in his abstract considerations and finally blends *Aufkläricht* into orthodoxy without managing to be really orthodox.

His trouble is that he has not understood what Jaspers calls *Liberalität*. Let us explain at once that this liberality stands on an entirely different plane from that of Protestant liberalism. The historical phenomenon which goes under the latter name remains altogether outside Jaspers' horizon in the present controversy, even though in fact he finds his way back to its basic principle. Liberality is a special theory of Jaspers': it means 'that unlimited openness to reason and communication which allows all true values to blossom, even those which can never co-exist in any one man' (KJRB, p. 42).

In describing liberality, Jaspers sets forth his own philosophy. The liberal attitude and liberal thought are those which we have been contrasting with Bultmann's since the beginning of this chapter. 'Liberality overcomes bodiliness and knowledge, without forswearing them, by a language that is fluid in character . . . In the midst of knowledge it preserves unknowing; in unknowing it gives ear to the language that the symbols of transcendence speak, and in the bodilinesses of faith it heeds the *Wirklichkeit* which is no such bodiliness but speaks through them, giving no guarantee in this world' (KJRB, p. 38). Orthodoxy, for its part, relying on a salvific event (the revelation of God in Jesus Christ) which is objective in character, which it treats as an absolute, and which spares men responsibility and decision, searches for guarantees.

Liberal faith draws sustenance from its own strength—that is, straight from transcendence, without the surety of anything (any revelation) that can be observed from without or that has been handed down by tradition. It stresses the responsibility of man, who is left on his own: only through his freedom does he become conscious of being a gift of transcendence. Liberality is a never-ending effort to shed light on the incomprehensible. It is a perpetual movement between knowing and unknowing. 'Where [this movement] hardens into knowledge we have orthodoxy; where it takes its natural course we have liberality. Any completion, any perfect certitude, is illiberality' (KJRB, p. 39). Orthodoxy is man's eternal temptation.

It is chiefly over the idea of revelation—we have just indicated as much—that the orthodox and the liberal part company. 'A faith which affirms that God has attached himself to one place and one age, once for all or by a series of acts, that there and there alone he has directly revealed himself, is a faith which ties God down to an object in the world. This scene in time and space is not only revered because of its historical bond with God; it takes on the absolute character of the divine itself. Revelation and the imparting of its grace are bodily present in the canonical books, in the profession of faith and in dogma, in the sacrament of priestly ordination, in the Church as the *corpus mysticum Christi*, and in other forms besides. Liberality believes in no such revelation' (KJRB, p. 41). Why? Because revelation as conceived of by orthodoxy has ceased to be a symbol in which transcendence both discloses and enshrouds itself.

Liberality knows that truth reveals itself only in leaps (*Sprünge*) made by the history of the spirit, as a perpetual mystery which is ever slipping through our fingers. It recognizes that the way men come to truth cannot be fathomed and that this incomprehensibility accounts for what still remains unfathomed within all revelation. Since orthodoxy and liberality use the word *revelation* to designate an absolute, static act of God, on the one hand, and the continuous, multiform revelation of truth, on the other, the use of the word must not becloud the 'radical' (KJRB, p. 42) difference in meaning.

Orthodoxy reproaches liberal faith with making man the judge of what God can and should do. In liberality (which the orthodox identify with unbelief) man speaks instead of letting God speak. The major issue therefore is this: has man with his intellect the last word on all that is, can be, and should be, or must he listen to what God says about the matter? Orthodoxy claims to be alone in professing faith in revelation—the 'preaching of him who was crucified and rose again'— and declares this profession to be a matter of eternal life and eternal death. Liberality answers the reproach in several ways:

(a) *How can revelation be identified?*—Orthodoxy asserts that there exists no criterion whereby revelation can be recognized; that it is *index sui*. To this we must reply that there is no direct revelation. Revelation always appears in earthly form and language, in the ideas and the acts of men. Liberality holds that anything is possible which God could do as absolute transcendence, but it sees nothing more than a human act, a human word, a human experience.

(b) *The hiddenness of God and what it means*—What matters first and foremost is God's hiddenness. Since Adam delved and Eve span, everything on earth that has tried to establish itself as God's absolute, universal deed and word has only been the word and deed of man decked out as God's. The truth is that God never reveals himself once and for all and for everybody. Kant judiciously recognized that God is eternal wisdom because he remains eternally hidden. If he appeared anywhere in his majesty we would be puppets, only moving on our strings. He has willed that we should use our freedom in order to find the road which leads to him. Our responsible reason notices hints and vague signs in the world, so that we may reach him by leading an authentic moral life.

Liberality refuses to give up this searching in exchange for a revealed doctrine that has been laid down for all time. It listens to the voice of God in *all* reality. If God is an eternal imperative to us, that is precisely because he only reveals himself by not revealing himself. Liberality will have none of absolute obedience to a holy scripture or to the authority of some ecclesiastical office, because it believes that every individual can make direct contact with God, thanks to human freedom and responsible human reason. What has been reverently received from tradition may be criticized and changed at any time. We have seen that myth argues against myth: therefore there exists no complete, direct, unique revelation of God. Because God is inexhaustible, unfathomable and hidden, he speaks in myths which complement each other or cancel each other out.

(c) *The meaning of objectivity in the whole*—When the orthodox accuse liberals of failing to recognize God's objective deeds and setting up the subject as final judge, they are on the wrong track altogether. They do not realize that there can be no object without a subject and no subject without an object. Light is shed upon the whole in which we exist and which we are, not by any divorce between subject and object but by the interaction of the two; not by the subject alone and not by the object alone. There is no *Dasein* without an *Umwelt*; no general awareness without any object; no existence without transcendence. Without our subjectivity transcendence, God, the whole of wholes, will never be elucidated.

We never know transcendence in itself but only as an object—that is, as connected with a subject. In other words, it presents itself to us only in the language of symbols; it has no reality except its reality for human life; it never exists apart from human life. God's deeds and words are symbols; they are the reality of transcendence for a subject which is possible existence. To affirm this is not in the least to control God; it is simply to acknowledge how objectivity figures in the structure of all that presents itself to us as being.

When my mind explores the whole, I grasp insofar as I am grasped; I think that which reveals itself to me as the other. I conceive of that other as independent of me, as existing even without me. I merely take note of the subjective conditions which are necessary in order for the various objective things to have their meaning. Thus empirical reality (*Realität*) reveals itself to me only insofar as I am a *Dasein*; the object of necessary and universal knowledge reveals itself to me only insofar as I am a general consciousness, and transcendence insofar as I am possible existence. Without its corresponding subject, the objective thing would never put in an appearance. The subject does not give rise to the object but is prerequisite for the appearance of the object, just as the object is prerequisite for constituting the subject.

Accordingly when orthodoxy represents God's revelation as an event which has happened in the world, it is muddling matters. It pictures a connection between this subject and object—that is, between existence and transcendence—like the connection there is between knowledge and its object; so that transcendence no longer speaks the vague language of symbols but reveals itself as the object of science does. This objective, clear-cut transcendence is not the real transcendence: it is only the transcendence set up by the Bible and the Church—only the assertion of men who as the witnesses and spokesmen of God demand from everyone an obedience they are pleased to call faith. Thus God's immediate and exclusive authority is put to work for an authority of this world, of mere men.

Is there then any revelation that can be considered a *Realität*, that is first perceived and then believed in? Must we not say, rather, that belief in revelation is the same thing as the revelation which calls it forth? Is not subject tied to object and object to subject in the case of revelation just as in every other case? And then must one not call revelation what always happens when a man believes, when he has faith in God? Then does this revelation not exist wherever it is affirmed, in the West (in Judaism, Christianity and Islam) and in Asia (in the Vedas and the sacred books of the Chinese)? Has any revelation a leg to stand on when it claims to be unique? Must we not widen the idea of revelation to the point of saying that every man has, in his freedom, the opportunity to experience himself as created and governed by transcendence, despite the vagueness which marks all signs in this world?

(d) *The historicity of what faith declares in the language of myth*— Liberality draws sustenance from the historical nature of its origins. We Westerners, for example, draw sustenance from the historicity of the Bible. But liberals will not openly profess their exclusiveness, setting it down in propositions as a truth valid for all men. They recognize that 'it is possible to draw near to God even without Christ, that Asians can find God even without the Bible' (KJRB, p. 46). They know how much historicity matters, know that faith cannot abstract from its origin or from the language which that origin has created.

We are in no way undermining faith when we discard the absolute, universal validity of its historical objectifications—that is, when we strip faith of any objective guarantee (*objektive Garantie*) in this world. Thanks to transcendental philosophy which, since Kant, has shown that being is not an object, we can avoid both infidelity and orthodoxy.

All tradition is a possible language of transcendence, not in general but in those historical situations which allow existence to find itself.

(e) *What follows from the mythical (symbolic) character of all revelation*— Since liberality does not admit an objective saving event (*ein objektives Heilsgeschehen*) which is anything absolute and necessary to all men for salvation, it considers the saving event a myth like any other myth. 'As such, it must be tested for the seriousness of an existentiell reality, by the power which radiates from its language and the truth which radiates from itself into real life' (KJRB, p. 47). Liberality accepts belief in a revelation, even in the saving event we were just finding fault with; but only belief in them as *possible* truth, which is valid solely for a man who believes in it and on condition that his words and actions do not destroy the freedom of those who stand in the immediate presence of God, on condition that he makes no attempt to coerce them.

(f) *The passionate conflict between liberality and orthodoxy*—Because of all that is at stake, the conflict between the claims of orthodoxy and the reactions of liberality has always been passionate in the extreme. For nearly two thousand years orthodoxy has censured our pride, accused us of deifying ourselves, consigned us to eternal damnation. But do we live a godless life? Are we deluded in trusting that God helps us in some (to us) incomprehensible, unforeseeable, incalculable way (*auf eine uns unbegreifliche und unvoraussehbare und unberechenbare Weise*),[14] insofar as we are men of goodwill? Doubtless Bultmann thinks so, since he says that in Christian eyes the idea of God without Christ is a delusion. But did God not side with Job against the orthodox theologians?

(4) *Is Bultmann liberal*[15] *or orthodox?*

Bultmann's position appears to be 'the quaintest mixture of sham *Aufklärung* and wild orthodoxy' (KJRB, p. 54). He is not really orthodox, because with his demythologization he throws articles of faith overboard by the handful, sparing only the essential thing: the event of Christ. And by rejecting all that does not fit in with his conception of modern science and scientific philosophy, he offends the orthodox. But he also gives umbrage to the liberals, precisely by upholding 'an inflexibly orthodox view of the event of salvation' (KJRB, p. 49). He fiercely defends justification by faith in a saving event—the Lutheran doctrine with the appalling implications absolutely alien to philosophic

---

14. That is, by way of signs; not as happens in orthodox revelation, which is an objective event 'both guaranteed and a guarantee'.

15. Need one explain that Jaspers does not ask if Bultmann is a 'liberal Protestant' but rather if he is a liberal such as I, Jaspers, mean and such as I am?

faith. In this respect Bultmann is orthodox to the backbone (*ganz und gar*). He is right, no doubt, in trying to shed philosophic light on faith, but forgets that the enemy must be beaten with their own weapons; instead of which he fights the *Aufklärung* in the old-fashioned way: he accepts it to the uttermost so as to turn round and assert orthodoxy with that much more force. How could he do otherwise when his philosophy is a false philosophy, of the scientific (existential) brand, which he suddenly drops halfway along the road in deference to the absurdest kind of faith. When all is said and done, with Bultmann a philosophy which explains *Dasein* as sheer despair (that is how *Sein und Zeit* can be read) seeks completion in deliverance by faith in a saving event. Rank sinner that I am, knowing myself for such by grace alone, I am offered this grace by an event which will save me if I believe in it.

The reply to be given is that the aforesaid analysis of *Dasein* is only a particular truth, in which many may recognize themselves but certainly not everyone will. Man as such is by no means made of a sin which can only be done away with by an event occurring at a given place and time. The religion of the Bible tells us quite a different story: that man is a *nobilitas ingenita* (to borrow the Pelagian phrase) and that he is humble because he knows he has not created himself and knows that he must be given to himself in order not to be damned. He knows he is in God's hands, but in virtue of the *direct* contact his personal freedom has with the deity and not thanks to any adventitious help given this freedom, which is the source (*Ursprung*) of all that he can be. He thinks he can do the will of the hidden God by an effort which is entirely his own responsibility. He believes that God helps him in a way which is incomprehensible, unforeseeable and incalculable.[16] This *nobilitas ingenita*, granted by God, the Bible calls 'Christ in me'. It is not a permanent possession, it is not given once for all, it must be conquered again and again. Such is liberality's view of man, his freedom and his task.

III

What foundation is there to the criticisms of Bultmann which Jaspers makes? Let us examine the matter, following the divisions of the foregoing section.

(1) *Scientific ontology and philosophic ontology*

The best thing to do here is to start with the comparison we have made

16. God's help does not, as orthodoxy imagines, take the form of an objective guarantee constituted by the saving event.

between Jaspers and Heidegger and the totally different ways in which they reject classical ontology, the one replacing it with philosophic faith and the other with the philosophy of being (see pp. 347–48, above). We have seen how Jaspers quarrels even with Heidegger's theory of existentials; how he accuses Bultmann of isolating this theory, which in *Sein und Zeit* was still linked with existence, and reproaches him with interpreting the Bible by means of scientific and philosophic ontology.

In complaining that Bultmann applies the Heideggerian existential to scripture, Jaspers grossly misjudges the nature of the existential to boot, identifying it outright with the ontology of modern science and *Professorenphilosophie*. Now we know that the basic theme of Bultmann's thought is precisely a *refusal* to use classical ontology and the categories of science for interpreting the Bible. In his reply to Jaspers he takes up this crucial idea once again. As to the charge that he is dazzled by the glamour of modern science, he succinctly recalls what we have already shown: that scientific *Begrifflichkeit*, whether in objective history or in the world-picture with which modern science presents us, is altogether unsuitable for understanding revelation (see pp. 69–80, and 312–13, above). As to the use he is supposed to have made of a philosophy existential in character (which for Jaspers means scientific), we have seen that he dismisses classical ontology as curtly as his critic does, for that ontology, whether in realist or in idealist form, represents the philosophy of natural man. The only business of theology (but a business of great weight) is to bring out in all its starkness the question 'that God asks man and that is a scandal to "natural man", because it demands the sacrifice of all the security one has sought' (KJRB, p. 61). As we know, Bultmann holds that classical ontology is nothing else than an effort on man's part to establish his security. That is why he judges it unfit to express revelation. Thus Jaspers' fundamental criticism of him, for having stuck at the stage of general consciousness, betrays a complete misunderstanding of Bultmann's thought.

The case is no otherwise when Jaspers makes his complaints in a slightly different way, accusing his adversary of divorcing subject from object and mistaking the true nature of appropriation (see pp. 351–2, above), for it is classical ontology which envisages the subject as an in-sistence. In Bultmann, man belongs to another realm of being, to *Verstehen*, to ec-sistence; for which reason he is essentially decision and 'appropriation'. Naturally enough, therefore, Bultmann chides his critic for failing to understand that the whole point of his work is precisely overcoming the old antinomy between subject and object (KJRB, p. 67). And he complains in general of Jaspers' *ex cathedra* pronouncements, the lack of any 'real communication' with him (KJRB, p. 59).

In a sense, however, one can understand Jaspers' error. Despite his desire to explain being to the utmost, the choice for him lies ultimately between ontology and the ineffable; whereas for Bultmann it lies between an objectifying ontology and an existential ontology. Far from repudiating all ontology, Bultmann proclaims the need for a *new* ontology. What that one is we have seen throughout this book, particularly in the preceding chapter: it is not a philosophy but the *Begrifflichkeit* appropriate to God's Word; it is revelation's sense of being. Here, then, we have the true nature of existentiality; and we cannot do without existentiality, as Bultmann stresses in his reply to Jaspers on the subject of myth.

(2) *Myth and ontology*

First of all it is well for us to note the sound elements in Jaspers' conception of myth. In particular he has partly revealed its true *Begrifflichkeit* by distinguishing between *Realität* and *Wirklichkeit* and, accordingly, denying that there is any *Realität* to the apparition on Sinai or the resurrection of Jesus. Like Jaspers, says Bultmann, I think 'that myth is misunderstood when the *Wirklichkeit* it speaks of is taken to be an "*empirische Realität*" and its language the language of a "bodiliness that is guaranteed and guarantees" ' (KJRB, p. 63, note 1). At the same time this objectification of myth is not, as Jaspers thinks, an adventitious phenomenon but part of its nature. Mythical thought is essentially ambiguous, and Christian revelation (if not scripture) steers clear of all objectification precisely because it is not a myth but the pure Word of God. But Jaspers above all has failed to see that it is not enough to declare myth a symbol of transcendence. We must go on to explore its structure, its ontology, its sense of being; otherwise the symbol becomes a magic word.

Myth can be defined as a symbol in the case of all mythologies (excepting aetiological myths). All alike speak of a *Wirklichkeit* that lies beyond empirical *Realität*, and of man's dealings with it. But are this *Wirklichkeit* and the idea of God, man and the world which it implies, interpreted everywhere in the same way—for example in Greek, Hindu and biblical mythology? In principle, to be sure, Jaspers sees 'spiritual combat' (p. 355, above) as a point of difference. But he seems to hold that such combat in the Bible, in Greek epic poems and tragedy, and in the sacred books of Asia, leads to the same transcendence.

Just as the concept of philosophy takes in very diverse things (in Jaspers and in Heidegger, say), so too does the concept of myth. Each myth has its own sense of being, each a set *Verständnis*, which fact Jaspers neglects to bring out because he locks himself up in the existentiell and refuses to conduct any ontological investigation. He states that to appropriate myth is to transform it by giving it an up-to-date, cogent meaning and speaks of the stable element in mythical truth which endures through all the transformations (KJRB, p. 34). What might this change and this stable element be? How would Jaspers interpret Rom 5:12–21 or 6:1–11? When he says that the event of salvation is a myth which 'must be tested for the seriousness of an existentiell reality, by the power which radiates from its language and the truth which radiates from itself into real life' (p. 360, above), one must ask: how shall that be done?

Again, he claims that appropriating the Bible is a business for the *Seelsorger*, who makes the mythical world present by the original spurting forth of appropriation (p. 355, above), who 'hazards hearing and speaking the language of transcendence as the language of God in the very *Wirklichkeit* of the community's life' (KJRB, p. 35). But, one must ask him, can the *Seelsorger* do without science? Must he not know Hebrew and Greek in order to understand the language of the Bible as God's language; or if he cannot read them, defer to the learned men who can? The *Seelsorger* cannot do without 'exact' knowledge.

Jaspers is right, of course, to emphasize that 'exact' knowledge or 'understanding of the understood' must be rooted in an 'original understanding', and Bultmann declares (KJRB, p. 65) that he has never said anything else. But, conversely, can I arrive at original understanding of a text, can I make value-judgments about it, accept or reject it existentielly, before I have understood it 'exactly'? Original understanding cannot dispense with scientific understanding, the existentiell cannot dispense with the existential. The interpreter of a text must try to gain a precise understanding of its content and present that to the reader. In no event may the interpreter decide anything in the reader's place, dissuade the reader from the yes or no which the text, exactly understood, demands of him. What applies to all interpretation applies to biblical interpretation. The interpreter of the Bible (be he scholar or *Seelsorger*) must indeed be in vital contact with it, but in order to grasp its 'precise' meaning and pass that on to the hearer, who alone can judge what response shall be given. All the interpreter does is faithfully convey the message, thus confronting the hearer with his responsibility.

Ontology, then, cannot be dispensed with. Jaspers himself, as we have seen, sets out to 'elucidate' existence. His philosophy is an *Existenzerhellung*. No doubt this elucidation differs from the Heideggerian analysis of *Dasein*, in that it occurs only in existence itself and cannot be divorced from 'existentiell communication'. But the fact remains that Jaspers cannot explain the major idea of his philosophy, *Existenzerhellung*, without making it universally intelligible—that is, without objectifying it as a doctrine. If he replies that objectification is done away with in authentic (existentiell) *Verstehen*, we must say that the same is true of the Heideggerian analysis. A man convinced that it holds good as a 'doctrine' is not excused from existentiell hazard, for this 'doctrine' shows him precisely that he is ec-sistence, responsibility, freedom; and therefore it can be fully equated with Jaspers' exhortation to man to 'be himself, to be straightforward, to be authentic, to . . . take seriously the problem of a hopeless situation' (KJRB, p. 12).

(3) *Revelation and ontology*

As we have seen, Jaspers repudiates the orthodox idea of revelation because it is the prisoner of objective ontology (and we know that to his mind no other ontology can be devised, since he identifies existential ontology with classical ontology). To the extent that he dismisses an objectifying idea of revelation, Bultmann falls in with him. As to Jaspers' statement, already quoted—'A faith which affirms that God has attached himself to one place and one age, once for all or by a series of acts, that there and there alone he has directly revealed himself, is a faith which ties God down to an object in the world'—Bultmann says: 'Quite so!' (KJRB, p. 38). It is unfortunately true, he goes on, that revelation has often been and often still is envisaged this way in the Christian churches. But how can Jaspers fail to perceive that this ever recrudescent objectifying idea has nevertheless always been exploded? Does he not realize that 'I fight precisely the tying down of God to an objective reality, the contempt which turns revelation into revealed data? Does he not see that the aim of my "demythologization" is to interpret the mythological eschatology of the New Testament in such a way that the event of revelation stands forth as the "eschatological" event in the authentic sense of the word?' (KJRB, pp. 68–9).

The incarnation of God's Word is not a *Mirakel* which took place about one thousand nine hundred and fifty years ago, but an eschatological event which began in the historical person of Jesus and continues ever-present in the preaching of the Church. Revelation is neither a system of dogma nor a system of ethics; liberal theology has every right to denounce its hardening into one form for good. Revelation is true only insofar as it is *event*. Again, liberal theology is quite right in denying that an objectifiable event in the remote past can avail to save all men. But we know that the 'objectivity' of the saving event is seated in its eschatological character. It will not do simply to say, with Jaspers, that we are in no way undermining faith when we discard the absolute, universal validity of its historical objectifications—that is, when we strip faith of any objective guarantee in this world (p. 359, above). We must go a step farther and say that only then does faith acquire its meaning and strength, because only then is it an *Entscheidung* (KJRB, pp. 70–71). This is the doctrine of justification by faith without works, which Jaspers so unfairly attacks. He has not realized that it is the noblest way in which one can repudiate the objectification of faith in one hard-and-fast form.

'Works' are the hallmark of natural man. If revelation is the rejection of that man, it must also be the rejection of works. The doctrine of justification by faith declares that revelation is the presence of the Wholly Other and therefore the death of all objectification; that revelation is not an idea of God (however sound) but God's *Anrede*, in which he reveals himself as *my* God speaking to *me*—that is, as the one who controls my life. Christ is not an historical phenomenon of the past but the ever-present Word of God, who annihilates man and by annihilating him brings him alive.

Although his dismissal of all objectification shows that he has a keen sense of transcendence, the fact remains that Jaspers stops halfway along his road. Witness his stubborn refusal to admit the absolute character of Christian revelation. We have seen how he puts the various symbols of transcendence all on the same plane, finding it alike in the Vedas, the sacred books of the Chinese, the Koran, and so forth. He declares that the way to God can be found without the Bible and without Christ, and takes Bultmann harshly to task for his orthodoxy on this vital point. How can he have failed to see that if there is a revelation of God it must be unique and absolute, and that that is the sense of its being? Does he not perceive that faith in any such revelation must necessarily claim to be absolute, because it considers itself the response to the 'I am the Lord your God, you shall have no other gods before me'? Of course, Bultmann goes on, 'a man is free to think faith in a revelation an absurdity. But if he does, then let us have no talk of revelation from him' (KJRB, p. 69). Jaspers asks: 'By what criterion are we to recognize the direct revelation of God?' (KJRB, p. 42; p. 357, above). He does not realize that revelation is necessarily *index sui*. One cannot satisfy oneself as to its truth until one has accepted it as true. Of its nature, it rules out all criteria. God need not justify himself to man. Those whom he summons cannot help affirming the absolute character of his Word; to act otherwise would be to deny the Word.

If Jaspers bungles the real ontology of revelation, it is because he bungles the real ontology of transcendence. He declares that the whole

prevents the subject from objectifying himself into a general consciousness and the object into an abstraction: in the bosom of the whole, the
objectivity of what is said and the subjectivity of him who says it
merge to form a single thing (see p. 352, above). But Bultmann disputes
the theory of the whole, which he says blocks one off from the
authentic idea of otherness and therefore from the authentic idea of
encounter.

Otherness and encounter exist only where there is an *Anrede*. 'To
push behind this latter by reflecting about the "whole" seems to me
not only shallow speculation but a failure to take summons and
encounter seriously. The notions of summons and encounter play no
part in Jaspers' thinking' (KJRB, p. 67). In other words, Jaspers has not
properly grasped the 'historicity' of the human being; he has not really
broken away from the category of the 'same'. So far as I can judge
from his text, Bultmann goes on, what he means by historicity is the
bare fact that man always finds himself at a certain point in time, that
he lives in accidental historical circumstances and is influenced by a
tradition (KJRB, pp. 68–9; p. 344, above).

The lame notion which Jaspers has of summons, encounter and
historicity prevents his arriving at an accurate *Begrifflichkeit* of transcendence. Does not the 'whole', or the 'whole of the wholes', remind
one of Schleiermacher's *Universum*, which Jaspers favours with an acid
remark in passing (KJRB, p. 32) but comes closer to than he imagines?
And does it not smack of Kant? Does he not believe in the possibility
(to use his own words) of 'a direct contact with God in personal,
responsible freedom through reason [which is present] in every man'?
(KJRB, p. 43; p. 357, above). Does he not also say that if man knows he
is in God's hands, that is 'only in virtue of the direct contact his personal
freedom has with the deity'? (KJRB, p. 50; p. 361, above). But then are
we not up to the eyes in immanence and is the 'transcendence' so dear
to Jaspers ultimately 'anything but what used to be called "spirit"'?
No doubt that spirit transcends bodiliness, but it remains immanent in
human reason. Is such "transcendence" the transcendence of God? If,
as Jaspers says, "the mystery of the revelation of truth" is unveiled "in
the leaps of the history of spirit" [p. 357, above], it would seem that
transcendence is likewise immanent in history' (KJRB, p. 68).[17]

17. As P. Ricoeur, for his part, has keenly observed, 'the secret difference between
religious faith and philosophic faith is that philosophic faith does not show the
world for what it is. In vain Jaspers keeps to Kierkegaardian language . . . I would
not hesitate to say that he has tried to work out a Kierkegaardian equivalent—all
subjective anguish and horror—of Spinoza's third type of knowledge, which
knows nothing beyond what the second type does but grasps all things, and itself,
in God' (P. Ricoeur, 'Philosophie et religion chez K. Jaspers' in *Revue d'histoire et
de philosophie religieuses* 37 [1957] p. 218). In other words the eminently Lutheran

IV

Jaspers replied to the foregoing in a long open letter (KJRB, pp. 77–117) dated April 1954 and written this time in a real spirit of communication. Bultmann acknowledged it very briefly, taking note of the readiness to dialogue, but put off detailed explanations to some later date. So far these have not been given[18] and therefore we can only conjecture what they may be.

(1) Jaspers' letter is first and foremost a reiterated and obstinate rejection of Christian transcendence. We know that he admits no transcendence beyond the world; to be more precise, beyond my freedom: my freedom is indispensable if transcendence is to be manifested—without freedom there can be no transcendence. On the other hand Jaspers exalts freedom as no one else does. I am the one who chooses and thereby determines his own being. What is more, I am fully myself in proportion to the vigour of my freedom: 'The more there is of will, the more there is of self', says Jaspers following Kierkegaard. I am answerable for myself, I make myself, I am the primal gushing forth of myself. In a word, what I am, I am *aus mir*. Nevertheless I am not what I am *durch mich*: I am given to myself by transcendence. 'Where I was authentically myself in my willing, I was simultaneously given to myself in freedom' (PH 2, p. 199). 'I am answerable for myself because it is I who will myself; in this way I am assured of being primal (*ursprünglich*) by being myself. Yet I am only given to myself, because in order to will myself I need help' (PH 2, p. 45).

How can experience of the gift of freedom (experience of the *durch*) be reconciled with experience of freedom's total responsibility (experience of the *aus*)? Jaspers never deals directly with this central problem because, as we have said, he does not concern himself with the theological subject of the connection between freedom and grace but with the philosophical subject of the world's metaphysical dimension. The question 'How does freedom fit in with transcendence?' abandons the field to this other question: 'How does transcendence manifest itself in immanence?'

---

or Augustinian problem of justification and freedom is overshadowed by the metaphysical problem of the world's absolute reality as a symbol—that is, as a manifestation of transcendence. 'Thus instead of offering a different solution to the same problem—the problem of reconciling freedom and God's omnipotence —Jaspers' religious philosophy really raises a new problem: the problem of reality's metaphysical dimension' (*ibid.*, p. 216).

18. As Bultmann confirms in a letter of 28 September 1960.

Jaspers is wrapped up in this properly philosophical question when he approaches Christianity, and therefore Bultmann criticizes his idea of transcendence, as we have seen. In his reply, Jaspers once more defends his thesis. First of all he rejoices at Bultmann's quoting him to the effect that man is given to himself by transcendence, and adds that he is indebted to Paul and Augustine for a clear understanding of what he experienced in himself even as a philosopher: 'helplessness in freedom' (KJRB, p. 78), or again 'the utter dependence of freedom on transcendence' (*ibid.*). Only an awareness that he is grounded in transcendence sets man free in the world.

Here the difference between Jaspers and Bultmann becomes evident. In Bultmann's eyes God's transcendence is correlative to man's sin. God's greatness shines forth in the forgiveness of sin. Such an abyss yawns between man and God that only forgiveness can fill it up. Man's helplessness takes the shape of guilt and God's omnipotence that of grace. Jaspers briskly dismisses these ideas; here, he repeats to Bultmann, 'I do not go along with you' (KJRB, p. 79). He takes up the theme, already familiar to us, of man as a *nobilitas ingenita* and adds in highly characteristic fashion that the only forgiveness he, Jaspers, knows of is forgiveness on the part of a man whom he has offended (KJRB, p. 80). But how can man offend transcendence? After all he is the symbol of transcendence, the *locus* where transcendence manifests itself. And therefore any notion of sin or forgiveness is so much rubbish in this context. Here we are struck full force with the consequence of Jaspers' slipping from the theological plane (that of Kierkegaard and Bultmann) to the philosophical, to concern with the absolute reality of the world as the manifestation of transcendence. We find ourselves a stone's-throw from Spinoza.

(2) Jaspers resumes his criticism of Christian revelation, denying its absolute newness, which Bultmann had stoutly affirmed in his reply. Here the thread of the philosopher's argument is his conviction that the ideas of absoluteness and objectivity are Siamese twins: whatever is absolute must be objective. As we know, Bultmann chided him for ignoring the whole point of his own work, which is an attempt to disobjectify Christianity. But how, Jaspers counters, can you talk of disobjectifying Christian revelation when you maintain that it is something absolute, when you assert the fact—in as 'disobjectified' and eschatological a form as you please—that God speaks to us only in Jesus Christ? Even if you say that revelation is not a *Mirakel* which took place twenty centuries ago but an eschatological event which only began with the New Testament and still remains present in the preaching of the Church, even if you claim that this event cannot be objectified in a dogmatic and ethical content, and so forth, but consists

in an *Anrede* of God that is every moment new—in short, if you make revelation a *Dass* instead of a *Was*—the fact does not alter that you are asserting a unique and absolute intervention on the part of God, which every human being is compelled to pass through in order to reach God. By so doing, whether you like it or not you objectify transcendence; by affirming that God's revelation stands or falls with Christ you make it 'a cast-iron objectivity' (KJRB, p. 81). You fail to see that man actually enjoys direct contact with God through his reason and through his freedom.

This view alone will fit in with Protestant thought, according to which there is no need of any mediator between God and man. By admitting only one 'symbol' of transcendence (Christ as God's Word ever present in the Church) you turn both symbol and transcendence into an object. If God reveals himself to Christians through Christ, Jaspers goes on, I have no objection to offer. But what of those who are not granted the grace to believe in Christ? Shall they be compelled to find God through this mediation which for them is altogether exterior? In that case we fall back into the objectification which Bultmann tried to avoid by his demythologizing, for the deity can only disclose himself in freedom. If Christ does not speak to all lives, he cannot be the revelation of transcendence to them all. To assert that only one road leads to God is to deny the historicity proper to each man (KJRB, p. 84). It is also to ignore the perpetual hiddenness of the deity, who never fully manifests himself in a given symbol. I may find God in Christ, but I cannot and must not conclude that therefore all men can find him only there. I am never entitled to speak or act in the name of *my* truth, to claim that God is against my enemy, though that enemy were the devil in person. God is always quite as much the God of my adversary. He infinitely overflows all particular revelations, all the motley and gainsaying of symbols (whether churches, nations or parties).

Moreover, Jaspers says in conclusion, the faith in God which the historical Jesus had (by which he means the Jesus of the synoptics, not the Johannine Jesus) was a philosophic faith and not that theological faith which claims to lay hold on total, absolute truth, to soar above all points of view, to be valid for everyone. When all is said and done, the historical Jesus was the exemplar of philosophic faith (KJRB, p. 86). Thus it is clear that when Jaspers finds fault with the claim of Christian revelation to absolute validity, not only Bultmann's theology is queried but Christianity itself. And Christianity can only give the answer which we shall presently give.

(3) Jaspers turns once more to the problem of myth (KJRB, pp. 88–94), saying at the utmost what he had already said in his lecture on

Bultmann. His conception of myth is wholly shaped by his theory of symbols, by his solicitude (more philosophic than religious) to discover the absolute dimension of reality. He will have none of demythologization because he holds that transcendence cannot exist without the world. He does not admit the *Jenseits der Welt*, whereas Bultmann, the Lutheran theologian, holds that God is essentially the *Jenseits der Welt*. In view of the necessary connection between the other world and this world, it is understandable that Jaspers should retain myth as the image, idea, figure, sign and symbol of transcendence. He does indeed reject the view which makes myth a *Realität*; but inasmuch as he rejects the Christian idea of creation, in its deepest meaning, God for him cannot exist without the *Wirklichkeit* of myth—in other words, without the myth which symbolizes him. Orthodox theologians who have sided with him against Bultmann would have done well to observe that his position on myth is wholly dictated by his philosophic faith—a faith that is immanentist when compared with Christianity.

At this point let us not be led astray by Jaspers' agnosticism. As has been remarked, he repudiates all ontology, including ec-sistential ontology, and maintains that transcendence is ineffable. Nonetheless he declares that in order for transcendence to exist, its symbol must exist. Bultmann, on the other hand, as we have seen, while affirming that true transcendence exists only where a *Jenseits der Welt* exists, thinks that this radical otherness does not lead to the absolutely unutterable. The *Dass* is also a *Was*, an 'essence'; it has an ontology of which man's *lumen naturale* gives him a *Vorverständnis*. God is not the unknowable and faith is not a lamentation. In his letter Jaspers deals again with the ineffability of transcendence, repeating that I can appropriate one myth and set aside another only through a struggle in my vitals.

Once again he faults Bultmann's concern for 'exactitude'. You ask me 'how is that done?', he says, which comes down to demanding a recipe. Would you question me the same way about a hymn to love? Do you not seem to think one can give a scientific seminar on myth? You also question me about what remains constant through the transformations of myth. I can give you no formal answer. What remains is the transcendent in the mythic symbol (KJRB, p. 92).

Plainly Jaspers rejects any difference between myths based on a difference in their nature or content; the criterion of choice is purely existentiell. With Bultmann it is both existentiell and existential: for example, there is no confusing the deity manifested in the sacred books of China with the deity who reveals himself in the Bible.

(4) Continuing his letter, Jaspers turns back to this very problem of the connection between the existentiell and the existential. Once more he denies that the existential approach can shed any light on the

existentiell (Let us remember, here, that he confuses existential ontology with scientific ontology, thus misunderstanding the thought of Bultmann, who contrasts them with each other.); that, only the transcendental approach can do. Nevertheless he admits that one can arrive at a 'valid universal knowledge', at a 'doctrine', at an 'agreement' as to the 'basic forms of being' which we are (KJRB, p. 98)—and on this head comes far closer to Bultmann than he realizes, by now taking existential ontology to mean what Bultmann thinks it means. Jaspers explains what these forms are by statements like the following: 'Our whole *Dasein* is a matter of understanding *Dasein*'; 'understanding is the mode in which the being that we are becomes present'; 'only what we find in our consciousness exists so far as we are concerned', and so forth. But he holds that *Existenz* can never be a knowledge that ought to be recognized as 'accurate' by every man who understands it. It does not belong to the sphere of 'accurate' knowledge; it gives existential analysis the slip. Beyond subject and object, which can give rise to an intellectual knowledge, there stands the whole, or transcendence, which only the existentiell can shed light on.

Jaspers cannot resist casting back to this idea of the whole. Bultmann's judgment of it has touched him on the raw. I do not think it is possible, he retorts, to affirm transcendence more roundly than I have done. All the same he concedes: I shall not gainsay you when you accuse me of not realizing what a serious business summons and encounter are, and therefore not perceiving the personal nature of the deity (*Persönlichkeit der Gottheit*). It is true that I have no acquaintance with the *Thou* of the deity, that I am familiar with summons and encounter only as they exist among men. I do not deny that transcendence may be experienced as a *Thou*; but I see the danger in the experience, which is that it may mean fleeing from the world (KJRB, p. 100). Once more we have that concern, more metaphysical than religious, which goads Jaspers to dismiss any transcendence defined as a *Jenseits der Welt*.

(5) As we have observed, Bultmann takes him to task for entertaining a milk-and-water idea of historicity. A being is historical, in Bultmann's eyes, if its existence can be determined by the other—which presupposes that the other is other to the core. Only a sheer otherness can make me become what I am not. Hence his fondness for dwelling on the categories of *Anrede* and encounter, which convey the other in its utter transcendence; hence the wariness with which he eyes the notion of the whole: it waters down the otherness and therefore the historicity of the *I*, which the *Thou* only half-determines because both are fused into the whole.

Jaspers, for his own part, thinks that to reject the whole—in other words, to believe that God reveals himself exclusively and for all men in Jesus Christ—is to deny historicity. As we know, he holds that the idea of revelation which orthodox theologians have objectifies transcendence. He says so once again here. Of course you own, he says to Bultmann, that revelation has no doctrinal content; but you declare it to be unique, absolute, valid for all men. By so doing you objectify it, for obviously many human beings cannot appropriate revelation by a free act in which it seems to them to be the symbol of transcendence. In cutting down the field of decision to the proportions of New Testament *Anrede* 'you wrongly identify historicity with something hard and fast which claims absolutely universal validity for an objective historical phenomenon' (KJRB, p. 101). You forget that people who do not believe in the New Testament may perfectly well be determined in their existence by God, thanks to countless other symbols of transcendence.

What will Bultmann the theologian reply to this die-hard criticism (which must not be made light of) from Jaspers the philosopher? No doubt simply this: that contrary to what Jaspers thinks (KJRB, p. 100), God offers the freedom of all men without exception the grace of believing in his revelation in Jesus Christ. The Word of God is an *Anrede* addressed to all mankind; it never ceases to be historical. Philosophic faith, we may be sure, will not make head or tail of this statement, but it constitutes precisely the scandal of Christian faith. There is no use asserting that I have not yet received God's call, because '*semper ita fit, ut opus nostrum intelligamus, antequam fiat, Dei autem opus non intelligimus, donec factum fuerit*' (Luther).

(6) Jaspers devotes two paragraphs of his letter to the *Seelsorger* and the theme of science and philosophy, without saying anything new. Let us note only that he declares himself incompetent, in a word, to answer Bultmann's question ('How would you interpret Rom 5:12–21 or 6:1–11?') and merely says that having done his best to make out Paul's purpose he would leave it aside and speak of these texts in such a way that 'a content of present-day faith should flow from them fit to be shared in communication' (KJRB, p. 104). Precisely because he knows that the thought of the biblical author is 'historically accurate', the *Seelsorger* is free to set it aside and 'recast the objectified faith [which the biblical texts contain] in a modern form which will be credible and therefore efficacious' (KJRB, p. 104). Thus we find Jaspers always interpreting scripture according to his theory of symbols.

In the same paragraph let us point out an absolutely wrong definition of existential analysis. With reference to Rom 5:12–21 and 6:1–11 he writes: I do not care to undertake any scientific existential analysis, any 'translation' (if I rightly understand your meaning) wholly shaped by my philosophic idea of man and the world (KJRB, p. 105). Now we know that Bultmann considers existential analysis to be the exact opposite: it consists in reading revelation with an appropriate *Begriff-lichkeit*--one, in other words, which clashes head-on with 'my philo-sophic idea of man and the world'.

(7) We have remarked that Bultmann had complained of his critic's obtuseness, *ex cathedra* pronouncmeents, and utter unreadiness for any exchange of views. At the end of the letter Jaspers goes to great lengths to explain his conduct in this matter and to apologize. Once more he admits the exasperation he feels, as a philosopher, at the absolute claims theologians put forward for Christian faith: this was the main reason for his onslaught (KJRB, pp. 112–13). He explains that he has no quarrel with Bultmann personally and recalls the contacts between them in the past, reaching as far back as the distant days when they were fellow-students at secondary school in Oldenburg. I dared not approach you then, he writes; 'I saw your eyes alight and rejoiced that you existed' (KJRB, p. 113).

Drawing to a close, he wonders what bearing his dialogue with Bultmann can have on the present state of the world—that is, on the struggle between freedom and every form of modern totalitarianism, whether it be Communism, Catholicism or technology. Inexorably the Catholic world waxes stronger. Its obvious kinship with political totalitarianism must stir up the free world to self-defence, today as in the past, against any supremacy for the Roman Church. Nevertheless if we did have to choose between Marxist totalitarianism and Catholic totalitarianism, the latter would be preferable by far because of the spiritual factors in it and because of the explosive energies which are always there in the Bible. If the Protestant form of biblical religion is to survive—not as Protestantism but as freedom—it cannot do so by aping Catholicism's liturgy, pomp, titles, hierarchy and centralized power. Nor can it do so by turning back to the 'Word', to the Lutheran or Calvinist outlook. That, Jaspers explains to Bultmann, is what my controversy with you was about. I see no hope, he goes on, except in liberality—that is, in a genuine Protestantism, 'which as such is able by tireless exertion to transform biblical religion in its every aspect' (KJRB, p. 116). My attack on you, he concludes, was unfair in that it obscures the bond between us two: our common battle with totalitarianism in all its forms. I wish I had brought out that bond more strikingly.

Bultmann's only reply to this very long letter was the following note:

'Thank you for your open letter. Today I can only tell you of my delight at the willingness to exchange views which I find in it. I must not enlarge at the moment. Nor must I decide at the moment whether to answer you directly or to comment on your views in some other context.

Yours,
Rudolf Bultmann'

As we have said, Bultmann has not yet elaborated this brief reply. Only one further allusion to Jaspers (though an important one) is to be found, in an article of 1958 (GV 3). Bultmann notices the philosopher's refusal to see God's revelation in an historical, temporal event, which would necessarily be an objectification of the divine. But that, Bultmann replies, is to adopt the standpoint of an observer and try to judge by one's own lights not only what sense of being is found in revelation at large but also what can or cannot be accepted in the concrete as divine revelation. That is to seek some criterion of God. One cannot give up all safety. And in reality one controls God thanks to a metaphysics which lays down beforehand where and when he may speak.

The charge Jaspers brings against Christian faith, therefore, must be fired back at him. 'What objectifies God's revelation is not identifying an historical event with an event that preaching ceaselessly makes present. For the historical event is not recalled as an event in the past; always it is present in the summons of preaching. What objectifies God's revelation, on the contrary, is claiming to be able to interpret human religions as symbols of "transcendence" ' (GV 3, p. 212).

CHAPTER EIGHTEEN

Bultmann and Barth

The contrast between Bultmann and Barth which we here outline stands entirely within the framework of Part Three of the present work, devoted to the links between theology and ontology. Keeping within this framework will best bring out the controversy between the two theologians.

I

Our first major text is a passage in *Die kirchliche Dogmatik* finding fault with the Modernist theology which holds that a potentiality of God exists within man. Barth ranges Bultmann with Schleiermacher because he admits there is a *Vorverständnis* of revelation, which Barth takes to be an 'ontological existentiell capacity' for faith. He thinks that Bultmann starts with a 'general ontology or anthropology' (TKD I, p. 35), with an '(existentiell) potentiality distinct from the actuality of revelation', with a ' "humanness-in-general" which the particular human being of faith [is] supposed to embody' (TKD I, p. 36). This ontological existentiell capacity, this existentiell potentiality, and this humanness-in-general are a 'prelusive notion of being in the Church' (TKD I, p. 34) and 'reduce faith to a mere piety' (TKD I, p. 36).

For his own part Barth declines 'to admit an ontological and existentiell human capacity for the Church's being', because that being is 'an *actus purus*, a deed of God's, an absolute beginning, intelligible only in itself and of itself, not a deed that anthropology can understand beforehand' (TKD I, p. 39). Faith is indeed a particular determination of man, but one that can issue 'only from something *outside* all human capacity—that is, from the doing of God' (TKD I, p. 37). It cannot 'explain its own history by means of some general potentiality or some general historicity of human life' (TKD I, p. 37). In short there is nothing pre-divine in man, as Barth also establishes in his extended controversy with Gogarten (TKD I, pp. 121–7).

The reader will already have picked out Barth's misunderstanding of Bultmann. In view of all we have been saying about the latter it must be obvious that he admits no 'existentiell capacity' for faith in man, only an existential capacity, by which he simply means that in order to receive revelation one must be a man and not a stone. There is no glimmer of the divine in man (ch. 1, above), no 'existentiell potentiality' for God's Word. When Barth talks of an 'ontological and existentiell capacity for the Church's being' he is confusing two completely different things. To admit an existentiell capacity in the sense he means would come down to modernism and liberalism, for it would amount to saying that man has a natural kinship with God—an idea Bultmann has always rejected quite as bluntly as Barth. But there must certainly be an *ontological* capacity for revelation, always provided we do not turn the word *existential* into a synonym of *existentiell*. To speak of man's existential, ontological capacity for revelation is to say that God can only address a freedom—one utterly fallen, no doubt, but a freedom all the same, not a thing or an animal.

When Barth said in his lecture of 1926, 'Sin has not so far destroyed the image of God in man as to leave God's kindness toward him objectless, as though man were no longer *man*, created and loved by God, something different from a stone or a stump',[1] he was saying nothing else than what Bultmann says (if people will but understand him aright). Again: 'If God's Word is not spoken to animals, plants and stones but to man and if determination by that Word is really the determination of human existence, what else could that mean but that in God's determination the self-determination whereby man is what he is meets something higher than itself and also, without being in any way adulterated, much less destroyed, is tidied up, set under judgment, and stamped with an unmistakable character' (TKD 1, p. 195). 'If the event of faith is the event of the Word's presence in man . . . this necessarily means that darkness *can* become light. Therefore man's power, insufficient of itself, *can* become the sufficient power of God' (TKD 1, p. 235). Finally: 'Once a believer, [man] cannot picture himself as the active subject of the business that is going on in him. And yet that business is his own experience and his own act, and in believing he does not behave at all like a block of wood or stone but instead like a man determining himself' (TKD 1, p. 37).

However Barth may dwell on God and the doings of God, he cannot deny and does not mean to deny that there exists within man what Bultmann calls an ontological capacity for understanding revelation—a capacity which a stone does not have. No doubt quoting Barth is always a hazardous enterprise, because of the dialectical nature of his thought. But put back into context the extracts we have adduced,

---

1. K. Barth, *Die Theologie und die Kirche*, p. 375.

in particular reread pages 181–239 of TKD 1, compare them with
KD 4, 1 (1953), pages 548ff and many a similar passage, and it will be
plain enough that their author in fact admits in man what he does not
care to call an ontological capacity but would gladly call so if he
understood the word 'ontological' in the sense Bultmann attaches to it.

II

We must now turn to a passage in KD 3, 2 (1948) which queries the
soundness of the existential interpretation. This interpretation Barth
always takes to be a humanist and subjective one. Commenting on the
major affirmations in the confession of faith he writes, against Bultmann: 'No doubt they all have a bearing on human existence. They
make possible, and undergird, the Christian view of it, thereby also
becoming—in a modified form—determinations of human existence.
But that is not what they are in the first place. In the first place they
determine the being and operation of God who is *different* from man
and *encounters* man—the being and actions of the Father, and the Son,
and the Holy Spirit. For this reason we must not reduce them to
propositions about the interior life of man' (KD 3, 2, p. 534).

Replying to his critic, Bultmann writes that 'that last sentence
betrays a total misunderstanding of the existential interpretation and
the sense of life which it conveys' (GV 2, pp. 233–4). For the ec-sistence
Bultmann talks of has nothing to do with the 'interior life' of man. On
the contrary, as we know, it is *outwardness*; it is determined by the
Anrede of a *Thou*; it can only be understood 'in abstraction from what
differs from it and encounters it (whether that be the world round
about, our neighbour or God)' (GV 2, p. 234). Ec-sistential analysis
studies that man who 'exists only in his live relations with what is
"different" from him, and in his encounters' (GV 2, p. 234). Barth
fancies that Bultmann's man is the man-subject of idealism and liberalism, of inwardness or religious experience. As Bultmann points out,
he thinks of existential analysis in terms of an anthropology borrowed
from Feuerbach, which he handsomely attributes to W. Herrmann
whereas even that thinker represented a departure from liberalism and
had some idea (a halting one, no doubt) of man as outwardness and
capacity for being.

On the whole Barth has paid too little heed to the crucial problem
of *Begrifflichkeit* and the import of the being of things. Thus he grants
me, Bultmann goes on (GV 2, p. 234), that the resurrection of Jesus is
not a fact which anyone could verify by the procedures of historical
science. But, he asserts, that does not mean that the resurrection never
happened: 'Can such a history not have really happened too and can

even such a history not be fitly acknowledged although for the sake of good taste, if nothing else, one refrains from calling it "historical fact" and although the historian in the modern sense can quite well call it a "tale" or a "legend" because it bilks his tools and procedures and tacit assumptions?' (KD 3, 2, p. 535).

Bultmann says: What, I ask you, does Barth mean by the words 'happen' and 'history'? What in the world can those events be which we are told 'happened in time with a far solider reality than anything that "historians" as such can prove'? (KD 3, 2, pp. 535f). In Barth we find something that amounts to the 'historical supra-history' and the 'supra-historical' history dear to the hearts of contemporary orthodox Lutherans, which we have already exposed as nonsensical and at the same time covertly rationalist (see ch. 9, §IV, above). If the resurrection of Jesus, as such and in its eschatological aspect, actually happened in time and in history, then what becomes of faith in it? We are left with a half-faith if the resurrection happened in time and history, even though science cannot verify its happening. Precisely as other-worldly it is this-worldly, hither-worldly. In short, Barth explains the resurrection through a halting *Begrifflichkeit* which he does not critically clarify. When he says that although we cannot take over the mythical view of the world wholesale, we can still make a judicious selection of elements to appropriate from it (KD 3, 2, pp. 536f), I can only reply, Bultmann says in conclusion, that he is being arbitrary. On what basis is his selection made (GV 2, p. 235)?

III

In 1952 Barth wrote a short work called *Rudolf Bultmann—Ein Versuch, ihn zu verstehen*. We shall now try to show that all he there offers are countless variations on one theme: the old theme of 1932 and 1948, that Bultmann puts the objective nature of revelation at hazard, that he humanizes and subjectifies it. All through his essay Barth defends the object against the subject, thereby bringing a whole philosophy into play, as we shall see.

(1) He would not do away with the subject. To me it is obvious, he says, that the New Testament can be soundly interpreted only insofar as one shares in the life of its message, insofar as one gives that message the obedience of faith and therefore believes in the message. But I do think it obviously follows that the *Verstehen* of my share can be rightly described only as an act of my *Selbstverständnis* (my understanding of *myself*; RB, p. 7).

Speaking more generally, Bultmann claims that the Christian message must be *translated* into the *Begrifflichkeit* and parlance of our time. New Testament *Begrifflichkeit* and parlance may be likened to the cradle that received the Word made flesh. We rid it of the cradle in which it is still lying. I think so too, says Barth, but there is a more important matter: trying to get deeper and deeper into the content instead of the container, the message itself rather than its husk and its rendering. Both must be done, of course; but first *cura prior* and then *cura posterior*. Do we really know *what* the New Testament is saying to us? Do we really know the One who encounters us there? In this regard we behave like *beati possidentes*! If I am told that the work of penetrating the message itself and the work of translating it are one and the same thing, my reply is that I do not find the identification convincing (RB, pp. 7–8).

I cannot make out how Bultmann has got into the posture of dwelling so on the translation of the kerygma. In their biographical sketch of him the Tübingen Faculty say that his theology derives from two sources: the Reformers, and the eighteenth- and nineteenth-century liberals. Rather than cast back to liberalism, I should think it more enlightening to observe that Bultmann was one of the founders of the *Formgeschichtliche Schule*. Now the special feature of that school was its looking beyond mere literary history, to concern itself with the '*Sachlichkeit*'[2] (the substance, the actual content) of the New Testament writings, seeking a better understanding of the message itself and as such. In those days we did not dwell on translating into a new *Begrifflichkeit* and language (unless Gogarten, perhaps, was an exception); and if Bultmann was already preoccupied with that business the fact escaped our notice. We observed nothing of the kind in the other exponents of form-criticism (M. Dibelius and K. L. Schmidt, for example). To this day I am at a loss to understand how Bultmann worked his way from the *Formgeschichtliche Schule* to the point of making New Testament translation a *cura prior*. In other respects he certainly follows in Luther's footsteps, but it is even more of a mystery to me how starting with Luther he has come to insist so on '*Verstehen*' and to give '*Auslegen*' ('interpretation') the sense of '*Uebersetzen*'[3] (RB, pp. 9–11).

Barth goes astray in asserting that Bultmann's underlying purpose is to translate the New Testament message into modern *Begrifflichkeit* and parlance. For we know that what Bultmann is about is not adapting God's Word to the man of today but rediscovering the very *Begrifflichkeit* of the New Testament; or rather, to be more precise, of revelation itself. Barth agrees that scripture is only the witness to

2. The inverted commas are Barth's.
3. The inverted commas are Barth's.

revelation, not revelation itself. 'When we study the Bible we are dealing in the first place with a written testimony which does not necessarily coincide with revelation but merely bears witness to it, and here we have the set bounds of the Bible' (TKD 5, p. 7). Hence the need for historical criticism: we must read the Bible 'taking the fullest account of its documentary and human character' (*ibid.*, p. 8).

Carefully as Barth may qualify the principle that scripture must be subjected to criticism and timidly as he may apply it, it should still have shown him that Bultmann is after nothing but the *Sachlichkeit* of the New Testament, would only pick out the wheat from the chaff— the wheat being God's Word and the chaff the all-too-human written witness. As we have seen, the biblical writers are not untainted with the sin of natural man and sometimes understand God's Word in terms of a naive rationalism—mythological rationalism—which is every bit as sinful as scholarly rationalism. Revelation itself must therefore be rediscovered so far as possible, though the task is never-ending because those who undertake it are men.

If Bultmann feels a deep concern for the man of today it is only insofar as we must confront him with the pure scandal of the gospel and not the sham scandal of mythology (see pp. 83–4, above). That is what Bultmann means by 'translation'. He has in no way questioned the twofold source that Barth points out. If the *Formgeschichtliche Schule* was taken up with the *Sachlichkeit* of the New Testament, Bultmann has never done anything but try to throw that *Sachlichkeit* into bold relief. If Bultmann started where Luther left off, it was only to carry forward Luther's underlying purpose (see pp. 82–3, above).

(2) Next Barth sums up Bultmann's view of fallen man, the man 'of this world', of the 'flesh', of sin and of death. All the terms which the New Testament uses to describe him underline the fact that he is a being bent on controlling himself. Fallen man is the man who belongs to the realm of the controllable. Now, says Barth, is this really the mind of scripture? Does the contrast between the seen and the unseen, the controllable and the uncontrollable, loom as large in scripture as Bultmann seems to think? Is the God of the Bible nothing more than the realm of the unseen and the uncontrollable? Can what God's Word tells us about the 'old man', his sin, his *servum arbitrium*, and his doom, really be watered down to these Platonist categories? Does not Bultmann's distinction stand squarely inside 'this world' and the 'flesh' (RB, p. 14)?

One must feel the same misgivings about Bultmann's view of the new man. According to him the believer is the man who gives up all safety, escapes from dread and care and is therefore free to love God and his neighbour; the man whose existence is 'deterrestrified', 'eschatological'. But can what scripture tells us about the new man be watered down to the idea of 'deterrestrification'? Does the New Testament not present 'eschatological existence' as a grateful response to the grace of God which has called it forth? Does that existence not thwart man? Is it not there antecedent to man? Does it not come from Christ who first of all thwarts man? Must we not therefore speak of Christ before we speak of his *beneficia* (RB, p. 15)?

Obviously what has Barth worried is the danger of immanence. Do Bultmann's notions of the seen and the controllable, the unseen and the uncontrollable, adequately convey the otherness of God and of the new life he brings us? Are they not simply subjectivism again? We know that they are nothing of the kind. Bultmann has often explained that the invisibility of the Christian God stands poles apart from the invisibility of the Greek godhead, which though spiritual remains a godhead immanent in the world when compared with the God of faith (GV 3, pp. 157–8; see ch. 6, §II, above). What is more, the category of the controllable answers precisely to the category of works as understood by Paul and Luther, and the category of the uncontrollable to that of grace. To say that God is the uncontrollable is to define him, more searchingly than Barth does, as the Wholly Other. To say that the new man is deterrestrified is to declare that having been pardoned by God's grace he is the new creature spoken of in the second Letter to the Corinthians.

There is no need to dwell on matters which we have fully set forth throughout this book. As to the main issue here, *why* Barth should think that Bultmann's description of the old man and the new man smacks of subjectivism (if only because of a philosophy which rules the more tyrannically for ruling unperceived), we shall begin to deal with it in the next section.

(3) Bultmann holds that the kerygma preaches (Barth goes on) and that it preaches the event of Christ. Thus one is given the impression that this event takes second place with respect to the preaching of it, thanks to which preaching the transformation of the old man into the new actually happens. The kerygma is history—that is, the transition from unauthentic life to authentic life, from yesterday to tomorrow. But if Christ depends on a kerygma which is the event of this transition, must he not by that very fact depend on the transition itself? Is he not the transition? And then have we not shifted our stress from the Christus*geschehen* to the *Christus*geschehen? Has not the event of Christ become subjectified, been made to depend on man—more precisely, on the event which is constituted by the transformation of the old man into the new?

Bultmann does admit of course that the event of Christ began with

Jesus of Nazareth, his life, death and resurrection. But is its real locus not in the kerygma and in the faith of those who attach themselves to the kerygma? The event of Christ, on this reading, seems to exist in and through the kerygma (that is, when all is said and done, in the transition from the old man to the new). That, says Barth, is what I cannot understand. I can quite well understand how *Christ* is the kerygma; but I cannot understand how Christ is the *kerygma*, which seems to be what Bultmann really means (RB, pp. 16–17). To put the matter in the language of classical theology, Barth goes on, I would say that clearly Bultmann's general aim is to fuse christology and soteriology and make out that the New Testament kerygma preaches this oneness. Thus far I can follow Bultmann, but I wonder how it escapes his notice that we are dealing with a oneness in *difference*, a oneness where christology, without breaking away from soteriology, yet goes *before* it and where soteriology comes *after* christology. The history which makes up the content of the kerygma (transition from the old man to the new) has its locus in the life and death of the man Jesus of Nazareth. He himself is the 'substance' (RB, p. 18) of the kerygma.

Bultmann, says Barth, thrusts Jesus Christ into the background (*ibid.*), making him the mere *Woher* (*terminus a quo*) for the transition from the old man to the new, so that christology is swallowed up by soteriology. Everything centres on man and his transformation from a sinful creature into a pardoned one. Christ has dwindled into a 'dim shape on the edge of things without any significance of his own' (RB, p. 18); he takes on meaning only to the extent that he enters the kerygma and is believed in by those who hear the kerygma. In short, how far does the kerygma as Bultmann interprets it still speak to us of any activity on God's part? Does it speak of anything else but activity on man's part, of a transformation which man brings about by his obedience? Are we not dealing here with an *imitatio Christi* (RB, p. 19)?

With the foregoing we begin to penetrate the marrow of our problem. Here, certainly, the only way to defend Bultmann is to attack Barth, showing that his criticism rests on philosophic assumptions—to be precise, on an ontology of the object. When he calls for the event of Christ to come first and afterwards the preaching of that event, Christ first and then the kerygma, christology first and then soteriology, God's activity first and then the transformation of man by that activity, when he upholds a 'significance of his own' for Christ, Barth is simply putting to work the philosophy of subject and object, the old philosophy of natural man, according to which otherness can only be the otherness of the object and genuine transcendence can only be objective.

Barth fails to see that Christ can have no 'significance of his own' for me until he transforms me and that he only becomes really independent of me, superior to me, transcendent with respect to me, when me makes me a new man. So long as he does not determine me, he is a being who does not control me, whom therefore I control, at least in the sense that I remain neutral towards him. But to take up an attitude of neutrality towards a being, towards God in particular, is to control him, is to deny him: 'He who is not with me is against me'. The only Christ who exists independent of me is the Christ of soteriology, the Christ who changes me, thereby—and only thereby—asserting his dominion over me. What makes him independent is not his objectivity but his lordship.

Only those who (consciously or unconsciously) uphold the philosophy of the object can think Bultmann guilty of subjectivism when he dwells on the transition from the old life to the new, on faith, on soteriology. Nothing is farther from his mind than asserting that Christ is an event of the Christian's interior life and that the transformation of man is not rooted in the absolute otherness of God. On the contrary, he means to safeguard the absolute otherness of Christ by showing that the other is not the other, for me, until the moment when it saves me. Christ is the Wholly Other when he makes me wholly other, when I allow him to be 'himself' by allowing him to determine my life, by ec-sisting towards him. Only then does he acquire a 'significance of his own'. As we have seen, this is how Paul envisages Christ's 'objectivity': in his eyes christology and soteriology are one and the same thing (see ch. 9, §IIc, above). Bultmann and Barth have the same purpose at heart—to defend the lordship of Christ. But Bultmann does so with a *Begrifflichkeit* which exactly suits (or at least more exactly suits) his purpose, whereas Barth thwarts his own real purpose by having recourse to a philosophy which was devised precisely to exalt man's supremacy and deny God's, as we shall see to better advantage in the ensuing sections.

(4) Barth applies his general criticism to Bultmann's view of Jesus's death and resurrection.

(a) I agree, he says, that the cross is more than an historical event, that it has, as Bultmann says, a 'cosmic' import—an import, that is, for every age; but I do not see how that import can attach to it simply by its becoming part of the kerygma and part of the faith of those who hear the kerygma. On the contrary, I hold that the cross is an event meaningful in itself (*in sich*), and that meaning of its own is what can and must make it meaningful in the kerygma and meaningful to the faith of those who hear the kerygma. Bultmann disturbs me when he stands that order on its head. I hold that what God did in the death of Jesus was done altogether outside the man who accepts the message;

without him; nay more, against him. I hold that the saving death of all men has taken place *already* in Jesus crucified, that their transformation from the old nature into the new has *already* been accomplished in him, their entrance into eschatological life *already* effected; and that all this business has not only been set on foot but brought to a close (RB, p. 21).

Bultmann—Barth goes on—has written this sentence: 'The cross is not salvific event because it is Christ's cross: it is Christ's cross because it is salvific event'. I should like to hear Bultmann himself give us the authentic interpretation of that statement. All my queries about his doctrine of the cross and, I daresay, about his general christology necessarily have their common root in my inability to understand that statement.

Here once more Barth entangles himself in the ontology of the object, which blinds him not only to Bultmann's thought but even (one may make bold to say) to his, Barth's, own underlying purpose. Making the cross the thing in itself that he talks of is turning it into a thing for man to control. As we know, the otherness of a thing in itself is a sham otherness. The only real otherness is that which calls me in question, thereby disclosing its lordship over me—in other words, its *real* being in itself.

Bultmann would not dream of denying that what God did in Christ crucified took place 'without' us and indeed 'against' us. That was bound to be so since man is a sinner through and through: 'Being the Word of God, Christ is *ante me* and *extra me*—but not as an objectively verifiable fact that could be dated *ante me*, rather as the Christ *pro me* who meets me as the Word' (KM 2, p. 206; see ch. 9, §IIb 2, above). When Christ acts against me he acts against me who am a sinner and for me who am pardoned. A relation of conflict is still a relation: if he is against me that is because I myself do exist. Only when I am saved or damned by him is Christ really my Lord—that is, really what he is 'in himself'. So long as he has no relation with me, either of friendship or enmity, he is only a being whom I control by my very indifference, whom I do not allow to be 'himself' because I neither assert nor renounce any *Anspruch* over him.

Barth's purpose is identical with Bultmann's. All that divides them is a matter of *Begrifflichkeit*, but one is entitled to think that the *Begrifflichkeit* Barth uses plays havoc with his underlying purpose and blinds him to the meaning of the famous Bultmannian dictum ('famous and ill-famed', Barth calls it) which he quotes. On pages 156–8, above, we have given it in full (which Barth unwisely neglects to do) and commented upon it. As to his averment that the salvation of men is wrought in the cross, what Christian will not accept it in *one* sense? But in another sense we must say with Père Bouillard, upholding

Bultmann against Barth: 'If there were no believers, neither would any
salvation have been wrought in the New Testament sense. The ἐφάπαξ
of Christ, on which Barth so dwells, would be emptied of its meaning.
How could we say that the life and death of Jesus were of crucial
import for the salvation of mankind if nobody believed in that import
and nobody lived by it? Without Christ, to be sure, there would be
no Christian faith, but without the faith of Christians Christ would not
be the ἐφάπαξ of salvation. The eschatological event of salvation
embraces both Christ and faith.'[4]

Even if there were no Christians it would still be true that God's
work involved men for him to save, and not simply the man Jesus of
Nazareth. Of its own nature it is relation to the freedoms for which
that work is done—and not simply to those freedoms insofar as the
man Jesus of Nazareth stands proxy for them. We shall come back to
this point in due course.

(b) Now let us turn to the resurrection. No doubt, Barth grants,
Bultmann declares that Jesus's resurrection is a deed of *God*, but a deed
of God which we can say nothing about except that it has found its
way into the kerygma and into faith. We can say nothing about its
nature as the foundation, object and theme of the kerygma; we can
assert nothing about the risen Christ in himself and as such (*an sich
und als solchen*), nothing about his own life after his death, nothing
about the actual meetings with his disciples *who did not yet believe* and
therefore could not be heralds of the kerygma, nothing about the
Christ who was seen 'within space and time' (RB, p. 22) after his
crucifixion. His resurrection seems to have taken place nowhere but
inside the kerygma and belief in the kerygma; it seems to be 'incarcerated' within them (RB, p. 23). Now this is what I cannot understand.
Does the New Testament not make everything, or practically everything, depend 'on the primacy of Jesus Christ's own resurrection . . .
on the fact that we have risen *in him*'? (RB, p. 23). Or do I fail to
perceive that that is just what Bultmann means to say? Heretofore,
I confess, I have understood (and precisely thereby *not* understood)
that Jesus Christ took precedence of his resurrection *in us*. So now the
cross is ontic and the resurrection is noetic; we learn what the cross
means, not from the objective fact that *tertia die resurrexit a mortuis* but
from the kerygma and from faith.

All the same, Barth says in conclusion, we must duly recognize that
Bultmann makes much of the Christus*geschichte*, thereby laying himself
open to be chided just as we are by the likes of Karl Jaspers and the
theologians who follow in his wake. No form of liberalism or neo-

4. H. Bouillard, *Karl Barth*, 3, p. 40.

liberalism will make head or tail of Bultmann. If only the embodiment of his purpose were as lucid as his purpose itself.

Barth's misgivings ('Do I not know perfectly well that Bultmann means to say the very thing I say?') are a credit to him. Yes, Bultmann does indeed mean to affirm the 'primacy of Jesus Christ's own resurrection'. Only this risen Christ *extra me* is not what Barth thinks. Being himself well and truly 'incarcerated' in the objective *Begrifflichkeit* of natural man, he fails to realize that the risen Christ exists *extra me* only to the extent that he exists *pro me*. Working from philosophic assumptions which seem to him axiomatic, he has laid it down that a thing can only be real if it is such quite independent of the subject who perceives it. Only subsequent to that reality can there be dealings between object and subject. The risen Christ 'in himself and as such' that Barth dreams of is only a sham otherness. To affirm his being *in se* is rank rationalism and subjectivism, because insofar as I know him *before* he becomes the determination of my life I control him exactly as I do any object. No doubt Barth grants Bultmann that the resurrection is not an historical fact like other historical facts (see §II, above); but he holds that nevertheless it is an event which happened quite apart from the kerygma and faith, since the risen Christ is supposed to have been seen by disciples who did not yet believe in him. But then, wherein does the resurrection differ from an ordinary historical fact?

The lameness of Barth's *Begrifflichkeit* becomes obvious here, as it does when he misunderstands the ontic and the neotic. He is trying to say that Bultmann regards the cross as a 'real' fact but one whose meaning becomes known only through the resurrection as an event that has occurred in the faith of believers. The resurrection (a subjective event) teaches us the meaning of the cross (an objective event). One need hardly say that this is barking up the wrong tree altogether: Bultmann has never distinguished between the noetic and the ontic, and he does not attach to the term 'ontic' anything like the meaning that Barth does. On the other hand this blunder of Barth's sheds considerable light upon the nature of his *Begrifflichkeit*. By identifying the ontic with the objective and contrasting the two with knowledge (the neotic), he shows that the waters he is swimming in are those of classical philosophy, where the major problem is to set forth the connection between subject and object.

(5) Next Barth turns to contemplate the fruits of demythologization. He begins by giving Bultmann's view of Jesus's virgin birth, the miracles, the expiatory death, the bodily resurrection, the parousia, Satan, the Church, the sacraments, and so forth. Then he remarks that Bultmann would throw some of these elements overboard (particularly

the image of a three-storey universe, Satan and the devils, the angels, the virgin birth, the empty tomb, and the ascension) and interpret the rest. Barth freely owns that we still find in Bultmann the marrow of the New Testament (translated): sin, death, God, his revelation in Christ and Christ alone, the Holy Spirit, the divine sonship of believers, the Church, the sacraments, eschatological hope. All these things are handled with a sobriety that could be taken to heart by many another who talks of them in more 'orthodox' vein.[5] Here again Bultmann is not a liberal, because what he tries to do is interpret, not perform sleight-of-hand (RB, pp. 27–8).

Why does he deem it necessary to interpret these elements of the New Testament? Because their content is clothed in mythological language. Myth terrestrifies what is not terrestrial, humanizes what is not human, objectifies what is not objective. Because there is nothing specifically Christian about its mythological trappings, the New Testament *can* be demythologized; and it *must* be demythologized, for in that guise its message defies comprehension. The mythical image of the world is as dead as a door-nail. To expect the man of today to accept it would be to demand of him a *sacrificium intellectus*. Moreover faith would be dragged down to the level of a work and its true scandal ignored. And after all, the business of demythologization was started by the New Testament itself, by Paul and John in particular.

I wish I could fall in with you, Barth goes on, but I am unable to do so. In the first place I ask: Can a man understand any text at all, ancient or modern, if he approaches it with his mind already made up as to how far the text can or cannot be understood, instead of waiting for it to disclose itself and patiently following wherever it may lead: if he thinks he has a criterion at his finger-ends for judging what is the evanescent form and what the abiding content? Must that criterion not be looked on as a purely tentative one, a mere working hypothesis? Does one not lock oneself out of a text if one approaches it with a ready-made yardstick, fished up somewhere outside the text, of what can be understood and what cannot; if before one has so much as read the text one thinks one knows exactly what is not real content but the mere categories and forms of thought in which the content lies wrapped? Has Bultmann's notion of myth the slightest bearing on the New Testament texts? Does a criterion exist which enables him to sift out mere representation in the New Testament from the thing represented? To which is the exegete accountable: to his contemporaries' way of thinking and his own, or to the spirit, the substance and the purpose of the text he has under examination (RB, pp. 30–31)?

5. The inverted commas are Barth's.

Barth shoots wide of the mark in declaring that Bultmann would throw parts of the New Testament overboard (the 'three storeys' of heaven, earth and hell; Satan and the devils; the virgin birth, the empty tomb, Christ's ascension) rather than interpret them. Bultmann has always said that *nothing* in the New Testament must be thrown away, that everything there has a meaning which need only be unearthed. As we have seen, the virgin birth, the empty tomb, and the rest, are later, mythologizing (rationalizing) images of Jesus of Nazareth's divine significance as the Word of God. We must hold fast to what they mean while discarding the way in which they say it, just as the most conservative of theologians stick to the meaning of the expression 'at the right hand of God' without imagining that Christ actually sits there.

As for the questions Barth asks Bultmann about his attitude towards the New Testament, doubtless the first thing to do is ask Barth those questions about his attitude towards Bultmann. Has Barth not approached the study of Bultmann with a 'mind already made up as to how far he can or cannot be understood' instead of 'patiently following' wherever he may lead? Does he not think he 'has a criterion at his finger-ends' (the Barthian criterion) for judging what in Bultmann will pass muster and what will not? Has he not approached Bultmann with a 'ready-made yardstick' fished up somewhere outside Bultmann, and chided him 'before he has so much as read him' in earnest—that is, with a readiness to test the categories of his (Barth's) own thought? Is he unaware of Bultmann's numerous articles on hermeneutics, or has he not learned from them that the basic rule of interpretation is to listen to a text in two ways—scientifically, by using the tools of the deepest possible familiarity with the language of the text, the age to which it belongs, and its spirit; and existentially, by being ready to give up all that one has and all that one is so as to 'let the newness, nay the strangeness, of the text exist' and bid it welcome?

Does Barth not know that Bultmann's one yardstick in his undertaking is the very intent of scripture, the Word of God himself; that he finds fault with the New Testament writers and their *Begrifflichkeit*, which here and there ill befits the reality they are trying to convey, in the name of that intent and that Word, not exclusively and not primarily in the name of modern man? Could he not credit Bultmann with having (like Barth himself) but one 'canon' of interpretation: God's revealed Word—whatever doubts one may be entitled to put forward about the way the canon is applied, just as one is entitled to do about Barth's theology, but without suspecting that he approaches the New Testament in the grip of preconceived ideas which are alien to it? Has he not read in Bultmann that 'the yardstick [of interpretation] can only be the underlying intent of the New Testament' (GV I, p. 315), 'the major purposes of the text itself' and not 'a modern *Weltanschauung* that does not query itself but instead sets itself up as the standard of criticism' (GV I, p. 262)? Has it escaped his notice that Bultmann by no means claims to have discovered the underlying intent of the New Testament? 'There is of course', he writes, 'no way to tell whether one has really found out the purposes of the text' (*ibid.*). For here we have to do with a task that 'is never definitely finished, never finished once and for all' (GV I, p. 263). Is Bultmann, then, one whit less unassuming than Barth?

(6) I now arrive, Barth goes on, at the crucial theological issue. Can we still talk of the New Testament kerygma after demythologization, when there remains no warrant for saying that God was pleased to lower himself, to become terrestrial (*weltlich*), hither-worldly (*diesseitig*), objective (*gegenständlich*) and '—*horribile dictu*—datable' (RB, pp. 32–3)? Or again when one is forbidden to confess that the kerygma springs from the fact that the first disciples saw not only the abasement of the Word made flesh upon the cross but also his glory in a resurrection which took place 'within space and within time'? If it is denied that 'they saw [the risen Christ] with their own eyes, heard him with their own ears, touched him with their own hands' (*ibid.*)? If it cannot be said that the resurrection of the Word made flesh occurred not only in 'an invisible, supra-historical, heavenly place but also in a truly visible, historical, earthly place—and therefore as humanly, as terrestrially, as "mundanely", as objectively as did the death of Jesus beforehand' (*ibid.*)? So that although faith can never point to the resurrection as its ground, the fact remains that 'there is not only a *Dennoch* [a 'nevertheless'] but also a *Darum* [a 'therefore']' (*ibid.*)? If it be denied that the death and resurrection of Jesus are a reality meaningful *in itself* (*in sich selbst*) and only then, and only as a result, 'for us'? If it be denied that this reality is 'what gives rise' to faith and the kerygma?

Must we not acknowledge Jesus Christ as 'him who lives for us *before* we believe in him, *without* our believing in him, *despite* our unbelief' (RB, p. 34), him 'in whom God *first* loved us' (*ibid.*)? I fear the demythologized New Testament gives off a pungent odour of docetism. Now is there not a connection here with the fact that Bultmann unduly neglects the Old Testament, so palpably 'earthly' and 'historical', and the Jesus of the synoptics, his preaching and his deeds, 'his road from the Jordan to Gethsemane' (RB, p. 33)?

We are familiar with Bultmann's theology of the incarnation. He holds that the incarnation is in no sense—at least in no sense such as

Barth means—a 'terrestrial, hither-worldly, objective' event (although, contrary to what Barth supposes, it is, *admirabile dictu*, 'datable': in Jesus of Nazareth and in him alone, Bultmann avows, the Word has become flesh). In the sense which Barth means, and which the Easter narratives meant before him, the disciples did not 'see [the risen Christ] with their own eyes, hear him with their own ears, touch him with their own hands'. Not only can no proof of faith be brought forward, there is not even any *Darum* for it; it is a sheer *Dennoch*.

No doubt certain passages of the New Testament (namely those to which Barth refers) do confound the incarnation of God's Word with its objectification. In other words they envisage it as more of a *Mirakel* than a *Wunder*. We have called attention to these naively rationalist passages in the context of the resurrection and seen how far they thwart the real purpose of the New Testament (ch. 9, §IIIb, above). We know that Paul and especially John rectify them and that what they substantially achieved must now be given the finishing touches. It is their underlying intent to declare that the Word became flesh in the soberest and most thoroughgoing sense of the term: the Word is in the flesh to such a degree that Jesus seems to be a man like other men and nothing more. There are no *Mirakel*, no wondrous birth, no empty tomb, no touching of the wounds, to serve as so many 'there-fores'. To use a phrase which does not quite befit this context, let us say that in Jesus the divine element shows 'neither hide nor hair' of itself. The incarnation of God is not his objectification.

It is therefore waggish to accuse Bultmann of docetism. What else is docetism but the theory that the Word only pretended to become flesh, so that Jesus Christ is not a man in the fullest sense of the term? Docetism is the theory of a fancy-dress incarnation. Now Bultmann, whose christology is that of Phil 2:5-8 and Jn 1:14, confesses that Jesus is so fully man that nothing in him gives any hint of the divine. The godhead hides away so well in him that no sign (no virgin birth, no empty tomb, or the like) betrays its presence—no sign such as *would* justify one in speaking of a docetist incarnation, in other words of a sham incarnation. If anyone be a docetist here it is Barth, who looks on the incarnation at least as a 'therefore', if not as a proof, whereas it is a sheer 'nevertheless'. Compared with Bultmann's intent and, we believe, the underlying intent of the New Testament—compared, that is, with revelation itself—his position is a rationalist one, because it admits that the divine in Jesus 'peeps out' and 'beckons' to man. Thus the incarnation becomes in some sense a disguise worn by the Son of God.

On the other hand Bultmann maintains that the *Logos* has utterly stripped himself of his divinity: not of course in the sense that he left it behind in heaven, but it exists in the flesh of the man Jesus of Nazareth to such a degree that nothing seems to distinguish him from other men so long as one has not made him one's *Verstehen*—in other words, so long as one has not become the 'new creation' of 2 Cor 5:17. True enough, Barth has always declared that faith is necessary for reading the signs and that they hold good as signs only for the believer. But the fact remains that they are 'terrestrial, hither-worldly, objective' signs, so that faith ceases to be a sheer *Dennoch*: it is a *Darum* as well. This *Darum* is what strikes Bultmann as a residue of rationalism and docetism. He holds that there is only *one* sign of God and the Holy Spirit: namely God and the Holy Spirit in actual 'bodily' presence. *Deus index sui.*

Barth is right in trying to safeguard the otherness of the *Christus-geschehen*. But we must ask him: What is otherness? Is it objectivity? What if objectivity turned out to be the negation of otherness? What if Barth, in order to safeguard otherness, used a whole *Begrifflichkeit* which destroys it? He looks on the risen Christ as an 'objective' being who has been 'seen, heard, touched'. All this parlance and all the ideas it embodies were concocted in order to express things of this world insofar as man masters them, wields them, exploits them—in short, *controls* them, whether by mere knowledge or by actual doings. And this is the very sense in which the Easter narratives understand them; for people wanted to be *sure* that Christ had indeed risen. The fact that these texts are of later date than faith in Easter and that there-fore they did not provide the basis for that faith, shows plainly enough that faith did not need the signs there related in order to come into being. Only afterwards was the risen Christ mythologized—that is, subjectified—little by little. He became the being whom men have finally made sure of, whom they have in their possession, since he eats bread and 'broiled fish before them' (Lk 24:38–43).

Of course Barth fully realizes that these passages are overdone and therefore, when he is not wrapped up in the effort to refute Bultmann, interprets them himself. Commenting on 1 Cor 15, he states that in verses 3–8 Paul has no intention of calling the resurrection a fact that can be verified and has been verified, but simply means to stress the identity of his preaching with that of the primitive community. The witnesses he speaks of are not men who saw an historical fact with their own eyes; it does not matter where or when the ὀφθῆναι occurred. This ὀφθῆναι refers neither to visions nor to objective realities; it is an event that can happen anywhere and at any time.[6] Bultmann replies that this exegesis of Paul's thought will not bear examination, that Paul

6. K. Barth, *Die Auferstehung der Toten* (1924), pp. 74ff.

means to declare the resurrection an historical fact and no bones about it. We must frankly admit that here, for once, the temptation to objectify sweeps him off his feet (GV I, pp. 54–5).

How did the Barth of 1924 turn into the Barth of 1952, who rationalizes the risen Christ by taking the Easter narratives as they stand? After all this same later Barth, who makes the Easter narratives a *Darum*, declares that we must see in them '*keinen "aufweisbaren" Glaubensgrund*' (RB, p. 33).[7] Therefore he still interprets them, for their obvious sense is that of 1 Cor 15:3–8: they are designed to prove that Jesus has risen from the dead. Only a personal theological prejudice of Barth's makes him deny them this *aufweisbar* character. But if a translation forces itself on us at all events, why not go all the way, as Bultmann does? Why half yield to the temptation of the object? Why come to a standstill half-way through what is an interpretation anyhow? Why not stride boldly on from the *Darum* to the sheer *Dennoch*?

Barth takes Bultmann to task for neglecting the Jesus of the synoptics. So far is Bultmann from doing any such thing that he has written a famous little book called *Jesus*, based exclusively on the synoptic tradition, which he happens to understand differently from Barth, that is all (see ch. 9, §IIIe, above).

(7) Not content with declaring that the New Testament must be interpreted, Barth goes on, Bultmann tells us what kind of interpretation it must be: an existential interpretation—in other words (Barth explains) an 'anthropological' one (RB, p. 35). 'Existential', he further specifies, 'means having to do with the interpretation of human existence. The ideas and terms which accurately sketch out human existence belong to another language, into which the affirmations of the New Testament, couched as they are in mythological language, need to be translated' (*ibid.*). Two great benefits follow from this undertaking. In the first place we clarify at last what the New Testament really means to say; and in the second place the man of today, who no longer thinks in mythological terms but in anthropological ones, is enabled to understand that on the three planes of exegesis, dogma and preaching the Christian message offers him no sham scandal but rather confronts him with the only real issue—the choice between belief and unbelief.

Before proceeding to attack them, Barth admits that he finds these views striking. How they simplify theology! What a concentrate of it they give us. What doors they open to *Sachkritik* of certain New Testament texts in the light of essentials, which we find first and foremost in Paul and John. How close they come to Luther's original

---

7. In 1924 Barth rejected not only any 'proof' but also any *Darum*.

ideas. What a vista for the theologian, being able to keep faith alike with the New Testament and with the modern world. How laughable we find the pious outcry of the orthodox against the negative side of Bultmann's undertaking, against the way he settles accounts with this or that assertion of the Bible or the Church, when we consider the power that radiates from the positive side of it.

Nonetheless, Barth goes on, I fear that Bultmann's hermeneutic rests on an assumption which does not seem to me unquestionably sound. So far as I can make out, the tremendous simplifications and condensations which theology has undergone in the course of its history have seldom happened when the impetus for them was sought in a deeper knowledge of the spirit, content and purpose of the New Testament, but rather as a rule when men had found a new philosophic principle and applied it to New Testament interpretation. Only in the latter case do we normally come upon such flashes. Now it is news to no one that Bultmann starts from a principle of this sort, that the yeast at work within his thinking is the existentialism of the younger Heidegger (whom Barth is fond of contrasting, here and elsewhere, with the latter-day Heidegger). From it he borrowed the idea that one must approach scripture with a particular '*Vorverständnis*'.[8]

First of all the New Testament is a certain *Vorverständnis* of '*Verstehen*'[9] at large whereby in one way or another any *Verstehen* at all involves a *Sichselbstverstehen* on man's part. And then, concretely, it is a particular *Verständnis* of this *Sichselbstverstehen*, which latter always consists in a clash between the authentic and the unauthentic, the past and the future. Thus the New Testament is supposed to be an anthropology, and an anthropology put together in the way I have just described. This is what one must have understood before approaching the New Testament; this is the *Vorverständnis* with which one must approach it.

How this scheme of things is applied we see at once by the notion Bultmann frames of man's sinful existence in unbelief and of his eschatological existence in faith. But by that very fact we also see how the event of Christ (the *Christusgeschehen*) only begins with Christ in person and then becomes the event of crossing over from the old life to the new, having no reality of its own apart from that crossing. So there is only one point on which Bultmann brings himself to break the Heideggerian pattern, namely the event of Christ insofar as it is God's deed. Here Bultmann speaks as a theologian standing on his own two feet. Except in this particular, everything positive he has to say about

8. The inverted commas are Barth's.
9. The inverted commas are Barth's.

the New Testament is locked up in the armour of the Heideggerian *Vorverständnis*. Thus anybody who would debate with him must be familiar with the knotty philosophy and knottier language of Heidegger; otherwise Bultmann will counter with a cold 'I do not understand' (RB, pp. 34–8).

For my own part I do not understand either. I do not see why I should have to wriggle into this suit of armour before I can cross the threshold of the New Testament. All honour to Heidegger, certainly; even to the early Heidegger of anthropology. But how can we receive his philosophy as though it were philosophy *as such*? At any rate he is of no such mind, and neither is Bultmann. No, only if it be taken for *the* philosophy of our time do there remain any grounds for setting it up as canonical. Bultmann seems to think that it *is* the philosophy of our time. But do we not also find the spirit of our age in quite different philosophical embodiments? Does not Heidegger himself, in his later writing, seem to have left behind the anthropological stage of *Sein und Zeit*, which was the formative influence on Bultmann? Does this philosophy represent a foundation so broad and so strong that we must install ourselves upon it, come to rest there—if only out of sympathy for modern man—that on principle we must be existentialists and must find in an existentialist notion the one *Vorverständnis* requisite to a sound *Verständnis* of the New Testament? I fail to see the binding force of such a claim.

I fail to see it if only because I am unable to believe that myth can be interpreted categorically, exclusively, in this totalitarian fashion so to speak, as the embodiment of a particular human '*Selbstverständnis*'.[10] No one will deny, of course, that it is this as well. But having regard to the endless variety of form which myth exhibits in the past and at present, how can we say that it is this and nothing else? What myth asserts that the human subject alone really 'exists',[11] so that the *only* thing which can properly be done with myth is to fit an 'existentialist, anthropological interpretation' onto it (RB, p. 39)?

But here we come to a graver theological issue. What becomes of the New Testament message if it is reduced categorically, exclusively and in totalitarian fashion to the human *Selbstverständnis* which finds voice in it? I repeat: it cannot and must not be probed for its anthropological content, for it relates an event which takes place between God and man, and in *form* is a human witness to that event. But are we not mutilating it if we tear from this witness what is 'primary and most unmistakable' in it (RB, p. 40), dubbing it the 'existential interpreta-

---

10. The inverted commas are Barth's.
11. The inverted commas are Barth's.

tion'[12]—the *Christusgeschehen* as the Christus*geschehen* on which everything is grounded, in which everything is steeped, by which everything
is overshadowed, so as to transform and interpret that in it which is
secondary and matters only because of a bearing on what is primary?
Let us honour and love Bultmann for breaking the Heideggerian
pattern on this head of the *Christusgeschehen*. But despite this blessed
inconsistency of his, the task of unearthing the New Testament message
in his existential interpretation as a whole staggers one if it does not
defeat one altogether.

Once more we are tempted to fire back at Barth the questions which
he puts to Bultmann. When he says that the tremendous 'simplifications
and condensations' which theology has undergone have 'seldom'
happened when the impetus for them was sought in a deeper knowledge
of 'the spirit, content and purpose' of the New Testament but rather
'as a rule' when men had found a new philosophic principle, we must
ask him what that tremendous 'simplification and condensation' is
which he has had Protestant theology undergo by setting it to rotate
on the axis of christology.[13] Has he not also hammered out, or rather
resuscitated, a philosophic principle for dealing with liberal subjectivism, namely the good old philosophy of the object, sugared over
with existentialism? Does the fact not cry aloud from all that we have
just said? Does not one of his former colleagues—and not the least
outstanding of them: E. Peterson—write that Barth has gone back 'to
the pre-idealist age of his Church', that is, to the ancient ontology?[14]
Does not Père Bouillard (who as a Catholic priest can hardly be sus-
pected of subjectivism and who is so fully alive to the problem of the
connection between theology and philosophy) take Barth to task for
insisting on 'an overly objective type of thought'[15] in his doctrine of
the relations between Christ and man?

Barth points out Bultmann's astonishing fidelity to the younger
Luther. Does this mean that the latter used a philosophic principle and
that the Reformation, when all is said and done, proves to be a
philosophy? If such is not the case with Luther, why should it be the
case with his disciple Bultmann? Why should not Bultmann too be
one of those 'rare' creatures (among whom Barth ranks himself) who
have brought about a 'simplification and condensation' of theology
based on 'the spirit, content and purpose' of the New Testament?

12. The inverted commas are Barth's.

13. In KD 4, 1, p. 858, Barth himself describes his theology as a *Konzentration auf
Jesus Christus*.

14. E. Peterson, 'Existentialisme et théologie protestante' in *Dieu vivant* 10, p. 47.

15. H. Bouillard, *Karl Barth*, 3, p. 40.

Because of his links with Heidegger? But what if Barth is barking up the wrong tree when it comes to those links?

He makes such an outlandish hotchpotch of *Verstehen, Verständnis* and *Selbstverständnis* as to obscure Bultmann's stand beyond recognition. His major blunder has been to interpret Bultmann's categories in terms of his own philosophic categories, which all derive from ordinary thought. The words 'understanding' and 'understanding of oneself' mean to him what they mean to Tom, Dick and Harry. They are apprehended through the traditional philosophy of subject and object, which is at once a scholar's philosophy and the philosophy of those who do *not* philosophize or who repudiate all philosophy.

When reading Bultmann, Barth should have been on his guard against his own ideas, even though he were to come back to them later; instead of querying Bultmann's *Begrifflichkeit* he should have scrutinized his own, if only to ask himself whether it did not prevent him from making contact with the mind of his opponent. But even when about the simple business of reading the other man, Barth has not got outside himself. Having been bent his whole life long on fighting subjectivism and restoring the objectivity of God's Word, he cannot understand that there is another way of posing the problem and safeguarding the otherness of revelation. Thinking as he does in terms of subject and object, he was bound to tilt Bultmann's ideas in the direction of the subject. For there is a subjective ring to these ideas (understanding, precomprehension, understanding of self) when they are taken according to common sense. It is the subject who understands and understands himself; *Verstehen* at large refers to the subject, not the object, and so do the existentiell and the existential.

In ordinary philosophy (whatever form, learned or spontaneous, it may take) existence always has to do with the subject; and in that philosophy existentiell certainties are contrasted with objective certainties. This fact explains why Barth has never grasped the difference between the existentiell and the existential, about which he waxes sarcastic and lets it go at that (RB, p. 35, note). He refers the existential and the existentiell to the subject alone, as anyone is bound to do who thinks in ordinary terms. Thus one can see why he goes on and on about the 'existential, anthropological' interpretation and declares that in Bultmann's eyes the New Testament reduces itself to an anthropology.

He has failed to understand three things:

(a) The first is that in Bultmann the words *Verstehen, Verständnis, Vorverständnis* and *Sichselbstverstehen* must not be taken in the sense which ordinary philosophy attaches to them. As we know, *Verstehen* is a category of encounter and otherness. To 'understand' the other is not to bring it back to oneself, to subjectify it. On the contrary, it is to let it call me in question, hearken to the *Anrede* which it directs to me—nay, which it *is*. So that *Sichselbstverstehen* is not an inward-looking business, a turning back upon oneself, much less a drawing of the other into oneself, but the receiving of a *new Selbst* which I have from it and which is the special favour it does me.

As to the precomprehension I have of the other, no more is it an arbitrary assumption of my own which I fit over the other so as to shape it in my image and likeness, but rather an anticipation of the other or, as Heidegger says, the *Vorstruktur* of the *Seiendes* (of the thing). As the word indicates, this prestructure is none of my own making; it is received from the being of the thing. When Bultmann keeps saying that we must approach the Bible with the *Vorverständnis* that is suitable to it, he leaves us in no doubt that we must approach it not with our own ideas in mind but with its. What matters is querying my way of thinking and looking at things, so as to take over the thinking and outlook of the text I have before me.

No doubt the *Vorverständnis* does convey my living bond with what the text is talking about, but the *lumen naturale* is not 'reason', or the 'intellect', or the 'mind' known to common sense and the classical philosophies; it is a light that comes to me from *being*, of which it is a participation. The *Vorverständnis* is something received. Of course, as we have often observed, it is not the thing itself. To have the mere idea (the *Vorverständnis*) of friendship or of God is to be the *lack* of friendship or of God. The *Vorverständnis* is not a *Dass* but a *Was*. It conveys the fact that I am the other in desire, in intaglio; which is to say that I am not the other insofar as it is other. Therefore the *Vorverständnis* in no way prejudices the other's otherness—or, in Barthian parlance, its 'objectivity'.

(b) Barth has never taken in the real nature of the existential and the existentiell. He identifies the existentiell—we may as well begin with it—with classical subjectivity, that which contrasts with objectivity. He has perceived that, to Bultmann's mind, man ec-sists only in his encounters, in the calls, that God, other men and the world direct to him. Far from being a species of inwardness, the existentiell is a category of outwardness.

'Against the digestive philosophy of "empirical criticism" [German positivism], of Neo-Kantianism, and every form of "psychologism", Husserl doggedly goes on insisting that things cannot be dissolved into consciousness . . . You knew that the tree was not you, that you could not get it into your stomach, and that knowledge could not in all fairness be likened to possession. At one and the same time conscious-ness has been scoured, it stands there as crystalline as a high wind, with nothing in it now but an urgency to flee itself, a stealing out of itself. If, to suppose the impossible, you stepped "inside" a consciousness you would be caught up in an eddy and flung out again at the foot of the tree, into all the dust; because consciousness has no "inside" to it, it is nothing but the outside of itself . . . Without more ado we have stamped "cancelled" on the cosy philosophy of immanence, where everything is done by compromise, by protoplasmic shufflings, by a lukewarm cellular chemistry. The philosophy of transcendence hurls you onto the highway, into a host of dangers, under a blinding glare. To be, Heidegger says, is to be-in-the-world. Understand this "being-in" in the sense of movement. To be is to burst into the world . . . Here we are, disenthralled of Proust, and at the same time disenthralled of the "inner life". It is futile for us to seek the caresses and coddling of our own privacy, like Amiel, like a child kissing its shoulder. Because in the end everything lies outside; everything, including even ourselves; outside, in the world, in the midst of others. We shall not come upon ourselves in some refuge, some den, but in the streets, in town, among the crowd'.[16] What Sartre says of Husserl and Heidegger must be said of Bultmann: for him, as for Husserl, Heidegger and Sartre, to ec-sist is to 'burst' forth.

Barth's idea of the ec-sistential is even murkier than his idea of the ec-sistentiell. Here his blundering arises from the fact that he thinks of things as standing on a single plane, with the subject at one end and the object at the other; whatever is not objective must be subjective and whatever is not subjective must be objective. First there comes the object, which exists in itself, and only afterwards comes the subject, who knows the object or shares in the life of the object. A man who thinks along these lines cannot understand the vital notion which is the sense of being—though the very people to whom it is a closed book make constant use of it, simply by distinguishing a chair from a table or an oak tree from a crocodile. The sense of being answers to the old idea of 'essence' but as regarded from the standpoint of being: being manifests itself as a chair, a table, an oak tree, or a crocodile. It discloses itself in a very special way in man.

To discover the ec-sistential structure of the human being is to set out his sense of being as the bursting forth we mentioned a moment ago. Therefore it is quite in order to equate the terms 'existential' and 'anthropological' as Barth does, but provided we reverse the sense in which he understands the position. Here anthropology must be taken to mean, not subjectivity, immanence, 'inner life', but outwardness,

16. J.-P. Sartre, 'Une idée fondamentale de la phénoménologie de Husserl: l'intentionalité' in *Situations* I (1939) 32–5.

transcendence, bursting forth. Bultmann has said so plainly enough: 'This interpretation [the existential interpretation] may be called "anthropological" provided one realizes that anthropology means ec-sistential analysis of the human being, and does not confuse it . . . with some anthropology of that objectifying school of thought which can only look on the human being as a phenomenon of this world' (KM 2, p. 184, note 1). Accordingly the term ec-sistential does not refer to man the subject, as Barth wrongly imagines, but to the essence of a being who is outwardness. Therefore to interpret scripture existentially is not to thimblerig its 'objectivity' for the behoof of the human subject but rather to let it exist in all its transcendence, to recognize that the Word of God, far from being determined by man, determines him through and through.

(c) Barth accuses Bultmann of getting himself incarcerated in the 'armour' of Heideggerian philosophy. What he does not ask is whether perchance he himself is not the prisoner of a philosophic suit of armour —that is, of the persuasion that no real otherness exists except the otherness of the object. Here again Sartre has well put the point that Barth misses. 'You see this tree', he says. 'But you see it on the very spot where it stands: at the edge of the road, in the middle of the dust, by itself, gnarled with the heat, fifty miles from the Mediterranean coast. It cannot step into your consciousness, being of a different nature from that consciousness.

'At this point you are put in mind of Bergson and the first chapter of *Matiére et mémoire*. But Husserl is no realist: he does not turn our tree, on its patch of crackled earth, into an absolute that will presently get in touch with us. Consciousness and the world are there at one and the same time. Standing outside consciousness by its very nature, the world by its very nature also relates to consciousness . . . To know is to tear ourselves away from the dank privacy of our own belly and nip down, outside ourselves, towards what is not ourselves, down beside the tree; and yet outside it too because it gives me the slip, holds me at arm's length, and I can no more melt into it than it can melt into me. I stand outside it and outside myself.'[17]

The delusion which the man in the street—and Barth—labours under is the idea that first the object exists and then the subject, who gets into touch with the object. He insists on the primacy of the object because he fancies that this means respecting the other in its transcendence, whereas in fact, as we have seen, objectivity is man's laying hold on otherness—his refusal to acknowledge it. Thus when Barth stoutly defends the objectivity of God's Word and the event of Christ,

17. J.-P. Sartre, *ibid.*

throughout his writing, the *Begrifflichkeit* he uses (or the *Denk-schematismus*, to take over one of his own terms) lays bare his underlying aim. True enough, he never sinks into the rank objectivism that marks Catholic theology as a whole. Here and there he finds fault with the *Begrifflichkeit* of the ancient Church. He rewrites the tractate on the Trinity in terms of modalities rather than persons. To a large extent his theology is 'eventist', 'existentiell', 'actualist'; but the objective strain which survives in it, the role it assigns—a more or less prominent one, unhappily—to traditional metaphysics, bursts forth in the controversy with Bultmann. That controversy acts as a reagent.

It is a remarkable circumstance that Barth also protests against Bultmann's 'ancestors', against all who have perceived that Christ 'in himself', without an accompanying relation to man, is mere guesswork. His writing is strewn with attacks on Luther, Melanchthon and Calvin himself, insofar as they stress the Christ of the *beneficia* rather than Christ in himself. There are passages which thus take them to task one after the other. Luther wrote: 'I have often said, and I do not weary of repeating it so that it may be remembered when I am dead and gone, that we must beware as we would the devil all those doctors who begin their teaching in heaven and set up to talk of God apart from Christ, as has been done until now in the upper schools where men abandon themselves to lofty speculations about who God is, what he thinks and does within himself in the heavenly world, and so forth'. Barth in his commentary waters down, tones down, muffles and whittles away the meaning of this text and others like it (TKD 2, pp. 114–15). He also quotes Melanchthon's statement that there seems to be precious little reason for bothering one's head over those '*loci supremi de Deo, de unitate, de trinitate Dei, de mysterio creationis, de modo incarnationis*', where the Scholastics entangled themselves in endless subtleties, thus beclouding the *beneficia Christi*. Their reasoning, which is '*e philosophia*', often came closer to heresy than to dogma and we must be on our guard against these '*disputationes frigidae et alienae a Christo*'.

Just as the physician must know more about the *vis nativa* of plants than about their nature, so we must know Christ first and foremost as *salutaris*. Here once again Barth does his best to weaken the force of these texts, which he says represent a 'momentary opinion', a 'fit of temper' against the abstract, unchurchmanlike method of the Scholastics, or some such thing (TKD 2, p. 113). He admits that Calvin runs down the authority and language of the ancient councils and creeds; that when called upon by Father Caroli to subscribe to them the Reformer declared it was a piece of 'tyranny', because true knowledge of Christ's divinity was nothing else than placing all one's trust in him:

*Quae practica notitia certior haud dubie est qualibet otiosa speculatione. Illic
enim pius animus Deum praesentissimum conspicit et paene attrectat, ubi se
vivificari, illuminari, salvari, justificari et sanctificari sentit.*[18] But here as
elsewhere Barth makes excuses, interprets, counterpoises, bowdlerizes,
belittles and pares down (TKD 2, pp. 113–14).

It is an historical fact that the Reformers had some second thoughts
about these statements, but far fewer ones than Barth says they did.
Moreover he himself admits in another context (RB, pp. 46–7) that the
elder Luther and Melanchthon stuck to the same basic train of thought
and that certain passages in the definitive edition of Luther's commentary on the letter to the Galatians seem to merge christology in
soteriology—passages which would supply Bultmann with 'wonderful' arguments for his existential method. As we know, Bultmann
does not neglect to invoke them. And after all, where the Reformers
did go back on their original statements the whole question is whether
they were not thereby offering sacrifice anew to what Luther still
called in the very year of his death '*die höchste Hure, die der Teufel hat*';[19]
and whether Barth, by having them retract even further than they did,
is not surrendering to her in still more perilous fashion.

Generally speaking it is Lutheran christology that he finds fault with,
as being too much centred on man, too 'noetic', not 'ontic' enough,
and he asks Lutherans: 'Does your christology attach due weight to
revelation considered as an event, as a *deed* of God?' (TKD 3, p. 158).
Always and everywhere we are confronted by this firm belief that
salvation lies in the object, this firm belief which finally turns into
Barth's real suit of armour.

The judgment he pronounces upon Heidegger is as wrong as the one
he pronounces upon Bultmann, for as we know, there are not two
Heideggers (ch. 16, footnote 17, above). Barth still lags at the stage
of thinking that *Sein und Zeit* is an anthropology, whereas all commentators on Heidegger long ago renounced that heresy, for which at
a pinch there may have been some excuse in 1927. Of course if a man
reads *Sein und Zeit* with the categories of ordinary thought in mind,
he will inevitably understand it in an anthropological sense. Barth's
trouble is that he has read Heidegger, just as he has read Bultmann,
without sufficiently detaching himself from the notions which are
dear to his heart. The pattern in his mind—the philosophy of subject
and object—blinds him to the real problem that Heidegger presents.

He is as much in the dark about the real bond between Bultmann and

---

18. See in ch. 8, § 113, above, the texts of Calvin which Bultmann quotes in his
commentary on John.

19. SW (Erlangen edition) 20 (2), 2, p. 475—The reference is to reason insofar as
it sets itself up as an authoritative standard.

Heidegger. Bultmann looks to Heidegger's philosophy, not in the least because he thinks it is 'the philosophy of our time' but rather because it helps us cleanse ourselves of the rationalism which is the distinctive nature of every man who comes into this world; because in its own way and on a different plane it carries on Luther's struggle against 'the devil's whore';[20] because it brings us not indeed into God himself but into God's 'native country'; because it teaches men to renounce every *Anspruch* over being and beings; because it schools men in long-suffering, expectancy, hearkening, lowliness and open-ness; because as an ontology it converges in an astonishing way with the *Begrifflichkeit* of the New Testament. It does not dwell on the Christian scheme of things (that is none of its business) but draws inspiration from the ontology which the Word of God brings into play—and therefore indirectly reveals.

The fact that Heidegger acknowledges Paul, John, Augustine, Luther and Kierkegaard as his masters is no accident. Not as though he took over their ontic scheme of things, but having clarified their ontological presuppositions he turns them into the foundation for a philosophy of being. Thus by following the guidance of Heidegger Bultmann in no way makes faith dependent on his philosophy (see pp. 331–3, above); and when there is need he does not shrink from criticizing that philosophy (see pp. 333–6, above).

Finally, when Barth thanks Bultmann for having broken the Heideggerian pattern on the crucial head of the *Christusgeschehen* he blunders once again. Bultmann holds, as we know, that man has a *Vorverständnis* of all things, including God and God's doings. Barth denies that this is so, because he seems to think that having a *Vorver-stehen* of a thing means controlling it. Here he has got the wrong sow by the ear. In the first place *Vorverständnis* is a *Was*, not a *Dass*; and in the second place it does not come from man the subject but from the *lumen naturale*—that is to say, from being. *Vorverstehen* is a category of outwardness, the pre-structure of a thing. To say that I have a pre-comprehension of what God does, does not in the least mean that I am subjectifying it. Moreover this precomprehension is absolutely necessary to enable me to grasp God's operation as a human being can and a stone or an animal cannot.[21]

---

20. 'Heidegger was much drawn to the younger Luther in particular, the Protestant whose stern faith branded the Schoolmen's "natural reason" a "whore"' (K. Loewith, 'Les implications politiques de l'existence chez Heidegger' in *Les temps modernes* 2 [1946] p. 348).—In a sermon preached the very year that he died, Luther was still flaying the strumpet reason, and more savagely than ever, as we have seen.

21. Père Bouillard also shows, refuting Barth, that in Bultmann's view 'we would be unable to recognize the event [of] Christ as God's doing if the quest for God

(8) Drawing to a close, Barth says that all the many questions he puts to Bultmann come down to this one problem: what is the *Verstehen* of the New Testament in particular and what is *Verstehen* in general?

(a) Is there a genuine New Testament *Verstehen* if we take for granted a changeless, normative image of what the reader 'can'[22] think possible, accurate and relevant; if we start with a '*Vorverständnis*'[23] that has been set up as canonical? Is man not encountered by the Word of God as by a truth and a reality ever alien and antagonistic to his power of comprehension? If I do not believe on the basis of my reason and my own powers how 'can' I understand anything? What does 'can' mean in a case where a *Verstehen* follows upon enlightenment by the Holy Spirit?

Obviously the attitude each of us takes toward the New Testament will be coloured by certain '*Vorverständnisse*', by each one's idea of what must be thought possible, accurate and relevant. No less obviously, the first thing we do when essaying to understand the Bible is always to put up our defences against its foreignness and 'domesticate'[24] it by means of our '*Vorverständnisse*'. But must this *Nostrifizierung* really be set up as a principle and a method, so that we confront the New Testament with a '*Vorverständnis*', a 'this-far-and-no-farther!', that are definitive and absolute? What standing have anthropologism and existentialism here, even though we were convinced that we must accept them as binding upon us? What standing have the idealism, the positivism, and the other systems of our fathers here?

Never mind how far we 'can' or cannot understand the New Testament, on what ground do we presume to bandy words with God in the name of such 'elements of this world'?[25] Shall we still hear his message if we set up such a *conditio sine qua non* between him and ourselves? If we shut ourselves up inside this suit of armour instead of striving for the utmost possible receptivity and openness towards the kerygma? Instead of making our own *Verstehenkönnen* (ability to understand) the catalyst of the New Testament, would it not be better to let the New Testament act as the catalyst of our *Verstehen-können*? Instead of reading the text within the framework of an

---

were not the driving agent behind our existence. In the sense Bultmann means, we actually have a precomprehension of what God does' (H. Bouillard, *Karl Barth*, 3, p. 57, note 3). This book of Père Bouillard's brings out as clearly as could be wished the way Barth goes on and on misconstruing Bultmann's thought.

22. The inverted commas are Barth's.

23. The inverted commas are Barth's.

24. The inverted commas are Barth's.

25. The inverted commas are Barth's.

allegedly normative self-understanding, does it not behoove us to understand ourselves as we find ourselves understood in the text, and then understand the text the better in the light of this sound self-understanding, even at the risk of thinking and speaking 'myth-ologically'[26] to a large extent? Does not Luther say: *Sacrae literae volunt habere humilem lectorem . . . qui semper dicit: Doce me, doce me, doce me?* Must not the modern reader, too, work from this 'ability'[27] to understand?

(b) Let us go on to consider *Verstehen* at large (RB, pp. 50–52). Far from being the application of a general hermeneutics, must not biblical hermeneutics act as the pattern and yardstick of *all* hermeneutics? Can I really expect to understand any text aright, even a mythical one, if I do not open myself with the utmost possible candour to its question-ing? Can I understand the other in general unless I am ready to let it tell me 'something brand new' (RB, p. 1), something that I was quite 'unable'[28] to tell myself before, something against which I had a prejudice, even many prejudices, and perhaps very well-grounded prejudices? Can I expect to understand the other so long as I think I automatically know just how far my *Verstehen* reaches with regard to it? Total *Verstehen* is difficult indeed for us. But it is one thing to be willing to have one's narrow-mindedness queried and its confines thrust outward, and quite another to enthrone that narrow-mindedness as a sacred duty and an inviolable law. Unless I can be limber in this way, it seems to me, not only can I not really understand any text aright, but any text at all will be Greek to me. What is more, I doom myself to being understood by no one.

If I wish a *Verstehen* to exist between the other and myself I must be capable of docility. But since this docility is not by any means a thing bred in the bone, whether I have to do with men or with texts; since I can no more summon it up in my dealings with other men than I can in my dealings with God; since it cannot be wrung from my own reason or any of my own powers (*aus eigener Vernunft und Kraft*)—a genuine *Verstehen* is only to be learned in the classroom of the Holy Spirit. Only in that classroom can the Bible be grasped as the witness of God's Word. Can a man understand myth, can he understand Goethe even, without docility, and therefore anywhere else but in the classroom of the Holy Spirit? As for this doctrine of a normative *Vorverständnis* which competes with the Holy Spirit by appointing him the bounds he must not overstep, this theory which underlies

---

26. The inverted commas are Barth's.
27. The inverted commas are Barth's.
28. The inverted commas are Barth's.

Bultmann's hermeneutic, does it not sound the death-knell of *any* genuine *Verstehen*? If we have any real communication at heart, must we not stop and think when confronted with this theory?

When we set sail, some thirty years ago, for new theological shores, the idea—at least my idea—was to turn inside out the notion of biblical '*Verstehen*'[29] and *Verstehen* in general which then prevailed, and ground 'human knowledge on a *becoming*-known and *being*-known which man owes to the *object* (*Gegenstand*) of his knowledge' (RB, p. 52). Our aim was to set biblical *Verstehen* (and thereby all *Verstehen*) free from the Egyptian prison in which one philosophy or another is forever trying to teach us what the Holy Spirit must say in order to be 'comprehensible'.[30] In those days we were trying to 'demythologize' the image man has of himself as the measure of his own *Verstehen* and of all *Verstehen*. We met with endless difficulties and we made mistakes, but all the same we were on the right road. If I am compelled to stop here in my essay to understand Bultmann, it is because I see him abandoning that road and backtracking with his theory of *Verstehen*. What brings a blush to my cheek is not so much his sweeping denials of the supernatural (RB, p. 53) as (what shall I call it?) his pre-Copernican behaviour.

Somewhere or other Père Bouillard mildly observes that Barth 'does not hesitate to repeat himself'. If he does indeed often repeat himself in *Rudolf Bultmann—Ein Versuch, ihn zu verstehen* at least it must be granted that he works his way round to a perfect siting of the problem and then cuts it down to its bare bones—the controversy over *Verstehen*.

To begin with, must we not once more ask Barth the basic questions he asks Bultmann? Finding himself face to face with a man whom he considers an antagonist, has he really been willing to 'have his narrow-mindedness queried and its confines thrust outward'? Has he not rather 'enthroned it as a sacred duty and an inviolable law'? Has he been willing to be told 'something against which he had prejudices, even many prejudices, and perhaps very well-grounded prejudices'? Can he 'really expect to understand Bultmann's thought aright' if he 'does not open himself with the utmost possible candour to its questioning'? Has he, for his own part, shown that 'docility' to which he so warmly exhorts us? Has it not come home to him that if Goethe cannot be understood without that docility, no more can Bultmann? Does he not approach Bultmann with a 'definitive and absolute *Vorverständnis* (in the sense which he, Barth, attaches to the term), with a 'this-far-and-no-farther'? Has he done his best to become a 'receptive, open' soul? Does he not

---

29. The inverted commas are Barth's.
30. The inverted commas are Barth's.

try to understand Bultmann by his own reason and his own powers? When reading Bultmann does he not 'set up *Nostrifizierung* as a principle and a method'? When all is said and done, has his attitude towards Bultmann not been 'pre-Copernican'?

Had Barth put into practice the splendid advice he lavishes on Bultmann, he would have perceived that Bultmann's *Verstehen* is no subjective, a priori principle with which its author attempts to 'domesticate' the New Testament but rather the very embodiment of 'the utmost possible receptivity and openness', because it is grounded precisely 'in a being-known'. He would have realized that *Verstehen* is the utter negation of acting 'by one's own reason and one's own powers' and that Bultmann's demythologization is the self-same one which he, Barth, says he has tried to bring about for thirty years—in other words, demythologization of 'the image man has of himself as the measure of his own *Verstehen* and of all *Verstehen*'.

His misconception of 'ability to understand' is typical. He identifies it with a negation, a 'definitive and absolute "this-far-and-no-farther",' a *conditio sine qua non*, a 'suit of armour', a 'catalyst', a 'competitor of the Holy Spirit'. In fact the 'ability' Bultmann speaks of is merely intended to point out that man, unlike a stone or an animal, *can* receive God's revelation. We have seen how Barth was first in stoutly maintaining that man, however fallen he may be, still remains man, because (to use his own words) sin does not turn man into 'a stone or a stump' (ch. 18, §1, above). As a consequence man is that being who *can* receive revelation. This the author of *Die kirchliche Dogmatik* declares in other texts, which we have quoted, notably the following: 'If the event of faith is the event of the Word's presence in man . . . that necessarily means that darkness *can* become light. Therefore man's power, insufficient of itself, *can* become the sufficient power' (*ibid.*) inasmuch as the human being does not behave, when believing, "like a block of wood or a stone"' (*ibid.*). Bultmann means to say nothing but this when he defines man as ability-to-be, as freedom, 'historicity' and temporality. Only he pushes on with much more exactitude than Barth, bewaring of any possible counter-attack on the part of the '*Gegenstand*'.

IV

In his preface to *Die kirchliche Dogmatik* 4, 1(1953), which deals with reconciliation, Barth gives warning that the subject matter of this volume forced him into a running dialogue with Bultmann, although (he says) I do not often mention him. Bultmann, he adds, has taken me to task for the fogginess of my *Begrifflichkeit*; but all the same I shall not follow his hermeneutic method, because I am not satisfied that it would enable me to set forth more clearly and with greater ease what I have to say. In fact, where Bultmann's doctrine of reconciliation and his own are concerned, Barth casts back to what he had already worked out in his book *Rudolf Bultmann—Ein Versuch, ihn zu verstehen.*

(1) How does Christ in himself come to us and how do we reach him? In view of what he is and what he does, how can we make bold to talk of our sin, of our justification, of ourselves as his community, of our faith? The truth is that before our faith exists he has already come to us and we are there with him; his being is in us and ours is in him. His being exists from the beginning; it belongs to us and ours belongs to him. As existing in himself, in his person and his work, he has already turned to us. Everything has been consummated in him, so that when a man becomes a believer nothing really new happens, nothing that rounds off the work of Christ. Our salvation is already won in him. He is not simply the possibility of our salvation, as though it became a reality through the obedience of our faith; he is himself that reality. How then can Bultmann write: 'Christ has created no more than the *possibility* of ζωή, which becomes a solid reality in the believer'?[31]

Here again Barth takes the word 'possibility' in the sense which ordinary thinking and parlance attach to it. Being an outsider to Bultmann's *Begrifflichkeit*, he does not perceive that we are dealing not with an abstract possibility but with a possibility of ec-sistence. In the relevant passage of his *Theologie des Neuen Testaments* Bultmann compares the race sprung from the first Adam with that sprung from the second. Paul teaches, he observes, that all men without exception are doomed to inherit death from the first Adam. But they do not receive life from the second Adam in the same way, as it were biologically. They do not all receive it automatically: only those receive it who have faith.

It is in this sense that Christ has won us only the possibility of life, which does not become a reality in a man until he accepts it by faith. Rom 5:1–11 means to show that the second Adam has given mankind life as surely as the first has bequeathed it death. But in the latter case, Paul says, that certainly was a fate that operated quite apart from the will of those who were born, whereas in the former case it does not really exist until a man cleaves to Christ by faith. Bultmann stresses the fact that Paul here turns his back on the naturalist view of redemption which the Gnostics entertained; salvation is not a phenomenon of nature but one of freedom; it involves a response on the part of man, in the sense that it is not wholly 'consummated' and 'real' for the individual (KD 4, 1, p. 313) before he believes in Christ. Barth, of course,

---

31. Bultmann, TNT, p. 252, quoted by Barth, KD 4, 1, p. 313.

has every right to say that faith does not 'round off' Christ's work. All the same the reconciliation which God effects is not an automatic thing; it calls for obedience on the believer's part. Does this obedience enter into the warp and woof of the eschatological event? That is a question we shall consider in due course.

(2) Farther on, when discussing faith and its object, Barth stoutly, nay passionately, dwells on the vital *pro me*. But then he says that what comes first is not the act whereby I acknowledge and testify that Jesus Christ exists for me, but rather the objective fact that he does exist for me. The fundamental thing is not the 'I believe' but the object of the 'I believe'. We must not set up the *pro me* as a principle. The sinews and sense of it are this: that *Jesus Christ* exists for me. I have no business singing the *Ich-Lied* unless I sing it as the *Christus-Lied*.

We must not expect to find God's nobility, truth and reality in what man feels able to acknowledge and confess as noble, true and real, and in what he 'existentielly'[32] fingers. We may not 'cut out' of God, for our sole attention, that which 'existentielly' interests us, by means of a '*Vorverständnis*' borrowed from some ontology or anthropology. The God who in Jesus Christ exists *pro me* may not be thrust into a procrustean bed so that we can mutilate him as the fancy strikes us. Christ is not a mere mathematical symbol denoting a power of the believing subject; he is the source and object of the subject's faith. All anthropologies and all ontologies find their measure and their law in him. Only by usurpation can a 'subjectivist philosophy' (KD 4, 1, p. 846) shoulder its way into theology. What must be demythologized is the 'I', as Paul demythologized it in Gal 2:20: 'It is no longer I who live, but Christ who lives in me.'

Bultmann's name never occurs in this passage, but he obviously provides the target throughout. This attack of Barth's, though hotter and clumsier, remains as humdrum as those that went before it. It lays bare his utter misconception of Bultmann's stand. He is sure that Bultmann uses a 'subjectivist philosophy'. Barth simply cannot get outside his philosophic credo, according to which anything that is not objective must be subjective and anything that is not subjective must be objective. Subjectivity becomes a procrustean bed for objectivity: whatever is given to the subject must be that much taken away from the object.

Barth cannot comprehend that the philosophy of ec-sistence is neither a philosophy of the subject nor a philosophy of the object, but something altogether different—a philosophy of *otherness*, which rejects the whole idea of the object, seeing in it the embodiment of the subject's

32. The inverted commas are Barth's.

will to be his own master, and the whole idea of the subject, holding that man as the subject is doomed to perpetual imprisonment inside himself. As envisaged by the ec-sistential interpretation, the *pro me* does not in the least make Christ a 'mathematical symbol denoting a power of the subject'; it makes him the Lord of man. Let Barth say what he likes, the act whereby 'I know, acknowledge and confess that Jesus Christ exists for me' is a crucial one, because only then Christ *is* my Lord. So long as I do not have faith, my attitude towards him is that of an observer and therefore of a critic and judge—in a word, the attitude of a master (lord). It is then that I put him into a procrustean bed (if we must use that metaphor, which hardly befits the theme we are discussing). Christ cannot possibly reign over me so long as I have not ec-sistentielly confessed him.

In view of all that we have said about *Vorverständnis* we may be pardoned for not casting back to that matter. As for demythologizing the 'I', that is precisely what Bultmann has at heart to do from one end of his work to the other. When Barth declares, in the preface to *Die kirchliche Dogmatik* 4, 1, that he is unwilling to take over Bultmann's *Begrifflichkeit* because it would not allow him to say what he has to say, we are entitled to think the opposite—that it would help him to convey his underlying intent a good deal better. It is hardly a paradox when Bultmann proves to be more Barthian than Barth.

(3) Considerable interest attaches to a further passage in *Die kirchliche Dogmatik*. Barth says that the act of faith does not refer to any 'doctrine, theory or theology' (KD 4, 1, p. 849) embodied in or by the community, nor yet to the profession of faith or to dogma; not even to the biblical 'stories' or to prophetic and apostolic theology as such. At its root, as an act of acknowledgment and free obedience, Christian faith is not in the least an 'acceptance-as-true' of certain narratives or propositions, whether their source be biblical or ecclesiastical, but an obedient 'acceptance-as-true' of him to whom the Bible bears witness and whom the Church then preaches in like manner: the living Christ himself, nothing else and no one else—of him whose place cannot be taken by the word of the prophets and apostles, of him whom that word can only serve.

Faith alone acknowledges him—not the texts of scripture which bear him witness nor the ecclesiastical preaching which makes him known. What faith holds to be true is this: that 'Jesus Christ is my Lord', says Barth quoting Luther. No doubt faith submits to the witness of scripture, and bears in mind the word of the Church; but its own object is solely that which we have specified—a 'that' which is not a 'that' at all, which towers above every 'that', which undergirds every 'that', and is the living Christ, the king of scripture and the head of the

Church. This is the point which must be driven home with the utmost vigour, against every pedestrian orthodoxy. Faith exists only in *direct* encounter with its object: it is not a matter of accepting as true the propositions which bear witness to or preach that object.

Here Barth asks himself: am I not at one with Wilhelm Herrmann and Rudolf Bultmann? Surely I am, he replies, on the *negative* side of what I put forward—that is, in my fight against popular orthodoxy, which considers faith to be accepting biblical texts or ecclesiastical pronouncements as true. But am I really and beyond all doubt at one with them in what I *positively* maintain, that the living Lord Jesus— whom scripture attests and the Church preaches—is the One whom faith must accept as true? Are Bultmann and I agreed that orthodoxy must be rejected on this basis and not on an ethico-anthropological one? I think the question had better be left open.

In very truth Barth never before came so close to Bultmann, not the one he generally pictures to himself but the real Bultmann, who insists day in day out that the object of faith (to use Barth's very words) is not a 'doctrine, theory or theology'; that the kerygma is not a set of abstract, universal, timeless truths but the *Anrede* of God speaking to us in Jesus Christ, the live encounter of the believer with his God; that faith maintains only one thing: that 'Jesus Christ is my Lord' (Luther). Nevertheless Barth shrinks from reaching an outright agreement once and for all. No doubt he is right, for it seems that he envisages the person of Christ as something in the nature of an object. True, he stoutly declares that Jesus Christ is not a 'that', but does he draw all the logical consequences from the fact? Does he not still fit Christ into the framework of the philosophy of subject and object? Has he really thought through the concept of encounter (which he uses again and again, especially here)?

It appears to us that Barth's failure to ponder sufficiently on the connection between theology and philosophy cries aloud from the passages we have just examined. His underlying intent is strikingly clear in them. By finding fault with orthodoxy he proclaims his refusal to objectify faith; he stresses the fact that objectification is only a way of bringing God to heel; he is full of praise for Luther's 'Jesus Christ is my Lord'. But no less obviously the categories and parlance he uses are impotent to convey at all effectively that intent of his, sound and ir-reproachably evangelic though it be. While washing his hands of any doctrinal *Fürwahrhalten*, he nonetheless calls faith an 'obedient *Fürwahrhalten*'.

Of course one is at liberty to give words whatever sense one chooses, but in any ontology that will hold water the two terms 'accept-as-true' and 'obedience' clash head-on. They hail from two different registers (in the musical sense) of thought and language: the first belongs to the philosophy of the object and the second to the philosophy of ec-sistence. In a metaphysics of *Fürwahrhalten* there is no room for obedience. So it would be better for Barth to clothe his intent in the language of ec-sistence (giving up, of course, the bad habit of confounding ec-sistence with ordinary subjectivity.)

Again, he states that Jesus Christ is the object (*Objekt*) of obedient *Fürwahrhalten*. But to look on Jesus Christ as an object[33] is to thrust him into the categories of natural man. The Lord whom Luther speaks of (this is the point) is not an object, because the object always refers to a subject who seeks to control it in one way or another. Here again, of course, one is at liberty to give words whatever meaning one chooses; but is one not better advised to refrain from giving them an unnatural meaning, and to express God's lordship in a *Begrifflichkeit* which befits it?

(4) Barth concedes that the obedient acknowledgment which constitutes faith is of an active nature, so far as concerns the subject; that it inevitably encroaches on himself, on his *Selbstverständnis*. It is an act which brings the whole man into play, turns his 'whole' being upside down, a 'thoroughgoing' decision about himself and about the world (KD 4, 1, p. 857). Be that as it may, Barth explains, I am speaking of an upset that is 'total' but not 'absolute', a decision that is 'thoroughgoing' but not 'eschatological', a free act of man that rests upon an act of God but is not 'God's very act as such' (*ibid.*).

True enough, he goes on, the event of faith could be thought of as a calling forth (*Vergegenwärtigung*) and re-enactment (*Nachvollzug*) in the believer of the salvific event which took place in Jesus Christ, so that the history of Jesus Christ, his death and resurrection, become the history of the believer himself. The whole reality of the *Christusgeschehen* would then consist in its being a new proffer of life made in the existence of the man who thereby describes the kerygma. Accordingly the truth and might of faith would be the act of the man who accepts this proffer, dying with Christ to himself and the world, so that he may become receptive to the future of his life. In that case we ought indeed to speak of an absolute upset, of an eschatological decision, of God's very act as such, which would all become event in the act of believing.

Time and again the attempt has been made to identify the history of Jesus Christ with the history of the Christian in this way, and vice versa. The theology of the younger Luther (until about 1519) represents a

---

33. When defining God or Christ as an object Barth uses the term *Objekt* rather than the term *Gegenstand*.

powerful thrust in that direction, which Bultmann merely carries forward. But we are unable to endorse either Luther or Bultmann. The true calling forth (or *repraesentatio*) of the history of Jesus Christ is the one that occurs in himself, making him the object and source of faith, which merely responds to that *repraesentatio* and is not its origin, so that God's salvific act cannot be identified with the free act of man. Jesus Christ still remains the object and source of faith. His death and resurrection are not received in faith. Faith is not a calling forth and re-enactment of his obedience, his sacrifice and his triumph.

Is Bultmann's idea anything else but the translation into existential language of the Roman Church's sacramental theology, which teaches that at the climax of the Mass, concurrently with the transmutation of the bread and wine, there occurs an 'unbloody repetition'[34] of Christ's sacrifice on Calvary—metaphysically identical with what happened then? A man who repudiates the doctrine of the Mass will not admit that the event which happened once and for all in Jesus Christ is renewed in the act of faith. With the elder Luther, he will see in faith a grasping (*comprehendere*) of Jesus Christ. He will not confuse this grasp with the death and resurrection of Christ nor, conversely, will he identify Christ's death and resurrection with it. Therefore when speaking of what happens in the act of faith he will not talk of an absolute upset, an eschatological decision, of God's act as such. Faith is merely a taking in (*Kenntnisnahme*) of what Jesus is and does for man; it is not the re-enactment of those things.

What Jesus is and does have no need to be repeated. They are present and efficacious in their own truth and power. Bultmann has not only crept up to the Mass but also to Catholic mysticism, to the idea that the saints relive the history of Christ in their own lives. When the Catholic theologian Hans Urs von Balthasar writes books about Thérèse of Lisieux or Elizabeth of Dijon he means to show that what Christ is and does becomes a present event in and through the life of these mystics, who relive, re-enact the history of Christ, so that he has ceased to be the object and source of their faith. In these circumstances does not sanctification become a self-sanctification, a work?

No doubt, Barth agrees, the life of a believer stands 'in very direct and close relation' (KD 4, 1, p. 859) to Christ, his death and resurrection. How shall we put this relation into words? Through the idea of analogy, which affirms neither too much nor too little. Faith changes man's existence, or rather the view and grasp he has of his existence, but only in such a way that they run parallel to him who as man's

34. The inverted commas are Barth's. He is quoting a time-honoured formula of Catholic theology.

Lord died in his stead: they enter into an analogy (*in Entsprechung*) with him to whom man cleaves. The believer can only live in the likeness (*im Gleichnis*) of Jesus who died and rose again for him. If anyone thinks this is saying too little, let him beware lest in saying more he say something worse. The eschatological event of our death and resurrection took place ages ago in the man Jesus; it is not repeated in us. Christ's death on Calvary was *ours*: that is how we died to sin, independent of our faith. Similarly our life is already real in the deed that Christ did once and for all, and that needs no rounding off by the event of our faith. Our faith does no more than bear witness to (*bezeugen*; KD 4, 1, pp. 325–6) the event of our death and resurrection, which took place in the man Jesus: in itself it is not an eschatological event.

Before scrutinizing these statements of Barth's we must recollect Bultmann's attitude towards the problem of the 'continued incarnation' —in other words, of tradition. The need for tradition follows from the purely gratuitous nature of the salvific event. Since man can in no way control it, that event must be handed down (*traditum*) to him, given to him from outside. For that reason it abides in the Church, present there in word and sacrament. It is in preaching and sacramental acts that Christ encounters men today. His work was not hemmed in by the few years he spent on earth: it is deathless, it is always going on. In preaching and in the sacraments 'the event of Christ takes place incessantly', 'goes on without a break' (GV 1, p. 289; see ch. 10, §1, above).

Such is the mind of Paul. When he proclaims the Word he knows that it is not himself, Paul, speaking, but Christ in person: 'We are ambassadors for Christ, God making his appeal through us' (2 Cor 5:20). If Christ proclaims himself in the preacher, no importance attaches to the preacher as a man: 'What we preach is not ourselves, but Jesus Christ as Lord, with ourselves your servants for Jesus's sake' (2 Cor 4:5). The strong points or failings of the apostle do not come into the picture, for it is as one entrusted with a mission that he serves men, as a 'steward of the mysteries of God' (1 Cor 4:1). Christians must no longer know anyone 'according to the flesh' (2 Cor 5:16; Greek text), least of all their preachers. Judging them according to the flesh and taking sides with Apollo or with Paul is precisely the sin of the Corinthians (1 Cor 1:10–16). But 'what then? Only that in every way, whether in pretence or in truth, Christ is proclaimed; and in that I rejoice' (Phil 1:18). Preachers are only servants, the 'ministers of a new covenant' (2 Cor 3:6), 'servants of God' (2 Cor 6:4), 'of Christ' (2 Cor 11:23; see 1 Cor 3:5); 'servants', nay 'slaves of Christ Jesus' (footnote in RSV to Rom 1:1; Gal 1:10; Phil 1:1).

Christ is not a bygone fact but the ever-living risen Lord at work through his ministers. A man becomes such a minister only insofar as he has ceased to be a man any longer, by dying and rising from the dead with Christ. The apostle bears about the dying of *Jesus* in his body, at the same time bestowing the life of Jesus on those to whom he preaches the gospel: 'Always carrying in the body the death of Jesus, so that the life of Jesus may also be manifested in our bodies. So death is at work in us, but life in you' (2 Cor 4:10–12). Has it struck Barth that Paul calls upon his hearers to follow not only in Christ's footsteps but also in his own? 'I urge you, then, be imitators of me' (1 Cor 4:16). Of course what they are to model themselves on is not Paul's human life but his eschatological life: 'Be imitators of me, as I am of Christ' (1 Cor 11:1). 'What you have learned and received and heard and seen in me, do; and the God of peace will be with you' (Phil 4:9).

What is more, it behooves Christians to imitate Paul's imitators: 'Mark those who so live as you have seen an example in us' (Phil 3:17). Paul calls on the Philippians to imitate him and his disciples because through the eschatological life and word of both it is Christ who summons men, that he may judge and save them. The preaching of the gospel spreads both death and life: such is the burden of 2 Cor 2:14–6:10. To one man the apostle is 'a fragrance from death to death, to the other a fragrance from life to life' (2 Cor 2:16). Because 'God . . . gave us the ministry of reconciliation' (2 Cor 5:18). Therefore just as Christ is 'the power of God' (1 Cor 1:24), the gospel preaching too is 'the power of God for salvation to everyone who has faith' (Rom 1:16). The event of preaching is the event of Christ and of salvation: 'Working together with him, then, we entreat you not to accept the grace of God in vain . . . Behold, now is the acceptable time; behold, now is the day of salvation' (2 Cor 6:1–2).

Paul does not blush to say: 'Christ is speaking in me' (2 Cor 13:3), because the apostle comes to men 'in the fullness of the blessing of Christ' (Rom 15:29), he speaks to them in the very power of the risen Lord who dwells in him: 'In dealing with you we live with him by the power of God' (2 Cor 13:4; Greek text [Tischendorf, eighth edition]).

Not in preaching alone does the eschatological event still go on but also in the sacraments. Baptism makes a man share in the death and resurrection of Christ (Rom 6:1ff; see ch. 10, §III, above). Those who take part in the Lord's Supper have κοινωνία with the κύριος bestowed on them (1 Cor 10:20f) because that meal is a καταγγέλειν of the eschatological event (1 Cor 10:20f; see ch. 10, §III, above). In short, the eschatological event 'still goes on' (TNT, p. 312) in the Church of the Word and the sacraments.

Does faith in that event actually form part of it? Paul has no doubt
that it does. In its character as a response to the word of preaching
(which, be it noted, is called ἀκοὴ πίστεως) faith forms part of the
eschatological event on the same footing as the Word itself. It is the
road to salvation, and as such Paul contrasts the 'law of faith' with the
'law of works'. He speaks of the 'coming' and the 'revealing' of faith
(Gal 3:23, 25); in other words, he speaks of it as he does of the event
of salvation itself, in the very same terms, so as to stress the fact that it
is of the very same eschatological nature. When so doing he does not
mean to deny the freedom of the act of faith, which must mark it
insofar as it is an 'obedience' (Rom 1:5).

We must go so far as to say that the concrete embodiment itself, in
the particular man's decision, of the capacity for faith also exhibits an
eschatological character. In the eyes of the believer his actual decision
is a gift of grace. He knows God as the One who gives rise in him to
will and deed alike—which does not mean that he (the Christian) is rid
of responsibility for his own act but rather that he is given the freedom
with which to do it, as we saw in the chapter devoted to predestination.
Left to himself, a man can only 'in-sist'—that is, do works. He remains
the bondsman of the world and of himself. Grace gives him manu-
mission, setting him free of himself for God. God gives rise to will and
deed alike, not by stepping into the man's shoes but by making him
ec-sist for God, by capacitating him for a free act oriented to God. The
man's act is every inch his own, but the fact that he can do it is a sheer
grace of God.

How the doing of God and the doing of man bear on each other is
a hopeless riddle in the *Begrifflichkeit* spawned by the philosophy of
subject and object, which has it that a man is endowed with freedom
as an attribute *before* his act of faith. On this reading it is impossible to
make out how God can give rise to will and deed alike without tramp-
ling upon human freedom and, conversely, how man can act freely
without denying grace. In this system faith can form no part of the
eschatological event because freedom is not a thing bestowed by grace
but instead, forsooth, possessed by a man before he ever makes an act
of faith—or, to be more precise, before he is summoned by God. Here
a vital point is ignored: by calling a man, Jesus Christ so transforms
him as to make his response possible, causing him to cross over from
slavery to the freedom of the sons of God, from in-sistence to ec-
sistence for God.[35] The eschatological freedom of the response is a gift

35. We say the freedom *of the sons of God* and ec-sistence *for God*, because obviously
enough God does not give man an *earthly* freedom and ec-sistence, with the
mere decisions and authenticity of this world in view, but an eschatological
freedom and ec-sistence which make possible the act of faith *in God*—that is to
say, an eschatological act. This, as we have seen, is precisely the vital issue over
which Bultmann makes a clean break with Heidegger (see pp. 333–6, above).

from God, but because it is a freedom the man receiving it remains fully answerable for his act of faith—and yet his act of faith is an eschatological event, because the freedom whence it comes forth remains a gift of grace and not an attribute which a man has by nature before ever making up his mind to believe.

When he refers to the 'coming' and the 'revealing' of faith and says that it has been 'granted' (Phil 1:29), Paul is stressing the fact that it forms part of the eschatological event. Again he firmly drives the same point home when discussing the act of faith in predestinationist terms (Rom 8:29 and 9:6–29). If these declarations about God's προγινώσκειν and προορίζειν (Rom 8:29), his ἐκλογή (Rom 9:11) and his σκληρύνειν (Rom 9:18), were to be taken at face value, no doubt they would be so many denials of what Paul affirms again and again, that faith is an obedience. God gives rise to will and deed alike in the sense which we have specified. These predestinationist texts have the virtue of making it crystal-clear that the decision of faith is not a human and earthly decision but an eschatological act.

Bultmann's idea only takes up the New Testament idea and pushes it somewhat farther. Barth would have it that Bultmann credits the believer's act of faith with the power to call forth the death and resurrection of Christ; that Christ, therefore, is no longer the sole and everlasting source of the eschatological event, which only begins in him since the believer repeats it, re-enacts it, in and through his faith. What happened the first time in Jesus Christ is as it were transferred to man: by his faith man is able to bring about the event of Christ anew in himself. Now if such be the case we must speak of an upset in his life that is not only 'total' but 'absolute', since he more or less becomes a second God; of a decision that is not only 'thoroughgoing' but 'eschatological', since the believer is able, through his own act, to accomplish the eschatological event anew. Therefore his act is 'God's very act as such'.

Need we say that this is giving a wrong-headed picture of Bultmann's stand? He has never said that the event of Christ is called forth by the power of faith; he says it is called forth by the power of God. It is neither actualized nor re-enacted by anything: it actualizes and re-enacts itself. But this language must be thrown overboard: properly speaking there is no *repraesentatio*, or *Vergegenwärtigung*, or *Nachvollzug*; there is continuance. The event of salvation is eschatological and eternal. It stands above time and space—which does not mean that it is cut off from them, like the Ideas in Platonism, but rather that its 'historical', unmetaphysical transcendence makes it present to all ages and all places, to the men of every civilization and every degree of culture. It is present of itself, not by dint of the faith which believers have. Thus there is no calling forth or re-enacting the event of Christ, there is only its abiding presence that presides over history although at the same time it stands within history and exists for it.

As Paul has established, the event of Christ is present in the Church of the Word and the sacraments as the unchanging source whence believers draw their faith. Accordingly to say that faith is eschatological in character is not in the least to claim that man has made it so. God is the one who gives rise to man's will and deed alike in the act of faith. Therefore the doctrine that the event of Christ still goes on in the life of believers neither humanizes the doing of God nor divinizes the doing of man, as such, in any way whatever. It only says what Barth wants said: that Christ not merely 'exists' but 'abides', or again that in the act of faith 'Christ's being and doing are present and efficacious in their own reality and their own might'. By all means we must declare with Paul that the event of Christ is continued by believers, but in the sense that it is the ever-living Lord who day in day out saves mankind through his ministers, through men who have become the new creation of 2 Cor 5:17, so that Paul can say without tainting himself in the slightest with subjectivism, 'Christ is speaking in me' (2 Cor 13:3).

Barth says that Bultmann's idea verges on the theology of the Mass. First of all let us take note that he seems to be a trifle hazy about that theology. He thinks that the sacrifice of Christ in the Mass is the Church's doing, just as he thinks that the believer (to Bultmann's mind) re-enacts the event of Christ by making an act of faith. Now it happens that according to Roman doctrine the sacrifice of the Mass is Christ's own doing, no less than the sacrifice of the cross is: *Idem nunc offerans . . . qui se ipsum tunc in cruce obtulit.*[36] True enough, the Council of Trent then goes on to explain that he does this *sacerdotum ministerio.*[37] But who can fail to see the gulf that separates the Catholic Church's view from the one Barth attributes to it? At Mass Christ himself is the chief agent; priests act only as his ministers. Paul too keeps saying that we are the ministers of Christ (see pp. 414-15, above) and Bultmann echoes him.

The difference between the theology of Paul and Bultmann, on the one hand, and Catholic theology on the other is that theirs is 'historical' in nature and the Catholic theology metaphysical. The Roman Church thinks of the ministry as a supernatural attribute infused into a man by God. By ordination the priest receives an indelible character.[38] The ministry is an institution instead of a ceaseless calling. Grace is something

36. *Conc. trid., sessio XXII, cap.* 2 (Denzinger 940).
37. *Ibid.*
38. *Ibid., sessio VII, can.* 9 (Denzinger 852).

the Christian possesses as an attribute. It is not 'forensic' but exists in him as an upper storey built on the same pattern as the lower storey—in other words, as a supernatural in-sistence.[39] So in refutation of Barth we must first of all give a fairer picture of what the Catholic Church maintains and second of all mark well that Bultmann stands as far from the Catholic position as do Paul and the Luther of 1519.

What are we to make of the theory which Barth sets up against Bultmann's? In *Die kirchliche Dogmatik* 4, 1, he sets forth his theology of faith with striking thoroughness. There, as we already know, he finds fault with Luther for harping too much on the idea of justification by faith alone. He thinks it better to dwell on the source and object of faith, namely Christ. The *articulus stantis et cadentis ecclesiae* is not the *sola fide* but its foundation: Jesus Christ and 'knowledge of *his* being, of what *he* does for us, in us, and with us' (KD 4, 1, p. 588). Man is justified in Jesus Christ. To put the matter in negative terms, justification destroys the fault man has committed and annihilates him himself insofar as he is its perpetrator. We can neither feel this change taking place nor imagine what it is like, because it takes place in the man Jesus and not in our own existence. In positive terms, justification restores man's birthright and lays the foundation for his new life. This again is an event which we can neither feel going on nor imagine, because it takes place in the man Jesus and not in our existence. It is something that happened to the son of God made man (KD 4, 1, pp. 616–21).

Our act of faith is in consequence simply a *knowledge* of the justification which we have undergone in and through Jesus Christ. Barth, of course, tacks the word *erkennen* onto the word *ergreifen* (*ibid.*, pp. 704, 709), but his commentary shows that this *ergreifen* is a matter of finding one's feet. Contrasting the 'objective' reconciliation that happens in Jesus Christ with the 'subjective' one that happens in the act of faith, he asserts that the 'subjective' one is brought about by our own fruitful and quickening knowledge of the 'objective' one (*ibid.*, p. 721). Faith is purely a matter of *knowing* something: the Christian recognizes and grasps what the unbeliever does not. Barth's doctrine of the sacraments fits in beautifully with his doctrine on faith. 'Our baptism does not *bring about* our salvation (any more than our faith does) . . . In

---

39. Nowadays many a Catholic theologian would not admit the sketch we have given of the position in the Roman Church, for modern Catholic theology is working its way towards a more 'eventist' view of things. The fact remains, however, that in the first place the official Roman doctrine has not changed and in the second place those Catholic theologians who come closest to Protestantism on this point still do not accept it, taking up a position somewhere in between it and the official orthodoxy of their Church, which moreover has often disowned them, either outright or by implication.

the case of baptism we are dealing with the *knowledge* of salvation, not with its cause.'[40] 'The power [of the sacramental event] must be understood in a cognitive sense rather than in a causal or originative sense.'[41] Baptism saves, sanctifies and cleanses in the sense that it 'genuinely acquaints us with all that'.[42]

Here again we see well enough what Barth is after: in season and out of season he would uphold God's lordship over man in Jesus Christ. But does the *Begrifflichkeit* he uses allow him to achieve that aim? Since the philosophy of subject and object is the level on which he never for a moment gives up thinking, the only way he can safeguard the object—that is to say Christ, the 'source and object of faith', as he reminds us—is by cutting down the role and import of the subject to an absolute minimum. This he does by having the act of faith dwindle into an act of knowledge. Faith and the sacraments are entirely 'a matter of cognition'. But is this going far enough? Does the free act of knowing not remain an act of the subject? When Barth says that faith is a *Kenntnisnahme* of Christ's being and doing, is that not still a *human* act and therefore a work? No, if one looks at matters from the philosophic standpoint, as in fact he does, there is only one way to safeguard the object and that is to get rid of the subject—which Barth, of course, will not hear of doing. But he fails to explain how the 'total' upset and 'thoroughgoing' decision which he still allows the believer in spite of everything, can co-exist with God's lordship and yet not encroach upon it. Normally a man's act of faith should be Christ's doing, Christ's act of faith. Despite all his efforts, Barth's quandary can be detected in the *argumentum ad hominem* we have quoted: 'Let anyone who thinks he can do better beware lest he do worse.'

Beyond a doubt it would be wiser to ask oneself whether the objectifying ontology one is using really befits what one has to say, and to confess that it does not because it pictures man as a being who is already free to accept or reject God *before* God saves him. So freedom exists independent of grace. On the other hand if we recognize man as a being who ec-sists, whose freedom is 'forensic', perpetually drawn from another than himself, then we can readily see why the first effect of God's action will be to give man the freedom with which he can respond. Then man no longer does anything of himself, not even a 'cognitive' act, which would still be a work. What he does comes wholly from God, although it remains his own doing since the gift

40. K. Barth, *La doctrine ecclésiastique du baptême*, p. 17 (French translation).
41. *Ibid.*, p. 19.
42. *Ibid.*

that grace gives is freedom. But if the act of faith is a gift of God, then it is not only a 'total' upset but an 'absolute' one, not only a 'thorough-going' decision but an 'eschatological' one. Set free, as he now has been, of all in-sistence, what a man does is no longer a 'work' (*Werk*) but an 'act' (*Tat*; see ch. 11, §11, above).[43]

The import of the sacraments is likewise more than cognitive. If Barth were not using an unsuitable *Denkschematismus* he would agree without turning a hair that a sacrament continues the event of Christ, since the whole thing is Christ's doing. There is no use alleging that the import of a sacrament is purely cognitive: this non-eschatological import still stands independent of Christ's eschatological work. Now how can we admit that autonomy in a sacrament? How can a sacrament be that which non-eschatologically apprises us of an eschatological event?

V

Barth has lucidly explained, in his book on Anselm,[44] why he will not base theology on philosophy or defend theology at the bar of philosophy. But he does not dream of forbidding the theologian to make use of philosophy within his thinking.[45] Without using a pattern of thought (*Denkschematismus*) we cannot read the Bible, much less study or write theology. 'Let us not stumble into the wild and insufferable error of those who accuse everybody on earth of having a mind coloured by some philosophical system or other whereas they themselves, they think, have kept virginally innocent of any such taint . . . Stuff and nonsense . . . Nobody can claim that he does not mix the gospel with some kind of philosophy' (TKD 5, p. 275).

The whole problem, therefore, is to decide how theology shall use philosophy. At least one major rule must be insisted on: the philosophy that we use can never be set up as an absolute. 'Any philosophy that is

43. As Bultmann puts it in a text where he does not have Barth in mind but where he shows that Paul makes faith a pre-condition for receiving righteousness, 'Paul seems unintelligible or paradoxical only to a mind which cannot picture fulfilling a condition as anything but a *Leistung* (a 'work'); whereas Paul holds that πίστις is precisely the sacrifice of *Leistung*, and therefore absolute obedience' (TNT, p. 317).

44. K. Barth, *Fides quaerens intellectum—Anselms Beweis der Existenz Gottes* . . . (1931).

45. The major texts dealing with this matter are TKD 5, pp. 273–81 (see also pp. 319–20) and *Credo*, pp. 229–32 (in the French translation). *Philosophie et Théologie* (separate reprint in French translation, of a study which appeared in *Philosophie und christliche Existenz*, 1960, published in honour of Heinrich Barth, Karl Barth's brother) does not deal with the theologian's use of philosophy but with the two contrasting procedures followed by the theologian and the philosopher respectively.

assumed to be an absolute necessarily ends by warping scripture'
(*ibid.*). The philosophy we pick out must serve as a mere hypothesis.
Accordingly one can perfectly well use several philosophies. Who
knows, other philosophies than mine may be sounder hypotheses.
When necessary—that is, when a better interpretation of the Bible is
at stake—I must be ready to give up my own philosophy in favour of
another, because it is always in a concrete situation that one way or
another of thinking will prove to be useful for explaining the Bible.
The Greek Fathers, like Luther and Calvin, were Platonists; medieval
theologians, like the orthodox Protestant theologians of the seventeenth century, were Aristotelians. Nowadays we turn instead to
Kierkegaard and existentialism. This is all well and good. But it would
be a very bad thing if we tried to use only one philosophy. 'How can
we enthrone one philosophy as being philosophy par excellence, how
can we turn it into a universal law without making an absolute of it—
which is to say, without thereby outraging and perverting the Word
of God?' (*ibid.*, 5, p. 279). No philosophy exists which the theologian
may allow to be thrust upon him as the normal *Vorverständnis* of
revelation. Though Bultmann is not mentioned by name, the word
Vorverständnis shows well enough that Barth has him in mind.

Such then is the Barthian view. What shall we think of it from
Bultmann's standpoint? First of all let us observe that the solution
Barth offers to the problem of the connection between theology and
philosophy follows from his own philosophic position. He is quite
right to say that philosophy must never become an absolute, which
would outrage and pervert the Word of God. But why is he so sure
that the only way to avoid making philosophy a 'second God', as he
puts it, is to use several philosophies? Because he thinks of philosophy
as standing on the purely ontic plane, as a particular scheme of God,
man and the world.

Barth always speaks of concrete philosophies: Platonism, Aristotelianism, idealism, existentialism. In his eyes philosophy can only be a
Weltanschauung. Nowhere—neither in the *Dogmatics* nor anywhere
else—does he distinguish between phenomenology and philosophy,
between the existential and the existentiell. As we have seen, this
distinction is so alien to him that all he can think of doing is to poke
fun at it (RB, p. 35, note). To be sure, he uses the words 'phenomenology'
and *Begrifflichkeit*, but he never attaches to them the strict meaning
they have in Bultmann. So far as he is concerned, they are virtually
synonyms for the word 'philosophy'. This being so, one can quite well
see why he will not hear of any special claims for a given philosophy
when it comes to interpreting the Bible. If we envisage philosophy as
Barth does, then indeed only particular philosophies exist and the only

way to avoid divinizing one of them is to use them all according to circumstances.

For his own part, Bultmann carefully distinguishes between phenomenological philosophy and philosophy in the strict sense. He holds that a 'correct', 'sound', 'accurate' philosophy exists. He does not talk of a 'true' philosophy, because that word hails from the ontic plane, but of a 'correct', 'sound', 'accurate' philosophy; and he puts the word *richtig* (which all the foregoing words render) in inverted commas. All of which means that this 'philosophy' stands on the plane of normal analysis and the sense of being that things have.

From this point of view there is only one sound philosophy. Nothing will ever turn man's sense of being into a stone's, that of sin into that of brotherhood, that of love into that of quantity. We could go on. When it comes to the sense of being, there is one truth and only one. No doubt it takes some looking for and will often be reckoned something else; that is another matter. The sense of being is 'historical', certainly; is never 'gets its finishing touches'; but it is always the same sense giving itself temporal form. Man will always be a freedom, he will never be a tree. Since God's Word speaks to men in human terms it behooves us to undertake a formal analysis of the categories used, to look for the 'accurate' *Begrifflichkeit* which suits them. Revelation does not mean to reveal that *Begrifflichkeit* but merely takes it for granted by using it; discloses it only by implication, as we have seen when studying such Pauline ideas as *soma* and *psyche*.

Ontological analysis in itself is the business of the *lumen naturale*. Do I hear a shout of 'the second God'? But what is the *lumen naturale* if not a share in God's light? Does Barth not confess that fallen man has become, to use his own words, neither 'a stone nor a stump' and that one need not be a Christian in order to avoid confusing the idea of God with the idea of a chair?

Besides, what are we after in this ontological probing? Are we out to thrust a *Vorverständnis* of revelation upon men, as Barth fancies? No, but to find the conceptuality which *suits* revelation. And therefore we throw our ideas and *Denkschematismus* overboard in order to be as docile as we can to the categories through which God speaks to us. True, those categories are not *what* he says; they are only that through which he says it; but we know that the *Was* cannot be split off from the *Dass*, the ontological from the ontic. As Heidegger says, not so much as a thread can be slipped between them. That, of course, is why the *Begrifflichkeit* used by revelation always reaches our minds more or less tinged with the philosophy of natural man, ingrained in us because we are sinners. The images the Bible uses always make common cause in us with our scheme of things—natural man's. We instinctively understand God, grace, love, and the rest in ordinary terms. We must cleanse our minds and use the ideas of God, grace, sin, and the rest as scripture does—that is, in accordance with the 'sound' sense of their being. So phenomenological analysis does not remotely resemble a 'second God'; it 'serves' the Word of God, just as Barth demands that philosophy do (TKD 5, p. 280).

It follows from what we have just said that, contrary to his impression, faith uses *no* philosophy in the sense he means—that is, no philosophy properly so-called. Barth is quite wrong in supposing that any philosophy can be the handmaid of revelation provided only that one uses it as an hypothesis and in a spirit of docility to faith. Such a use does nothing to change the godless nature of all philosophies. All of them without exception are *human* schemes of God, man and the world, and as such imcompatible with faith—and the worst offender is the philosophy of subject and object so dear to Barth's heart. Every one of them is a 'second God'. As to the *Begrifflichkeiten* involved in these philosophies, they suit the Word of God no whit better, because not so much as a thread can be slipped between the existential and the existentiell. We know what havoc has been wrought in theology by the ontologies that the various philosophies have spawned. Even Heidegger's thought is far from blameless in this respect, for the philosopher's scheme of things taints the existential analysis itself. Faith must not use any philosophy at all; all it may use is the ontology which revelation itself uses, which is the 'sound', 'accurate' *Begrifflichkeit*.

True enough, God's Word did not create the categories it brings into play, but—apart from mythological perversions for which the biblical writers alone must bear the blame—it uses them in their *sound* meaning and in accordance with the truth of their 'nature'. These ideas are God's creation by the very fact that he created man and his *lumen naturale*; but thanks to the ontic scheme of things cherished by a creature in rebellion against his Creator, they are not to be found incorrupt in any culture of any age, in any philosophy. Man sees them as coloured by his sinful scheme of things and to a greater or lesser extent mistakes the real sense of their being. That is why, de facto if not de jure, the genuine ontology of God, man and the world can be found in Christian revelation alone.

When he claims that any philosophy can be used—even though he adds the basic condition that it must be done in obedience to scripture —is not Barth making philosophy a 'second God' in spite of himself? To use his own words, is he not 'warping' the Word of God, as was more or less done by those theologians whose use of philosophy he indorses—the Greek Fathers with their Platonism, the Schoolmen and orthodox Protestants with their Aristotelianism, and the rest? Luther trod no such path: his own genius consisted in trying to shake off *any Begrifflichkeit* that was borrowed from any philosophy whatever. As for himself, he settled for the *Begrifflichkeit* of the object.

There can be no doubt that the historical circumstances in which Barth found himself were the major factor shaping his choice. The great concern of his whole life was to react against what he calls the liberal and modernist 'heresy', which issued from idealist philosophy. Liberal theologians kept harping on man the subject, on psychology, the 'inner life' and piety. Against all that Barth tried to bring back the dignity and primacy of the 'object'. But while so doing he remained imprisoned in his opponents' formulation of the problem. He did not give enough thought to setting the question (of how philosophy and faith are connected) on another plane. His rich and nimble mind (as no one can gainsay) ranged far beyond the *Begrifflichkeit* of the object. It is well known, for instance, how much of his work deals with existentialism; but that is a philosophy in the strict sense. Never has he centred his thinking on ontology as we define it in this book.

One of the main points of interest in this essay on Bultmann is its disclosure of how firmly he keeps the object playing first fiddle. By the very nature of his undertaking, and although he had not a shadow of any direct intent to do so, Bultmann left Barth without a leg to stand on and, reagent-like, produced a 'chemical' change in him. As we have seen, all the passages in the *Dogmatics* which refer to Bultmann bristle with Barth's objectivism. Always he takes his stand on the same ground—the philosophy of subject and object. His whole endeavour is, not indeed to stamp out the subject, but to make it come to terms with the object, the primacy of which he never wearies of vindicating. In his lecture of 1956 on 'God's humanity' he refers once more to Bultmann, whose thought he perceives to be based on transcending the whole 'pattern of subject and object'.[46] But what, he goes on, does this transcendence mean until it has been established beyond doubt that Bultmann's enterprise does not take us back again to anthropocentric myth? Thus we find Barth still wedged fast inside his suit of armour, the issue of subject and object.

At the end of his essay, as we have seen, he admits that what most distresses him about Bultmann is the 'pre-Copernican' nature of his work. He wistfully takes note that the younger generations, who never knew the 'Egyptians'—that is, the age of Ritschl, Harnack and Troeltsch and the times before that—now have no inkling of the deliverance which he and his followers wrought. Of course, he says, I would not try to make our enterprise the yardstick and law of all things; but if

46. K. Barth, *L'humanité de Dieu*, p. 39.

the theology of the latter half of this century becomes a 'demythizing' and 'existential'[47] one—that is, a theology of hidebound 'pre-comprehension'—may the Christian people not be chastised for it as the children of Israel were in the wilderness when they fell to sighing for the flesh-pots of Egypt!

But who, in all honesty, is the more 'pre-Copernican'—Bultmann or Barth? In making theology revolve round the object, does Barth not make it revolve round *man* as surely as if he set it revolving round the subject? Does not the objective road he has taken lead as straight 'to Egypt' as ever the subjective road of the Ritschls, the Harnacks and the Troeltsches did? When Barth makes shift with firmly standing at the other pole of their philosophy, has he shaken off its chains? Is it not heart-rending that this philosophy should have entangled him in a hopeless misjudgment of Bultmann's real thinking? Is it not much to be wished that theology in the second half of this century should desert the arena of subject and object once and for all, turn its back without a qualm on that 'flesh-pot of Egypt' to push farther on into the promised land of God's one revelation in Jesus Christ and of the *Begrifflichkeit* which befits it?

47. The inverted commas are Barth's.

CHAPTER NINETEEN

Conclusion

'If demythologization is demanded in the first place by the clash between the mythological picture of the world [which is that] of the Bible and that picture of the world which scientific thinking has painted, it will also be immediately clear that demythologization is likewise demanded by faith itself. Faith insists on being freed from its bondage to any world-picture put forward by objectivist thought, whether it be the thought of myth or the thought of science.

'This clash proves that faith has not yet found the kind of expression which befits it, that it has not become aware of its specifically unverifiable nature, has not clearly perceived that its motive and its object are identical, has not yet fully grasped the transcendence and hiddenness of God's doings; and that by turning a blind eye to its specific "*Dennoch*" [its 'nevertheless'] it objectifies God and God's doings in the realm of earthly affairs. When in the name of the modern world-picture critics protest against the mythological world-picture [which is that] of the Bible and of the Church's traditional preaching, they are doing faith a very good turn by rousing it to serious reflection on its real nature. Now what demythologization tries to do, precisely, is answer that call.

'God's invisibility rules out any myth which would make God and his doings visible. But being the invisibility of *God*, it likewise rules out any notion of invisibility and mystery that is framed in terms of the *Begrifflichkeit* of objectivist thought. God eludes the objectifying eye; he can only be believed in in spite of appearances—precisely as the sinner's justification can only be believed in in spite of an accusing conscience.

'And indeed thoroughgoing demythologization runs parallel to the Pauline and Lutheran doctrine of justification by faith alone, without the works of the law—or rather, it is the logical completion of that doctrine in the realm of knowledge. Like the doctrine of justification, it shatters all false security and every misguided craving for security on man's part, whether the security which is based on good deeds or that which is based on objective knowledge.[1]

1. *Sein konstatierendes Erkennen*: Bultmann means objective, rational knowledge in general—that of common sense, science and philosophy.

'The man who would believe in God as his God must realize that he has nothing in hand on the basis of which he can believe; that he finds himself as it were in mid-air and can demand no proof that the Word which summons him is true. The motive of faith and its object are one and the same. Only he who gives up all security will find security— only he who is ready (as Luther says) to plunge into inward darkness. Just as that faith in God which is faith in justification will not define that certain given acts sanctify, so that faith in God which is faith in creation will not define that certain given areas in the world, and in worldly events, are holy. Thus we have learned from Luther that there are no holy places in the world, that the whole world is a profane place—always saving the *terra ubique Domini*, which too can only be believed in in spite of appearances.

'What makes the house of God holy is not its consecration by a priest but solely the preaching of the Word. Similarly nature and history are profane through and through, and only in its character as the preaching of the Word does anything that has happened or happens in nature and history become, for the believer, an act of God, a *Wunder*, in spite of appearances. Precisely for the sake of faith the world is made profane and restored to its specific determinism[2] as the sphere of man's labour. But as a result the believer's relation to the world and the world-picture [which is that] of science constitutes the paradox of the ὡς μή' (κμ 2, pp. 207–8).

These lines admirably convey the underlying aim of Bultmann's work. Most men of our time who still believe in God and his revelation—especially, perhaps, the more cultured of them—are prey to a schizophrenia which is all the deadlier for passing unnoticed. Whether they know it or not, whether they like it or not, they live in a world completely different from the one which witnessed the birth of Christianity. Religious-minded men of antiquity did not suffer from dual personality because at that time the supernatural order and the natural order were one and the same thing.

The cosmos was looked on as divine and the divine as cosmic. Commonplace phenomena were put down to the interposition of heaven, and divine phenomena were thought of as unusual natural phenomena. No doubt the underlying purpose of myth was to tell men about a realm that was the realm of the 'Wholly Other'; but in actual fact heaven skimmed so close to earth that the two seemed to merge in one. This happened in the New Testament, because the men who wrote it were unable to rise above their age in every respect. Now ancient times are dead and buried. In our days (to use Heideggerian

2. Its *Gesetzlichkeit* or 'lawfulness'.

terms) being 'historicizes' itself, 'shapes' itself, in an entirely different way.

A gulf yawns between heaven and earth. Man no longer has a supernatural knowledge of the world, but a philosophic, scientific, technical one instead. The universe has gone profane. Its structure and laws have been scrutinized. Science is not a set of theories; it is a way of proceeding. To be familiar with nature is to use and change it. The world has turned into a human scheme of things which leaves no room for any idea of mythological meddling in earthly affairs on the part of heaven.

What we must do here is point out that no one nowadays can accept or reject this view of things as he happens to choose. Just as ancient man could not shake off the outlook which was his own, just as the Greek or Jew of the fifth century did not in the least mind doing without the wireless and the cinema but quaked at an eclipse of the sun, so the man of today must accept the modern world-picture whether he likes it or not. Those of our contemporaries who are most addicted to superstitition, miracles and the occult sciences still use the telephone and the automobile and can witness a total eclipse of the sun without turning a hair.[3] In short, they behave as though the world were entirely profane. But what they do, jeers at what they think.

For level-headed and educated Christians, of course, this popular mythology is beneath contempt. They accept science and technology, defending their attitude on the grounds that science and faith stand on two completely different planes. But though they reject magic, spiritualism and every kind of heathen miracle, they still countenance Christian miracles, only demythologizing the grossest of them. They no longer believe that unworthy reception of the Eucharist can cause physical death (1 Cor 11:30) nor that Christ sits at the right hand of God in the naive literal sense, as the first Christians did. But they accept his virgin birth, his resurrection, his ascension, and his coming at the end of the world as the New Testament presents them. Generally speaking they have a 'supra-intra-terrestrial' idea of God and what he does. They are theologians of the school which has been most waggish about Bultmann's statement that 'nobody can use electric light and the wireless, and accept modern clinics and medical techniques when ill, and at the same time believe in the world of spirits and the miracles of the New Testament' (KM I, p. 18).

3. We mention a total eclipse of the sun because this phenomenon, which happens in France only once or twice a century, was seen in the Midi on 15 February 1961, providing the historian of culture with as much food for thought as the astronomer. Many an eye-witness made it perfectly clear, for instance, how the least educated man of our time simultaneously realized what a deliverance science brought him and what holy terror the ancients must have felt when confronted with this strange event.

It answers no purpose to turn up one's nose and say that this statement is 'naive'. That is only running away from oneself so as not to
have to query one's pet opinions. It would be better to twit oneself and
ask whether one's cocksureness does not mask the anguish gnawing at
one's vitals and that craving for security which is the hallmark of *homo
religiosus*. That anguish and craving give rise to a misguided idea of
faith. Men confuse the incarnation of the divine with its objectification.
They do not perceive that if God has really become flesh, then no
earthly sign (no miracle) can avail to disclose him and Jesus must be
'profane' from head to foot. It is only in spite of every appearance to
the contrary that anyone can believe this utterly human man to be the
Word of God.

Our opponents plead that the New Testament presents a different
picture of the incarnation. They belittle all that sets Paul apart from the
synoptics and John from Paul. They want to have their cake and eat it.
Because the New Testament is scripture they are afraid to study it
critically. But since it cannot possibly be accepted, either, just as it
stands, the various Christian orthodoxies spin a web of more or less
skilful compromises designed to hide the schizophrenia that we have
spoken of.

Official Catholicism at least has a certain logic in its favour, for it
demythologizes as little as may be. In it the mythological elements of
the New Testament have found one of their safest redoubts. The
Roman church does not tolerate thoroughgoing biblical criticism and
it is well known how warily Catholic exegetes must step when setting
forth their ideas. Moreover the Catholic view of the supernatural rules
out any de-objectification of dogma, morals, worship or ecclesiastical
institutions.

The same must be said *mutatis mutandis* of eastern Orthodoxy.
Protestant fundamentalism bends even less to the 'reigning fashion',
though its followers (by the most astonishing intellectual gymnastics)
use every up-to-date technique in the service of faith as they understand
it, without so much as batting an eyelid. If we leave liberalism out of
consideration (it having no bearing on the matter under discussion
here), the major Protestant denominations generally profess an 'open'
orthodoxy—which is to say that they are always up to the eyes in
large-scale salvage operations; always busy as bees, working out huge
compromises meant to reconcile the mythological elements in the New
Testament with modern thought. A good number of typical examples
will be found in the series of volumes entitled *Kerygma und Mythos*,
where a motley band of theologians query Bultmann's undertaking
and set forth their own solutions.

Barth's theory of the sign is the subtlest attempt that has been made to protect scripture from criticism and 'hold on to everything'. As we have seen, it is no more 'faithful' to the thinking of the biblical writers than Bultmann's demythologization is, because the men of the New Testament regard the miracles as proof of something. Ever since 1926 Bultmann has chided Barth for faint-heartedness in what is an *interpretation* and has begged him to understand Paul better than Paul understood himself (GV 1, pp. 57 and 63).

The same appeal should be made to all Christians today. Luther masterfully sifted out the essence of revelation by saying that there are no holy places; or, as Bultmann says, no 'holy areas in the world and in worldly events'. The truth is that orthodox Christians are terrified by the radicalism of the cross, which they turn into a 'supra-intra-terrestrial' thing (a sacrifice of expiation) whereas it fairly shouts that there is nothing sacred in the world, that the divine can never manifest itself there as a 'holy area', because it is the judgment and annihilation of everything here below. There is no splitting off the resurrection from the cross, nor the incarnation of the divine from the annihilation of the human.

In order to see God a man must die to every objective sign of God in the world, which God's work leaves looking exactly as it looked before. Revelation does not mythologically change the course of nature and history. No miraculous star leads men to Christ: the cross makes the miraculous star a star exactly like every other. Miraculous stars are still part of natural man. God is above the stars, and a man believes in him in defiance of all stars, just as the Christian believes in his justification in defiance of his sin. The two things are one and the same. Thus the real charge that must be brought, to one degree or another, against every Christian denomination is the '*Nondum considerasti quanti ponderis sit peccatum*'.

The resurrection hides away so deep in the cross that one can only reach it through the cross. To look on God's incarnation in Jesus as his objectification in a virgin birth, miraculous deeds, a visible resurrection, ascension and parousia, is the *religious* way (in other words, the most guilty way) of jettisoning the cross. It is using God to lay hold on God, displacing the real scandal of the cross with the sham scandal of a faith that is 'human, all too human'. In an article of 1948 on the present state of theology, Bultmann condemns the retrograde movement (*Reaktion*) of Christianity these days, which expresses itself in the craving for orthodoxy of some sort, or in casting back to a fundamentalism which will brook no historical or theological criticism of the Bible. He observes that this retrograde movement is corrupting faith, because 'it pretends to offer men security where there can and must be no security'.

'Christian faith is no *Weltanschauung* that clears up the riddle of life and frees men from responsible decision in the moment. Christian faith is the strength and daring to utter the *"Dennoch"* even though we are lost in the riddle and the pitch-black night . . . It is that strength and daring because it is trust in the grace of God which has called man to life and gives life a meaning, even though he does not see the meaning yet. Not a scrap of security undergirds this trust, because it is the Word of grace spoken to man. God's Word gives scandal by being at once the Word of grace and the Word of the cross, by making the promise of life depend on a readiness to step over the threshold of death' (GV 3, pp. 191–2).

By asserting God's transcendence, of course, we do not deny his presence. Luther denies that there are any holy places and in the same breath preaches the *terra ubique Domini*. Precisely because the world and man are judged, they are pardoned. Whenever we picture God as a supra-intra-terrestrial being, whenever we take his doings for a *Mirakel*, whenever we envisage the incarnation of his Word in Jesus Christ on the pattern we have criticized, not only do we mythologize the divine but by that very fact we deny that *God* is present among men. By destroying the remote God we destroy the intimate God. By rationalizing God we rob men of him. It is no longer God who encounters them but an *Ersatz* for God, the wraith of a Saviour. By laying violent hands on the transcendence of God we debar God from being immanent. Throw the cross overboard and you throw the resurrection overboard. Divinize the earth and you profane heaven.

Having cut God down to his own stature, religious man now stands face to face with nothing but himself. The more or less mythological idea of the incarnation which the Christian churches entertain is the living proof that they refuse to stand before the true God, will not allow themselves to be wholly determined by him. To hanker after holy areas in nature and history is to flee God, to get rid of the resurrection by getting rid of death—and that is shutting the door to salvation. Christians who repudiate the lofty idea of God which Bultmann puts forward, thinking thereby to safeguard the divine presence among men, should realize that all they are talking about is a God made to their own measure. In short they are talking about themselves, which means death and nothingness. There is no choice to be made between the absolutely other God and the absolutely intimate God: he is absolutely intimate only because he is the Wholly Other. Only if he is sheer otherness can God be my life. If a God who looks rather like me is the God who saves me, then I save myself. But we know that 'whoever would save his life will lose it' (Mk 8:35). Only the eschatological God who destroys man and the world can be man's Saviour and the world's.

In conclusion we must note the bearing which demythologization has on the ecumenical movement. The divisions among Christian churches do not come from the God they all have in view but from the objectifications of God which they hatch. Only when it has been contaminated by the thinking of natural man does revelation sink to the level of a supra-intra-terrestrial phenomenon. The churches are divided because they have set themselves up as orthodoxies. Orthodoxy turns faith into a *Weltanschauung*—that is, a system of thought—and an institution. If Christians had a noble enough idea of God they would really confess that 'Jesus is Lord' (1 Cor 12:3); they would see that he cannot be tied down to any earthly pattern—to any dogma, any ethics, or any organization. What the churches call truth is in reality a compromise between God and sinful man, who always itches to fit the Wholly Other into his own thoughts and deeds—that is, to rationalize him. Rationalism alone keeps the churches asunder. They all have the same underlying purpose but thwart it with objectifications of one kind or another, according to the various cultures and traditions. Cultures and traditions are all schemes of natural man and by interpreting revelation in terms of these, Christians wall themselves in from each other.

If God is thought of as a *Dass*, as the One who is ever coming, ever judging and destroying natural man and all the patterns of his thinking and behaviour then what issue can go on dividing us? The only choice that is left is the choice between God and the world, faith and unbelief, salvation and damnation, eternal life and eternal death. Nothing is left but the real scandal of revelation which Jesus himself put into words: 'Blessed is he who takes no offence at me' (Mt 11:6).

INDEX